The Nature and Context of Minority Discourse

The Nature and Context of Minority Discourse

Edited by
Abdul R. JanMohamed and David Lloyd

Oxford University Press
New York, Oxford

Oxford University Press
Oxford New York Toronto Delhi Bombay
Calcutta Madras Karachi Petaling Jaya
Singapore Hong Kong Tokyo Nairobi
Dar es Salaam Cape Town Melbourne Auckland

and associated companies in
Berlin Ibadan

First published as Numbers 6 and 7 of *Cultural
Critique* by Oxford University Press, Inc., 200
Madison Avenue, New York, New York 10016

Oxford is a registered trademark of Oxford
University Press

Library of Congress Cataloging-in-Publication Data

The nature and context of minority discourse.
  edited by Abdul R. JanMohamed and David Lloyd.
  p. cm.
  ISBN 0-19-506702-9 (cloth)
  ISBN 0-19-506703-7 (paper)
  1. Literature—Minority authors—History and
  criticism. 2. Ethnic attitudes in literature.
  3. Minorities in literature.
  I. JanMohamed, Abdul R., 1945– . II. Lloyd,
  David, 1955– .
PN491.5.N38 1990
809′.8920693—dc20   90-34838

                                        CIP

Cover art: Nora Pauwels

The Nature and Context of Minority Discourse

vi

Preface

In 1986, a conference entitled "The Nature and Context of Minority Discourse" was held at the University of California, Berkeley. In publishing the conference papers, along with some additional relevant essays, in two issues of *Cultural Critique*,[1] our intention was twofold: to define a field of discourse among various minority cultures and to intervene in the politics of cultural education in the United States.

By "minority discourse," we mean a theoretical articulation of the political and cultural structures that connect different minority cultures in their subjugation and opposition to the dominant culture. This definition is based on the principle that minority groups, despite all the diversity and specificity of their cultures, share the common experience of domination and exclusion by the majority. The common experience does not induce any kind of homogenization, but it does provide the grounds for a certain thinking in solidarity across the boundaries of different identities—which, as often as not, are imposed rather than autonomously constructed. We conceived the conference as a means of "marginalizing the center"—of permitting a theoretical and potentially practical work among minorities that did not require passage through hegemonic culture, a passage that is always ultimately assimilative and tends to restore the canonical forms of majority domination. The dialogue that could take place among minorities would entail displacing the insistent "core–periphery" model and redrawing intellectual agendas at all levels.

Our attempt to initiate a dialogue about minority discourse was quite successful. The intensity of debate during the course of the

---

1. A. R. JanMohamed and D. Lloyd, eds., "The Nature and Context of Minority Discourse" and "The Nature and Context of Minority Discourse II" [Special issues], *Cultural Critique* 6 and 7.

conference and subsequently, as we can infer from the demand for the two issues of *Cultural Critique* jointly republished here, far exceeded our expectations. The wealth and variety of the discussions at the conference are only partially represented by the papers published here. The papers republished in this volume address the often disparate immediate concerns of a variety of communities but nonetheless reflect collectively on the nature and context of minority discourse: on the construction of "minorities" as such; on the particularities of the cultural struggles waged by minority groups, in the effort to "represent themselves"; and, by way of developing a theory of minority discourse, on the epistemological, political, and cultural consequences that any struggle with the hegemonic culture entails. All the papers, in spite of their diversity, explore and articulate different aspects of minority cultures that have been ignored until recently by an educational system dedicated to the reproduction of the dominant ideology.

We could not have known that the conference and these papers would join a constellation of publications and events that inaugurated what has become nationally known as the "Western Cultures" or the Canon Debate, although the conference and the final response of the National Endowment for the Humanities (cited in the Introduction) already contained the nucleus of the debate. Juxtaposed against the possibility of a dialogue among minorities that might expand the questioning of dominant values is a stereotyping of that dialogue as Babel, a confusion of tongues disruptive of the orderly architecture of state and university. The same terms and stereotypes are evident, over and over again, in attacks on multiethnically conceived curricula, on interdisciplinary or cultural studies, and even on the fairly innocuous expansion of existent canons. Despite such obstacles, the initial stages of our attempt to provide an occasion and a space for the exploration of minority discourse have proved relatively easy to fulfill. In contrast, our attempts to intervene in the politics of cultural education have turned out to be a small part of what promises to be a large and prolonged struggle.

Like minority discourse itself, this volume is the product of sustained collective effort. We would like to thank the University of California, Berkeley, for supporting the original conference, all those who participated formally or informally at the conference, *Cultural Critique* for publishing the essays, and Donna Przybylowicz, the editor of *Cultural Critique,* without whose collaboration and editorial support the two issues on minority discourse would not have been possible. We hope this anthology will be the first of many volumes in the continuing struggle toward an "unfiltered" minority discourse.

—*Abdul R. JanMohamed and David Lloyd*

Introduction:
Toward a Theory of Minority Discourse:
What Is To Be Done?

Abdul R. JanMohamed and David Lloyd

I

At a moment when the liberation and celebration of differences and polyvocality are central features of critical endeavors, it is perhaps best to begin by defining the term "minority discourse" and justifying its singularity. In the past two decades, intellectuals involved in ethnic and feminist studies have enabled fresh examinations of a variety of minority voices engaged in retrieving texts repressed or marginalized by a society that espouses universalistic, univocal, and monologic humanism. Although this archival work has generated provocative theoretical analysis (in the best instances dialectical), it still remains true that the dispersal of the intellectuals in underfunded "special programs" has perpetuated and reinforced the fragmentation and marginalization of nonhegemonic cultures and communities in academic as well as in other spheres. Thus various minority discourses and their theoretical exegesis continue to flourish, but the relations between them remain to be articulated. Such articulation is precisely the task of minority discourse, in the singular: to describe and define the common denominators that link various minority cultures. Cultures designated as minorities have certain shared experiences by virtue of their similar antagonistic relationship to the dominant culture, which seeks to marginalize them all. Thus bringing together these

1

disparate voices in a common forum is not merely a polemical act; it is an attempt to prefigure practically what should already be the case: that those who, despite their marginalization, in fact constitute the majority should be able collectively to examine the nature and content of their common marginalization and to develop strategies for their reempowerment.

The need for such forums for comparative studies of minority cultures and for the definition of a common political agenda cannot be overemphasized, because the denial of such spaces and of any but a negative value to minority cultures continues to be central to the agenda of Western, Eurocentric humanism. For instance, in one chapter Henry Louis Gates, Jr., provides a fascinating example of a minority intellectual. Alexander Crummell accepted Euro-American hegemony so thoroughly that, after learning Greek to prove that he was civilized, he dismissed all African languages as "the speech of rude barbarians" and as "marked by brutal and vindictive sentiments, and those principles which show a predominance of the animal propensities." To the extent that we minority intellectuals still communicate professionally in European languages and within the "truth" of Western discourse rather than in our own languages and discourses, we are heirs of Crummell. Every time we speak or write in English, French, German, or another dominant European language, we pay homage to Western intellectual and political hegemony. Many such examples of how minority intellectuals were subjugated and "subjectified" by Western "humanistic" discursive practices can be adduced. Usually, however, we tend to distance such "subjectification," either historically—it used to happen in the past—or spatially—it happens to other people.

Given this tendency to repress the current political context of minority cultures, one cannot overemphasize that Western humanism still considers us barbarians beyond the pale of civilization; we are forever consigned to play the role of the ontological, political, economic, and cultural Other according to the schema of a Manichaean allegory that seems the central trope not only of colonialist discourse but also of Western humanism. The hegemonic pressures that forced Crummell to reconstruct his entire world in accordance with the values of the Manichaean allegory— that allowed him to define the African past in totally negative terms and the European past in totally positive ones—are just as prevalent today, in spite of what we have been led to believe by the abolition of slavery, the "success" of the Civil Rights movement, and the admission of a handful of minorities and women to the academy. Apt evidence of this state of affairs was ironically provided by the negative response of the National Endowment for the Humanities (NEH) to our application for funding the 1986 conference "The Nature and Context of Minority Discourse."

Documents furnished by NEH clearly show the determining criterion for its decision to reject our application. Of the external reviews solicited by NEH, five were to be returned to NEH by November 7, 1985, and one was to be returned "ASAP." Some of the initial five reviewers had minor reservations about our proposal, but all recommended funding the conference. However, the review solicited in haste recommended rejection, and the summary of the NEH panel discussion makes clear that our proposal was indeed rejected on the basis of this evaluation. After praising the credentials of the conference organizer, the "ASAP" reviewer provides fascinating reasons for his negative evaluation.

> I cannot but feel that a conference that would bring together in a few days of papers and discussion specialists on Chicano, Afro-American, Asian-American, Native-American, Afro-Caribbean, African, Indian, Pacific island, Aborigine, Maori, and other ethnic literature would be anything but diffuse. A conference on ONE of these literatures might be in order; but even with the best of planning, the proposed conference would almost certainly devolve into an academic tower of Babel. It is not at all clear that a specialist on Native-American literature, for example, will have much to say to someone specializing in African literature. It is also unlikely that the broad generalizations Professor JanMohamed would have them address would bring them any closer.

The ideological implications of this evaluation are self-evident. First, when Europeans come together to discuss their various national literatures, they are seen as being able to communicate coherently across linguistic barriers, and such coherence is not only encouraged in conferences but even institutionalized in the form of comparative literature departments in various universities across the country; in contrast, when ethnic minorities and Third World peoples want to have similar discussions, their dialogue is represented, according to the ideology of humanism, as incoherent babble, even though they propose to use a single dominant European language for this purpose. Second, Western humanists find it inconceivable that Native-Americans, Africans, and others who have been brutalized by Euro-American imperialism and marginalized by its hegemony can have anything relevant to say to each other. Third, ethnic minorities must be prevented from getting "close" to each other, through broad generalizations or any other means. Eighteenth-century statutes in South Carolina and other states made the desire of black Americans to acquire literacy a criminal offense, and various colonialist educational policies systematically repressed native education, as South Africa still does. We are now allowed to learn the master's language, but our use of it to discuss the issues that most concern us is still defined as babble, an "incoherence" that Eurocentric humanist discourse still needs to pose as a foil to its own civilized coherence.

II

Given such a historically sustained negation of minority voices, we must realize that minority discourse is, in the first instance, the product of damage—damage more or less systematically inflicted on cultures produced as minorities by the dominant culture. The destruction involved is manifold, bearing down on variant modes of social formation, dismantling previously functional economic systems, and deracinating whole populations at best or decimating them at worst. In time, with this material destruction, the cultural formations, languages, and diverse modes of identity of the "minoritized peoples" are irreversibly affected, if not eradicated, by the effects of their material deracination from the historically developed social and economic structures in terms of which alone they "made sense." With a certain savage consistency, this very truncation of development becomes both the mark and the legitimation of marginalization. The diverse possible modes of cultural development that these societies represent are displaced by a single model of historical development within which other cultures can only be envisaged as underdeveloped, imperfect, childlike, or—when already deracinated by material domination—

inauthentic, perverse, or criminal. From this perspective, such cultures are seen as capable of development toward a higher level of cultural achievement only through assimilation to that already attained by those of European stock. Even the majority culture's recognition of the damage already inflicted can be converted, with a *frisson* of charitable pathos, into a stimulus toward the more rapid assimilation of "disadvantaged" minorities to the dominant culture's modes of being.

It is crucial, especially in the context of a volume that seeks in a sense to celebrate the positive achievements and potential of minority discourse, to stress the real and continuing damage inflicted on minorities. The pathos of hegemony is frequently matched by its interested celebration of differences, but only of differences in the aestheticized form of recreations. Detached from the site of their production, minority cultural forms become palatable: a form of practical struggle like *capoeira,* a form of defense developed by Brazilian slaves whose physical movements were severely restricted by chains, becomes recuperable first as a Hollywood spectacle of break dancing and then as a form of aerobics. Attending to minority cultural forms requires accordingly a double vigilance, both with respect to their availability for hegemonic recuperation and to their strategies of resistance (strategies that will always be referable to the specific material conditions from which such forms are produced). Minority discourse is in this respect a mode of ideology in the sense in which Marx in "On the Jewish Question" described religion—at once the sublimation and the expression of misery—but with the critical difference that in the case of minority forms even the sublimation of misery needs to be understood as primarily a strategy for survival, for the preservation in some form or other of cultural identity, *and* for political critique. For example, the Afro-American culture, to the extent that African slaves were deprived of their own cultures and prevented from entering white American culture, can function as a paradigm of minority cultures. Houston Baker, Jr., has pointed out that in Afro-American culture this sublimation and expression of misery—a comprehension and a critique—find their unique form in the blues matrix, "a mediational site where familiar antinomies are resolved . . . in the office of adequate cultural understanding." This sublimation and expression, then, are not imposed from above by the dominant culture, nor are they the form in which that culture misrecognizes or legitimates its oppressive practices. Rather, cultural practices are an intrinsic element of the economic and political struggles of Third World and minority peoples. Indeed, exactly to the extent that such peoples are systematically marginalized vis-à-vis the global economy, one might see the resort to cultural modes of struggle as all the more necessary, even within the framework of a Marxist analysis of such struggles. For many minorities, culture is not a mere superstructure; all too often, in an ironic twist of a Sartrean phenomenology, the physical survival of minority groups depends on the recognition of its culture as viable.

One aspect of the struggle between hegemonic culture and minorities is the recovery and mediation of cultural practices that continue to be subjected to "institutional forgetting," which, as a form of control of one's memory and history, is one of the gravest forms of damage done to minority cultures. Archival work, as a form of counter-memory, therefore is essential to the critical articulation of minority discourse. Since ethnic and women's studies departments and programs were instituted in the late sixties, such archival work has continued apace. However, if the previously marginalized production of minority cultures is not to be relegated by the force of dominant culture to the mere repetition of ethnic or feminine exotica, theoretical reflection cannot be omitted. Such theory would be obliged to provide a sustained critique of the historical conditions and formal qualities of the institutions that have continued to legitimize exclusion and marginalization in the name of universality. One must always keep in mind that the universalizing humanist project has been highly selective, systematically valorizing certain texts and authors as *the* humanist tradition while ignoring or actively repressing alternative traditions and attitudes.

The "inadequacy" or "underdevelopment" ascribed to minority texts and authors by a dominant humanism in the end only reveals the limiting (and limited) ideological horizons of that dominant, ethnocentric perspective. Because the dominant culture occludes minority discourse by making minority texts unavailable— either literally through publishers and libraries or, more subtly, through an implicit theoretical perspective that is structurally blind to minority concerns—one of the first tasks of a reemergent minority culture is to break out from such ideological encircle-ment. In such an endeavor, theoretical and archival work of mi-nority culture must always be concurrent and mutually reinforc-ing: a sustained theoretical critique of the dominant culture's apparatus both eases the task of recovering and mediating mar-ginalized work and permits us to elucidate the full significance of the specific modes of resistance—and celebration—those works contain. However, neither the theoretical nor the archival work can afford to stop with establishing the validity of the achieve-ments and values of marginalized cultures. The danger remains that these cultures will thus be recuperated, as Deleuze and Guat-tari put it, into "performing a major function." Unmediated by a theoretical perspective, the mere affirmation of achievement lends itself too easily to selective recuperation into the dominant culture, which always regards individual minority achievement as symptomatic of what (given a certain level of "development") a depoliticized "humanity" in general is capable.

As the affirmation of a universal humanity, which is always an ideological postulate insofar as its real conditions are not yet given, such premature integration is exactly what is to be avoided. Those who argue for the creation of canons of various ethnic and feminist writings do so with the full awareness that the formation of different canons permits the self-definition and, eventually, self-validation that must be completed before any consideration of integration. To date, integration and assimilation have never taken place on equal terms, but always as assimilation by the domi-nant culture. In relations with the dominant culture, the syncretic movement is always asymmetrical: although members of the dom-inant culture rarely feel obliged to comprehend various ethnic cultures, minorities are always obliged, in order to survive, to master the hegemonic culture (without thereby necessarily gain-ing access to the power that circulates within the dominant sector). To believe otherwise is either naive or self-serving and denies the fact that cultural struggle continues at every level, in many ways, and, most importantly, at the theoretical level. For example, to argue that one has never considered oneself "minor" and then to complain that ethnic literatures have traditionally been mar-ginalized is to confuse cultural pride with the nature of current political reality (for, surely, it is the political situation of an ethnic literature, not the strength or weakness of one's pride, that renders it "minor"). This kind of conflation can be avoided when theory works in conjunction with archival projects: the theoretical and archival struggle must continue jointly so long as the culture of domination persists globally.

Minority discourse must similarly be wary of "pluralism," which, along with assimilation, continues to be the Great White Hope of conservatives and liberals alike. The semblance of pluralism disguises the perpetuation of exclusion insofar as it is enjoyed only by those who have already assimilated the values of the dominant culture. For this pluralism, ethnic or cultural difference is merely an exoticism, an indulgence that can be relished without significantly modifying the individual who is securely embedded in the protective body of dominant ideology. Such pluralism tolerates the existence of salsa, it even enjoys Mexican restaurants, but it bans Spanish as a medium of instruction in American schools. Above all, it refuses to acknowledge the class basis of discrimination and the systematic economic exploitation of minorities that underlie postmodern culture.

However, an emergent theory of minority discourse must not be merely negative in its implications. Rather, the critique of the apparatus of universalist humanism entails a second theoretical task permitted by the recovery of excluded or marginalized practices. The positive theoretical work involves a critical-discursive articulation of alternative practices and values that are embedded in the often-damaged, -fragmentary, -hampered, or -occluded works of minorities. This is not to reassert the exclusive claim of the dominant culture that objective grounds for marginalization can be read in the inadequacy or underdevelopment of "minority" work. On the contrary, it is to assert that even the very differences that have always been read as symptoms of inadequacy can be reread transformatively as indications and figurations of values radically opposed to those of the dominant culture. A theory of minority discourse is essential precisely for the purposes of such a reinterpretation, for, in practice, the blindness of dominant theory and culture towards the positive values of minority culture can easily engulf us. Because we, the critics of minority culture, have been formed within the dominant culture's educational apparatus and continue to operate under its (relatively tolerant) constraints, we are always in danger of reproducing the dominant ideology in our reinterpretations unless we theoretically scrutinize our critical tools and methods and the very categories of our epistemology, aesthetics, and politics. In the task of reevaluating values, our marginality can be our chief asset.

For example, in rejecting the premature avowal of humanist pluralism, the theory of minority discourse should neither fall back on ethnicity or gender as an a priori essence nor rush into inculcating some "nonhumanist" celebration of diversity for its own sake. Rather, ethnic or gender differences must be perceived as one of many residual cultural elements; they retain the memory of practices that have had to be (and still have to be) repressed so that the capitalist economic subject may be more efficiently produced. The theoretical project of minority discourse involves drawing out solidarities in the form of similarities between modes of repression and struggle that all minorities experience separately but experience precisely as minorities. "Becoming minor" is not a question of essence (as the stereotypes of minorities in dominant ideology would want us to believe) but a question of position: a subject-position that in the final analysis can be defined only in "political" terms—that is, in terms of the effects of economic exploitation, political disenfranchisement, social manipulation, and ideological domination on the cultural formation of minority subjects and discourses. The project of systematically articulating the implications of that subject-position—a project of exploring the strengths and weaknesses, the affirmations and negations that are inherent in that position—must be defined as *the* central task of the theory of minority discourse.

Deleuze and Guattari's observation that "minor" literature is necessarily collective here gains its validity. Out of the damage inflicted on minority cultures, which, as Fanon so clearly recognized, prevents their "development" according to the Western model of individual and racial identity, emerges the possibility of a collective subjectivity formed in practice rather than contemplation. For the collective nature of minority discourse is due not to the scarcity of talent, as Deleuze and Guattari claim, but to other cultural and political factors. In those societies caught in the transition from oral, mythic, and collective cultures to the literate, "rational," and individualistic values and characteristics of Western cultures, the writer more often than not manifests the collective nature of social formation in forms such as the novel, thus transforming what were once efficacious vehicles for the representation of individually, atomistically oriented experiences into collective modes of articulation. However, more importantly, the collective nature of all minority discourse also derives from the fact that minority individuals are always treated and forced to experience themselves generically. Coerced into a negative, generic subject-position, the oppressed individual responds by transforming that position into a positive, collective one. Therein lies the basis of a broad minority coalition: in spite of the enormous differences among various minority cultures, which must be preserved, all of them occupy the same oppressed and "inferior" cultural, political, economic, and material subject-position in relation to the Western hegemony. Just as it is vitally important to avoid the homogenization of cultural differences, so it is equally important to recognize the common political basis of a minority struggle. The minority's attempt to negate the prior hegemonic negation of itself is one of its most fundamental forms of affirmation.

The theory of minority discourse raises yet another question: what does the "becoming minor" of theory and pedagogy entail? Clearly, it necessitates far-reaching transformations of cultural or "humanist" education. At the level of content, what is required in the way of introducing new material to syllabi and new courses to major programs is simple enough to outline but in practice significantly difficult to achieve, as any who have made the attempt will testify. At the level of form, the emerging theoretical synthesis entails not only the study of different material but also the effective transgression of current disciplinary divisions. For example, the study of minority cultures cannot be conducted without at least a relevant knowledge of sociology, political theory, economics, and history; otherwise, the specifics of the struggles embodied in cultural forms remain invisible. The ground for such changes in the form of pedagogy is the refusal of the assumption of the timeless universality of cultural products and of the concomitant tendency to read cultural texts exclusively for their representation of "aesthetic" effects and "essential" human values. For the premature claim to represent a realm of aesthetic freedom and disinterest has time and again legitimated the political quietism of academic institutions. That claim must be rejected as masking the very real damage inflicted by dominant culture on its minorities.

III

In this inevitably gradual process of revaluing values, which perforce advances only by glimpse and paradox toward systematic formulations, the role of the intellectual becomes doubly problematic, for the intellectual is twice marginalized by the institutional structures within which he or she must work (and which are as much a part of the quotidian world of practice in contemporary Western society as factory or home). The intellectual appreciates the collective nature of minority cultures yet is cut off from those cultures by virtue of the relative privilege offered by educational institutions as part of their hegemonizing function. More often than not, the minority intellectual is also marginalized within the institution, in part individually as a direct result of continuing racial or sexual discrimination, but more importantly (since it is here a question of an effect of structure) as a result of the systemic relegation of minority concerns to the periphery of academic work. No moral pathos attaches to this double alienation of the minority intellectual, unpleasant as its effects may be, for both forms of alienation spring as inevitably from the modes of late capitalist society as do the systematic exploitation of less-privileged minority groups, the feminization of poverty, the demonization of Third World peoples, and homophobic hysteria. The dual alienation of minority intellectuals derives not from the universal anomie of spirits in the material world nor even from the intrinsic "difficulties" of the theoretical work in which they may be engaged. Both aspects derive, rather, from the division of labor required by economic rationalization and by the need to denigrate alternative modes of rationality as, in Sylvia Wynter's phrase, the "ontological Other."

Unfortunately, an alienation so systematically produced cannot be overcome simply by wishful identification with an abstractly idealized "minority collective," because both the alienation of the minority intellectual and the collective identity that can emerge in the struggle against domination are recto and verso of the same process of rational division of labor—two complementary modes of the damage it inflicts. To overcome the situation will entail a mutually complementary work of theoretical critique and practical struggle, which clearly will take different forms in different spheres. Although the intellectual cannot prescribe what is to be done in other spheres, within the academic sphere there are transformations to be effected that will necessarily complement those undertaken by minorities elsewhere.

The foremost of these transformations is the critique and reformulation of the traditional role of humanist intellectuals and of the disciplinary divisions that sanction that role. The systemic function of the traditional humanist intellectual has always ultimately been the legitimation of the sets of discriminations required for economic and social domination. The very claim to universality that humanism makes, while utopian in itself, is annulled by the developmental schema of world history through which it is to be achieved. Accordingly, actual exploitation is legitimated from the perspective of a perpetually deferred universality. Although the phenomena of exploitation may without doubt be criticized well-meaningly on individual grounds, a critique of the rationale underlying the distinctions that legitimate exploitation cannot be produced systematically out of traditional humanism.

Herein lies the specific difference between the objective alienation, which the minority intellectual seeks to overcome, and the pathos of alienation, which afflicts the traditional humanist: the minority intellectual is situationally opposed to the alienation, while the traditional intellectual seeks either to make the characteristics of the alien prefigurative of deferred universality or (in a recent, insidiously logical development of the former version) to accept positivistically as merely given the alienated conditions of labor in the glorified form of "professionalism." Knowing that exploitation and discrimination are neither the inevitable products of universal history nor rationally justifiable but, rather, are the products of concrete and contestable historical developments, the minority intellectual is committed to the critique of the structures that continue to legitimate them.

The minority intellectual must also be committed to a reappraisal of "affirmative action," which in the humanities has meant either the creation of special units—separate departments of ethnic studies, women's studies, and (with conspicuous scarcity) gay-lesbian studies—that have been relegated to the margins of the universities or the employment of one or two minority individuals in a large department. At best, such action has confined itself to the quantitative level; it has resulted in a few more minority intellectuals in the academy. However, we must now move beyond numerical presence and special programs. What we must require from the institutions and from ourselves is the intellectual equivalent of "affirmative action." In the first place, we must see that a "humanism" that systematically ignores all issues concerned with the relations of domination, as it has done at least since Matthew Arnold consigned the dominated to the realm of anarchy, is in a sense profoundly bankrupt. Because relations of domination permeate every facet of our personal and social lives as well as of our literature and culture, a critique of culture that ignores such relations can be, at best, a distorted one. From a minority viewpoint, a viable humanism must be centered on a critique of domination. In the second place, it follows that most of those who hold power and those whose subject-positions are protected by the prevailing hegemony will be more interested in the efficacious use of power than in examining its misuse. In contrast, those who are dominated will understand the devastating effects of misused power; they are in a better position to document and analyze, as the contemporary resurgence in black women's writing illustrates, how relations of domination can destroy the "human" potential of its victims. The concerns of the victims of domination must be at the center not only of a minority discourse but also of non-Eurocentric, non-aestheticizing "humanism"—that is, of a Utopian exploration of human potentiality.

IV

Minority discourse implies that it is the perpetual return of theory to the concrete givens of domination, rather than the separation of culture as a discrete sphere, that militates against the reification of any dominated group's experience as in some sense "privileged." Just as domination works by constant adjustment, so the strategies of the dominated must remain fluid in their objects as in their solidarities. Apposite here is Sylvia Wynter's critique in her chapter of the various "isms" that single out particular specifications of "ontological otherness" as a unique field of political action: the tactical necessities that determine such maneuvers ossify only too rapidly into new domains of relative privilege, leaving, as the racial bias of even the feminization of poverty indicates, a bottom line of discrimination and exclusion that imposes all the more on those who suffer from it. This critique of former and current practices of minority groups implies, on the one hand, that minority groups need constantly to form and to re-form ever-more-inclusive solidarities and, on the other, that the material and intellectual formations by which "minorities" are constituted must be put under ever-increasing pressure. The two programs are complementary of course; the critique of the current basis of disciplinary divisions within the academic institutions and the consequent, at first experimental, production of other syntheses or bodies of knowledge will lead inevitably to the erosion of those structures by which the marginalization of "special programs" is justified. In time, the experimental nature of these new syntheses will give way to an increasingly systematic refutation of the pseudoscientific and pseudorational formulations on whose basis minorities continue to be oppressed.

From the present, necessarily limited perspective, it seems sure that, whatever shifts of this nature minorities will prove capable of effecting, they will at least be unsatisfactory insofar as they do not permit a far greater real acceptance of difference and diversity than is currently evident in any sphere of Western society. The realization of the goal of true acceptance will depend not on an epochal rupture at the discursive level—a hope that would retain a large element of idealism—but on radical transformations of the material structures of exploitation. The effectiveness of any new formations we can intellectually project could be predicated on such transformations alone, and to think otherwise in the context of continuing genocide, exploitation, and technological destruction is to risk an impermissible disproportion. But this is not, at the other extreme, to relegate intellectual work to perpetual adventism, an idealistic waiting for some historically inevitable precipitation of a class formation powerful enough to "smash the system." Openings for intervention are various and multiple at any moment, and indeed most of the terms of a critical minority discourse have been forged precisely in the practices of engaged minority groups. To cling solely to the role of an "intellectual" as to a singular and determinate identity would be fatuous where the process of the rational division of labor has made of every modern subject a fragmented or multiple identity, who functions now as a professor, now as one among women, now as a tenant, now as a black employee, now as a lesbian feminist. The gain that can be located in this situation by a critical minority discourse lies in the recognition that these multiple identities are neither reducible nor impermeable to one another, that there is no sphere of universal and objective knowledge or of purely economic rationality, that what is worked out in one sphere can be communicated in another, and that institutional boundaries will always need to be transgressed in the interests of political and cultural struggle. Insofar as the practices that emerge in any of these spheres remain referable to the fundamental goal of a society based on the possibility of uncoerced *economic* self-determination (the only foundation on which effective political or cultural self-determination can be based), they do not become isolated and abstract Utopian activities.

The effort of critical minority discourse to produce social and cultural formations genuinely tolerant of difference and to critique the dominant structures that tend to reduce the human to a single universal mode accounts for its apparent affinities to poststructuralism and postmodernism. It is essential not to collapse the distinction between the discourses of minorities and Third World groups and those of Western intellectuals; above all, apparently postmodern minority texts must not be seen as representations of the dissolving bourgeois subject. Certainly there is an overlap, especially in the realm of gender issues, and virtually without exception the contributors to this volume owe much methodologically to the critical reading of poststructuralist writings. But where the point of departure of poststructuralism lies within the Western tradition and tries to deconstruct its identity formations "from within," the critical difference is that minorities, by virtue of their very social being, must begin from a position of objective nonidentity that is rooted in their economic and cultural marginalization vis-à-vis the "West." The nonidentity that the critical Western intellectual seeks to (re)produce discursively is for minorities a given of their social existence. But as such a given, it is not yet by any means an index of liberation, not even of the formal and abstract liberation, which is all that poststructuralism, in itself and disarticulated from any actual process of struggle, could offer. On the contrary, the nonidentity of minorities remains the sign of material damage to which the only coherent response is struggle, not ironic distance. To be sure, the fact that the material damage is legitimated by humanist institutions and their universal claims entails as its logical corollary the demystification of "the figure of man." And to be sure, the nonidentity experienced by minorities as the oppressive effects of Western philosophies of identity is the strongest reason that a rigorously critical minority discourse, in its positive transformation of the discourses emerging from that nonidentity, should not merely fall back on the oppositional affirmation of an essential ethnic or gender identity. In minority discourse, the abstract philosophical questions of essence and ethics are transformed into questions of practice; the only meaningful response to the question, "What is or ought to be?," has to be the question, "What is to be done?"

Rethinking Modernism:
Minority vs. Majority Theories

Nancy Hartsock

W omen's studies is in many ways a curious academic field. With
the exception of ethnic studies, we owe a great deal more than
other academic disciplines to social movements off campus. The large
exception here, of course, is ethnic studies. Indeed, we owe much of our
very existence in academia to the struggles of those who did not have as
their goal the creation of a new scholarly field; rather, they were interested in a much more general social transformation. Moreover, many of us
in women's studies remain committed to doing academic work—both
research and teaching—in ways that are indebted to the politics and
organizational forms of the activist women's movement. The issue of
the relation of academics to activists is, in consequence, a more critical
one for women's studies than for the other academic disciplines in
which many of us also take part.

What has been the relation of academics and activists? It is not too
harsh to say that there has been a history of misunderstandings, failed
expectations, and bitterness. I doubt that either side has much real
sense of what the other does. Activists have often been very critical of
academics. Activists tend to see themselves as doing more than they

I would like to thank Donna Haraway and Ric Olguin for their detailed comments.

can, with less money and resources than they need, often living on subsistence wages, and working very long hours. Activists are likely to see academics as very privileged: not only do many of the university women make several times the wages that many activists work for, but the university also gives them access to all sorts of other privileges— including insurance, space, duplicating facilities, having their way paid to conferences, teaching only a few hours a week, working only for nine months a year. Moreover, activists have questions about the research academics do: academics involve themselves in the oddest and often most irrelevant-sounding concerns. As one activist put it, the academy's predisposition is to regard anything dead as good and anything living as suspect.

The view from within the academy is, of course, quite different. Our programs are often underfunded; the faculty have had to teach women's studies courses as an overload; and the problems of time and money within the university seem very similar to those outside—being asked, and trying, to do too much with too little. As academics involved in women's studies we often see ourselves as occupying a very tenuous ground within the university. Despite the appearance of teaching only a few hours a week and having (many of us) summers "off," we see ourselves as putting in very long hours. The institutions at which we work have their requirements. From within the university, academics often perceive activists as having much more freedom—as being without institutional constraints and responsibilities and as asking for resources the women's studies faculty either don't have or cannot spare.

Both these views have some truth, but both sides of these accusations point to the issue I want to raise here—namely that where we are located in the social structure as a whole and which institutions we are in and not in have effects on how we understand the world. We need close collaboration between academics and activists outside the university—we need it in order to do both better scholarship and better organizing. Activism needs to be informed by theory. Theory can help us understand which issues are shared by all women and which issues affect different women differently. In addition, theory can give us some perspective on the significance of any particular effort. One of the dangers of political activity in the absence of a more theoretical understanding of women's situation is that such activity can lead to a submersion in the day to day struggle, and to a consequent failure to address the hard questions of what real difference these struggles will make for women. Thus, for example, one can be led to argue for the need for abortion rights without recognizing that reproductive rights have other important dimensions, especially for women of color; or one become absorbed in single issue, dead-end work, as NOW did on the ERA.

But if theory is an important resource for activists, what is the situation of academics? We face our own set of problems—one of the most important is that, if we become cut off from the political perspectives provided by links with activists, we are more likely to be caught up in the questions that move other academics who have never shared our political commitments. We need to inquire of our research and teaching: Who is it for? To whom are we ultimately accountable? How can we recognize and assess the political stakes involved in seemingly irrelevant academic distinctions. What are the political issues on the agenda for feminist academics?

Most important, I would argue, are questions about difference, especially differences among women. We need to develop our understanding of difference by creating a situation in which hitherto marginalized groups can name themselves, speak for themselves, and participate in defining the terms of interaction, a situation in which we can construct an understanding of the world that is sensitive to difference. Clearly, this is a task for academics and activists alike. Here, however, I want to concentrate on the academic side.

What might such a theory look like? Can we develop a general theory, or should we abandon the search for such a theory in favor of making space for a number of heterogeneous voices to be heard? What kinds of common claims can be made about those of white women and women and men of color? About the situations of Western peoples and those they have colonized? For example, is it ever legitimate to say "women" without qualification? These kinds of questions make it apparent that the theoretical crisis we face not only involves substantive claims about the world but also raises questions about how we come to know the world, about what we can claim for our theories—questions of epistemology. I want to ask, what kinds of knowledge claims are required for grounding political action by different groups? Should theories produced by "minorities" rest on different epistemologies than those of the "majority"? Given the fact that the search for theory has been called into question in majority discourse, do we want to ask similar questions of minority proposals?

In our efforts to find ways to include the voices of marginalized groups, we might expect helpful guidance from those who have argued against totalizing and universalistic theories such as those of the Enlightenment. Many radical intellectuals have been attracted to an amalgam of diverse writings, ranging from literary criticism to the social sciences, generally termed "postmodernism." These postmodernist writers, among them figures such as Foucault, Derrida, Rorty, and Lyotard, argue against the faith in a universal reason we have inherited from Enlightenment European philosophy. They reject accounts that claim to encompass all of human history: as Lyotard puts it, "Let us wage a war on totality."[1] In its place they propose a social criticism that is ad hoc, contextual, plural, and limited. A number of feminist theorists have joined in the criticism of modernity put forward by these writers. They have endorsed their claims about what can and cannot be known or said or read into/from texts.

Despite their apparent congruence with the project I am proposing, these theories, I contend, would hinder rather than help its accomplishment. Despite the postmodernists' own desire to avoid universal claims, and despite their stated opposition to such claims, some universalistic assumptions creep back into their work. Thus, postmodernism, despite its stated efforts to avoid the problems of the European modernism of the eighteenth and nineteenth centuries, at best manages to criticize these theories without putting anything in their place. For those of us who want to understand the world systematically in order to change it, postmodernist theories at their best give little guidance. (I should note that I recognize that some postmodernist theorists—Foucault, for instance—are committed to ending injustice. But this commitment is not carried through in their theories.)[2] Those of us who are not part of the ruling race, class, or gender, not a part of the minority which controls our world, need to know how it works. Why are we—in all our variousness—systematically excluded and margin-

---

1. Jean-François Lyotard, *The Postmodern Condition: A Report on Knowledge*, trans. Geoff Bennington and Brian Massumi, Theory and History of Literature, vol. 10 (Minneapolis: University of Minnesota Press, 1984), 82.

2. My criticism is that this commitment rests on what appears to be an ungrounded hope, as is evidenced by my discussion of Rorty below.

alized? What systematic changes would be required to create a more just society? At their worst, postmodernist theories merely recapitulate the effects of Enlightenment theories—theories that deny marginalized people the right to participate in defining the terms of their interaction with people in the mainstream. Thus, I contend, in broad terms, that postmodernism represents a dangerous approach for any marginalized group to adopt.

The Construction of the Colonized Other

In thinking about how to think about these issues, I found the work of Albert Memmi in *The Colonizer and the Colonized* offered a very useful structure for understanding both our situation with regard to postmodernist theorists and the situation of some postmodernist theorists themselves: those of us who have been marginalized enter the discussion from a position analogous to that which the colonized held in relation to the colonizer.[3] Most fundamentally, I want to argue that the philosophical and historical creation of a devalued Other was the necessary precondition for the creation of the transcendental rational subject outside of time and space, the subject who is the speaker in Enlightenment philosophy. Simone de Beauvoir has described the essence of the process in a quite different context: "Evil is necessary to Good, matter to idea, and darkness to light."[4] While this subject is clearest in the work of bourgeois philosophers such as Kant, one can find echoes of this mode of thought in some of Marx's claims about the proletariat as the universal subject of history.

Memmi describes the bond that creates both the colonizer and the colonized as one which destroys both parties, though in different ways. As he draws a portrait of the Other as described by the colonizer the colonized emerges as the image of everything the colonizer is not.

---

3. My language requires that I insert a qualification and clarification at this point: I will be using a "we/they" language. But while it is clear who "they" are, the "we" refers to a "we" who are not and never will be a unitary "we," a "we" artificially constructed by the totalizing, Eurocentric, masculine discourse of the Enlightenment. I do not mean to suggest that white Western women share the material situation of colonized peoples but rather that we share similar positions in the ideology of the Enlightenment.

4. Simone de Beauvoir, *The Second Sex*, trans. and ed. H. M. Parshley (New York: Knopf, 1953), 74.

Every negative quality is projected onto her/him. The colonized is said to be lazy, and the colonizer becomes practically lyrical about it. Moreover, the colonized is both wicked and backward, a being who is in some important ways not fully human.[5] As Memmi describes the image of the colonized, feminist readers of de Beauvoir's *Second Sex* cannot avoid a sense of familiarity. We recognize a great deal of this description.[6]

Memmi points to several conclusions drawn about this artificially created Other. First, the Other is always seen as Not, as a lack, a void, as deficient in the valued qualities of the society, whatever those qualities may be (*CC*, 83). Second, the humanity of the Other becomes "opaque." Colonizers frequently make statements like "You never know what they think. Do they think? Or do they instead operate according to intuition?" (Feminist readers may be reminded of some of the arguments about whether women had souls, or were capable of reason, or of learning Latin.) Memmi remarks ironically that the colonized must indeed be very strange, if he remains so mysterious and opaque after years of living with the colonizer (*CC*, 85). Third, the Others are not seen as fellow individual members of the human community, but rather as part of a chaotic, disorganized, and anonymous collectivity. They carry, Memmi states, "the mark of the plural" (*CC*, 85). In more colloquial terms, they all look alike.

I am not claiming that women are a unitary group, or that Western white women have the same experiences as women or men of color, or as colonized peoples. Rather, I am pointing to a way of looking at the world characteristic of the dominant white, male, Eurocentric ruling class, a way of dividing up the world that puts an omnipotent subject at the center and constructs marginal Others as sets of negative qualities.

What is left of the Other after this effort to dehumanize her or him? S/he is pushed toward becoming an object. "As an end, in the colonizer's supreme ambition, [the Other] should exist only as a function of the needs of the colonizer, i.e., be transformed into a pure colonized. An object for himself as well as for the colonizer"(*CC*, 86). The colonized ceases to be a subject of history, and becomes only what the colonizer is not. After having shut the colonized out of history and having

---

5. Albert Memmi, *The Colonizer and the Colonized* (Boston: Beacon Press, 1967), 82; all further references to this work, abbreviated as *CC*, will appear in the text.

6. For example. compare de Beauvoir's statement that "at the moment when man asserts himself as subject and free being, the idea of the Other arises" (*The Second Sex*, 73).

forbidden him all development, the colonizer asserts his fundamental immobility (*CC*, 92, 95, 113). Confronted with this image as it is imposed by every institution and in every human contact, the colonized cannot be indifferent to it. Its accusations worry the colonized even more because s/he admires and fears the powerful colonizing accuser.

We can expand our understanding of the way this process works by looking briefly at Edward W. Said's account of the European construction of the Orient. Said makes the political dimensions of this ideological move very clear: he describes the creation of the Orient as an outgrowth of a will to power. "Orientalism," he states, "is a Western style for dominating, restructuring, and having authority over the Orient."[7] (Interestingly enough, in the construction of these power relations, the orient is often feminized.) There is, however, out of this same process, the creation of the opposite of the colonized, the opposite of the Oriental, the opposite of woman, the creation of a being who sees himself (I use the masculine pronoun here purposely) as located at the center and possessed of all the qualities valued in his society. Memmi describes this process eloquently:

> The colonialist stresses those things that keep him separate rather than emphasizing that which might contribute to the foundation of a joint community. In those differences, the colonized is always degraded and the colonialist finds justification for rejecting his subjectivity. But perhaps the most important thing is that once the behavioral feature of historical or geographical factor which characterizes the colonialist and contrasts him with the colonized has been isolated, this gap must be kept from being filled. The colonialist removes the factor from history, time, and therefore possibly evolution. What is actually a sociological point becomes labeled as being biological or, preferably, metaphysical. It is attached to the colonized's basic nature. Immediately the colonial relationship between colonized and colonizer, founded on the essential outlook of the two protoganists, becomes a definitive category. It is what it is because they are what they are, and neither one nor the other will ever change. (*CC*, 71-72)

---

7. Edward W. Said, *Orientalism* (New York: Random House, 1978). Interestingly enough, one can find this same will to power in the emerging European science developing during the same period.

Said points to something very similar. He argues that "European culture gained in strength and identity by setting itself off against the orient as a sort of surrogate and even underground self."[8] Orientalism is part of the European identity that defines "us" vs. the non-Europeans. To go further, the studied object becomes another being in relation to whom the studying subject becomes transcendent. Why? Because, unlike the oriental, the European observer is a true human being.[9]

But what does all this have to do with theory and the search for an adequate epistemology? I want to suggest that in each of these cases—and the examples could be multiplied—what we see is the construction of the social relations, the power relations, which form the basis of the transcendent subject of Enlightenment theories—he (and I mean he) who theorizes. Put slightly differently, the political and social as well as the ideological/intellectual creation of the devalued Other was *at the same time* the creation of the universalizing and totalizing voice postmodernists denounce as the voice of Theory.

These social relations and the totalizing voice they constitute are incorporated as well in the rules of formal logic. As Nancy Jay points out, the rules of logic we have chosen to inherit from Aristotle must be seen as principles of order. She calls attention to the principle of identity (If anything is A, it is A), the principle of contradiction (Nothing can be both A and not-A), and the principle of the excluded middle (Anything and everything must be either A or not-A). "These principles are not representative of the empirical world; they are principles of *order*. In the empirical world," she notes, "almost everything is in a process of transition: growing, decaying, ice turning to water and vice versa."[10]

These logical principles of order underlie the pattern of thought I have been describing, a pattern which divides the world into A and not-A. The not-A side is regularly associated with disorder, irrationality, chance, error, impurity; indeed, not-A is *necessarily* impure, a catchall, negative category. The clue to this division of categories, Jay notes, is the presence of only one positive term. Thus, men/women/children is one form of categorizing the world, while men/women-and-children is

<hr/>

8. Ibid., 3; and see 8.
9. Ibid., 97, 108; see also the reference to the "tyrannical observer," 310.
10. Nancy Jay, "Gender and Dichotomy," *Feminist Studies* 7, no. 1 (Spring 1981); 42.

quite another in implication.[11] Radical dichotomy, then, functions to maintain a certain kind of order. The questions posed eloquently in the literature I have been examining are these: In whose interest is it to preserve dichotomies? Who experiences change as disorder?[12] The central point I want to make is that the creation of the Other is simultaneously the creation of the transcendent and omnipotent theorizer who can persuade himself that he exists outside time and space and power relations.

The social relations which express and form a material base for these theoretical notions have been rejected on a world scale over the last several decades. Decolonization struggles, movements of young people, women's movements, racial liberation movements—all these represent the diverse and disorderly Others beginning to speak and beginning to chip away at the social and political power of the Theorizer. These movements have two fundamental intellectual/theoretical tasks—one of critique and one of construction. We who have not been allowed to be subjects of history, who have not been allowed to make our history, are beginning to reclaim our pasts and remake our futures on our own terms.

One of our first tasks is the construction of the subjectivities of the Other, subjectivities which will be both multiple and specific. Nationalism and separatism are important features of this phase of construction. Bernice Reagon (civil rights movement activist, feminist, singer with Sweet Honey in the Rock, and social historian with the Smithsonian) describes the process and its problems eloquently:

> [Sometimes] it gets too hard to stay out in that society all the time. And that's when you find a place, and you try to bar the door and check all the people who come in. You come together to see what you can do about shouldering up all of your energies so that you and your kind can survive . . . . That space should be a nurturing space where you sift out what people are saying about you and decide who you really are. And you take the time to try to construct within yourself and within your community who you would be if you were running society . . . . [This is] nurturing, but it is also nationalism. At a certain stage, nationalism is crucial to a

---

11. Ibid., 47.
12. This is Jay's question; see Ibid., 53.

people if you are ever going to impact as a group in your own interest.[13]

Somehow it seems highly suspicious that it is at this moment in history, when so many groups are engaged in "nationalisms" which involve redefinitions of the marginalized Others, that doubt arises in the academy about the nature of the "subject," about the possibilities for a general theory which can describe the world, about historical "progress." Why is it, exactly at the moment when so many of us who have been silenced begin to demand the right to name ourselves, to act as subjects rather than objects of history, that just then the concept of subjecthood becomes "problematic"? Just when we are forming our own theories about the world, uncertainty emerges about whether the world can be adequately theorized? Just when we are talking about the changes we want, ideas of progress and the possibility of "meaningfully" organizing human society become suspect? And why is it only now that critiques are made of the will to power inherent in the effort to create theory? I contend that these intellectual moves are no accident (but no conspiracy either). They represent the transcendental voice of the Enlightenment attempting to come to grips with the social and historical changes of the middle to late twentieth century. However, the particular forms its efforts have taken indicate a fundamental failure of imagination and reflect the imprisonment of dominant modes of thought within Enlightenment paradigms and values. Let us examine more closely one effort to describe the tasks we are advised to engage in if we adopt the postmodernist project.

Richard Rorty's Conversational Alternative

Richard Rorty's contribution to postmodernist work deserves attention as a model for an account of what theorists might do. Fundamentally, Rorty is arguing against the epistemology of the Enlightenment—something he terms simply "Epistemology." (I read this move as a statement that there always has been only one way of knowing, such that to question this way of knowing is to question the project of knowing itself.)

---

13. Bernice Reagon, "Coalition Politics: Turning the Century," in *Home Girls*, ed. Barbara Smith (New York: Kitchen Table/Women of Color Press, 1983), 357.

Rorty argues that the desire for a theory of knowledge is simply a desire for constraint. Moreover, it reflects the "overconfidence of theory." We must instead "free ourselves from the notion that philosophy must center around the "discovery of a permanent framework for inquiry."[14] Rather than view even normal science as the search for objective truth, he argues that we should see it as one discourse among many. One must reject the "tacit and self-confident commitment to the search for objective truth on the subject in question"; it was simply an error of systematic philosophy to think that such questions could be answered by some new transcendental and singular discourse (382, 383). In addition, he argues against the notion of epistemology that assumes all contributions to a discourse are commensurable (one might substitute the notion of mutual intelligibility here). Rather, he argues for a recognition of cacaphony and disorder. Epistemology told us that to be rational, i.e., to be fully human, we must find agreement. But this assumes that such a common ground exists (316). Rorty is confident, however, that it does not. Thus, hermeneutics, his preferred mode of philosophizing, will redefine rationality as a willingness to abstain from epistemology, that is, to abstain from the idea that to be rational is to find the common set of terms into which all contributions should be translated if agreement is to become possible (318).

Hermeneutics is not to be a successor subject to Epistemology; rather, it represents the hope that the cultural space left by the demise of Epistemology will not be filled (315). Thus, it represents the abandoning of certain values—rationality, disinterestedness, the possibility of floating free of educational and institutional patterns of the day (331).

Accordingly, we must give up the notion that there is a human essence. We must give up the idea of a search for the truth and simply try to redescribe ourselves yet again. This entails, as part of the project, giving up the idea that any vocabulary has a privileged attachment to "reality," and accepting the contention that sentences are more strongly related to other sentences than they are to "truth." That is, we must abandon the notion of correspondence to reality in the case of sentences as well as ideas. We must see sentences as "connected with other sentences rather than with the world" (357, 358, 361, 363, 372).

---

14. Richard Rorty, *Philosophy and the Mirror of Nature* (Princeton: Princeton University Press, 1979), 315, 381, 380; all further references to this work will appear in the text.

In addition, Rorty argues that philosophers should give up the task of being constructive. Instead, they should take up an oppositional and reactive stance, should be skeptical about systematic philosophy (366).

Rorty, then, is proposing an interesting but dangerous mix of ideas. He is attacking the transcendental knower who exists outside time and space and has privileged access to true knowledge. Those of us who were marginalized by our very act of speaking have attacked this same figure of the transcendental knower—whether we were conscious of it or not. Rorty, thus, would seem to be involved in a project which is friendly to those we have been involved in.

To get a better sense, however, of whether the approach he advocates can be of use to us, let us examine the positive content of what he is suggesting. How would a hermeneutic approach work? Rorty proposes the notion of culture as a conversation rather than as a structure erected upon foundations (319). The conversation is to be about what he terms "edification"—"finding new, better, more interesting, more fruitful ways of speaking." The point of doing philosophy, then, should be seen as continuing a conversation that is developing a program rather than discovering truth. We must avoid the self-deception that comes from believing that we know ourselves by knowing a set of objective facts, and we must likewise avoid the notion that we are really different from "either inkwells or atoms" (373). Inquiry, then, should proceed on the ground that persons in conversation are simply those whose paths through life have fallen together, united by civility rather than by a common goal, much less common ground (318).

Using an analogy to Thomas Kuhn's distinction between normal and revolutionary science, Rorty proposes a distinction between normal and "abnormal" discourse. Normal science is the practice of solving problems against the background of a consensus about what counts as a good explanation and about what it would take for a problem to be solved. Revolutionary science, in contrast, represents the introduction of a new paradigm indicating what is to count as a good explanation. By analogy, abnormal discourse is what happens when someone joins the conversation who is ignorant of its "normal" conventions—or who chooses to set them aside. What results could be nonsense, or it could be intellectual revolution (320-21). (One wonders how one could tell the difference in Rorty's system.) Hermeneutics, then, is the study of these abnormal discourses through the creation of another abnormal discourse. As such, it must be reactive and must dread the possibility of being institutionalized. "Great edifying philosophers are reactive and offer satires, parodies, and aphorisms. They know their work loses its point when the period they were reacting against is over. They are intentionally peripheral" (353, 369).

Rorty argues that edifying philosophers should avoid having views, should "decry the notion of having a view while avoiding having a view about having views" (371). The proper image is one of conversational partners rather than of individuals holding views on subjects of common concern. Moreover, the edifying philosopher wants to use the conversation to expand the community—that is, to see knowledge connected with solidarity rather than with power. One should, he argues, operate from an "ungroundable but vital sense of human solidarity," an aspiration based on moral hope rather than on claims about what we may know of the world.[15]

This, then, is his critique of the transcendental subject and his alternative project for philosophy. It would seem to be a project that might provide the underpinnings for an account of the world that would allow all conversational partners to participate. Yet, I believe that this form of argument is, in fact, dangerous to those of us who have been marginalized. It cannot accomplish the tasks we have in front of us. Indeed, despite its appearance of allowing space for many voices in the conversation, the effect of ideas like this is to smuggle back in the authority of the transcendental ego.

I have several problems with Rorty's argument. There are a number of internal inconsistencies in his proposal—more interesting to me as a philosopher than for our purposes here. But for our immediate purposes, my objections to this methodology as something of value to minority discourse rest on several points. First, Rorty ignores power relations: we are not all in a position now to participate as equals in a conversation. Many of us have not yet even had a chance to name ourselves and to theorize our situations. Second, Rorty sets out to be reactive, unconstructive, and peripheral. But those of us who have been marginalized are all too familiar with the powerlessness that limits our options to these stances. Rorty is, in a sense, choosing to be

---

15. Rorty, *Consequences of Pragmatism (Essays: 1972-1980)* (Minneapolis: University of Minnesota Press, 1982), 208.

marginal—(a good thing for someone at the center but not for those at the margins who have of necessity been reactive, unconstructive and peripheral).

Third, and related, his substitution of "abnormal discourse" for Kuhn's concept of "revolutionary science" represents an important shift: it is a retreat from the idea that we are seeing historical agency and action. Fourth, Rorty chooses to defend the values of the Enlightenment on the basis that they have produced good outcomes. Yet, these values cannot be defended without again dragging in the omnipotent subject created by the Enlightenment.

Let us take up these objections in turn. Rorty invites us to join his conversation, but he has, in a style reminiscent of the transcendental subject he inveighs against, set the rules of the discussion in a way inappropriate to those of us who have been marginalized. Moreover, the notion of a conversation implies that we are all equally able to participate, that we are not marked by culturally and historically constructed difference. One is reminded of Bell Hooks's point about racism in feminist writing: "The force that allows white authors to make no reference to racial identity in their books about 'women' that are in actuality about white women is the same one that would compel any author writing exclusively on black women to refer explicitly to their racial identity." She continues that "it is the dominant race that reserves for itself the luxury of dismissing racial identity while the oppressed race is made daily aware of their racial identity. It is the dominant race that can make it seem that their experience is representative."[16]

From having been constructed as void and lack, and from having been forbidden to speak, we are now expected to join in equal conversation with someone who has just realized that philosophy has been overconfident. Rorty, with other postmodernists, is the inheritor of the disembodied, transcendent voice of reason. It is certainly a good thing for him to abandon the project of defining the world for everyone and instead to propose a conversation. But it will not work: conversation implies the presence of subjects—contingent, historically limited subjects, to be sure, but subjects who can speak. The silenced Others, however, are now involved in theorizing the world from their own perspective and in making this naming "stick." Conversation on Rorty's

---

16. Bell Hooks, *Ain't I a Woman: Black Women and Feminism* (Boston: South End Press, 1982), 138.

terms would only reinforce previous power relations.

Let us turn to Rorty's second prescription for philosophy: the effort to be reactive, peripheral. Here, too, this is a good strategy for the inheritor of the voice of the transcendental ego. Becoming marginal is an important strategy for those of us who are privileged by race, class, gender, or heterosexuality. It is a strategy we should undertake. But to the extent that we have been constituted as Other, it is important to insist as well on a vision of the world in which we are at the center rather than at the periphery. The "center" will obviously look different when occupied by women and men of color and white women than it does now, when occupied by white men of a certain class background. Indeed, given our diversity, it may cease to look like a center at all. But, as for being peripheral, we've done that for far too long. Let those who have put themselves at the center practice moving to the margins now.

Third, and related to this, Rorty proposes the idea of abnormal discourse as a modification of Kuhn's normal vs. revolutionary science. While he intends this to counter the hegemonic, normal discourse of the supra-historical subject, the substitution of "abnormal" for "revolutionary" is not innocent. Revolutionary science, or the more precise parallel, revolutionary discourse, would not remain peripheral but rather would transform normal discourse. This, in fact, is a much more appropriate formulation of our task. We should undertake the construction of revolutionary discourses which would not remain "abnormal" or peripheral but would have the effect of transforming "normal" discourse.

Fourth, Rorty chooses to defend the values of the Enlightenment on the ground that they have produced good outcomes. Thus he demonstrates his commitment to the project of the Enlightenment—in other words, he brings the project of the Enlightenment in through the back door while claiming to get rid of it. These values have a homogenizing effect: they produce a homogeneous equality which fails to recognize the specificity of different communities.

The overall result is that the Others constructed by the Enlightenment are once again silenced, but this time in the name of a rejection of the methods, if not the values, of the Enlightenment. To return to the terms that Memmi uses, Rorty perhaps can be described not so much as the colonizer who consents, as the citizen of the metropolis who says, "But we gave them their independence—Why do they keep complaining about neocolonialism? Why do they keep bringing up questions of power?"

Foucault's Refusal

I believe similar cases could be made about other postmodernist figures. Foucault represents another figure from Memmi's landscape, a figure who also fails to provide an epistemology which is usable for the task of revolutionizing, creating, and constructing. Foucault is more like Memmi's colonizer who refuses, and thus exists in a painful ambiguity.[17]

Memmi states that as a Jewish Tunisian he knew the colonizer as well as the colonized and so "understood only too well (the difficulty of the colonizer who refuses—) their inevitable ambiguity and the resulting isolation: more serious still, their inability to act" (*CC*, xiv-xv). He notes that it is difficult to escape from a concrete situation and to refuse its ideology while continuing to live in the midst of the concrete relations of a culture. The colonizer who attempts it is a traitor, but he is still not the colonized (*CC*, 20-21). The political ineffectiveness of the Leftist colonizer comes from the nature of his position in the colony. Has any one, Memmi asks, ever seen a serious political demand that did not rest on concrete supports of people, or money, or force. The colonizer who refuses to become a part of his group of fellow citizens faces the difficult political question of who he might be (*CC*, 41).

This lack of certainty and power infuses Foucault's work. He is clearly rejecting any form of totalizing discourse: reason, he argues, must be seen as born from chaos, truth as simply an error hardened into unalterable form in the long process of history. He argues for a glance that disperses and shatters the unity of man's being through which he sought to extend his sovereignty.[18] That is, Foucault appears to endorse a rejection of modernity. Moreover, he has engaged in social activism around prisons. His sympathies are obviously with those over whom power is exercised, and he suggests that many struggles can be seen as linked to the revolutionary working class movement. In addition, his empirical critiques in works such as *Discipline and Punish* powerfully unmask coercive power. Yet they do so, on the one hand,

---

17. My general remarks here are taken from a much more lengthy and nuanced chapter on Foucault in my forthcoming *Post-Modernism and Political Change*.

18. These are arguments he makes in "Nietzsche, Genealogy, History," in *Language, Counter-Memory, Practice*, ed. Donald F. Bouchard (Ithaca: Cornell University Press, 1977).

by making use of the values of humanism that he claims to be rejecting: as Nancy Fraser points out, the project gets its political force from the "reader's familiarity with an commitment to modern ideals of autonomy, dignity, and human rights."[19] Moreover, Foucault explicitly attempts to limit the power of his critique by arguing that unmasking power can have only destabilizing rather than transformatory effects.[20]

But the sense of powerlessness and the isolation of the colonial intellectual resurfaces again and again. Thus, Foucault argues: "Humanity does not gradually progress from combat to combat until it arrives at universal reciprocity, where the rule of law finally replaces warfare; humanity installs each of its violences in a system of rules and thus proceeds from domination to domination."[21] Moreover, Foucault sees intellectuals as working only alongside, rather than with, those who struggle for power, working locally and regionally. Finally, in opposition to modernity, he calls for a history that is parodic, dissociative, and satirical, and thus a history that is directed against reality, identity, and truth. History, then, is not knowledge but countermemory and, thus, a transformation of history. Genealogy, the form of history he calls for, accordingly, should be seen as a form of concerted carnival.[22]

We must view this as a positive step, just as many of Rorty's oppositions to modernity must be considered as important and useful modifications of a paradigm. In the end, though, Foucault appears to endorse a one-sided wholesale rejection of modernity as such, and to do so without a conception of what is to replace it. Moreover, some have argued persuasively that, because Foucault refuses both the ground of foundationalism and the "ungrounded hope" endorsed by Rorty, he stands on no ground at all, and thus fails to give any reasons for resistance. Indeed, he suggests that if our resistance succeeded we would simply be changing one discursive identity for another, and in the

---

19. Nancy Fraser, "Foucault's Body Language: A Post-Humanist Political Rhetoric?" *Salmagundi*, no. 61 (Fall 1983): 59.

20. See Charles Taylor, "Foucault on Freedom and Truth," *Political Theory* 12, no. 2 (May 1984): 175-76.

21. Michael Foucault, "Nietzche, Genealogy, History," *Language, Counter-Memory, Practice: Selected Essays and Interviews*, ed. Donald F. Bouchard, trans. Bouchard and Sherry Simon (Ithaca, N.Y.: Cornell University Press, 1977) 151.

22. Ibid. 160-61.

process would create new oppressions.[23]

But precisely the most pressing question for those of us committed to social change is what we can replace modernism with. This is crucial for those of us who have been marginalized. The so-called "majority" can probably perform the greatest possible political service by resisting and by refusing the overconfidence of the past. But the message we get from them is either that we should abandon the project of modernity and substitute a conversation or that we should simply take up a posture of resistance as the only strategy open to us. However, if we are not to abandon the project of creating a new and more just society, neither of these options will work for us.

Toward Minority Theories

Those of us who have been marginalized by the transcendental voice of universalizing Theory need to do something other than ignore power relations, as Rorty does, or resist them, as figures such as Foucault and Lyotard suggest. We need to transform them—and to do so, we need a revised and reconstructed theory, indebted to Marx, among others, and incorporating several important features.

First, rather than getting rid of subjectivity or notions of the subject, we need to engage in the historical and political and theoretical process of constituting ourselves as subjects as well as objects of history. We need to recognize that we can be the makers of history and not just the objects of those who have made history until now. Our nonbeing was the condition of being of the "majority," the center, the taken-for-granted ability of one small segment of the population to speak for all; our various efforts to constitute ourselves as subjects (through struggles for colonial independence, struggles for racial and sexual liberation, etc.) were fundamental to creating the preconditions for the current questioning of universalistic claims. But, I believe, we need to sort out who we really are. Put differently, we need to dissolve the false "we" I have been using into its real multiplicity and variety and, out of this concrete multiplicity, build an account of the world as seen from the margins, an account which can transform these margins into

---

23. See Gad Horowitz, "The Foucaultian Impasse: No Sex, No Self, No Revolution," *Political Theory* 15, no. 1 (February 1987): 63-64.

centers. The point is to develop an account of the world which treats our perspectives not as subjugated knowledges, but as primary.

It may be objected that I am calling for the construction of another totalizing and falsely universal discourse. But that is to be imprisoned by the alternatives posed by Enlightenment thought and postmodernism: either one must adopt the perspective of the transcendental and disembodied voice of Reason, or one must abandon the goal of accurate and systematic knowledge of the world. Other possibilities exist and must be (perhaps can only be) developed by hitherto marginalized voices. Moreover, our history of marginalization will work against creating such a totalizing discourse. This is not to argue that oppression creates "better" people; on the contrary, the experience of domination and marginalization leaves many scars. Rather it is to note that marginalized groups are far less likely to mistake themselves for the universal "man." We know that we are not the universal man who can assume his experience of the world is the experience of all. But if we will not make the mistake of assuming our experience of the world is the experience of all, we still need to name and describe our diverse experiences. What are our commonalities? What are our differences? How can we transform our imposed Otherness into a self-defined speccificity?[24]

Second, we must do our thinking on an epistemological base that indicates that knowledge is possible—not just conversation or a discourse on how it is that power relations work. Conversation as a goal is fine; understanding how power works in oppressive societies is important: but if we are to construct a new society, we need to be assured that some systematic knowledge about our world and ourselves is possible. Those who are (simply) critical of modernity can afford to call into question whether they ever really knew the world. But we will not have the confidence to act if we believe that we do not know the world. They are, in fact, right that they have not known the world as it is rather than as they wished and needed it to be: they created their world not only in their own image but in the image of their fantasies. To create the world in our various images, we need to understand how it works.

Third, we need an epistemology that recognizes that our practical

---

24. See my "Difference and Domination in the Women's Movement: The Dialectic of Theory and Practice," in *Class, Race, and Sex: the Dynamics of Control*, ed. Amy Swerdlow and Hanna Lessinger (Boston: G. K. Hall, 1983).

daily activity contains an understanding of the world—subjugated, perhaps, but present. Here I am reaffirming Gramsci's argument that all men are intellectuals and that all of us have an epistemology. The point, then, for "minority" theories is to "read out" the epistemologies in our various practices. I have argued elsewhere for a "standpoint" epistemology—an account of the world with great similarities to Marx's fundamental stance.[25] While I would modify some of what I argued there, I would still insist that we must not give up the claim that material life (class position in Marxist theory) not only structures but sets limits on the understanding of social relations and that, in systems of domination, the vision available to the rulers both will be partial and will reverse the real order of things.

Fourth, our epistemology needs to recognize the difficulty of creating alternatives. The ruling class, race, and gender actively structures and envisions the world in a way that forms the material-social relations in which all parties are forced to participate; their vision, therefore, cannot be dismissed as simply false or misguided. In consequence, oppressed groups must struggle for their own vision, which will require both theorizing and the education that can come only from committed political struggle to change those material and social relations.

Fifth, as an engaged vision, the understanding of the oppressed exposes the relations among people as inhuman, and thus there is a call to political action. That is, the critique is not one that leads to a turning away from engagement but rather one that is a call for change and participation in altering power relations.

The critical steps are, first, using what we know about our lives as a basis for critique of the dominant culture and, second, creating alternatives. When the various "minority" experiences have been described, and when the significance of these experiences as a ground for critique of the dominant institutions and ideologies of society is better recognized, we will have at least the tools with which to begin to construct an account of the world sensitive to the realities of race and gender, as well as class. To paraphrase Marx, the point is to change the world, not simply to redescribe ourselves or reinterpret the world yet again.

---

25. I have made an extended case for such an epistemology in *Money, Sex, and Power: Toward a Feminist Historical Materialism* (New York: Longman, 1983; Boston: Northeastern University Press, 1984), ch. 10.

The Race for Theory

Barbara Christian

I have seized this occasion to break the silence among those of us, critics, as we are now called, who have been intimidated, devalued by what I call the race for theory. I have become convinced that there has been a takeover in the literary world by Western philosophers from the old literary élite, the neutral humanists. Philosphers have been able to effect such a takeover because so much of the literature of the West has become pallid, laden with despair, self-indulgent, and disconnected. The New Philosophers, eager to understand a world that is today fast escaping their political control, have redefined literature so that the distinctions implied by that term, that is, the distinctions between everything written and those things written to evoke feeling as well as to express thought, have been blurred. They have changed literary critical language to suit their own purposes as philosophers, and they have reinvented the meaning of theory.

My first response to this realization was to ignore it. Perhaps, in spite of the egocentrism of this trend, some good might come of it. I had, I felt, more pressing and interesting things to do, such as reading and studying the history and literature of black women, a history that had been totally ignored, a contemporary literature bursting with originality, passion, insight, and beauty. But unfortunately it is difficult to ignore this new takeover, since theory has become a commodity which helps determine whether we are hired or promoted in academic institutions — worse, whether we are heard at all. Due to this new orientation, works (a word which evokes labor) have become texts. Critics are no longer concerned with literature, but with other critics' texts, for the critic yearning for attention has displaced the writer and has conceived of himself as the center. Interestingly in the first part of this century, at least in England and America, the critic was usually also a writer of poetry, plays, or novels. But today, as a new generation of professionals develops, he or she is increasingly an academic. Activities such as teaching or writing one's response to specific works of literature have, among this group, become subordinated to one primary thrust, that moment when one creates a theory, thus fixing a constellation of ideas for a time at least, a fixing which no doubt will be replaced in another month or so by somebody else's competing theory as the race accelerates. Perhaps because those who have effected the takeover have the power (although they deny it) first of all to be published, and thereby to determine the ideas which are deemed valuable, some of our most daring and potentially radical critics (and by *our* I mean black, women, third world) have been influenced, even coopted, into speaking a language and defining their discussion in terms alien to and opposed to our needs and orientation. At least so far, the creative writers I study have resisted this language.

For people of color have always theorized — but in forms quite different from the Western form of abstract logic. And I am inclined to say that our theorizing (and I intentionally use the verb rather than the noun) is often in narrative forms, in the stories we create, in riddles and proverbs, in the play with language, since dynamic rather than fixed ideas seem more to our liking. How else have we managed to survive with such spiritedness the assault on our bodies, social institutions, countries, our very humanity? And women, at least the women I grew up around, continuously speculated about the nature of life through pithy language that unmasked the power relations of their world. It is this language, and the grace and pleasure with which they played with it, that I find celebrated, refined, critiqued in the works of writers like Morrison and Walker. My folk, in other words, have always been a race for theory — though more in the form of the hieroglyph, a written figure which is both sensual and abstract, both beautiful and communicative. In my own work I try to illuminate and explain these hieroglyphs, which is, I think, an activity quite different from the creating of the hieroglyphs themselves. As the Buddhists would say, the finger pointing at the moon is not the moon.

In this discussion, however, I am more concerned with the issue raised by my first use of the term, *the race for theory*, in relation to its academic hegemony, and possibly of its inappropriateness to the energetic emerging literatures in the world today. The pervasiveness of this academic hegemony is an issue continually spoken about — but usually in hidden groups, lest we, who are disturbed by it, appear ignorant to the reigning academic élite. Among the folk who speak in muted tones are people of color, feminists, radical critics, creative writers, who have struggled for much longer than a decade to make their voices, their various voices, heard, and for whom literature is not an occasion for discourse among critics but is necessary nourishment for their people and one way by which they come to understand their lives better. Cliched though this may be, it bears, I think, repeating here.

The race for theory, with its linguistic jargon, its emphasis on quoting its prophets, its tendency towards "Biblical" exegesis, its refusal even to mention specific works of creative writers, far less contemporary ones, its preoccupations with mechanical analyses of language, graphs, algebraic equations, its gross generalizations about culture, has silenced many of us to the extent that some of us feel we can no longer discuss our own literature, while others have developed intense writing blocks and are puzzled by the incomprehensibility of the language set adrift in literary circles. There have been, in the last year, any number of occasions on which I had to convince literary critics who have pioneered entire new ares of critical inquiry that they did have something to say. Some of us are continually harassed to invent wholesale theories regardless of the complexity of the literature we study. I, for one, am tired of being asked to produce a black feminist literary theory as if I were a mechanical man. For I believe such theory is prescriptive — it ought to have some relationship to practice. Since I can count on one hand the number of people attempting to be black feminist literary critics in the world today, I consider it presumptuous of me to invent a theory of how we *ought* to read. Instead, I think we need to read the works of our writers in our various ways and remain open to the intricacies of the intersection of language, class, race, and gender in the literature. And it would help if we share our process, that is, our practice, as much as possible since, finally, our work *is* a collective endeavor.

The insidious quality of this race for theory is symbolized for me by the very name of this special issue — Minority Discourse — a label which is borrowed from the reigning theory of the day and is untrue to the literatures being produced by our writers, for many of our literatures (certainly Afro-American literature) are central, not minor, and by the titles of many of the articles, which illuminate language as an assault on the other, rather than as possible communication, and play with, or even affirmation of another. I have used the passive voice in my last sentence construction, contrary to the rules of Black English, which like all languages has a particular value system, since I have not placed responsibility on any particular person or group. But that is precisely because this new ideology has become so prevalent among us that it behaves like so many of the other ideologies with which we have had go contend. It appears to have neither head nor center. At the least, though, we can say that the terms "minority" and "discourse" are located firmly in a Western dualistic or "binary" frame which sees the rest of the world as minor, and tries to convince the rest of the world that it *is* major, usually through force and then through language, even as it claims many of the ideas that we, its "historical" other, have known and spoken about for so long. For many of us have never conceived of ourselves only as somebody's *other*.

Let me not give the impression that by objecting to the race for theory I ally myself with or agree with the neutral humanists who see literature as pure expression and will not admit to the obvious control of its production, value, and distribution by those who have power, who deny, in other words, that literature is, of necessity, political. I am studying an entire body of literature that has been denigrated for centuries by such terms as *political*. For an entire century Afro-American writers, from Charles Chestnutt in the nineteenth century through Richard Wright in the 1930s, Imamu Baraka in the 1960s, Alice Walker in the 1970s, have protested the literary hierarchy of dominance which declares when literature is literature, when literature is great, depending on what it thinks is to its advantage. The Black Arts Movement of the 1960s, out of which Black Studies, the Feminist Literary Movement of the 1970s, and Women's Studies grew, articulated precisely those issues, which came *not* from the declarations of the New Western philosophers but from these groups' reflections on their own lives. That Western scholars have long believed their ideas to be universal has been strongly opposed by many such groups. Some of my colleagues do not see black critical writers of previous decades as eloquent enough.

Clearly they have not read Wright's "Blueprint for Negro Writing," Ellison's *Shadow and Act*, Chesnutt's resignation from being a writer, or Alice Walker's "Search for Zora Neale Hurston." There are two reasons for this general ignorance of what our writer-critics have said. One is that black writing has been generally ignored in this country. Since we, as Toni Morrison has put it, are seen as a discredited people, it is no surprise, then, that our creations are also discredited, but this is also due to the fact that until recently dominant critics in the Western World have also been creative writers who have had access to the upper middle class institutions of education and until recently our writers have decidedly been excluded from these institutions and in fact have often been opposed to them. Because of the academic world's general ignorance about the literature of black people and of women, whose work too has been discredited, it is not surprising that so many of our critics think that the position arguing that literature is political begins with these New Philosophers. Unfortunately, many of our young critics do not investigate the reasons *why* that statement — literature is political — is now acceptable when before it was not; nor do we look to our own antecedents for the sophisticated arguments upon which we can build in order to change the tendency of any established Western idea to become hegemonic.

For I feel that the new emphasis on literary critical theory is as hegemonic as the world which it attacks. I see the language it creates as one which mystifies rather than clarifies our condition, making it possible for a few people who know that particular language to control the critical scene — that language surfaced, interestingly enough, just when the literature of peoples of color, of black women, of Latin Americans, of Africans began to move to "the center." Such words as *center* and *periphery* are themselves instructive. *Discourse, canon, texts*, words as latinate as the tradition from which they come, are quite familiar to me. Because I went to a Catholic Mission school in the West Indies I must confess that I cannot hear the word "canon" without smelling incense, that the word "text" immediately brings back agonizing memories of Biblical exegesis, that "discourse" reeks for me of metaphysics forced down my throat in those courses that traced *world* philosophy from Aristotle through Thomas Aquinas to Heidegger. "Periphery" too is a word I heard throughout my childhood, for if anything was seen as being at the periphery, it was those small Caribbean islands which had neither land mass nor military power. Still I noted how intensely important this periphery was, for U.S. troups were continually invading one island or another if any change in political control even seemed to be occurring. As I lived among folk for whom language was an absolutely necessary way of validating our existence, I was told that the minds of the world lived only in the small continent of Europe. The metaphysical language of the New Philosophy, then, I must admit, is repulsive to me and is one reason why I raced from philosphy to literature, since the latter seemed to me to have the possibilities of rendering the world as large and as complicated as I experienced it, as sensual as I knew it was. In literature I sensed the possibility of the integration of feeling/knowledge, rather than the split between the abstract and the emotional in which Western philosophy inevitably indulged.

Now I am being told that philosophers are the ones who write literature, that authors are dead, irrelevant, mere vessels through which their narratives ooze, that they do not work nor have they the faintest idea what they are doing; rather they produce texts as disembodied as the angels. I am frankly antonished that scholars who call themselves Marxists or post-Marxists could seriously use such metaphysical language even as they attempt to deconstruct the philosophical tradition from which their language comes. And as a student of literature, I am appalled by the sheer ugliness of the language, its lack of clarity, its unnecessarily complicated sentence constructions, its lack of pleasurableness, its alienating quality. It is the kind of writing for which composition teachers would give a freshman a resounding F.

Because I am a curious person, however, I postponed readings of black women writers I was working on and read some of the prophets of this new literary orientation. These writers did announce their dissatisfaction with some of the cornerstone ideas of their own tradition, a dissatisfaction with which I was born. But in their attempt to change the orientation of Western scholarship, they, as usual, concentrated on themselves and were not in the slightest interested in the worlds they had ignored or controlled. Again I was supposed to know *them,* while they were not at all interested in knowing *me*. Instead they sought to "deconstruct" the tradition to which they belonged even as they used the same forms, style, language of that tradition, forms which necessarily embody its values. And increasingly as I read them and saw their substitution of their philosphical writings for literary ones, I began to have the uneasy feeling that their folk were not producing any literature worth mentioning. For they always harkened back to the master-pieces of the past, again reifying the very texts they said they were deconstructing. Increasingly, as *their* way, *their* terms, *their* approaches remained central and became the means by which one defined literary critics, many of my own peers who had previously been concentrating on dealing with the other side of the equation, the reclamation and discussion of past and *present* third world literatures, were diverted into continually discussing the new literary theory.

From my point of view as a critic of contemporary Afro-American women's writing, this orientation is extremely problematic. In at-tempting to find the deep structures in the literary tradition, a major preoccupation of the new New Criticism, many of us have become ob-sessed with the nature of reading itself to the extent that we have stopped writing about literature being written today. Since I am slight-ly paranoid, it has begun to occur to me that the literature being produced *is* precisely one of the reasons why this new philosophical-literary-critical theory of relativity is so prominent. In other words, the literature of blacks, women of South America and Africa, etc., as overtly "political" literature was being preempted by a new Western concept which proclaimed that reality does not exist, that everything is relative, and that every text is silent about something — which indeed it must ne-cessarily be.

There is, of course, much to be learned from exploring how we know what we know, how we read what we read, an exploration which, of necessity, can have no end. But there also has to be a "what," and that "what," when it is even mentioned by the new philosophers, are texts of the past, primarily Western male texts, whose norms are again being transferred onto third world, female texts as theories of reading proliferate. Inevitably a hierarchy has now developed between what is called theoretical criticism and practical criticism, as mind is deemed superior to matter. I have no quarrel with those who wish to philoso-phize about how we know what we know. But I do resent the fact that this particular orientation is so privileged and has diverted so many of us from doing the first readings of the literature being written today as well as of past works about which nothing has been written. I note, for example, that there is little work done on Gloria Naylor, that most of Alice Walker's works have not been commented on — despite the rage around *The Color Purple* — that there has yet to be an in-depth study of Frances Harper, the nineteenth-century abolitionist poet and novelist.

If our emphasis on theoretical criticism continues, critics of the future may have to reclaim the writers we are now ignoring, that is, if they are even aware these artists exist.

I am particularly perturbed by the movement to exalt theory, as well, because of my own adult history. I was an active member of the Black Arts Movement of the sixties and know how dangerous theory can become. Many today may not be aware of this, but the Black Arts Movement tried to create Black Literary Theory and in doing so became prescriptive. My fear is that when Theory is not rooted in practice, it becomes prescriptive, exclusive, élitish.

An example of this prescriptiveness is the approach the Black Arts Movement took towards language. For it, blackness resided in the use of black talk which they defined as hip urban language. So that when Nikki Giovanni reviewed Paule Marshall's *Chosen Place, Timeless People*, she criticized the novel on the grounds that it was not black, for the language was too elegant, too white. Blacks, she said, did not speak that way. Having come from the West Indies where we do, some of the time, speak that way, I was amazed by the narrowness of her vision. The emphasis on *one way* to be black resulted in the works of Southern writers being seen as non-black since the black talk of Georgia does not sound like the black talk of Philadelphia. Because the ideologues, like Baraka, come from the urban centers they tended to privilege their way of speaking, thinking, writing, and to condemn other kinds of writing as not being black enough. Whole areas of the canon were assessed according to the dictum of the Black Arts Nationalist point of view, as in Addison Gayle's *The Way of the New World*, while other works were ignored because they did not fit the scheme of cultural nationalism. Older writers like Ellison and Baldwin were condemned because they saw that the intersection of Western and African influences resulted in a new Afro-American culture, a position with which many of the Black Nationalist idealogues disagreed. Writers were told that writing love poems was not being black. Further examples abound.

It is true that the Black Arts Movements resulted in a necessary and important critique both of previous Afro-American literature and of the white-established literary world. But in attempting to take over power, it, as Ishmael Reed satirizes so well in *Mumbo Jumbo*, became much like its opponent, monolithic and downright repressive.

It is this tendency towards the monolithic, monotheistic, etc., which worries me about the race for theory. Constructs like the *center* and the *periphery* reveal that tendency to want to make the world less complex by organizing it according to one principle, to fix it through an idea which is really an ideal. Many of us are particularly sensitive to monolithism since one major element of ideologies of dominance, such as sexism and racism, is to dehumanize people by stereotyping them, by denying them their variousness and complexity. Inevitably, monolithism becomes a metasystem, in which there is a controlling ideal, especially in relation to pleasure. Language as one form of pleasure is immediately restricted, and becomes heavy, abstract, prescriptive, monotonous.

Variety, multiplicity, eroticism are difficult to control. And it may very well be that these are the reasons why writers are often seen as *persona non grata* by political states, whatever form they take, since writers/artists have a tendency to refuse to give up their way of seeing the world and of playing with possibilities; in fact, their very expression relies on that insistence. Perhaps that is why creative literature, even when written by politically reactionary people, can be so freeing, for in having to embody ideas and recreate the world, writers cannot merely produce "one way."

The characteristics of the Black Arts Movement are, I am afraid, being repeated again today, certainly in the other area to which I am especially tuned. In the race for theory, feminists, eager to enter the halls of power, have attempted their own prescriptions. So often I have read books on feminist literary theory that restrict the definition of what *feminist* means and overgeneralize about so much of the world that most women as well as men are excluded. Nor seldom do feminist theorists take into account the complexity of life — that women are of many races and ethnic backgrounds with different histories and cultures and that as a rule women belong to different classes that have different concerns. Seldom do they note these distinctions, because if they did they could not articulate a theory. Often as a way of clearing themselves they do acknowledge that women of color, for example, do exist, then go on to do what they were going to do anyway, which is to invent a theory that has little relevance for us.

That tendency towards monolithism is precisely how I see the French feminist theorists. They concentrate on the female body as the means to creating a female language, since language, they say, is male and necessarily conceives of woman as other. Clearly many of them have been irritated by the theories of Lacan for whom language is phallic. But suppose there are peoples in the world whose language was invented primarily in relation to women, who after all are the ones who relate to children and teach language. Some Native American languages, for example, use female pronouns when speaking about non-gender specific activity. Who knows who, according to gender, created languages. Further, by positing the body as the source of everything French feminists return to the old myth that biology determines everything and ignore the fact that gender is a social rather than a biological construct.

I could go on critiquing the positions of French feminists who are themselves more various in their points of view than the label which is used to describe them, but that is not my point. What I am concerned about is the authority this school now has in feminist scholarship — the way it has become *authoritative discourse*, monologic, which occurs precisely because it does have access to the means of promulgating its ideas. The Black Arts Movement was able to do this for a time because of the political movements of the 1960s — so too with the French feminists who could not be inventing "theory" if a space had not been created by the Women's Movement. In both cases, both groups posited a theory that excluded many of the people who made that space possible. Hence one of the reasons for the surge of Afro-American women's writing during the 1970s and its emphasis on sexism in the black community is precisely that when the ideologues of the 1960s said *black*, they meant *black male*.

I and many of my sisters do not see the world as being so simple. And perhaps that is why we have not rushed to create abstract theories. For we know there are countless women of color, both in America and in the rest of the world to whom our singular ideas would be applied. There is, therefore, a caution we feel about pronouncing black feminist theory that might be seen as a decisive statement about Third World women. This is not to say we are not theorizing. Certainly our literature is an indication of the ways in which our theorizing, of necessity, is based on our multiplicity of experiences.

There is at least one other lesson I learned from the Black Arts Movement. One reason for its monolithic approach had to do with its desire to destroy the power which controlled black people, but it was a power which many of its ideologues wished to achieve. The nature of our context today is such that an approach which desires power singlemindedly must of necessity become like that which it wishes to destroy. Rather than wanting to change the whole model, many of us want to be at the center. It is this point of view that writers like June Jordan and Audre Lorde continually critique even as they call for empowerment, as they emphasize the fear of difference among us and our need for leaders rather than a reliance on ourselves.

For one must distinguish the desire for power from the need to become empowered — that is, seeing oneself as capable of and having the right to determine one's life. Such empowerment is partially derived from a knowledge of history. The Black Arts Movement did result in the creation of Afro-American Studies as a concept, thus giving it a place in the university where one might engage in the reclamation of Afro-American history and culture and pass it on to others. I am particularly concerned that institutions such as Black Studies and Women's Studies, fought for with such vigor and at some sacrifice, are not often seen as important by many of our black or women scholars precisely because the old hierarchy of traditional departments is seen as superior to these "marginal" groups. Yet, it is in this context that many others of us are discovering the extent of our complexity, the interrelationships of different areas of knowledge in relation to a distinctly Afro-American or female experience. Rather than having to view our world as subordinate to others, or rather than having to work as if we were hybrids, we can pursue ourselves as subjects.

My major objection to the race for theory, as some readers have probably guessed by now, really hinges on the question, "for whom are we doing what we are doing when we do literary criticism?" It is, I think, the central question today especially for the few of us who have infiltrated the academy enough to be wooed by it. The answer to that question determines what orientation we take in our work, the language we use, the purposes for which it is intended.

I can only speak for myself. But what I write and how I write is done in order to save my own life. And I mean that literally. For me literature is a way of knowing that I am not hallucinating, that whatever I feel/know *is*. It is an affirmation that sensuality is intelligence, that sensual language is language that makes sense. My response, then, is directed to those who write what I read and to those who read what I read — put concretely — to Toni Morrison and to people who read Toni Morrison (among whom I would count few academics). That number is increasing, as is the readership of Walker and Marshall. But in no way is the literature Morrison, Marshall, or Walker create supported by the academic world. Nor given the political context of our society, do I expect that to change soon. For there is no reason, given who controls these institutions, for them to be anything other than threatened by these writers.

My readings do presuppose a need, a desire among folk who like me also want to save their own lives. My concern, then, is a passionate one, for the literature of people who are not in power has always been in danger of extinction or of cooptation, not because we do not theorize, but because what we can even imagine, far less who we can reach, is constantly limited by societal structures. For me, literary criticism is promotion as well as understanding, a response to the writer to whom there is often no response, to folk who need the writing as much as they need anything. I know, from literary history, that writing disappears unless there is a response to it. Because I write about writers who are now writing, I hope to help ensure that their tradition has continuity and survives.

So my "method," to use a new "lit. crit." word, is not fixed but relates to what I read and to the historical context of the writers I read *and* to the many critical activities in which I am engaged, which may or may not involve writing. It is a learning from the language of creative writers, which is one of surprise, so that I might discover what language I might use. For my language is very much based on what I read and how it affects me, that is, on the surprise that comes from reading something that compels you to read differently, as I believe literature does. I, therefore, have no set method, another prerequisite of the new theory, since for me every work suggests a new approach. As risky as that might seem, it is, I believe, what intelligence means — a tuned sensitivity to that which is alive and therefore cannot be known until it is known. Audre Lorde puts it in a far more succinct and sensual way in her essay "Poetry is not a Luxury":

> As they become known to and accepted by us, our feelings and the honest exploration of them become sanctuaries and spawning grounds for the most radical and daring of ideas. They become a safe-house for that difference so necessary to change and the conceptualization of any meaningful action. Right now, I could name at least ten ideas I would have found intolerable or incomprehensible and frightening, except as they came after dreams and poems. This is not idle fantasy, but a disciplined attention to the true meaning of "it feels right to me." We can train ourselves to respect

our feelings and to transpose them into a language so they can be shared. And where that language does not yet exist, it is our poetry which helps to fashion it. Poetry is not only dream and vision; it is the skeleton architecture of our lives. It lays the foundations for a future of change, a bridge across our fears of what has never been before.[1]

---

1.   Audre Lord, *Sister Outsider* (Trumansburg, N.Y.: The Crossing Press, 1984), 37.
Lloyd

Ethnic Identity and
Post-Structuralist Differance

R. Radhakrishnan

Ethnic "identity" and "differance": surely an untenable conjunction. Well, the purpose of my essay is to suggest that such a conjunction is not only tenable, but also desirable and, in a sense, ineluctable. My paper then articulates the intersection of "ethnicity" with "differe(a)nce" and goes on to suggest ways in which this reciprocal "identification" can, on the one hand, historicize and situate the radical politics of "indeterminancy" while, on the other, situate the politics of empowerment as a transgression of the algorithm of "identity."

The constituency of "the ethnic" occupies quite literally a "prepost"-erous space where it has to actualize, enfranchize, and empower its own "identity" and coextensively engage in the deconstruction of the very logic of "identity" and its binary and exclusionary politics. Failure to achieve this doubleness can only result in the formation of ethnicity as yet another "identical" and hegemonic structure. The difficult task is to achieve an axial connection between the historico-semantic specificity of "ethnicity" and the "post-historical" politics of radical indeterminacy. A merely short-term affirmation of ethnicity certainly leads to a substitution of the "contents" of history but leaves untouched the very forms and structures in and through which historical and empirical contents are legitimated. On the other hand, an avant-gardist advocacy of "difference as such" overlooks the very possibilities of realizing, through a provisionally historical semantics, this "difference" as a worldly and consequential mode. I posit the notion of the "radical" or the "post-ethnic" as the moment that materializes the temporality of the "post-" as a double-moment that is as disruptive as it is inaugural. My elaboration of the "post-" also works itself through such historically determinate issues as Jesse Jackson's "rainbow-coalition," in the context of binary (two-party) politics, and the nature of the "intellectual-constituency" relationship. I conclude with the claim that Post-Structuralist politics will not allow us any kind of return to naive empiricism or historicism. What it does, instead, is to transform the very meaning of the term "political."

My title then represents my choice to conceptualize "ethnicity" through Post-Structuralism. Why such a choice? My reasons are that I believe it is possible to do the following: to generate through Post-Structuralism a "radical ethnicity" even as we legitimate "programmatic and short-term ethnicity"; to prevent the discussion of ethnicity from relapsing into such pre-critical modes as naive empiricism, naive historicism, and unself-reflexive praxis; to disallow, in the process, the notion of theory as mastery and, instead, to enable an articulation of historically determinate and intentional, but non-authoritarian, attitudes to "reality" and "knowledge." I hope this prefatory statement of intention makes it clear that my paper does *not* seek to effect the hierarchic subsumption of ethnicity under Post-Structuralism.

In a recent article on the situation of the Black intellectual, Cornel West offers the following diagnosis:

> In addition to the general anti-intellectual tenor of American society, there is a deep distrust and suspicion of the black community toward black intellectuals. This distrust and suspicion stem not simply from the usually arrogant and haughty disposition of intellectuals toward ordinary folk, but, more importantly, from the widespread refusal of black intellectuals to remain, in some visible way, organically linked with Afro-American cultural life. The relatively high rates of exogamous marriage, the abandonment of black institutions, and the preoccupation with Euro-American intellectual products are often perceived by the black community as intentional efforts to escape the negative stigma of blackness or viewed as symptoms of self-hatred. And the minimal immediate impact of black intellectual activity on the black community and American society reinforces common perceptions of the impotence, even uselessness, of black intel-

lectuals. In good American fashion, the black community lauds those black intellectuals who excel as *political Activists* and *cultural Artists*; the life of the mind is viewed as neither possessing intrinsic virtues nor harbouring emancipatory possibilities — solely short term political gain and social status.[1]

West goes on to draw some conclusions:

> And, to put it crudely, most black intellectuals tend to fall within the two camps created by this predicament: "successful" ones, distant from (and usually condescending toward) the black community, and "unsuccessful" ones, disdainful of the white intellectual world. But both camps remain marginal to the black community — dangling between two worlds with little or no black infrastructural bases. Therefore, the "successful" black intellectual capitulates, often uncritically, to the prevailing paradigms and research programmes of the white bourgeois academy, and the "unsuccessful" black intellectual remains encapsulated within the parochial discourses of Afro-American intellectual life. The alternatives of meretricious pseudo-cosmopolitanism and tendentious, cathartic provincialism loom large in the lives of black intellectuals. And the black community views both alternatives with distrust and disdain — and with good reason.[2]

The critical and theoretical unpacking of the many issues that West raises so brilliantly and perspectivally in his piece will provide the momentum for my own reflections. Here, then, are the questions that I wish to generate and in some sense resolve during the course of my essay. What is the nature of "constituency" and how does it co-implicate the intellectual and the community? What are the connections between "representational" politics and the "organicity" of the intellectual/theoretical enterprise? Is the relationship of the ethnic intellectual to the ethnic community an isomorphic reproduction of the relationship that holds between the so-called "non-ethnic" intellectual and her community? That is, does "organicity" have the same incidence in

---

1. Cornel West, "The Dilemma of the Black Intellectual," *Cultural Critique* (Fall 1985): 112-13.
2. Ibid., 113.

both cases? How generalized a category is or should ethnicity be in light of the demystified understanding that even the so-called "white" constituency has always been "ethnic?" What is the nature of the *topos* occupied by the intellectual and how is this space structurally coordinated, on the one hand, and determined, on the other, by semantic/historical specificity? And finally, what is the status of a specific "ethnic" intellectual, for example, the "black" intellectual within the "rainbow" of the "ethnic-in-general?" — Is it exemplary? representative? of heuristic value? In other words, what bearing does the mode of self-empowerment of one ethnic constituency have on ethnicity as constituency, ethnicity, as heterogeneity, that is, ethnicity as such?

Even if we grant the intellectual as theorist (for my purposes here, I am making an equational connection between the role of the intellectual and that of the theorist, an identification that might well need differentiation in another context) the credentials of being well-intentioned, the paradox still remains: whereas the intellectual perceives theory to be an effective intervention on behalf of ethnicity, the people/masses that are the constituency are deeply skeptical and even hostile to the agency of the theorist. The circumstantial reality of this problem forces open the occluded connection between theory and history, and theory and experience; that is, it argues for the "medial" function (as against the "autonomous function") of theory. Does theory then by definition operate pre-emptively both of history and experience? If her commitment to theory is what renders the intellectual suspect and duplicitous in the perception of her constituency, and if, furthermore, popular consciousness detects in theory an intrinsic drive towards self-mastery, identity, and rarefaction that renders it amoral and apolitical, on the one hand, and disinterested and meritocratic, on the other, then surely the very historicity of theory needs to be examined and perhaps called into question. It is even conceivable that the very meaning of theory is to be transformed, revolutionized in the context of "ethnicity as emergence." The theory we are looking for may have to fulfill all of the following requirements: it must divest itself from economies of mastery and yet empower the "ethnic" contingently and historically; it must generate critical statements even as ethnicity is affirmed, endorsed, and legitimated; and it must be able to conceptualize the "post-ethnic" as a radical and necessary extension of the "ethnic."

How should theory express ethnicity especially when its own history is at organic variance with the phenomenon of the "ethnic"? Does theory have a place in the ethnic program? One possible option is to assume that the historical experience of the ethnic as such is its own unmediated theory. Another option is to discredit the very notion of ethnicity as unmediated, as an experiential given, and, consequently, to accord theory the task of reading ethnicity as a socio-political-cultural construct caught up in the connectedness of its own history to prehistories and other histories. Or, theory could engender itself as a meta-critical mode with an avant-gardist momentum all its own that founds its own autonomous and autotelic discourse and, in the process, abdicates its referential commitment to history and experience. It is this last tendency in some versions of Post-Structuralist theory that is rightly perceived by political activists as self-serving and in the ultimate analysis as *status quo* politics. What is at stake here is the representative and representational connection between theory and constituency. Should the ethnic theorist be empowered to speak on behalf of the collectivity? To put it crudely: do the interests of the ethnic theorist, who teaches, publishes, and disseminates theory culturally and institutionally and academically, coincide with the interests of the collectivity? Does not the academic/institutional affiliation of the theorist always already dispose her towards a trans-ethnic network? Is the theorist a friend or foe, a mercenary, an opportunist, or a supercilious patron?

I feel that even before we can begin to ask any of these questions, we need to come to grips with the very representational algorithm, historicize it, and make distinctions between modes of representation. Broadly speaking, there are two possible attitudes to representation: the axiomatic and the problematic. In the first instance, representation is reliable, and in the other it is suspect: organic or Post-Structuralist. Here I wish to bring in two of the most consequential, adversarial theorists in recent history and pit them against each other: Antonio Gramsci and Michel Foucault. Rightaway we can see drastic differences: Gramsci rotted away and died in an Italian Fascist prison and wrote so much of his powerful theory while incarcerated, whereas Foucault was one of the most privileged and overdetermined thinkers of his time, dominating the French scene along with such others as Jacques Lacan, Jacques Derrida, and Roland Barthes. I am not sug-

gesting that Gramsci's life in itself authenticates his revolutionary theory whereas Foucault as theorist stands to lose because of his academic
and institutional legitimation. But I am saying that beween the two
models lies a world of difference: differences in historicity, nationalistic
situation, and differences in what was at stake. Given these differences,
Gramsci advocates the model of the organic intellectual, while Foucault
rejects the very framework of representation.

For Foucault, nothing is more ignominious than being spoken for.
He sees representation as disciplinary, panoptic, and coercively theoretical and, therefore, argues for struggles that can only be regional,
singular, and nomadic. The best that an intellectual can do is to
thematize her own marginality and not presume to speak for the other. And yet, the fact is that, more than any other Post-Structuralist
thinker, it was Foucault who tried to voice the "other" in project after
project. How then does one valorize such works? Are these attempts
progressive or are they merely symptomatic of the deficiencies of the
empowered point of view from which they are undertaken? (We cannot but recall in passing here Derrida's critique of Foucault's representation of madness). If it is the case that the ethnic intellectual straddles
two temporalities, the organically representational and the post-
representational, then what can be expected from such a position? Let
us now juxtapose two passages, one from Foucault and the other from
Gramsci. First we will look at Foucault in the context of a published
conversation with the French philosopher, Gilles Deleuze:

> In the most recent upheaval, the intellectual discovered that the
> masses no longer need him to gain knowledge: they *know* per-
> fectly well, without illusion; they know far better than he and
> they are certainly capable of expressing themselves. But there
> exists a system of power which blocks, prohibits, and invali-
> dates this discourse and this knowledge, a power not only
> found in the manifest authority of censorship, but one that pro-
> foundly and subtly penetrates an entire societal network.
> Intellectuals are themselves agents of this system of power —
> the idea of their responsibility for "consciousness" and
> discourse forms part of the system.[3]

---

3.   Michel Foucault, "Intellectuals and Power," *Language, Counter-Memory, Practice*,
trans. Donald F. Bouchard and Sherry Simon (Ithaca: Cornell Univ. Press, 1977), 207.

Gramsci in his elaboration of the organic intellectual dispels the mythic status of the "traditional intellectual" and deconstructs the categorical distinction between the intellectual and the "non-intellectual":

> All men are intellectuals, one could therefore say; but all men do not have the function of intellectuals in society.
>
> When we distinguish intellectuals and non-intellectuals we are in fact referring only to the immediate social function of the category of professional intellectuals, that is to say, we are taking account of the direction in which the greater part of the specific professional activity, whether in intellectual elaboration or in muscular-nervous effort, throws its weight. This means that, if we can speak of intellectuals, we cannot speak of non-intellectuals, because non-intellectuals do not exist.[4]

Earlier on in the same essay, "The Formation of Intellectuals," Gramsci demystifies the notion of the "true," ideal, and transcendent intellectuals who speak a non-specific, non-perspectival truth. Such traditional intellectuals deny history and the many breaks in history, and they also naturalize their ideological investment in their own class, constituency, etc.

Gramsci is arguing for a situation where all human beings are intellectuals, a situation that provides a structural and ideological continuity between what I call the "general" intellectual and the "professional" or specific intellectual. What we are seeking here is a conjuncture where there is not only the availability of a socio-politico-cultural infrastructure but the continuous and homogeneous expression of this infra-structure in the professional super-structure as well. It is significant that Cornel West in his analysis of the contemporary black situation in the U.S. identifies the increasing non-availability of such a consistent infra-structure as one of the determining causes of the alienation of the black intellectual from the black constituency.

To paraphrase Gramsci further, the traditional intellectual inheres in a "timeless" and therefore pre-revolutionary *episteme* and is inimical to revolutionary emergence. As the agent of a true and timeless order

---

4. Antonio Gramsci, "The Formation of Intellectuals," *The Modern Prince & Other Writings*, trans. Dr. Louis Marks (New York: International Publishers, 1957), 121.

that claims to be culturally autonomous of specific modes of production, exchange, and elaboration, the traditional intellectual is a leveller, that is, she homogenizes, neutralizes, and defuses the circumstantial reality of oppositions. and contestations for dominance and hegemony. The reality of the organic intellectual, on the contrary, is co-eval and co-extensive with the reality of the class to which she belongs. The locus of the intellectual is but a specific elaboration of the general intellectuality of the entire class or constituency. The professionalization of a few intellectuals does not result in the betrayal of their representative function.

However attractive and emancipatory Gramsci's analysis, two questions need to be raised: first, does "professionalization" in our contemporary context have the same meaning as it did for Gramsci? One of our problems in the post-industralist information society is "professionalism" itself and with it the problem of "institutionality." (I am aware that here I am guilty of a totalization, for the Third World represents a very different temporality where the reification of the "institutional" has not yet taken place. We could then say, following Gramsci's line of thought, that institutionality itself is specific to a certain society). But in spite of this reservation, the value-free, self-serving logic of the institution, we must admit, has been one of the chief agents of depoliticization. To such an extent, indeed, that to say that someone or some philosophy has been "institutionalized" has come to mean an academic and not a political legitimation. What Gramsci could not have foreseen, then, is the extent to which the Institution, the Academy, the University, the Government, and Multi-National corporate structures function across semantic and ideological territories, thus reducing the intellectual to a pre-determined structural space within the macro-space of the "institutional." The confidence that Gramsci exudes as he talks about the capacity of the intellectual to control intentionally the elaborations of her program sounds to me quite naive in its optimism when applied to the present context. My point here is that the present context has to include, but also go beyond, the Gramscian paradigm. The disciplinary apparatuses and the "microphysical" inscriptions of power, about which Foucault cautions the intellectuals, need to be taken seriously.

The second question that should be raised concerns the relationship of the organic intellectual to her own traditional pre-history and, analogously, the manner in which the "ethnic" intellectual is implicated in the "colorless" and to many, the "colored" or pre-ethnic past? The question of genealogy remains to be answered. Is there a pure and radical "break" between the two regimes? If the "ethnic" is the emergent mode, where is it emerging from? How does the "emergent" mode emerge counter-mnemonically (to use Foucault's telling concept) from the dominant and the hegemonic models? And crucially, how does the "ethnic" name itself? What kind of identity is asserted through this name? The problem here is as ethnic as it is theoretical and epistemological. "Naming," "identity," and the "self" already have a sedimented history of their own, and, therefore, it becomes crucial to ask how this present historical instance of "naming" repeats or recuperates the general economy of the "name." Is it possible or even politically feasible to isolate the protocol or the morphology of the present instance from the algorithmic logic of the general? It is true that the present historical context is anything but the semantic repetition of an earlier content, and yet it remains complicitous with the exclusionary logic of the "self." In an essay entitled, "I yam what I am: the topos of un(naming) in Afro-American literature," Kimberly Benston emphasizes this very problematic of the "name," and the active interplay within the "name" of the negative and the affirmative:

> Social and economic freedom — a truly new self — was incomplete if not authenticated by self-designation. The *unnaming* of the immediate past ('Hatcher's John', etc.) was reinforced by the insertion of a mysterious initial, a symbol of the long-unacknowledged, nascent selfhood that had survived and transcended slavery. On the other hand, the association with tropes of American heroism ('Lincoln,' 'Sherman', etc.) was also an act of *naming*, a staging of self in relation to a specific context of revolutionary affirmation.[5]

Having situated the socio-political and historico-economic specificity of the occasion of "naming" and "unnaming," Kimberly Benston "remembers" the theological and metaphysical origins of the impulse to "unname," that is, to be nameless, ineffable, and sublime:

---

5. Kimberly Benston, "I yam what I am: the topos of un(naming) in Afro-American literature," *Black Literature and Literary Theory*, ed. Henry Louis Gates, Jr. (New York: Methuen, 1984), 153.

... the refusal to be named invokes the power of the Sublime, a transcendent impulse to undo all categories, all metonymies, and reifications, and thrust the self beyond received patterns and relationships into a stance of unchallenged authority. In short, in its earliest manifestations the act of unnaming is a means of passing from one mode of representation to another, of breaking the rhetoric and 'plot' of influence, of distinguishing the self from all else — including Eros, nature and community.[6]

But isn't this precisely the kind of ahistorical fundamentalism about which Post-Structuralist thought warns us? The program of naming and unnaming takes the following historically determinate steps (different phases of a developmental sequence): ethnic reality realizes that it has a "name," but this name is forced on it by the oppressor, that is, it is the victim of representation; it achieves a revolution against both the oppressor and the discourse of the oppressor and proceeds to unname itself through a process of inverse displacement; it gives itself a name, that is, represents itself from within its own point of view; and it ponders how best to legitimate and empower this new name. The last phase brings up a complex problem: the problem of the "second or 'meta-' order." I call it the problem of "in the name of." In whose name is this new name being authorized, authenticated, empowered? This appeal to an authority that "enables" but is extrinsic to the immediate or historical name betrays the desire for the Absolute and the irrefragable Self. The assumption that there exists an essence (African, Indian, feminine, nature, etc.) ironically perpetrates the same ahistoricism that was identified as the enemy during the negative/critical or "deconstructive" phase of the ethnic revolution. Doesn't all this sound somehow familiar: the defeat and overthrow of one sovereignty, the emergence and consolidation of an antithetical sovereignty, and the creation of a different, yet the same, repression? What the appeal to the "nameless" forgets is first, that any emancipatory, emerging movement of the "self" carries with it a set of repressive mandates that are the obverse of the emancipatory directives, which is to say that the legitimate affirmation of any identity cannot but constitute in the long run another determinate alterity unless this very problematic is critically

6. Ibid., 153.

thematized in the very act of affirmation; and second, that the very immediacy of felt, lived, historical, and existential reality does not obviate the need for an analysis of the forms in which this reality is packaged, comprehended, accounted for, and judged. In other words, there is a place, and a necessary one at that, for a critical analysis of the morphology of historical content in conjunction with its real effects. Disregard of the mediated nature of these historical realities (and the consequent neglect of what Foucault calls the *historical apriori* that enables and conditions discursive possibilities, in other words, an *apriori* that in its very epistemic constitution of historicity denies history its primordiality as well as its plenitude) can only result in mystified assumptions about "freedom" and the propriety of the "revolutionary self."

But there is yet another problem: the attempt to shore up authority for the revolutionary self "namelessly" perpetrates a monologic ideologization, that is, the valorization of a "unitary" or "monothetic" revolutionary identity that is insensitive to what I term the "axial" or heterogeneous momentum of the revolutionary emergence — a point that is tellingly made by Medvedev/ Bakhtin in *The Formal Method in Literary Scholarship*:

> For in the ideological horizon of any epoch and any social group there is not one, but several mutually contradictory truths, not one but several diverging ideological paths. When one chooses one of these truths as indisputable, when one chooses one of these paths as self-evident, he then writes a scholarly thesis, joins some movement, registers in some party. But even within the limits of a thesis, party, or belief, one is not able to "rest on his laurels." The course of ideological generation will present him with two new paths, two truths, and so on. The ideological horizon is constantly developing — as long as one does not get bogged down in some swamp. Such is the dialectic of real life.[7]

The error in monologic ideology is not just formal or theoretical. The fault lies in that it betrays and falsifies "the dialectic of real life." (I will not get into the problem of whether or not the dialectic inheres in real-

---

7.   P.N. Medvedev/M.M. Bakhtin, *The Formal Method in Literary Scholarship*, trans. Albert J. Wehrle (Baltimore: The Johns Hopkins Univ. Press, 1978), 19-20.

ity.) The ideologization, in the name of an affirmative programmatic, of heterological, heteroglossic, and heterogeneous realities into a single/identical blueprint is just not in touch with lived reality. But this does not mean that lived realities can be expressed without formal mediation; such an assumption can only lead to mysticism or an immanent phenomenology. Realities are always mediated, but what needs radical transformation is the mode of mediation: from the "mono-" to the hetero-." I will be dealing with the problem of the politics of the "hetero-" a little later in my essay in the context of "axial temporality," a category that I claim has the capacity both to express the "heterogeneous" and at the same time move towards legitimation and contingent empowerment.

The concern expressed by Medvedev/Bakhtin is not just academic, for some of our Post-Structuralist political and cultural anxieties fall within the problematic raised by Medvedev/Bakhtin. A recent essay by Deborah E. McDowell on Black Feminist criticism makes a very similar diagnosis:

> Not only have Black women writers been "disenfranchised" from critical works by white women scholars on the "female tradition," but they have also been frequently excised from those on the Afro-American literary tradition by Black scholars, most of whom are males. For example, Robert Stepto's *From Behind the Veil: A Study of Afro-American Narrative* purports to be "a history . . . of the historical consciousness of an Afro-American art form — namely, the Afro-American written narrative." Yet, Black women writers are conspicuously absent from the table of contents.[8]

It is clear that the model of "identity" and its corollary, the representational algorithm, are inadequate when the realities, exclusions, and jeopardies that we are experiencing are, at the very least, multiple. To speak, then, unproblematically of a single Black, Feminist, or Third World model of revolution is as repressive as it is naive. These emergences are pressing for a different language, a different politics and temporality, for an infinitely complex program of action that has to fulfill

---

8.   Deborah E. McDowell, "New Directions for Black Feminist Criticism," *The New Feminist Criticism*, ed. Elaine Showalter (New York: Pantheon Books, 1985), 187.

the following objectives: empowerment and enfranchisement of contingent "identities," the overthrow of the general hegemony of Identity, and the prevention of the essentialization/hypostasis and the fetishization of "difference."

How then do we reconcile "short-term ethnicity" with "radical ethnicity," that is, "present ethnicity" with "post-ethnicity"? The two programs, while not antithetical ideologically, do seem discontinuous; they occupy different planes of resistance. What I recommend, then, is a critical interaction between Post-Structuralism, in particular the politicized practice of "difference" and the strategy of "counter-mnemonic" practice, and short-term ethnic activism.[9] Such interaction, I believe, can point the way not merely to the achievement of imminent objectives but to the coordination and creation of a different historico-epistemic *topos* where heterogeneous realities (all of which have one structural similarity, that is, they have all been victims of "identical" representation) may be lived, expressed, and "legitimated" heterogeneously. This articulation cannot but be "double" (i.e., in the sense in which Derrida talks about the "double session," which when politicized is not all that different from the "Manichean" *episteme* as invoked by Abdul JanMohamed),[10] in so far as it has to invoke two temporalities: that of oppression, memory, and enforced identity, and that of emergence after the "break," the counter-memory, and heterogeneous difference. Emerging movements, then, straddle two historicities: that of the oppressor and that which is "their own," and besides, within their own "territory," these movements experience the structural synchronicity imposed by their common aetiology and a "heterochrony" that is expressive of different historical densities and circumstantialities. Thus, feminism, post-Colonialism, ethnicity, homosexuality, and lesbianism, to name just a few constituencies,

---

9.   For a more substantive analysis of the nature and the deployment of the "post-," see my forthcoming article, "The Epistemics of the Future in the Age of the Post-."

10.   I am referring here to Abdul JanMohamed's ground-breaking work, *Manichean Aesthetics: The Politics of Literature in Colonial Africa* (Amherst, Ma.: The Univ. of Massachusetts Press, 1983), and his more recent piece, "The Economy of Manichean Allegory: The Function of Racial Difference in Colonialist Literature," *Critical Inquiry* 12, no. 1 (Autumn 1985): 59-87. I am not claiming that the Derridean "double-session" and the category of the "Manichean" as developed by JanMohamed are identical or synonymous. But I am suggesting that the "doubleness" or the ambi-valence that characterizes both structures can be used strategically in the context of the Post-Colonialist emergence and its attitude to is own pre-history.

are both singular and isomorphically irreducible multiple expressions. Both along a horizontal and a vertical axis, the identity of these movements is marked by "difference."[11] What is necessary, then, is a critical tactic that will call into question both the economy of identity and the axiology of binarity that underwrites the nomology of identity. To demonstrate this point, I choose two seemingly unconnected examples but which on deeper reading turn out to be obverse expressions of the same intention: first, Jacques Derrida, and second, Jesse Jackson's "rainbow-coalition" politics.

When Derrida keeps insisting that the critic/activist has to make a "deep-structure" diagnosis and detect the logocentric (and its other versions, the phallogocentric, the photo- and the phonocentric, and in short the "centric" itself) imperative that undergirds even the most local oppression, he definitely steps beyond Gramscian notions of resistance. But precisely because he transcends the Gramscian problematic, he also overlooks what is significant within the Gramscian framework. Let me explain with the help of an *ad hoc* mock allegory. Imagine this scenario: vast crowds of people protesting apartheid with placards and slogans that read, "Abolish apartheid"[12] "Down with Racism," and imagine also a "canonical"

---

11.   I am thinking here of the many serious problems confronting the theoretical and practical formulation of the feminist programmatic. Third World feminists, for example, have been raising questions which they believe cannot be adequately dealt with if the feminist movement is privileged in the name of the white woman. The reality that identity is constituted along multiple axes (race, gender, nationality, sexual preference, etc.) makes any univocal or representative solution unacceptable.

12.   Jacques Derrida's recent piece, "Racism's Last Word," *Critical Inquiry* 12, no. 1 (Autumn 1985): 290-99, is a good example of the kind of strategy I am discussing here. While Derrida's discussion of racism in this essay is neither irrelevant nor lacking in political perspectivity, it is pitched at a level of theory and formalization that comes close to overlooking the historical specificity of apartheid. One gets the feeling that here was another pretext for Jacques Derrida to "instantiate" his gestural radicality which is never inopportune but, by the same token, is never, so to speak, "right on." A much earlier piece of Derrida's, "The Ends of Man," displays the same rhetorical orientation. While being, in my evaluation, one of his brilliant deconstructive essays, "The Ends of Man" does only token justice to its occasionality, the occasion of U.S. involvement in Vietnam. Derrida makes it a point to refer to his critical attitude towards American foreign policy, but does not develop it any further. This "gestural" or "citational" mode of invoking socio-political and historical reality and refusing to take it seriously, I maintain, itself needs to be historicized. I would also submit that in the context of apartheid, the Derridean gesture is at best effete, at worst, seriously objectionable.

Derridean in the midst of this large group with a placard in her hand
that reads, "Death to Binarity, End Logocentrism." It would be
quite appropriate if everyone else looks at this person and the placard quizzically, even suspicously, as if to ask, "Friend, or Foe?" The
politics of the placard is as unclear as it is indeterminate. The slogan
rarefies the protest into a structural shibboleth. First, I will raise the
political objections to this slogan, and then I will construct the
Derridean objection to these objections.

Even if it is the case that apartheid is, in the ultimate analysis, the
expression of a more generalized malaise, that is, logocentrism and
binarity, the slogan makes its point at a level of abstraction and generalization that is of no significance whatsoever. It is generalized to
the point of tautologous emptiness; in other words, to say that apartheid is logocentrism is to say "nothing" at all, and besides, the very
choice to represent and semanticize the significance of apartheid at a
certain syntactic/structural remove that pre-empts the semantic/his-
torical specificity of apartheid posits its own politics of a distantiated
and Olympian wisdom that in turn becomes one with *status quo* politics exactly because it resists local, circumstantial, and historical
identification. The Derridean would retort (and it is as amusing as it is
frustrating that the anti-Derridean will find the Derridean apolitical
on precisely those grounds on which the Derridean rests her case of
political radicality) by saying that it is myopic to separate the politics of
apartheid from the politics of logocentrism and that unless the mode
of production known as "binarity" is confronted *as such* (for Derrida,
binarity, and in general, the structures of the past cannot be "stepped
beyond"; they can only be turned against themselves for purposes of
"revolution," in other words, there can be no pure "breaks" or *ex
nihilo* formations that are organic[13] with themselves), we will be "always already" co-opted into the very regime that we are opposing (a

---

13. The term "organic" that to Gramsci represents a socio-political vitality has
come to mean, in the Post-Structuralist discourse, conservatism of the worst kind. In
so far as the term "organic" is complicitous with the logic of the "natural" and the
"primordial," it is construed by Post-Structuralists as ahistorical, but it may well have
other connotations and cognate implications that are missed by the Post-Structuralist
critique. The "organic" as *construct* may well represent the kind of collectivity and the
consequent de-centerings that are so central to the Post-Structuralist enterprise. The
refusal to historicize the very genealogy of words that turn authoritative, I submit, often results in imprecise differentiations. Another concept in question is "theory" itself,

fear that Gramsci, armed as he is with the notion of "organicity," does not take seriously — if anything, he might suggest quite the opposite competence, that is, the competence of the "organic" to convert and transform the "traditional"). What is at stake here is the correctness of strategy locked within binarity: a syntactic strategy[14] as against a semantic strategy. But, does it have to be one or the other? Can we not define the very *topos* of political struggle as the determinate tension between the syntactic and the semantic, the critical and the affirmative, the radically indeterminate and the intentionally determinate?

Now to my second example. My focus is on three aspects of Jackson's campaign for the Democratic nomination to run for President: "the rainbow-coalition," the radicality of the slogan, "our time has come," and the positionality of Jackson's politics within the binary

---

for this word used totalizingly covers up the presence of different temporalities. Therefore, to be "for theory" or "against theory" does not really reveal much unless we also specify "what kind of theory." Both Ronald Reagan and Michel Foucault are opponents of "theory," but surely they do not have the same kind of theory in mind.

14.   Jacques Lacan's "allegory of the signifier," based on this reading of Edgar Allan Poe's *The Purloined Letter*, proves its point by dealing with the letter syntactically, that is, without ever having to ascertain what the "semantics" or the "contents" of the letter might have been. I am in full support of this revolutionary way of accounting for meaning-production in so far as it calls into question the metaphysical conspiracy of "meaning" as pure interiority. My critique of the Lacanian model, however, is that it entirely does away with "semantic" or "historical" significance. The insight that meaning is produced through a structural relay does not have to negate the possibility that these very structural or algebraic slots can be differentiated on the basis of the "contents" therein. Both the privileging of algebra and the detective imagination indicate a certain "disinterest" in historical and existential specificity. The detective we know is "interested" in crime in its capacity as "case"; for the detective imagination, the rarefaction of a story into the algebra of analysis is all that matters. In the Lacanian context, I would like to propose a speculation somewhat along the following lines: what if we were told that the contents of the purloined letter had to do with political intrigue, an attempt at conspiracy or usurpation from within, or the queen's collusion with a foreign power to topple the present regime, or the queen's complicity with an anti-royalist, pan-national, global movement, etc., would it still not make a difference? Of course, Lacan would still be correct in maintaining that the resolution of the problem, that is, the problem of how to find the letter, can still be reached in abeyance of the actual contents of the letter. But this insistence is really the insistence of tautology, for the letter's content is being understood as belonging to the category known as "with potential for blackmail," something which we have always known from the very beginning of the narrative. Such an *askesis* of interest in a very real sense prevents the production of a new knowledge. I believe I would not be too wrong in calling this state of affairs "the narcissism of the signifier."

space of the two-party system. I shall begin, then, with the last of the three areas since that is immediately relevant to my critique of binarity. A critical point that Jesse Jackson kept making throughout the campaign was that his politics and his constituency would work with and work through the logic of the Democratic party and its binarily constituted opposition to the Republican party. This approach set apart Jackson's candidacy from that of Walter Mondale and Gary Hart, both of whom, in spite of many adventitious differences, were exemplary of the Democratic party rhetoric. The singularities of their positions could be ideologically and hierarchically subsumed under the Democratic party logic which in its turn is determined by its binary relationship to the rationale of the Republican party. Jackson's reality, in many ways, is not expressible within this binary space. He could only work with and within the more progressive of the two parties while at the same time interrogate and *not* fetishize the identity of the Democratic party. The socio-political and historical reality of the cry "our time has come" and the strategy of the "rainbow-coalition" can at best, by way of an opportune *bricolage*, make use of the institutionality known as the two-party system, but it cannot afford to be "identified" within the binary grid. Jackson's purpose was to transform the very nature of the Democratic party from within, destabilize it from within so as to make it more sensitive to "interests" that lie outside its framework. One could say that Jackson's strategy *vis à vis* the Party was that of the Derridean "double-session." For after all, even within the Democratic party, whose loyal and card-carrying member Jesse Jackson is, he was identified and found not genuinely representative because he was the spokesperson of "special interests," a term that is of "special interest" to the Post-Structuralist intellectual. If Jackson's interests are "special interests," the implication is that certain interests are "natural," "general," "representative," and ideologically neutral and value-free. Corporate, military, business, male, "white," non-ethnic interests are general and representative to the point of being non-ideological, objective, axiomatic, and even "dis-interested," whereas the axis of constituencies represented by Jackson are distortions of political reality. Should we be surprised, then, that the "rainbow-coalition" is in an ec-centric and differential relationship to the authority of the Democratic party and also to the space of binary politics? If "our time is to come," in its own way, then, the "rainbow-coalition" will have to situate itself subversively within the exigencies of binary politics.

All of this brings us to that continuum that collocates the theoretical with the political task, that of living, expressing, formalizing, and legitimating heterogeneity in a heterogeneous way. Another way of saying it would be to transform "our time has come" into "the time of 'our times have come' " or, better still, "our times have come." The two real dangers here are the cognitive and theoretical homogenization of the heterogeneous, and the celebration of heterogeneity as deliquescence, as non-purposive and indeterminate. Again, we have to look for the answer in the determinate-indeterminate, in a historically contextualized application of the "double session." Before that, we need to make a thematic connection between the "ethnic" and the "heterogeneous," that is, if we are to take radical ethnicity seriously.

What the ethnic self, the non-self, has to contend with is the reality of its entrapment in multiple temporalities and histories. It has to empower itself as "identity" and, at the same time, realize its potential to be a site, the *topos* of a revolution that is also its own meta-revolution. What do I mean by different histories and temporalities?

First, we have the history of the self which is also obversely the history of the silence of the non-self. These two histories are synchronic and simultaneous, and yet semantically they occupy different temporalities. But they are identical in a way since they are co-implicated, periodized, and historicized within the logic of binarity that founds both the Self and the Other. The relationship of the "self" to the "identity of binarity" and that of the "other" to this same "identity of binarity" opens up yet another threshold. Furthermore, there is the rarefied and "nomologized" identity of the very binary structure and its putative temporality that has a juridical hold over all the historical deployments of the "self" and the "other." In other words, we cannot but come to terms with the canonicity of the binary mode. The task for radical ethnicity is to thematize and subsequently problematize its entrapment within these binary elaborations with the intention of "stepping beyond" to find its own adequate language. My point here is that the emancipation of the "ethnic" from the "pre-ethnic" is both semantically specific and an instance of the differential emergence of "difference" from the hegemonic grid of "identity." The politics of the ethnic becomes radical only when it is situated within the emergence of "difference." To suggest how crucial this is, I would like to quote from Foucault:

Difference is transformed into that which must be specified within a concept, without overstepping its bounds. And yet above the species, we encounter the swarming of individualities. What is this boundless diversity, which eludes specification and remains outside the concept, if not the resurgence of repetition?[15]

Foucault's concern in this essay is not overtly political, but the consequences of his articulation are indeed deeply political. The attempt to enfranchise difference "differentially" is but another name for the politics of heterogeneity.

We must, of course, make clear distinctions between heterogeneity as bohemianism, anarchism, and political indifference and heterogeneity as political destiny. We must also distinguish between a categorical heterogeneity, that is, a heterogeneity construed by the homogeneous logic of the "category," and an a-categorical heterogeneity that finds its "self-expression" through the breakdown of the "categorical." In its efforts to inaugurate its own kind of language, heterogeneity is bound to face two types of dangers, one from without and the other from within. First, the danger from without would take the form of heterogeneity considered as a lapsarian version of homogeneity (the danger that Foucault anticipates in the passage quoted above). Second, the danger from within would actualize itself in the ascendancy of one of the "heterogeneous" elements into a position of hegemonic dominance. This would result in acute contestations among different versions of heterogeneity, a total violation of the decentered and non-authoritarian spirit of heterogeneity. To schematize this situation a little, we seem to have the following options: heterogeneity or difference as an expressive or phenomenological reality with no clearly articulated political strategy for survival; heterogeneity as a limited secession from the rhetoric of the "homogeneous," that is, heterogeneity as expressively and experientially and historically disjunct from the norm of the homogeneous but whose "official" reality is to be constituted within the framework of centrist and representational articulation; the celebration of heterogeneity as the pluralization of effective identities within the normativity of Identity so that we will have as many official and

---

15. Michel Foucault, "Theatrum Philosophicum," *Language, Counter-Memory, Practice*, 182.

empowered versions of heterogeneity as there are heterogeneous elements, for example, Jewish, Black, Feminist, Post-Colonialist heterogeneities. My recommendation is that none of the above are adequate and that what we are in need of is the practice of "axial temporality."

There is nothing new about the idea of the axis; it is as old as political struggle. What is new, however, is the conceptualization of axial reality in opposition to identical reality. The valorization of the "axial" as an interrogation of the integrity of the "identical" initiates a countermnemonic break from the regime of a certain identical history. The dynamics of Post-Structuralist thought and the trajectory of radical ethnicity can be seen in the convergence at the point where "axis" replaces identity. Both radical ethnicity and Post-Structuralist reality warrant the space opened by the conceptualization of the "post-": the space after the "break" where radical ethnicity and Post-Structural discourse can come into their own, now that "representation" and "identity" have been pre-historicized. The politics of the "post-" may now enable the generous production of non-authoritarian and non-territorial realities/knowledges whereby boundaries would be recognized and transcended, limitations accepted and transformed.

The strategy of "Post-Politics" is double, that is, it conjoins in a relationship of complementarity the twin tasks of semanticizing the indeterminacy of the temporality of the "post-" and radicalizing the ethnic momentum beyond authoritarian closure. Having done this, my essay too will have come full circle, for we began with a brief reflection on the appropriateness of my title, and I will end with the reiteration that "theory" and "ethnicity" cannot and should not be conceived as antithetical modes.

The term "post-" has assumed substantive and autonomous significance in the Post-Structuralist context. I say "substantive" and "autonomous" since Post-Structuralist thought in many ways has liberated the prefix "post-" from its position of semantic heteronomy and enabled it as the "substance" of "difference" and "differance."[16] When we think of such coinages as Post-Feminism, Post-Representation, Post-

---

16. My reference here is to Jacques Derrida's virtuoso essay, "Differance," [*Speech and Phenomena*, trans. David B. Allison (Evanston: Northwestern Univ. Press, 1973)] where he coins the formation "differance" to suggest the radical, "unheard" (for the *a* in "differance" can only be seen and not heard) and non-conceptualizable play of "difference."

Marxism, Post-Ethnic, etc., and think about it seriously, we realize that what is being proposed is a new and differential temporality: the deferred temporality of the "after." In the traditional understanding, the prefix "post-" is a relational and non-nominal term that occupies the non-space between an anterior knowledge that has a "name" and a future knowledge that has as yet no name. The "post-" is the non-description of an anomie which in the fullness of time it is hoped will acquire a proper name and with it a proper temporality, history, and periodic identity. The tacit philosophic assumption here is that periods, histories, phenomena, and names are characterized intrinsically by the potential for an ideal and identical development marked sequentially by a before and an after. With the advent of Post-Structuralist thought, the term "post-" has taken on an adversarial and phantasmal[17] meaning whereby one always occupies a position of radical contingency in the wake of identity-formation. In its very relational and differential disposition, the "time of the post-" makes perennial pre-histories of grounded, authoritative time. The flow of the "post-" is hence the transformational and critical momentum of a certain way of knowing that is incompatible with knowledge as conservation.

The rhetoric of the "post-" indicates a kind of mercurial, theoretical progression that is constantly marking out new thresholds, frontiers, and boundaries, and in this very marking keeps crossing, traversing, and transcending these frontiers through a momentum that is irrepressibly indeterminate, nameless, and anomic. But it also represents the discovery of a temporality that deconstructs the authority of such structures as "genre," "period," "epoch," "episteme," "canonicity," etc. Here again, there is the need to proceed with caution. The easy option is to submit to avant-gardism and remain indifferent to the pressures and urgencies of "fleshing out" the structures opened up by critical thought. The more difficult and the more meaningful choice is to in-mix this critical energy with the convictions and intentional commitments of affirmation. To restate this in the context of my entire presentation, if the "ethnic" were to remain purely ethnic it would still

---

17.   The term "phantasmal," initially for Deleuze and derivatively for Foucault, is symptomatic of an a-categorical thinking that reproposes, in opposition to philosophic thought in its various guises, an entirely different orientation to time and thinking. Also relevant is the concept of the "meaning-event" in Foucault.

be trapped within the many larger and general economies of repression that I have been problematizing so far. The "Post-Ethnic," on the contrary, is the moment or the *topos* that dramatizes, I could almost say, allegorizes its own doubleness. As the radically ethnic, it is the last in an entire series of Identity that by virtue of choosing to be terminal in that series inflicts fatality to the entire series and, in that very breath, inaugurates the time of the "after." The "ethnic" that is exemplary of "that which comes after" decelebrates the logic of priority, primogeniture, primordiality, etc., and founds the timeless time of the "after" divorced from the temporality of the "before." In Derridean terms, "radical ethnicity" is that "dangerous supplement" that demonstrates that "it," i.e., "identity" (and the identity of authority as in "in the name of"), is pre-post-erous. The momentous undertaking that radical ethnicity is entrusted with is the creation of a future where oppression will be not just be immoral or unconscionable, but virtually "unthinkable." The "time-after," I hope, will be such a future.

Authority, (White) Power, and the (Black) Critic; It's All Greek to Me

Henry Louis Gates, Jr.

I want to address the first topic of this conference in three parts: first, I want to present a parable about canon-formation at crucial moments of cultural liminality in the black tradition, a parable in which the figures of Alexander Crummell, John C. Calhoun, Greg Tate, and Wole Soyinka play their parts. I have chosen to share this parable because I believe that we are at just such a moment of literary liminality in the African-American tradition; at that old crossroads—presided over by Esu-Elegbara—where tradition and the present, Africa and the West, Afro-America and America, black, indeed, and white face each other in confrontation. The potential at such a moment of liminality is wondrous, and I believe that such a moment must be named. After narrating this parable, I next want to discuss, briefly, three previous attempts—of several attempts—at canon-formation in the Afro-American tradition. I choose to do so by discussing the idea of the black anthology as canon-formation, and I have four anthologies in mind. The first is William G. Allen's 1849 volume, entitled *Wheatley, Banneker, and Horton.* The second is *Negro Caravan,* published in 1941 and edited by Sterling Brown, Arthur Davis, and Ulysses Lee. Third is *Black Fire,* published in 1968 by Amiri Baraka (LeRoi Jones) and Larry Neal.[1] Finally, I want to

---

1. William G. Allen, *Wheatley, Banneker, and Horton; With Selections From the Poetical Works of Wheatley and Horton, and the Letter of Washington to Wheatley, and of Jefferson to Banneker* (Boston: Daniel Laing, Jr., 1849); Sterling A. Brown, Arthur P. Davis, Ulysses Lee, eds., *The Negro Caravan: Writings by American Negroes* (New

discuss in broad outline the editing of the Norton Anthology of Afro-American Literature, a project commissioned by Norton and still in an early stage of organization.

I

Alexander Crummell, a pioneering nineteenth-century pan-Africanist, statesman, and missionary who spent the bulk of his creative years as an Anglican minister in Liberia, was also a pioneering intellectual and philosopher of language, founding the American Negro Academy in 1897 and serving as the intellectual godfather of W.E.B. Du Bois. In his first annual address as president of the academy, delivered on December 28, 1898, Crummell selected as his topic "The Attitude of the American Mind Toward the Negro Intellect."[2] Given the occasion of the first annual meeting of the great intellectuals of the race, he could not have chosen a more timely or appropriate topic.

Crummell wished to attack, he said, "the denial of intellectuality in the Negro; the assertion that he was not a human being, that he did not belong to the human race," assertions, he continued, which set out "to prove that the Negro was of a different species from the white man" (p. 10). Crummell argues that the desire "to becloud and stamp out the intellect of the Negro" led to the enactment of "laws and statutes, closing the pages of every book printed to the eyes of Negroes; barring the doors of every school-room against them!" This, he concludes, "was the systematized method of the intellect of the South, to stamp out the brains of the Negro!", a program which created an "almost Egyptian darkness [which] fell upon the mind of the race, throughout the whole land" (p. 10).

Crummell next shared with his audience a conversation he had

York: The Citadel Press, 1941); LeRoi Jones and Larry Neal, eds., *Black Fire: An Anthology of Afro-American Writing* (New York: William Morrow, 1968). All subsequent references to these works will be given parenthetically in the text.

2. Alexander Crummell, "The Attitude of the American Mind Toward the Negro Intellect," Occasional Papers, No. 3 (Washington, D.C.: The American Negro Academy, 1898). All subsequent references will be given parenthetically in the text.

overheard in 1833 or 1834, when he was "an errand boy in the Anti-slavery office in New York City":

> A distinguished illustration of this ignoble sentiment can be given. In the year 1833 or 4 the speaker was an errand boy in the Anti-slavery office in New York City.
>
> On a certain occasion he heard a conversation between the Secretary and two eminent lawyers from Boston,—Samuel E. Sewell and David Lee Child. They had been to Washington on some legal business. While at the Capitol they happened to dine in the company of the great John C. Calhoun, the senator from South Carolina. It was a period of great ferment upon the question of Slavery, States' Rights, and Nullification; and consequently the Negro was the topic of conversation at the table. One of the utterances of Mr. Calhoun was to this effect—"That if he could find a Negro who knew the Greek syntax, he would then believe that the Negro was a human being and should be treated as a man." (pp. 10–11)

"Just think of the crude asininity," Crummell concluded rather generously, "of even a great man" (p. 11). For John C. Calhoun— who held during his lifetime the offices of U.S. congressman, secretary of war, vice president, senator, and secretary of state, and who stood firmly to his dying day a staunch advocate of states' rights and a symbol of an unreconstructed South—the person of African descent would never be a full member of the human community, fit to be anything but a slave, until one individual black person—just one—demonstrated mastery of the subtleties of Greek syntax, of all things! Perhaps fearing that this goal would be too easily achieved, Calhoun later added mastery of the binomial theorem to his list of black Herculean tasks.

The salient sign of the black person's humanity—indeed, the only sign for Calhoun—would be the mastering of the very essence of Western civilization, of the very foundation of the complex fiction upon which white Western culture had been constructed, which for John C. Calhoun turned out to have been Greek syntax. It is highly likely that "Greek syntax," for Calhoun, was merely a hyperbolic figure of speech, a trope of virtual impossibility, the first to leap to mind during an impassioned debate over states' rights and the abolition of slavery. Calhoun, perhaps, felt driven to the hyperbolic mode because of the long racist tradition, in Western letters, of demanding that black people *prove* their full humanity, a tradition to which Calhoun was heir. We know this tradition all too well, dotted as it is with the names of great intellectual Western racialists, such as Francis Bacon, David Hume, Immanuel Kant, Thomas Jefferson, and Hegel, to list only a few. Whereas each of these figures demanded that blacks write poetry to prove their humanity, Calhoun—speaking in a post–Phillis Wheatley era—took refuge in Greek syntax.

And, just as Phillis Wheatley's mistress and master had urged her to write poetry to refute racialists such as Hume and Kant, Calhoun's outrageous demand would not fall upon the deaf ears of an inarticulate intellectual inferior. In typical Afro-American fashion, a brilliant black intellectual accepted Calhoun's challenge, just as Wheatley had accepted her challenge almost a century before. The anecdote that Crummell shared with his fellow black academicians, it turns out, was his shaping scene of instruction. For Crummell, Calhoun's challenge was his reason for jumping on a boat, sailing to England, and matriculating at Queens College, at the University of Cambridge, where he mastered the intricacies of Greek syntax in a broader field of study, theology. Calhoun, we suspect, was not impressed.

But even after both John C. Calhoun and racial slavery had been long dead, Alexander Crummell never escaped the lesson he had learned as an errand boy at the anti-slavery office. Crummell never stopped believing that mastering the master's tongue was the *sole* path to civilization and to intellectual freedom and social equality for the black person. It was the acquisition of Western "culture," he argued, which the black person "must claim as his rightful heritage, as a man: not stinted training, not a caste education, not," he concludes prophetically, "a Negro curriculum" (p. 16). As he argues so passionately in his well-known speech of 1860, entitled "The English Language in Liberia,"[3] the acquisition of the English language, along with the simultaneous acquisi-

---

3. Alexander Crummell, "The English Language in Liberia," in *The Future of Africa* (New York: Charles Scribner, 1862), pp. 9–57. All subsequent references will be given parenthetically in the text.

tion of Christianity, is the wonderful sign of God's providence encoded in the nightmare of African enslavement in the racist wilderness of the New World:

> The acquisition of [the English language] is elevation. It places the native man above his ignorant fellow, and gives him some of the dignity of civilization. New ideas are caught up, new habits formed, and superior and elevating wants are daily increased. (p. 35)

Crummell accepted fully an argument central to the Enlightenment, that written and spoken language-use was the tangible sign of reason; and it was the possession of reason, as Francis Bacon put it in *The New Organon,* "that . . . made man a god to man." Crummell's first anonymous epigraph states this relation clearly:

> Language in connection with reason, to which it gives its proper activity, use, and ornament, raises man above the lower orders of animals, and in proportion as it is polished and refined, contributes greatly . . . to exalt one nation above another, in the scale of civilization and intellectual dignity. (p. 8)

English, for Crummell, was "in proportion . . . polished and refined" in an *inverse* ratio as the African vernacular languages were tarnished and unrefined. And, while the fact that black people spoke English as a first language was "indicative of sorrowful history," a sign of "subjection and conquest," it was also "one of those ordinances of Providence, designed as a means for the introduction of new ideas into the language of a people; or to serve as a transitional step from low degradation to a higher and nobler civilization" (p. 18).

English, for Crummell, was "the speech of Chaucer and Shakespeare, of Milton and Wordsworth, of Bacon and Burke, of Franklin and Webster," and its potential mastery was "this one item of compensation" which "the Almighty has bestowed upon us" in exchange for "the exile of our fathers from their African homes in America" (p. 10). English was "a transforming agency, which is gradually subverting the native languages of our tribes," he maintains with great approval, as the imperialistic forces of

Great Britain "introduce trade and civilization, pioneer letters and culture, and prepare the way for the *English Language* and Religion" (pp. 34, 32; Crummell's emphasis). It is "this noble language," he concludes on an unmistakable air of triumph, which is "gradually lifting up and enlightening our heathen neighbors" (p. 32). In the English language are embodied "the noblest theories of liberty" and "the grandest ideas of humanity" (p. 51). By the slave mastering the master's tongue, these great and grand ideas will become African ideas, because "ideas conserve men, and keep alive the vitality of nations. . . . With the noble tongue which Providence has given us, it will be difficult for us to be divorced from the spirit, which for centuries has been speaking through it" (p. 52). "And this," Crummell proclaims, "is our language," and it is "upon the many treasures of this English tongue" that he has "dwell[ed] with delight" (p. 29).

In direct and dark contrast to the splendor and wonders of the English language, Crummell pits the African vernacular languages. "The refined and cultivated English language" is "alien alike from the speech of [our] sires and the soil from whence they sprung" (p. 11). "Let us," he continues, inquire "into the respective values of our native and acquired tongue. . . . The worth of our fathers' language, will, in this way, stand out in distinct comparison with the Anglo-Saxon, our acquired speech" (p. 19). Black vernacular languages, for Crummell, embody "definite marks of inferiority connected with them all, which place them at the widest distances from civilized languages." Crummell then lists these shared "marks of inferiority" of the black vernacular:

> Of this whole class of languages, it may be said, in the aggregate that (a) "They are," to use the words of Dr. Leighton Wilson, "harsh, abrupt, energetic, indistinct in enunciation, meager in point of words, abound with inarticulate nasal and guttural sounds, possess but few inflections and grammatical forms, and are withal exceedingly difficult of acquisition." This is his description of the Grebo; but it may be taken, I think, as, on the whole, a correct description of the whole class of dialects which are entitled "Negro." (b) These languages, moreover, are characterized by lowness of ideas. As the speech of rude barbarians, they are marked by brutal and vindictive sentiments, and those principles which show a pre-

dominance of the animal propensities. (c) Again, they lack
those ideas of virtue, of moral truth, and those distinctions of
right and wrong with which we, all our life long, have been
familiar. (d) Another marked feature of these languages is
the absence of clear ideas of Justice, Law, Human Rights, and
Governmental Order, which are so prominent and manifest
in civilized countries. And (e) lastly—Those supernal truths
of a personal, present Deity, of the moral government of
God, of man's immortality, of the judgment, and of Everlast-
ing Blessedness, which regulate the lives of Christians, are
either entirely absent, or else exist, and are expressed in an
obscure and distorted manner. (pp. 19–20)

So much for the black vernacular!

Any attempt even to render the master's discourse in our own
black discourse is an egregious error, Crummell continues, because to do so is merely to translate sublime utterances "in broken
English—a miserable caricature of their noble tongue" (p. 50).
Such was the case when the English, in the West Indies, translated
the Bible from the rich cadences of King James into the "crude,
mongrel, discordant jargon" of the black vernacular. No, translation just won't do, because "a language without its characteristic
features, stamp, and spirit, is a lifeless and unmeaning thing."
The attempt to translate from English to the black vernacular is
"so great a blunder." We must abandon forever both indigenous
African vernacular languages as well as the neo-African vernacular languages that our people have produced in the New World:

All low, inferior, and barbarous tongues are, doubtless, but
the lees and dregs of noble languages, which have gradually,
as the soul of a nation has died out, sunk down to degradation
and ruin. We must not suffer this decay on these shores, in
this nation. We have been made, providentially, the deposit of
a noble trust; and we should be proud to show our appreciation of it. Having come to the heritage of this language we
must cherish its spirit, as well as retain its letter. We must
cultivate it among ourselves; we must strive to infuse its spirit
among our reclaimed and aspiring natives. (p. 50)

I cite the examples of John C. Calhoun and Alexander Crummell as metaphors for the relation between the critic of black

literature and the broader, larger institution of literature. However, lest anyone believe that the arguments of Calhoun, Kant, Jefferson, Hume, or Hegel have been relegated to their proper places in the garbage can of history, she or he need only recall the recent works of Japanese prime minister Nakasone, when he remarked that America will *never* be the intellectual equal of Japan because the presence of Chicanos, Puerto Ricans, and blacks lowers the country's collective IQ! (To which Ronald Reagan responded, when queried, that before responding he needed to see Nakasone's remarks "in context"!)

Calhoun and Crummell are my metaphors for acts of empowerment. Learning the master's tongue, for our generation of critics, has been an act of empowerment, whether that critical language be New Criticism, so-called humanism, structuralism, Marxism, poststructuralism, feminism, new historicism, or any other "ism" that I have forgotten. Each of these critical discourses arises from a specific set of texts within the Western tradition. At least for the past decade, many of us have busied ourselves with the necessary task of learning about these movements in criticism, drawing upon their modes of reading to explicate the texts in our tradition. This has been an exciting time for critics of Afro-American literature, producing perhaps not as much energy as did, say, the Harlem Renaissance or the Black Arts movement, but certainly producing as many critical essays and books about black literature, and yes, even jobs and courses in white English departments. Even with the institutionalization of the racism inherent in "Reaganomics" and with the death of black power, there have never been more jobs available in Afro-American literature in white colleges and universities than there are today, as even a cursory glance at the MLA job list will attest. (Last year alone, thirty-seven such positions were advertised.) In a few years, we shall at last have our very own Norton anthology, a sure sign that the teaching of Afro-American literature already has been institutionalized and will continue to be so, as only the existence of a well-marketed, affordable anthology can ensure. Our pressing question now becomes this: in what languages shall we choose to speak, and write, our own criticisms? What are we now to do with the enabling masks of empowerment which we have donned as we have practiced one mode of white criticism or another?

In the December 9, 1986, issue of the *Voice Literary Supplement,* in an essay entitled "Cult-Nats Meet Freaky-Deke,"[4] Greg Tate argues cogently and compellingly that

> black aestheticians need to develop a coherent criticism to communicate the complexities of our culture. There's no periodical on black cultural phenomena equivalent to *The Village Voice* or *Artforum,* no publication that provides journalism on black visual art, philosophy, economics, media, literature, linguistics, psychology, sexuality, spirituality, and pop culture. Though there are certainly black editors, journalists, and academics capable of producing such a journal, the disintegration of the black cultural nationalist movement and the brain-drain of black intellectuals to white institutions have destroyed the vociferous public dialogue that used to exist between them. (p. 5)

While I would argue that *Sage, Calaloo,* and *BALF* are indeed fulfilling that function for academic critics, I am afraid that the truth of Tate's claim is irresistible. But Tate's real and very important contribution to the future of black criticism is to be found in his most damning allegation: "What's unfortunate," he writes,

> is that while black artists have opened up the entire "text of blackness" for fun and games, not many black critics have produced writing as fecund, eclectic, and freaky-deke as the art, let alone the culture, itself. . . . For those who prefer exegesis with a polemical bent, just imagine how critics as fluent in black and Western culture as the postliberated artists could strike terror into that bastion of white supremacist thinking, the Western art [and literary] worlds. (p. 5)

To which I can only say, echoing Shug in *The Color Purple,* "Amen. Amen." Only by reshaping the critical canon with our own voices in our own images can we meet Tate's challenge head-on, because the black tradition theorizes about itself in the vernacular.

Before I return to those metaphors of progress, elevation, and intellectual equality with which I began, John C. Calhoun and Alexander Crummell, let us consider another example of the

---

4. Greg Tate, "Cult-Nats Meet Freaky Deke," *Voice Literary Supplement,* December 9, 1986. All subsequent references will be given parenthetically in the text.

black artist at the peculiar liminal crossroads where the black world of letters meets the white. If mastering the forms of Western poetry to refute the racist logocentrism epitomized by John C. Calhoun motivated Phillis Wheatley to break forever the silence of the black voice in the court of Western letters, and motivated Crummell to sail to Cambridge to master Greek syntax, how did Wole Soyinka respond to becoming the first black recipient of the Nobel Prize in literature, that sacred icon of Western intellectual and artistic attainment which many of us thought would be withheld from us for still another century, and which many of us take to be another nuclear warhead dropped upon the last bastion of white racism—that is, their theories of our intellectual inferiority? Soyinka, born in Abeokuta, Nigeria, which Crummell had predicted to be one of the places in West Africa at which the English language would reach perfection as spoken by black people (p. 36), responded not as Crummell did to the racism which led him to Cambridge, by extolling the virtues of the English language over the African vernacular languages, which Crummell thought to reflect the animal propensities of an inferior, barely human intellect, but by recalling the irony that this single event in the history of black literature occurred while Nelson Mandela was languishing in prison and while Western capitalism was guaranteeing the survival and indeed the growth of the prison-house of apartheid. Dedicating his laureate speech to Nelson Mandela, Soyinka proceeded to attack the existence of apartheid and the complicity of the West in its continuation, as a nervous Swedish Academy shifted its weight uneasily.

Soyinka was most concerned to analyze the implications of African artistry and intellect being acknowledged before the white world, at long last, through this curious ritual called the Nobel Prize, endowed by the West's King of Dynamite and weaponry. Soyinka refused to address his black audience; rather, he addressed his white auditors and indeed the racist intellectual tradition of Europe as exemplified by Hegel, Hume, Locke, Voltaire, Frobenius, Kant, and others, who "were unabashed theorists of racial superiority and denigrators of the African history and being" (p. 10).[5]

---

5. Wole Soyinka, "This Past Must Address This Present," Nobel Laureate Address, December 8, 1986. All citations are taken from the manuscript, and will be given parenthetically in the text.

The blacks of course are locked into an unambiguous condition: on this occasion I do not need to address *us*. We know,
and we embrace our mission. It is the *other* that this precedent
seizes the opportunity to address, and not merely those who
live outside, on the fringes of conscience. . . .

Some atavistic bug is at work here which defies all scientific
explanation, an arrest in time within the evolutionary man-
date of nature, which puts all human experience of learning
to serious question! We have to ask ourselves then, what event
can speak to such a breed of people? How do we reactivate
that petrified cell which houses historic apprehension and
development? Is it possible perhaps that events, gatherings
such as this might help? Dare we skirt the edge of hubris and
say to them: Take a good look. Provide your response. In
your anxiety to prove that this moment is not possible, you
have killed, maimed, silenced, tortured, exiled, debased and
dehumanized hundreds of thousands encased in this very
skin, crowned with such hair, proudly content with their very
being. (pp. 8–9)

Soyinka's brilliant rhetorical gesture was to bring together an
uncompromising renunciation of apartheid and a considered indictment of the racist tradition in Western letters which equates
the possession of reason with the reflection of the voice and the
face of the master, a tradition which overwhelmed Alexander
Crummell, standing as he did at a point of liminality between
Western culture and African culture. Citing the work of Locke,
Hume, Hegel, Montesquieu, and a host of others as "dangerous
for your racial self-esteem!" (p. 19), Soyinka marshalled a most
impressive array of citations to chart the racist tradition in Western letters which would deny to the black world the particularity
of its discourse, as typified for Soyinka by the following sentiment
of the expressionist Johannes Becher: "Negro tribes, fever, tuber-
culosis, venereal epidemics, intellectual psychic defects—I'll van-
quish them" (p. 16). To underscore the failure of the Western
intellectual to escape his or her own myopic racism in even the
most sublime encounters with the Black Other, Soyinka compares
Becher's exhortation with the commentary of Leo Frobenius
upon encountering the most sacred, and most brilliantly rendered, bronze of the Yoruba people:

And was it by coincidence that contemporaneously with this
stirring manifesto, yet another German enthusiast, Leo

Frobenius—with no claims whatever to being part of, or indeed having the least interest in the Expressionist movement, was able to visit Ile-Ife, the heartland and cradle of the Yoruba race and be profoundly stirred by an object of beauty, the product of the Yoruba mind and hand, a classic expression of that serene portion of the world resolution of that race. In his own words: "Before us stood a head of marvelous beauty, wonderfully cast in antique bronze, true to the life, encrusted with a patina of glorious dark green. This was, in very deed, the Olokun, Atlantic Africa's Poseidon." Yet listen to what he had to write about the very people whose handiwork had lifted him into these realms of universal sublimity: "Profoundly stirred, I stood for many minutes before the remnant of the erstwhile Lord and Ruler of the Empire of Atlantis. My companions were no less astounded. As though we had agreed to do so, we held our peace. Then I looked around and saw—the blacks—the circle of the sons of the 'venerable priest,' his Holiness the Oni's friends, and his intelligent officials. I was moved to silent melancholy at the thought that this assembly of degenerate and feeble-minded posterity should be the legitimate guardians of so much loveliness." A direct invitation to a free-for-all race for dispossession, justified on the grounds of the keeper's unworthiness, it recalls other schizophrenic conditions which are mother to, for instance, the far more lethal, dark mythopoeia of [the Nazis]. (pp. 16–17)

"He is breaking an open door," one member of the Swedish Academy said to me while Soyinka spoke. "Why would he choose to indict apartheid at an historic moment such as this?" Soyinka chose to do so to remind the world that no black person can be truly free until we are freed from even the *probability* of racial oppression, and that even Nobel Prizes in literature are useful only when its first black recipient reminds the world of that fact, and of the history of the use of race and reason as tropes of oppression in Western letters. As critics and Artists, Soyinka argues, we must utilize the creative and critical tools at hand to stomp racism out. This is our first great task.

But what else contributes to the relation, then, between (white) power and the (black) critic? Soyinka's terms, and my title, might suggest that ours is the fate of perpetual negation, that we are doomed merely to "oppose," to serve within the academy as black signs of opposition to a political order in which we are the subjugated. We must oppose, of course, when opposition is called for. But our task is much more complex. Again, to define this task, I can do no better than to cite Soyinka: "And when we borrow an alien language to sculpt or paint in, we must begin by co-opting the entire properties of that language as correspondences to properties in our matrix of thought and expression."[6] And this, it seems to me, is the challenge of black canon-formation at the present time. Soyinka's own brilliant achievement in the drama is to have done just this, to have redefined the very concept of "tragedy" by producing a synthesis of African and European tragic forms. At all points, his "English" is Yoruba-informed, Yoruba-based. To assume that we can wear the masks, and speak the languages, of Western literary theory without accepting Soyinka's challenge is to accept, willingly, the intellectual equivalent of neocolonialism, placing ourselves in a relationship of discursive indenture.

It is the challenge of the black tradition to critique this relation of indenture, an indenture that obtains for our writers and for our critics. We must master, as even Jacques Derrida understands, how "to speak the other's language without renouncing [our] own."[7] When we attempt to appropriate, by inversion, "race" as a term for an essence—as did the negritude movement ("We feel, therefore we are," as Leopold Senghor argued of the African)— we yield too much: in this case, *reason* as the basis of a shared humanity. Such gestures, as Anthony Appiah observes, are futile and dangerous because of their further inscription of new and bizarre stereotypes. How do we meet Soyinka's challenge in the discourse of criticism?

The Western critical tradition has a canon, as the Western literary tradition does. I once thought it our most important gesture to *master* the canon of criticism, to *imitate* and *apply* it, but I now believe that we must turn to the black tradition itself to develop theories of criticism indigenous to our literatures. Alice Walker's revision of Rebecca Cox Jackson's parable of white interpretation

---

6. Cited in "Nigeria: The New Culture," *New York Post,* February 17, 1987, Supplement, p. 1.

7. Jacques Derrida, "The Last Word in Racism," in *"Race," Writing, and Difference,* ed. H. L. Gates, Jr. (Chicago: University of Chicago Press, 1986), p. 333.

(written in 1836) makes this point most tellingly. Jackson, a Shaker eldress and black visionary, claimed like John Jea to have been taught to read by the Lord. She writes in her autobiography that she dreamed a white man came to her house to teach her how to *interpret* and understand the word of God, now that God had taught her to read:

> A white man took me by my right hand and led me on the north side of the room, where sat a square table. On it lay a book open. And he said to me. "Thou shall be instructed in this book, from Genesis to Revelations." And then he took me on the west side, where stood a table. And it looked like the first. And said, "Yea, thou shall be instructed from the beginning of creation to the end of time." And then he took me on the east side of the room also, where stood a table and book like the two first, and said, "I will instruct thee—yea, thou shall be instructed from the beginning of all things to the end of all things. Yea, thou shall be well instructed. I will instruct."
>
> And then I awoke, and I saw him as plain as I did in my dream. And after that he taught me daily. And when I would be reading and come to a hard word, I would see him standing by my side and he would teach me the word right. And often, when I would be in meditation and looking into things which was hard to understand, I would find him by me, teaching and giving me understanding. And oh, his labor and care which he had with me often caused me to weep bitterly, when I would see my great ignorance and the great trouble he had to make me understand eternal things. For I was so buried in the depth of the tradition of my forefathers, that it did seem as if I never could be dug up.[8]

In response to Jackson's relation of interpretive indenture to "a white man," Walker, in *The Color Purple*, records an exchange between Celie and Shug about turning away from "the old white man" which soon turns into a conversation about the elimination of "man" as a mediator between a woman and "everything":

---

8. Rebecca Cox Jackson, "A Dream of Three Books and a Holy One," *Gifts of Power: The Writings of Rebecca Cox Jackson, Black Visionary, Shaker Eldress*, ed. Jean McMahon Humez (Amherst: University of Massachusetts Press), pp. 146–47.

Still, it is like Shug say, you have to git man off your eyeball, before you can see anything a'tall.

Man corrupt everything, say Shug. He on your box of grits, in your head, and all over the radio. He try to make you think he everywhere. Soon as you think he everywhere, you think he God. But he ain't. Whenever you trying to pray, and man plop himself on the other end of it, tell him to git lost, say Shug.[9]

Celie and Shug's omnipresent "man," of course, echoes the black tradition's synechdoche for the white power structure, "the man."

For non-Western, so-called noncanonical critics, getting the "man off your eyeball" means using the most sophisticated critical theories and methods available to reappropriate and redefine our own "colonial" discourses. We must use these theories and methods insofar as they are relevant to the study of our own "colonial" discourses. We must use these theories and methods insofar as they are relevant to the study of our own literatures. The danger in doing so, however, is best put by Anthony Appiah in his definition of what he calls "the Naipaul fallacy":

It is not necessary to show that African literature is fundamentally the same as European literature in order to show that it can be treated with the same tools; . . . nor should we endorse a more sinister line . . . : the post-colonial legacy which requires us to show that African literature is worthy of study precisely (but only) because it is fundamentally the same as European literature. [10]

We *must* not, Appiah concludes, ask "the reader to understand Africa by embedding it in European culture" (S, p. 146).

We must, I believe, analyze the ways in which writing relates to race, how attitudes toward racial differences generate and structure literary texts by us *and* about us. We must determine how

---

9. Alice Walker, *The Color Purple* (New York: Harcourt Brace Jovanovich, 1982), p. 179.

10. Anthony Appiah, "Strictures on Structures: The Prospects for a Structuralist Poetics of African Fiction," in *Black Literature and Literary Theory*, ed. H. L. Gates, Jr. (New York: Methuen, 1984), pp. 146, 145. All subsequent references to this work, abbreviated as "S," will be included in the text.

critical methods can effectively disclose the traces of ethnic differences in literature.

But we must also understand how certain forms of difference and the *languages* we employ to define those supposed differences not only reinforce each other but tend to create and maintain each other. Similarly, and as important, we must analyze the language of contemporary criticism itself, recognizing especially that hermeneutic systems are not universal, color-blind, apolitical, or neutral. Whereas some critics wonder aloud, as Appiah notes, whether or not "a structuralist poetics is inapplicable in Africa because structuralism is European" (S, p. 145), the concern of the Third World critic should properly be to understand the ideological subtext which any critical theory reflects and embodies, and the relation which this subtext bears to the production of meaning. No critical theory—be it Marxist, feminist, post-structuralist, Kwame Nkrumah's "consciencism," or whatever—escapes the specificity of value and ideology, no matter how mediated these may be. To attempt to appropriate our own discourses by using Western critical theory uncritically is to substitute one mode of neocolonialism for another. To begin to do this in our own tradition, theorists have turned to the black vernacular tradition—to paraphrase Jackson, they have begun to dig into the depths of the tradition of our foreparents—to isolate the signifying black difference through which to theorize about the so-called discourse of the Other.

Even Crummell recognized that Western economic and political subjugation has inflicted upon us a desire to imitate, to please, to refashion our public discursive images of our black selves after that of the colonizer: "he will part," Crummell with great satisfaction concludes of the colonized African, "at any moment, with the crude uncouth utterances of his native tongue, for that other higher language, which brings with its utterance, wealth and gratification" (pp. 34–35).

Thus, it seems to me, is the trap, the tragic lure, to which those who believe that critical theory is a color-blind, universal discourse, or a culturally neutral tool like a hammer or a screwdriver, have unwittingly succumbed. And by succumbing to this mistake, such critics fail to accept the wonderful opportunity offered to our generation of critics as heirs to the Black Arts movement, the great achievement of which, as Greg Tate correctly concludes, was to define a "black cultural *difference*" and "produce a post-liberated black aesthetic [which is] responsible for the degree to which contemporary black artists and intellectuals feel themselves heirs to a culture every bit as def [sic] as classical Western civilization. This cultural confidence," he concludes, "has freed up more black artists to do work as wonderfully absurdist as black life itself" (p. 5).

As Tate concludes, where is the black critical theory as great as this greatest black art? Our criticism is destined merely to be derivative, to be a pale shadow of the white master's critical discourse, until we become confident enough to speak in our own black languages as we theorize about the black critical endeavor.

We must redefine "theory" itself from within our own black cultures, refusing to grant the racist premise that theory is something that white people do, so that we are doomed to imitate our white colleagues, like reverse black minstrel critics done up in whiteface. We are all heirs to critical theory, but we black critics are heirs as well to the black vernacular tradition. Our task now is to invent and employ our own critical theory, to assume our own propositions, and to stand within the academy as politically responsible and responsive parts of a social and cultural African-American whole. Again, Soyinka's words about our relation to the black tradition are relevant here:

> That world which is so conveniently traduced by Apartheid thought is of course that which I so wholeheartedly embrace—and this is my choice—among several options—of the significance of my presence here. It is a world that nourishes my being, one which is so self-sufficient, so replete in all aspects of its productivity, so confident in itself and in its destiny that it experiences no fear in reaching out to others and in responding to the reach of others. It is the heartstone of our creative existence. It constitutes the prism of our world perception and this means that our sign need not be and has never been permanently turned inwards. If it were, we could not so easily understand the enemy on our doorstep, nor understand how to obtain the means to disarm it. When this society which is Apartheid South Africa indulges from time to time in appeals to the outside world that it represents the last

bastion of civilization against the hordes of barbarism from its North, we can even afford an indulgent smile. It is sufficient, imagines this state, to raise the spectre of a few renegade African leaders, psychopaths and robber barons whom we ourselves are victims of—whom we denounce before the world and overthrow when we are able—this Apartheid society insists to the world that its picture of the future is the reality that only its policies can erase. This is a continent which only destroys, it proclaims, it is peopled by a race which has never contributed anything positive to the world's pool of knowledge. A vacuum, that will suck into its insatiable jaw the entire fruits of centuries of European civilization, then spew out the resulting mush with contempt. How strange that a society which claims to represent this endangered face of progress should itself be locked in centuries-old fantasies, blithely unaware of, or indifferent to the fact that it is the last, institutionally functioning product of archaic articles of faith in Euro-Judaic thought. (pp. 11–12)

As deconstruction and other post-structuralisms, or even an aracial Marxism and other "articles of faith in Euro-Judaic thought," exhaust themselves in a self-willed racial never-never land in which we see no true reflections of our black faces and hear no echoes of our black voices, let us—at long last—master the canon of critical traditions and languages of Africa and Afro-America. Even as we continue to reach out to others in the critical canon, let us be confident in our own black traditions and in their compelling strength to sustain systems of critical thought that are as yet dormant and unexplicated. We must, in the truest sense, turn inward even as we turn outward to redefine every institution in this profession—the English Institute, the MLA, the School of Criticism—in our own images. We must not succumb, as did Alexander Crummell, to the tragic lure of white power, the mistake of accepting the empowering language of white critical theory as "universal" or as our own language, the mistake of confusing the enabling mask of theory with our own black faces. Each of us has, in some literal or figurative manner, boarded a ship and sailed to a metaphorical Cambridge, seeking to master the master's tools, and to outwit this racist master by compensating for a supposed lack. In my own instance, being quite literal-minded, I booked passage some fourteen years ago on the *QE II!* And much of my early work reflects my desire to outwit the master by trying to speak his language as fluently as he. Now, we must, at last, don the empowering mask of blackness and talk *that* talk, the language of black difference. While it is true that we must, as Du Bois said so long ago, "know and test the power of the cabalistic letters of the white man," we must also know and test the dark secrets of a black and hermetic discursive universe that awaits its disclosure through the black arts of interpretation. For the future of theory and of the literary enterprise in general, in the remainder of this century, is black, indeed.

II

How does this matter of the black canon of criticism affect our attempts to define canon(s) of black literature? I believe, first of all, that until we free ourselves of the notion that we are "just Americans," as Ellison might put it, and that what is good and proper for Americanists is good and proper for Afro-Americanists, we shall remain indentured servants to white masters, female and male, and to the Western tradition, yielding the most fundamental right that any tradition possesses, and that is the right to define itself, its own terms for order, its very own presuppositions. If we recall the etymology of the word "theory" from the Greek *theoria*, we can understand why the production of black text-specific theory is essential to our attempts to form black canons: theoria, as Wlad Godzich points out in his introduction to Paul de Man's *The Resistance to Theory*, "is a public, institutional act of certification which assumes the authority to 'effect the passage from the seen to the told'; and provides the basis for public discourse. Theory, then, is—like rhetoric—a form of cognition modeled upon (public) utterance rather than upon (private) perception."[11] When we mindlessly borrow another tradition's theory, we undermine this passage from the seen to the told—from what we see to how we tell it—this basis for our own black public discourse, this relation between cognition and utterance.

---

11. Wlad Godzich, "Foreword," in Paul de Man, *The Resistance to Theory* (Minneapolis: University of Minnesota Press, 1986), pp. xiv–xv, cited in Barbara Jones Guetti, "Resisting the Aesthetic," forthcoming in *Diacritics*.

Lord knows that this relationship between the seen and the told—that gap of difference between what we see among and for ourselves and what we choose to tell in (a white, or integrated) public discourse—has been remarkably complex in our tradition, especially in attempts to define the canon of black literature at any given time.

Curiously enough, the very first evidence of the idea of the "canon" in relation to the Afro-American literary tradition occurs in 1849, in a speech delivered by Theodore Parker. Parker was a theologian, a Unitarian clergyman, and a publicist for ideas; Perry Miller described him as "the man who next only to Emerson . . . was to give shape and meaning to the Transcendental movement in America." In a speech on "The Mercantile Classes" delivered in 1846, Parker had lamented the sad state of "American" letters:

> Literature, science, and art are mainly in [poor men's] hands, yet are controlled by the prevalent spirit of the nation. . . . In England, the national literature favors the church, the crown, the nobility, the prevailing class. Another literature is rising, but is not yet national, *still less canonized.* We have no American literature which is permanent. Our scholarly books are only an imitation of a foreign type; they do not reflect our morals, manners, politics, or religion, not even our rivers, mountains, sky. They have not the smell of our ground in their breath.[12]

Parker, to say the least, was not especially pleased with American letters and their identity with the English tradition. Did he find any evidence of a truly American discourse?

> The real American literature is found only in newspapers and speeches, perhaps in some novel, hot, passionate, but poor and extemporaneous. That is our national literature. Does that favor man—represent man? Certainly not. All is the reflection of this most powerful class. The truths that are told are for them, and the lies. Therein the prevailing sentiment is getting into the form of thoughts.

---

12. Theodore Parker, *Social Classes in a Republic,* ed. Samuel A. Eliot (Boston: American Unitarian Association, 1907), p. 32. Emphasis added.

Parker's analysis, of course, is "proto-Marxian," embodying as it does the reflection-theory of base and superstructure. It is the occasional literature, "poor and extemporaneous," wherein "American" literature dwells.

Three years later, in his major oration on "The American Scholar," Parker at last found an entirely original genre of American literature:

> Yet, there is one portion of our permanent literature, if literature it may be called, which is wholly indigenous and original. The lives of the early martyrs and confessors are purely Christian, so are the legends of saints and other pious men; there was nothing like this in the Hebrew or heathen literature, cause and occasion were alike wanting for it. So we have one series of literary productions that could be written by none but Americans, and only here; I mean the Lives of Fugitive Slaves. But as these are not the work of the men of superior culture they hardly help to pay the scholar's debt. Yet all the original romance of Americans is in them, not in the white man's novel.[13]

Parker was right about the originality, the peculiarly *American* quality, of the slave narratives. but he was wrong about their inherent inability to "pay the scholar's debt"; scholars had only to learn to *read* the narratives for their debt to be paid in full, indeed many times over. As Charles Sumner said in 1852, the fugitive slaves and their narratives "are among the heroes of our age. Romance has no storms of more thrilling interest than theirs. Classical antiquity has preserved no examples of adventurous trial more worthy of renown."[14] Parker's and Sumner's views reveal that the popularity of the narratives in antebellum America most certainly did not reflect any sort of common critical agreement about their nature and status as art. Still, the implications of these observations for black canon-formation would take three-quarters of a century to be realized. The first attempt to define a black canon that I have found is that by Armand Lanusse, who edited

13. Theodore Parker, *The American Scholar*, ed. George Willis Cooke (Boston: American Unitarian Association, 1907), p. 37.

14. Charles Sumner, cited in *The Slave's Narrative*, ed. Charles T. Davis and H. L. Gates, Jr. (New York: Oxford University Press, 1985), p. xv.

Les Cenelles, an anthology of black French verse published at New Orleans in 1845—the first black anthology, I believe, ever published. Lanusse's "Introduction" is a defense of poetry as an enterprise for black people, in their larger efforts to defend the race against "the spiteful and calumnious arrows shot at us," at a target defined as the collective black intellect (p. xxxviii).[15] Despite this stated political intention, these poems imitate the styles and themes of the French Romantics and never engage directly the social and political experience of black Creoles in New Orleans in the 1840s. *Les Cenelles* argues for a political effect—that is, the end of racism—by publishing apolitical poems, poems which share as their silent second texts the poetry written by Frenchmen three thousand miles away. We are like the French—so, treat us like Frenchmen. An apolitical art was being put to uses most political.

Four years later, in 1849, William G. Allen published an anthology in which he canonized Phillis Wheatley and George Moses Horton. Like Lanusse, Allen sought to refute intellectual racism by the act of canon-formation. "The African's called inferior," he writes. "But what race has ever displayed intellect more exaltedly, or character more sublime?" (p. 3). Pointing to the achievements of Pushkin, Placido, and Augustine, as the great African tradition to which Afro-Americans are heir, Allen claims Wheatley and Horton as the exemplars of this tradition, Horton being "decidedly the superior genius," no doubt because of his explicitly racial themes, a judgment quite unlike that which propelled Armand Lanusse into canon-formation. As Allen puts it:

> Who will now say that the African is incapable of attaining to intellectual or moral greatness? What he now is, degrading circumstances have made him. Past clearly evinces. The African is strong, tough and hardy. Hundreds of years of oppression have not subdued his spirit, and though Church and State have combined to enslave and degrade him, in spite of them all, he is increasing in strength and power, and in the respect of the entire world. (p. 7)

---

15. Armand Lanusse, ed., *Les Cenelles: A Collection of Poems by Creole Writers of the Early Nineteenth Century,* translated and edited by Regine Latortue and Gleason R. W. Adams (1845; reprint, Boston: G. K. Hall, 1979). The original publisher was H. Lauve.

Here, then, we see the two poles of black canon-formation, established firmly by 1849: is "black" poetry racial in theme, or is black poetry any sort of poetry written by black people? This quandary has been at play in the tradition ever since.

I do not have the time here to trace in detail the history of this tension over definitions of the Afro-American canon and the direct relation between the production of black poetry and the end of white racism. I want merely to point to such seminal attempts at canon-formation in the twenties as James Weldon Johnson's *The Book of American Negro Poetry* (1922), Alain Locke's *The New Negro* (1925), and V. F. Calverton's *An Anthology of American Negro Literature* (1929), each of which defined as its goal the demonstration of the existence of the black tradition as a political defense of the racial self against racism. As Johnson put it so clearly:

> . . . the matter of Negro poets and the production of literature by the colored people in this country involves more than supplying information that is lacking. It is a matter which has a direct bearing on the most vital of American problems.
>
> A people may be great through many means, but there is only one measure by which its greatness is recognized and acknowledged. The final measure of the greatness of all peoples is the amount and standard of the literature and art that they have produced. The world does not know that a people is great until that people produces great literature and art. No people that has produced great literature and art has ever been looked upon by the world as distinctly inferior.
>
> The status of the Negro in the United States is more a question of national mental attitude toward the race than of actual conditions. And nothing will do more to change that mental attitude and raise his status than a demonstration of intellectual parity by the Negro through the production of literature and art.[16]

Calverton's anthology made two significant departures from this model, both of which are worth considering, if only briefly.

---

16. James Weldon Johnson, ed. *The Book of American Negro Poetry, Chosen and Edited with an Essay on the Negro's Creative Genius* (New York: Harcourt, Brace, 1922), p. vii.

Calverton's was the first attempt at black canon-formation to provide for the influence and presence of black vernacular literature
in a major way. "Spirituals," "Blues," and "Labor Songs" each
comprise a genre of black literature for him. We all understand
the importance of this gesture and its influence upon the editors
of *The Negro Caravan*. Calverton, as well, announces in his intro-
ductory essay, "The Growth of Negro Literature," that his selection principles have been determined by his sense of the history of
black literary forms, leading him to make selections because of
their formal "representative value," as he puts it. "Certain
nineteenth-century poems, for instance," he explains, "which
have been included are pathetically naive and sentimental; yet in
the development of Negro literature they undoubtedly have their
place, and therefore, have been used . . . to represent what the
Negro in America has achieved in the art of literary forms."
These forms, he continues, are *black* forms, virtually self-
contained in a hermetic black tradition, especially in the vernacular tradition. It is worth repeating Calverton's conclusions at
length:

> The Negro, in the eyes of the critics, is an oddity, and as an
> artist and intellectual is stranger far than fiction. Their expla-
> nation of his recent success is based mainly upon what they
> consider an aspect of patronage on the part of the reading
> public and the publisher. His work is greeted from the point
> of view of race and not of art. He is pampered as a Negro,
> and his work is praised often when it ought to be attacked. As
> a consequence, they are convinced that in a few years, as this
> illusion in reference to his work has begun to vanish, the
> interest in Negro literature will cease, and the urge in favor of
> its creation will correspondingly disappear.
>
> Upon close analysis, these interpretations are seen to be at
> once irrelevant and futile. . . . his contributions to American
> art and literature are far more free of white influence than
> American culture is of English. Indeed, we may say that the
> contributions of the Negro to American culture are as indige-
> nous to our soil as the legendary cowboy or gold-seeking
> frontiersman. And, in addition, it is no exaggeration what-
> soever to contend that they are more striking and singular in
> substance and structure than any contributions that have
> been made by the white man to American culture. In fact,

they constitute America's chief claim to originality in its cultural history. In song, the Negro spirituals and to a less extent the Blues; in tradition, Negro folk-lore; and in music, Negro jazz—these three constitute the Negro contribution to American culture. In fact, it can be said, that they constitute all that is unique in our cultural life. . . . After all, the Negro, in his simple, unsophisticated way, has developed out of the American *milieu* a form of expression, a mood, a literary genre, a folk tradition, that are distinctly and undeniably American. This is more than the white man has done. The white man in America has continued, and in an inferior manner, a culture of European origin. He has not developed a culture that is definitely and unequivocally American. In respect of originality, then, the Negro is more important in the growth of American culture than the white man. His art is richer, more spontaneous, and more captivating and convincing in its appeal.

The social background of Negro life in itself was sufficient to inspire an art of no ordinary character. Indeed, the very fact that the Negro, by the nature of his environment, was deprived of education, prevented his art from ever becoming purely imitative. Even where he adopted the white man's substance, as in the case of religion, he never adopted his forms. He gave to whatever he took a new style and a new interpretation. In truth, he made it practically into a new thing. There were no ancient conventions that he, in his untutored zeal, felt duty-bound to respect, and no age-old traditions that instructed him, perforce, as to what was art and what was not. He could express his soul, as it were, without concern for grammar or the eye of the carping critic. As a result, his art is, as is all art that springs from the people, an artless art, and in that sense is the most genuine art of the world. While the white man has gone to Europe for his models, and is seeking still a European approval of his artistic endeavors, the Negro in his art forms has never gone beyond America for his background and has never sought the acclaim of any culture other than his own. This is particularly true of those forms of Negro art that come directly from the people. It is, of course, not so true of a poet such as Phillis Wheatley or of the numerous Negro poets and artists of to-day, who in more ways than one have followed the traditions of their white contemporaries rather than extended and perfected the original art forms of their race. Of course, in the eighteenth century,

when Phillis Wheatley wrote, these Negro art forms were
scarcely more than embryonic. Today, on the other hand,
their existence has become a commonplace to the white writer
as well as the black.[17]

Return, or turn, to the black vernacular, Calverton argues, to
unearth the veiled structures of black difference.

If Calverton's stress upon the black vernacular heavily influenced the shaping of *The Negro Caravan*—certainly one of the
most important anthologies in the tradition—his sense of the
black canon as a formal, self-contained entity most certainly did
not. As the editors put in the Introduction to the volume:

> The editors therefore do not believe that the expression
> "Negro literature" is an accurate one, and in spite of its con-
> venient brevity, they have avoided using it. "Negro literature"
> has no application if it means structural peculiarity, or a
> Negro school of writing. The Negro writes in the forms
> evolved in English and American literature. "A Negro novel,"
> "a Negro play" are ambiguous terms. If they mean a novel or
> a play by Negroes, then such works as *Porgy* and *The Green
> Pastures* are left out. If they mean works about Negro life,
> they include more works by white authors than by Negro, and
> these works have been most influential upon the American
> mind. The editors consider Negro writers to be American
> writers, and literature by American Negroes to be a segment
> of American literature. They believe that it would be just as
> misleading to classify Clifford Odet's play about Jewish life as
> "Jewish literature" or James T. Farrell's novels of the Chicago
> Irish as "Irish literature" or some of William Saroyan's tales as
> "Armenian literature."
>
> The chief cause for objection to the term is that "Negro
> literature" is too easily placed by certain critics, white and
> Negro, in an alcove apart. The next step is a double standard
> of judgment, which is dangerous for the future of Negro
> writers. "A Negro novel," thought of as a separate form, is too
> often condoned as "good enough for a Negro." That Negroes
> in America have had a hard time, and that inside stores of

17. V. F. Calverton, "The Growth of Negro Literature," in *An Anthology of
American Negro Literature*, ed. V. F. Calverton (New York: The Modern Library,
1929), pp. 3–5.

Negro live often present unusual and attractive reading matter are incontrovertible facts; but when they enter literary criticism these facts do damage to both the critics and the artists. The editors do not hold that this anthology maintains an even level of literary excellence. A number of the selections have been included as essential to a balanced picture. Literature by Negro authors about Negro experience is a literature in process and like all such literature (including American literature) must be considered as significant, not only because of a body of established masterpieces, but also because of the illumination it sheds upon a social reality. (p. 7)

And later, in the Introduction to the section entitled "The Novel," the editors elaborate upon this idea by pointing to the relation of revision between *Iola Leroy* and *Clotel,* a relation of the sort central to Calverton's canon, but here defined in most disapproving terms: "There are repetitions of situations from Brown's *Clotel,* something of a forecast of a sort of literary inbreeding which causes Negro writers to be influenced by other Negroes more than should ordinarily be expected" (p. 139). The black canon, for these editors, was that literature which most eloquently refuted white racist stereotypes (p. 5) and which embodied the shared "theme of struggle that is present in so much Negro expression" (p. 6). Theirs, in other words, was a canon that was unified thematically by self-defense against racist literary conventions, and by the expression of what the editors called "strokes of freedom" (p. 6). The formal bond that Calverton had claimed was of no political use for these editors, precisely because they wished to project an integrated canon of American literature. As the editors put it,

In spite of such unifying bonds as a common rejection of the popular stereotypes and a common "racial" cause, writings by Negroes do not seem to the editors to fall into a unique cultural pattern. Negro writers have adopted the literary traditions that seemed useful for their purposes. They have therefore been influenced by Puritan didacticism, sentimental humanitarianism, local color, regionalism, realism, naturalism, and experimentalism. Phillis Wheatley wrote the same high moralizing verse in the same poetic pattern as her contemporary poets in New England. While Frederick Douglass brought more personal knowledge and bitterness into his antislavery agitation than William Lloyd Garrison and Theodore Parker, he is much closer to them in spirit and in form than to Phillis Wheatley, his predecessor, and Booker T. Washington, his successor. Frances E. W. Harper wrote antislavery poetry in the spirit and pattern of Longfellow and Felicia Hemans; her contemporary, Whitfield, wrote of freedom in the pattern of Byron. And so it goes. Without too great imitativeness, many contemporary Negro writers are closer to O. Henry, Carl Sandburg, Edgar Lee Masters, Edna St. Vincent Millay, Waldo Frank, Ernest Hemingway and John Steinbeck than to each other. The bonds of literary tradition seem to be stronger than race. (pp. 6–7)

So much for a definition of the Afro-American tradition based on formal relationships of revision, text to text.

At the opposite extreme in black canon-formation is the canon defined by Amiri Baraka and Larry Neal in *Black Fire*, published in 1968. This canon, the blackest canon of all, was defined by both formal innovations and by themes: formally, individual selections tended to aspire to the vernacular or to black music, or to performance; theoretically, each selection reinforces the urge toward black liberation, toward "freedom now" with an up-against-the-wall subtext. The hero, the valorized presence, in this volume is the black vernacular: no longer summoned or invoked through familiar and comfortable rubrics such as "The Spirituals" and "The Blues," but *embodied, assumed, presupposed,* in a marvelous act of formal bonding often obscured to some readers by the stridency of the political message the anthology meant to announce. Absent completely was a desire to "prove" our common humanity to white people by demonstrating our power of intellect. No, in *Black Fire*, art and act were one.

III

I have been thinking about these strains in black canon-formation because a group of us are editing still another anthology, which will constitute still another attempt at canon-formation.

W. W. Norton will be publishing the Norton Anthology of

Afro-American Literature. The editing of this anthology has been a great dream of mine for a long time. I am very excited about this project. I think that I am most excited about the fact that we will have at our disposal the means to edit an anthology which will define a canon of Afro-American literature for instructors and students at any institution which desires to teach a course in Afro-American literature. Once our anthology is published, no one will ever again be able to use the unavailability of black texts as an excuse not to teach our literature. A well-marketed anthology—particularly a Norton anthology—functions in the academy to *create* a tradition, as well as to define and preserve it. A Norton anthology opens up a literary tradition as simply as opening the cover of a carefully edited and ample book.

I am not unaware of the politics and ironies of canon-formation. The canon that we define will be "our" canon, one possible set of selections among several possible sets of selections. In part to be as eclectic and as democratically "representative" as possible, most other editors of black anthologies have tried to include as many authors and selections (especially excerpts) as possible, in order to preserve and "resurrect" the tradition. I call this the Sears Roebuck approach, the "dream book" of black literature.

We have all benefited from this approach. Indeed, may of our authors have only managed to survive because an enterprising editor was determined to marshall as much evidence as she or he could to show that the black literary tradition existed. While we must be deeply appreciative of that approach and its results, our task will be a different one. Our task will be to bring together the "essential" texts of the canon, the "crucially central" authors, those whom we feel to be indispensable to an understanding of the shape, and shaping, of the tradition. A canon is the essence of the tradition: the connection between the texts of the canon reveals the tradition's inherent, or veiled, logic, its internal rationale.

None of us are naive enough to believe that "the canonical" is self-evident, absolute, or natural. Scholars make canons. Keenly aware of this—and quite frankly, aware of my own biases—I have attempted to bring together as period editors a group of scholar-critics, each of whom combines great expertise in her or his period with her or his own approach to the teaching and analyzing of Afro-American literature. I have attempted, in other words, to bring together scholars whose notions of the black canon might not necessarily agree with my own, or with each other. I have tried to bring together a diverse array of ideological methodological, and theoretical perspectives, so that we together might produce an anthology which most fully represents the various definitions of what it means to speak of the Afro-American literary tradition, and what it means to *teach* that tradition.

I can say that my own biases toward canon-formation are to stress the formal relationship that obtains among texts in the black tradition—relations of revision, echo, call and response, antiphony, what have you—and to stress the vernacular roots of the tradition, contra Alexander Crummell. Accordingly, let me add that our anthology will include a major innovation in anthology production. Because of the strong oral and vernacular base of so much of our literature, we shall include a cassette tape along with our anthology. This means that each period will include both the printed and spoken text of oral and musical selections of black vernacular culture: sermons, blues, spirituals, R & B, poets reading their own "dialect" poems, speeches, and other performances. Imagine having Bessie Smith and Billie Holiday singing the blues, Langston Hughes reading "The Negro Speaks of Rivers," Sterling Brown reading "Ma Rainey," James Weldon Johnson "The Creation," C. L. Franklin "The Sermon of the Dry Bones," Martin speaking "I Have a Dream," Sonia Sanchez "Talking in Tongues"—the list of possibilities is endless, and exhilarating. So much of our literature seems dead on the page when compared to its performance. Incorporating performance and the black and human voice into our anthology, we will change fundamentally not only the way that our literature is taught but the way in which any literary tradition is even conceived.

Negating the Negation as a Form of Affirmation in Minority Discourse: The Construction of Richard Wright as Subject

Abdul R. JanMohamed

> This battle with Mr. Covey was the turning point in my career as a slave . . . . I now resolved that, however long I might remain a slave in form, the day had passed forever when I could be a slave in fact. I did not hesitate to let it be known of me, that the white man who expected to succeed in whipping, must also succeed in killing me.
>
> In learning to read, I owe almost as much to the bitter opposition of my master, as to the kindly aid of my mistress. I acknowledge the benefit of both.
> —Frederick Douglass, *Narrative of the Life of Frederick Douglass*

I

Writing and death stand as the two determining parameters of Douglass's as of Richard Wright's life and career, and the twin imperative of the former can be used to elucidate the latter's self-representation. In light of Douglass's experience and Orlando Patterson's definition of "social death" as a mode of oppression through which slaves, and by extension those who grew up under the control of Jim Crow society, are coerced and controlled, Richard Wright's first autobiographical work, *Black Boy*, can be seen as a complex exploration of his successful attempt to survive the rigors of a racist Southern hegemony and to escape from that confinement through writing. The content of *Black Boy* describes how Wright managed to resist Jim Crow society's attempt to limit his development to that of a "black boy," a sub-human creature devoid of initiative and entirely compliant to the will of white supremacy, whereas the very existence of *Black Boy* as an articulate and penetrating discursive text demonstrates his ability to overcome that drastically limiting formation. In short, *Black Boy* is a testament to the struggle over the formation of black subjectivity in a racist society.

As I hope to demonstrate in this paper, Wright's autobiography illustrates the value of a sustained negation of the attempted hegemonic/ideological formation—a negation that seems to me paradigmatic of all negation that lies at the center of minority discourse. According to Gilles Deleuze and Félix Guattari the three salient characteristics of minority literature are: 1) the deterritorialization of the dominant or major language by the minor literature that uses that language as a vehicle, 2) the fundamentally political nature of all minor literature, and 3) its tendency to represent collective values. This description, though limited by the fact that it is based on the study of one European writer, Kafka, is quite accurate.[1] Yet it seems to me that Deleuze and Guattari do not trace the genealogy of minority discourse all the way back to its phenomenological source in the relations of domination that constitute the antagonism between dominant and minority groups. I would argue that the three characteristics are based on the minority's prior will to negate the hegemony. Such a will takes precedence because the hegemonic formation of minorities is itself based on an attempt to negate them—to prevent them from realizing their full potential as human beings and to exclude them from full and equal participation in civil and political society—and because minorities cannot take part in

---

1. Gilles Deleuze and Félix Guattari, *Kafka: Toward a Minor Literature*, tr. Dana Polan (Minneapolis: University of Minnesota Press, 1986): see particularly chapter three.

the dominant culture until this hegemonic negation is itself negated. The most crucial aspect of resisting the hegemony consists in struggling against its attempt to form one's subjectivity, for it is through the construction of the minority subject that the dominant culture can elicit the individual's own help in his/her oppression. One of the most powerful weapons in the hands of the oppressor is the mind of the oppressed; without control of the latter's mind the dominant culture can enforce compliance only through the constant use of brute force.

Wright's major tactic in resisting hegemonic formation consisted of establishing a specular relation with society's attempt to negate him; he turned himself into a mirror that reflected the negation back at the hegemony: "in what other way had the South allowed me to be natural, to be real, to be myself," he asks rhetorically, "except in rejection, rebellion, and aggression."[2] In a paradox that typifies his life, Wright thrived on resisting all attempts to coerce or break him—his stubbornness gained strength from opposition, and he managed to find virtue in negation. Yet in defining the positive value of literature, the cultural formation that provided him with the only possibility of escape from racist confinement, Wright was partially blind to the relation between the negative and positive components of his subjective formation. Toward the end of his autobiography Wright ponders how he, a young man in many respects as ordinary as hundreds of other black boys in the South, had managed not to succumb to the racist hegemony—why had he retained, indeed cultivated, a consciousness of open possibilities, of larger horizons, of freedom while the white *and* black people surrounding him had "demanded submission." His unequivocal answer points to redeeming the value of literature:

> It had been only through books—at best, no more than a vicarious cultural transfusion—that I had managed to keep myself alive in a negatively vital way. Whenever my environment had failed to support or nourish me, I had clutched at books. (*BB*, 282)

While there is no doubt, judging from the evidence he furnishes, that literature did simultaneously provide him with information about the external world and with an inner, symbolic space wherein he could

---

2. Richard Wright, *Black Boy*, (New York: Harper and Row, 1945), 284. All further references to this autobiography will be included in the text.

keep alive the hope of a less constrained life, his endorsement of literature begs the question. Why was he, out of all the other black boys, predisposed to this influence of literature? Why did he find it valuable while others did not and why did he approach it in such a a way that it did not become simply a realm of escapist fantasy for him but rather a combative political and aesthetic tool, one that he later used in order to investigate the ideological world of an oppressive society? As he himself admits, and as I shall show later, literature initially played a negative function for him; he had clutched at it more from desperation than from an abiding sense of its intrinsic, independent value. But even this negativity, part of a much larger, sustained negativity, does not provide a sufficient explanation of his unique ability to survive the overwhelming restrictions of racist confinement. No doubt the final explanation is overdetermined, and it is probably impossible to formulate a precise equation governing the various contributing factors. Nevertheless, it is clear that both personality and circumstances conspired to create in Richard Wright a fundamental resistance to the racist attempt to fit him into the hegemonic mold reserved for "niggers."

Among the socio-political circumstances that contributed to Wright's formation the most significant is the Jim Crow extension of the fundamental structures of slave society. According to Orlando Patterson all forms of slavery are characterized by three constitutent elements: the slave's "social death," his utter powerlessness, and his overwhelming sense of dishonor.[3] Defeated in battle, the slave is permitted to live in captivity rather than being killed on the battlefield. Thus the slave's status is a substitute for his death, and his powerlessness and dishonor are direct products of that status. His "social death" has two important dimensions: 1) the slave is not absolved from the prospect of death; rather death is conditionally commuted and can be revoked at the master's whim; and 2) he is incorporated into the new society as an internal enemy, as a non-being. He can possess none of the legal, moral, or cultural rights that his masters enjoy. In fact, slave cultures are structured in such away that the slave has no socially organized existence except that which is allowed him by his master, who becomes the sole mediator between his own living community and the living death his

---

3. Orlando Patterson, *Slavery and Social Death*, (Cambridge, Ma.: Harvard University Press, 1982).

slave experiences. The slave's condition is perpetual and inheritable, a condition that Patterson calls "natal alienation." Ultimately, honor depends on an individual's ability to impose himself on or assert himself against another within culturally accepted terms. In this sense, honor rests on personal autonomy and power, attributes which the slave lacks.

II

The most elemental and persistent manifestation of social death in Wright's life was hunger. By constantly holding the black/slave on the verge of death through virtual starvation, Jim Crow society could exploit and syphon off the entire production of his "life," including his labor, as surplus value. Starvation thus became the most efficacious means of confining the black within the realm of social death. Wright's father's ill-paid work as a sharecropper and later as an itinerant laborer, followed by his desertion of the family, the series of crippling strokes suffered by his mother, the poverty of his maternal grandparents, the inability of a black boy to earn decent wages in the South, and other circumstantial factors forced Wright to exist on the verge of starvation. The most telling evidence of the effect of this hunger on Wright's formation is the psychosomatic link that the child forges between his deep hatred for his father and physical deprivation:

> As the days slid past the image of my father became associated
> with my pangs of hunger, and whenever I felt hunger I thought of
> him with a *deep biological bitterness*. (*BB*, 22; emphasis added)

The absence of the father and food, of protection and nurture, together form a physical and psychic lack that comes to symbolize for Wright an essential feature of the condition of social death.[4] Hunger eventually becomes a metaphor for the intellectual deprivation, the

---

4. Not until the publication of *The Long Dream* in 1958, when Wright himself had become a father, was he able to return to this theme with greater equanimity and insight and to show the devastating effects of the inability of the black father to play the symbolic role of the lawgiver and protector in a white racist culture. As I hope to show in my forthcoming study of Wright, his brilliant insights make this novel at least as significant as *Native Son*.

isolation, and the "eternal difference" that are experienced as both personal and racial phenomena by Wright and other black boys in the South: "To starve in order to learn about my environment was irrational, but so were my hungers" (*BB*, 140). The intellectual and physical starvation imposed by the Jim Crow society becomes such a fundamental feature for Wright that he had originally intended to entitle his autobiographical work *American Hunger*. However, when he agreed to publish it in two parts, the title of the first part, *Black Boy*, designating the generic reductive manner in which all black men are perceived by a racist society, in effect became a kind of synomym, an external mark for the title of the second book, *American Hunger*, designating the inner affliction suffered by all blacks. Through the generic markers that constitute his titles, Wright implies that the external categorization of black men as "boys" is accompanied by an intellectual deprivation, by a systematic attempt to prevent them from coming to consciousness about the relations of domination in a racist society.

Eventually, the "biological bitterness" toward his father comes to include a subdued horror of the barely conscious condition under which his father existed. When Wright meets him some twenty-five years after the father had deserted the family, Wright marvels at this man "with no regrets and no hope":

> how completely his soul was imprisoned by the slow flow of the seasons, by the wind and the rain and the sun, how fastened were his memories to a crude and raw past, how chained were his actions and emotions to the direct, animalistic impulses of his withering body. (*BB*, 43)[5]

This stark contrast between Wright, who had not only managed to break out of the confinement of Southern society but who had made his reputation precisely by bringing to consciousness the destructive effects of its culture, and his father, who seems to have capitulated entirely to that culture and whose consciousness had been all but extinguished, marks the kind of social and paternal negation that Wright had to over-

---

5. Wright's portrayal of his father is dangerously close to a racist stereotype of the primitive, barely conscious black. Yet as *Native Son* demonstrates, Wright's strategy requires that such stereotypes not be denied through simple negation but rather that they be exploded through a demonstration of how racist society forces blacks to conform to these stereotypes.

come. The culture of social death also forced Wright to develop a deep and abiding familiarity with suffering, which he experienced at a very young age through his mother. After surviving one of her more severe strokes, his mother called him to her one night and confessed her unbearable torment and her desire to die, which elicited from him a painful response: "That night I ceased to react to my mother; my feelings were frozen. I merely waited upon her, knowing that she was suffering." As he had combined his hunger and his hatred for his father into a metaphor, so at this point he was able to cope only by turning his love and her suffering into a symbol:

> My mother's suffering grew into a symbol in my mind, gathering to itself all the poverty, the ignorance, the helplessness; the painful, baffling, hunger-ridden days and hours; the restless moving, the futile seeking, the uncertainty, the fear, the dread; the meaningless pain and the endless suffering. Her life set the emotional tone of my life, colored the men and the women I was to meet in the future, conditioned my relation to events that had not yet happened, determined my attitude to situations and circumstances I had yet to face. (*BB*, 111)

His symbolic appropriation of her suffering, however, had a dual effect on his personality. On the one hand, he transformed the tension between affection and suffering from a static symbol into the central purpose of his life; he became an unrelenting and unflinching explorer of human suffering in general: her illness invoked in him "a conviction that the meaning of living came only when one was struggling to wring a meaning out of meaningless suffering," and it made him "want to drive coldly to the heart of every question and lay it open to the core of suffering that I knew I would find there" (*BB*, 112). On the other hand, it strenghtened his predisposition to withdraw from a harsh world into a brooding, meditative isolation. Because, as a poor, black child he found himself powerless to change the external racist world, he turned to an inner, imaginative world of "unlimited possibilities," to fantasies that "were a moral bulwark that enabled me to feel I was keeping my emotional integrity whole, a support that enabled my personality to limp through days lived under the threat of violence" (*BB*, 83-84). This inner world of feelings and fantasies grew more rapidly than the external world of facts and opportunities until Wright felt that at the age of thirteen he had a far better understanding of his feelings than he had a command of external facts (*BB*, 136). The two facets of his personality—the retreat into an inner world of fantasies that became "a culture, a creed, a religion" and the dedication to expose the causes of suffering—combined to form the driving impulse of his career as a writer.

The chronological development of negation in Wright's life begins with these two experiences that are captured in the figuration of hunger and suffering. While society forms Wright "indirectly" through these experiences, it attempts to control him more directly through the pervasive violence of Jim Crow culture. The underlying violence, which is in fact the horizon of hegemonic formation within that culture, is accurately captured by the aesthetic structure of "The Ethics of Living Jim Crow," the autobiographical preface to *Unle Tom's Children*. The understated, casual acknowledgments of violence at the beginning and end of the sketch emphasize how physical brutality profoundly brackets black social formation in the Southern context. The first paragraph describes the house and yard behind the railroad tracks where Wright lived as a young boy. It is not the absence of the greenery of white suburban lawns that Wright laments; instead, the child delights in the cinders that cover the yard because they make "fine weapons" for the war with the white boys, an activity that the child considers "great fun."[6] In contrast to this opening, where the world is unproblematically perceived as an arsenal, the end of the preface represents the world in a latent state of siege. In his speculations on how blacks feel about racial oppression, Wright offers the answer of one of his acquaintances: "Lawd, Man! Ef it wasn't fer them polices 'n' then ol' lynch mobs, there wouldn't be nothin' but uproar down here!" (*UTC*, 15). Thus racist hegemony and the marginalization of blacks, along with the distortion of their psyches, are based on the daily use of the threat of overwhelming violence, based indeed on the ever-provisional deferral of their death sentences, which the blacks, in order to survive, eventually have to accept as a pedestrian fact of life. That is, they have to learn to live "normally" in what Wright calls the culture of "terror."

---

6. "The Ethics of Living Jim Crow," preface to *Uncle Tom's Children* (New York: Harper and Row, 1940), 3. All further references to this preface will be incorporated in the text.

Even as a young child, his political precocity enabled him to understand, in a vague, emotional way, the fundamental structure of this culture. His early attitudes to death and fate were no doubt aided by his
sympathy for the prolonged suffering of his mother, by her confessed
desire to die, and by his grandmother's religious preoccupation with
death—which made him "so compassionately sensitive toward all life
as to view all men as slowly dying"—and her otherworldly notion of
fate, which "blended with the sense of fate that I had already caught
from life" (*BB*, 123-24). Wright's insight into the fundamental structures of his political situation and his incipient decision to negate the
hegemony in an uncompromising manner manifest themselves in his
resolution not to accept the master/slave contract. While pondering
the mysteries of his youthful, rather mythic comprehension of racial
segregation and oppression—as well as the apparent anomaly of his
grandmother, who looked "white" but, unlike other whites, lived with
the rest of his "black" family—Wright reacts to his vague fear and
knowledge of racial conflict by deciding to adhere to a basic rule: "It
would be simple. If anybody tried to kill me, then I would kill them
first" (*BB*, 58). The following apocryphal tale, which demonstrates his
increasing commitment to the above rule and which later informs his
short stories, also illustrates the dialectical relationship between the
formation of Wright, as represented in his autobiographical works,
and his investigation of the culture of social death in his fiction. The
tale concerns a black woman who avenges the death of her husband at
the hands of a white mob. Under the pretext of retrieving the body,
she makes her way into the white throng; as the members of the mob
stand around gloating over her and her husband's body, she pulls a
gun and shoots four of them. Wright does not know whether the story
is factually accurate or not, but he senses that "it was emotionally true
because I had already grown to feel that there existed, *men against whom
I was powerless, men who could violate my life at will.*" This tale, which gives
"form and meaning to confused defensive feelings that had long been
sleeping" in Wright's mind, reinforces his resolve, and he decides that
in a similar situation he would emulate the woman so that he could
"kill as many of them as possible before they killed me" (*BB*, 83-84,
emphasis added). Wright thus demonstrates his clear understanding of
the terms under which Jim Crow society obliges blacks to live:
powerlessness, the conditional, instantly revocable commutation of a

death sentence, and, of course, the dishonor that accompanies these conditions. This tale provides the plot of his story "Bright and Morning Star," while the decision to "kill as many of them as possible before they killed me" becomes Big Boy's fantasy in "Big Boy Leaves Home" and the actual principle on which Silas acts in "The Long Black Song." Thus the meaning of the tale is worked out in the symbolic realm of the stories and is then utilized for a better understanding of Wright's own life in his autobiographical works.

However, between the young child's vague understanding of the culture of social death and the mature writer who begins to investigate that world in *Uncle Tom's Children* lay the vast and pernicious world of social death, the most brutal and dispiriting aspects of which he had yet to experience and which were to become the subject matter of his fiction. In his entrance into that world, he was handicapped not only by being trapped within the harsh environment of his family but also by the chronic transitoriness, which was partly responsible for his poor education: before he reached the age of thirteen he had had only one year of continuous education. Wright's "real education," however, had little to do with standard academic learning. *Black Boy* is virtually silent about the details of his pedagogical life; judging from his autobiographical writings and the various biographies about him, his keen intelligence and attention were focused elsewhere. Thoughout his life in the South his mind was forced to concentrate primarily on physical and intellectual survival. At first Wright's energies were occupied with enduring his maternal family, which sought to break his independent spirit and make him conform to a Southern way of life and to the code of the Adventist religion. However, as Wright later realized, his family, without being conscious of it, had been "conforming to the dictates of the whites above them" in its attempt to mold him: his formation by the hegemony had been unwittingly mediated by his family (*BB*, 284).

III

Wright represents and examines the most concrete and pivotal aspects of the culture of social death and the mechanisms of hegemonic formation in those portions of *Black Boy* that depict his life from the end of his formal education to his departure from the South, that is, the years between May 1925 and November 1927. These vignettes depict the ways in which the desires and aspirations of a young black person are restricted by racist dominance and hegemony; under such constraints the boundaries of the self are so limited that rarely, if ever, can he succeed in becoming a full member of civil society. Wright's anecdotes demonstrate how the individual is so effectively coerced into internalizing the external, social boundaries that he learns to restrict himself "voluntarily." Wright shows that hegemony seeks to inform the very self-conception of the young man (and his view of reality, knowledge, possibility of progress, and so forth) in order to create a subject who will become identical to the limited view of him that the ideological apparatus itself has constructed. From the hegemonic viewpoint, the external construction of the subject should, ideally, coincide with self-construction. No luxury of choice is available in this process of self-construction; rather, hegemony forces the developing black individual to accommodate himself to the very absence of choice. The black boy must be taught to reify himself and the world; that is, he must perceive his liminality and the social and political restrictions that surround him not as the historical products of social relations but as natural and even metaphysical facts. The poignancy of Wright's anecdotes lies in the narrative juxtaposition of the graphic descriptions of the hegemonic process with acute representations and analyses of his subjective reactions. The contrast between the violence, persecutions, daily limitations, and narrow horizons and Wright's rage, frustration, humiliation, and bitterness reveals the wrenching tensions that a sensitive individual undergoes when he is being subjugated by a racist society.

When Wright enters the black work force serving the Southern whites, he finds himself constantly subjected to violence designed to teach him to assume "voluntarily" the subservient place reserved for "niggers" or slaves: he witnesses black people's acceptance of white violence and its effects on them, he soon becomes a victim of casual violence intended to teach him his "place," and, most dishearteningly for him, he finds his ambitions crushed by the threat of violence. While his black friends have learned to accommodate themselves or at least give a convincing appearance of accommodation, Wright is unable to master his reactions. His inability to prevent his resentment from registering on his face or in his demeanor results in his dismissal from various jobs because his employers do not like his "looks." When he forgets to address white boys as "sir," he is hit on the head with a bottle and thrown off a moving car. His assailants consider themselves benign teachers: had he made that mistake with other white men, they insist, he might have quickly become "a dead nigger" (*BB*, 200).

Such routine brutality seems to disturb Wright less than the threat of more serious violence that forces him to curb his professional ambition. Having been lucky enough to be hired by an enlightened "Yankee from Illinois" who wants to give him the chance to learn a skilled job in his optical company, Wright soon finds himself forced out—the white employees resent this attempt at professional desegregation and, fabricating a charge against him, threaten to kill him.[7] In compelling him to resign, his white colleagues win a dual victory. First, within the symbolic economy of racial segregation they correctly interpret his aspiration to learn a "trade" as equivalent to a desire to become "white," that is, as an attempt to overcome racial difference and to work his way out of the world of social death, and in successfully blocking his ambition they maintain the boundaries of that world. Second, in insisting to him that suicide is the most logical solution for the dilemma of being black ("If I was a nigger," one of the white workers tells him, "I'd kill myself," [*BB*, 207]), they provide him with a choice between actual death, embodied in their threat to kill him, and social death, implicit in his resignation. Thus Wright can either "voluntarily" throttle his ambition and humanity or face a violent physical death. This process of "education" is designed to ensure that ultimately the black man should deeply internalize the hegemonic system, that he should accept the distinctions between himself and whites as "natural," "ontological" species differences. As we will see, the hegemony insists that such differences have to be accepted not just at the conscious level but even at the preconscious one.

This episode also illustrates the manner in which Wright is forced to "collaborate" in his own negative formation. The white workers force him to resign by putting him in a double bind: one of the workers, Reynolds, accuses Wright of not using the appellation "Mr." when referring to the other white man, Pease. Before Wright can even respond

---

7. Michel Fabre (*The Unfinished Quest of Richard Wright* [New York: William Morrow & Co., 1973]) does not discuss this episode at all in his biography of Wright. However, whether or not the occurrence is factually verifiable, it does seem to possess what Wright would call an "emotional truth."

to this charge, Reynolds warns him that if he denies the allegation he will be calling Reynolds a liar. Thus by either accepting or refuting the charge Wright violates a cardinal rule of the Southern timocracy: a black man can never challenge the honor of a white. This ritual, accompanied by a beating and the threat of death, succeeds in enforcing all aspects of the syndrome of social death. First, Wright is forced to acknowledge the white man as a "master" ("Mister") and, by implication, himself as a slave; second, he has to relinquish all personal dignity to his white assailants; and finally, in agreeing to resign, he has to accept both the death of his professional ambition and by implication, his own social death—he must, in a sense, commit suicide. The mortification (both shame and death) and the utter dejection produced by such an encounter would not usually be available for conscious scrutiny. However, in this case the enlightened owner's good intentions painfully foreground the effects. In his attempt to investigate the causes of Wright's resignation, he exhorts Wright, in front of Pease and Reynold, to identify the assailant. Wright attempts to speak:

> An impulse to speak rose in me and died with the realization that I was facing a wall that I would never breech. I tried to speak several times and could make no sounds. I grew tense and tears burnt my cheeks. (*BB*, 221)

Wright weeps not only because of the professional disappointment but also because of his "complicity" in his defeat: this encounter, he says, left "[me] drenched in shame, naked to my soul. The whole of my being felt violated, *and I knew that my own fear had helped to violate it*" (*BB*, 212, emphasis added). His fear thus becomes a part of his formation in a dual sense: as the title of the first part of *Native Son*, "Fear," testifies, the subjugated man carries his anxiety with him in every encounter with his masters; and to the extent that he allows his fear to "violate" his own being, he becomes an agent of the hegemony that is dedicated to negating him.

Although he *intellectually* understands the rules of Jim Crow society and the contradictions that engulf him and although the racist regulations and his predicament have a profound effect on him, Wright is still unable to transform these into an *emotional* acceptance of the hegemony. This state of mind is revealed to him at his next job, where a minor accident that would have led to a mundane reprimand turns into another dismissal and a discovery of how profoundly Wright must negate himself in order to live in the South. When Wright is scolded for having broken a bottle, each response he gives seems to infuriate the manager; when he is finally told that he has been employed for a trial period, his reply, "Yes, sir. I understand," leads to his dismissal (*BB*, 214-215). It seems that Wright's replies reveal greater self-possession than Jim Crow society can tolerate from a black, for in this system inferior creatures, that is, slaves, are not supposed to possess dignity or honor, which might imply a form of equality with the masters. The implications of this incident are drastic: in order to survive in the South, Wright must in fact *become* inferior, he must relinquish *all* vestiges of pride and self-esteem.

However, with each discovery of what is required of him, Wright seems to get more deeply mired in the conflict between his desire for intellectual understanding and the society's demand for emotional submission. Each confrontation fuels his internal struggle: "I could not make subservience an *automatic* part of my behavior. I had to feel and think out each tiny item of racial experience in the light of the race problem, *and to each item I brought the whole of my life*" (*BB*, 215; emphasis added). Having lived on the edge of this contradiction and suffered its effects over a long period, Wright's insight into his own dilemma becomes brilliantly penetrating. In order for subservience to be *automatic* it cannot be conscious; it has to become a part of one's pre-conscious behavior pattern: precisely at the point where one's behavior is unconsciously controlled by a prevailing ideology, one has succumbed to a cultural hegemony. Wright's personal imperative is diametrically opposed to this demand: he wants to *understand* each racial incident that he experiences in light of the entire social, political, and ideological system of racism and slavery. And to each incident he devotes his entire *consciousness*. Thus, whereas ideology demands an emotional, unconscious acquiescence, Wright's project entails becoming perfectly aware of the unconscious pattern of behavior. The two, it would seem, cannot exist in the same universe. It finally becomes impossible for Wright to deny that the contradiction is irreconcilable. He often wishes that he could be like "the smiling, lazy, forgetful black boys" working with him in the hotel, who had "no torrential conflicts to resolve":

> Many times I grew weary of the secret burden I carried and longed
> to cast it down, either in action or in resignation. But I was not
> made to be a resigned man and I had only a limited choice of ac-
> tion, and I was afraid of all of them. (*BB*, 220)

The fundamental contradiction that tortures Wright is finally laid out
with syllogistic clarity: action against Jim Crow restrictions would
probably lead to physical death, and resignation would certainly lead
to social death. Some sixty years after the end of the Civil War, Wright
and all other blacks in the South were still facing the original contract
between master and slave. Afraid that if he stayed in the South he
would lose control of his emotions sooner or later and "spill out words
that would be my sentence of death," Wright decides to leave the
South.

Thus Wright finds himself under enormous pressure, both from the
white and the black communities, to conform to the rules of Jim Crow
culture. Society not only expects him to follow the rules but to
internalize them until he becomes totally resigned to the prevailing
distribution of power. However, since he refuses to accept those restrictions, he is faced with both an external battle with society and an
internal struggle with himself that fully exposes the contradictory and
explosive nature of his subject position. On the one hand, he must
contend against his own nature and consciousness so as not to reveal
the slightest resentment, frustration, or implied criticism to his white
employers; on the other hand, he must avoid capitulating to Jim Crow
society while pretending to have acquiesced. Thus he has to remain
constantly poised on a thin edge between feigned acceptance and silent opposition.

Yet such a contradiction, to the extent that it can be confined to an
intellectual or conscious realm, can be handled relatively easily in
comparison to the one that Wright subjects himself to in order to understand the structure of this culture. For him to understand thoroughly the system and the effects of racial oppression and to bring
them to the light of full consciousness, he has to be entirely open to
that system, he has to internalize it fully while maintaining a space
within his mind that remains uncontaminated by the racist ideology—
he has to retain a vantage point from which he can observe, critique,
and oppose white ascendancy. To allow oneself to be subjected to the
indignities and deprivations of Jim Crow society, to think constantly

about the restriction of the culture of social death and yet not be able to express one's feelings or be able to rebel against the system, is to hold together a highly explosive subject position. It is precisely this site that Wright explores in *Uncle Tom's Children* and, more systematically, in *Native Son*, after which he is able to describe and examine his own formation in the South with greater equanimity. Thus *Black Boy* is remarkable not so much for its rebellion as for the control that Wright had to exercise and the internal struggle that he had to wage against being engulfed by the racist sovereignty. Thus the autobiography charts the growth of a double consciousness, of a "duplicity" that turns the consciousness of its own condition into a cunning weapon. It is a remarkable document of Wright's total absorption of the racist attempt to negate him and his own total negation of that attempt.

Rejection of the hegemony, Wright learns before he is able to leave the South, has to be as total as possible under the given circumstances. Even feigned acceptance, he finds, is in danger of becoming real. While working in Memphis, Wright reluctantly allows himself to be persuaded to fight another young black man for the entertainment of whites. Wright and his opponent agree that they will pretend to fight. However, to his great horror the boxing match suddenly becomes quite real as each fighter begins to vent his frustrations on the other. But more significantly, hatred of the racist society is turned against another black: "The hate we felt for the [white] men whom we had tried to cheat went into the blows we threw at each other." (*BB*, 265). Almost all forms of dissemblance, Wright finds, are treacherous.

IV

Only one mode of dissemblance, literature, turns out to be productive and "constructive" for Wright. Literature eventually serves his purposes not only because it is the realm of "as if," a space in which one can investigate human potentiality in ways that are immediately unconstrained by the contingencies of actual life, but also because it provides the space within which one can attempt to resolve the actual contradiction of a constrained and frustrating life. Yet Wright could gain access to this zone of symbolic dissemblance only through a prior act of social dissemblance. Southern culture had barred all blacks from entry into high culture. Not only were blacks prohibited from discussing a whole set of subjects (see *BB*, 253) but more crucially they could not borrow books from the Memphis public library. Wright managed to circumvent this restriction by borrowing a library card from a sympathetic white Northerner and by pretending that the books were requested by his white master. Yet even this resourceful and cunning "triumph" contains a profound negation of Wright. He finds that within or outside the library he cannot afford to exhibit his literacy or his interest in literature: he can borrow books only on the assumption that he cannot and will not read them. In his attempt to possess any form of knowledge, he has to lead a double existence: while trying to play the role of a genial and happy black, content with his place in society, he has to satisfy his intellectual hunger, cultivate his sensibility and the consciousness of his condition, and nurture his rage in secret. After this experience whenever he brought a book to work, he "wrapped it in newspaper—a habit that was to persist for years in other cities and under other circumstances" (*BB*, 273).

Thus his subjectivity must always be hidden; it can never be displayed in public or be recognized by most whites who surround him. Not only does racist society negate Wright, but he too must negate himself, at least in public. Orlando Patterson argues that the slave can never be the subject of property, only its object; we should add that the black in Jim Crow society, like his enslaved ancestor, can never be the subject of (white) culture, only its object.

V

Yet paradoxically, Wright was able to save himself through another form of dissembling. As we have seen, Wright attributes his ability to survive the Jim Crow restrictions to his love of literature, and, as we have also seen, he was able to understand and experience the demands of the hegemony without emotionally capitulating to its control; that is, while he fully experienced himself as a degraded being, he had managed to retain a space in his mind where his *potential* humanity remained intact. Given this mode of rebellion, given his quiet but determined nurturing of his human potentiality in the abstract spaces of his mind, it is not surprising that he found an outlet in literature, which is precisely an area where the *potentiality* of human endeavour can be rehearsed and explored. When Wright, disguised as an errand boy, discovered in the segregated Memphis public library H. L. Mencken's *Prefaces*, and through it a much larger literary world, he was already predisposed to this particular mode of simulation. But because his conception of his human potential was devoid of positive content the initial function of literature for him was as negative and empty as his "humanity."

The sustained negation that he had been nurturing is first thrown into relief by the guilt that the reading of Mencken and other modern writers provokes: "I could not conquer my sense of guilt, my feeling that the white men around me knew that I was changing, that I had begun to regard them differently" (*BB*, 273). This guilt, then, becomes an index of how deeply Wright has internalized the Southern ideology and how precariously dependent upon the racist Other his negation must have been. But literature was also negative in that it depressed him. While opening up new horizons of human potentiality to him, it showed him how much he had missed by growing up in the South, and it confirmed his own view of the culture of social death: "I no longer *felt* that the world about me was hostile, killing; I *knew* it." His entire life had been shaping him, he says, to understand the realist and naturalist novel, and his complicated experience of his mother's senseless suffering was revived by reading Dreiser's *Jennie Gerhardt* and *Sister Carrie* (*BB*, 274). Literature thus functions as a mirror that reflects his own negation and experience of suffering.

His reading provokes him to contemplate once again his prospects in the South. He ponders various alternatives—armed rebellion, playing the Sambo role, taking out his frustrations on other blacks, escaping through sex and alcohol, and attempting to become a professional—but rejects them all as unfeasible because they would all kill something in him. To stay in the South, he knows, means to stifle his consciousness, means accepting social death at some level. Caught between the negation of his own life and the negation and distance provided by his reading, Wright implicitly opts for the only possibility that he has ever known—to use his mind as a mirror that will bring his predicament to consciousness: "I held my life in my mind, in my consciousness each day, feeling at times that I would stumble and drop it, spilling it forever" (*BB*, 277). In thus affirming his predisposition, literature mirrors his own mirroring mind. Having finally decided to leave the South, Wright boards the train from Memphis to Chicago and allows himself en route to think more fully about the role of literature in his life. In a highly controlled and impoverished world, where both whites and blacks had "demanded submission" and refused to affirm Wright's belief in himself, it was only through literature that he manages to keep himself *"alive* in a *negatively* vital way" (*BB*, 282; emphasis added). On his way North, which symbolized a utopian space where one might be able to lead a fuller and freer life, Wright could now afford to meditate more explicitly on his negative existence and the manner in which literature had helped him to bring his negation into sharper focus.

Although the South had attempted to crush his spirit, Wright feels that he had never capitulated; he had never accepted that he was "in any way an inferior being," and nothing the Southerners had said or done to him had ever made him "doubt the worth of my own humanity." But at a more concrete level, the environment had allowed him to manifest his humanity only in a negative form. He had lied, stolen, fought, struggled to contain his seething rage, and it was only by accident that he had never killed. The South had only allowed him to be himself through "rejection, rebellion, and aggression" (*BB*, 283-84). It had given him only the choice of becoming either a slave or rebel; he had chosen the latter, because that was the only way he could affirm his humanity. It had been an entirely negative assertion of his humanity, but he had devoted himself entirely to it:

> In a peculiar sense, life had trapped me in a realm of emotional rejection; I had not embraced insurgency through open choice. Existing emotionally on the sheer, thin margin of southern culture, I had felt that nothing short of life hung upon each of my actions and decisions. (*BB*, 282)

Since this culture could not provide him with any landmarks by which "I could, in a positive sense, guide my daily actions," Wright converted his "emotional rejection," his negation, into the very essence of his "life." Wright thus transformed himself into a dialectical negation of the culture of social death, and in each confrontation with the racist hegemony what was at stake was not some abstract notion of human dignity or freedom but his very life-as-a-negation. By carefully nurturing himself as negation and by presenting this negation in the form of his autobiographical work, *Black Boy*, Wright makes a double impact. In the first place, the *publication* and the literary success of *Black Boy* becomes an affirmation, a vindication of his strategy of negating the racist negation. In the second place, by choosing for the title of his autobiography the generic marker of racist objectification, "black boy," Wright correctly implies that he is describing the formation of all those who have been "subjectified" by racism. As Houson A. Baker Jr. implies, ontogeny in *Black Boy* recapitulates phylogeny.[8] Only if we see that the confrontation, at the individual as well as at the collective level, is between life and death, either social or actual death, can we begin to appreciate why Wright repeatedly describes his life and that of his characters such as Bigger as charged with an enormous tension. In his existential mood, with his life as an embodiment of negation constantly on the verge of extinction, Wright reads authors "like Dreiser, Masters, Mencken, Anderson, and Lewis," and finds in them an echo of his own life and "vague glimpses of life's possibilities."

At this point literature represents for Wright a world of possibilities, and it lures him into the paradoxical realm of potentialities and actualities. Jim Crow society, he says, "kept me from being the kind of person I might have been," and in leaving the South and experiencing a different kind of life he "might learn who I was, what I might be" (*BB*, 284). The paradox, of course, is that who he might be, his future potentiality, is entirely predicated on who he is, on his actuality; he would never have been concerned with his own potentiality if he were not already an embodied negation constructed around abstract potentiality. In his own way, Wright is aware of this paradox, for he immediately follows his speculations by arguing that he is leaving the South not in order to forget it, but so that he can understand it better and determine what it has done to its black children: "I fled so that the numbness of my defensive living might thaw out and let me feel the pain—years later and far away—of what living in the South had meant" (*BB*, 284). This, of course, is exactly what he accomplishes in *Uncle Tom's Children* and *Native Son*: his fictional works, written years later and far away from the South, constitute the cries of pain. He knows that he cannot really leave the South, that it has formed him and is an

---

8. See Houston A. Baker, Jr., *Blues, Ideology, and Afro-American Literature: A Vernacular Theory* (Chicago: The University of Chicago Press, 1984), 147.

indelible part of himself. However, he hopes that by transplanting his experience of it to a different soil it might bloom differently:

> And if that miracle ever happened, then I would know that there was yet hope in that southern swamp of despair and violence, that light could emerge even out of the blackest of the southern night. I would know of the blackest of the southern night. I would know that the South too could overcome its fear, its hate, its cowardice, its heritage of guilt and blood, its burden of anxiety and compulsive cruelty. (*BB*, 284-85)

Wright is thus clearly aware that his potentiality consists of bringing to consciousness in symbolic form his experiences of the racist attempt to negate his actuality. His positive potentiality will manifest itself precisely in his success in bringing to consciousness his negating actuality. Thus the passage cited above embodies the twin imperatives of his life and fiction. To the extent that he is an emblem of the negation that issues from the culture of social death, his fictional rendering of his own experiences reflects that deep, deterministic connection between the environment and the individual that is a hallmark of naturalism. And to the extent that, unlike Bigger, Wright is able to transcend the limitations of his environment, his fiction represents the slave's dialectical overcoming of his condition by bringing to consciousness the structures of his social death in the symbolic realm of literature.

VI

Wright's autobiography and fiction can be best appreciated as an archaeology of negation and freedom. That is, by excavating the repressed layers of his consciousness and by insistently expressing his discoveries in the predominantly "negative" forms of his novels he defines his own negation of the prior hegemonic negation as the most fundamental form of self-affirmation: in his work racist negation becomes the opposite of what it is initially—it becomes a site of freedom. The power and the value of Wright's sustained negation is captured aptly in Baker's metaphor of the "black (w)hole." Wright, it seems to me, had dedicated himself precisely to absorbing all negation in order to negate it, and his commitment to this task was unrelenting. A hasty affirmation, a premature sense of being accepted and affirmed as a full subject by the hegemony, he seems to have felt, is always in danger of being appropriated once again by the processes of hegemonic formation. In his article in this issue of "Minority Discourse," Henry Louis Gates, Jr. argues that we must not think of ourselves as being condemned to "the fate of perpetual negation . . . doomed merely to 'oppose,' to serve within the academy as black signs of opposition to a political order in which we are subjugated. We must oppose, of course, when oppositon is called for. But our task is so much more complex." No doubt the task of affirming is complex and important, and Gates's diverse interventions in the discursive field of the black literary diaspora is an excellent embodiment of that complexity. But as the NEH response, cited in the introduction, to the grant application for the "Minority Discourse" conference illustrates, the guardians of hegemony still consider "vernacular" literature, even though these are "English vernaculars," to be barbaric babble. From Crummell's view of African languages to the priorities of the NEH, the dominant ideology still attempts to negate minorities and therefore must be met with a similarly sustained opposition: we cannot afford the luxury of defining negation as an occasional tactic to which one resorts reluctantly. In her article, also included in this issue, Sylvia Wynter rightly warns us that the category "minority" is a discursive construct and not a "brute fact." However, we must also remember that Wright's most negative protagonist, Bigger Thomas, feels so oppressed that he can hardly breath. If hegemonic formation is so powerfully negating that it can even control one's autonomous nervous system, one's ability to breath, then we must face the empirical "fact" that some, if not all, of us are indeed reduced, some, if not all, of the time, to experiencing ourselves, ideologically and physically if not ontologically, as brute, oppressed "facts." Thus sustained negation of the hegemony may be necessary not only for the liberation of our minds but also of our voices and bodies. We must remember that not only is there a Bigger Thomas somewhere in all of us, but also a Richard Wright, whom we must allow to come to consciousness in us.

Politics, Patriarchs, and Laughter

Renato Rosaldo

In an influential essay called "What is a Minor Literature?," Gilles Deleuze and Felix Guattari have asserted that minority discourse can be distinguished from great literature by three features: deterritorialization, an emphasis on politics, and a collective value.[1] *Deterritorialization* refers both to writers' positions (outside their homeland and using a language not their own) and to their extreme modes of expression (either excessive and inflated, in the manner of James Joyce, or sparse and intensified, in the manner of Franz Kafka). The *emphasis on politics* affirms that in a minor literature individual dramas become political rather than Oedipal as in a great literature. *Collective value* refers to the writer's terrain where utterances reflect a community's usage, rather than being sharply individuated.

Deleuze and Guattari's political project as well as their reverse snobbism become evident when they exclaim: "Only the minor is great and revolutionary."[2] Their reverse snobbism becomes condescending when they affirm that the paucity of talent among the producers of a minor literature enables the latter to have political and collective value. A minor literature without individuated masters, they claim, can be based in a community, and because it is based in a

* This paper was completed during my tenure as a Fellow of the Stanford Humanities Center. I am grateful for comments on an earlier draft of this paper by Hector Calderón, Abdul JanMohamed, José Limón, Kathleen Newman, Mary Pratt, José Saldívar, and Tom Vogler.
1. Gilles Deleuze and Felix Guattari, "What is a Minor Literature?" *Mississippi Review* 11, no. 3 (1983): 13-33.
2. Ibid., 26.

community it is great. A transvaluation of values follows: with regard to traditions, the great is minor, and the minor is great.

In a more sober vein, Deleuze and Guattari justify their conception of a minor literature as follows:

> . . . 'minor' no longer characterizes certain literatures, but describes the revolutionary conditions of any literature within what we call the great (or established). Everyone who has had the misfortune to be born in the country of a major literature must write in its tongue, as a Czech Jew writes in German, or as an Uzbek Jew writes in Russian. To write as a dog who digs his hole, a rat who makes his burrow. And to do that, to find his own point of underdevelopment, his own jargon, a third world of his own, a desert of his own. There has been a great deal of discussion on: What is a marginal literature? — and also: What is a popular literature, a proletarian literature, etc.? Evidently the criteria are very difficult to define so long as we do not work first in terms of a more objective concept, that of a minor literature.[3]

Deleuze and Guattari argue that a minority's use of a major language is the enabling condition for literatures called popular, marginal, and proletarian. For this reason, they go on to urge that the term minor literature be elevated to the status of a master concept that subsumes, or at any rate precedes, the other terms in its family.

Deleuze and Guattari, as I have said, exemplify their argument with such European writers as Franz Kafka and James Joyce. Exceptional in having been canonized among the great, Kafka and Joyce hardly exhaust the range of minor writers. Aside from appearing Eurocentric and elitist, exemplifying an argument with such writers makes one suspect the validity of Deleuze and Guattari's generalizations about minor literatures. One wonders to what extent their analysis holds when applied to less recognized voices among American minorities. Does their figure of a Czech Jew writing in German correspond, for example, with that of a south Texan of Mexican ancestry writing in English?

What follows contests Deleuze and Guattari's generalizations by discussing two quite different Chicano writers: Américo Paredes,

---

3. Ibid., 18.

who has been in succession a singer, a poet, a journalist, and a folklorist at the University of Texas at Austin; and Ernesto Galarza, who has been concerned, as a scholar-activist, with union organizing and agribusiness. Neither Paredes nor Galarza has devoted himself primarily to imaginative fiction, but their social descriptions, fundamentally shaped by a political vision, are worthy of literary analysis. Moreover, their writings provide grist for my project because they do not readily fit the mold of a minor literature as proposed by Deleuze and Guattari.

Perhaps my critique can begin with an anecdote. One spring afternoon I found myself in a heated discussion with a person who violently objected to what I said in an earlier incarnation of this paper.[4] My paper had contested, as it will again in what follows, the application of Deleuze and Guattari's notions to Chicanos. Instead of deterritorialization, I suggested that the creative space of resistance for Chicanos be called the *border*, a site of bilingual speech, rather than English only. For Chicanos, the border is as much a homeland as an alien environment. Instead of a simple collective vision, Paredes and Galarza imagined their communities as a line of *patriarchs*, emblematic simultaneously of collectivity and Oedipal relations. Instead of an earnestness enveloping politics, I found a *politics of laughter*, where chuckles and wit became subversive.

What had given most offence was my emphasis on the interplay of politics and laughter. The move from majority to minority, my interlocutor insisted, was deadly earnest: if Américo Paredes and Ernesto Galarza thought immigration to America was a laughing matter, they had a lot to learn about human degradation. Think, the person said, about the Czech general who was forced to leave his homeland, and eventually found himself working as a janitor in Chicago. He was pathetic. He lived in misery all week long and on Sundays put on his military uniform and reminisced with old friends about bygone days. His life was no joke.

---

4. My interlocuter remembers our exchange rather differently. This person recalls recognizing from the outset the distinctive character of Chicano history, but insisting that Deleuze and Guattari's argument applies to eastern European immigrants to the United States. Despite failures of communication, we do seem to agree that Chicano history comprises an exception to Deleuze and Guattari's rule. My point is that American minority history should neither be ignored nor reshaped and assimilated to Eurocentric models of a minority literature.

Paredes, I tried to explain, was not an immigrant. His Mexican ancestors never moved; instead, the border itself had moved, through conquest. He grew up in what had become south Texas, close to the border, in the region that was his ancestral homeland. He was forced to live, as his ancestors were not, under a dominant, aggressive group that spoke a language not his own, but they were the immigrants, not he. Not unlike the experiences of blacks and Native Americans, Chicano history cannot readily be assimilated to a tale of immigration and displacement. Among other things, these differing histories distinguish the immigrant Czech general from Américo Paredes. Indeed the metamorphosis of the general into the janitor simply is unthinkable as a Chicano tale of the movement north from Mexico. My interlocutor came to understand something of these differing histories and told me this should have been made clear from the very beginning. Maybe next time, I replied.

Politics, Parades, and Wit

My discussion of Américo Paredes will revolve around a key figure, "The Patriarch," and three episodes: "The Primordial Society," "The Fall," and "The Conflict." To anticipate, the key figure and the three episodes will be gradually dismantled over the course of what follows.

Consider initially the primordial terrain and its coherent social order. The latter establishes certain standards against which more contemporary social life can be judged. Then comes "The Fall," the disruption and alteration of "The Primordial Society." Through American conquest, the primordial homeland is torn asunder, becoming the border. No longer dominant, but dominated, the Mexican people enter into "The Conflict" with Anglo-Texans. Sung and remembered in ballads, border conflict between Mexicans and Anglo-Texans becomes Paredes's central preoccupation. Throughout these three episodes, Mexican resistance to domination is guided by patriarchs embodying a distinctive version of manhood. (The less public, but equally significant, role of matriarchs requires another paper.)

Let me consider Paredes's first book, *"With His Pistol in His Hand": A Border Ballad and Its Hero*, which was published in 1958.[5] (More

---

5. Américo Paredes, *"With His Pistol in His Hand": A Border Ballad and Its Hero* (Austin:

recently, by the way, this book has become a movie, *The Ballad of Gregorio Cortez*, starring James Edward Olmos, otherwise known for his roles in *Zoot Suit* and *Miami Vice*.) The book concerns a man who, through a misunderstanding, shoots a Texas sheriff and becomes the object of a manhunt. The manhunt, of course, raises political issues about majority domination and minority resistance between Anglos and Chicanos in south Texas. Ahead of its time, the book embodies a sophisticated conception of culture where conflict, domination, and resistance, rather than coherence and consensus, are the central subjects of analysis.

"With His Pistol in His Hand" was without precedent. Neither the Chicano political movement nor the discipline of Chicano Studies was conceived until about a decade later. As a result, Chicano scholars worked in isolation, and often literally did not know one another (as was the fate of Paredes and Galarza).

During the late fifties, anti-Mexican prejudice throughout the southwest and California was even more evident than today. In south Texas, where this prejudice was particularly extreme, it took courage to challenge the dominant ideology of Anglo-Texan racial superiority. It is within this context that one should understand Paredes's devastating yet understated critique of J. Frank Dobie and Walter Prescott Webb's influential work. In their work Dobie and Webb present an academic version of popular Anglo-Texan racial ideology; their writings celebrate Anglo-American Texans and denigrate their fellow citizens of Mexican ancestry. The pertinent circumstances of the publication of Paredes's work have been described by José Limón as follows:

> [I]n the late 'fifties the then chief editor of the University of Texas Press refuses to publish *With His Pistol in His Hand* unless Paredes deletes all critical references to Walter Prescott Webb.

University of Texas Press, 1958). All further references appear in the body of the paper. I have discussed Paredes's work in more abbreviated form elsewhere — "Chicano Studies, 1970-1984," *Annual Review of Anthropology* 14 (1985): 405-27; "When Natives Talk Back: Chicano Anthropology Since the Late 60s," *Renato Rosaldo Lecture Series Monograph* (Tucson: Mexican American Studies and Research Center, 1986), 2:3-20; "Where Objectivity Lies: The Rhetoric of Anthropology" in *The Rhetoric of the Human Sciences*, John Nelson, Donald McCloskey, and Alan Megill, eds. (Madison: Univ. of Wisconsin Press, 1987).

When the book does appear, an ex-Texas Ranger actually tries to get Paredes' address from the Press so that he can "shoot the sonafabitch who wrote that book."[6]

Apparently, Paredes had touched a nerve. It is little wonder that, in recognition of the humorous integrity that distinguishes the man's scholarship and his politics, Chicano scholars now honor him by speaking of him as don Américo.

1. The Primordial Society

For my present purposes, the beginning of the book is most critical because it introduces "The Primordial Society," "The Fall," and "The Conflict." Writing in a manner sparse, modest, and understated, Paredes uses a nostalgic mode to describe "The Primordial Society" set in a mythic territory. The territory is south Texas from the arrival of Mexican settlers in 1749 to the Mexican-American War of 1848. In a culturally distinctive instance of Frederick Jackson Turner's version of frontier democracy, Paredes asserts that this area was marked by egalitarian relations where patriarchs maintained a cohesive and bounded social order. Women of strong character could, as individuals, inspire the same respect as men, but their achievements were not sanctioned by social expectations. Paredes describes this primordial social order as follows:

> Social conduct was regulated and formal, and men lived under a patriarchal system that made them conscious of degree. The original settlements had been made on a patriarchal basis, with the "captain" of each community playing the part of father to his people.
>
> Town life became more complex, but in rural areas the eldest member of the family remained the final authority, exercising more real power than the church or the state. There was a domestic hierarchy in which the representative of God on earth

---

6. José Limón, "The Return of the Mexican Ballad: Américo Paredes and His Anthropological Text as Persuasive Political Performance," SCCR Working Paper No. 16 (Stanford, Ca.: Stanford Center for Chicano Research, 1986), 29. See also José Limón, "Américo Paredes: A Man From the Border," *Revista Chicano-Riqueña* 8 (1980): 1-5.

was the father. Obedience depended on custom and training
rather than force, but a father's curse was thought to be the most
terrible thing on earth. (11)

If taken literally, Paredes's view of the frontier social order seems
more mythic than descriptive. How could any society function so
smoothly, without rifts, inconsistencies, and contradictions? Did
everyone conform with "The Patriarch's" expectations? Did "The
Patriarch"--quite unlike, for example, Juan Rulfo's Pedro Paramo--
never use force in gaining compliance?

Arguably, Paredes's myth of "The Primordial Society" thriving
under a patriarchal order plays an analytical role in his work that is
more tropological than anthropological. The patriarchal order establishes
the terms for constructing a figure of resistance more than it describes
Rio Grande society's historical past. It enables Paredes to develop a conception of manhood mythically endowed with the rhetorical capacity to
combat Anglo-Texan anti-Mexican prejudice.

2. The Fall

"The Fall" results from the War of 1848 which abruptly shatters
the mythic epoch of primordial pastoral patriarchy. After nearly a
century of peaceful existence, the united land was divided: a border
was imposed and the patriarchs were deposed. The Mexicans fell
from innocence, their Edenic paradise split asunder. Paredes describes the opening of the new era as follows:

> It was the Treaty of Guadalupe that added the final element to
> Rio Grande society, a border. The river, which had been a focal
> point, became a dividing line. Men were expected to consider
> their relatives and closest neighbors, the people just across the
> river, as foreigners in a foreign land. A restless and acquisitive
> people, exercising the rights of conquest, disturbed the old
> ways. (15)

The intrusive border definitively brings the old ways to an end. They
survive more as an ideal of manhood than as an ongoing social order.

His tone then shifts from unadorned description to deadpan

humor. When it comes to folklore, he says in the following, those of Mexican ancestry have it all over the Anglo-Texans:

> In "The Conflict" along the Rio Grande, the English-speaking Texan (whom we shall call the Anglo-Texan for short) disappoints us in a folkloristic sense. He produces no border balladry. His contribution to the literature of border conflict is a set of attitudes and beliefs about the Mexican which form a legend of their own and are the complement to the *corrido*, the Border-Mexican ballad of border conflict. (15)

In his social criticism Paredes speaks obliquely, deftly, pointedly, bilingually. Mexicans, he says, sing fine *corridos* of border conflict, and Anglo-Texans counter, not with song, for on this subject they have none, but with attitudes and beliefs. Doomed to lose the shooting wars, Mexican singers of tales use their *corridos* to resist brute Anglo-Texan racial prejudice.

3. The Conflict

As he speaks in more detail about the third phase, "The Conflict," Paredes plays with ironic parallel constructions. He begins with the Anglo-Texan legend about Mexicans. In this view, Mexicans are cruel, cowardly, treacherous, thieving, and generally, due to their mixed blood, degenerate. Mexicans supposedly recognize the superiority of Anglo-Texans, especially the finest of their breed, the Texas Rangers. This legend has circulated less in folklore than in actual practice, ideologically supported by the printed word, extending in an all-too-continuous line from nineteenth-century war propaganda to twentieth-century scholarly works. In Paredes's words:

> The truth seems to be that the old war propaganda concerning the Alamo, Goliad, and Mier later provided a convenient justification for outrages committed on the Border by Texans of certain types, so convenient an excuse that it was artificially prolonged for almost a century. And had the Alamo, Goliad, and Mier not existed, they would have been invented, as indeed they seem to have been in part. (19)

Gradually unrolling his punch-line, he obliquely says Anglo-Texan scholars reshaped, in fact partially invented, their history. Their re-membered, indeed celebrated, past — "remember the Alamo" — served to justify abuses of the Mexican population in south Texas.

Mexican perceptions of Anglo-Texans appear not in authoritative print, but in sayings, anecdotes, and ballads about the Texas Rang-ers. Rangers, for example, are said to plant rusty old guns on the un-armed Mexicans they kill. Armed Mexicans, on the other hand, are shot in the back or in their sleep. Without American soldiers, the sayings go, Rangers would not dare enter the border region. Many a tale tells of how Rangers shot innocent Mexicans, but claimed to have killed them while in pursuit of thieves. Paredes is quick to say that such perceptions were partisan:

> I do not claim for these little tidbits the documented authenticity that Ranger historians claim for their stories. What we have here is frankly partisan and exaggerated without a doubt, but it does throw some light on Mexican attitudes toward the Ranger which many Texans may scarcely suspect. And it may be that these atti-tudes are not without some basis in fact. (25)

His rhetorical tactic nicely parallels and opposes that used to sum-marize Anglo-Texan perceptions, for he once again ends by revers-ing himself, but this time he accents the significant grain of truth, rather than the invention, in Mexican perceptions.

In his own good time, Paredes settles down to tell the ballad of Gregorio Cortez. His beginning, strikingly told without distance or humor, rather like his version of "The Primordial Society," displays the ancient ideal of manhood in the following manner:

> That was good singing, and a good song; give the man a drink. Not like these pachucos nowadays, mumbling damnfoolish-ness into a microphone; it is not done that way. Men should sing with their heads thrown back, with their mouths wide open and their eyes shut. Fill your lungs, so they can hear you at the pas-ture's further end. And when you sing, sing songs like *El Corrido de Gregorio Cortez*. There's a song that makes the hackles rise. You can almost see him there--Gregorio Cortez, with his pistol in his hand. (34)

These are the country men of old, descendants of the primordial patriarchs, not the degenerate urban boys of the late 1950s, the *pachucos*. Unaided by microphones, their voices carry across the pasture, making their listeners feel *muy gallo*, literally very rooster, very male like a fighting cock, with rising hackles.

This mythic, nearly parodic masculine figure should be viewed within the context of border conflict, rather than taken too literally. For Paredes, men of mythic integrity can resist and transcend — at least in cultural terms — Anglo-Texan anti-Mexican prejudice. Not unlike Gregorio Cortez, the singer of *corridos* himself stands as a figure of resistance to Anglo-Texan domination.

4. "The Conflict" in the Academy

More recently, Paredes has done battle against Anglo anthropologists whose writings (probably unwittingly) have perpetuated popular stereotypes of the Mexicans of south Texas. In a trilingual text, wit as a political weapon opens the critique, which at once dismantles prejudice and constructs a positive sense of Chicano culture, in this manner:

> The main target of Chicano wrath has been anthropologist William Madsen, Romano's erstwhile colleague, who has become a sort of *bête blanche* of the *movimiento*. Madsen's little book *Mexican-Americans of South Texas* is Exhibit A, to which all Chicanos point with disgust. Ethnic studies instructors risk censure by their students if they use *Mexican Americans of South Texas* as a text or even assign it for outside reading.[7]

The paper goes on to show how ethnographers have systematically erred by taking literally jokes, metaphors, and apochryphal stories. In so doing they have turned the Mexicans of south Texas into one-dimensional parodies of themselves. Paredes puts it succinctly: "Madsen's Chicanos are not only literal-minded, they never crack a joke."[8] With its peculiar double vision and sense of incongruity, humor itself is consti-

---

7. Américo Paredes, "On Ethnographic Work Among Minority Groups: A Folklorist's Perspective," in *New Directions in Chicano Scholarship*, R. Romo and R. Paredes, eds. (La Jolla: Univ. of California, San Diego, Chicano Studies Program, Chicano Studies Monograph, 1978), 1-32.
8. Ibid., 5.

tutive of Chicano culture and its political vision.

Paredes's battle against a pernicious ideology, present both among the ordinary Anglo-Texans and in official university culture, has been conducted with courage, dignity, and wit. *"With His Pistol in His Hand"* is marked by reflexivity.[9] Its author, its singer of *corridos*, and its hero embody a certain culturally distinctive masculine heroics of resistance to Anglo-Texan prejudice. The figure of masculine heroic resistance certainly requires critique from a present day feminist perspective, but this particular late fifties border conflict, with its dynamic of Anglo-Texan domination and Mexican resistance, required challenge by a persona who was larger than life. Even today, anti-Mexican prejudice among Anglo-Texans remains something of a legend among Chicanos.[10]

Politics, Galarza, and the Mockery of Patriarchs

Ernesto Galarza, who died recently, was a scholar-activist. He too has been a revered figure among Chicano scholars and activists. His lifetime concern was farming, both the political economy of agri-business and the struggles of the workers. Without holding an academic position, he distinguished himself as a writer and as an organizer. In conjunction with organizing in elementary schools, he even wrote children's stories. Late in his career and after the Chicano movement was already underway, in 1971 Galarza published his bilingually entitled autobiography, *Barrio Boys*.[11]

Let me concentrate on the beginning of *Barrio Boy* where "The Patriarch" appears along with "The Primordial Society," "The Fall," and "The Conflict." Galarza treats the central figure and the three episodes in a manner that parallels, as it plays against, Paredes's work. For Galarza, "The Patriarch" plays a central role, but one

---

9. See Limón, op. cit.

10. Recently, for example, a Chicano member of Stanford's Medical School faculty half-jokingly, half-seriously remarked that local Bay Area prejudice seems relatively benign compared with that in south Texas "where they shoot you."

11. Ernesto Galarza, *Barrio Boy* (New York: Ballantine Books, 1972). All further references appear in the body of the paper. For another reading of *Barrio Boy* see José Saldívar, "Caliban and Resistance: A Study of Chicano-Chicana Autobiography" (Paper delivered at Chicano Colloquium Series, Stanford Center for Chicano Research, 22 March 1986).

marked more by gentle mocking than solemn reverence. His version of "The Primordial Society" is disrupted as soon as it is constructed. "The Fall" is produced by his own whimsical recollection, not by immigration across a divisive border. In "The Conflict," patriarchs as emblems of political authority, whether they be Mexican or Anglo, are more subverted than celebrated. Due to their differing political visions, the historical chasm between the assimilationism of 1958 and the mobilized Chicano community of 1971 and the distance between Galarza's eventual home in Sacramento and Paredes's natal south Texas (justly celebrated among Chicanos, as I have said, for its anti-Mexican prejudice), the enemy for Galarza appears less racial than capitalistic and bureaucratic.

1. The Primordial Society

Galarza's work can be read with solemnity, as if it were written in a flat earnest manner. Yet the work is marked by heteroglossia, a play of English and Spanish, and by an understated, often self-deprecating deadpan humor through which his political vision becomes apparent.

Barrio Boy opens soberly enough, with a scene of Mexican rural life viewed through rose-tinted glasses.

> The pine kindling was marvelously aromatic and sticky. The woodsmen of the pueblo talked of the white tree, the black tree, the red tree, the rock tree —*palo blanco, palo negro, palo colorado* and *palo de piedra*. Under the shady canopies of the giants there were the fruit bearers —*chirimoyas, guayabas, mangos, mameyes*, and *tunas*. There were also the coffee bushes, volunteers that straggled here and there in an abandoned coffee patch. (6)

Life is peaceful. Nature is aromatic, colorful, and abundant. "The Primoridal Society" appears fully present as the mountain tropics are eulogized in Galarza's pastoral opening.

2. The Fall

The pastoral opening is abruptly interrupted by the following meditation on the turkey buzzard, the *zopilote*:

But of all the creatures that came flying out of the *monte* — bats, doves, hawks — the most familiar were the turkey vultures, the *zopilotes*. There were always two or three of them perched on the highest limb of a tree on the edge of the pueblo. They glided in gracefully on five feet of wing spread, flapping awkwardly as they came to rest. They were about the size of a turkey, of a blackish brown color and baldheaded, their wrinkled necks spotted with red in front. Hunched on their perch, they never opened their curved beaks to make a sound. They watched the street below them with beady eyes. Sometime during the day, the *zopilotes* swooped down to scavange in the narrow ditch that ran the length of the street, where the housewives dropped the entrails of chickens among the garbage. They gobbled what waste the dogs and pigs did not get at first. (6)

As ugly in appearance as it is graceful in flight, this scavenger becomes a mock national bird for Galarza's natal village of Jalcocotán, Nayarit, México.

Governed by male heads of family, or *jefes de familia*, Jalcocotán formally resembles Paredes's primordial Rio Grande society ruled by benevolent patriarchs. Yet Galarza introduces the term *jefe de familia* by talking, not about "The Patriarch," who in following passage has long since died, but about a vital diminutive matriarch with twinkling eyes:

Dona Esther, my Aunt Tel, as I called her, was a small person. Something over five-feet-five, she was fair-skinned and hazel-eyed. She seldom laughed, for when we came to Jalco she had already had enough grief to last a person a lifetime, the least of which was the responsibility for two younger brothers and a sister after the death of Grandfather Félix. He, too, had been a rigid *jefe de familia*. She had lived all her life under authority but it had not bent her will; standing up to it she was more than a person — she was a presence. When she was alone in the cottage with us she told jokes about animals and foolish, stuck-up persons. She smiled mostly with her eyes. (17)

Endurance, resiliance, and joy make the matriarch Aunt Tel an inspiring presence in young Ernesto's life.

In his tender yet impious mockery of patriarchs, Galarza moves from Aunt Tel to Coronel, the dominant rooster of Jalcocotán. To be *muy gallo*, literally very rooster, very male like a fighting cock, as Paredes suggested in his depiction of the ballad singer, is to be a real man. Roosters, especially fighting cocks, are widely celebrated as symbols of manhood in Mexican speech and song. Galarza introduces Coronel, who challenges all within earshot, as follows:

> Strutting in the sun, Coronel flashed the ochre rainbow of his feathers — orange red, brick red, ruby red, geranium red, and blood red. Coronel always held himself like a ramrod, but he stood straightest when he was on top of the corral wall. From up there he counted his chickens, gave the forest a searching look, and blasted out a general challenge to all the world. With his flaming red crest and powerful yellow spurs, Coronel was the picture of a very *jefe de familia*. (23)

If Jalcocotán's national bird is a mock eagle, the turkey buzzard, its dominant head of family is a mock patriarch, the rooster Coronel.

3. The Mock Conflict

"The Conflict" pits Coronel against the turkey buzzard in a mock cockfight. After a vivid description of the fight, Galarza describes how word spread through the village:

> Up and down the street the alarm spread. "Coronel is fighting the *zopilote*."
> "He is killing Coronel."
> "Get him, Coronel. *Éntrale, éntrale*."
> A ring of small children, women, pigs, and dogs had formed around the fighters. (31)

The parodic fight, of course, has no adult male witnesses. In any case, it is all over in a moment. The turkey buzzard flies off with his prize, and the rooster claims victory:

> As suddenly as it had started, the fight was over. The *zopilote*, snatching at the heap of chicken guts that had tempted the hen, wheeled and spread his great wings, lifting himself over the crowd. He headed for a nearby tree, where he perched and finished his spoils.

Coronel, standing erect among the litter gave his wings a powerful stretch, flapped them and crowed like a winning champ. His foe, five times larger, had fled, and all the pueblo could see that he was indeed *muy gallo*.

Seeing that Coronel was out of danger, Nerón and I dashed to tell the epic story. We reported how our rooster had dashed a hundred times against the vulture, how he had driven his spurs into the hugh bird inflicting fatal wounds. Nerón, my dumb witness, wagged his tail and barked. (31)

The cockfight mocks the village's established authorities so obliquely and gently that its humor can be missed. Such are childhood memories and the apparent innocence they confer. Despite their self-deprecating postures and their unadorned plain speech, neither Galarza nor Paredes has written an innocent narrative.

When Galarza describes a *corrido* songfest, his account must be taken tongue-in-cheek. It has none of the solemnity of Paredes's depiction of a man who throws his head back as he belts out the *corrido* of Gregorio Cortez. In Galarza's words:

When some of the *compadres* got drunk, usually on Sundays, there was singing in some corral or in the plaza. Women and children took no part in these affairs, which sometimes ended in fights with machetes. We couldn't help hearing the men's songs, which became louder with the drinking. They sang the *corrido* of Catalino, the bandit who stood off hundreds of *rurales*, the mounted police who chased him up and down the Sierra Madre year in and year out. In his last battle, Catalino was cornered in a canyon. From behind a boulder he picked off dozens of rurales with his Winchester, taking a nip of *aguardiente* between shots, and shouting to his persecutors: "Acérquense, desgraciados, aquí está su padre." The rurales, like anybody else, did not like to be called wretched punks especially by an outlaw who boasted he was their father. In Mexico for such an insult you paid with your life. They closed in until Catalino lay dead. They chopped off his head and showed it in all the pueblos of the Sierra Madre, which made Catalino hero enough to have a ballad composed about him. It was generally agreed that he was from Jalcocotán where the bravest men were to be found, especially on Sunday nights when they were drunk. (48-49)

Nobody's masculine reputation escapes Galarza's parodic gaze. The rurales are insulted by Catalino. Catalino himself can become a hero only by having his head chopped off. The village men become the best and bravest in the region, particularly during their Sunday night drunken songfests. Galarza's humor deflates a certain masculine ethic but leaves the men's humanity quite intact. Not unlike this essay, Galarza's mocking critique of Mexican patriarchs remains androcentric and thus incomplete.

4. The Conflict

When the autobiography nears its end, "The Conflict" and the target of Galarza's political attacks come more clearly into focus. His central subject is not patriarchy but the Chicano struggle against Anglo-American domination. If Paredes's primordial patriarchs can be regarded as models for creating mythic figures of resistance, Galarza's mockery of Mexican patriarchs provides a critical idiom for resisting Anglo-American figures of authority. The former valorizes ancient Rio Grande patriarchs in order to endow them with mythic potency in fighting Anglo-Texan prejudice against Mexicans; the latter mocks rural Mexican patriarchs in order to develop the terms for undermining Anglo-American figures of authority. Both inflated and deflated patriarchs become displaced, as the analyses proceed, into figures of resistance to Anglo-American oppression.

As an educated boy, by then living in Sacramento and fluent in English, Galarza translates and otherwise helps his elders in their struggles with established Anglo authorities:

> When troubles made it necessary for the *barrio* people to deal with the Americans uptown, the *Autoridades*, I went with them to the police court, the industrial accident office, the county hospital, the draft board, the county clerk. We got lost together in the rigamarole of functionaries who sat, like *patrones*, behind desks and who demanded licenses, certificates, documents, affidavits, signatures, and witnesses. (252)

In this passage, if young Ernesto reminds one of the *gallo*, the rooster Coronel, the functionaries bring to mind the *zopilote*, the turkey buzzard. The sense for incongruities, the whimsy informing his political vision, still is evident as Galarza deploys the heteroglossia of a bilingual text to Mexicanize Anglo-American bosses. In being Mexicanized, these bosses are verbally assimilated to what they probably most abhor: *Autoridades* and *patrones*.

Shades of "The Patriarch," the parodic rigid Mexican *jefe de familia*, give a peculiar penumbra to Galarza's perception of American authorities with their multiple bureacratic offices and their innumerable Latinate documents. One Anglo-American *Autoridad* deepens the incongruities by urging young Ernesto "to tell the people in the camp to organize. Only by organizing, he told me, will they ever have decent places to live" (260). By then young Ernesto had already started his lifetime career in organizing.

Fathers, Sons, Politics, and Laughter

All this talk about *Autoridades* and *jefes de familia* makes me want to say two words about my father by way of a half-serious, half-playful way of further dismantling "The Patriarch," "The Primordial Society," "The Fall,", and "The Conflict." But I hardly know what to say. If I can speak at all, especially in a dismantling mode, it is only because others have come before me, and the struggle has reached a different phase than it had for Paredes and Galarza.

Let me begin by saying that when my father was about twenty he came north from Mexico City to Chicago where he completed high school. He continued his education, and (to make a long story short) now has retired from the University of Arizona where he headed the Romance Languages Department for some fifteen years or so.

1. Collapsing "The Primordial Society" and "The Fall"

In my father's lifetime "The Fall" preceded his knowledge of "The Primordial Society." His primordial terrain was an *hacienda* near Minatitlán, a small town on the coast of Vera Cruz. His stories about the *hacienda* seemed peculiarly vague, more from the imagined than the remembered past. To tell the truth, I never really believed in the *hacienda*. Recently, however, my understanding of the magical realism in his *hacienda* stories has changed. Within two years of my father's birth during the Mexican Revolution, he lost his own father, his paternal uncle, and his paternal grandfather. The *hacienda* was once real enough, but not in his lifetime. Nor did he ever assume his seemingly destined place in the familial line of patriarchs. He once told me that he grew up surrounded by women; he never spoke about primordial patriarchy, neither with Paredes's solemnity nor with Galarza's mocking tones. By the time of his earliest memories, "The Primordial Society" had been destroyed. He knew it only after "The Fall," in the form of tales told to him of what once had been.

In the United States he married an Anglo woman who was direct, funny, engaging, and instrumental. His marriage allowed him to retain a modest, plain-spoken, self-deprecating humor also shared by Paredes and Galarza. The possibility of border discourse, marked by bilingual heteroglossia, understatement, and humor, seems quite at odds with Deleuze and Guattari's model of a minor literature.[12]

2. "The Primordial Society," "The Fall," and "The Conflict"

Where there are fathers, there are sons, so perhaps I should say a word about myself. In high school I probably resembled, not Gregorio Cortez, but one of those *pachucos* scornfully depicted by Paredes mumbling into a microphone. As a professor's son I was nicknamed Conchukus, a combination of *pachuco* and Confucious. For me, "The Primordial Society" was never pristine; it came after "The Fall," and included "The Conflict," for it straddled the border with a fluid biculturalism that not only tolerated, but happily incorporated and played upon incongruities.

Perhaps the flavor of our bilingual border world can be conveyed by a couple of stanzas from Jose Montoya's well-known poem, his tender parodic portrait of the *pachuco*, "El Louie":

En Sanjo you'd see him
      sporting a dark topcoat
      playing in his fantasy
      the role of Bogart, Cagney
      or Raft.
. . . . .

---

12. Paredes's and Galarza's work can highlight qualities of humor and heteroglossia in Joyce and Kafka that have been overlooked by Deleuze and Guattari. The Chicano writers remain distinctive in having neither the exhuberance of Joyce nor the intensity of Kafka. Their work instead is low-key, modest, self-deprecating, and understated.

An Louie would come through —
melodramatic music, like in the
mono — tan tan taran! — Cruz
Diablo, El Charro Negro! Bogart
smile (his smile as deadly as
his vaisas!) He dug roles, man,
and names — like "Blackie," "Little
Louie . . . "

Ese, Louie . . .
Chale, man, call me "Diamonds!"[13]

This poem can be read with too much solemnity. As the *pachuco*
plays his roles, the poem invites commentary on existential emptiness
or degenerate individualism. At the other extreme, but perhaps more
plausibly, "El Louie" can appear to be engaged in cultural resistance.
Rather more modestly, the poem can be understood as accenting the
playful heteroglossia of border culture.[14] El Louie, for example, enacts
roles from the dominant society, "Bogart, Cagney, or Raft," and in a
ludic leap juxtaposes them with the heroes of Mexican *charro* or cowboy
films, "Cruz Diablo" and "El Charro Negro." Montoya's poem recalls
both Paredes's suggestion that humor deeply informs Chicano
resistance and Galarza's mocking Mexicanization of Anglo-American
Autoridades.

The fantasy of Mexicanization has its dark side. Probably most
Anglo-Americans have encountered this dark side as a manufactured
anxiety about the Latinization of the United States, a vision which
informs *Miami Vice*, the new immigration bill, and Ronald Reagan's
rhetoric.

---

13. José Montoya, "El Louie," *Rascatripas*, vol. 2 (Oakland, Ca., 1970).
Reprinted in Antonia Castañeda et al., *Literatura Chicana, Texto y Contexto* (Englewood
Cliffs, N. J.: Prentice-Hall, 1972), 173-76; Luis Valdes and Stan Steiner, *Aztlán: An
Anthology of Mexican-American Literature* (New York: Random House, Inc., 1972), 333-37;
Arturo Madrid-Barela, "In Search of the Authentic Pachuco: An Interpretive Essay,"
Aztlán 4, no. 1 (1973): 31-59, (poem, 53-55).

14. The potential affinities of heteroglossia and political resistance have most
recently been confirmed in the distinctively Filipino carnivalesque overthrow of the
seemingly all-powerful Marcos dictatorship. In one moment, Filipinos wept in fear for
their lives as they stood firm before tanks; in the next moment, they turned to buy ice
cream or joke with friends.

Anxiety about Mexicanization has also been known to surface in the academic homeland. Recently, for example, a transcript of a University of Arizona Faculty Senate meeting recorded the speech of a Spanish Professor. After protesting too much about having been called a racist, the Professor went on to say the following:

> Despite my devotion to Hispanic civilization, I find that that culture has two institutions that are models well worth avoiding — its forms of government and of higher education. The truth of the matter is that my unfortunate department was thoroughly Mexicanized back in the sixties. The university's president and provost would apparently like to make that mistake universal. I call upon all my colleagues with the least care for scholarly integrity to extirpate a deep rooted evil in one department to prevent its spread through the entire institution.[15]

Whatever qualities of Hispanic civilization the Spanish Professor may admire, they do not extend to placing Chicanos in positions of authority in government and education. Here, the Professor puts up an invisible sign: "No Mexicans Allowed."

Unlike Galarza's formally comparable whimsical bilingual fantasy, this man's earnest nightmare of Mexicanization — contagious, spreading, virulent, like a cancer — has been inscribed in a decidedly monolingual (English only) space whose Anglo-American borders must be defended. Outsiders must be kept out and insiders in. Life on the border where El Louie's ludic spirit can bring together Bogart and El Charro Negro, Cagney and Cruz Diablo has unfortunately not intruded upon the Spanish Professor's purist imagination. Alas, others with similarly constrained imaginations have played out their visions in wider social arenas — mass media, national policy, presidential mandates — with even more dire consequences for Chicanos.

---

15. Transcript of statement made to faculty senate, 20 January 1986 (mimeograph), 4. A briefer passage from the same text has also been cited in Scott Heller, "Language, Politics, and Chicano Culture Spark Battle at U. of Arizona," *Chronicle of Higher Education* 31, no. 22 (22 February 1986): 1, 24-26, 26.

Summary

(1) Deleuze and Guattari have presented their concept of a minor literature with canonical European examples which do not readily apply to Chicanos. In discussing two Chicano writers, I have argued for the political centrality of humor, a degree of authorial individuation, and the border as a heterogeneous space of bilingual cultural creativity.

(2)   My critique of "The Patriarch" remains androcentric and limited. Perhaps a deeper critique can be suggested by citing the following brief passages from Lorna Dee Cervantes's poem, "Beneath the Shadow of the Freeway":

> Myself — I could never decide.
> So I turned to books, those staunch, upright men.
> I became Scribe, Translator of Foreign Mail,
> interpreting letters from the government, notices
> of dissolved marriages and welfare stipulations.
> I paid the bills, did light man-work, fixed faucets, insured
> everything
> against all leaks.
> . . . .
> in the night I would hear it
> glass bottles shattering on the street
> words cracking into shrill screams
> inside my throat a cold fear
> as it entered the house in hard
> unsteady steps stopping at my door
> my name bathrobe slippers
> outside a 3am mist heavy
> as a breath full of whiskey
> stop it go home come inside
> mama if he comes here again
> I'll call the police[16]

After the woman narrator tries on male roles, she encounters "The Patriarch," but this time the man's drinking is no joke. He has not

---

16. Lorna Dee Cervantes, "Beneath the Shadow of the Freeway," *Latin American Review* (Spring-Summer 1977). Reprinted in Dexter Fischer, ed., *The Third Woman: Minority Women Writers of the United States* (Boston: Houghton Mifflin, 1980), 378-81.

come as a singer of *corridos*, but as a staggering, sterile figure, more a victimizer than a victim, more a destroyer than a creator. The figure of "The Patriarch" ranges from the warrior hero of *With His Pistol in His Hand* to the abusive drunk depicted by a number of Chicana writers of the 1980s. Ultimately, it is against a reading of these recent feminist texts that the warrior heroes of pioneering Chicano writers must be discussed. For Chicanos to project our heritage into the future, we must attempt the delicate and vexed task of recuperating courageous early works without reifying them.

(3) Lorna Dee Cervantes's poem takes place in Silicon Valley, just south of Stanford University. The other writers discussed here have resided in Texas, California, and Arizona. The fear of Mexicanization is happening here at home, not someplace else. When read in Los Angeles, this paper stimulated discussions of Kafka, Baudelaire's writings on humor, and other reflections on distant times and places. Perhaps the topic comes too close to home, for the 1980 Los Angeles population was over 27% of "Spanish origin."

(4)   The central subject of this paper has been an attempt to characterize a minor literature which should be understood in the context of Chicano struggles against anti-Mexican prejudice by a dominant Anglo-American majority. Not unlike this paper, Chicano narrative form is often deadpan, unadorned, and self-deprecating; its understated humor can readily be missed, but it is barbed. This humor, along with other rhetorical modes, constitutes Chicano culture, both as a positive identification and as a form of resistance.

Defining Asian American Realities Through Literature

Elaine H. Kim

There were some letters in the "Dear Abby" column recently that reflect a gulf between Asian Americans and the descendants of European immigrants. Two Irish Americans wrote that they could not understand why an American of "Oriental" descent would complain about being asked "what are you" within five minutes of being introduced to a "Caucasian." One wrote, "I don't think it's rude... I think it's a positive component of international understanding." Abby says that the "Oriental" readers, "without exception," responded like the following letter writer:

> ... What am I? Why, I'm a person like everyone else . . . . 'Where did you come from?' would be an innocent question when one Caucasian asks it of another, but when it is asked of an Asian, it takes on a different tone . . . . When I say, 'I'm from . . . Portland, Oregon!' they are invariably surprised . . . because they find it hard to believe that an Asian-looking person is actually . . . American . . . . Being white is not a prerequisite for being . . . American . . . and . . . it's high time everyone realized it.

Significantly, Abby concludes the column with the other Irish American letter: "The Irish are so proud of being Irish, they tell you before you even ask. Tip O'Neill never tried to hide his Irish ancestry."[1]

---

1. "Dear Abby," *San Francisco Chronicle*, 28 April 1986.

So much writing by Asian Americans is focused on the theme of claiming an American, as opposed to Asian, identity that we may begin to wonder if this constitutes accomodation, a collective colonized spirit — the fervent wish to "hide our ancestry," which is impossible for us anyway, to relinquish our marginality, and to lose ourselves in an intense identification with the hegemonic culture. Or is it in fact a celebration of our marginality and a profound expression of protest against being defined by domination?

Today, as we study the power of "otherness" and the celebration of marginality, we must pause to think about the complexity and diversity of minority discourse in order to understand why the political concerns expressed in Asian American literature are unique. Tied to issues of gender, social stratification, racial oppression, and the need to restore the foundations of our history and culture, the most recurrent theme in our writing is what I call claiming America for Asian Americans. That does not mean disappearing like raindrops in the ocean of white America, fighting to become "normal," losing ourselves in the process. It means inventing a new identity, defining ourselves according to the truth instead of a racial fantasy, so that we can be reconciled with one another in order to celebrate our marginality. It is this seeming paradox, the Asian American claim on America, that is the oppositional quality of our discourse.

In this article, I have deliberately chosen to provide a roughly chronological survey of various Asian American literary works, because our literature is still unfamiliar to most scholars and because it represents diverse nationalities and different class backgrounds, nativities, generations, historical moments, and genders, factors that often make quite contradictory demands. In general, though, I think it is fair to say that the literature reflects an overarching collective concern, the invention of an American identity.

Asian Americans may seem squarely placed in the so-called hegemonic stage of domination. Our literature is written primarily by American-born, American-educated Asians whose first language is English, whether we concur and collaborate or resist. The Asian American writer exists on the margins of his or her own marginal community, wedged between the hegemonic culture and the non-English-speaking communities largely unconcerned with self-definition. Nor has the transformation of our communities during the last two decades brought with it a legion of new writers: for the most part, they continue to be second and third generation American born Chinese and Japanese. They cannot be expected to speak in the voices of the vast numbers of immigrants and refugees whose stories have never been well represented in our literature, past or present.

Inscriptions of Asians in U.S. Popular Culture

Although we are no longer under direct colonial domination, clumsy racial fantasies about Asians continue to flourish in the West, and these extend to Asian Americans as well. The Vietnamese in Japanese army uniforms, the sinister villains and brute hordes of faceless masses found in films like "Rambo" are not much different from the business-suited New York Chinatown gangland mobsters in "Year of the Dragon." Familiar representations of Asians — always unalterably alien — as helpless heathens, comical servants, loyal allies and, only in the case of women, exotic sex objects imbued with an innate understanding of how to please, serve, and titillate, extend directly to Asian Americans and exist in all cases to define as their dialectical opposite the Anglo man as heroic, courageous, and physically superior, whether as soldier, missionary, master, or lover.

These racial romances so characteristic of the dominant phase of colonization may be part of the baggage of Western imperialist penetration into Asia; nevertheless they are extended to us, who have not been allowed a separate identity. Asian America is after all itself a creation of white racism that groups nationalities and nativities together, making it possible to blame — and murder — a Chinese American out of frustration over competition from Japanese auto manufacturers.

We can see how the notions about Asians and Asian Americans overlap in the "middleman minority" function for both. British and American scholarship traditionally placed Asians between blacks and whites on a racial continuum: if whites were born to lead, blacks were best at hard labor, and Asians were suited to carry out orders. This notion has been sedimented into our interpretations of economic development in Asia today: the "little tigers," South Korea, Taiwan, and Singapore, are sandwiched between the industrialized nations of the West and the countries of Africa and Latin America. Only Japan presents a classification problem. In this country, Asian America is a buffer zone between whites and blacks or Hispanics: supposedly obedient, docile, efficient at carrying out the mandates of the decision makers, Asian Americans are increasingly visible in low middle management, high clerical, and small business occupations. Ideologically, we occupy the position of "model minority," living proof that racism is not what keeps other people of color down.

Views Of The Literary Critics

Racist and culturally hegemonic views of Asians and Asian Americans are inscribed in works by well-known Anglo American writers like Jack London, as well as a plethora of lesser writers, like the creator of Charlie Chan, Earl Derr Biggers, whose caricatures have survived him. That both Biggers and his British counterpart, Arthur Sarsfield Ward, creator of Fu Manchu, received recognition and honorary degrees at Harvard demonstrates how extensive has been the penetration of these views of Asians and Asian Americans into the American intelligentsia. Indeed, it is difficult for Anglo American literary critics to remain unaffected by the same notions embedded in the minds of Dear Abby's readers. Contemporary Chinese American playwright Frank Chin has noted that New York critics of his play, *Chickencoop Chinaman*, complained in the early 1970's that his characters did not speak, dress, or act "like Orientals."

Certainly reviews of our literature by Anglo-American critics reveal that the criteria used to assess their literary merit have been other than literary and aesthetic. Reviewers of Etsu Sugimoto's *A Daughter of the Samurai* (1925) praised the writer because she "pleads no causes, asks no vexing questions"[2] at a time when the controversial issue of Japanese exclusion was being spiritedly discussed. Critics of *The Grass Roof* (1931) lauded Younghill Kang's Korea, which is described as a "planet of death," its brilliant colors, haunting music, and the magic of its being fading into an "infernal twilight" of decay commanded by the inability to modernize. But when Kang depicts the arrogance and race prejudice of the American missionaries in Korea, the critics are indignant:

---

2. *New York Tribune*, 22 November 1925.

> Mr. Kang does not, I think, give a full account of American missionaries. Doubtless these are blundering human beings, just like the rest of us. He accuses them of lack of education, yet he longed ardently to come to their country for the kind of education they receive. He was desperately eager to receive the benefit of their escort to America.[3]

During the World War II era, the American public became widely aware of broad distinctions among Asian nationalities, at least between Japanese and all others. China and the Philippines became known as allies in the Pacific, and popular magazines like *Life* and *Time* carried feature articles on how to tell the Chinese from the Japanese. In 1943 and 1950, the first books by second generation Chinese Americans were published by major houses. Promoters of Pardee Lowe's *Father and Glorious Descendant* suggested that the book might be worth reading because Lowe's enlistment in the U.S. Army showed him to be "one of America's loyal minorities."[4] Jade Snow Wong's *Fifth Chinese Daughter*[5] was valued primarily as evidence that American racial minorities have only themselves to blame for their failure in American life. Such a view, expressed by a member of a racial minority group, was important during the Cold War period, when charges of race discrimination in the United States were circulating in developing countries which, having recently been freed from direct colonial rule, were questioning the value of American world leadership. The U.S. State Department in fact negotiated the rights to publish Wong's book in a number of Asian languages and arranged a tour for her in 1952 to forty-five Asian locales from Tokyo to Karachi, where she was to speak about the benefits of American democracy from the perspective of a Chinese American.

During the Civil Rights movement of the late 1960s and the period of increased ethnic awareness immediately ensuing, several books by Japanese Americans were brought out by major publishers. Critical reception was shaped by political concerns at a time when people of color vociferously seeking justice and equality could be shown the

---

3. Lady Hosie, "A Voice From Korea," *Saturday Review of Literature*, 4 April 1931, 707.

4. Pardee Lowe, *Father and Glorious Descendant* (Boston: Little, Brown and Co., 1943), book jacket.

5. Jade Snow Wong, *Fifth Chinese Daughter* (New York: Harper and Row, 1950).

example of the non-militant approach of the "model minority." Jeanne Wakatsuki and James D. Houston's *Farewell to Manzanar*[6] was celebrated for its "lack of bitterness, self-pity, or solemnity."[7] in portraying the wartime incarceration of Japanese Americans. Daniel Okimoto's *American in Disguise*[8] was appreciated by critics for having been written with "restraint" during "the current racial uproar."[9] One reviewer praised him for talking of "the Negro problem sympathetically and yet not without the racial pride of one from a subculture which always worked hard and had a devotion to education as a spur to achievement."[10] Ironically, what the reviewers call "racial pride" can also be seen as racial self-hatred: *American in Disguise* illustrates that the price for such "success" is rejection of both Japanese and Japanese American identity. Okimoto thus finds white women "personally as well as physically" appealing, because they have the "seductive attraction" of being able to provide him with "[c]rowning evidence of having made it." The "key to final assimilation," Okimoto notes, is intermarriage, and the book ends with the writer's reference to his own children, for whom "[p]hysically, at least, half the disguise I have worn will be lost." Even in the end, his own face is still an unfortunate "disguise."[11]

The barriers to understanding Asian American literature posed by the blinders of culturally hegemonic interpretations can be seen in other non-literary criteria. In *Publisher's Weekly*, one critic praises Maxine Hong Kingston's *The Woman Warrior*[12] for its "myths rich and varied as Chinese brocade" and its prose manifesting "the delicacy and precision of porcelain": "East meets West with . . .charming results" in the book.[13] A closer look would have revealed its deliberately anti-exotic, anti-nostalgic character:

---

6. Jeanne Wakatsuki and James D. Houston, *Farewell to Manzanar* (San Francisco: San Francisco Book Company/Houghton Mifflin, 1973).

7. *Saturday Review World*, 6 November 1973; *Library Journal*, 1 November 1973, 3257.

8. Daniel Okimoto, *American in Disguise* (New York: Walker-Weatherhill, 1971).

9. Phoebe Adams, "Short Reviews: Books," *Atlantic Monthly* 227, no. 4 (April 1971), 104.

10. J.J. Conlin, *Best-Seller* 31, no. 9 (1 April 1971).

11. Okimoto, *American in Disguise*, 206.

12. Maxine Hong Kingston, *The Woman Warrior* (New York: Vintage Books, 1977).

13. *Publisher's Weekly* 212 (September 1976): 72.

The old man opened his eyes wide at us and turned in a circle, surrounded. His neck tendons stretched out. "Maggots!" he shouted. "Maggots! Where are my grandsons? I want grandsons! Give me grandsons! Maggots!" He pointed at each one of us, "Maggot! Maggot! Maggot! Maggot! Maggot! Maggot!" Then he dived into his food, eating fast and getting seconds. "Eat, maggots," he said. "Look at the maggots chew."
"He does that at every meal," the girls told us in English.
"Yeah," we said. "Our old man hates us too. What assholes."[14]

A critic notes with approval that Kingston's name indicates that she is married to an "American," that is, a white, implying that she herself is not "American" and that her marriage has some bearing on the critical approach to her book.[15] In the *National Observer*, one reviewer defends his interpretation by mentioning that his wife is Chinese Canadian. Even Kingston's portrayal of ambiguity as central to the Chinese American woman's experience is misconstrued: "It's hard to tell where her fantasies end and reality begins," the critic complains. He is confused by her depiction of some Chinese women as aggressive and verbal and others as docile, as if there can only be one type of Chinese woman. These confusions are "especially hard for a non-Chinese," he concludes, "and that's the troubling aspect of the book."[16] One of the main points of *The Woman Warrior* is that a marginal person indeed derives power and vision from living with paradoxes. The narrator says: "I learned to make my mind large, as the universe is large, so that there is room for paradoxes."[17]

Though truly universal, Asian American literature exists outside the canon of American literature and is considered narrow and specialized work penned by aliens to whom the English language and the culture it represents can never really belong. Thus, despite the place we are supposed to occupy as an assimilated "model minority," it's hard to think of an Asian American writer who is not immediately identified as such, attesting to the continuing marginality of our literature.

---

14.   Kingston, *The Woman Warrior*, 222-23.
15.   Jane Kramer, "On Being Chinese in China and America," *New York Times Book Review*, 7 November 1976, 19.
16.   Michael Malloy, " 'The Woman Warrior': On Growing Up Chinese, Female, and Bitter," *National Observer*, 9 October 1976, 25.
17.   Kingston, *The Woman Warrior*, 35.

Early Immigrant Writers: A Class Perspective

The first Asian American writers in English were acutely aware of common misconceptions about Asia and Asians. These early immigrant writers were not representative of the general population of Asian Americans, who were predominantly laborers recruited for agricultural and construction work in Hawaii and on the Pacific Coast. Consumed in struggles for their livelihood in a hostile environment and segregated in field labor camps and ethnic urban enclaves, they usually did not speak or write in English. Even Filipino immigrants were mostly illiterate, since recruiters in search of a docile labor force preferred those without formal education. Then too, autobiographical writing and popular fiction were not found in the traditional cultures that produced the first immigrants. In China and Korea, writing and literature were the domain of the literati, who traditionally confined themselves to classical poetry and essays. Autobiography as such was unknown, since for a scholar to write a book about himself would have been deemed egotistical in the extreme. Fiction was considered frivolous and was usually written under pen names. Farmers and peasants performed as master storytellers, dramatic dancers, and singers but rarely expressed themselves through the written word.

Scholars and diplomats, who had been exempted from exclusion legislation aimed at restricting the entry of Asian laborers into the United States, comprised a disproportionately large part of the early Asian American voice. Addressing an Anglo American audience, they tried to win sympathy for the people of the educated elite of which they were part. Their portrayals of Asia are focused on high culture, and their criticisms of American society are tentative and apologetic.

Probably the best known interpreter of Asia to the West is self-styled cultural envoy Lin Yutang, whose *My Country and My People*[18] enjoyed enormous popularity in the West, although Chinese critics have pointed out that Lin was "out of tempo with the Chinese people," indulging as he does in "chitchat on the moon, rocks and gardens, dreams, smoke and incense" while Chinese were dying by the millions

---

18.   Lin Yutang, *My Country and My People* (New York: John Day Co., 1937).

in their struggle against foreign domination. "No wonder," writes one critic, "many Chinese called his book 'My Country and My Class' or, resorting to a pun . . . .'Mai Country and Mai People,' mai being the Chinese word for selling and betraying."[19] Ironically, Lin spent most of his life in the United States as a Chinese expatriate; the place he won for himself here was made possible only if he remained Chinese.

The writings of Younghill Kang and Carlos Bulosan illustrate the transition from sojourner to immigrant searching for a permanent place in America. Kang and Bulosan paint vivid portraits of the lives of Korean and Filipino exiles — their work, their aspirations, their exclusion from American social and intellectual life. Searching for entry into that life, first through books and then through American women, both discover that the America of their aspirations does not yet exist: it must be invented, brought into being.

Not one of the characters in Kang's *East Goes West*[20] achieves his American dream. Reading Shakespeare in his unheated room, the narrator is only able to think of food, and the young American woman he so eagerly hopes to befriend moves away, leaving no forwarding address. The story ends with his dream of being locked in a dark cellar with some black men as torch-bearing whites are about to set them all on fire. His only hope is a Buddhist interpretation of the dream, that he will be reincarnated into a better life.

Bulosan's *America is in the Heart*[21] describes the lives and work of the Filipino migrant workers who followed the harvest, working in fields and canneries from the Mexican border to Alaska during the 1920s and 1930s. Although Bulosan is attempting to claim America for the thousands of farmworkers and menial laborers for whom he seeks to give voice, it is an America of the heart, a dream, a promise, an ideal forged from loneliness and suffering.

> We must be united in the effort to make an America in which
> our people can find happiness . . . . We are all Americans that have

---

19.   Chan Wing-Tsit, "Lin Yutang, Critic and Interpreter," *College English* 8, no. 4 (January 1947): 163-64.

20.   Younghill Kang, *East Goes West* (New York: Charles Scribner's Sons, 1937).

21.   Carlos Bulosan, *America is in the Heart* (Seattle: Univ. of Washington Press, 1946 and 1973).

toiled and suffered and known oppression and defeat, from the first Indian that offered peace in Manhattan to the last Filipino pea-pickers. . . . America is a prophecy of a new society of men . . . the nameless foreigner, the homeless refugee, the hungry boy begging for a job and the black body dangling from a tree.[22]

The war era's paternalistically friendly attitudes towards certain Asian nations has passed, Bulosan died in poverty and obscurity, and Asian Americans are eternal aliens once again, periodically reminded that we have no right to "complain" about anything. Instead, we should be grateful. "If you don't like it here," even third generation Asian Americans would be told, "you can always go back."

The contemporary Southeast Asian refugee claim on America is captured in Wendy Law-Yone's *The Coffin Tree*,[23] which is the story of a Burmese refugee woman who can never "go back." The contrast between her life in Burma and America provides us with a profound understanding of why she almost loses her mind. Her brother, who had been the vital one in Burma, fails to thrive here. After he dies and she hears of the death of her father, her last link to Burma, she is totally alone in the world, having lost the continuity between past and future provided by her family in the traditional culture. Unless she can adapt herself to a hostile and terrifying new world, with its bitter loneliness, its telephone answering machines, and its asylums for the insane, unless she can survive the transplant and set down roots in American soil, she will disappear from the face of the earth.

Community Portraits

In our communities, the wish to "disappear" by being fully assimilated into white society has always been resisted in fervent attempts to preserve cultural integrity within the American context. Although Louis Chu's *Eat a Bowl of Tea*[24] never achieved popularity or financial success during his lifetime, the novel is now viewed as a cornerstone in the Asian American literary tradition. The book is set in New York

22.   Ibid., 188-89.
23.   Wendy Law-Yone, *The Coffin Tree* (New York: Alfred A. Knopf, 1983).
24.   Louis Chu, *Eat A Bowl of Tea* (New York: Lyle Stuart, 1961).

Chinatown in the late 1940's, the characters aging men who have spent their lives in laundry and restaurant labor. Their contacts with American society are limited to harassment by police and immigration officials and brief encounters with American prostitutes. Their lives have been sustained by fantasies about China and by the profound warmth of their friendships with each other. The central contradiction is the conflict between the old community of bachelor sojourners and the young immigrants who will make America their permanent home. Chu's Chinese American community is on the threshhold of change: forced by the Chinese Revolution to face the likelihood that they may never return to their homeland after all, the old men find that the community structure they have built in New York is all that is left to them. The uncertain future belongs to the youth, represented by Ben Loy, whose sexual impotence is a reflection of the social powerlessness of generations of Chinatown bachelors constricted by genocidal American laws and policies. The bitter tea he must drink is his willingness to compromise in order to obtain a new life in America. The tea is Chinese medicine, and the move he makes is from New York to San Francisco Chinatown. Although he will not raise his son as he was raised, he will not forsake his Chinese roots. The vital quality of Chu's prose comes from his ability to appreciate the language spoken around him by a people to whom verbal skill and witty exchanges were valued as a social art. Instead of the "pidgin English" invented for comic effect by Anglo-American writers about the Chinese, Chu translates the idioms and images from Cantonese dialects, presenting them in skillfully crafted dialogues. In these, he gives us a vivid picture of the social relationships and attitudes that governed Chinatown life for many decades.

By deliberately not addressing Anglo American readers, Chu is able to present a non-hegemonic view of his own community within the context of American society — that is, as Milton Murayama says, "setting the record straight . . . with love, with all the warts showing."[25] At the same time, he is able to use the English language in new ways.

Because of differential treatment of Japanese Americans under American laws, American-born, American-educated, English-speaking second generation Japanese *nisei* comprised about half of the

---

25. Interview, Louis Chu, 7 December 1979.

Japanese population in the United States by 1930, resulting in the publication of more Japanese American literary work in English earlier than those found in other groups. This work appeared first in ethnic print media. Addressed to fellow *nisei*, it unself-consciously attempts to appropriate the English language and literary forms for Japanese American use. The essential quality in these writings is a balance made possible by the writers' biculturalism, which gives them two pairs of eyes through which to see both their communities and their American context without distortion or romanticism. By the 1950's, some of this work was published outside the newsprint ghetto.

John Okada's *No-No Boy*[26] was probably rejected by the Japanese American press and community in the 1950s because it depicts both American society and the post-war Seattle Japanese American community in an intensely unflattering light. The characters have little in common with the "model minority" that picks itself up by the bootstraps: incapacitated by self-hatred, their relationships have been distorted by the internment experience. Parents and children, husbands and wives, brothers and friends are pitted against each other in bitter conflicts caused by their collective shame. The protagonist searches desperately for a way to put together the pieces of his own fragmented life. Despite his pain and alienation, he retains his profound faith in the promise of American justice and equality. *No-No Boy* is an indictment of race hatred and a testament to the strength and faith of the oppressed.

Nor is the view of the pre-war Japanese American family and community and its American context a pretty one in Milton Murayama's *All I Asking For Is My Body* (1959).[27] The *nisei* stagger under the combined weight of Japanese family traditions and the uniquely American plantation system of Hawaii. The book challenges unquestioning acceptance of tyranny and hierarchy as impediments to human freedom.

Murayama's dialogues are carefully crafted to express the bicultural realities of the characters in standard and pidgin English and in standard and colloquial Japanese, which is translated into

---

26. John Okada, *No-No Boy* (Rutland, Vt.: Charles E. Tuttle Co., 1957).
27. Milton Murayama, *All I Asking For Is My Body* (San Francisco: Supa Press, 1959, 1968, 1975).

standard and informal English. Murayama decided to print the book himself with the help of a linotype setter from Hawaii because he felt that commercial editors would "correct the English and kill the pidgin."[28]

Gender perspectives in the critique of pre-war Japanese American family and community life on the West Coast are contained in half a dozen remarkable short stories published between 1949 and 1961 by Hisaye Yamamoto.[29] The focus is on the changing roles of women imprisoned with well-meaning but weak and insensitive husbands and on the bleakness and isolation of rural toil. Ultimately, the women are vanquished. The men are never condemned, but they remain in the shadows as guardians of the prison doors, for the most part conventional and colorless in comparison to the women who are the central figures. The women's strength comes from surviving sorrow. They also pass a legacy to their daughters, who as a result may not be subdued in the end. Characteristic of Yamamoto's style is subtle irony and understatement, usually through the juxtaposition of two currents that reflect the quintessential quality of Japanese American life: beneath a placid and respectable surface, there are dark hints of hidden tragedy, tinged with death and violence. Yamamoto accomplishes this by presenting the stories through the eyes of an ingenuous young American-born narrator who understands less about what she is describing than what readers can guess.

Alienation and Loss

The contemporary generation of Japanese American writers, most of whom are of the *sansei* or third generation, grandchildren of the immigrants, is feeling the effects of the internment and dispersal of the Japanese American community Okada and Yamamoto depicted with such familiarity and confidence. Although most returned to

28.   Interview, Milton Murayama, 7 December 1979.
29.   "The Legend of Miss Sasagawara," *Kenyon Review* 12, no. 1 (Winter 1950): 99-115; "Yoneko's Earthquake," *Furioso* 6, no. 1 (Winter 1951): 5-16; "Las Vegas Charley," *Arizona Quarterly*, no. 4 (Winter 1961): 303-22; "The Brown House," *Harper's Bazaar*, no. 2879 (October 1951): 166; 283-84 and in *Asian American Authors*, ed. Kai-yu Hsu and Helen Palubinskas (Boston: Houghton Mifflin Co., 1972):114-22; "Seventeen Syllables," *Partisan Review* 16, nos. 7-12 (July-December 1949): 1122-1134 and in *Ethnic American Short Stories*, ed. Katharine D. Newman (New York: Washington Square Press, 1975), 89-103.

California after the U.S. government's largely unsuccessful attempt to scatter them across the United States at the end of the war, they never regained their hold on Pacific Coast agriculture, and the Japantowns that had flourished all along Highway 99, the road that cuts through the fields and past the canneries of Asian America, have disappeared. Nationally, more than half of today's *sansei* marriages are outmarriages. Ronald Tanaka traces the path toward cultural annihilation in a poem about a book of photographs on Japanese American internment :

> the people who put out that book,
> i guess they won a lot of awards.
> it was a very photogenic period
> of california history, especially
> if you were a white photographer
> with compassion for helpless people.
>
> but the book would have been better,
> I think, or more complete, if they
> had put in my picture and yours, with
> our hakujin wives, our long hair and
> the little signs that say, "what? me
> speak japanese?" and "self-determination
> for everyone but us." and then maybe
> on the very last page, a picture of
> our kids. They don't even look like
> japanese[30]

In the decade between 1965 and 1975, playwright Frank Chin and short story writer Jeffery Paul Chan focused their attentions on a search for a viable new identity for Chinese American men, an identity that would link them to the cowboys who settled the American West and the nameless men who built the transcontinental railroad with their bare hands. The identity crises of the young in Chin and Chan's work stems in part from the complicity of older generations of Chinese immigrant men who cling to "mildewed memories" of

---

30.   Ronald Tanaka, "Appendix to Executive Order," *Ayumi: A Japanese American Anthology* (San Francisco: Japanese American Anthology Committee, 1980), 240.

China and to Chinese American women who cater to tourists' exotic fantasies. The failure of fathers is a favorite theme: in Chin's *Chickencoop Chinaman*,[31] Tam Lum's father is a dishwasher who bathes in his underpants because he fears that little old white ladies might peek at him through a keyhole. Women are represented as insensitive and unsophisticated or else as seekers after white "racist love." The only possible survival is escape from the suffocating environment — escape, ironically, into the culture that invented the fantasy in the first place. After lashing out at the emasculating effects of racial oppression, Chin and Chan accept the oppressors' definition of "masculinity." The result is unresolved tension between contempt and desire to fight for their Asian American characters. Cynicism, sexism, alienation, and preoccupation with death and decay have led not to a new identity but to the conclusion that we are doomed. In 1978, Chin said:

> There is no doubt in my mind that the Asian American is on the doorstep of extinction. There's so much out-marriage now that all that is going to survive are the stereotypes. White culture has not acknowledged Asian American art. Either you're foreign in this country, or you're an honorary white. I hope we can create work that will add to the human estate, but then I think we'll die out.[32]

Reconcilation

Most contemporary Asian American writers do not share Chin's pessimism. By weaving connections between us and our history, our forebears, each other, other people of color in this country and the world, these writers are inventing Asian American identities outside the realm of racial romance and externally imposed definitions.

Much contemporary Asian American literature expresses kinship with other people of color in America, especially blacks and Native Americans, who frequently appear in the works. "Soon the white

---

31.   Frank Chin, *The Chickencoop Chinaman and The Year of the Dragon* (Seattle: Univ. of Washington Press, 1981).

32.   Nikki Bridges, "Conversations and Convergences," Asian American Women Writers' Panel, Occidental College, January 1978, 16.

snow will melt," writes poet Al Robles, and "the brown, black, yellow earth will come to life."[33]

Our self-invention was stimulated by U.S. involvement in Asia, creating links with Asia on our own terms. Because we had been defined historically by race, it was difficult for many of us not to respond to the racial character of the war in Vietnam. Stunned by graphic news coverage of war-torn hamlets, we sometimes saw the faces of our friends and relatives in the visages of Vietnamese peasants. We were susceptible to the argument that U.S. foreign policy in Asia had always been racist and genocidal, that profits had been more important to government policymakers than Asian lives. We perceived the parallels between the war in Vietnam and the conquest of the Philippine resistance during the Spanish American War, in which an estimated one-sixth of the population of Ilocos was exterminated in the name of democracy. We concluded that the use of the atomic bomb on Japanese civilians during World War II evidenced the racist attitudes of military officials and policy makers toward the entire race.

In "The New Anak" (1975), Sam Tagatac writes of a Filipino American soldier in Vietnam who thinks of the land of his birth and his countrymen when he sees the tropical sun and rains, the distant hills, and the peasants with their water buffaloes as they are strafed by American bombers:

> I remember the light of that lagoon, the mythical sound of
> the flying dragon, spitting fire, one pass, one strafing gun
> across water for what is water from the sight of the gods,
> the crosshair splitting in the forming of a real image, so
> distant the face of . . . your face, my face.[34]

In Maxine Hong Kingston's *China Men*,[35] the Chinese American brother is haunted by nightmares of himself as a soldier in the rescuing army, walking among enemy corpses.

---

33. Alfred Robles, Untitled Poem, *Aion* 1, no. 2 (Fall 1971): 81 (Asian American Publications) (ed. Janice Mirikitani).

34. Sam Tagatac, "The New Anak," in *Aiieeeee! An Anthology of Asian-American Writers*, ed. Frank Chin, Jeffery Paul Chan, Lawson Fusao Inada, and Shawn Hsu Wong (Washington D.C.: Howard Univ. Press, 1974), 248.

35. Maxine Hong Kingston, *China Men* (New York: Alfred K. Knopf, 1980).

Laundry tubs drain beneath the bodies. The live women and children on the ironing tables, the last captured, are being dissected. He takes up the sword and hacks into the enemy, slicing them; they come apart in rings and rolls . . . . When he stops, he finds that he has cut up the victims too, who were his own relatives. The faces of the strung-up people are also those of his own family. Chinese faces, Chinese eyes, noses, and cheekbones.[36]

Dedicating her poems to dead heroes of Latin America and Africa like Orlando Letelier and Steven Biko, *sansei* poet Janice Mirikitani reflects on the connections between the wars waged by the U.S. in the Third World, the bombing of Japan, and the internment of Japanese Americans.

if you're too dark
they will kill you
if you're too swift
they will buy you
if you're too beautiful
they will rape you

watch with eyes open
speak darkly
turn your head like the owl
behind you[37]

Restoring the Foundations

Recognizing our kinship with others who struggle against domination, we must also claim our own identity as Americans. Asian American writers must piece together and sort out the meaning of our past, distorted and omitted by racism, from shreds of stories heard in childhood or from faded photographs that have never been explained. In Wing Tek Lum's "A Picture of My Mother's Family" (1974), the poet searches for the significance of each detail of an old photograph: he must try to make the story of his half-forgotten an-

---

36. Ibid. , 291.
37. Janice Mirikitani, "Japs," *Awake in the River* (San Francisco: Isthmus Press, 1978).

cestors relevant to himself. Like many Asian Americans, he does not even know their names, where they were born, or anything about their childhood in a distant land. The photograph is tantalizingly unrevealing.

> It is perhaps morning, the coolness
> captured now in such clear light; they seem
> somehow illuminated by beams from the moon,
> ... my grandfather...
> looks on...
> towards his right far away. I imagine a dark rose
> has caught his proud eye, though I do not know
> if such flowers have ever grown there.[38]

Taking up as their task the restoration of the foundations of Asian American history in the U.S., contemporary writers are locating, translating, and publishing work by previously little-known writers in their native languages, literature that illuminates our American roots. *Island: Poetry and History of Chinese Immigrants on Angel Island 1910-1940* (1980) is an anthology of poetry carved in Chinese by unknown immigrants on the walls of the Angel Island Detention Center barracks. They give voice to the spirit of our forebears:

> How many people ever return from battles?
> . . . . .
> Leaving behind my writing brush and removing my
> sword, I came to America.
> Who was to know two streams of tears would flow upon arriving here?
> If there comes a day when I will have attained by ambition and become successful
> I will certainly behead the barbarians and spare
> not a single blade of grass.
>
> Don't say that everything within is
> Western styled.
> Even it if is built of jade, it has turned into a cage.[39]

---

38. Wing Tek Lum, "A Picture of My Mother's Family," *Yardbird Reader*, vol. 3, ed. Frank Chin and Shawn Hsu Wong (Berkeley: Yardbird Publishing Company, 1974), 141.
39. Him Mark Lai, Genny Lim, and Judy Yung, eds., *Island: Poetry and History of Chi-*

By penetrating and occupying the consciousness of his shadowy forbears, Lawrence Yep contributes to the effort to repair the foundations of the Asian American heritage in *Dragonwings*,[40] a historical novel about nineteenth-century Chinese in America who invented a biplane. Rewriting our history from an Asian American perspective has brought to light new cultural heroes. The two characters in David Henry Hwang's play, "The Dance and the Railroad,"[41] are Chinese railroad workers in the 1867 strike. Many contemporary Japanese American writers focus on the internment. In "Family Album for Charlotte Davis," Lonnie Kaneko searches for the meaning of the word "Minidoka" only to discover that the name of that desert camp means water.

> Yesterday Charlotte asked, 'You mean there is still
> a bitterness?' Something wormed its way through my blood
> Snake. Water. Earth. 'It is a thirst,' I say.[42]

Sensitive to the foreboding certainty that the elderly and their life experiences will vanish before they can be understood and appreciated, Asian American writers portray the old with a sense of urgency. Bienvenido N. Santos, himself a Filipino expatriate who has lived in the United States since the declaration of martial law in the Philippines, says that his attention continually returns to the Filipino manongs who are the unsung heroes of American labor.

> . . . old timers among our countrymen who sat out the evening of
> their lives before television sets in condemned buildings . . . .
> Then the grin in both story and writer kept getting twisted in a gri-
> mace of pain close to tears . . . . now I realize that perhaps I have also
> been writing about myelf.

The preservation of the oldtimers' tales is important to the young be-

---

nese Immigrants on Angel Island 1910-1940 (San Francisco: Chinese Culture Center Hoc Doi Project, 1980), 84-85, 134-35.

40.   Lawrence Yep, *Dragonwings* (New York: Harper and Row, 1975).

41.   David Henry Hwang, *Broken Promises: Four Plays By David Henry Hwang* (New York: Avon Books, 1983).

42.   Lonnie Kaneko, "Family Album for Charlotte Davis," *Amerasia Journal* 3, no. 1 (Summer 1975): 135.

cause through the "transmission of grief from father to son we realize that it is the son who is singing and leading the dance in the end."[43]

Claiming America requires reconciliation with our fathers and forefathers in this country, Shawn Hsu Wong's short novel *Homebase* opens with a garden book reference to a Chinese tree planted a century ago in California gold country: "Often condemned as a weed tree . . . it must be praised for its ability to create beauty and shade under adverse conditions."[44] The narrator is haunted by the ghosts of the men of his great-grandfather's generation, men who built the railroads over the High Sierras, setting down roots deep in the earth like sharp talons clinging close to the heart of the land. He imagines letters his great-grandfather might have written home to China: "I do not want the seasons to run over my back, letting the days and night, the weather ride me, break me. I will find a piece of land to work where I can remain . . . and watch the seasons ease on that place, root down in this difficult soil, and nurture my land."[45] But the Chinese were "motherless and wifeless . . . in a country that hated [them]." They worked their way from the hinterland to the ocean's edge; Rainsford imagines that they tried to swim home to China and that the desert sands and the white surf are made of their bones, bleached by the sea and sun. Rainsford has been an orphan, living on the fringes of America, speaking Chinese or English like a ventriloquist's dummy through the grimace of clenched teeth. He dreams of traveling across the country with a patronizing, whining, "cheerleader-teaser" white girl who is the "shadow, the white ghost of all my love life . . . the dream of my capture of America . . . she tells me things about me that I am not . . . that I am the product of the richest and oldest culture in the history of the world . . . when in fact I have nothing of my own in America."[46] When Rainsford finally rejects her "love," she becomes irritated and tells him to go back where he came from. Driving on in the dark night, he sees his grandfather in the mountain fog and smells his clothes in the redwood trees as he travels through the canyons

43. Bienvenido N. Santos, "Preface," *Scent of Apples* (Seattle: Univ. of Washington Press, 1979), xx; "The Filipino as Exile," *Greenfield Review* 6, nos. 1-2 (Spring 1977): 51.
44. Shawn Hsu Wong, *Homebase* (New York: I. Reed Books, 1979), 1.
45. Ibid., 27.
46. Ibid., 31-32.

and cascades where his forefathers once worked and are buried. An American Indian tells him that he must find out where his people have been and see the town after which he is named, so that he can claim his home, his history, and the legacy of his forefathers. By reaffirming the love that connects his life to the lives of his father and forefathers, and thus his links to Chinese America, he can affirm his American identity: "[I]dentity is a word full of home. Identity is a word that whispers, not whispers, but GETS you to say, 'ever, ever yours . . . .' Dear Father, I say, I write, I sing, I give you my love, this is a letter, whispering those words, 'ever, ever yours.' "

Immigrant fathers and American roots are brought together in Maxine Hong Kingston's *China Men.* Arriving in five different ways, by way of Cuba, Angel Island, or Ellis Island, the father is the "legal" and the "illegal" immigrant, the "father from China" and the "American father." By "banding the nation north and south, east and west" with the transcontinental railroad, these fathers have established their legitimacy as the "binding and building ancestors of this place."[47] Their spirits unbroken by the treatment they face in America, they remain, planting trees that will take years to bear fruit. Each China man claims America in his own way: by bringing his wife, by buying a house here, by insisting that a Chinese explorer discovered America first. The narrator's "American father" has "the power of . . . making places belong to him."[48] He claims America by donning Fred Astaire clothing and admiring himself in hubcap reflections along Fifth Avenue in New York City.

For Kingston's China men, claiming America is an aggressive act; it means refusing to be broken. Although he is worked like an animal on the sugar plantations of Hawaii, Bak Goong seethes with rebellion and a burning desire to break the silence imposed by labor foremen. He camouflages his talk in curses coughed at his oppressors, avenging himself with a sword forged of his words as he sings to his fellow workers:

> "If that demon whips me, I'll catch the whip and yank him off
> his horse, crack his head like a coconut. In an emergency a hu-

---

47.   Kingston, *China Men,* 146.
48.   Ibid., 238.

man being can do miracles — fly, swim, lift mountains, throw them. Oh, a man is capable of great feats of speed and strength."[49]

Gender Perspectives

Claiming America also means reconciliation between men and women. Racism has created a haunting distance between the sexes in our literature and culture. Certainly the absence of significant female characters in Asian American men's writing reflects the harsh realities of the bachelor life created by exclusion and anti-miscegenation laws. Carlos Bulosan, for example, wrote at a time when Filipino men outnumbered women in some American cities by as many as forty-seven to one. The inscription in American popular culture of Asian men as sexless automatons is complemented by the popular view of Asian women as only sexual beings, which helps explain the phenomenal success of Singapore Airlines, the enormous demand for X-rated films featuring Asian women in bondage, the demand for "oriental" bath house workers in U.S. cities, and the booming business in mail order marriages. There is no doubt that the rift between our men and women caused by racism is reflected in our literature. We can detect, however, an intense yearning for reconciliation. The narrator in Wakako Yamauchi's "That was all" (1980) is haunted by her vision of the slim brown body and mocking eyes of a man she sees only in a fleeting dream as an aging woman.[50] In "The Boatmen on River Toneh" (1974), the narrator is "swept against the smooth brown cheeks of a black-haired youth . . . and into his billowing shirt" only in death.[51] There are no lovers among Kingston's *China Men*. But perhaps a mending of the rift is at hand: the narrator in Shawn Hsu Wong's *Homebase* dreams of the woman he loves: "she is the summit I must return to in the end."[52] In David Henry Hwang's "FOB",[53] it is not only the gap between the immigrant and Ameri-

---

49.   Ibid., 101.
50.   Wakako Yamauchi, "That Was All," *Amerasia Journal* 7, no. 1 (Spring 1980): 115-120.
51.   Wakako Yamauchi, "The Boatmen on Toneh River," *Counterpoint: Critical Perspectives on Asian America*, ed. Emma Gee (Los Angeles: UCLA Asian American Studies Center, 1976), 533.
52.   Wong, *Homebase*, 79.
53.   David Henry Hwang, "FOB," in *Broken Promises*.

can-born Chinese that is bridged; the legendary woman warrior Fa Mu Lan teaches Gwan Kung, god of warriors and writers, how to survive in America, and Grace goes off with Steve, the immigrant, at the end of the play. With her, he can claim a new American identity.

Community

Without the reconciliation of the self to the community we cannot invent ourselves. This "community" begins with but extends beyond the boundaries of our families, far beyond Chinatown to wherever resistance to domination is taking place. While the narrator in *The Woman Warrior* has to "get out of hating range"[54] of a community that hates women, that community is the curse and blessing of her life. The escape into the "American-normal" world gives her a new, antiseptic way of seeing things, but it has diminished her. Now when she peeks into the basement window where the villagers say they see a girl dancing like a bottle imp, she no longer sees a spirit in a skirt made of light; instead, concrete pours out of her mouth to cover forests with freeways and sidewalks, replacing the vibrant world she left with plastics, periodical tables, and "TV dinners with vegetables no more complex than peas mixed with diced carrots."[55] It is not the colorless world she seeks refuge in that has taught her who her enemies are, the "stupid racists" and "tyrants who for whatever reason can deny my family food and work." These are easily recognizable, "each boss two feet taller than I am and impossible to meet eye to eye . . . if I took a sword, which my hate must surely have forged out of the air, and gutted [him], I would put color and wrinkles into his shirt."[56] She has temporarily traded the glorious identity of Fa Mu Lan, who could be both woman warrior and model of filial piety, for a "slum grubby" American reality. All she can do in America is get straight As and become a clerk-typist. The question is whether or not her heritage and the tradition of Fa Mu Lan can serve her here. Although she has left the immigrant community, she longs to return:

The swordswoman and I are not so dissimilar. May my people un-

---

54.   Kingston, *The Woman Warrior*, 62.
55.   Ibid., 237.
56.   Ibid., 58.

derstand the resemblance so that I can return to them. What we have in common are the words at our backs . . . . And I have so many words — 'chink' words and 'gook' words too — that they do not fit on my skin.[57]

If we read Cathy Song's poetry as Asian Americans, we can see that the most effective poems in *Picture Bride*[58] are not the ones replete with images of jade and sour plums or that compare children to dumplings wrapped in wonton skins or describe a girl's cheeks as being like tofu, but the ones that explore the relationship between the persona and her family, from whom she ventures forth and with whom she is eventually reconciled. The volume as a whole traces the strength of kin communion and the ties between the generations. The narrator-character dreams of freedom from the constricted world of her mother, whose vision is limited like that of a seamstress to the piece of cloth she is working on at the moment beneath her fingers. The older woman sleeps in "tight blankets" and catches strands of her daughter's braids in her gold ring. But after the narrator moves across a series of landscapes that carry her ever further away from her family, she comes to rest finally at her mother's feet.

> It has taken me all these years
> to realize that this is what I must do
> to recognize my life.
> When I stretch a canvas
> to paint the clouds,
> it is your spine that declares itself:
> arching,
> your arms stemming out like tender shoots
> to hang sheets in the sky.[59]

This is not an urge to disappear into the ocean of American society. This is a reaffirmation of our invention of ourselves. In *Dangerous Music* (1975), Jessica Tarahata Hagedorn's America is the "loneliest of countries," where the Filipino immigrant can lose her sanity and forget who she is among bottles of foot deodorant, mouthwash, and

57. Ibid., 62-63.
58. Cathy Song, *Picture Bride* (New Haven, Conn.: Yale Univ. Press, 1983).
59. Ibid., 48.

vaginal spray, where she can die a "natural death" encased in Saran Wrap on the beach. She must "stay crazy all the time"

> with songs inside
> knifing the air of sorrow
> with our dance
> a carnival of spirits
> shredded blossoms
> in the water[60]

However impermeable, Asian American literature is universal. That it is opaque is the source of its strength and vision. What Asian American writers express is the desire to remain as "others" by defining our own "otherness," not as foreigners but as American "others." Our claim on America, then, is part of our resistance to domination.

---

60. Jessica Hagedorn, "Something About You," *Dangerous Music* (San Francisco: Momo's Press, 1975).

The Native-American Tradition and Legal Status: Tolowa Tales and Tolowa Places

Allogan Slagle

The Tolowa Nation of Indians is an Athapaskan-speaking community whose aboriginal range once included all of what is now Del Norte County, California. As of March, 1987, there were 337 enrolled Tolowas. There are also at least 200 other persons of Tolowa descent who are not on the Tolowa Nation roll, including the members of the Big Lagoon Rancheria of Smith River Indians, the Smith River Rancheria, and the Elk Valley Rancheria. This American Indian tribe is engaged in the process of seeking recognition by the United States government. As their attorney and principal researcher for their federal recognition case, I completed and submitted their brief to the Bureau of Indian Affairs for active consideration through the Federal Acknowledgment Staff in May, 1986, submitted additions in July 1986, and submitted the base roll in March, 1987. Having taken particular interest in the status clarification problems of unrecognized and terminated American Indian tribes since my admission to the California State Bar in 1979, I serve as principal investigator for the recognition projects of the Tolowa Nation and Yokayo tribe, the Mono Lake Indian Community, Chuckchansi-Yokuts, the Hayfork Norelmuk Band of Wintu and other tribes of California. The Yokayo petition was submitted to the Bureau of Indian Affairs, Department of the Interior, in February 1987.

In these undertakings, it has become apparent that information culled from the oral traditions of unrecognized American Indian tribes, as transcribed and studied since contact and conquest, may be critical in many cases for status clarification. Part of the Tolowa federal recognition case, for example, hinges on proof that the tribe had a distinct Athapaskan culture. Pliny Earle Goddard's *Tolowa Tales and Texts*, transcribed from interviews with Tolowa consultants between 1902 and 1911, comprise the most important set of manuscripts for this aspect of my investigation.[1]

Some Tolowa tales and texts have been collected in other works, most recently and notably in *The Tolowa Language* and occasional publications of the Center for Community Development at Humboldt State University in Arcata, California, and in Austin Warburton and Joseph Endert's *Indian Lore of the North California Coast*.[2] Anecdotal accounts with folkloric elements and legendary accounts of historical Tolowa figures are often useful. Ephraim Musik's tales of the "Legend of Dead Lake," based on a quasi-historical rebellion in a Tolowa town, and his "biography" of Boy-Die, Nah-Yu-Mah, or Yu-E-Noh (1797-1897), the great Tolowa Indian Doctor, are important examples which have moldered until now.[3] The Tolowa Tales are important to the Tolowas' federal recognition case, as I shall indicate in some detail below, in identifying their culture and distinguishing it from those of other Indian cultures.

The Tolowas, as a distinct political body, had made three unratified treaties with governments on both federal and local levels by 1857, and in 1935 the tribe accepted recognition under the terms of the Indian Re-

---

1. Important unpublished manuscripts on the Tolowas have been kept for seventy-five years in the Archives of the University of California, Berkeley; Pliny Earle Goddard, *Tolowa Tales and Texts*, with partial index by A. L. Kroeber and table of contents by Dale Valory, 311 pages with free and interlinear translations; and *Unpublished Tolowa Myths and Texts Collected at Smith River, California*, 2 vols. with partial index by Kroeber and table of contents by Valory, 24 texts with interlinear translations, 33 texts with no interlinear translations, and 10 texts and tales with free translations.

2. See Austin D. Warburton and Joseph F. Endert, *Indian Lore of the North California Coast* (Santa Clara, Calif.: Pacific Pueblo Press, 1966).

3. See the issues of the *Del Norte Record* of August and September 1880.

organization Act (1934), in a federally supervised election. Despite their long relationship with the United States the tribe was never federally recognized. Then, in 1978, the Tolowas got another chance for recognition when the United States Congress created a new process, in 25 CFR 83.1, *et seq.* (1978, Rev.'d. 1 April 1985) for clarifying the status of unrecognized tribes. Recognition is important for the Tolowas: acknowledgment under the present criteria does not determine whether an ethnographic Indian tribe exists, but acknowledgment is a prerequisite to the protection, services, and benefits of the federal-Indian relationship, with all the privileges, immunities, and responsibilities other tribes enjoy. Acknowledgment also affords the community the active protection and privileges of the guardian-ward relationship, and when such acknowledgment is granted, the United States defines the tribe's sovereignty as that of a "dependent domestic nation." The criteria for recognition require, among other things, a showing by preponderance that the Tolowas have been identified historically and continuously until the present as "American Indian, Native American, or aboriginal"; that they presently inhabit, and for the past two centuries have more or less continuously inhabited, a specific geographic range; and that they have a system of self-government that has evolved from aboriginal sources. The existence of the Goddard manuscripts suggests the Tolowa Nation's continuous historical possession of a clearly defined territory in what is now Del Norte County, California, whose leaders, the Tolowa Headmen (or Richmen), dominated the political, social, economic, and religious lives of the Tolowa people through 1911.

The Tolowas had an origin myth that Headmen, singers, and dancers told through song and dance cycles, prayers, and oral narratives at all World Renewal ceremonies. Tolowa spiritual leaders taught that the material world and all things in it emerged from the hill at the center of the town of Yontocket. Pacific Athapaskans themselves believed that their ancestors originated where they were residing at the time of white contact. Tamie Tsuchiayama investigated the question of whether there is any folkloric basis for the widespread belief that Athapaskan-speaking groups now in California and the Southwest, including the Tolowas, were once connected to Athapaskan tribes in the McKenzie Basin

---

4. See the Tamie Tsuchiayama, "A Comparison of the Folklore of the Northern, Southern and Pacific Athapaskans: A Study in Stability of Folklore within a Linguistic Stock," Ph.D. diss., University of California, Berkeley, 1947.

and were involved in a mass migration southward; he found that little connection was apparent or provable.[4] The question of the Athapaskan migration affects the Tolowas because they were presumably a part of that migration, and their case for long-term residence at their present site hinges on evidence that their own particular exodus happened before non-Indians arrived in the New World or at least in pre-contact times. Fortunately, recent linguistic and archaeological studies strengthened the Tolowas' aboriginal claim to most of Del Norte County.

Great diversity exists in Pacific Athapaskan languages. Located on the drainage of the Smith River in Del Norte County, the northwesternmost California county, the Tolowas' closest Athapaskan-speaking neighbors were the Tututni and Chetco of the region extending from the lower Rogue River to Gold Beach in southwestern Oregon, and the Hupa in the lower Trinity River area. Non-Athapaskan speakers with whom the Tolowas had close geographic, cultural, political, and genealogical relationships included the Takelmás in the Waldo-O'Brian area in southwestern and south-central Oregon, the Karuks west of Gasquet, and, of course, the Yuroks of the Klamath River. It is not at present feasible to prove the Tolowas' origins far to the north in Alaska or Canada. It is feasible, however, and of critical importance to the Tolowas' case, to demonstrate that the Athapaskan-speaking Tolowas have long resided in their present range and also that they were politically distinct from their present neighbors. Kenneth Whistler placed the entry of Athapaskan language speakers in Del Norte County at 1100-1300 A.D. on the basis of the Point St. George findings, adding that, "from approximately 650 B.P. [before the present date], there should be evidence of distinctive Tolowa occupation in the far north end of the [Redwood National Park] and of Chilula occupation of the Redwood Creek drainage."[5]

Corroborating this assertion are Goddard's transcriptions of Tolowa tales (1902-1911), which A. L. Kroeber organized in 1958. In support of my contention that the telling of these tales is still an important aspect of Tolowa culture, I have indicated the tellers of these tales to the present generation, according to Loren James Bommelyn:[6]

1. Securing Fire: Sam Lopez, Sr., Amelia Julia James Lagoon Brown

---

5. Kenneth Whistler, cited as a source and contributor, in Polly Bickel, *Study of Cultural Resources in Redwood National Park* (Denver: National Park Service, Denver Service Center, 1979), 161-71.

6. Author's unpublished Tolowa field notes, 1984.

(both of Howonquet), and Laura Scott Coleman (of Nelechun-dun) told this story to the present generation. This story is one of a type found among the Jicarilla, Lipan, Chiricahua, San Carlos, and White Mountain Apaches in the Southwest, among the Chilcotin and Carrier of the North, and among the Sinkyone and Kato of the Pacific group, in which fire is wrested from its hoarders by a trickster. In this story, there are actually several tricksters who suffer for taking the fire in various ways.[7]

2. Spearing the Pitchy Sea Lion. A pitch-covered sea lion lands some miles off the shore of Howonquet, on the other side of the earth, where there are giant waterfalls.

3. Sea Otter Pet Carries Off the Baby. A kidnapping story, the title of this tale is self-explanatory. There were other stories which warned against leaving pets alone with children.

4. The Tenth Brother.

5. Catching the White Bird. Characters arrive at the Winchuck River, then the hero quests on a high mountain above the river. Finally, he proceeds to a beach north of Howonquet (Smith River).

6. The Boy and His Mother. Amelia Brown carried this story. Point St. George is the setting, then the action moves to the Klamath region.

7. The Brothers. Point St. George and Pebble Beach are settings for this story.

8. The Pet Snake. This story carried another warning against leaving children alone with pets.

9. The Flood. Sam Lopez, Eunice Henry Bommelyn (of Nelechundun), Laura Scott Coleman, Amelia Brown, Berneice Brown Coughlin Humphreys (Amelia's daughter) all knew this story. This tale describes the destruction and recovery of the world and of a hilltop, Emily-Enli, that moved down from Oregon to land on another hill near Howonquet. Holt analyzed flood myths in Oregon and California, reporting: "The typical California picture is of animals and people running from the flood, swimming or flying about in search of an unsubmerged spot; while in Oregon and Washington tales people take in panic to their canoes, drift about to come to rest on high points of land or tie canoes to high mountain peaks or tall trees."[8] The Tolowa and Chetco versions combine

---

7. See, generally, Tsuchiayama, "A Comparison of the Folklore of the Athapaskans."

8. Holt quoted in Ibid., 103.

elements of both the California and Oregon models of the story. Steven Powers found the following version at Crescent City. In this version of the story, "En-Mi" is Mount Emily, a peak on the Chetco River, and "Whut" is a village at the mouth of the Chetco River:

> There was a time when the people did not obey the laws of God. The World was flooded with a great tidal wave, then torrential rains. Only a young man and a woman made it, by order of their adopted grandmother, to the top of En-Mi. The animals also gathered for their lives at En-Mi. The mountain top floated upon the waters. It came to rest in Elk Valley. The animals ran away and the couple returned to Whut. There they found nothing of their prior life. Many lay dead upon the Earth. They built a simple hut to live in. One day while fishing, a woman came paddling from the South. With these three people the new generations began.[9]

Similar tales appear among neighboring tribes. The Tolowas continued to pass down this story to the present generation. Through studies of the Ghost Dance, the Indian Shaker Church, and their other revivalistic activities, it has become evident that the Tolowas believed that their world would be remade in some sense and that the coming of the whites had heralded this purgation and renewal. To the Tolowas, the whites represented the Waugies, the white race which had formerly inhabited their lands and had vanished one night, but whose return was promised in an old Tolowa prophecy.

The Flood tale continues to provide the model for the Tolowas' survival today. Each person of any character and quality, male or female, was supposed not only to cultivate the arts, skills, and knowledge needed to survive as a Tolowa man or woman, but also to learn all that was required to revive the whole culture from a single mated pair, if necessary. The Flood tale was carried by the leaders of the Tolowa Ghost Dance, who had been the leaders of the Tolowas' World Renewal Religion. Lineal descendants of these leaders, attaining to religious and secular leadership themselves, employed this tale for its prophetic purposes in fostering

---

9. Steven Powers, "Tribes of California," *Contributions to North American Ethnology* 3 (1877): 70.

acceptance of the Indian Shaker Church and Methodist Mission among the Tolowas.

The flood tale gave hope and a promise of renewal in the darkest days of Tolowa history. To the modern Tolowas, who continue to carry and tell this story to their young, the flood tale is an important moral lesson, a portent, and a model for all people. It is a story of exemplary behavior and triumph under excruciating hardships. It is the one story Tolowas would share with non-Indians. It is said that the old keepers of the Tolowa World Renewal ceremony—Kweltnesat and Lossegingno—told this story at Yontocket, the holiest and oldest of Tolowa towns, during religious festivals. They continued to relate it after Yontocket was burned to the ground in 1853, at the Klamath River Reservation while in exile there and when they fled the Klamath River Reservation in the 1860s and returned to live in and to rebuild their home at the ruins of Yontocket, which whites called Burnt Ranch. They taught this story in the 1870s, during the Tolowa Ghost Dance, for the flood tale presaged the Ghost Dance, in which the Tolowas restored their World Renewal religion. The story continued to be a part of religious festivals when the Tolowas joined the Indian Shaker Church in large numbers. They see the reflection and pattern for all their old prophecies of destruction and restoration in the flood tale.

10. The Children Who Lived in the Woods. This tale describes the sacred mountains to the east of Tolowa villages (Signal Peak, High Divide, Low Divide, Doctor Rock).
11. Frog He Wanted a Pet. Point St. George and Yontocket are settings for this tale.
12. The Young Man Who Married Frog Girls.
13. The Young Man Who Got Money from a Bird. The young hero succeeds in his quest for riches with the help of a great white spirit-bird. Much of the action takes place on or near the Tolowas' shoreline.
14. She Was Married in the South. A young Tolowa girl finds a husband in Yurok country.
15. Panther and His Wives.
16. The Girl Who Burned Her Child.
17. The Girl Who Brought Riches to Her Father.
18. Revenge of the Twins. Amelia Brown told this story of Musl-

Ye. The village of Musl-Ye (Gasquet) was the next-to-last town on the middle fork of the Smith River. The Go'-T'si-Ne or Takelma Indians from the Waldo-O'Brian region in southern Oregon were Musl-Ye's attackers in this story, which was based on a battle that actually occurred in the generation before the conquest.

19. The Western World. Point St. George, a rock five miles out to sea, near the shore of the western Pacific, is the scene of this story.

20. She Was Always Weaving Baskets. The Tolowas' account of how basket making began at Point St. George.

21. Panther and His Brother.

22. Origin of the Hupa. Apparently, the first Hupas came from Yontocket, though some of the action in the story occurs at Achulet ("rich village").

23. Coyote and His Wife.

24. Coyote's Marriage. Ernest Scott (of Nelechundun) keeps this tale.

25. Gold Beach Young Man. The town of Gold Beach marked the boundary of Tolowa and Chetco territories.

26. Dancing in a Rock. Eunice Henry Bommelyn (of Nelechundun) and her family keep this tale. The story takes place at Ta-At-Tun, near Crescent City and near Howonquet (Smith River).

27. Coyote and His Five Sons.

28. Securing the Sun. This story describes five worlds under the sea.

29. Limiting the Tides. All the action occurs on the Tolowas' beaches.

30. Wild Woman. Laura Coleman (of Nelechundun) passed on this story before her death in the 1970s. It is about the children of Yontocket (Burnt Ranch).

31. Woman of the Woods. This story from Yontocket resembles other Athapaskan "Bear Woman" narratives.[10]

32. The Abducted Woman. The site of this story is Howonquet (Smith River).

33. Coyote Dancing. The setting is on and near Arch Rock, north of Howonquet. This is also a tale recounted in Austin Warburton and Joseph Endert's *Indian Lore* (1986).

34. Cottontail Rabbit a Doctor. The tale refers to a particular town, perhaps Ta-At-Tun.

---

10. See Tsuchiyama, "A Comparison of the Folklore of the Athapaskans," 34ff.

There are pieces of evidence much more important to the Tolowas' case for federal acknowledgment than the information furnished in these texts. As I mentioned earlier, the Tolowas negotiated three treaties: two with the United States government and one with the citizens of Del Norte County and Crescent City. In 1935, the Crescent City Tolowas had a federal election, in which they accepted federal recognition as an Indian tribe under the terms of the Indian Reorganization Act of 1934. Still, many aspects of these tales provide support for the Tolowas' case for federal acknowledgment that evidence of treaties and tribal elections cannot. Goddard collected most of the Tolowa tales surviving today between 1902 and 1911, when most Tolowas were landless and lived in or around Crescent City, Pebble Beach, Smith River, Gasquet, Lake Earl, and other scattered settlements. The Smith River Reservation had been eliminated in 1868, but Elk Valley and Smith River Rancherias were not established until the late 1920s. Ironically, at this date Goddard's consultants had no idea that their stories could be of use in a case for status clarification, yet the *Tales and Texts* mentions places, concepts, and characters which are useful in establishing the Tolowas' case on several counts. The criteria for acknowledgment in 25 CFR 83.7 require information in several categories. These criteria do not apply to groups that have already been established (25 CFR 83.7 a, b); hence, no federally recognized tribe is required to meet these criteria in order to *continue* to be recognized. The burden of meeting these evidentiary requirements falls only on those tribes toward whom the United States has failed or refused to recognize a fiduciary responsibility.

According to 25 CFR 83.7 a,

> "Evidence to be relied upon in determining the group's substantially continuous identity shall include one or more of the following:"
> "(5) Identification as an Indian entity by anthropologists, historians or other scholars."
> "(6) Repeated identification as an Indian entity in newspapers and books."
> "(7) Repeated identification and dealings as an Indian entity with recognized Indian tribes."

The Goddard manuscripts clearly supply such identification. Goddard is justly celebrated for his scholarship on the Tolowas, the Hupas, and other tribes. His credentials as an anthropologist, ethnographer, and

folklorist are well known; and once published, the Goddard manuscripts will supply such repeated public identification more clearly
than in their recognized and cited but largely unpublished state.

The Tales are of definite ethnological interest in that neighboring
tribes had many similar tales. The *Tales and Texts* place the Tolowas as
one of the distinct and autonomous tribes which shared the classic
northwestern California culture. Tale 6, "The Boy and His Mother," is
almost identical to a Dug-Out Boy narrative Goddard attributed to the
Hupas, though the Tolowas' version places the scene of the tale at
Point St. George.[11] Tale 9, the flood narrative, is quite similar to that of
the Chetcos. Tale 18, concerning Musl-Ye, or Gasquet, the next-to-last
town on the middle fork of Smith River, describes a historical (1840s)
battle with the Takelma tribe (Goh'-T'si-Ne) of the Waldo-O'Brian
area. Tale 22 describes the Origin of the Hupa from a nucleus of lost
Tolowa children from the central ancient town of Yontocket. Interestingly, the Hupa take credit for founding the Tolowas in a very similar
tale. My Tolowa ethnography, *Huss: The Tolowa People*, includes names
and short biographies of all the Tolowa carriers of these tales in contemporary times.[12] The ethnohistoric section includes a discussion of
all the Tolowa and Yurok narratives which identify Tolowa sites, sacred
heroes, demigods, and deities, and the like. Numerous publications
describe the literatures of the Tolowas' neighbors.[13] Today, the Yuroks,
Hupas, and the Tututni, Chetco, and Takelma survivors at Siletz all
recognize the Tolowas as an American Indian tribe, just as their ancestors did according to the *Tales and Texts*.

The stipulations of 25 CFR 83.7 b requires evidence that a substantial portion of the petitioning group inhabits a specific area or lives in a
community viewed as American Indian and distinct from other populations in the area and that its members are descendants of an Indian

11. See "Dug from Ground," in Goddard, *Hupa Texts* (Berkeley and Los Angeles:
University of California Press, 1904), 146ff; rpt. in Stith Thompson, *Tales of the North
American Indians* (Bloomington, Ind.: Indiana University Press, 1973), 97-100.

12. See Slagle, *Huss: The Tolowa People* (Arcata, Calif.: Humboldt State University,
Center for Community Development, 1986).

13. For important examples, see Kroeber, *Yurok Narratives*, University of California
Publications in American Anthropology and Archaeology, vol. 35, no. 9 (1942); and
Yurok Myths (Berkeley and Los Angeles: University of California Press, 1976); Phillip
Drucker, "The Tolowa and Their Southwest Oregon Kin," University of California
Publications in American Archaeology and Ethnology, vol. 36, no. 4 (1937) 221-300;
Cora Dubois, *The 1870 Ghost Dance*, University of California, Berkeley, Anthropological
Records no. 3 (1939): 1; and L. Farrand and L. J. Frachtenberg, "Shasta and
Athapaskan Myths from Oregon," *Journal of American Folklore* 28 (1915): 224-42.

tribe which historically inhabited a specific area. Taken as a whole, the *Tales and Texts* offer such evidence very effectively. Most of the tales are associated with particular sites, and they explain the powers and functions associated with those sites as actual geographic possessions and as sacred places. Further, contemporary consultants carry these tales today, or versions of them, which suggests the continuity as well as lines of heirship to and dispersion of the tales in Tolowa country. Thus, these tales identify as part of their secular and sacred geography the following important sites in the Tolowa world: to the far north, on the actual border of Tolowa territory to that of their Chetco Kin, the Winchuck River, Mount Emily, and Gold Beach, all in Oregon; the most northerly settlement and the second largest town, Smith River (Howonquet), and the neighboring Lopez Beach and Arch Rock, just off the California-Oregon border in the Pacific Ocean; the sacred mountains on the eastern perimeter of Tolowa country, High Divide; the most easterly Tolowa settlement and important trading town, Musl-Ye (Gasquet), in a tale showing it was consequently vulnerable to attack from northern Takelma neighbors; the southernmost border of actual Tolowa settlement and northernmost region of Yurok settlement, the Klamath River; and northeast, the Hupas' country. Turning again to the north, Ta-At-Tun is now the coastal town of Crescent City; nearby, at Point St. George, the village of Point St. George (Doh-Ding-Tun), only fairly recently abandoned, but clearly very ancient, and important as a cultural and trade center; Pebble Beach (Mesltetltun), just north of Point St. George; Yontocket, the sacred center and approximate midpoint of the major coastal settlements. Both the Smith River and the Klamath River, as well as the Pacific Ocean and the beach, figure prominently in the stories. There are unnamed islands and lands to the west in the tales, perhaps mythological, as is the set of five subterranean worlds below the Tolowa land. Thus, one can see that the "known Tolowa world" prior to contact and conquest is economically defined in this remnant of Tolowa myth, legend, and folklore. Loren Bommelyn told me of a tale in which Fish Duck starts at the Winchuck River, continues at Smith River, moves to Lopez Beach, and ends at Yontocket (Burnt Ranch).

In addition, 25 CFR 83.7 c requires the candidate tribe to include a statement of facts which establishes that the petitioner has maintained tribal influence or other authority over its members as an autonomous entity throughout history up until the present. The Tolowas' tales at least suggest such a continuity of influence and leadership. That they have continued to serve in the moral instruction and entertainment of the Tolowa youth is a fact which can be used to establish a case on the latter issue.

The published or unpublished oral accounts of tribal histories and tales may be crucial in establishing cases for federal acknowledgment. The future of such tales and accounts as significant contributions to the body of minority literatures and world literature is certainly assured, to the extent that their existence can be used to prove the continuous cultural and political existence of the tribes which created them. Minority literatures such as those of the 104 or more unrecognized Indian tribes of the United States often manifest the aboriginal concepts of sovereignty, religion and philosophy, and law and morality in these nations' consciousnesses. Yet, the use of tribal folklore and mythology as in the Tolowa case is unusual in a petition for federal acknowledgment.

My task has been to present all available data about the client tribe in the strongest light, resolving ambiguities in favor of the presumption that the Tolowas have been since pre-contact, and now are, an Indian tribe as defined by 25 CFR 83.1, *et seq.* I have done so, ever mindful that the burden lies on the Tolowas in the first instance to prove that these conclusions are reasonable, by preponderance. I also have been painfully aware that, in its obstinate avoidance of this issue of national honor, the United States has refused to recognize the tribe as a whole until now. Indeed, the aboriginal sovereign identity and rights of many tribes of California Indians have been ignored more persistently and destructively, on the whole, than those of tribes in most other regions. The attitude of the federal government has been that California Indian rancherias were little more than "homes for homeless California Indians," since many tribes were so reduced in numbers and circumstances that they retained no sovereignty as communities, no independent identities, no distinctively identifiable aboriginal culture.

The passions and prejudices of many minds and several generations have brought us to the present point in clarifying Tolowa sovereign status. The effect of these human feelings and reactions must be weighed in every instance where, as here, ethnohistoric and ethnographic data must supply the basis of an argument that may have a binding effect on the sovereign rights and responsibilities of a community. In the 1970s and 1980s, in controversies between American Indian tribes and the United States over the tribes' retained natural resource rights, sovereignty, cultural rights, and entitlements, it became painfully evident that such data, depending on how they are interpreted and by whom, can determine the destinies of Indian tribes for the worse. Those scholars who fear that their efforts in such a cause may interfere with the balance and life of the community, or that it could lead to distress in their own disciplines, might recall that other scholars have been quite willing to serve as hired expert witnesses for the federal government, state and local governments, and for recreational and commercial special interests against tribes, regardless of the effect on the Indians, and without concern about antagonizing colleagues.

With a tribe's future as a federally recognized sovereign entity at issue, I have had to question the assumptions of my predecessors. Richard Gould reported finding only ten "traditionally oriented Tolowa Indians" in Del Norte County with whom he could have useful interviews, but one might speculate from the facts my own work shows that he could find only ten consultants whose qualifications suited his own research needs. It is not necessary to conclude anything about the actual number of Tolowa Indians or "traditionally oriented" Tolowa Indians based on this unquestionably competent scholar's statements, for other investigators have stated similar things.[14] Suffice it to say that the Tolowas themselves have shown me evidence that there are more Tolowas, even more people that still speak at least some

---

14. Richard Gould, "Tolowa," in *Handbook of North American Indians* 8 (1976), 128-36. No less problematic are views of nineteenth-century observers and commentators (not ethnographers) of the Tolowas and other California Indians who dealt with first-generation consultants. Warning flags should rise on reading H. H. Bancroft's peculiar impressions of California Indians:

> The Californians wear no clothes, they build no houses, do not cultivate the soil, they have no boats, nor do they hunt to any considerable extent; they have no morals, nor any religion worth calling such. The missionary fathers found a virgin field whereon neither god nor devil was worshipped. We must look, then, to other causes for a solution of the question why a nobler race is not found in California. *(The Native Races of the Pacific,* vol. 1 of *The Works of H. H. Bancroft* [1882]: 325-27)

Many writers and scholars of the late 1800s shared the bias that Christian non-Indians could lay moral and legal claims to "Digger" land and resources without regard to their prior rights, particularly to property.

As a matter of first impression, Phillip Drucker put the Tolowas low on his scale of California's northern coastal tribes. Yet he failed to consider the degree of desolation Tolowas experienced at the hands of their new neighbors, or the steps they had made toward recovery through transformation by the time of his encounter with them. He wrote that the Tolowas:

Tolowa, than one might suspect from such statements. I have had to ask questions no one has had the *incentive* to ask before about the nature and continuity of Tolowa leadership from pre-contact to the present, recalling that the obligations of an advocate, though not always the skills of an *attorney*, per se, are required of one who undertakes a study of this kind.

I intend that my work on the Tolowas should stand as a challenge to all academics, disciplines, and institutions, especially those which support programs and research in American Indian studies, to *address* more aggressively the failure of the federal government to acknowledge the scores of unrecognized tribes. There are definite advantages to federal recognition (including the tribe's ability to run its own economic programs with certain tax and other advantages, and to exercise aspects of retained sovereignty), which might otherwise lie forever beyond the reach of tribes like the Tolowa Nation. Additionally, U.S. policy today favors relations only with acknowledged tribes. Members of the Tolowa Nation at present are only individually recognized as California Indians. Given the present trends in administrative policy, all members of tribes that are not federally recognized may soon be denied services available to other Indians.[15]

> were culturally marginal to—that is to say, in many respects pallid imitations of—the civilizations of the lower Klamath River. [They] shared a set of cultural patterns modified from the basic motifs of the Northwest Coast and elaborated in a number of unique ways. Their civilization, simple and poor as it may seem in comparison with that of the northern tribes, was complex indeed as compared to that of their Oregon coastal neighbors and most of the native groups of Oregon. (Phillip Drucker, *Indians of the Northwest Coast* [New York: American Museum of Natural History, 1955], 13)

It is hard to guess what the state of southern Oregon culture was like even five years before contact with whites, for the Tolowas devastated that region in a war in about 1850. Homer Barnett, on the strength of Drucker's Tolowa fieldnotes, concluded:

> The Tolowa yield a greater number of traits (1,342) than all but two other groups. This I attribute to two causes: first, they doubtless had a more complex culture; and second, if I am not mistaken, Drucker has supplied information, not from one informant (as data for the others have been gathered), but from his knowledge of Tolowa derived from several sources, so that what we have is a composite total, an amalgamation of all that is known of them. (Homer Barnett, "Oregon Coast," University of California, Berkeley, Anthropological Records no. 1 [1987], 157)

15. Proposed revisions of regulations governing eligibility of California Indians for Indian health services may effectively terminate services to unrecognized California Indians by 1991. See the current regulations at 25 C. F. R. 704, *et seq.*

It remains morally incumbent on the United States as trustee of Indian tribes to deliver on its generations-old obligations to those tribes and their individual members. Federal-Indian policy, and the federal tribal intergovernmental relationship, existed from the beginning for the benefit of all Americans, not only for Indians and Indian tribes. It is in the best interests of the United States as well as the Tolowas to recognize the relationship that has arisen by force of federal action and inaction. As the U.S. Supreme Court has observed since the *Cherokee* cases in 1831 and 1832, the United States has, through treaties, contracts, and course of conduct, assumed an equitable obligation to the tribes, equal to the extent of "plenary" federal authority over them.

After submitting a recognition petition, the work of the principal investigator is that of an advocate and administrator, providing organization and direction in completing the process of exhausting administrative remedies associated with status clarification and assisting in securing the professional technical assistance required until the project is complete. The use of the narrative ethnography, tribal history, and other data included in the petition has been decided in concert with the consultants and the Tribal Council. The publication of the petition or portions thereof is, by agreement with the Tribal Council, to be through the media and is not expected to produce significant royalties, since the aim is to make the information available to the tribe, to the interested lay or scholarly reader, as well as to the staff of the federal acknowledgment project. The success of the narrative which the Tolowas have submitted to the Bureau of Indian Affairs will continue to depend heavily on the group's interactions with its social, political, and natural environments.

The financial resources available for such work have always been limited, despite the urgent need. Scholars wishing to do this kind of research will find surprisingly little support from their academic institutions; this is because this kind of research produces scholarship which is frankly and openly partisan; many scholars, reflecting a current trend against applied anthropology, will dismiss it as an attempt to revive a tribe that some academics and politicians prefer to classify as "extinct." Such research, then, can offer the typical scholar little hope of material reward and will always demand a willingness to search for a truth others with conflicting agendas simply do not want to hear.

The petition may succeed as scholarship but may fall short of its goal as advocacy. On the other hand, if it is found to be better advocacy than scholarship and helps achieve the goal of federal acknowledgment for the Tolowa Nation, perhaps it will have brought us all a step closer to recognizing the sovereign rights of an aboriginal community which has the purpose of surviving *as a community* whatever may befall it. I have operated under the assumption that it deserves to succeed as advocacy only if it is good scholarship. Many would agree that the world's great powers and intellectual leaders need greater respect for the sovereignty and natural rights of indigenous peoples and for the strength and survival capability of their enduring communities. Working for socially responsible goals as defined by the immediate client Indian community as well as for the various disciplines whose tools one uses, is a necessary effect and aim of researching and composing a case for status clarification. This work must also be found to serve needs of the United States as a whole, recognizing that the federal-Indian relationship would not exist if it did not serve social, political, and economic interests common to all American citizens.

Regardless of the result of the recognition process, the Tolowa Nation may outlast the case, the argument, the disciplines whose professors argue the matter, and the forums in which they argue it. That would be a fitting vindication of their claim to tribal identity, indeed.

Dialogue as Conquest:
Mapping Spaces for Counter-Discourse*

José Rabasa

> Muley:
> Valiente eres español
> y cortés como valiente
> tan bien vences con la lengua
> como con la espada vences.
> —Calderón de la Barca,
> *El príncipe constante*[1]

> siempre publiqué y dije a todos los naturales de la tierra, asi
> señores como los que a mi venían, que vuestra majestad era
> servido que el dicho Muctezuma se estuviese en su señorio,
> reconociendo el que vuestra alteza sobre el tenía, y que
> servirían mucho a vuestra alteza en le obedecer y tener por
> señor, como antes que yo a la tierra viniese le tenían.
> —Hernán Cortés, *Segunda Carta a Carlos V*[2]

The *Historia del Abencerraje y la hermosa Jarifa* (c. 1561) is generally credited for inaugurating a fashionable commonplace in

*For helpful critical readings of earlier drafts I would like to thank the following, while
noting my own sole responsibility for the final form: Danny Anderson, Amy Burce,
James Clifford, Sidney Monas, and Hayden White. Parts of the essay were presented
on different occasions at the Department of Anthropology and the Department of
Spanish and Portuguese, University of Texas at Austin. I received valuable comments
in both contexts. This essay is a revised version of the paper I read at "The Nature and
Context of Minority Discourse" conference, where I learned a great deal from the discussions of papers and conversations with other participants.
1.   Pedro Calderón de la Barca, *El príncipe constante*, ed. Alberto Porqueras Mayo
(Madrid: Espasa-Calpe, 1975), I, xi, 705-6. [Courageous you are, Spaniard,/and
courteous as well as courageous;/As well you conquer with the tongue/as with the
sword you conquer.] Translation is the author's.
2.   Hernán Cortés, *Cartas y Documentos* (Mexico: Editorial Porrúa, 1963), 63. [I al-

Golden-Age Spanish Literature.[3] Following this novel, numerous ballads, histories, and plays tell of a Christian narrator who addresses and represents the image of a valiant Moor under defeat. What opens with an exaltation of the Moor's courage moves to a description of him sighing. Since captivity could not be the source of sorrow, the Spaniard presses the Moor to reveal the secret of his affliction: a love story lies at the core. In the above epigraph, Muley equates tongue with sword. This dispersion of violence opens the Moorish genre not only to a new reading, but also to the study of the representation of "alien" cultures.

The equation *discourse is violence*, obviously pertinent to the question of dialogue as conquest in Cortés's correspondence with Charles V, refines the commonplace *knowledge is power*; it displaces the formulation of the problem from misuse of information to an integral view of knowledge as a form of domination, of control. Johannes Fabian has pointed out in *Time and the Other*, apropos of the uses of time by anthropology, that "Anthropology's claim to power originated at its roots. It belongs to its essence and is not a matter of accidental misuse."[4] In the context of anthropology, dialogue with informants in the field is the most prevalent form of acquiring information. Thus power relations can be traced, beyond the uses of time in the representation of alien

---

ways published and declared to the natives, both chiefs and those who came to see me, that your majesty wished that Muctezuma should retain his dominion, recognizing that which your majesty held over him, and that they would be serving your highness by obeying him and considering him as their lord as they had before I came to their land.] All further references will appear in the body of the paper. The English versions of quoted passages from the *Letters* are my translations. I have, however, consulted *Letters from Mexico*, trans. A.R. Pagden (New York: Grossman Publishers, 1971) and *Five Letters of Cortés to the Emperor*, trans. J. Bayard Morris (New York: W.W. Norton, n/d). Since some terms in Bayard's as well as Pagden's translation deviate from the Spanish lexicon of conquest, I have considered it necessary to provide my own translations.

3.   For a study of the *Abencerraje* as a prototype of the Moorish genre, see Claudio Guillen, "Literature as Historical Contradiction: *El Abencerraje*, the Moorish novel, and the Eclogue," in *Literature as System: Essays toward the Theory of Literary History* (Princeton, N.J.: Princeton Univ. Press, 1971), 159-217. My observations on Calderón's lines, and the tradition that draws from the *Abencerraje*, I owe to Israel Burshatin, "Power, Discourse, and Metaphor in the *Abencerraje*," *M.L.N.* 99 (March 1984): 195-213. Also of interest in Burshatin, "The Moor in the Text: Metaphor, Emblem, and Silence," *Critical Inquiry* 12 (Autumn 1985): 98-118.

4.   Johannes Fabian, *Time and the Other: How Anthropology Makes Its Object* (New York: Columbia Univ. Press, 1983), 1.

cultures, to the initial production of "raw" data. In the case of Cortés we find an openly stated understanding of the uses of dialogue for conquest as well as a comprehension of the power of knowledge. In contrast, modern anthropology, despite the ambiguous roles functionalism played in the theorization of British Indirect Rule, resists the image of the anthropologist as conqueror.[5]

An apparent exception, from within a French tradition, would be Marcel Griaule's use of militaristic metaphors to convey the process of gaining access to another culture. The two main metaphoric structures of Griaule's ethnographic method are, as James Clifford sums them up, "a documentary system (governed by images of collection, observation, and interrogation) and an initiatory complex (where dialogical processes of education and exegesis come to the fore)."[6] Thus an ongoing, long-term penetration into the secrets of the culture complements a panoptic representation of the whole. But again, Griaule's metaphors of conquest pertain not to a direct filiation with a colonial power, but to an unabashed acknowledgment of power and the manipulation of informants: "We'd make him smile, spit up the truth, and we'd turn out of his pockets the last secret polished by the centuries, a secret to make he who has spoken it blanch with fear."[7] The quote speaks for itself. One cannot simply dismiss this statement as a breach of objectivity (though to speak thus is certainly a breach of the post-colonial ethic of fieldwork). It expresses a will to sift biased information in the pursuit of a neutral account.

By paying attention to the power dynamics of dialogue and representation, I will attempt to gauge the distance separating the *interested* conqueror from the *neutral* anthropologist. The point is not to reduce these enterprises to a common project or intentionality, but to understand how conquest displays forms of colonial encounter and epistemological limits that haunt the intended good faith of ethnography.

---

5. For an assessment of functional anthropology as an aid to colonial administration, see the essays included in *Anthropology and the Colonial Encounter*, ed. Talal Asad (London: Ithaca Press, 1973). The polemic argued in these essays is centered on such issues as direct filiation or the misuse of knowledge.

6. James Clifford, "Power and Dialogue in Ethnography: Marcel Griaule's Initiation," in *Observers Observed: Essays on Ethnographic Fieldwork. History of Anthropology*, vol. 1 (Madison: Univ. of Wisconsin Press, 1983), 131.

7. Quoted by Clifford, "Power and Dialogue," 141.

One readily grasps the image of the anthropologist as conqueror in the equation *knowledge is power*. But even before the misuse of knowledge for imperialistic purposes, the production of knowledge already entails conquest. In the spirit of Neitzsche's assertion that the concept of "liberty is an invention of the ruling classes,"[8] this paper will show how dialogue was an invention of the conquistadores. It aims to elaborate an experimental, perhaps perverse, genealogy of the conventional anthropological enterprise and of recent dialogical experiments as well.

In the first part of this essay, I will briefly outline some of the most outstanding features of conventional anthropology and its critique by dialogical alternatives. This exposition is geared around the question of Cortés as a proto-anthropologist, indeed, as an inventor of dialogue. The second part analyzes Cortés's objectification of Mexican civilization and the place of knowledge and dialogue in the Conquest. A third part examines the dialogue between Moctezuma and Cortés in light of a passage from Hegel's *Phenomenology of Mind* on the Master/Slave relation. And beyond Cortés's recorded speech of the Mexican ruler, the Florentine Codex exemplifies the indigenous narrative of the Conquest. In the concluding remarks, I will return to the question of anthropology's descent.

I must point out that the overall project attempts to dismantle the "Europe and its others" complex overhanging the master discourses of conquest and modern anthropology. In Deleuze and Guattari's terms,[9] this essay aims to deterritorialize the latter by opening up margins and interstices in the master narratives (as it were, to constitute a context) where minor discourses may emerge. Thus, it will contribute to what James Clifford has defined as the necessity "to imagine a world of generalized ethnography,"[10] where a dispersion of authority and a mishmash of idioms would make it increasingly difficult to formulate dichotomous Self/Other definitions of independent cultures.

---

8. Quoted by Michel Foucault, "Nietzsche, Genealogy, History," in *Language, Counter-Memory, Practice*, trans. Donald F. Bouchard and Sherry Simon (Ithaca, New York: Cornell Univ. Press, 1977), 142.

9. I am drawing the notion of deterritorialization and its application to minor discourse from Gilles Deleuze and Félix Guattari, "What Is a Minor Literature?" trans. Robert Brinkley, *Mississippi Review* 22, no. 3 (Spring 1983): 13-33.

10. James Clifford, "On Ethnographic Authority," *Representations* 1, no. 2 (1983): 119.

Cortés as Proto-Anthropologist

The second epigraph, drawn from Cortés's *Second Letter* (1520) to Charles V, purveys an ideal sense of conquest in which Moctezuma (or better, Motecuhzoma) would remain a master while serving Charles V. This ideal formulation seeks to retain the ancient order intact. But it is plagued with a paradox since Tenochtitlan had become accessible through the formation of hostile collaborators, which already implied the dissolution of the political structure of Moctezuma's dominions. It can be read as an early expression of what the British would call Indirect Rule. Before discussing functionalism in the context of Indirect Rule, a description of Cortés's writings will help us to visualize the range of topics, the multiple facets of his personality, and thus to assess their proximities and distances to the modern anthropological enterprise.

In what has been called the *Corpus cortesianum* (1519-1526), commonly known to English speaking audiences as the *Five Letters of Cortés to the Emperor* in the 1928 abridged translation by J. Bayard Morris, the *Second Letter* stands out with its vivid descriptions of the cultures encountered in the ascent to Tenochtitlan from the Gulf of Mexico, of the topography of central Mexico, and of the urban complexity of Tenochtitlan. In addition, we can mention two lasting motifs in the literature of colonial encounters that first crystallized in this letter. The first is the destruction of the ships, that, despite the falsification of the event, gave rise to the image of "burning the ships behind him." The second motif is the identification of Cortés with the god Quetzalcoatl in the dialogue with Moctezuma (according to native history, this semi-divine figure had been banished in a distant time and place and had prophesied his return in the form of a conqueror). First printed in Seville in 1522, the *Second Letter* had several printings and translations in the sixteenth century. The most notable is the Latin version printed in Nuremberg in 1524, which is important not only because of its broad circulation, but also because it included a map attributed to Cortés, known in English as the "Map of Mexico City and the Gulf."[11]

---

11.   For a study of the different versions, printings, and possible draftsmen of the map, see Manuel Toussaint, "El plano atribuido a Cortés," in Manuel Toussaint, Federico Gómez de Orozco, and Justino Fernández, *Planos de la ciudad de México siglos XVI y XVII: estudio histórico, urbanístico y bibliográfico* (Mexico: Instituto de Investigaciones Estéticas de la Universidad Nacional Autónoma de México, 1938), 91-105.

This edition also included the *Third Letter* (1522). As it has often been remarked, the love and admiration for Mexico in the *Second Letter* is replaced by hate, terror, and the display of military strategies that led to the capture and destruction of Tenochtitlan. But the tone is epic, and Cortés praises the courage, intelligence, and greatness of the enemy. One might argue that the image of Cortés as a Conquistador depends on the image he fabricates of the conquered — the enemy must be a worthy contender in order to infuse a chivalric tone into his narration. A long tradition in Spanish letters that alternates between "vilified" and "idealized" Moors mediates Cortés's representation of his Mexican opponents.[12]

The *Fourth Letter* was first printed in Toledo in 1525 and had a second edition in Zaragoza in 1526. It did not have the diffusion in Latin of the *Second* and *Third Letters* and was not printed outside Spain until 1779 in a German edition. This letter dwells mostly on the organization of the new colony as well as on the reconstruction of Mexico City. Cortés appears at the peak of his political and military career.

Though the *First Letter* was written by the *cabildo* — the Judiciary and Council of Veracruz — it forms part of the five major letters. This letter was discovered in the Imperial Archives of Vienna during the last century by William Robertson and was never printed in Spain until 1844. This letter gives an account of the earlier explorations of the Gulf of Mexico by Francisco Fernández de Córdova and Juan de Grijalva. But more importantly, this letter justifies the disobedience of the trade-oriented instructions of Diego de Velázquez, the governor of Cuba. It argues that the continuation of trade, specifically of slaves, would be detrimental to the interest of the Empire. Access to what is described as a vast, highly sophisticated civilization ruling from the hinterland would be curtailed by following Velázquez's policies.

In the *Fifth Letter* (1526), also discovered during the above-mentioned search and never published until the nineteenth century, Cortés narrates the main events of his expedition to Honduras and illustrates his travels for Charles V with an indigenous map of the territories. Thus this letter is highly revealing of how Cortés appropriated native texts.

In addition to these major letters (of approximately 40,000 words

---

12. See Burshatin, "The Moor in the Text."

each, with the exception of the first and third with 10,000 and 20,000 words respectively), Cortés wrote other shorter letters, ordinances, and instructions. One may further complement the corpus with the letters of Charles V to Cortés. This essay is mainly concerned with the policies expressed in those documents written between 1519 and 1526. As Marcel Bataillon has pointed out, Cortés became a forbidden author in 1527.[13] The "honeymoon" with Charles V ended, Cortés's power was undermined, and the correspondence increasingly pleaded for the value of his former deeds. It was indeed during these years that a concept of conquest, centered on dialogue, was jointly elaborated in their exchange of letters.

From the correspondence we can derive an image of Cortés that combines the functions of soldier, administrator, jurist and, more important for the purpose of the essay, of a proto-ethnographer. Cortés's early elaboration of Indirect Rule allots a place to the natives that closely parallels the one given them later within the structure of the British Empire, and more poignantly so, parallels the contributions made by functionalist anthropology to an efficient administration. But functionalism should not be reduced to a handmaiden of colonial authority. In keeping with its specialization as a discipline during the first half of the twentieth century, the scientific observation by academic anthropology of alien cultures was defined as objective and neutral (value-free). Such scientist claims set the ethnographer apart from the missionaries, administrators, and other practical types. And it was precisely on account of these claims that anthropologists were able to appeal to the Colonial Office, without this fact necessarily jeopardizing the autonomy of the discipline. After World War II, mainly as a consequence of changes in the colonial world, there was a rearrangement of the cadre and, perhaps, a reformulation of the ethics of the discipline. We may note that the claims of objectivity and neutrality were further reinforced. In a recent article Marcus and Cushman have pointed out how the American and British traditions, despite their different theoretical orientations (cultural vs. social structural), consolidated ethnographic realism as "*the* literary institution' serving positivistic scientific goals."[14]

---

13.   Marcel Bataillon, "Hernán Cortés, autor prohibido," in *Libro jubilar de Alfonso Reyes* (Mexico: Universidad Nacional Autónoma de México, 1959), 77-83.

14.   George E. Marcus and Dick Cushman, "Ethnographies as Texts," *Annual Review of Anthropology* 11 (1982): 30 (emphasis by Marcus and Cushman).

Ethnographic realism sets the backdrop for the recent experiments in ethnographic writing. Among the most notable changes are the inclusion of the encounter in fieldwork and the substitution of dialogue for the us/them division implicit in an omniscient point of view. The above schema of twentieth-century anthropology is far from complete, and I might add that it is subordinate to my main purpose: to read Cortés as a proto-ethnographer whose writing manifests the determining historical structure of the "Europe and its others" complex that haunts the anthropological project.[15]

The same criteria of objectivity and neutrality, and the formulation of universal laws to explain social life which have defined anthropology as a positive science, have constituted the basis for the traditional histories of the discipline. Thus genealogies are set in motion where premodern figures state "felicitous" phrasings that anticipate the more rigorous propositions of modern anthropology.[16] Within this perspective there is no room for Cortés or even for Fray Bernardino de Sahagún among the other missionaries. They are either by-passed or dismissed as furnishing aberrant forms of knowledge. Historians proceed as if to exorcise the discipline from the demons of colonialism by excluding forms of inquest candidly posed as modes of gaining dominion.

Muley's words furnish a motif that testifies to the "yoking of force and discourse."[17] They also suggest a clearing in the power of representation that Edward Said's *Orientalism* analyzes in terms of the concomitant production of a Western omniscient self and a silent other.[18] Calderón's other not only speaks, but deconstructs, the textual violence effected on the Moor by an "abencerraje-inspired tradition of romantic and noble Moors."[19] As a self-deconstructive passage, it un-

15.   For a detailed overview of contemporary anthropology, see Sherry B. Ortner, "Theory in Anthropology Since the Sixties," *Society for the Comparative Study of Society and History* 26, no. 1 (1984): 126-66.
16.   See M.T. Hodgen, *Early Anthropology in the Sixteenth and Seventeeth Centuries* (Philadelphia: Univ. of Pennsylvania Press, 1964); Urs Bitterli, *Los "salvajes" y los "civilizados": el encuentro de Europa y Ultramar* (Mexico: Fondo de Cultura Económica, 1981). For a critique see James A. Boon, "Comparative De-enlightenment in the History of Ethnology," *Daedalus* 109 (1980): 73-91. Also of interest is Michael T. Ryan, "Assimilating New Worlds in the Sixteenth and Seventeenth Centuries," *Society for Comparative Study of Society and History* 23, no. 4 (1981): 519-38.
17.   Burshatin, "Power, Discourse and Metaphor," 207.
18.   Edward W. Said, *Orientalism* (New York: Vintage Books, 1979).
19.   Burshatin, "Power, Discourse and Metaphor," 207.

masks the violence of representation; moreover, the motif also conveys an intratextual referential plane where communication itself corresponds to a mode of conquest. Thus we may associate the two primordial elements of ethnography — fieldwork and writing — with domination.

Kevin Dwyer and Vincent Crapanzano, among others, have expressed that within a Moorish tradition, there is the need to include the confrontation with informants in the written text.[20] Against a monological approach that construes the reality of the other out of field notes or experiences, they propose a dialogical model where the voices of the interlocutors would reveal the joint construction of a shared reality. I cannot do justice here to the complexity and sophistication of Dwyer's and Crapanzano's proposals. It is not a question of writing them off, but of pointing out some shortcomings in what one may call the "becoming minor" of anthropology's master discourse. Dialogue is but one mode among others of ethnographic authority. As James Clifford has recently pointed out, Dwyer's and Crapanzano's texts "remain representations of dialogue," where the possibility of escaping typifications "depends on their ability fictionally to maintain the strangeness of the other voice and to hold in view the specific contingencies of the exchange."[21] Given the present discussion, the overriding control of the writer in the textualization of the encounter does not come as a surprise, but my point is to trace it back to the exchanges in the field.

"As Tuhami's interlocutor," writes Crapanzano, "I became an active participant in his life history, even though I rarely appear directly in his recitation." Crapanzano goes on to mention how "my presence and questions not only prepared him for the text he was to produce, but they produced what I read as a change of consciousness in him. They produced a change of consciousness in me, too."[22] Both change for sure, and

---

20.   Kevin Dwyer, *Moroccan Dialogues: Anthropology in Question* (Baltimore and London: Johns Hopkins Univ. Press, 1982); "The Dialogic of Ethnology," and "On the Dialogic of Field Work," *Dialectical Anthropology* 4, no.3 (1979): 205-24, and 2, no. 2 (1977): 143-51. Vincent Crapanzano, *Tuhami: Portrait of a Moroccan* (Chicago: Univ. of Chicago Press, 1980); "On the Writing of Ethnography," *Dialectical Anthropology* 2, no. 1 (1977): 69-73. For a discussion of dialogical authority, see James Clifford, "On Ethnographic Authority," 133-35, and passim. I would not have been able to conceptualize this essay without Clifford's study.
21.   Clifford, "On Ethnographic Authority," 134-35.
22.   Crapanzano, *Tuhami*, 11.

accordingly the text implies a critique of timeless, ahistorical ethnographies that silence the other. But who is the master puppeteer in the interview? Let us exemplify the mastery of the ethnographer with Dwyer. In what follows Dwyer reflects upon the virtues of his own text, a "direct" record of a taped dialogue: "I reject the Faqir's attempts to provide initial formulations of otherness." Only on the basis of such guided interrogatories can the project achieve the following results: "what emerges for the Faqir is a greater potential for self-realization, for me of self-transcendence; for one the development of self, for the other its mutation."[23] The ethnographer, once more, retains the stronger role in the communication as he fashions himself as a vehicle for the self-realization of Faqir. Indeed, Dwyer defines what is real in his rejection of Faqir's answers. This perhaps explains the Faqir's falling asleep during the last interview that closes Dwyer's book. It certainly testifies to Dwyer's honesty by displaying the limits of his enterprise.[24]

A theoretical point will help us understand the shortcomings of dialogical ethnography. Insofar as communication requires that an addresser and an addressee recognize a referent in the interior of a message, dialogue corresponds to a form of "worlding," of constituting unmotivated signs.[25] The becoming unmotivated of signs implies a stronger discourse that ultimately defines a sense of reality. Moreover, the above definition of communication is specifically a western invention. Roy Wagner has drawn the following distinction: "we should not be surprised to discover that urban Westerners stress the use of language as control, whereas tribal, peasant, and lower-class peoples control language through expressive formulations (through

---

23.   Dwyer, "On the Dialogic," 147,148.

24.   See Paul Rabinow, "Discourse and Power: On the Limits of Ethnographic Texts," *Dialectical Anthropology* 10, nos. 1/2 (1985): 1-13; esp. 7.

25.   I am here modifying the definition of communication given by Roman Jakobsen, "Linguistics and Poetics," in *Style in Language*, ed. Thomas A. Sebeok (New York and London: Technology Press & John Wiley, 1960), 350-77. Following Jacques Derrida we may add that: "It is therefore *the game of the world* that must first be thought; before attempting to understand all forms of play in the world" (*On Grammatology*, trans. Gayatri Spivak [Baltimore and London: Johns Hopkins Univ. Press, 1976], 50). On the notion of worlding and colonial discourse, see Gayatri Spivak, "The Rani of Sirmur," in *Europe and Its Others*, vol. 1, ed. Francis Barker, et. al (Colchester: Univ. of Essex, 1985), 128-51. Also informing the notion of dialogue as violent and power-ridden are Bakhtin's reflections on dialogism in "Discourse and the Novel," in *The Dialogic Imagination: Four Essays*, trans. Caryl Emerson and Michael Holquist (Austin: Univ. of Texas Press, 1981), 314-15, and passim.

their use of the world, we might say)."[26]

Whenever these two modes of relating to language are dominant, it necessarily implies a breakdown in communication. Referents can never be recognized as long as two different contexts or discourses mediate their significance. As such, dialogue with an other is an illusion. There is only dialogue among the same, and indeed it is power-ridden. Since going native forecloses the possibility of representing the other, control by means of translation seems to be the other alternative. Logical as well as rhetorical constructs, however, thwart the project of translation. But perhaps the same forms of inquiry from which ethnography dissociated itself might suggest another alternative. Whereas the university-trained ethnographer posits resistance at the limits of the enterprise, the missionary and the colonial administrator reveal the spaces of counter-discourse. The former sublates the confrontation by straightening out the natives' misapprehensions; the latter open the text to mockery, parody, and hybridization whereby the natives question authority.[27] Paradoxically, domination provides for a keener display of invention by the native.

The Garden in the Ideal City of the Conquistador

Hernán Cortés's "Map of Mexico City and the Gulf" (fig. 1) juxtaposes an outline of the gulf coast to a plan of Tenochtitlan. From this map one can derive the basic elements that differentiate a discourse of conquest from one of exploration. The Map provides as well a point of entry for a more elaborate analysis of the discourse of conquest in Cortés's correspondence with Charles V.

In a nutshell, the New World of the explorer corresponds to an idyllic Garden whose contours need to be mapped and its specimens de-

---

26. Roy Wagner, *The Invention of Culture*, rev. ed. (Chicago: Univ. of Chicago Press, 1981), 107.

27. See the stimulating discussions of hybridization in Homi Bhabha, "Of Mimicry and Man: The Ambivalence of Colonial Discourse," *October* 28 (1984): 125-33; "Signs Taken for Wonders: Questions of Ambivalence and Authority Under a Tree Outside Delhi," in *Europe and Its Others*, vol. 1, 89-106. In reading Bhabha, one must take into account Abdul JanMohamed's critique in "The Economy of Manichean Allegory: The Function of Racial Difference in Colonialist Literature," *Critical Inquiry* 12 (Autumn 1985): 59-87, esp. 56-61.

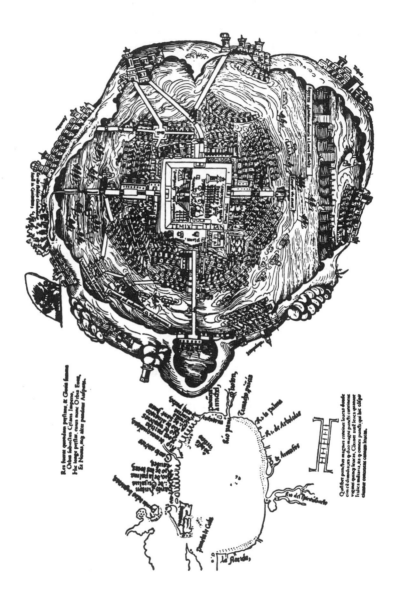

FIGURE 1 — Hernán Cortés, "Map of Mexico City and the Gulf Coast" (1524)

scribed and named; on the other hand, the New World city of the Conquistador contains the secrets of the land, and thus learning the native text undermines the value of direct description.

The figure of Cortés and the event of the Conquest of Mexico are well known, and I do not believe they need a recapitulation here. I will not be concerned with cataloguing further the cruelties, ideological manipulations, and negative attitudes towards Mesoamerican civilization that the partisans of the so-called Black Legend have been busily comprising from Las Casas and de Bry up to W. Arens and Tzvetan Todorov.[28] Inevitably, they succumb to a reterritorialization of the event with a totalizing interpretation. It seems to me that the apologists of the conquest, and Cortés in particular, pose a more complex question to examine:

> Ya sus contemporáneos comenzaron la enumeración de sus
> defectos, tarea que se ha proseguido hasta hoy; pero que no se

---

28. For Las Casas consider the ample circulation and translation of the *Brevísima relación de la destrucción de Indias* (1552), facsim. ed. Manuel Ballesteros Gaibrois (Madrid: Fundación Universitaria Española, 1977). On de Bry's translation of Las Casas and the Black Legend in general, see M.S. Giuseppi, F.S.A., "The Work of Theodore de Bry and his Sons, Engravers," *Proceedings of the Huguenot Society of London* XI (1915-1917): 204-27; Rómulo D. Carbia, *Historia de la Leyenda Negra Hispano-Americana* (Buenos Aires: Ediciones Orientación Española, 1943). For a recent example of a denunciation of ideological manipulation, see W. Arens's interpretation of cannibalism as an invention for the justification of the Conquest in *The Man-Eating Myth: Anthropology and Anthropophagy* (New York: Oxford Univ. Press, 1979). With respect to the validity of Arens's hypothesis, see *The Ethnography of Cannibalism*, ed. Paula Brown and Donald Tuzin (Washington, D.C.: Society for Psychological Anthropology, 1983). Insofar as Todorov's point of departure for a semiotic and moral explanation of the Conquest consists of an evaluation of attitudes and a reduction of its success to the superiority of phonological writing, the benevolent facade of the Conquest is undermined in *The Conquest of America: The Question of the Other*, trans. Richard Howard (New York: Harper and Row, 1984), esp. 57-139. Todorov's classification of Mesoamerican culture as presymbolic because of a lack of phonological writing defeats the moral question of dialogue — the *Other* ends up engrossed in a monologue where symbols cannot be differentiated from reality. For Todorov the success of the conquest is a result of the technological superiority of phonetic writing. It is not only questionable that there was a lack of phonetic writing in Mesoamerica, but more importantly so, the supposedly inferior understanding of symbolism that Todorov ascribes to Mexican culture betrays, in the final analysis, a refusal to account for the native's creativity. For a discussion of writing in pre-Columbian America and Todorov's position, see Gordon Brotherston, "Towards a Grammatology of America: Lévi-Strauss, Derrida and the Native New World Text," in *Europe and Its Others*, vol. 2, esp. 63.

olvide un factor esencialisimo en la valoración de Cortés. El armo
y a estimación de que gozaba entre los indios.
[Already his contemporaries began the enumeration of his defects, a task that has been continued until today; but an essential
factor for the appraisal of Cortés must not be forgotton: the love
and esteem he had among the Indians. (My translation)][29]

Ramón Iglesias's brilliant observation obviously implies Cortés's love
for Mexico. But why do I call this move by Iglesias brilliant? Simply
because I take the "love of Cortés" as a crucial aspect of the Conquest.
A number of approaches can be derived from Iglesias's point. On the
one hand, one could accentuate the natives' desire for a conqueror,
while on the other, one could also insist on the motif of the conquered
conquistador. I have chosen instead to observe how "love" has a strategic place in the program of conquest. In brief, dialogue and communication constitute an integral component of the Conquest, and
not an extrinsic factor to be evaluated. In what follows, we will examine the terrain where the ordinary definition of discourse as dialogue
emerges as a rule within a discursive formation that frames the performance of the Conquistador and the production of Mexico.[30]

The circular form of the plan of Tenochtitlan, its location on a lagoon on a par with Venice, its broad avenues and open spaces reveal
the projection of an ideal city onto the fabric of a real one. The ideali-
zation follows Cortés's verbal descriptions not on a one-to-one basis,
but as an imaginary representation of the different indigenous codes
contained within the city. Little is to be gained by denouncing the distortion when the import of the plan is symbolic.

For the Conquistador, the city constitutes not only an object of dis-

---

29.   Ramón Iglesias, "Hernán Cortés, in *Cronistas e historiadores de la conquista de
México*, ed. Juan A. Ortega y Medina (Mexico: Sep/Setentas, 1972), 119.
30.   On the notion of discursive formation, see Michel Foucault, *The Archaeology of
Knowledge*, trans. A.M. Sheridan Smith (New York: Harper Torchbooks, 1972), esp.
31-39. For the ordinary notion of discourse, see Emile Benveniste, "The Nature of
Pronouns," in *Problems in General Linguistics* (Coral Gables: Univ. of Miami Press,
1971), 217-22. Also of interest are Roman Jakobson's observations about discourse
with respect to communication and reference in "Linguistics and Poetics." Hayden
White, in *Tropics of Discourse: Essays in Cultural Criticism* (Baltimore and London: Johns
Hopkins Univ. Press, 1978), provides a useful definition of discourse in the etymolog-
ical sense of *discurrere*, "to move back and forth, to and fro," for understanding the
tropological forms that forge the familiar out of the unfamiliar, and vice versa, in
Cortés's production of Mexico (3-4).

course in need of codification, but a new mode of discursivity as well. The plan of Tenochtitlan bears a duplicity in its representation. On the surface both maps (the plan of Tenochtitlan and the chart of the coast) would seem to fulfill an analogous informative function about two distinct geographic objects requiring different forms of representation. The two maps can also be seen as clarifying each other: while the map of the coastline locates particular features in a broader geographic context, the plan of the city defines the novelty of the region. But under closer inspection, the plan of the city does not denote a real object; the plan is an ideal reconstruction of a city by then in ruins. The pluperfect *fuerat* (had been) in the legend establishes the plan as an imaginary projection that fulfills a purpose other than cartographical accuracy. As an imaginary reconstruction, the plan is a *sine qua non* for the *Gloria Summa* expressed in the legend. It provides a mirror for the Emperor wherein the effigy of the Conquistador surfaces as a faithful and bold servant pushing further the bounds of the Empire. The codification of the exotic city of the New World depends on a metaphorical transposition of the known for its depiction, but the city is also equivalent to an indigenous encyclopedia and a power structure that reduces the world beyond its confines to a spatial text. For instance, in the *Second Letter* Cortés mentions *pinturas* (paintings, indigenous maps) of the political structure of the Mexican dominions and a *pintura* of the gulf that provides the initial data for the chart of the coast: "Otro día me trajeron figurada en un paño toda la costa . . ." ["The next day they brought me a cloth with a figuration of the whole coast . . ."](67). Quite literally the city contains all the secrets.

But the plan of Tenochtitlan bears the imprint of the historical momentum of the Conquistador; it portrays the strategic benefits of the site and an urban structure whose avenues, open spaces, and the unrepresented debris of the city in ruins provide a material substratum for imagining a new city. The plan bespeaks a spatialization of native history and the infusion of a new historical temporality. On the ruins of the ancient city, Mexico City arises and preserves indelible traces of the ancient order for the present. This transformation of reality may be likened to a palimpsest where the text of the conquered furnishes and retains its formal structure in the text of the conqueror. It is not the explorer's accidental and fortuitous mushrooming of colonial entrepots on a landscape that murmurs an extraneous language. The *fuerat*, the had-been of Tenochtitlan, retains a ghost-like presence in a mnemonic deposit of information about the land despite its destruction.

Thus the city is not opposed to the garden of the explorers since it contains in it the forms of the zoo and the botanical garden. The market in the city and the indigenous library further complement the mimicry of nature (the artificial garden) with a native code that registers economic, political, historical, nutritional, and medicinal secrets. The destruction of the city obviously does not imply the disappearance of Mesoamerican civilization. The codes registered within the plan continue to exist, though in a dismembered form. And it is precisely in the interstices of this objectification of the city that a whole array of the oppositional practices of everyday life proliferates in an invisible mode.[31]

The force of the plan is obviously strategic in the sense defined by Michel de Certeau as the mastery of places by vision: "the look transforms strange forces into objects which one can observe and measure, therefore controlling and 'including' them in one's vision."[32] In addition, the proper place of *strategy* implies a mastery of time as well as the transformation of the uncertainties of history into readable spaces. On the other hand, *tactics* belongs to oppositional practices. For de Certeau, *tactics* is defined by the absence of a proper place; it is wily and creates surprises. It operates in time and scrambles the proper places of mastery by changing the very organization of space. Sahagún's *Historia de la cosas de la Nueva España*, the Spanish title of what is commonly known as the *Florentine Codex*, further elaborates Cortés's program with an encyclope-

---

31.   I derive the term "oppositional practices" from Michel de Certeau, "On the Oppositional Practices of Everyday Life," *Social Text* 3 (Fall 1980): 3-43. The above essay summed up for an English audience some of the main arguments developed in his *L'invention du quotidien: Arts de faire*, vol. 1 (Paris: Union Général d'Editions, coll. 10/18, 1980). There is an English version with the title *Practices of Everyday Life* (Berkeley and Los Angeles: Univ. of California Press, 1984). As de Certeau points out in *The Practices of Everyday Life*, he draws his inspiration from the Amerindians who, "even when they were subjected, indeed even when they accepted their subjection, the Indians often used the laws, practices, and representations that were imposed on them by force or by fascination to ends other than those of their conquerors; they made something else out of them; they subverted them from within — not by rejecting them or by transforming them (though that occurred as well), but by many different ways of using them in the service of rules, customs or convictions foreign to the colonialization which they could not escape. They metaphorized the dominant order; they made it function in another register" (31-2). I believe that one might further illuminate the above, much studied question with de Certeau's categories.

32.   De Certeau, "On the Oppositional," 5.

dic compendium of the various codes registered in the plan. Sahagún builds his *Historia* in order to reconstruct Nahuatl language before the Conquest so as to preserve what he considers valuable and also to provide a semiotic repertoire for identifying superstitious practices. I must add that the informants themselves produce the original Nahuatl version of the text. As we will see shortly, it is an invaluable document for tracing the other side of the dialogue and its tactical interventions.

As a panoptic overview, the plan entails a dialogical process that sought to retain Moctezuma as a Master in servitude and in the long run to preserve the native order. Dialogue is at once a mode of controlling the Spaniards and of gaining knowledge; it is also an imperceptible mode of conquering. Dialogue indeed establishes what is proper and obviously mediates the recognition of Charles V. It is beyond the scope of this study to quote and fully comment on passages exemplifying dialogue. Let is suffice to point out that one can open the Cortés-Charles V correspondence at random and find numerous passages that insist on love and elaborate on what they call *conversación* (conversation in the sense of social intercourse) and *plática* (talk in the context of inquiries) as modalities of conquest. Instead, I will delineate some general characteristics.

The process of learning about the other not only produces data but introduces dialogue into a web of practices ranging roughly from the exchange of goods to conversion. For Charles V and Cortés, fairness and love are the ways to conversion and the recognition of lordship. Though with metaphors opposite to Marcel Griaule's, Cortés complements the panoptic with dialogue. Cortés's letters elaborate a clear understanding of cultural differences and the need to establish a common ground of discourse, a third order that would not dissolve the specific cultures. Inquiries into the kinds of tributes the natives paid in the past, trade equivalences, forms of slavery, and so on, conjoin the dialogical paths of "treating, trading and conversing" as modes of gaining a deeper understanding of the codes contained within the city. The Conquistador becomes a mediator for introducing the new order and effecting what Charles V calls the "reconocimiento del vasallaje que me deben" ["the recognition of the vassalage they owe me"] (587). Moroever, Charles V constantly prohibits war and any other form of unfair treatment "porque de miedo no se alboroten ni se levanten." ["so that out of fear they do not riot or rebel"] (588).

Conversation suggests an imperceptible mode of conquering; it would transform the consciousness of the natives by immersing them in a new order comprising the Conquistador as well. It implies at once a fairness and a remittance of the old order into the past. The pluperfect *fuerat* (had been) in the legend of the map does not merely refer to a time that had passed, but also to the stoppage of native history that the momentum of the conquest imposes from the beginning.[33] This stoppage operates under two paradoxes. On the one hand, it seeks to retain the ancient order intact, but ignores the transformation of the object in the process of gaining power. On the other, it ignores an ongoing historical consciousness in the subjectivity of the natives requisite for a recognition of Charles V. We can trace a glimpse of the latter illusion in the concerns Charles V expresses in the previous quote about the precariousness of domination. Revolt remains a possibility.

The Dialogue with Moctezuma

A series of precautions and detailed instructions manifest a long-term conquest and an elaborate process by means of which Charles V would be recognized as the Supreme Lord. Most of the letters were written after the fall of Tenochtitlan — under truce, as it were. They can be seen as immersed in a contradiction deftly posited by Hegel in a famous passage on the Master/Slave relation in *The Phenomenology of Mind*:

> But for recognition proper there is needed the moment that what the master does to the other he should also do to himself, and what the bondsman does to himself, he should do to the other also. On that account a form of recognition has arisen that is one-sided and unequal.

Hegel goes on to mention how the master depends on the slave. But in the end, Hegel dismisses the independence of the slave "as a piece of cleverness which has mastery within a certain range, but not over the universal power nor over the entire objective reality."[34] Hegel, of

---

33.   See Fabian's critique of Benveniste's study of temporal verb forms in *Time and the Other*, 82.

34.   G.W.F. Hegel, *The Phenomenology of Mind*, trans. J.B. Baillie (New York: Harper Torchbook, 1967), 236, 240. My usage of this passage is inspired by the

course, announces here the coming of Reason as the next stage in the development of *mind*. We need not discuss the "magical solution" of the contradiction, nor what elsewhere Hegel calls *the cunning of reason* — the belief in progress beyond the surface of historical events.[35] Let us observe, instead, how the contradiction and incomplete recognition arise from the initial proposition about self-consciousness wherein the truth of each adversary depends on the other:

> Self-consciousness has before it another self-consciousness; it has come outside itself. This has a double significance. First it has lost its own self, since it finds itself as an *other* being; secondly, it has thereby sublated that other, for it does not regard the other as essentially real, but sees its own self in the other.[36]

The relationship partakes of two illusions, that of the master and that of the slave; hence the truth of the relationship reveals itself as a precarious truce where a future resurgence of strife is inherent in the unfolding of the illusions. The unfolding of the subjectivities implies a mutual process of translation and appropriation. Not only must the slave speak the language of the master, but he must also speak from the representation the master renders of the adversary's language.

Let us examine in this light some instances of the representation of the initial encounter between the two cultures and observe how the textual production of the conquistador is indissolubly bound to that of the conquered. Our concern will reside in the representation and

---

poststructuralist readings of Jacques Lacan, "Aggressivity in Psychoanalysis" and "The Subversion of Subject and the Dialectic of Desire in the Freudian Unconsciousness," in *Ecrits*, trans. Alan Sheridan (New York: W.W. Norton, 1977), 292-325; Jacques Derrida, "From Restricted to General Economy: A Hegelianism Without Reserve," in *Writing and Difference*, trans. Alan Bass (Chicago: Univ. of Chicago Press, 1978), 251-77; André Glucksmann, *Le discours de la guerre: théorie et stratégie* (Paris: l'Herne, 1967). Glucksmann's reading of Hegel in the light of Roman Jakobson, Emile Benveniste, and Jacques Lacan has been particularly useful. As Glucksmann points out: "La lutte á morte ne fait que décrire les conditions apriori de toute communications, que ce soit celle du mot d'amour ou de l'injonction la plus scabreuse" (80). Beyond the idealism of the linguists, war without respite lies in the horizon of Hegel's formulation. My point for bringing in Hegel is to chart a terrain for arresting the dialectic, and thus warding off the "cunning of reason."

35.   G.W.F. Hegel, *The Philosophy of History*, trans. J. Sibree (New York: Dover Publications, 1956), 33.

36.   Hegel, *The Phenomenology of Mind*, 229. Emphasis by Hegel.

not with straightening out the actual events. Since the purpose is not to retell the story but to analyze the discursive exchange, I do not follow the sequence of events.

Under the ideal conceptualization of the Conquest given in the epigraph to this essay from the *Second Letter*, a temporal stoppage of native discourse seeks to retain Moctezuma as a master in servitude. Charles V figures as a master over both Cortés and Moctezuma. But mastery depends solely on the role Charles V might play as Quetzalcoatl in the historical narrative of Moctezuma. The primal dialogue of the two cultures, as represented in the *Second Letter* by the meeting of Cortés and Moctezuma at the gates of Tenochtitlan, reveals an appropriation of native history that precludes an assimilation of the slave into the language of the master. In other works, Moctezuma's illusion is indispensable for the representation of the master and mastery in the truce:

> Yo le respondí a todo lo que me dijo, satisfaciendo a aquello que me paració que convenía, en especial en hacerle creer que vuestra majestad era a quien ellos esperaban . . .
> [I replied to all that he said, satisfying him in those things I thought most fitting, especially in making him believe that your majesty was he whom they were expecting . . .] (60)

In the speech of Moctezuma, Cortés exposes justifications for the Conquest and for Moctezuma's belief that Charles V is the *subject* of a narrative that prefigures the place of the conquest in native history. The representation of the dialogue with Moctezuma is in itself a mode of communicating with Charles V; it ultimately legitimates conquest and Cortés's proceedings. But it also reveals the frailty of the discursive exchange.

Cortés's strategem of leading Moctezuma to see the intruders as the protagonists of a narrative sorely decries the belief that the truce will last the span of this illusion. Cortés's personification of Quetzalcoatl cannot be sustained for long since it contradicts the missionary character of the Conquest. Yet the appropriation of the narrative provides the vehicle for representing "natural" servitude and the illusion of the slave *qua* his own language.

But Moctezuma's voice quivers, and he previews his own death as well as the imminent end of the truce when he pleads with Cortés not to believe the collaborators about the wealth of Tenochtitlan; moreover, Moctezuma feels obliged to raise his clothes in order to prove to Cortés that he is not a god: "A mí véisme aquí que soy de carne y hueso como vos y como cada uno, y que soy mortal y palpable . . ." ["You can see that I am of flesh and blood like you and all other men, mortal and tangible . . ."] (59). The raising of the clothes could be seen as emblematic of an absolute submission — providing one's body for the inscription of a new order.[37] A deep sigh, which echoes the chivalric effect of Boabdil's sigh after the fall of Granada, must be heard in Cortés's representation of Moctezuma's submission to Charles V. Moctezuma expresses a stoic resignation in contemplating the tragic unfolding of events. Recognition is nothing but a tenuous truce that ultimately depends on a stoppage of native history. Mesoamerican civilization is reduced to the significance it has in the temporal frame of the Empire —it is a *thing* without subjectivity.

Historical records tell us about the natives and a taciturn Moctezuma who sees the intruders as *teules*. The meaning of this term (that is, what is a "god" in the Nahua pantheon?) remains far from clear.[38] An amusing passage from Bernal, where he describes Cortés and Moctezuma's chuckling and "elbowing each other" about their common attribute, *teule*, should have cautioned historians about drawing far-fetched and totalizing explanations of the Conquest on this misnomer. Delusion does not preclude knowledge, nor can myth and religion be reduced to ideologies.

Let us observe from the other side of the dialogue how minor knowledges concur with misnomers and misrepresentations in delusion. In Book XII of the *Florentine Codex* (ca. 1585) the Spaniards are represented as an absence and inversion of culture in the context of a history of the Conquest written from a native point of view. It is the *vision de los vencidos* (vision of the vanquished) in Miguel León-Portilla's words;[39] it is also a subversion and appropriation of Spanish forms of culture. The Conquistador exists on account of the illusion of the conquered where the insistence on calling them *teules* implies retaining an indige-

---

37.   On writing and the inscription of the law on the body, see Michel de Certeau, *The Practice of Everyday Life*, 131-53.
38.   See Alfredo López Austin, *Hombre-Dios, Religion y política en el Mundo Náhuatl* (Mexico: Universidad Nacional Autónoma de México, 1973).
39.   See Miguel León-Portilla, "Introducción general," in *Visión de los vencidos. Relaciones indígenas de la conquista*, trans. Angel María Garibay K. (Mexico: Universidad Nacional Autónoma de México, 1972), xxiii, "Quetzalcoatl-Cortés en la conquista de México," *Historia Mexicana* XXIV, no. 1 (1974): 13-35.

nous narrative of the event. The end of the *teule* interpretation would entail an end of the Nahua understanding of history and the world. Book XII forges a memory of an atrocious event that intends to prevent its dissipation into forgetfulness. It constitutes a register which perpetuates a form of memorizing in the process of inventing the Spaniard. Beyond a version of *mestizo* culture where the two cultures merge into a new one, we should take it as a form of hybridization and adopt Homi Bhabha's phrase — "less than one and double." As Bhabha defines it: "hybridity intervenes in the exercise of authority not merely to indicate the impossibility of its identity, but to represent the unpredictability of its presence."[40] This ambivalent space certainly troubled Sahagún.

Passages and vignettes reveal the adaptation of alphabetic writing, of "hispanic" forms of life, and of moral criteria for constructing a nefarious Spaniard:

> And when they had given them these (golden banners, precious feather streamers, and golden necklaces), they appeared to smile; they were greatly contented, gladdened. As if they were monkeys they seized upon the gold. It was as if their hearts were satisfied, brightened, calmed. For in truth they thirsted mightily for gold; they stuffed themselves with it; they starved for it; they lusted for it like pigs.[41]

From all appearances the syntactical doubling of metaphors is a characteristic trait of prehispanic poetry.[42] Whereas the Franciscans would comply with the moral outrage expressed in this passage, they would not express it as such. The fixation on gold, as revealed in its monotonous repetition in the text, implies a native view wherein the Europeans are mocked ("like monkeys," "like pigs") and wherein gold is seen as a lowly object of desire. I am not qualified to evaluate the accuracy of Anderson and Dibble's translation of the Nahautl. Nor does it matter if we simply observe the surface of the text. The translation certain-

---

40. Homi Bhabha, "Signs Taken for Wonders," 99.
41. Fray Bernardino de Sahagún, *Florentine Codex, General History of New Spain. Book 12. The Conquest of Mexico*, 13 vols., trans. Arthur J.O. Anderson and Charles E. Dibble (Sante Fe: Univ. of New Mexico Press, Monographs of the School of American Research, 1975), 13:31.
42. See Angel María Garibay K., *Panorama literario de los pueblos náhuas* (Mexico: Editorial Porrúa, 1975), 35-41.

ly captures the intensity of the passage; its doubling of metaphors actually upturns and makes redundant any pursuit of a figurative meaning as it marks an insistence on expression over content. Paraphrasing Deleuze and Guattari, we might add that just as the Spaniards become pigs and monkeys, so the pigs and monkeys become Spaniards.[43] Thus the characterization of the Spaniards as savages, *popolcas* (those who cannot speak Nahuatl), gains intensity with their animal behavior and the suggestion that they eat gold. The attributes *teule* and *popolca* do not contradict each other but reinforce each other with the image of an uncouth god that brings about the destruction of culture; after all, the Spaniards melt down artifacts in order to devour gold.

On the other hand, the pictorial version of the Conquest in the *Florentine Codex* (fig. 2) is not an illustration of the text, but a mode of writing the event. The pictorial version antecedes the written both in terms of the order of research followed by Sahagún and with respect to the innumerable stories that could be told about frame 25, second from the top in the right hand column, which tells about the gifts Moctezuma sent to Cortés on his way to Tenochtitlan. Indeed the written portion illustrates the pictorial with intensive images. It all suggests that the transformation of the Spaniards into animals does not imply a reterritorialization but a deterritorialization of alphabetic writing and its privileged domain of the signified. As a form of counter-discourse, it produces effects rather than objects by altering the Spanish system of representation.

Likewise the dominant three-dimensional representational space of the vignettes is deterritorialized. The fanciful mountain in the right hand corner is not merely a background scenario but a glyph denoting the location of the event near Popocatepetl, "smoking mountain." Thus, stylized prehispanic pictographs furnish captions to a version of the Conquest expressed by means of a clash of forms of life and pictorial conventions.[44] Indeed landscape (a European trait) becomes an element for writing glyphs. In a less obvious place we find this prac-

---

43.   Deleuze and Guattari, 22.

44.   Cf. Donald Robertson, *Mexican Manuscript Painting of the Colonial Period* (New Haven: Yale Univ. Press, 1959), 21-2. Although not concerned specifically with the Florentine Codex, the following provide suggestive ways for approaching the clash of forms in post-conquest pictorial manuscripts: Joaquin Galarza and Abraham Zemsz, "Le 'portrait-royal' dans l'écriture aztéque 'tableaux' du codex Tovar," *Communications* 29 (1979): 15-56; Rolena Adorno, "On the Pictorial Language and the Typology of Culture in a New World Chronicle," *Semiotica* 36, nos. 1/2 (1982): 1-31.

FIGURE 2 — Scenes from the Conquest of Mexico in Book XXI of the *Florentine Codex* (ca. 1585)

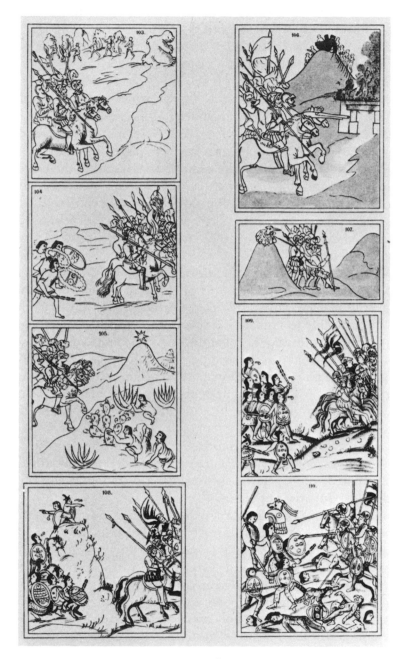

FIGURE 3 — Scenes from the Conquest of Mexico in Book XXI of the *Florentine Codex* (ca. 1585)

tice recurring in frame 105 (fig. 3), second from the bottom on the left-hand column, where the toponym of the town Citlatepetl, "star mountain," remains invisible to all but the trained eye. Other frames on the right-hand column further exemplify the use of glyphs to caption events and the clash of forms of life. Frames 89 to 92 (fig. 4) on the right-hand column vividly portray the confrontation of pictorial conventions in a movement that concludes with the amorphous depiction of the battle on the bottom vignette. As it were, it mocks the representation of war itself. The opposing forms reemerge in the pursuit of the Spaniards and allies depicted in frame 93, second from the bottom in the left-hand column. Again three-dimensional space becomes a place for inscribing signs from the old order; notice the floating headdress and insignia. In the words of de Certeau, we may sum up the above observations by stating that "memory does its work in a locus which is not its own."[45]

In the interstices of alphabetic writing and three-dimensional space we have traced a casual insertion of pictorial details and forms of storytelling that metonymically transforms the plot of the Conquest from military defeat of the natives to an endless discursive struggle. As I have pointed out above, Sahagún's project had two purposes: to build, on the one hand, a classic repertoire of Nahuatl texts that would eventually give place to a dictionary for arresting what he viewed as a deterioration of Nahuatl language and to reconstruct, on the other, the ancient order for the identification of superstitious beliefs in everyday practices. But this dual intent of Sahagún also opens a space for tactical interventions by the informants. The so-called spiritual conquest reiterates Cortés's stoppage of native history. Innovation cannot be anticipated, nor enclosed in a proper place — strategy finds its match in the surprises of tactics.

On the basis of Cortés's "Map of the Mexico City and the Gulf," we have seen how the definition of the New World as an ideal garden was replaced in the discourse of the Conquistador by the city which contained the secrets of the land. From there we have observed how Cortés's use of dialogue entailed an overcoding of the native text. The formation of a palimpsest imposes a stoppage of indigenous history as well as the introduction of a new narrative time. Beyond a question of representation, the superimposition of a new historical temporality

---

45.   De Certeau, "On the Oppositional," 40.

FIGURE 4 — Scenes from the Conquest of Mexico in Book XXI of the *Florentine Codex* (ca. 1585)

on the indigenous structure brings forth a material transformation of Mesoamerican civilization despite the intention to keep the old order intact. The Conquistador was thus caught up in two paradoxes: one ignored the continuity of an indigenous discourse outside the representation of the the Conquistador; the other disregarded the transformation of the object in the process of gaining knowledge. A blatant example of the latter would be the fact that the city became accessible by the formation of hostile collaborators. Furthermore, this implies that the appearance of the Conquistador and the notion of a *conquista* by a handful of men is nothing but a textual illusion.

Cortés's *Letters* seem to encapsulate the limits as well as the possible variation of colonial discourse. They thus constitute a sort of ur-dialogue of encounters between Europeans and alien cultures. Our question has not been Cortés's genius nor the origin of colonialism, but the emergence of a particularly modern form of colonial power and corresponding forms of resistance. This essay has attempted to elaborate an experimental genealogy. In Foucault's words, our concern with descent has sought "to identify the accidents, minute deviations — or conversely, the complete reversals — the errors, the false appraisals, and the faulty calculations that gave birth to those things that continue to exist and have value for us."[46]

As we have read Cortés, we have traced passages that indicate a will to objectivity and neutrality. Knowledge introduces a closure of native history, but this transformation of the other into a *thing* is not an exclusive practice of conquest. We find it prescribed by the best intended anthropologists. Remember Lévi-Strauss's famous proposal: "I believe the ultimate goal of the human sciences to be not to constitute, but to dissolve man."[47] Dialogical ethnography responds to this proposition; nevertheless, it cannot elude the shortcomings of dialogue. Ideal communication requires mutual recognition, but the representation of the encounter (already a form of power) must exclude the violence of the dialogical process. Muley's words cannot be represented without serious consequences for professional ethics.

Since I am not an ethnographer in the strict sense of the term, I need not be concerned with the ethics of the discipline. But I do have a posi-

46.   Michel Foucault, "Nietzsche, Genealogy, History," 146.
47.   Claude Lévi-Strauss, *The Savage Mind*, trans. George Weidenfelf (Chicago: Univ. of Chicago Press, 1966), 247.

tive proposal — one that has inspired this essay — to contribute to the conceptualization of a world of generalized ethnography. Perhaps, something is to be gained by dispersing the confrontation beyond crass, culturally defined dichotomies of Self-Other (which reproduce *ad nauseum* the "Europe and its others" complex), and by starting to wonder about the inner Other — that all too Eurocentric Self that haunts the ethnographer's most venerable intentions. Evidently, Eurocentrism is not an "out there" that we can identify, but the locus where minor discourses intervene.

The Politics of the Possible

Kumkum Sangari

The nonmimetic narrative modes of Gabriel García Márquez and Salman Rushdie inhabit a social and conceptual space in which the problems of ascertaining meaning assume a political dimension qualitatively different from the current postmodern skepticism about meaning in Europe and America. Yet such nonmimetic, non-western modes also seem to lay themselves open to the academized procedures of a peculiarly western, historically singular, postmodern epistemology that universalizes the self-conscious dissolution of the bourgeois subject, with its now characteristic stance of self-irony, across both space and time. The expansive forms of the modern and the postmodern novel appear to stand in ever-polite readiness to recycle and accommodate other cultural content, whether Latin American or Indian. The ease with which a reader may be persuaded to traverse the path between such non-western modes and western postmodernism—broadly defined here as the specific preoccupations and "sensibility" of both contemporary fiction and of poststructuralist critical discourse may

This essay is the revised version of a piece written for the conference on "Márquez and Latin America" held in Hydrabad in September 1984, subsequently published in the *Journal of Arts and Ideas* (Delhi) 10-11 (January-June 1985). It would not have been possible without the help of Ranjan Batra, Anuradha Kapur, Badri Raina and Sudesh Yaid.

216

well lead us to believe they were indeed made for each other. There is not much to be gained by surveying the literature on the subject or in quibbling with individual readings, since the question here is obviously much larger than the "misreading" of any single writer. The question concerns the way the writings of the "Third World" (a term that both signifies and blurs the functioning of an economic, political, and imaginary geography able to unite vast and vastly differentiated areas of the world into a single "underdeveloped" terrain) are consumed in the West (a term produced to opposite effect by the same procedures). My intention here is to examine the politics of this conjuncture by locating those aspects of their narratives that provide, or at least seem to provide, a *mode of access* for the at once diverse and homogeneous discourse of poststructuralism, and which enable their habilitation as texts of a near canonical Euro-American postmodernism.

I

Márquez's marvellous realism is a mode of perception grounded in the political and historical formation of Latin America. Not just the inscription of the marvellous in the real is produced by the colonial history and cultural heterogeneity of Latin America—the disjunctures in the *understanding* of the real are equally mediated by and refracted through the apparatus of various kinds of domination, colonial and neocolonial, underwritten by feudal survivals and reactive nationalisms.

The cultural heterogeneity of Latin America is at once different from and determined by the "linear" history of the West, which both nests inside and shapes Latin American history, often by erasure. The simultaneity of the heterogeneous is a matter of historical sedimentation that results from the physical coexistence over time of different ethnic groups (native American-Indian, Arab, African, Indochinese, Asian, Spanish), each laden with its respective cultural freight of myth, oral narrative, magic, superstition, Roman Catholicism, Cartesian education, and Western rationalism. Simultaneity is the restless product of a long history of miscegenation, assimilation, and syncretization *as well as* of conflict, contradiction, and cultural violence. It is also the unique history of colonization by the Spanish colonizer who, as cultural hybrid, faces across a timelag the changed configuration of those social forces that once produced the conquistadores. Although a hybrid social formation has an unusual and resistant retentiveness, it would be a mistake to read this as simply the inert absence of change, succession, and continuity. The piecemeal assimilation of European (and American) culture is difficult either to reject or to homogenize: first, because in a contradictory way it is both something that is *owned* as well as something to be *resisted,* and, second, because of an "uneven" material development that, contrary to the unidirectional laws of "progress," enforces the coexistence of primitive agriculture with advanced technology and export economies.

In a complex way Latin American history *secretes* the history of Europe and in turn renders it ironic. Márquez's intent is obvious when he points out in his Nobel Lecture that "the statue of General Francisco Morazán [1792-842, the last president of the Central American Federation] erected in the main square of Tegucigalpa is actually one of Marshall Ney [1769-1815, one of Napoleon's commanders], purchased at a Paris warehouse of second-hand sculptures."[1] It is thus a history that forbids (or ought to) either a simple relation to or a linear interpretation of the past and that insistently raises the question of *how* it is to be known. If the Latin American coastline saw the simultaneous influx of black African slaves and Swedish, Dutch, and English pirates, then surely it is more than merely symbolic for the patriarch to see from his window the ships of Christopher Columbus and the ships of the U.S. Marines anchored simultaneously in his harbor. Within this context it is not surprising that Márquez does not set up the real and the marvellous as antithetical realms.[2] He neither construes himself as the "other" nor indulges in a simple-minded rejection of rationalism: he refuses to consent unthinkingly to parallel and essentialist categories such as primitive and modern, tribal and rational. For Márquez "even the most seemingly arbitrary creation has its rules. You can throw away the fig leaf of rationalism only if you don't descend into chaos and irrationality."[3] So in *The Autumn of the Patriarch* the "sainthood" of the dictator's mother is rationally exposed as fraud, shown to be a lucrative part of several illusions imposed on him even as other "miracles"

1. Gabriel García Márquez, 1982 Nobel Lecture, "Latin America's Solitude," *Le Nouvel Observateur* (8 January 1983): 60.

2. Irlemar Chiampi Cortez, "In Search of a Latin American Writing," *Diacritics* 8, no.4 (Winter 1978): 7.

3. Márquez, *The Fragrance of Guava*, trans. Ann Wright (London: Verso, 1982), 31.

are instated as "real," for instance, the dictator's secret knowledge of a salt that can cure lepers and make cripples walk. The *margin* for arbitrariness, the casting up of the strange, the incongruous, the peripheral, is the *product* of a historical situation. At this level marvellous realism embodies a *specific* social relation. The apparent "novelty" of marvellous realism results from its immersion in the social matrix wherein improvisation is not merely a formal literary reflex but a function of living in the world.

Finally, the cultural simultaneity of Latin America must be distinguished from the cultural synchronicity of the "First World." Here it is a matter of historical conjuncture in which different modes of production, different social formations, and different ways of seeing overlap as the ground of conflict, contradiction, change, and intervention, both indigenous and foreign. Not only is Big Mama an emblematic figure in this respect—her power is described in "Big Mama's Funeral" as being at once seignorial, manorial, papal, electoral, *and* mercantile (she runs a financial empire)—but the feudal forms and practices implanted by Spanish colonialism are shown to be reappropriated by emerging power structures. Thus the cruelest killer in *The Autumn of the Patriarch* is José Ignacio Saenz de la Barra, the last scion of aristocracy and a sort of medieval prince of darkness.[4]

In contrast, the synchronic time of the modern and of the postmodern in the West is an *end* product of the now discredited linear time of modernity and progress. The synchronic vision of culture in the West takes shape through the conglomerative modality of collage as "different times and different spaces are combined in a here and now that is everywhere at once."[5] Synchronicity, as it inhabits dominant

---

4. ". . . But Saenz de la Barra had made him note that with every six heads sixty enemies are produced and for every sixty six hundred are produced and then six thousand and then six million, the whole country, God damn it, we'll never end, and Saenz de la Barra answered him impassively to rest easy, general, we'll finish with them when they're all finished, what a barbarian" (Márquez, *The Autumn of the Patriarch*, trans. Gregory Rabassa [London: Picador, 1978], 162; further citations from this work will be included in the text).

5. Octavio Paz, *Alternating Current*, trans. Helen R. Lane (New York: Viking Press, 1967), 21. Geoffrey Hartman describes the "cultural supermarket": "a liberation not of men and women, but of images, has created a *theatrum mundi* in which the distance between past and present, culture and culture, truth and superstition is suspended by a quasi-divine synchronism" (*The Fate of Reading* [Chicago: University of Chicago Press, 1975], 104).

institutions and discourses, is the joint apogee of a cultural modernism and a consumer culture, the instant availability effect of the spatialization of the museum and of the push-button archive, as well as a matter of the recurring renovation of style through new juxtapositions. It must, of course, be said that the cultural heterogeneity produced in the west through class stratification and ethnic difference also has both an oppositional and vulnerable relation to the influential apparatus and dominant discourses of "high" culture.

The double disjunction of a hybrid simultaneity and of the economic and ideological deformations of neocolonialism is the condition within which the real is perceived and also the condition within which both authors and texts are produced. Consequently, the problems of meaning and representation that beset the "Third World" are very different from the slippage of meaning and of the "real" which currently confronts *academic* discourses of Europe and America. To say this is not to claim the possibility of arriving at some essential indigenous truth by a more tortuous route, but to insist that the epistemological problem is *itself* a historical one. Both meaning and the need for locating meaning are conjunctural; and it is useful to maintain a distinction between the realized difficulty of knowing and the preasserted or a priori difficulty of knowing. And if we agree, then surely the problem of meaning for the "Third World" is also at bottom entangled in the problems of social and political aspiration and reconstitution whereas the tenuousness of meaning in the "West," equally a product of this historical conjuncture, is one in which the felt absence of the will or the ability to change things as they are can become the voice of epistemological despair. For us, the difficulty of arriving at "fact" through the historical and political distortions that so powerfully shape and mediate it leads not to dismember finally either the status or the existence of fact. Rather, it tends to assert another *level* of factuality, to cast and resolve the issues of meaning on another, more dialectical plane, a plane on which the notion of knowledge as provisional and of truth as historically circumscribed is not only *necessary* for understanding, but can in turn be made to *work* from positions of engagement within the local and contemporary. For me, this is the precise function of Márquez's marvellous realism as a cognitive mode.

II

Márquez's marvellous realism not only emerges from the contingent, simultaneous, polyphonic contours of his material world, it is also a transformative mode that has the capacity both to register and to engage critically with the present and to generate a new way of seeing. Though he digs beneath the rational encrustations of colonialism to uncover ways of storytelling that existed before or that have subcutaneously survived, he avoids the familiar "Third World" bind, the swing from disillusionment with an inadequate rationalism to an easily available mysticism—in some sense mutually constitutive categories brought into play by colonialism. Marvellous realism answers an emergent society's need for renewed self-description and radical assessment, displaces the established categories through which the West has construed other cultures either in its own image or as alterity, questions the Western capitalist myth of modernization and progress, and asserts without nostalgia an indigenous preindustrial realm of possibility. In *One Hundred Years of Solitude* the "almost" two-hundred-year-old Francisco the Man sings the news in songs he has composed, "accompanying himself with the same archaic accordion that Sir Walter Raleigh had given him in the Guianas." In these songs he "told in great detail the things that had happened in the towns along his route . . . so that if anyone had a message to send or an event to make public, he would pay him two cents to include it in his repertory."[6] In fact it becomes impossible to idealize a folk culture which on examination proves not only to be crafted from the contingent but to be hybrid as well!

As a mode, marvellous realism is attached to a real *and* to a possible. The seamless quality of this mode, the difficulty of distinguishing between fact and invention, brings an enormous pressure to bear upon the perception of reality. For example, do the incipient rebels in *The Autumn of the Patriarch* actually slice up and dine on the cooked corpse of their comrade? Are two thousand children really kidnapped and massacred because they have discovered how the general rigs the lottery so that he can win every time? The unanswerability of the questions

---

6. Márquez, *One Hundred Years of Solitude*, trans. Gregory Rabassa (Harmondsworth: Penguin, 1970), 52-53; further citations from this work will be included in the text.

throw them onto another plane.[7] If the real is historically structured to make invisible the foreign locus of power, if the real may thus be other than what is generally visible, if official versions are just as visible and visibly "real" as unofficial versions, and if even the *potentially* real is a *compound* of the desired and the undesirable, then marvellous realism tackles the problem of truth at a level that reinvents a more acute and comprehensive mode of referentiality. The brutality of the *real* is equally the brutality and terror of that which is *immanent,* conceivable, potentially possible.[8] Besides, if the furthest reaches of imaginary construction alone can equal the heinous deformations of the real, then marvellous realism must exceed mimetic reflection in order to become an interrogative mode that can press upon the real at the point of maximum contradiction. The difficulty of fixing meaning itself is located as a part of social transactions and of ideology. In this sense the difficulty of distinguishing between fact and fiction becomes a *political* difficulty that bears upon the ethical difficulty of functioning as "real" human beings.

Marvellous realism discovers a figurative discourse that produces a knowledge inseparable from its performance in language, image, and metaphor and that can be understood in its total configuration but not necessarily explained. Through it Márquez legitimizes the status of the possible as valid knowledge. He realigns the notion of history as a set of discoverable facts with the notion of history as a field of diverse human and cultural possibility. His narratives figure a dynamic relation of past to future in which the present is seen in terms of its potential and in which the varied creative abilities of his culture are embodied in the very capaciousness of the narrative itself. The act of perception is relative yet historically determined; indeed, reality is alterable *only because* it is both relative and determined. The recognition of such relativity

---

7. During "The Violence," or *La Violencia*, in Columbia between 1946 and 1953 certain techniques of torture and death were so common that they were given names; thus *picar para tamal* referred to cutting up a living person into small pieces.

8. In an interview with Gene Bell-Villada, Márquez discusses the strike sequence in *One Hundred Years*: "That sequence sticks closely to the facts of the United Fruit strike of 1928, which dates from my childhood . . . . The only exaggeration is in the number of dead, though it does fit the proportions of the novel. So instead of hundreds dead, I upped it to thousands. But it's strange, a Columbian journalist the other day alluded in passing to 'the thousands who died in the 1928 strike.' As my Patriarch says: 'It doesn't matter if something isn't true, because eventually it will be!' " (*South* [January 1983]: 22).

is precisely the recognition that the world is open to change: it is necessary to prevent a foreclosure by a single meaning so that different meanings may become possible.

There is nothing purely formal in Márquez's choice of mode. In one sense the performative aspect of the style lies outside the text in already existing ways of seeing[9] and relies not on the shock of novelty but on shared structures of knowledge and belief. Even in its most "excessive" moments the intent of the style is neither to surprise nor to draw attention to its own uniqueness (as in Euro-American modernist fiction) but to convey the *shared* social basis of the extraordinary or singular effect.[10] Thus metaphor is treated literally: torrential tropical rain is a downpour that lasts for several years, old age and physical decay are manifest as green slime on the teeth, Colonel Buendia's distance from reality is a white chalk circle demarcating ten feet of space around him, Amaranta Ursula leads her devoted husband into Macondo "by a silk rope tied around his neck." Metaphor is turned into *event* precisely so that it will *not* be read *as* event, but folded back into metaphor as disturbing, resonant image. This is a technique that can make palpable a whole range of natural and social phenomena, and can mime the operative modalities or political effectiveness of an ideology without recourse to the mimetic mechanics of "exposure." A good example of the "naturalization" of an "unnatural" relation as well as of the necessary *re*-presentation of the already known is the collection of the sea by the Americans (not in repayment but as "surety for the interest" on unpayable debt), which is neatly parcelled and transported to Arizona. The perverse fertility of the dictator who allows this to happen—mani-

---

9. It is illuminating to see how Márquez can be read in Latin America. When he decided he would not publish another book until Pinochet quit as Chile's president, political prisoners at a detention camp near Valparaiso decided to give him a gift: "They would recreate *One Hundred Years of Solitude* in popular verse—the traditional form of verses of ten lines each. The book would be illustrated with woodcuts, a technique used by Chilean popular engravers since the nineteenth century, The wood came from used tea chests. The only tool was a small knife made from an old metal saw. The inking roll was an empty shampoo bottle filled with sand," One woodcut, done by historian Leonardo Leon, shows Innocent Erendira's wicked grandmother being carried by skeletons who represent "the exploitation of the ill-fed, ill-clothed masses" (interview in *South*: 23).

10. Márquez says, "I know very ordinary people who've read *One Hundred Years* . . . carefully and with a lot of pleasure, but with no surprise at all because, when all is said and done, I'm telling them nothing that hasn't happened in their own lives" (*The Fragrance of Guava*, 36).

fested in the algae and lichen, sea flowers and sea animals that grow on his body—portends the barrenness of the seabed. And yet I must add that the literalization of metaphor is neither an arbitrary trick nor a homogenizing device but capable of fine discriminations. The obliterated banana company workers who vanish with no trace and are declared never to have existed are the exact opposite of the nude saint, Remedios the Beauty, who ascends to heaven along with the sheets hung out to dry—just as the protean Mr. Brown of the banana company is the opposite of Melquíades with his many lives. Different kinds of gullibility and "magic" are at work here: the first kind signifies the official (alien) extinction of human value; the second represents some of the indigenous exigencies of survival.

III

Márquez's narratives direct attention to the *social, collective, performative*, and *manifold processes* by which *meaning* is *generated*, to *parole* instead of *langue*. Unlike Euro-American postmodern fiction, which directs attention to the abstract processes whereby meaning is either generated but never found or is lost in the finding (for example, Italo Calvino's *Invisible Cities*), the self-conscious textuality in Márquez's narratives is grounded in an overplus of meaning, a barely controlled semantic richness. The conscious technical complexity of the texts does not ask to be read as an effect either of the autonomy of language or text or even as a gesture toward the auto-referentiality of art. Rather, the narratives gesture toward the *autonomy* of the *story* in its *semantic* aspect: stories exist above and beyond the storytellers who relate them, the language in which they are told, and the narrative structures in which they are held; stories are as protean as the people who tell and retell them, remember and forget them, repeat or improvise them. Stories are as malleable as human history. Márquez's fiction is not encumbered by the myth of the originality either of the author or of the narrative. Stories exist inside a continuous social space within which they can be remodeled and recombined. Little stories drop from long narratives to become full-fledged tales, or full-fledged tales are compressed into cameos and reinserted into long narratives.

Márquez's marvellous realism, then, is an interactive mode based on a notion of collectivity (a social relation) which the narratives *figure forth* in several ways. The storyteller *and* the stories have a shared existence in the social matrix that is always prior to their telling. Though the narrative voices change, neither these voices nor the voice of the narrator is highly individuated in the bourgeois sense of being authored/authorized by a singular subjectivity or a single perspective. *The Autumn of the Patriarch* enacts the polyglot dialogue of different social voices in a hybrid, power-riven culture. There is a polyphony of voices—the dictator, his mother, soldiers, commanders, soothsayers, many nameless women and men—which are to be deciphered at the dialogic and representative level, not at the level of individual motivation or internal psychological consistency. The long sentence in *Autumn* contains "multiple monologues"[11] that shift between first, second, and third person, singular and plural speech, that both address and answer. A single sentence (like Spanish as a language) may incorporate, though never proportionately, the socially disparate voices of both oppressor and oppressed. In the episode of the general and the beauty from the dogfight district, the two voices are meshed, they *make* each other's separate reality. The interactive narration replicates the way in which people construct and are mutually constructed by their social relations. It also allows for a comparative standpoint which gives free "permission to narrate" from a number of places within the narrative rather than privileging any one place. No place in the narrative is exempt from scrutiny.[12] The narrative is "open" in the sense that it creates a figurative space for "interventions on the part of those represented."[13] However, this method also *controls* the generation of meaning without preempting it; by providing multiple voices within the narrative, it *fixes* the social locus of the production of meaning. This heterogeneity constitutes the particular mode of the text's orientation toward the listener/reader—a heterogeneity that telescopes but does not set out to efface the contradictions between contending social voices.

The function of the long sentence in *Autumn* is not to achieve a

---

11. Márquez claims that "the multiple monologue allows several unidentifed voices to interrupt, just as it happens in real history. For example, think of those massive caribbean conspiracies, full of endless secrets which everyone knows about" (*The Fragrance of Guava*, 86).

12. I owe this point to Ruth Frankenburg who develops it in her essay "The Challenge of *Orientalism* for Feminist Theory" (1984; unpublished).

13. Edward Said, "In the Shadow of the West," *Wedge* 7/8 (Winter/Spring 1985): 4.

higher degree of individualization and formal sophistication but to pile up stories, all part of the same story told by different voices. Each sentence is a story or even a series of stories: the sentence cannot stop because all the stories are *connected*. In Henry James's fiction syntactical elaboration is an endorsement of uncertainty and the site for the formation of an aristocratic bourgeois consciousness. In Joseph Conrad's fiction, syntactical complexity gestures toward an ineffable universe wherein mystery begins to underwrite and overdetermine imperial history. In William Faulkner's fiction the long sentence becomes a sign of the incestuous involution of the American South and simulates the relentless claustrophobia of oppression that leaves no space to breathe or time to punctuate and is impossible to stem or stop. The style of *Autumn* is closest to Faulkner; however, the ideological locus of the long sentence is finally different from all these writers. The long sentence is an index of the *fecundity* of the repressed, of the barely begun and unfinished—*not uncertain*—stories simmering beneath the strident sounds and tight enclosures of dictatorship, and so gestures toward unopened possibilities. From within the loops and whorls of narrative bursts the recognition that the stories people tell will never finish, will strain and break through the controlling constraints of grammar. The speech of many unnamed storytellers gels, coheres, contradicts, overlaps, and is retold. The long sentence shows that heteroglossia—the genuine plurality of unmerged and independent voices—is not an achievement, but a continuing struggle between contending social forces that, like the sentence, has no "natural" culmination. The sentences accumulate into a narrative that displays the collective, digressive quality of an oral narrative, which invokes the submerged life of a ravaged people and marks their glimpsed resilience. Within a hybrid culture like Latin America (unlike sealed tribal formations) the traffic between oral forms and written forms is not necessarily one-way. Though subject to the mediation of colonial and class relations, the written too finds its *way back* into orality;[14] since the

---

14. Alejo Carpentier describes hearing an illiterate black poet recite "the wonderful story of Charlemagne in a version similar to that of the *Song of Roland*" in a small fishing village on the Caribbean coast, and points out how the search for an " authentic" regional essence reveals that a "particular folkloric dance was only the contemporary manifestation of an age-old ritual or liturgy which . . . had travelled from the Mediterranean to the New World via Africa," or that "a peasant folksong was almost word for word an old frontier ballad from the days of the Moorish occupation

written and the oral are both interdependent and improvisatory, neither is simply at one with itself. Together they *begin* to describe a field within which "values are not reified but volatile"[15] and have to be returned to the whole business of living.

Further collectivity is infused at the level of the *subject* itself, in the "I" just as it is infused in the single sentence. Individuality is a truly connective definition—that which connects the subject to a collectivity—so that it is the richness of contextualization that *sets off* the notation of personal particularity and differentiates the individual, rather than the social collectivity itself as being subject to the unique perception of the bourgeois individual. The solitary ageless dictator is a "composite character[16]," the sum of several Latin American dictators, as well as an infinitely divisible character, held together by his function. The complexity of the dictator is the complexity of his contradictory social construction (as agent and pawn, protector and destroyer) and revealed interaction rather than of an "internalized" individuality wherein the full connection between private and public then needs to be wrested from the unconscious or from other "concealed" realms. This composite and divisible mode of characterization is able to show the individual shapes of tyranny and to represent dictatorship itself as a complicit social institution, diffused throughout the social fabric, both supported from within the country and propped up from without.

The ideological space Márquez's texts occupy is composed of a series of openings and closings. Causality is complex; the narratives are composed simultaneously at many levels and literally held together by repetition and retelling. The narratives return to fixed points again and again from different directions. Repetition is the mnemonic glue that binds the stories as well as that which allows the stories a point from which to depart in a *different* direction. It both preempts surprise and encodes a desire to totalize, to resist fragmentation, and to structure the new through the familiar[17] and builds upon the notion of impro-

---

of Spain," or how a researcher recently heard "peasants deep in the Cuban interior reciting past Hindustani eulogies to Count Lucanor and even a version of *King Lear*" ("The Latin American Novel," *New Left Review* 154 [November/December 1985]: 100, 106).

15. Geeta Kapur, "Art and Internationalism," *Economic and Political Weekly* 13, no. 19 (13 May 1978): 803.

16. Márquez, interview in *South*: 22.

17. Françoise Gründ also discusses the artistry of many Third world performances

visation wherein each performance is at once exceptional and also obedient to a given structure; each performance can be repeated, yet no two performances are identical, for each is always open to the transformations of a particular context. Thus repetition is the ground of both the *new* and the *same*. The stillness of repetition, even in an early piece like "Leaf Storm," is not just a sign of fatalism and despair.[18] At one level, the style pulls out onto the surface and lays bare—in conjuncture rather than in essence—the fatalistic way in which events are perceived and enacted in the consciousness of the town folk. At another level, the same memory that enables the closures of repetition also proves to be the agent of historical sense and of political understanding, that is, it provides the openings. In *One Hundred Years* José Arcadio Secundo's persistent memory is the only record that remains of the banana company massacre; the plague of insomnia which leads to collective loss of memory is equivalent to the loss of historiography, of a usable past, indeed of historical agency.[19] So Pilar Ternera reads the past in the cards. Memory functions as flexible, collective, material practice open to improvisation and personal reminiscence (but not dependent on it) and is different from the kind of memory which is central to the modernism of Eliot and of Proust. For them memory becomes the often conservative, always individuated organizing principle of poems and narratives designed to cope with cultural fragmentation, to authorize singular visions (which ironically intensify the experience of

---

that "rests assuredly in the interpretative quality of repetition" in contrast to Western theater which is "based on the sudden discovery of the unknown, the 'taking' of the spectator by surprise. The western artist and dramatist must be a master of surprise, must be a perpetual innovator, a novelist"("Ali Baba's Cave," *Semiotext(e)* 4, no. 3 [1984]: 55-56).

18. Like a slowed down whirl of the leaf storm,the story revolves around the death of the doctor through repeated narratives.The arrival of the banana company is perceived as a leaf storm which rearranges the human and material "dregs" and " rubble" of other towns into a "different and more complex town" (Márquez, *"Leaf Storm" and Other Stories*, trans. Gregory Rabassa [N.Y.: Harper and Row, 1979], 1).

19. C. V. Subbarao writes: " It is through oral traditions that the peasants preserve their history . . . . History is for them not discontinuous. Each insurgency brings not only fresh history but also fresh ways of remembering and preserving it. And it is a history as remembered by them that can help change history. The peasant is thus not only the subject of history but also a historian, presumably with his own historiography" (unpublished review of Ranajit Guha's *Elementary Aspects of the Peasant Insurgency*,1984). See also Jean Franco on the radical role of oral narratives, especially for the Indians in Latin America, in "Dependency Theory and Literary History: The Case of Latin America," *Minnesota Review* 5 (Fall 1975): 68-69.

fragmentation), to preserve a "monumental civilization" as "heritage" through quotation, and to relive it through nostalgia.

Collectivity in-forms the thematic and structural preoccupation with the enigma or the unsolved puzzle in Márquez's narratives. What is problematized is not meaning "itself," but the recovery of meaning in specific contexts. The emphasis is on why, in a particular situation, an unequivocal answer cannot be found. The lampoons of *In Evil Hour* reveal what everybody knows, the familiar becomes unfamiliar and takes on the character of a revelation, but the authorship of the lampoons remains a mystery. The priest says that the lampoons are a "terrorism of the moral order;" Cassandra the soothsayer finds out that they are written by everybody and nobody; Judge Arcadio, the self-styled detective, knows that the clues are so varied that it cannot be individuals or even a conspiracy; the mayor simply uses the opportunity to reimpose a fascist rule on the town. The lampoons (like the subversive leaflets) are an efflorescence of the submerged life of the town—what is known has to be continually brought to the surface and reunderstood.

The Chronicle of a Death Foretold is also structured as an unsolved enigma: the whole town is shown trying to understand *why* Santiago Nasar is murdered *after* the virtual complicity of the entire town in not preventing the murder has been previously established. People gather in strange surrender to witness a murder that has been announced; though the murderers wish to be prevented, even the priest does not stop them. Guilt is collective. The town wants to understand its own role and responsibility in the matter: "None of us could go on living without an exact knowledge of the place and mission assigned to us by fate."[20] And even as people claim to understand the motive for the murder— honor in a male chauvinist society which requires brides to be virgins—the murder obviously remains senseless. The narration, with its attentive, "factual" rendering of many voices by a single narrator, and its scrupulous reconstruction of the movements of both the victims and the killers, consciously attempts to compensate for its own inadequacy. The inability of the narrator or of the town *finally* to understand becomes in this case equivalent to the townspeople's inability to change. The unsolved enigma, at this level, is not an index of an indeterminable reality, but the failure of the historical will of a people.

---

20. Márquez, *The Chronicle of a Death Foretold*, trans. Gregory Rabassa (New York: Alfred Knopf, 1983), 96; further citations from this work will be included in the text.

At another level, the text exploits the colonial notion of the enigmatic "native" (for instance, the mysterious Arab or the inscrutable Chinese). The enigmatic native is a familiar Orientalizing trope that encodes, first, the incapacity of the Western consciousness to apprehend the "native" save as alterity, and, second, the reserve, resistance, interested information, or secrecy that the colonizer repeatedly encountered and that probably indicated both a recalcitrance and a conscious strategy on the part of the "natives." The stereotype of the enigma—in its origin, if not in its use—is at bottom dialogic. Again the colonizers' notations of the enigmatic " other" are systematically accompanied by vigorous attempts (by missionaries, anthropologists, ethnographers, and administrators)[21] to penetrate into the substratum of truth. So the links between the female (the powerless and the colonized), chastity (the hitherto unconquered and unknown), enigma (the impenetrable object of scrutiny), and colonization are deep historical ones. The very form of *Chronicle of a Death* is *gendered*: structured as female, the form becomes a critique of the content (the subjection of women to the violating codes of a chauvinist society), and functions to protect the already violated woman from further violation or further surveillance. The question of whether Santiago Nasar is guilty and, if not, then who deflowered Angela Vicario ("raised to suffer") remains unanswered. The unanswered question is not an invitation to further guesswork, but addresses itself to whether the question itself is worth asking or is necessary to answer, whether the question itself is not the first in a series of violations of which the murder is a culmination.

At a third level, to maintain the text as enigma is also to maintain a resistance to being construed as an object of scrutiny. The enigma produces strain and anxiety in those who seek to inspect and understand it, and it rejects the instrumentality of Western "sight"; it exercises power by sustaining insecurity and by openly refusing to surrender its "meaning." Enigma, as structure, endures by virtue of what it withholds, retains the attention it has caught, and acquires a political stamina. The structure of the unsolved enigma in *Chronicle of a Death* is more than a mode of collectivity: it is crafted both as a *resistant* mode and as an *interrogative* mode, both as an *outer* imposition (the way whole continents may

---

21. See James Clifford, "Power and Dialogue in Ethnography," in *Observers Observed: Essays in Ethnographic Fieldwork,* ed. George Stocking (Madison, Wis.: University of Wisconsin Press, 1983), 147.

remain subject to dominant ways of seeing and not seeing) and as an *inner* imposition (to maintain oneself as an enigma *for* oneself is to fail in political understanding and social will). Such a structure can convey simultaneously a sense of latent energy and of lethargy; it can bring the pressure of *not knowing* to bear with a certain intensity on the problems of *not doing*. To not see is to abnegate responsibllity, not to be seen is to be isolated or to be left to perish, a fate that may not be merely individual but collective. The investigating magistrate, tracing the sequence of events leading to the death of Santiago Nasar (a man whom all were watching but never quite seeing), writes *"Fatality makes us invisible"* (113).

IV

The preoccupation with circular time and the rejection of linear time in Márquez's narratives are often read as evidence either of his fatalism or of his primitivism. However, the absence of a single linear time need not be read as the absence of a historical consciousness but rather as the operation of a different kind of historical consciousness. The play of linear time with circular time achieves its cognitive force through marvellous realism's capacity to generate and manage various kinds of alignments, tensions, and discontinuities between sequential and nonsequential time.

Márquez's critique of the linear time of rationality and progress in *One Hundred Years* is leveled from inside the suspicion, well-founded in the Latin American context, that the development of science and technology within the structures of neocolonialism may guarantee continuous dependence. There is a "marvellous" passage where bananas become the fruit of empiricism and thence the fruit of empire. After eating a bunch of bananas, Mr. Herbert assesses Macondo's potential:

> When he finished the first bunch he asked them to bring him another. Then he took a small case with optical instruments out of the toolbox that he always carried with him. With the suspicious attention of a diamond merchant he examined the banana meticulously, dissecting it with a special scalpel, weighing the pieces on a pharmacist's scale, and calculating its breadth with a gunsmith's calipers. Then he took a series of instruments out of the chest with which he measured the temperature, the level of humidity in the

atmosphere, and the intensity of the light . . . but he did not say anything that allowed anyone to guess his intentions. (211)

The talismanic notion of technology as a type of "magic" art or as the required miracle that will bring with it the wonders of prosperity is played off against the possibility of an indigenous alternative science which does not materialize. Local attempts to construct such a science—the attempts to use magnets to discover gold or to use the daguerreotype to establish the existence of God—are shown to be romantic failed attempts that can, at best, offer only a utopian faith in the possibility of rediscovering one's own reality.

However, the wonders of technology that "dazzle" the inhabitants of Macondo—the "frightful" train that is "like a kitchen dragging a village behind it," the bulbs, the phonographs, and the telephones—are not presented merely as an instance of primitive naiveté, but as a historical irony. Western technology does not cross the seas as a mere emblem of "progress," but as a broker of profit that easily represents itself as magical and opportunely insinuates its own calculable properties as miraculous. Christopher Columbus has no qualms about representing his scientific knowledge of the stars as shamanistic power:

> With a solemnity worthy of the adventures in boys' books, he takes advantage of his knowledge of the date of an imminent lunar eclipse. Stranded on the Jamaican coast for eight months, he can no longer persuade the Indians to bring him provisions without his having to pay for them; he then threatens to steal the moon from them, and on the evening of February 29, 1504, he begins to carry out his threat, before the terrified eyes of the caciques . . . .
> His success is instantaneous.[22]

Cortes's conquest of Mexico is no doubt made easier by his claim that his information comes not from human informers, but from the supernatural realm that communicates with him through a ship's chart and a compass.[23] Mr. Herbert and his captive-balloons (a business "which takes him halfway around the world with excellent profits") belong to this hoary tradition of magical invention and intervention; he gets his come-

---

22. Tzvetan Todorov, *The Conquest of America*, trans. Richard Howard (New York: Harper and Row, 1984), 19.
23. Ibid. 111-12.

uppance when the inhabitants of Macondo, working on a different cultural logic of exposure to magic, come to consider his "invention *backward*" after having seen and tried the gypsies' "flying carpets" (211; my emphasis).

Through the expansion of time beyond linearity, Márquez moves beyond the simplifying oppositions of rational and irrational, and attempts to introduce the notion of time as a structure of values, as in his treatment of death. There are two kinds of death in *One Hundred Years:* first, the horrible brevity of the massacres of the civil war, colonial rule, and the imperial fruit company, and, second, an older, integrated, more acceptable way of dying. The first José Buendía dies slowly, publicly under a chestnut tree. Deaths are expected, accompanied by premonition and warning. Prudencio Aguilar is killed in a duel; and when, after dying, he seeks his assassin for company, the living understand and accommodate him:

> When he finally identified him [Aguilar], startled that the dead also aged, José Arcadio Buendía felt himself shaken by nostalgia. "Prudencio" he exclaimed. "You've come from a long way off!" After many years of death the yearning for the living was so intense, the need for company so pressing, so terrifying the nearness of that other death which exists within death, that Prudencio Aguilar had ended up loving his worst enemy. (76)

This older form of death bears remarkable similarities to the prebourgeois, medieval forms of dying in Europe described so brilliantly by Philip Ariès in his book *In the Hour of Our Death.* The natural and daily presence of the dying and the dead among the living, the popular belief in an intermediate space between death and the definite conclusion of life—in sum, a death that is neither a complete separation nor a total annihilation is, with the emergence of the "secular" individual in Europe, replaced by a notion of dying as anxious and privatized and of death as an end, as decomposition, and as stigma. In *One Hundred Years* the prebourgeois (or "marvelous") death functions along an axis of value that it also betokens; it comes to signify a collective management of the time of mortality and cannot be taken literally as a gullible inability to distinguish the real from the not real. The same people who write letters and send verbal messages through Amaranta to their dead, refuse to accept the "resurrection" of a dead actor in a new role in a different film; and when it is explained that cinema is an illusion, they refuse to waste time "to weep over the acted out misfortunes of imaginary beings" (209).

Further, Márquez attempts to develop a mode that can take cognizance of time as it is experienced. Prophecy, the structural obverse of memory, is not merely a means of self-enclosure within a relentless circularity, but part of a complex notion of causality that takes into account both the perceived concurrence of mythic time within a cultural simultaneity and the felt experience of enclosure within a seemingly deterministic logic. Prophecy, as notation, may be taken to signify the popular perception of events to be one in a series of extra-economic determinations that make up what we call history.

The narratives are obsessed with the quality of time and derive a special intensity from prolonging stagnation, oppression, decay. On a political level the stagnant time in *One Hundred Years* is imposed by a determining history that puts Latin America out-of-date, keeps it in thrall, fixes it in another time. Stagnant time is both indigenous time *and* alien time, in the sense that it is *re*-imposed by foreign domination. Further, since linear time is also embedded in Macondo as the history of Euro-American intrusions in some form, and so as its *own* history, there is no such thing as pure or uncontaminated indigenous time. It is significant that the concurrent or circular time of Macondo is not only invaded or interrupted by the gypsies who bring alchemy, but also exists in dialectical relation with the several entries of linear time. Thus the banana company builds a separate enclave within Macondo, fences off circular time in order to exploit it. Linear time is as "impure" and as oppressive as circular time.

Finally, if circular time is a metaphor for historical inevitability, then it is important to notice that it does come to an *end.* Pilar Ternara perceives incest as a cyclic retardation of linear time: "the history of the family was a machine with unavoidable repetitions, a turning wheel that would have gone on spilling into eternity, were it not for the progressive and irremediable *wearing* of the axle" (365; my emphasis). If circularity wears out, becomes bankrupt like other historical fates, so does linearity. The conclusion of *One Hundred Years* at once images and ironizes a decadent European apocalypticism, described by Vyacheslav Ivanov as the "feeling, at once oppressive and exalting, of being the last in a series."[24] The

24. Vyacheslav Ivanov, "Correspondence from Opposite Corners," quoted by Renato Poggioli in *The Theory of the Avant-Garde,* trans. Gerald Fitzgerald (Cambridge, Mass.: Harvard University Press, 1968), 75.

conclusion is poised in a liminal space and in an in-between time, which, having broken out of the binary opposition between circular and linear, gives a third space and a different time the chance to emerge. Similarly, the end of the dictator's life in *The Autumn of the Patriarch* is described as "the good news that the uncountable time of eternity has come to an end" (206). The end of eternity is the end of *known*, even conceivable time; it comes out on the other side of both the cyclic and the linear. The irrevocability of this end as end insists on a new beginning, but the modalities of the new or clues as to how it will come about are absent.

The power of Márquez's narratives lies in the insistent pressure of *freedom* as the *absent horizon*—which is neither predictable nor inevitable. The way marvellous realism figures collectivity and takes metaphor to excess indicates a reality that exceeds the space allotted to it by its own history. The excess of meaning bursting out of its present time into an imaginable (or probable) time exerts immense pressure on his narratives. This may be an absent freedom, but it is not an abstract freedom: it is precisely that which is made present and possible by its absence—the lives that people have never lived *because* of the lives they are forced to live or have chosen to live. That which is desired and that which exists, the sense of abundance and the sense of waste, are dialectically related.

V

Salman Rushdie's narratives may employ a comparable nonmimetic mode, but they can neither be bracketed with Márquez nor seen as continuous with Western postmodernism, and need to be "contextualized" separately. Here I can undertake no more than to sketch in his problematic historical location. If Márquez creates a subsuming and transformative mode that, drawing on substantive indigenous narrative modes, can also rework and relegate the epistemologies of both realism and modernism, Rushdie's narratives play provocatively with disparate ways of seeing, yet are riven by the strain of double coding for different audiences. Further, drawing on culturally distinct modes, they are caught between different ideological systems, pressured by different demands. In the attempt to negotiate two terrains Rushdie's narratives confirm and unsettle much on either side.

The diverse, diffuse, and class-divided relationships with colonial culture and the English language, in part the product of a mode of colonization unaccompanied by any large-scale influx of British settlers in India, make Rushdie's insider/outsider position both representative and precarious. The resident middle class in India can be similarly Anglicized, alienated or isolated, and equivocal about its cultural alignments. In some sense Rushdie represents a postcolonial middle-class ethos and is shaped by its contradictions. The introduction of first realist, then modernist modes under the aegis of colonialism in nineteenth-century India occurred in contradictory combination with insistent reconstructions of precolonial culture. These latter were necessitated as much by the cultural formation of this class as by the political economy of imperialism, which has since prolonged the moment of "uneven" development long after the end of direct political rule. The notable cultural diversity of India was and remains subject both to fabricated divisions and to imposed homogeneities in the interests of political control. Rushdie also undertakes an archaeological (and necessarily distanced) excavation of an emigré's past, working from within a contingent modernism imposed by cultural displacement and compelled to accept its hybrid identity. In his use and remaking of English as an Indian vernacular, as well as in his conscious arrogation of an "international" literary ancestry, he attempts to break from both unconsious influence (the site of more devious cultural insinuation) and a parochial nationalism (often tied in binary relation to its adversary Western modes.)

The social formation of the Indian subcontinent, then, is in many ways amenable to Rushdie's fabulous realism. Rushdie draws on extant narrative modes—the epic and the folktale. The informality of the epic structure—the scope for interpolation, digression, accretion, in addition to its self-ascribed status as history or *itihaas* (for example, the *Mahabharata*)—has allowed it in the past to represent ideological collectivities as well as to permit the expression of contesting world views. The serial character—that is, stories nesting inside and/or leading to each other—of folktales (for example, the *Panchatantra* or the *Katha Sarit Sagar*) and their improvisatory, ingenuous yet generic, underindividuated "oral" narrators are a significant indigenous resource for Rushdie. Further, his fabulation finds a fertile ground not just in classical and oral culture but also in the social perception of art.

This perception does not always constitute the real and the not-real as a binary opposition, but as coexistent; and in it, sacred and secular art forms can be read as miracle or *chamatkar*, signifying not the presence of the miraculous per se but an elasticity and a capacity for wonder on the part of the listener/viewer/reader that can give the quality of a revelation. As an aesthetic of creativity and response this is quite different from the consciously engineered "surprise" of the unexpected juxtaposition that is central to Euro-American modernism. Modernism in fact derives its energy from a steady opposition to realism: realism is the implied or habitual mode of perception that has to be countered or subverted.

In *Midnight's Children* Rushdie attempts to play with these two ways of seeing and so, perforce, with two different conceptions of the subject. The form of the narrative has an epic intention; unfinished stories give a sense of unending possibility; the narrator's choice of story is presented as merely one of several. The totalizing yet open epic structure exists cheek-by-jowl with an epistemological mode (based, like Western modernism, on an acknowledged yet decentred realism) that privileges faulty sight, peripheral or incomplete vision, limited perception, deliberate fallibility, and the splinter effect—in short, with a covertly totalizing quasi-modernist aesthetic of the fragment. To some extent, the narrative finds its dynamic in the modernist challenge to premodern forms and vice versa.

The narrator, Saleem Sinai, is also split through the center. On the one hand, he is a scribe and storyteller, and his favorite god is Ganesh—not surprising considering Saleem's nose and occupation. His narrative method combines the compendious knowledge of a pundit with a preauthorized orality: he reads out what is written to the nonliterate Padma, as well as writes what he hears, and so attempts to forge a conscious relation between the oral and the written. The narrator and the narration toy with the idea of the writer as expressing a transindividual consciousness. The narrator humbly makes repeated attempts to establish the story as larger than himself. But the narrator and the narration also make different kinds of moves and are imbricated in a different kind of "self" consciousness. The narrative incorporates the criteria by which the text might be judged, speculates on the narrator's motivation, biographical formation, and "role, " and ponders the status of fiction vis-à-vis the "real"—displays the characteristic modernist preoccupation with the composition, fictiveness, and self-reflexiveness of narrative.

The conflation of an "oral" narrator with a modernist narrator leads to an interesting parodic result—they send up each other. If Ganesh breeds with Tristram Shandy to hatch Saleem Sinai, then who is the butt of the joke? The ineffectual Shandyesque Saleem, who despite asserted humility makes repeated attempts to establish himself as more important than the story, to present himself as the agent of history, parodies both the historical aggrandizement of the (impotent) individual—the paradigmatic protagonist of nineteenth century realist fiction—and the vaunted epicality of his own narrative. The often indulgent autoreferentiality of the postmodern idiom is opened up for inspection and irony, especially as the narrative's own substantive alignment is with the specificity of colonial and contemporary experience on the Indian subcontinent. Finally, by wearing its technique on the sleeve, as it were, the narrative is able to display to an Indian middle class the doubleness of its own parentage, the making of its urban habitat, of its popular culture, and of its "despair"—an image of its own peculiar hybrid formation wherein too many things have "leaked" into each other. However, somewhere in this region where two ways of seeing intersect lies the curious desire of the narrative to confirm both ways of seeing. While the parodic mode works at the expense of both epistemologies, the allegorical mode (albeit problematized and contested), which sets up the narrator as both child and fate of independent India, attempts to conjoin the two. Saleem Sinai is to be at once the voice of the individual and of a collectivity, to be spectator and participant, to be unique and representative.

Such a position is precarious precisely because neither parodic rejection nor large-hearted assimilation is a sufficient confrontation of the formation of the Indian middle-class subject, which, though hybrid, is not identical with the "classic" formation of the Western bourgeois subject. Even within the Anglicized section of the middle class the bourgeois subject is but tenuously in place. Its alienations have a different cultural, social, and political genesis and so are of a different order. The repetitive, obsessive quality of a fragmented individual consciousness, though grafted on, does not always stick, as in the amnesiac Sunderbans episode where Saleem, in Buddha-like apathy, regresses into an inner landscape. The strain of negotiating the treacherous terrain between two worlds surfaces in the way the Sunderbans episode tropes the journey through the jungle/hell as an outer projection of inner torment, and almost falls into the psychologizing metaphors, which go at least as far back as Conrad, where the darkness within the imperial bourgeois consciousness becomes identical with the fetid darkness of the jungle. Again the narrative embraces all mythologies in an effort to activate an essentially plural or secular conception of Indianness; it even appears at times to grasp Indianness as if it were a torrent of religious, class, and regional diversity rather than a complex articulation of cultural difference, contradiction, and political use that can scarcely be idealized. Through the diversity of its narrative techniques and the diversity it seeks to record, *Midnight's Children* effects something that verges on an indigenized "tropicalization" of the subcontinent.

Rushdie's is a fertile project. It relies on the received or preexisting transformative capacity of indigenous narratives and readers; but can it be said to be itself transformative, to effect a different mode of understanding, to offer to remake the reader? Running aground on the shoals of parody and allegory, he scarcely uses his freedom as a professed fabulist. The totalizing potential of his chosen form cohabits uneasily with a modernist epistemology of the fragment, the specific perspectivism of the bourgeois subject. However, in the ability and attempt to play both with different conceptions of the subject and with different ways of seeing, a play licensed by this historical moment as well as by the intersection between the non-Western and the postmodern, his narratives open the way toward more incisive descriptions of interpenetrative cultural formation.

VI

What are the modes of access into such nonmimetic fiction for contemporary Euro-American, academic, poststructuralist discourse? In what sense are the openings provided by the fiction itself and in what sense are they constructed by the critical discourse?

As my argument maintains, the hybrid writer is already open to two worlds and is constructed within the national and international, political and cultural systems of colonialism and neocolonialism. To be hybrid is to understand and question as well as to represent the pressure of such historical placement. The hybrid, lived-in simultaneity of Latin America, both historical and contradictory, is also the ground for political analysis and change. And yet for these same reasons, hybridity as a position is particularly vulnerable to reclassification. The "modern" moments of such nonmimetic fiction emerge in fact from different social formations and express or figure different sets of social relations. Though forged within the insistent specificity of a localized relation, the very differences of such fiction are read as techniques of "novelty" and "surprise" in the West. Novelty guarantees assimilation into the line of postmodern writers not only because the principle of innovation is also the principle of the market in general,[25] but also because the postmodern obsession with antimimetic forms is always on the lookout for new modes of "self" fracture, for new versions of the self-locating, self-disrupting text. From this decontextualizing vantage point various formal affinities can easily be abstracted from a different mode of cognition; the nonmimetic can be read as antimimetic, difference can easily be made the excuse for sameness. The transformative spaces in a text—that is, those which do not readily give up their meaning—are the crucial node of its depoliticization. The enigma in Márquez's narratives can be read as a radical contextual figure or can be recuperated as yet another self-reflexive instance of the postmodern meaning/representation problematic. The synchronic time-space of postmodernism becomes a modality for collapsing other kinds of time—most notably, the politically charged time of transition. And further, since postmodernism both privileges the present and valorizes indeterminacy as a cognitive mode, it also deflates social contradiction into forms of ambiguity or deferral, instates arbitrary juxtaposition or collage as historical "method," preempts change by fragmenting the ground of praxis.[26]

However, it is difficult to understand postmodernism without at the same time understanding the appropriative history of Western "high" modernism. Raymond Williams points out that modernism is governed by the "unevenness . . . of a class society," and this—along with its mobility and dislocations, which find a home within the "imperial

25. Nicos Hadjinicolaou, "On the Ideology of Avant-gardism," *Praxis* 6 (1982): 56.
26. For a more detailed discussion, see Kumkum Sangari, "The Changing Text," *Journal of Arts and Ideas* 8 (July-September 1984): 73-74.

metropolis"—leads to the characteristic experience of "estrangement and exposure."[27] Nonetheless, modernism also enters into and is governed by another set of relationships. Modernism is a major act of cultural self-definition, made at a time when colonial territories are being reparceled and emergent nationalisms are beginning to present the early outlines of decolonization. As a cultural ensemble, modernism is assembled, in part, through the internalization of jeopardized geographical territory—which is now incorporated either as "primitive" image/metaphor or as mobile nonlinear structure. Though intended as a critique, such incorporation often becomes a means for the renovation of bourgeois ideology, especially with the institutionalization of modernism. Ironically, the "liberating" possibilities of an international, oppositional, and "revolutionary" modernism for early-twentieth-century "Third World" writers and artists came into being at a time when modernism was itself recuperating the cultural products of non-western countries largely within an aesthetic of the fragment. The modernism they borrowed was already deeply implicated in their own history, being based partly on a random appropriation and remodeling of the "liberating" and energizing possibilities of their own indigenous "traditions."[28] Not only have the critical practices which have developed around modernism been central to the development of an assimilative bourgeois consciousness, a powerful absorptive medium for transforming colliding realities into a cosmopolitan, nomadic, and pervasive "sensibility," but the freewheeling appropriations of modernism also coincide with and are dependent on the rigorous documentation, inventory, and reclassification of "Third World" cultural products by the museum/library archive.[29] Modernism as it exists is inconceivable without the archive, and the archive as it exists is inconceivable without the political and economic relations of colonialism.

The modernist problems of knowing and representation continue to

---

27. Raymond Williams, *Writing in Society* (London: Verso, 1984), 221-23.

28. K. V. Akshara demonstrates how "traditional Indian theatre techniques were exported from India and are now being imported in the form of post-colonial influences," in "Western Responses to Traditional Indian Theatre," *Journal of Arts And Ideas* 8 (July-September 1984).

29. For a documentation and critique of some aspects of this process, see James Clifford "Histories of the Tribal and Modern," *Art in America* 73, no. 4 (April 1985) 164-77, and Hal Foster, *Recodings: Art, Spectacle, Cultural Politics* (Port Townsend, Wa.: Bay Press, 1985), 181-209.

inform postmodernism. Though the organizing role of individual perception—which could legitimate perspective—and the cohesive role and concept of "art" have lost their ability to bind the aesthetic of the fragment into a "whole" and are indeed challenged and "unmade" by postmodernism, there are distinct ideological and historical continuities between the two. Not only has the destabilizing of the image that modernism effected now been extended into the prose of postmodern critical theory and refined anew, but a postmodern aesthetic continues to raid the "inarticulate" cultural forms of the "Third World," to "textualize" a geographically lost terrain (for example, Roland Barthes's *Empire of Signs*).

Postmodern skepticism is the complex product of a historical conjuncture and is constructed as both symptom and critique of the contemporary economic and social formation of the West. But postmodernism does have a tendency to universalize its epistemological preoccupations—a tendency that appears even in the work of critics of radical political persuasion. On the one hand, the world contracts into the West; a Eurocentric perspective (for example, the post-Stalinist, anti-teleological, anti-master narrative dismay of Euro-American Marxism) is brought to bear upon "Third World" cultural products; a "specialized" skepticism is carried everywhere as cultural paraphernalia and epistemological apparatus, as a way of seeing; and the postmodern problematic becomes *the* frame through which the cultural products of the rest of the world are seen. On the other hand, the West expands into the world; late capitalism muffles the globe and homogenizes (or threatens to) all cultural production[30]—this, for some reason, is one "master narrative" that is seldom dismantled as it needs to be if the differential economic, class, and cultural formation of "Third World" countries is to be taken into account. The writing that emerges from this position, however critical it may be of colonial discourses, gloomily disempowers the "nation" as an enabling idea and relocates the impulses for change as everywhere and nowhere. Because it sees the West as an engulfing "center," it perpetuates the notion of the "Third World" as a residue and as a "periphery" that must eternally palpitate the center. This center-periphery perspective is based on a homology

---

30. See, for example, Frederic Jameson, "Literary Innovation and Modes of Production: A Commentary," *Modern Chinese Literature* 1, no. 1 (1984): 76.

between economic and cultural domination, and like the discursive structure of self and other, cannot but relegate the "Third World" to the false position of a permanent yet desired challenge to (or subversion of) a suffocating Western sovereignty.[31] From there it continues to nourish the self-defining critiques of the West, conducted in the interest of ongoing disruptions and reformulations of the self-ironizing bourgeois subject.

Such skepticism does not take into account either the fact that the postmodern preoccupation with the crisis of meaning is not everyone's crisis (even in the West) or that there are different modes of de-essentialization which are socially and politically grounded and mediated by separate perspectives, goals, and strategies for change in other countries. Postmodern skepticism dismantles the "unifying" intellectual traditions of the West—whether liberal humanism or Marxism—but in the process denies to all the truth of or the desire for totalizing narratives. There is no necessary or obvious connection, as is often assumed, between the decentering of unitary discourses (or, the projects of the Enlightenment and modernity) and an "international" radicalism. To believe that a critique of the centered subject and of representation is equal to a critique of colonialism and its accoutrements is in fact to disregard the different historical formation of subjects and ways of seeing that have actually obtained from colonization; and this often leads to a naive identification of all nonlinear forms with those of the decentered postmodern subject. Further, the crisis of legitimation (of meaning and knowledge systems) becomes a strangely vigorous "master narrative" in its own right, since it sets out to rework or "process" the knowledge systems of the world in its own image; the postmodern "crisis" becomes authoritative because it is inscribed within continuing power relations and because, as an energetic mode of "acquisitive cognition,"[32] it is deeply implicated in the structure of institutions. Indeed, it threatens to become just as imperious as bourgeois humanism, which was an ideological maneuver based on a series of affirmations, whereas postmodernism appears to be a maneuver based on a series of nega-

---

31. This is in fact the resounding note on which Hal Foster concludes (*Recodings*, 208).

32. See Jean-Christophe Agnew, "The Consuming Vision of Henry James," in *The Culture of Consumption: Critical Essays in American History*, eds. Richard Wrightman Fox and T. J. Jackson Lears (New York: Pantheon, 1983), 74.

ations and self-negations through which the West reconstrues its identity as "a play of projections, doublings, idealizations, and rejections of a complex, shifting otherness."[33] Significantly, the disavowal of the objective and instrumental modalities of the social sciences occurs in the academies at a time when *usable* knowledge is gathered with growing certainty and control by Euro-America through advanced technologies of information retrieval from the rest of the world.[34] In a somewhat pontifical diagnosis of the crisis of legitimation and the loss of credibility in the "grand narratives" of emancipation, beginning with the French Revolution and culminating in Marxism, Lyotard concludes that "our role as thinkers is to deepen our understanding of what goes on in language, to critique the vapid idea of information, to reveal an irremediable opacity at the very core of language."[35] To take such postmodern skepticism seriously may well entail stepping outside it in order to examine how, on the one hand, the operations of neo- colonialism (based on such vapid information) continue to be confidently carried out abroad and, on the other, "return" as the crisis of meaning/representation/legitimation at home. Postmodernism, like modernism, may well turn out to be, in some respects, another internalization of the international role of the West. If the appropriation and internalization of the unknowability (or undecidability) produced in the contested and contradictory social space of gender, class,[36] and imperial relations in nineteenth-century Euro-America provided both models of the self and grounds for the epistemological and ontological preoccupation of modernism, then perhaps the question of the *present locales* of undecidability is an urgent one.

The history of the West and the history of the non-West are by now irrevocably different and irrevocably shared. Both have shaped and been shaped by each other in specific and specifiable ways. The linear time of the West or the project of modernity did not simply mummify

33. James Clifford, review of *Orientalism*, by Edward Said, in *History and Theory* 12, no. 2 (1980): 220.

34. See Arturo Escobar, "Discourse and Power in Development: Michel Foucault and the Relevance of his work to the Third World," *Alternatives* 10, no. 3 (Winter 1984-85): 387.

35. Jean-François Lyotard, "Rules and Paradoxes and a Svelte Appendix," *Cultural Critique*, no. 5 (Winter 1986-87): 216.

36. Kumkum Sangari, "Of Ladies, Gentlemen, and the Short Cut: *The Portrait of a Lady*," in *Women/Image/Text*, ed. Lola Chatterjee (Delhi: Trianka, 1986).

or overlay the indigenous times of colonized countries, but was itself open to alteration and reentered into discrete cultural combinations. Thus the history of Latin America is also the history of the West and informs its psychic and economic itinerary. The cultural projects of *both* the West and the non-West are implicated in a larger history. If the crisis of meaning in the West is seen as the product of a historical conjuncture, then perhaps the refusal either to export it or to import it may be a meaningful gesture, at least until we can replace the stifling monologues of self and other (which, however disordered or decentered, remain the orderly discourses of the bourgeois subject) with a genuinely dialogic and dialectical history that can account for the formation of different selves and the construction of different epistemologies.

Minority Discourse and the African Collective: Some Examples from Latin American and Caribbean Literature

Josaphat Bekunuru Kubayanda

1. Origins and Definitions

Historically the seeds of Caribbean and Latin-American minority discourse and the African collective can be said to have been sown when Fray Bartolomé de Las Casas, by a spectacular (mis)use of what Césaire calls "Christian pedantry,"[1] recommended to the Spanish crown the importation of "more robust" native Africans to replace the "weaker" American Indians on the harsh plantations and mines in the New World. That single and singular (mis)judgement for which Las Casas later repented was, nevertheless, generally in keeping with the insensitivities of an expansionist Europe for which Africa and the rest of the then so-called "unknown" world represented something outside the possibilities of human civilization. Soon enough and in the long run, Las Casas's solution to the Indian labor problem was to have all kinds of complex consequences of a racial, moral, economic, sociopolitical and, least expected, literary nature. This article deals with some of the literary developments arising from that early European encounter with Africa in the New World. What is the nature of the imaginative writing in the present century of the descendants of those Africans who were, by the nature and effect of the colonial legal and political discourses, marginalized

---

1. Aimé Césaire, *Discourse on Colonialism*, trans. Joan Pinkam (New York: Monthly Review Press, 1972), 11.

and thus denied access to the Spanish language, Spanish official history, and Spanish power? In what ways can this literature be characterized as "minor" in the context of post-independence Latin America, a sub-continent which is in and of itself on the periphery? Why and how is this Black literary production different from dominant discourse?

One way to respond to these questions is to return in a general sense to Las Casas's formulation and to its impact on Black consciousness in Latin America. It seems to me that in theory, at least, there is almost no way a Black minority discourse of the Americas can be separated from the historical collective memory of the propositions of some of the learned secular and religious humanists of Spain, or from the specific legacies of slavery, dispersal, and other forms of marginalization. There is little chance that it can be divorced altogether from protest thought.[2] The union of writing, memory, and protest is what Césaire, for instance, suggests in his seminal study, *Discourse on Colonialism*: this, too, is the major concern of the novel *Chombo* (1981) by the Panamanian Carlos Guillermo Wilson, the son of immigrant parents from the West Indies for whom Spanish remains, to a large extent, the language of the majority culture.[3] The novel is about the experiences of those West Indians and their offsprings who were brought to build the Panama Canal. There is in it a particular passage which Wilson himself considers to be central to his preoccupations as a novelist.[4] It has to do with a female character, Abena Mansa Adesimbo, whose origins can be traced back to Jamaica and further back to the Gold Coast (modern Ghana). Like all the 100,000 Panamanian West Indians who helped to construct the canal, Abena's identity, her "africanidad,"[5] is portrayed as threatened with fragmentation and extinction by the dominant social and political discourse of the majority that is represented textually by the Catholic Church and by a secular Eurocentric order. Contrary to the wishes of the old woman Nenén, and in compliance with the pressures of the dominant society, Abena symbolically rejects the African

---

2. See, for instance, August Meier et al., eds., *Black Protest Thought in the Twentieth Century*, 2nd ed. (Indianapolis: The Bobbs-Merrill Company, 1971).

3. Carlos Guillermo Wilson, *Chombo* (Miami: Ediciones Universal, 1981).

4. At the thirty-nineth Kentucky Foreign Language Conference, 24 April 1986, Wilson read this piece from his novel and commented upon it extensively.

5. Wilson, *Chombo*, 59.

name given to her child on the grounds that it would make integration problematic for her baby. Thus, the latter is baptized against the wishes of Nenén whose voice throughout the novel is strengthened by the African collective, by the consciousness of the African element within a text and context where it is, as it were, under siege:

> On the eve of the Catholic baptism of the child, Nenén again showed her rejection of a religion which had allowed the bloody invasion of Ethiopia, and worse still, she rejected the priest of that religion — Bartolomé de las Casas — who had ruled in favor of the enslavement of Africans in the sugar plantations of the Americas.[6]

Thus it seems that a primary concern of this minority writing is with the apprehension of African humanity within particular spatio-temporal coordinates in which "no one colonizes innocently,"[7] in which the "threat to person and personality remains a complex arrangement of absurd hostilities and fateful consequences,"[8] in which the African is scathed and bruised in multiple ways.

> Between colonizer and colonized there is room only for forced labor, intimidation, pressure, the police, taxation, theft, rape, compulsory crops, contempt, mistrust, arrogance, self-complacency, swinishness, brainless elites, degraded masses. No human contact, but relations of domination and submission . . .[9]

Evidently the concept of the African collective as source of a Black Latin American minority utterance will not be properly grasped without a reference to this Césairean idea of "relations of domina-

---

6. Ibid., 59.
7. Césaire, *Discourse*, 17.
8. Lemuel A. Johnson, "The Dilemma of Presence in Black Diaspora Literature: A Comparativist Reading of Arnoldo Palacios' *Las estrellas son negras*," *Afro-Hispanic Review* 1, no. 1 (Jan. 1982): 3.
9. Césaire, *Discourse*, 27. Minority theory of discourse in general has, of necessity, to do with a critique of domination. One of the European theorists with something of direct relevance to minority discourse is Michel Foucault. Foucault sees and grasps the complexities of our present and our past, points out the power relations of our past and of our present, and suggests, like Césaire, the need to construct discourses of resistance.

tion and submission." The African collective is coextensive with historical referentiality and with both the real and preceived processes of discriminatory differentiation that Césaire's words suggest, that is, the New World type of social relationships in which cultural and racial differences sometimes appear harmful rather than helpful.

Minority discourse necessarily reflects cultural contacts and the problems that they generate and nurse.[10] When some of the problems of the real world of cultural contacts are translated into imaginative writing, as they are in the multiple texts in the Black Latin American literary tradition, we as real readers are invited, as it were, to consider the protagonists or the poetic voices, themselves nearly always completely "drained of their essence,"[11] as they pose and examine crucial group questions on genealogy, identity, and existential anguish. Who are *we*? What have *we* done? What has been done to *us*? What can *we* do? Where are *we* going? These are some of the major questions an Afro-Latin minority discourse addresses. As Deleuze and Guattari have convincingly argued, dominant discourse need not and usually does not pose these types of collective questions, the reason being that its cultural terrain has been relatively stabilized and "universalized" through colonial conquest and propagation.[12] In fact, Richard Terdiman also argues, with good reason, in his book *Discourse/Counter-Discourse* that "the dominant *remains dominant*," and even seemingly absorbs its antagonists into its fold.[13]

Minority literary discourse inhabits a traumatized and traumatizing world. We sense this in theory from many sources, particularly Edward W. Said's *The World, the Text, and the Critic*: we learn that there is no opposition between the text, with all the elements of textuality it may contain, and the world.[14] The discursive situation, continues

---

10.   Melville J. Herskovits's writings, especially *Acculturation: The Study of Culture Contact* (New York: J.J. Augustin, 1938) and *The Myth of the Negro Past* (1941; New York: Beacon Press, 1958), provide an early theoretical background from an anthropological perspective.

11.   Césaire, *Discourse*, 21.

12.   Gilles Deleuze and Félix Guattari, "What Is a Minor Literature?" *Mississippi Review* 22, no. 3 (Spring 1983): 15-33.

13.   Richard Terdiman, *Discourse/Counter-Discourse: The Theory and Practice of Symbolic Resistance in Nineteenth-Century France* (Ithaca: Cornell Univ. Press, 1985), 73.

14.   Edward W. Said, *The World, the Text, the Critic* (Cambridge, Mass.: Harvard Univ. Press, 1983), 49-50.

Said, reflects the gap between superior and inferior, colonizer and colonized, and, one might add, dictator and citizen. Language itself contains the world, and minority discourse borrows the language of the dominant world, which in its purely dominant form negates or diminishes the minority subject. What, then, does the minority literature do with such a dominant tongue? Shakespeare's Caliban is admittedly the supreme example in the Western literature of the minority subject crushed by the language of the majority. But Caliban saves himself through a counter-discourse which "deterritorializes" the borrowed English tongue with curses.

Nearly every Caribbean writer of note has commented upon the centrality of language in the expression of a Caribbean Self. Thus, for Roberto Fernández Retamar of Cuba, Caliban becomes, in cultural terms, the appropriate symbol of the islands.[15] For Césaire, as for Frantz Fanon, the minority writer eventually must attempt to cast away the cultural burden that the language of the majority, like French, imposes. This can be done, they propose, through a rebellious *don de sabotage*[16] or through a recontextualizing, reframing, or destruction of, in Guillén's words, "the purity of academe / the purity of grammarians / the purity of those who insist they have to be pure, pure, pure."[17] Should a new grammar be created? Can it be done, the perceptive reader wonders, when dominant discourse seems indestructible, when language, despite its apparent neutrality and innocence is, as Bernard Henri Levy writes in *Barbarism with a Human Face*, the pillar that supports dominant power and behavior? "Language *is* simply power, *the very form of power, entirely shaped by power*." "We know that the regulation of language is the best preparation for the regulation of souls."[18]

I believe, then, that "the regulation of the souls" and the official prescriptions of history are among the most significant marks of the master discourse against which the minority literature of Afro-Latin

---

15. Roberto Fernández Retamar, *Caliban: Apuntes sobre la cultura en nuestra América*, 2nd ed. (Mexico: Editorial Diogenes, 1974).

16. Aimé Césaire, *Cahier d'un retour au pays natal/Return to My Nativeland*, pref. André Breton and trans. Emile Snyder (Paris: Editions Présence Africaine, 1971).

17. Nicolás Guillén, "Digo que no soy un hombre puro," *La rueda dentada* (La Habana: UNEAC, 1972), 8 (my translation).

18. Bernard-Henri Lévy, *Barbarism with a Human Face* (New York: Harper & Row, 1979), 32-33.

America pits itself. Minority discourse is circumstantially a counter-hegemonic discourse; it thrives on a counter-hegemonic vision also, which is not to suggest, as the reader might expect, that it is far from rational. My point is that minority discourse sounds dialectically rational. This is because it claims that the languages of power and the historical assumptions and distortions they have engendered endow their users, potentially at least, with a power-based vision of the world and with a consciousness that tends to devalue those who are different and less powerful. But I must point out that minority literature is not just jettisoned against the dominant canon and its hegemonic centers, but also is immersed in those substratum African/African-American linguistic forms customarily thought to be outside the possibilities of creativity.

I chose this topic because Black Latin America is a minority area par excellence, historically and culturally. It has produced minority writers (who write in the major European languages) of considerable importance, some of whom rank among the best in the Spanish language. Among them are Zapata Olivella, Nicolás Guillén, Arnoldo Palacios, Adalberto Ortiz, Jorge Artel, and others. Reading them one can observe their marginality within the larger Latin American society and within the Spanish tradition, a marginality sometimes promoted by critical neglect and by a cultural stress on the "Latin" to the exclusion of the non-Latin in Latin America. To counter-balance this, Black minority discursivity provides a linkage with Africa, although this again is often ignored by those who fail to appreciate what is being done cross-culturally in Third World letters. Indeed, one of the fascinations for me of this topic is what it has to say about writing and, by implication, about critical reading and about our knowledge of the cultural realities of Latin America. The rest of my essay, then, is divided into two major sections which investigate the nature, context, and function of minority texts from Afro-Latin America.

2. Discourse, Power, and the African Continuum

Because colonial language legitimized the colonial and neocolonial orders, because in Latin America and the Caribbean, in particular, the colonial language (be it French, Spanish, or Portuguese) reinforced the hierarchical relationships between the colonials, the white *criollos* (creoles), and the Indian and African populations, and because the colonial functions of language were carried over into the post-independence period, the language question was/is taken very seriously. There was almost bound to develop among the *conquistadores*, and later the *caudillos* (political bosses) and dictators of Latin America, a hegemonic rhetoric. At the same time that this was happening in the dominant culture, there emerged among the minorities a counter-hegemonic discourse. Examples would include Indian (both oral and written), Jewish, Chicano, and Afrocentric literatures, the latter of which is my primary concern here.

How does a Black Latin American counter-discourse work? First, as in Césaire's *Return to My Nativeland* and Juminer's *Bozambo's Revenge*,[19] it takes the metropolitan language and "deterritorializes" it by creating with it a style almost unrecognizable within the standard discursive practices of the metropolitan centers and the administrative strongholds of Latin America. Its function is clearly one of reversal at the level of speech; however, it also raises and nurtures a combative consciousness through linguistic subversiveness. Second, a Black minority counter-discourse introduces a new set of discursive features, which include the cohesive and symbiotic relationships of oral and written discourses, the presence in print of paralinguistic cues usually denied to the writer in the formal linear tradition of Europe, the use of "regularitites" and other sociolinguistic patterns from the African continuum rather than from the standard reservoir of the culturally and historically dominant discourse of the crown, cross, *conquistador*, or *caudillo*.[20] Here its function is the affirmation of the roots of a minority culture. It has a collective value because its goal is to arouse and nourish a collective sensibility.

Negritude's role in all this is not small. It liberated the creative minds of the Black writers so that they could create literary ironies to counteract some of the monolithic formulations of the dominant

---

19. Césaire, *Return*, and Bertène Juminer, *Bozambo's Revenge*, trans. Alexandra B. Warren (Washington, D.C.: Three Continents Poem, 1976.)

20. For further reading, see J.B. Kubayanda, "The Linguistic Core of Afro-Hispanic Poetry: An African Reading," *Afro-Hispanic Review* 1, no. 3 (Sept. 1982): 21-26.

discourse. For the African minorities, or lettered minorities in the Latin world, the dominant discourse — from the *conquistadores* to Conrad and Kipling — presented itself as political discourse or, as González Echevarría better phrases it, "the voice of the masters."[21] This was particularly the case whenever the dominant discourse was confronted with the phenomenon of the Other, especially the so-called African *tabula rasa*, the cheap African slave labor market, and the mystery of the African jungle. *Bozambo's Revenge* confronts the dominant discourse and savagely strips it of its logic by turning its tide backwards so that primitive Europe is colonized by civilized Africa. Language use as we know it through formal education thus breaks down almost completely, as the dream of the minority group takes over the structure of the text. Like Juminer, Césaire takes that unilinear, monocausal master view of Africa and of things African, deflates its certainties, and projects the possibilities for a multi-dimensional reality beyond the imperial dreams of the master discourse of France and colonial Martinique.

The desire and the quest for a genuinely plural reality are at the heart of minority discourse. The African presence in the New World, according to Césaire, not only undermines mainstream monolithism but makes possible, theoretically at least, a unique multifacetedness which admits to collective or multiple existence in America. This in itself represents a sociocultural and humanistic attempt at innovation by those who, ironically, have invented nothing and humiliated no other race. Very often readers have failed to see this ironic twist of language in Césaire, and therefore have missed one of the salient characteristics of Caribbean minority discourse in general.

To underscore my thesis, one also has to look in a very special way at the Dominican Pluralist movement in poetry since 1975, especially Manuel Rueda's *Con el tambor de las islas*.[22] Going beyond the earlier tradition of drum poetry (cultivated by Guillón, Palés Matos of Puerto Rico, and Jorge Artel of Colombia), *Con el tambor* uses the multi-

---

21.   Roberto González Echevarría, *The Voice of the Masters: Writing and Authority in Modern Latin American Literature* (Austin: Univ. of Texas Press, 1985).

22.   Manuel Rueda, *Con el tambor de las islas* (Santo Domingo: Editora Taller, 1975). The Pluralist movement in the Dominican Republic of which Rueda is chief advocate is essentially experimentalist in nature. Its purpose is to force a new way of reading upon us and, thus, to suggest a new way of looking at the world.

vocal sounds of the Caribbean drum to great creative advantage: to represent the Caribbean people, to create a complex counter-linearity, a network of plural forms and of poetic "blocks" in one semantic or structural unit, calligraphs and *dragramas* (the drama of the word and the human person), all of which function as signs of several currents in the text and in the world. By implication, Rueda sees drum language, the language maligned and persecuted almost incessantly by the colonial discourse and order, as the medium not only for a new poetic discourse, but for a new voice against absolutism in writing and reading. Set in the mountains of Santo Domingo, *Con el Tambor* takes us to the beginning of things when there was the drum which produced a pure, primeval language of several sounds, realities, and possibilities. But that was before writing and its one-dimensional representation of time and space, as well as its support for dominance, came into being. Drum language came from the gods and therefore puts no limits on truth, whereas writing is a human creation and, therefore, an extension of human folly and limitations. However, when drum music is mixed, in a particular discursive space, with the written word, it provokes a response from us; it shocks us into participating and into seeing the simultaneity of things. The architecture of the poem *Con el tambor* is clearly a mixture of musical forms and writing: the words shout or sing to us with different letter sizes and colors and without the spatial crowding that we observe in linear writing.

I have said that the Black minority literature of Latin America introduces fresh Afrocentric discursive features for an affirmation of a "minor self" against the possibilities of cultural disappearance. Langston Hughes's famous poem "I Too Am America" is most demonstrably paradigmatic of that legacy of self-affirmation, which is partly what Henry Louis Gates describes as "integrity."[23] To complete that sense of self, Black minority literature, even when it uses a European language, seeks rhythmic reintegration into the signs and substance of

---

23.   Henry Louis Gates believes and has argued, contrary to scholars like Wayne Booth, that writing has never been "neutral," that in fact it has nearly always served some definite purpose. To this extent, Black writing, for Gates, is not value free; rather it serves to preserve the "whole" from being destroyed. See Gates, "Criticism, Integrity and the Black Idiom," conference on "The Nature and Context of Minority Discourse," Univ. of California, Berkeley, 26 May 1986.

the Afro-American and African traditions. It is fundamentally a written expression of reconnection and reappropriation. And this takes many forms. As argued in another paper, African rhetoric, whether oral-traditional or written-modern, relates to ancestry and to the natural agencies of revitalization or integrity (the baobab or palm trees, for example), and to textual categories like play jokes, riddles and proverbs, ritual narratives, mortuary or lament rites (dirges), musical formulae, and occasionally ideophonic sequences.[24]

It is neither possible nor desirable here to go into the details of each of these elements, but I would like briefly to mention what I believe to be a veritable *magnum opus* in Latin American letters of the present age. I am referring to *Changó, el gran putas* (1983) by Manuel Zapata Olivella of Columbia.[25] *Changó* is an ancestral novel, a novel in search of integrity. Written over a twenty-year period, *Changó* is the stunning result of novelistic maturation, the embodiment of a ritualistic and epic language in Spanish that belongs to and celebrates the Yoruba cosmogony, especially the god Shango (Changó), god of life, dance, and war, the three elements of blackness that Zapata Olivella himself says he sees in Colombia and in Latin America.[26] For this reason no New World novel is closer to the African utopian core than *Changó*. The falsely vulgar word *"putas"* in the title has confused Zapata Olivella's readers, but it really refers to something other than "Holy Fucker." This "something" is a textual entity almost more powerful than the Christian God or Devil and, because of its resilience, is seen by Zapata Olivella to be "applicable to the Blacks who have managed to survive the slave raids in Africa, the tremendous conditions of misery and hunger to which they were subjected during the Middle Passage, and who managed to survive all the slave regimes in this continent."[27] Thus, we have the coalition of two "divine" images, one from the Columbian Pacific Coast (*putas*), the other of African origin (Shango). This coalition at the imaginative level

---

24. J.B. Kubayanda, "Notes on the Impact of African-Oral-Traditional Rhetoric on Latin American and Caribbean Writing," *Afro-Hispanic Review* 3, no. 3 (Sept. 1984): 5-10.

25. Manuel Zapata Olivella, *Changó, el gran putas* (Bogotá: Editorial Oveja Negra, 1983).

26. Interview, Yvonne Captain-Hidalgo, "Conversación con el Doctor Manuel Zapata Olivella," *Afro-Hispanic Review* 4, no. 1 (January 1985): 26-32 (my translation).

27. Ibid., 30.

seems to produce the New World ideal, or the minor writer's desire for a genuine cultural synthesis, an enduring new wholeness, rather than an acculturative structure (that is, a movement from inferiority to superiority), which is the cornerstone of dominant discourse when it encounters minority voices. *Changó* shows in a unique way that minority literary discourse, being naturally pluralistic in conception and form, does feed on and is, in turn, fed by more than one tradition. This, I believe, is a major advantage for a minority discourse — an advantage, because it is connected to a kind of cultural heroism which eschews narrowness.

3. Minor Literary Reconstructions of History

Earlier I claimed that Afro-Latin literary discourse is embedded in a particular sociopolitical and historical context. Its primary function is not to make an accurate description of historical events, but rather to raise the national conscience by addressing questions that have to do with the minor self *vis-à-vis* the national identity or sovereignty, and with the perceived conflicts between freedom and autocracy, between Utopia and reality. Its purpose is not to record the "facts" but to reach a deeper *meaning* and to project a minority ethos. It indirectly argues against the anti-meaning movement in literary or critical scholarship. And one can understand why a literature congruent with a culture of questioning, of resistance, of the recuperation of one's roots, and of self- and national renewal, will be involved with definitions and significations. The Black Latin American idiom is therefore deconstructionist only to a point: it deconstructs the binary space in chronological history that allows "the master," as Fanon said of colonial Algeria, to laugh at "the slave." But its tendency, in symbolic terms, to destroy the negative constructions of history or of repressive power is underscored by a corresponding desire for "bio-power" (Foucault), that is, the "solidaristic" means to manage the repressed self throughout history, the harrowing effects of domination notwithstanding.[28]

A clear example of what I am talking about is the maroon novel in Spanish which, briefly stated, redefines and rejects the standard

---

28. François Ewald, "Bio-Power," *History of the Present* 2 (Spring 1986): 8-9.

structures of the dominant historical discourse. I regard the maroon narrative as a good illustration of minority discourse in Latin America for the reasons that follow. Maroon narrative or poetry deals with marooning and with an underground discursive scheme unfamiliar to dominant discourse. The term "marooning" refers to the guerrilla resistance movements among Blacks that spanned the seventeenth, eighteenth, and nineteenth centuries in the Americas, especially the Haiti of Macandal, the Brazil of the *quilombos* (African encampments), the Jamaica of Cudjoe, the Surinam of Baron and Araby, the Cuba of José Antonio Aponte, the Mexico of the Mandingo rebels, the Ecuador (specifically Esmeraldas) of Illescas, and the Virginia of Nat Turner.[29] Marooning enabled the runaway slaves both to challenge and to escape the plantation or post-plantation order. But it was also intended to articulate, as independently as possible and within the colonial structure, the sociocultural and spiritual modes of being of the minority activists. It made it impossible for the dominant order to assume complete control of the discursive world. Today, marooning is considered an important minor historical paradigm for minorities in certain Latin American and Caribbean countries, particularly Cuba and the French Caribbean, who are reexamining their histories in order to redefine themselves without the perspectives of the metropolitan hegemonies. As a result, marooning is increasingly being given a new place in both the historical and intellectual domains of the Caribbean, and the maroon figure is becoming, in imaginative literature, protagonist rather than object of history. My thesis is that there is a correlation between this maroon discovery and the concerns, content, and context of the minority texts examined below.

Although certain works, like *Juyungo* by Adalberto Ortiz, *Cuando los*

---

29. On this subject see, among other studies, Eugene D. Genovese, *From Rebellion to Revolution* (Baton Rouge: Louisiana State Univ. Press, 1979); Sally and Richard Price, *Afro-American Arts of the Surinam Rain* (Berkeley: Univ. of California Press, 1981); Mary Jane Hewitt, "An Overview of Surinam," *Black Art* 5, no. 1 (1981): 4-28; José Luciano Franco, "Palenques de Frijol, Bumba y Muluala," in *Plácido y otros ensayos* (La Habana: Ediciones Unión, 1964); Thomas Flory, "Fugitive Slaves and Free Society: The Case of Brazil," *The Journal of Negro History* 64, no. 2 (Spring 1979): 116-130; and Patrick J. Carroll, "Mandinga: The Evolution of a Mexican Runaway Community, 1735-1827," *Comparative Studies in Society and History* 19, no. 4 (October 1977): 488-505.

guayacanes florecían by Estupiñán Bass, and *Chombo* by Carlos Guillermo Wilson, are set mainly in the twentieth century, Hispanic-American maroon novels often take place in the nineteenth century. Diaz Sanchez's *Cumboto* is situated in a Venezuelan community of fleeing Blacks; Miguel Barnet's *Biografía de un cimarrón* focuses on an ex-maroon's recollections of nearly one hundred years of personal marooning; and César Leante's *Los guerrilleros negros* deals with the period immediately following the 1812 widespread slave revolts throughout the island of Cuba.[30] This nineteenth-century setting is not without explanation. As evidenced by several studies of the plantation economy, the 1800s saw the emergence of fully-fledged slave societies in the Latin regions, especially Cuba and Brazil, which profitably turned from precapitalist toward capitalist development by becoming world producers and suppliers of sugar and coffee. That economic boom, however, contributed much to a dramatic worsening of the social conditions and race relations in Latin America. At the same time that the social rigors became pronounced internally, Latin American countries were either intensifying their emancipation drives against Spain or consolidating their newly-won freedom. Thus, the maroon consciousness, essentially a minority consciousness in the context of Latin America, was seemingly alert to what appeared to be a great historical paradox, that is, the white *criollo's* increasing drive for independence set alongside a continually potent chattel slavery and system of social injustice. In addition, as witnessed by the observations of the main maroon speakers in the works mentioned earlier, the maroon consciousness appeals to a new discourse vital to a new thinking and to the expression of a revolutionary stream of writing in Latin America. As the paragraphs which immediately follow will confirm, that vitality of the maroon creative act almost corresponds to the indomitable spirit or ethic of authentic liberation.

Nothing testifies more tellingly to that minority spirit of disso-

---

30. The principal maroon texts used here are: Adalberto Ortíz, *Juyungo* (Buenos Aires: Americallee, 1943); Miguel Barnet, *Biografía de un cimarron* (Buenos Aires: Editorial Galerna, 1968); Ramón Diaz Sánchez, *Cumboto* (Santiago: Editorial Universitaria, 1967); César Leante, *Los guerrilleros negros* (Mexico: Siglo XXI, 1979); Estupiñán Bass, *Cuando los guayacanes florecian* (Quito: Editora Casa de la Cultura Ecuatoriana, 1954); and Carlos Guillermo Wilson, *Chombo*.

nance than the numerous discursive units concerning the clearly conflictive relationships between the national covenant and the African maroon presence. For example, in one such dissident discourse, the protagonist-narrator in *Los guerrilleros* states: "I did not know the word fatherland . . ." ("Desconocía la palabra patria . . .").[31] The speaker's psychic anguish and self-confession seem to be rooted, as I have argued earlier, in the maroon view that there is a fundamental historical contradiction in Latin America. This view undermines simple readings of reality and deconstructs, as it were, those monological forms of nationhood which the maroon narrator confronts. Barnet describes this as "the false myth of a unified nation."[32] Esteban Montejo, the maroon protagonist of *Biografía* who is similar to the narrative voice in *Los guerrilleros*, lives by an ethic of refusal:

> When slavery was ended, I ceased being a maroon. From the people's shouting I knew that slavery was over and I came out (of my hiding place.) They shouted: "Free at last." But I didn't really believe it. For me it was (all) a lie.[33]

This skeptical view that official history is no more than a deception was underscored early enough by some nineteenth-century Cuban cultural historians, such as Martin Morúa Delgado, who advocated a genuine unification and an open extention of sovereignty to all the Cuban nationals. This, he hoped, would turn Cuba away from the "tortuous paths" of the colonial era.[34] The maroon text's commitment to the principle of full emancipation constantly comes to the fore through a language that contradicts the textual and political claims of the old *raison d'état*, or those of the nascent *criollo* superstructure. The Blacks talked about full emancipation because there was a great uncertainty about the social implications of unfettered freedom. Indeed, uncertainty bred fear which in turn led to a nearly schizophrenic conditioning of the *criollo* mind regarding the Black

31. Leante, *Los guerrilleros negros*, 11.
32. Miguel Barnet, "The Culture That Sugar Created," *Latin American Literary Review* 18, no. 16 (Spring/Summer, 1980): 40.
33. Barnet, *Biografía*, 62.
34. Martin Morúa Delgado, *Integración cubana y otros ensayos*, ed. Alberto Baeza Flores (La Habana: Editorial Comisión Nacional Del Centenario de Martin Morúa Delgado, 1957), 64 and 196.

minorities. According to the Cuban essayist, del Valle, any African assertiveness in the nineteenth century was considered one of the two most serious misdemeanors that could be committed against the Hispanic-American public policy and administration, the other being any form of agitation of sociopolitical significance.[35]

Yet, against this backdrop, maroon writing throbs with ideals of self-government and is striking for its language of strident probing and resoluteness. In context, it is subversive of the dominant order in that it looks for its own truth beyond that of established reality; it addresses not only the question of the unilateral projections of the pre-independence period but also the *criollo* ideological articulations of post-independence including those of the so-called revolutionary eras. To the maroon frame of mind, a questioning deconstructionist mind, the old-time servitudes seem to reappear in the new society as part of a real or perceived stasis, that is, as the constancy of things, which is the base of "black rage."

This textual pinning of a note of cruel immutability on official history and historiography does not degenerate into resignation as may be expected; rather it leads in literature to modes of rupture with the modalities of the past, such as the sugar culture of Cuba, the Canal culture of Panama (*Chombo*), or the peonage of Ecuador (*Juyungo; Cuando los guayacanes florecían*). In consequence one often finds in maroon literature not just forms of protest but plain *licentia* which Cicero, long before the emergence of modern society, described as a "figure of diction and thought" or "a frankness of speech" occurring when a subordinate reprehends her superior for an ethical transgression.[36] Its literary focus is on verbal reversions and inversions; its functions include an undermining of the conventional formalities and orthodoxies and a broadening of our horizon of questioning. A good example of *licentia* is found in *Los guerrilleros* where the maroon captain, Gallo, lampoons the Catholic priest who acts as mediator between the government

---

35. Francisco G. del Valle, *La vida literaria en Cuba (1936-1940)* (La Habana: Cardenas, 1938), 8. Also see Charles Minguet's unpublished study, "Le Noir dans la Sensibilité et l'Idéologie des Creoles Americains à l'Epoque de l'Independance (1780-1816)," Colloquium on Negritude in Latin America, Dakar, Senegal, 7-12 Jan. 1974.

36. See Cicero, *Ad C. Herpennium Libri IV*, trans. Harry Caplan (Cambridge, Mass.: Harvard Univ. Press, 1954), 371.

forces and the rebel maroon troops.[37]

The expressive militancy I have been discussing is often high-lighted by symbolic weaponry. Textually, the machete functions al-most like the sword in the epic of Old Europe. Historically, it was the maroon hero's weapon of war, his companion, a powerful arm ar-rayed against the guns, hounds, and horses of the slave captors and conquistadors. The machete, to some extent, is turned into the sym-bolic agent that orders the literary worlds of Barnet and Leante, and those of Carpentier (*En reino de este mundo*), Ortiz (*Juyungo*), Olivella (*Chambacú* and *Cuentos de muerte y libertad*), Bass (*Cuando los guayacanes florecían*), and Wilson (*Chombo*).

The reason for the prevalence of this warring symbol in the texts of Black minorities in Latin America can be found in unofficial history: throughout colonial Africa and Latin America certain "natives," like the Asante warriors of the Golden Stool, the Afro-Cuban and Afro-Peruvian maroons, and the Saramaka of Surinam, frequently re-sorted to the machete as a major weapon of freedom. In the Cuban Wars of Independence, Montejo recalls in the *Biografía*, "the machete was the weapon for battle. Our commanding officers (Maceo and Maximo Gómez) would tell us: Upon arrival raise your machetes"[38] But there is in all this widespread use of the machete a fairly strong suggestion that the maroon experience of life, an experience going back to the beginnings of the New World, had itself opened up all of America to the possibility of liberation. To this extent, the machete has been transformed from a simple, ethnic weapon of self-protec-tion to a broader sign of new trends of thought and action; it has be-come, in Barnet's words, "the epic of our nation (Cuba)."[39]

Maroon literature, it is suggested here, comes alive in epic narra-tive or heroic ballad; it is energized not just by machetes alone, but also by fictional and historical figures who are almost always fired by flights of moral ambition and activism. The maroon narrative or poem, however, scarcely indulges in the types of fantasied feats that mark most European epics from the *Iliad* to *Paradise Lost* (one excep-tion being the Spanish *El Mío Cid*). All the same, the maroon text of-

---

37.   Leante, *Los guerrilleros*, 200.
38.   Barnet, *Biografía*, 164.
39.   Barnet, "The Culture," 53.

ten takes a biographical or autobiographical form, portraying minority children and youths, male and female, as sources of national energy, as symbols of revolt against injustice, and as agents of some virtue. Natividad in *Cumboto* supplies corroborative testimony. Unlike the adult Roso and his West Indian ancestors who founded Cumboto, Natividad physically cannot oppose the enslaving structures at hand. Nevertheless, his mission in the story reflects an epic consciousness and a psycho-ethical awareness germane to the poetics of marooning: Natividad is resolved and succeeds in influencing the secluded aristocratic world of his master and friend Federico, thereby deconstructing the simple binary master-servant opposition which the politics of the story and the facts of history seem to uphold. It is true that the one event in the novel that kindles the imagination of Natividad is the heroic flight from the Caribbean and the resettlement on the Venezuelan coast long before the arrival of the European planter class. But unable to trace his blood parents and thus unable to fix meaning in exclusive terms, Natividad, as speaking person, becomes the voice of the entire community and ends up being Federico's only reliable companion and spiritual adviser. His success seems to signify for him an overall defeat of the monolinear expectations that his world has laid upon him. There is thus not an irreconcilable conflict between his sign and that of others; rather there is only an obvious *différance*, a trace of the substance of his sign in the other.

Conclusion

What conclusion can one draw about Black Latin American minority discourse? What will become of it? Will it get absorbed by the dominant discourse? Will it disappear on its own? I think that the problem is epistemological, that is, it has to do with the organization and dissemination of knowledge. Thus, to paraphrase Said again, the answer lies more with the readers and critics of minority literature than with the creators of that literature: " . . . critics create not only the values by which art is judged and understood, but they embody in writing those processes and actual conditions in the *present* by means of which art and writing bear significance."[40] In other words, all liter-

---

40. Said, *The World*, 53.

ary discourse, including minority discourse, is dependent upon a certain critical responsibility. I believe there is a real Black Latin American literary tradition, just as there is a distinct Black North American literary tradition. One of the dangers that arises is what happens if minority *critical* discourse ignores the minority *literary* discourse which continually interacts with both the dominant and marginal cultures. Another possible danger might be a failure to apply to minority literature the critical theories now being developed by Said, Spivak, Gates, and other scholars who are concerned with literary works and cultural objects outside the dominant canons set up by the West. In any case, Black Latin American minority discourse is an important one that will play an increasingly significant role in Latin American scholarship. As argued above, and as corroborated by other readers,[41] it has all kinds of possibilities. First, Black Latin American minority discourse forces us as readers to reconsider some of the so-called "universals" of history, to abandon monolithic reading, and to open our minds to multiple readings of reality. Second, it nourishes and is nourished by some of the most cogent cultural values of traditional Africa. Third, it is inseparable from the integrity of the race, but it does not attempt to raise the latter above all others; it simply affirms and reclaims its roots where the dominant culture overrides or tries to override the marginal groups. Finally, it rejects the politics of control, especially where this control is cultural. This is because minority discourse operates from the awareness that, as Kenyan writer Ngugi wa Thiong'o has put it, "once you control how a people look at themselves, you can in fact make a move in any other direction."[42]

---

41.   I am thinking, for instance, of Richard Jackson's already extensive scholarship on the literature of Black Latin America, especially his book *Black Writers in Latin America* (Albuquerque: Univ. of New Mexico Press, 1979).

42.   Hansel Ndumbe Eyoh, "Language as Carrier of People's Culture: An Interview with Ngugi wa Thiong'o," *UFAHAMU* 14, no. 3 (1985): 156.

Hebrew in an Israeli Arab Hand:
Six Miniatures on Anton Shammas's *Arabesques*

Hannan Hever

1. The Majority as Minority

In a recent interview a question was asked of the Israeli writer Amos Oz:

> Anton Shammas's new novel *Arabesques* has been published to great critical acclaim. Do you consider the presence of this novel, written by an Israeli Arab in Hebrew, to be a turning point in Israeli society?

Oz responded:

> I think of this as a triumph, not necessarily for Israeli society, but

Earlier versions of this paper were presented in Berkeley to the Group for the Study of Colonial Discourse at the University of California, and at the Graduate Theological Union. I would like to express my thanks to Abdul JanMohamed, both for his personal support and for his help and advice in the preparation of this paper.

for the Hebrew language. If the Hebrew language is becoming attractive enough for a non-Jewish Israeli to write in it, then we have arrived.[1]

Oz recognizes the great importance of this book. He is less sure, though, in assessing how central a place it occupies in a particularly *Israeli* context. Yet despite his slightly patronizing tone—as if admission to "Israeli-ness" were his to give or deny—Oz is, at the same time, publicly acknowledging a certain lack of strength in the Hebrew language. His words can be interpreted, if taken literally, as setting Shammas apart as an Arab and not according him his full cultural rights as a member of Israeli society. But at the same time, Oz's answer sounds almost like a direct quotation from decades of Zionist writings expressing the unflagging hope that the persecuted Jewish minority would someday achieve the status of a majority, and with it political sovereignty in Israel. Oz is presenting the Hebrew language in two lights: as the language of the ruling majority and as the language of a minority compelled to fight for cultural and political recognition.

Anton Shammas's *Arabesques* can be read as a protest, aimed principally at the ambiguous multiplicity that is perhaps *the* paramount characteristic of Israeli public discourse today. A wealth of examples could be mustered to prove that Israel, though behaving like a nation of rulers and conquerors, still relies heavily on the argumentation and rhetoric of a minority struggling for its very existence. Undoubtedly contributing to this phenomenon is the speed with which Israeli Jews made the transition, immediately after the Holocaust, from a persecuted minority to a ruling majority in their own state. But other considerations enter in as well—for example, the way Jewish history, steeped in suffering, figures so intensely in the worldview of present-day Israel or in the Israeli "fortress mentality" vis-à-vis a largely hostile Arab world. What has developed, as a result, is an astonishingly elastic mode of public discourse, able to adapt itself to almost any dialogical

---

1. David Twersky, "An Interview with Amos Oz," *Tikkun* 1, no. 2 (1986): 26. The interviewer gives the title of Shammas's novel in the singular (i.e., *Arabesque*), as it appears (in English) on the copyright page of the Hebrew edition. I will refer to the book in the plural (i.e., *Arabesques*), as in the Hebrew title. All citations from *Arabesques* (Tel Aviv: Am Oved, 1986) will be from this Hebrew edition, and will be included in the text. An English translation of *Arabesques* is forthcoming; in the present essay all translations from the Hebrew are those of Orin D. Gensler.

situation. Depending on the requirement of the particular confrontation, it can speak in the voice of an impotent minority, in need of reas-
surance, or in the voice of a confident majority, sure of itself and its
power. In one way or another, then, almost any text found in present-
day Israel is liable to fall into the same mode: a blindness to the fundamentally asymmetrical power relationships it enunciates. This holds
even—and perhaps chiefly—for texts expressing sympathy or solidarity with the Palestinian cause.[2]

Anton Shammas, as an Israeli Christian Arab, has published a Hebrew novel, a text written in the language of the conquerors. The reaction of the Israeli Jewish writer Oz, on the other hand, is based in large
measure on the historical fact that Hebrew is the language of Zionism,
the national liberation movement of a Jewish minority which founded
the State of Israel. The Arab Shammas was born after Israeli independence, an Arab and an Israeli citizen, in the village of Fasuta in the Galilee, and linked his destiny and his literary career to Hebrew literature
and culture. *Arabesques* is his first novel, though he has also published a
book of poetry and a children's book—as well as translations from Arabic. He is an active contributor to Israeli newspapers and periodicals.

The identity of an Israeli Christian Arab does not line up in any simple
way with the main political forces at work in Israel and the Middle East
and in fact stands somewhat apart from them. From this special viewpoint, Shammas has constructed a novel that represents a real challenge
to his Hebrew-speaking readers. As an "Israeli Arab," Shammas is a
member of a minority group—but as a Christian, he falls outside the
Islamic mainstream of the minority that, at least according to the prevalent Israeli conception, tends more "naturally" to be identified with the
Palestinians. On the other hand, he writes in Hebrew, the language of
the dominant Jewish culture, which is itself a minority within the predominantly Arab Middle East. This peculiar position, which Shammas
likens to the image of a Russian babushka doll,[3] gives him a unique
perspective on Israeli public discourse from the inside and the outside
at once. With this spiritual and political flexibility, Shammas can develop

2. Hannan Hever, "An Extra Pair of Eyes: Hebrew Poetry under Occupation,"
Tikkun 2, no. 2 (May 1987): 84-87, 122-26.

3. Anton Shammas, "Al Galut Ve-Sifrut" [On Exile and Literature], *Igra* 2 (1987): 67-
70; Shammas, "Ashmat Ha-Babushka" [The Guilt of the Babushka], *Politika* 5-6
(February-March 1986): 44-45.

an authorial voice that forces his readers to take a fresh look at their cultural assumptions and expectations. The principal alternatives for critical and popular response to Shammas would tend to represent him as either an *Arab* author writing in *Hebrew* or a *Hebrew* author of *Arab* extraction. Shammas, however, sees himself as neither: he defines himself as someone unable to decide whether Israel represents homeland or exile. For an Arab author to be writing in Hebrew at all is highly unusual in the Israeli cultural landscape—a phenomenon undoubtedly connected with a blurring of the traditional boundaries of Israeli national culture. As a writer, Shammas rejects these polarized images that have been bestowed on him. He responds, instead, on another plane entirely and puts forth his own *Israeli* identity as his personal utopian resolution to the dilemma.

As has been frequently remarked, Shammas may well have created the most truly Israeli novel yet written. But that Israeli essence is imagined through an intricate web of negations. From an *Israeli* viewpoint, at once Jewish and Arab, great significance attaches to this analytical and demystifying negationist stance. The member of a minority within a minority within a minority, Shammas has used the figure of the arabesque as a richly articulated vehicle for minority discourse; such richness is indispensable considering the complexity of the Israeli reality with which Shammas is grappling. As we shall see, this figure has two principal aspects: the one negative, a striving for demystification, and the other positive, an attempt to develop a language adequate to the problems of a minority. This duality will reveal how Shammas's decision to write in the Other's language provides a glimmer of hope, a possible way out of the political and cultural dead end in which Israeli society now finds itself.

As an analysis of Anton Shammas's *Arabesques,* this essay will attempt to respond to the challenge presented by the novel's negationist stance. The comparison between the textual flow of the novel itself and our paraphrases of it will illustrate that the opposition between Shammas's *Arabesques* and any attempt to restate it synoptically is fundamental. The extent to which this opposition is politically charged is quite apparent: we need only note the asymmetry of a Jewish-Israeli text passing judgment on a Hebrew text by an Israeli Arab. And, in fact, a dual consciousness underlies this essay. On the one hand, there is an awareness of the power implications of the hermeneutic acts we perform in imposing hierarchies of meaning on the text. On the other hand, paraphrase is inevitable, even if one takes for granted the irreducible heterogeneity and uniqueness of the text.[4] The division of this essay (sometimes quite abrupt) into chapters, the discontinuous shifts of topic, the fragmentary nature of the exposition, and the avoidance of any sort of harmonious, well-rounded interpretation all constitute a partial response to the unique challenge of the arabesque as a vehicle for minority discourse.

2. Who Are You, Anton Shammas?

The status of the narrator—his identity, values, potentialities, and especially his relation to the narration—is one of the focal points of this semiautobiographical novel. As part of the "communicative contract" that he offers his readers, Shammas deliberately undermines the authority and unity of the narrative voice in his novel. A sharp formal split differentiates those chapters whose titles mark them as belonging to the "narrative" portion of the book from those chapters comprising the "narrator's" portion. The *narrative* sections unfold the history of the multi-branched Shammas family, starting from the early nineteenth century (when the patriarch of the family moved to the Galilee from Syria) on through the period prior to the founding of the State of Israel in 1948 and up to the present-day Israeli occupation of the West Bank and the Gaza Strip. The "narrator" portions relate the journey of the author, Anton Shammas, from Israel to America, to take part in the International Writing Program held annually in Iowa City. This formal thematic split signals the possible absence of conventional, causal links between the narrator and his narrative.

In no small measure, Shammas's novel is organized like a detective story. The Israeli Christian Arab Anton Shammas and his Palestinian döppelganger Michael Abayyad, from the Center for Palestinian Studies in Beirut, are in effect trying to track each other down. Shammas the narrator is named after his cousin Michel Abayyad, who himself had been named Anton Shammas but, soon after birth, was kidnapped from his

---

4. On this fundamental tension and attempt to resolve it through the problematization of paraphrase, especially in the writing of intellectual history, see Martin Jay, "Two Cheers for Paraphrase: The Confessions of a Synoptic Intellectual Historian," *Stanford Literary Review* 3, no. 1 (Spring 1986): 47-61.

natural mother, Almaza, to be raised by a childless couple from "the old Arab nobility" in Beirut (232). From a newspaper article, Shammas the narrator learns of a certain Surayya Sa'id, a blond-haired Christian woman who had converted to Islam and married the son of Abdallah Al-Asbah, one of the heroes of the Great Arab Revolt of 1936. Shammas surmises that she is none other than Layla Khouri, the same woman his father had brought in 1936 from the village of Fasuta in the Galilee to Beirut to live with the Baytar family and who had later been a servant in one of the wealthy neighborhoods of that city. In 1948, Layla Khouri had paid a very brief visit to Fasuta, only to be expelled to the West Bank by the Israeli army. Surayya Sa'id, that is, Layla Khouri, had been a servant in Michel Abayyad's house when the adopted boy was growing up, and was secretly in love with him. On the very night in 1948 when Layla returned to Fasuta from Beirut, Michel Abayyad's parents were blackmailed into revealing the terrible secret of their adopted son and were forced to send the young Michel to America.

Shammas himself labels all this an "Arab soap opera" (52). But in the "narrator's" portion of the book, the story reappears. During Shammas's emotional meeting with Michael Abayyad in Iowa City, Abayyad tells his own life story, a story very similar to the one Shammas had extracted from Layla Khouri. But Abayyad's version is not precisely the same as the "narrative" version—it is set a year later (in 1949, instead of 1948), and the servant in the Beirut house of his childhood is identified not as Layla Khouri but as Shammas the narrator's own aunt Almaza.

Abbayad's narrative casts the entire book in a new light. Michael Abayyad had returned from America to Beirut in 1978 to join the staff of the Center for Palestinian Studies in Beirut. There he made the acquaintance of Nur, Anton Shammas's cousin, who suggested to Abayyad that he try to locate his natural mother—the same woman who had suddenly appeared at his adoptive parents' house years ago in 1949 to claim her missing child. But the Beirut of 1978, caught up in a civil war, was not the ideal place for such a search. And on the other hand, the fact of having grown up with Almaza, the bereaved mother, influenced Abayyad so strongly that he came to identify completely with her lost son, Anton. On the basis of Nur's stories, Abayyad decides to write the fictitious autobiography of Anton Shammas and to inject himself into the story in the role of Anton, Almaza's dead child. And now the reader is given a hint that the "narrative" portion of the novel referred to above, including the whole Abayyad-Shammas affair as told by Layla Khouri, is the invention of Michael Abayyad the writer. Here, at least, we seem to have reached a secure epistemological ground: the "narrative" portions of the novel are to be taken as a fabrication. But Shammas the author has not yet exhausted his Chinese puzzle of boxes-within-boxes. The chapter summarizing the "narrator's" section of the novel not only reveals that the "narrative" portion is a fiction—it also includes a statement by Shammas the author that the "narrator's" portion is itself a fiction. Shammas strips Abayyad of the authority of the reliable narration and reveals his own authorial presence even in passages spoken directly by Abayyad. Thus any identity between the "narrative" parts of the novel and the fictitious autobiography written by Abayyad is represented as, at best, an uncertain possibility. And so the novel acquires yet another topmost layer of reliability, undermining in turn the reliability of all the layers beneath.

By this point, the notion of a causal link between the two portions of the novel has been so seriously undercut that it is impossible to tell who is the "authentic" Shammas: the Shammas of the "narrative" part or the Shammas of the "narrator's" part. There is, of course, a temporal discrepancy between the two versions, regarding the moment at which Shammas becomes acquainted with Abayyad's story: relatively early in the "narrative" version, quite late in the "narrator's" version. And yet the two are presented as separate events. In fact, any differences between the two versions can be taken equally well as a contradiction or as a simple matter of mutual indifference. Each story line has its own claim to reality, and the reader has no way of determining which reality is "genuine."

There are in fact two Anton Shammases in the novel. Both appear in the book as protagonist-narrators; both are writers by profession; each calls the other's authority into question. It would be hard to overestimate the importance of this literary gesture. Here the very composition of the novel mirrors Shammas's ambivalent position vis-à-vis the question of his own personal and national identity. And here too he takes an important step forward in encountering the fundamental tensions of Israeli public discourse: the dual representation of the Jews as majority and minority calls for the creation in the novel of a new type of literary subject, a subject who, confronting this duality, is capable of taking steps toward determining its real nature. Indeed, given the absence of such a determination, he can turn even this weakness to his advantage, using it as an analytical tool to crack into the duality and attempt to change it.

3. The Israeli Arab as Palestinian; The Palestinian as the Israeli Jew's Jew

The self-identity of the Israeli was formed by Jews who were trying to build a state with a Jewish majority that would, at the same time, in the framework of a liberal democracy respect the identity and rights of *all* Israelis, Jews, and Arabs alike. This formula included both the ideal of a democratic state and the ideal of a Jewish state with a Jewish majority and a Jewish character, a place of refuge for the Jewish people. The seeds of a contradiction are all too evident here, and they sprouted and grew over the years. The Arab inhabitants of Israel, in fact, never were citizens with truly equal rights. Confiscation of lands, constant pressure from the security forces, neglect of education in the Arab sector—these are only a few examples from a long history of discrimination. The temporary and partial compromises that attempted to reconcile the contradictions became more and more unworkable over the years. The problem was exacerbated by reduced Jewish immigration, with demographic projections indicating that the Jews were likely to lose their majority status in the not-too-distant future. The dramatic climax came, of course, in 1967, when Israel conquered Gaza and the West Bank. The desire to strengthen the ideal of a Jewish state was now reinforced by the desire to hold onto the occupied territories (though inhabited by over a million Arabs)—and the inevitable result was to undermine Israeli democracy while suppressing the Palestinians and their national aspirations.

With the Israeli sense of self-identity caught in this dynamic and contradictory situation, the very act of writing an *Israeli* novel becomes a highly complex cultural process. And given the bewildering array of sides and opinions in the current Israeli scene, all charged with emotion and almost totally politicized, any attempt at genuine criticism becomes extremely difficult. It is not easy to carry on an incisive political dialogue in a charged situation where all the interlocutors are interested parties automatically slotted into this or that political pigeonhole. Nor is it any easier to carry on a struggle against an occupying power whose past history and present consciousness preclude any neatly categorical analysis in terms of simple categories such as strong-weak or ruler-ruled. Indeed, Israeli public discourse disguises the power of the dominant majority precisely by adopting the linguistic and behavioral style of a minority—one way to circumvent temporarily the contradiction alluded to above, where the image of a small democratic Israel fighting for a homeland for the oppressed Jewish people conflicts with the image of a great Israel engaged in deliberate suppression of the Palestinians. An outrageous expression of this ambivalent imagery can be seen in the protests of the Jewish settlers in the occupied territories at their "abandonment" by the Israeli government and in the rhetoric of self-styled persecuted victims that accompanies their anti-Palestinian activities.

The occupation has created a cultural matrix in which these contradictions have become blurred. One measure of how deeply rooted this culture now is can be seen in the overwhelming use in Israel of Arab workers for manual labor, which has in turn led to a large measure of rhetorical overlap in Israeli discourse between the categories of class and nationality. The ideological and cultural aspects of these phenomena, especially their literary manifestations, evince an opposition between minority and majority—which does not always coincide with the opposition between weakness and strength.[5] The dynamic flexibility of the opposition minority/majority—the mutual dependence between minority and majority, their relative degrees of power as well as a special sensitivity to the link between cultural and linguistic identity, on the one hand, and sovereignty and political legitimacy, on the other, all find expression through the discourse of the arabesque. The importance of this dynamic opposition can be seen most of all in the great strength it imparts to a minority confronted with the defense

5. For an analysis of the categories of weakness and strength throughout Jewish history, see David Bial, *Power and Powerlessness in Jewish History* (New York: Schocken Books, 1986). Bial shows, among other things, how post-1967 Zionism was mistakenly considered an organic continuation of Jewish history rather than a break in it. This, he suggests, is the background for the widespread tendency to identify anti-Zionism with anti-Semitism; it likewise explains the characterization of Israeli sovereignty as a contradictory mixture of exaggerated fear and grandiose ambition (146).

mechanisms of a majority that, however powerful, feels itself perfectly entitled to minority status and consciousness.

A very special way of seeing and reacting must be developed in order to crack open this smooth and flexible battery of defense mechanisms, to criticize the presuppositions of the dominant discourse from the outside without losing the vantage of a participant involved personally in events from the inside. To do this in a *novel*, it is crucial to determine first what identity and authority are available to its narrator. Shammas makes these issues the central focus of his novel and tries in it to delineate the true Israeli image through a dialectical juxtaposition of an Arab image and a Jewish image.

The mutual undermining of the "narrative" and the "narrator's" segments of the novel is largely responsible for the uncommon dual effect Shammas has created: on the one hand, powerful emotional involvement in *each* of the two segments; on the other, the abstract viewpoint from which *both* parts are formulated. It is from this same viewpoint that Shammas formulates his own identity, through a systematic dialectical negation, almost to the point of absurdity, of the national significance of his own ancestral roots. In one of the most entertaining parts of the novel (15-16), Shammas presents his family's ancestry as an utter hodge-podge of periods, religions, and nationalities. The founder of the family, who immigrated from southwestern Syria to the Galilee only at the beginning of the last century, did so chiefly because the rival family in his old village was trying to kill him. The Christian inhabitants of Fasuta in the Galilee had been persecuted and oppressed by the Moslem inhabitants of nearby Dir El-Qasi, which was renamed Moshav Elqosh after the Israeli War of Independence. The village of Fasuta itself was built not only on the ruins of the Crusader fortress Pasova, but also on the still earlier ruins of the ancient Jewish village Mifshata, where a number of priests had settled after the destruction of the Second Temple. Thus any attempt at any positive statement, made on the basis of a present-day political interpretation of the past, contains the seeds of its own negation. Shammas has created a text that parodies the genre of dynastic political genealogy. And so the text, in purporting to do justice to the political interests of all the parties involved, actually satisfies none of them. In this way Shammas sidesteps the traditional terms of the debate, which has conventionally focused on stating and comparing the historical rights claimed by each of the parties.

Shammas thus exposes the distorted conception of time underlying Israeli public discourse. And he criticizes this conception from a perspective for which he must pay a certain political price. Shammas rejects the whole framework of historical privileges and justifications, and structures the debate instead in futuristic and utopian terms. In this he assumes a risk, evincing a certain weakness, given a volatile political situation articulated precisely in terms of historical questions such as "Who was there first?" One could doubtless regard this as a lack of sensitivity, on Shammas's part, to the concrete political realities of the conflict. But, on the other hand, one could also see it as a concrete exercise in political tactics, crediting Shammas for relinquishing one position of strength to gain a better one.

In his political essays Shammas returns again and again to the demand that the Jewish state should finally adopt the political agenda of an *Israeli* state, a democratic homeland for Jews and Arabs alike.[6] Yet at the same time he demonstrates a sensitivity to the legitimate fears and aspirations of Israeli Jews. His call for an Israeli state as opposed to a Jewish one is actually more a call for a reversal of priorities, an inversion of the hierarchy whereby Jewish considerations automatically take precedence over democratic ones. But the challenge announced in Shammas'ss novel, a challenge aimed in part at the Israeli Left, involves something more: a special sensitivity to the dialogue he is conducting with the presuppositions underlying even the leftist point of view. Shammas develops his Israeli identity as an Arab by confronting his own identity with the Israeli-ness of the Jews. In fact, his primary demand of Israeli Jews is that they change the rules of the game—that, as Jews, they reexamine the function that keeping old scores and accounts has in confusing the issues of their political and moral situation today. This is, however, no more than he demands of himself as he develops his own Israeli identity by rejecting much of the contemporary significance of his own historical and genealogical roots.

In the novel the essence of Shammas's confrontation with the Israeliness of the Jews is embodied in the confrontation between Shammas, the protagonist-narrator, and Yosh (Yehoshua) Bar-On, the Jewish

---

6. Anton Shammas, "Milhamti Be-Tahanot Anshe-Ha-Ruah" [My Fight against the Windmills of the Intellectuals], *Moznayim* 60, no. 3 (September 1986): 26-27; Anton Shammas, "Ashmat Ha-Babushka," 45.

Israeli author who travels with Shammas to Iowa City. Shammas has hardly bothered to hide the fact that the prototype for Bar-On is the Israeli author A. B. Yehoshua. He is presented satirically in the novel and, indeed, is seen in much the same light as Shammas saw Yehoshua during the stormy debate between the two which was carried on in the Israeli press about a year ago. The Israeli author Bar-On appears in the novel as a somewhat ridiculous figure, with racist beliefs and impulses, engaging in inner monologues strung together out of colloquial or literary clichés. One of the highpoints of the real-world debate between Shammas and Yehoshua came in a newspaper interview when the "liberal" Yehoshua, who is identified with the moderate-liberal wing of Israeli political opinion, made the following suggestion: after the creation of a Palestinian homeland in the occupied territories—of which he approves—Yehoshua proposed that Shammas find full expression for his nationalism by packing up and moving to the newly formed Palestinian state. In a series of replies that drew many others into this ongoing debate, Shammas tried to show Yehoshua that his suggestion is quite akin to Meir Kahane's proposal to ensure the Jewishness of Israel through an organized expulsion of the Arab population. The unwillingness of Yehoshua, and of many other Israeli liberals, to acknowledge the Arab Shammas as a full-fledged Israeli, whose native land is Israel just as theirs is, was proof for Shammas that the majority is not inclined to relinquish the Jewish primacy of the State of Israel, even at the risk of sacrificing its democratic character. In the novel Shammas focuses on the way liberals fall into the trap of racist discourse patterns. It is precisely for this reason that he conducts the satire with considerable sophistication—the better to expose the two-faced nature of Israeli public discourse.

In Paris, en route to Iowa City, Bar-On wonders what Shammas's reaction would be "if he only knew that to myself I think of him—proud Palestinian-Israeli-Arab that he is—as 'my Jew' " (72). In fact both of these epithets, "Palestinian" and "Jew," belong here to the same discursive universe of stereotyping and discrimination. It is crucial that Shammas refuses to label himself a Palestinian. In the novel, he rebuts attempts to define him as a Palestinian by noting, among other things, that as far back as the 1948 war his father did not consider himself a Palestinian refugee. Bar-On does define Shammas as a Palestinian, thus feeding the discriminatory stereotype of the Israeli Arab as having "alien" loyalties. To be sure, Bar-On is presented as wishing to show empathy for the plight of an Israeli Arab writer. However, as the satire brings out clearly, Bar-On's inner monologue reveals *both* his feeling of genuine empathy with a fellow-minority—an empathy based on the similarity between Shammas's situation and that of the Jews as a national minority—*and* the racist stance of a superior majority, in the unconsciously derogatory use of the phrase "my Jew."

4. Arabesques in Time, Arabesques in Space

Does the novel open with Shammas speaking of the death of his grandmother Alya on 1 April 1954, in the village? Or is he instead speaking of the death of his father in Haifa, in April 1978? In fact, Shammas is doing both at once—a fact that has profound implications for his treatment of time in the novel. The simultaneous interweaving of earlier and later events is a structural principle of the novel; Shammas exploits it chiefly as a concrete means of realizing his cyclical conception of time. The numerous digressions, the twists and turns, the sudden predestined meetings all conform, in one way or other, to the Arabian iconography of the arabesque. This phenomenon stands out particularly in the "narrative" parts, which revolve mostly around the village of Fasuta. But a careful reading of the "narrator's" portion, which describes the trip to Iowa City, also reveals the figure of the arabesque. Even in such a straightforward matter as Shammas's travel journal, things are not what they seem: for one, the entries are not always in chronological order! The connections among events within each part are highly complex, as is the relationship between the two parts. The static arabesque frees the chronological flow of time in the plot from any necessary involvement with such notions as redemption or progress. As mentioned above, Shammas questions the validity of relying on his own family genealogy as a basis for present-day political judgments; and, at the same time, he stands opposed to present-day manifestations of Zionism. Instead, he offers his own Israeli-ness as an alternative, embodying a more modest and far less apocalyptic conception of time.

The traditional figure of the arabesque, pervading the structure of the novel at every level, brings Shammas's representational mode close to a pure statement of formal relations. In the arabesque, Shammas has found a way to relate to the past without falling victim to its nondialectical universalism. Thus he describes the hardships of the Arab refugees of 1948—he attempts to shift the moral debate from considerations of precedence, of who or what came first, to confrontations with undeniably concrete instances of human suffering. The two-dimensional nature of the arabesque motivates the description of the oppression of the Palestinian woman without minimizing its urgency or gravity within the overall web of political oppression depicted in the novel. Thus, for example, in describing the hardships endured by Layla Khouri, Shammas has interwoven her mistreatment by Israeli soldiers in 1948 and 1981 with her misfortunes at the hands of Arab society (for example, her betrayal by a member of Shammas's family, and her sexual and apparently financial exploitation by the woman Sa'ada). Layla the Palestinian is portrayed in the novel as a commodity, passed from hand to hand, from government to government. In this respect, her existence parallels another arabesque, the cyclical course taken by Abayyad, the boy who was kidnapped into adoption and was himself treated as a commodity, whose loss first brought misery to his poverty-stricken natural parents just as it would later to his wealthy adoptive parents. Thus the arabesque takes the fetishization of the individual and the dominance of exchange value and weaves them into a fabric of human relationships existing in a context of social and political repression.[7] This unfolds against the background of the Zionist revolution, with the political realignments and the social and economic modernization which accompanied it, all culminating in the abandonment of the village and its noncommercialized way of life based upon use value.

The arabesque does not serve only a negative, critical function; it also bears a positive, utopian message. It acts as an analogue, in the area of the visual arts, to the position of Islamic "contractualism" in the social sphere. The distinction between Islamic contractualism and Western corporativism is a close parallel to the distinction between the collective *Gemeinschaft,* based on personal relationships, and the impersonal and achievement-oriented *Gesellschaft* usually associated with

---

7. Abdul R. JanMohamed, "The Economy of Manichean Allegory: The Function of Racial Difference in Colonialist Literature" in *Race, Writing, and Difference,* ed. Henry Louis Gates, Jr. (Chicago: University of Chicago Press, 1986), 79.

modern technological society. In contrast to western corporativism, with its preference for hierarchical structures in which a limited number of conclusions are drawn from a limited number of premises (on the model of geometry), the cyclical rhythms of the arabesque could well be said to characterize an "indefinitely expandable" structure. The arabesque provides a framework within which it becomes possible to reduce the apparently "chaotic variety of life's reality" to manageable proportions, yet without "arbitrarily setting bounds to it." The novel's arabesque style displays the general features of Islam's traditional atomism, an atomism representing an "equal and co-ordinated responsibility of all possible individuals for the maintenance of moral standards."[8]

This moral atomism and, in particular, the special kind of reduction that does not stifle the individuality of certain details are the key to understanding Shammas's arabesque discourse. In a striking passage in the novel, Shammas writes:

> That was Uncle Yusef. On the one hand a believing Catholic, whose heart, like that of Saint Augustine, was firm and secure, as if the Virgin herself had promised him that his years were but links in a chain leading to salvation and redemption. And on the other hand he believed, as if to keep an escape hatch open, that if dust were to return unto dust, and the jaws of death were gaping, that the twisting, elusive, cyclical periodicity of things would have the power to withstand death. But he was unaware of these two opposing aspects coexisting within himself; he saw them only as a unitary whole. (204)

Shammas's novel forces these two types of discourse, linear and cyclical, into a confrontation involving not synthesis but an attempt to extract the best from each. Shammas presents himself in the novel as someone in a position both to clarify this temporal duality—the coexistence of Christian time and quasi-pagan time in Uncle Yusef—and to enter into the Christian conception of time as a path leading to salvation (204). But this intermediate stance, in fact a continuation of Uncle

---

8. Marshall G. S. Hodgson, *The Venture of Islam: Conscience and History in a World Civilization* (Chicago: University of Chicago Press, 1974), 344-47. This book approaches the specific arabesque mode of reduction by viewing it in opposition to geometry, drawing an analogy between the arabesque and the nature of a historical report.

Yusef's position, represents a source from which Shammas draws strength. From within this static arabesque of time, but with one foot already on the outside, Shammas is in a position to continue striving toward his goal of a utopia, without paying the price of a nondialectical universalization of the past. Undoubtedly, dehistoricization can be made to serve the purposes of those interested in perpetuating the status quo of oppression, through a deliberate confusion of the notions of development, contingency, and the potential for change.[9] But the arabesque, whose cyclicity has the power "to withstand death," enables Shammas to keep a firm grasp on the absolute reality of suffering and of human existence, whose universal validity is not altered or obscured by its relative position in time. The arabesque creates the effect of static motion, motion without progress. This is its way of "withstanding death" and of undermining attempts to develop a rigidly teleological concept of "national time." It must be emphasized that the great flexibility of the arabesque does not disconnect it from the process of generalization and reduction involved in the creation of a "national subject." But it is never committed to a rigid representation of a national subject, fixed in space and time, and is therefore free to become an *autonomous* critical tool, endowed with its own absolute and self-sufficient validity. With its power thus not contingent upon the exclusive authority of some national subject, it becomes an effective weapon for the minority.

Standing both inside and outside the arabesque, Shammas freezes history; he does this to forge a critical dialogue in which both sides are precluded, in their argumentation, from appealing to selective generalizations based on decontextualized bits of history. Shammas denies Israeli Jews the right to justify present wrongdoings by past grievances, and he holds himself to the same standard. Others have not been so careful. Edward W. Said, for example, rightly criticizes the distortion of history implicit in Zionist claims about the Palestinians, but he falls into the same trap himself in his discussion of the enactment of the Law of Return (which imparts automatic Israeli citizenship to any Jewish immigrant) when the State of Israel was established. He views the law as racist, as a reflection of the inherently discriminatory character of the State of Israel, ignoring the fact that the Law of Return, like affirmative action in the United States, was enacted in an attempt to discrimi-

---

9. JanMohamed, "The Economy of Manichean Allegory," 77.

nate in favor of a disadvantaged minority, persecuted and uprooted Jews everywhere.[10] Shammas, too, is conscious of the law's racist implications. But he expresses this awareness in a completely different way than Said, and with sensitivity to its dialectical dimensions, by proposing that the law in its present form be repealed in the not-too-distant future and remain in force only for immigrants from distressed Jewish communities.

The nonmimetic geometrical abstractions of the arabesque are intimately linked to the function of *spatial* patterning in the novel. The entire journey to America in fact shows clear elements of a search for roots and spiritual identity. But here too the cyclical arabesque is brought into play, the same motion without progress wherein every destination immediately becomes the take-off point for a new quest. The writers participating in the International Writing Program are housed in a dormitory suggestively called the Mayflower, a name which hints at a connection between Shammas's ideal conception of Israeli identity and the model of a society of immigrants embodied in America and its young history. Yet, at the same time, Shammas has come full circle: he comments, while discussing a letter to his Jewish lover Shlomit in Israel, that only now in Iowa City, "over twenty years after I left my childhood house, do I feel, for the first time in many years, that I can conjure up my childhood house in the village, its smells and sights and sensations, for I am able for the first time to describe it to Shlomit, who never set foot there" (133).

Shammas invests his layover in Paris en route to Iowa City with a special function. First of all, during this intermezzo the novel introduces the figure of Amira, the Jewish writer from Egypt. In fact, the images of women in the novel—including Shammas's Lebanese cousin, his Jewish Israeli lover Shlomit, and Layla Khouri, the Christian woman converted to Islam—make up a representative sample of Middle East geography. There is a large degree of overlap here with the range of male figures. All these serve to lay out, in effect, a map of the different local and national images constituting the cardinal terms in the system of oppositions that collectively define Shammas's Israeli identity. A planned reunion in Paris with Shammas's female cousin from Lebanon represents a new possibility for Shammas to express his identity as an

---

10. Edward W. Said, "An Ideology of Difference" in *Race, Writing, and Difference*, 40. See also Shammas, "Ashmat Ha-Babushka," 45.

Arab. But at first the meeting does not come off. This fact is another example of the dialectical process—where a possibility is presented only to be rejected—by which Shammas develops his own identity. Indeed, as a "replacement" for his cousin, Shammas immediately makes contact with her opposite: the Jew Bar-On, who is also staying over in Paris.

5. The Gospel According to Uncle Yusef; or, Hebrew as the Language of Redemption

Uncle Yusef's arabesque tales are described by Shammas in these words:"They flowed about him in a stream of illusion which linked interior and exterior, beginning and ending, reality and fiction" (203). The arabesque, which makes no claim to represent any reality outside itself, is by that very token a fine vehicle for conveying a variety of heterogeneous materials. This constant confusion of domains and categories characterizes the lesson Shammas learns from his uncle's legacy. As he puts it, his uncle has given him all the keys to extricate himself from the arabesque and enter another existence—all the keys but the final one. The key to salvation lies in bringing together the two halves of a single whole—a juncture that comes only once. But the incompleteness in Shammas prevents him, as he puts it, from relying with confidence on any possibility of salvation whatsoever. Like the almost inextricable confusion between fiction and reality, epitomized in the contradiction between the two halves of the story, the novel presents a series of illusory solutions in the form of sets of twins, or near twins, who are intended to complement and complete one another. All this illustrates the novel's clear-sighted appreciation of the political potential of the arabesque. The bond between Shammas the Christian Arab and Bar-On the Jew should be sought not in some sort of messianic eschatology but rather in a close analysis of the Israeli experience and the utopian elements already present in it.

The stories told by Shammas's Christian Arab family from Fasuta depict a static existence, a dimension highlighted even more by the orality of these stories telling of family life in the village in the years before (and even after) the founding of the State of Israel. Oral literature acquires its cultural significance in relation to the time frame in which it is told. Here the time frame of the storyteller is also the political and moral time frame in which Shammas the author wrote and published his book. In this way Shammas simultaneously emphasizes the oral sources of his stories and the radical change that he himself introduces in moving from a traditional oral tale to a written story. Only rarely in the novel does he deny his identity as an Israeli writer and pretend to be a naive folk narrator. Over and over again, Shammas stresses the tension between his connection to oral tradition and his commitment to writing. Indeed, sometimes the very act of storytelling, as in Layla Khouri's case, can undermine the stability of reality. Shammas needs both types, both oral and written narrative, in order to come to terms with his own national literary tradition and to open a gateway to the utopian conception of modern Israeli nationhood outlined in his novel. What he does, in fact, is to rework in writing those stories he heard orally from Uncle Yusef in order to formulate through them a present reality. As remarked earlier, the atemporal, arabesque rhythms of the oral tradition serve as a touchstone for evaluating the nondialectical attitude toward time found in Israeli public discourse. With this in mind, it is noteworthy that Israeli critics reacting to the book have largely ignored the revolutionary function which Shammas gives to the blending of oral and written modes—they delight in the folklore and reject those parts having contemporary political relevance.

The duality with which Shammas displays his oral sources, a blend of estrangement and closeness, parallels the duality of his relationship to Hebrew literature and indeed complements it. In distancing himself from his oral sources, Shammas is forcing his way into written Hebrew literature as an outsider demanding equal rights with the insiders. The conceptual framework that best illuminates the relationship between Bar-On and Shammas is the world of literature and books, a world epitomized by the gathering of writers participating in the International Writing Program. Bar-On, at work on a book about an Israeli Arab, asks to make use of the figure of Anton Shammas. He wants to portray the Arab in his story with real empathy and not reduce him to a stereotype. But the motives underlying this—for example, his desire that his Arab character should play a leading role in a study of the image of the Arab in modern Hebrew literature—only accentuates Bar-On's own stereotypical attitudes toward his Arab characters. The stereotype, of course, is in general an extreme expression of domination. And so, as

Shammas shows us, Bar-On's desire to change the surface formulation of the stereotype without addressing the presuppositions of his own discourse leads him, at best, into a new variation on the same stereotype. At one point Bar-On announces his intention to write "about the isolation of the Palestinian Israeli Arab, an isolation greater than any other" (84). This would appear to reveal a special sensitivity to the fate of his protagonist—but the larger context of Shammas's novel makes it clear that it is just another indication of Bar-On's unwillingness to give up control over the representational moulds available for the depiction of this fate.

Bar-On's highly practical, utilitarian attitude toward the Other is illustrated by his reaction to Shammas's attempts to preserve his own independence in the face of Bar-On's domination. Bar-On proposes to treat Shammas's private life as an object to be exploited in the creation of his novel. Even when Bar-On gives up on Shammas, he still clings to the same Palestinian stereotype. And so, at one point, he seeks a functional replacement for Shammas, finding it in a Palestinian writer also taking part in the Writing Program; and when things fail to work out with this Palestinian substitute, he leaves America and returns to Israel. But just as the fictional autobiography of Shammas written by Abayyad the Palestinian does not count in the novel as *the* definitive text determining Shammas's identity, so too Shammas provides Bar-On the Jew with misleading information about his life. Shammas develops his own Israeli identity by liberating it from the various political interpretations threatening to swallow it up. And thus he keeps both Abayyad the Palestinian and Bar-On the Jew at a distance, allowing neither to gain control over the representation of his life story.

A number of Bar-On's comments on his own forthcoming novel are strikingly applicable to the novel *Arabesques* as well. And the deliberate obscurity which beclouds the whole matter of textual interrelationships, in comparing Shammas's own text with other texts developed within it (that of the Palestinian and that of the Jew), emphasizes their predominant status as mere collections of images rather than as representations of some external reality. In this way, through the world of literature and books, the ideological dilemma of Shammas's identity is translated into a struggle between texts. The arabesque novel, in its rejection of the authority of all representation, focuses our attention on the *internal* dynamics of the political, national, and cultural images involved.

Shammas is contrasted with Bar-On in the context of the Writing Program, at a time when both authors are at work on their own new books. At the same time, though, Shammas was also engaged in a confrontation with Bar-On's real-life counterpart, the Israeli writer A. B. Yehoshua, author of the well-known Hebrew short story "Facing the Forests."[11] The central episode of this story concerns the burning of a forest, forests being one of the paramount symbols of Zionist reconstruction. This particular forest was planted on the ruins of an Arab village destroyed in 1948, and it is set on fire by an old Arab villager with the silent cooperation of an eccentric Jewish fire warden.

The arabesque binds literature and metaliterature, the literary text itself and the critical discourse responding to it. And so Yehoshua's story enters into Shammas's novel, along with the important article written in response to it by the critic Mordechai Shalev.[12] Shalev criticizes the fact that the figure of the Arab in the story, with its political and moral overtones, fulfills a much more general oedipal function: the Arab serves as a means for the young man to carry out an oedipal revolt against the generation of his fathers. In essence Shalev claims that the moral issue, the eviction of the Arabs from their land, is only a pretext for raising the real question: Whose life has the greater vitality, the Jew's or the Arab's? Shammas portrays Bar-On (Yehoshua) as trying, in his new novel, to accommodate the critic Shalev. But Bar-On is unable to see that the attack against him was directed largely against the imposition of individual psychology on what is properly a political and collective matter. Yehoshua's story is thus seen as exploiting the figure of an oppressed Arab in order to fulfill the spiritual needs of an Israeli Jew. The same point is further emphasized by the fact that Yehoshua's Jewish protagonist is an antihero, an eccentric existing on the fringes of society. Even in the protests of the younger generation of Israelis against the injustices accompanying the realization of the Zionist dream—even here, Shammas tells us—the image of the Arab is exploited when a dominant majority ignores its responsibility to examine its own past with maturity and integrity.

---

11. A. B. Yehoshua, "Facing the Forests," in *Three Days and a Child*, trans. Miriam Arad (London: Peter Owen, 1971), 131-74.

12. Mordechai Shalev, "Ha-Aravim Ke-Pitaron Sifruti" [The Arabs as a Literary Solution], *Ha-Aretz*, 30 September 1970.

6. Which One Is the Other's Ventriloquist?

In principle, what we are dealing with here is a variation on the Hegelian paradigm of the master-slave relationship, whereby the master's consciousness of himself as master is conditioned by the slave's acknowledgment of the master's superior status. Yehoshua's story "Facing the Forests" and Bar-On's clinging to the stereotype of the Palestinian both emphasize the role played by the figure of the Arab as the key to the identity of the Israeli Jew. But a situation whereby the Israeli "master" draws on a dual consciousness—as minority and majority at once—complicates considerably any attempt at interpretation. And it renders equally problematic: the strategies open to those condemned to the role of "slave" in this dialectic. For the Israeli "master," in conformity with the Hegelian paradigm, has attained this status only after winning a life-and-death struggle for independence, and continues to derive its self-consciousness and legitimacy from its still-recent past as an oppressed minority.

But the Hegelian "slave" in the novel, that is, the Israeli Arab, is just as dependent on the Israeli "master" for his own consciousness. His confrontation with Bar-On is especially relevant here. After Bar-On's hurried departure from Iowa City and return to Israel, Shammas is beset by guilt and the sense of having missed an opportunity. Despite the struggle he wages against Bar-On, with Bar-On ultimately recast as his satirical victim, Shammas's life is fundamentally dependent upon Bar-On's. Shammas is afraid that his meeting with Abayyad could be taken by Bar-On as an attempt to enlist Shammas in the PLO; he interprets this as an important clue to his own identity, which cannot exist without the presence, at once threatening and soothing, of Bar-On the Jew. Just as he feels betrayed when Bar-On prefers the Palestinian to himself (152), so he reflects: "How could I react without Bar-On breathing down my neck? How could there even *be* a situation, good or bad, where Bar-On was not breathing down my neck?" (232).

The fact that Shammas is set in opposition to a master who is himself a slave—namely, the Israeli Jew—limits the spiritual and revolutionary power that normally accrues automatically to the slave. It is hardly an accident that the blatant materialistic dimension of Arab life in Israel and the occupied territories, with the Arabs visible and prominent as manual laborers, finds as little genuine political expression in the novel as it does in real life. As an Israeli Arab, Shammas too must confront the dual consciousness of the Israeli-Jewish master-slave, and in consequence he has difficulty in crystallizing any sort of revolutionary consciousness. As Fredric Jameson has said, there is a certain advantage to having an overall map of a given situation, a map drawn from the realistic materialist viewpoint of someone who fulfills it in his own work. Shammas has such a map but cannot take advantage of it. Neither Yehoshua nor Shammas can allow himself to take advantage of the national allegory that characterizes the materialism of Third World literature, an allegory "where the telling of the individual story and the individual experience cannot but ultimately involve the whole laborious telling of the experience of the collectivity itself."[13]

As mentioned above, Shalev has criticized the story "Facing the Forests" for substituting an external political dimension for its oedipal concerns. Shalev's attack can now be reinterpreted as an attack on Yehoshua's deviation from the national allegory that is permitted him as an Israeli author belonging to the majority culture. For Shammas the arabesque, with its flexibility and "freedom from any myth-based symbolism," is the appropriate vehicle for coping with the problematic status of allegory in this literary and political situation.[14] He is suspicious of the validity of the Israeli national allegory, both for the Israeli Jew, with his uncertain identity as master, and for himself as a half-slave whose role and identity are no less uncertain; and his suspicion finds expression in the novel in a heterogeneous and discontinuous arabesque of allegorical patterns, many of them Christian, interwoven with passages of local documentary narrative. For Shammas, the allegorical image of the New Testament cock—the image of the cock before it crowed at dawn to signal that Peter had denied his Lord Jesus—introduces in the novel a fascinating blend of mutually incompatible interpretations reflecting both Eastern and Western traditions. The reality depicted in the novel rejects over and over again the promise of redemption implicit in this mythic image. The arabesque blends fact and fiction, realism and romance, tragedy and soap opera, with bits of the real-life biography of the author Anton Shammas thrown in. All

---

13. Fredric Jameson, "Third-World Literature in the Era of Multinational Capitalism," *Social Text* 15 (Fall 1986), 69, 85-86. Jameson makes use here of the Hegelian paradigm of the master-slave relationship.

14. Hodgson, *The Venture of Islam*, 510.

this alerts the reader over and over not to expect the ideological satisfaction which a traditional, fixed literary genre is able to supply.

In several senses, Anton Shammas's *Arabesques* both falls into and deviates from the patterns of a "minor literature" as defined by Gilles Deleuze and Felix Guattari.[15] In accordance with this pattern, *Arabesques* is not subject to the authority or the conventions of standard literary genres. First, this Hebrew novel written by an Arab "doesn't come from a minor language; it is rather that which a minority constructs within a major language" (*KML*, 16). At the hands of the Israeli Arab Shammas, Hebrew, the mythic language of Zionism, undergoes a process of *deterritorialization*—the first definitional component, according to Deleuze and Guattari, of a minor literature. Yet this characterization, which at first glance appears to fit the case of Shammas rather well, is somewhat deceptive. For, although Shammas does carry out a process of deterritorialization of Hebrew, at the same time he is reterritorializing it as the language of the *Israeli*.

The second component of a minor literature, whereby *everything* (including the individual) is viewed in *political* terms, also marks a divergence between Deleuze and Guattari's definition and Shammas's novel with the special situation from which it springs. For Deleuze and Guattari, the "political" means a liberation from the unified authority of an autonomous subject, a notion which they apply to Kafka. Politicization undoubtedly plays a significant role in Shammas's novel too: it is a major effect of the mutual undercutting performed by the narrators of the two halves of the novel. Shammas, however, does not politicize everything. His intermediate stance here can be seen both in the novel's critical response to Yehoshua's politicization of the oedipal pattern in "Facing the Forests" and in its refusal to see itself as a national allegory.

Nor does Deleuze and Guattari's third definitional component, whereby "everything takes on a collective value" (*KML*, 17), make the case of Shammas any easier to pigeonhole. This notion of collectivity is to be understood in terms of the opposition between a non-reductionist "collective assemblage of enunciation" and the reductionist concept of a (national) subject (*KML*, 18). In fact, "collectivity" in Deleuze and

---

15. Gilles Deleuze and Félix Guattari, *Kafka: Toward a Minor Literature,* trans. Dana Polan, foreword by Réda Bensmaia, (Minneapolis: University of Minnesota Press, 1986); all further references to this work, abbreviated as *KML*, will appear in the text. Bensmaia's introduction was especially helpful in the following discussion.

Guattari's sense is at variance with the dual effect of the arabesque, which simultaneously preserves the independence and particularity of atomic bits of experience while carrying out a reduction, albeit open-ended, which organizes and unites them. Deleuze and Guattari's anti-reductionist stance carries a price: a disconnection from the inherently reductionist, utopian project of nation making. Indeed, in their discussion of the collective component of a minor literature, they suggest that an author on the margins of the community is all the more able "to express another possible community and to forge the means for another consciousness and another sensibility" (*KML*, 17). By contrast, Shammas does not construct his Israeli utopia from some totally Other consciousness or sensibility, but from the existing, contradiction-ridden inventory of present-day Israeli reality.

But all these differences shrink into insignificance as Deleuze and Guattari proceed to expand the scope of their definition enormously, claiming that the term *minor* "no longer designates specific literatures but the revolutionary conditions for every literature within the heart of what is called great (or established) literature" (*KML*, 18). From here it is only a step to their conception of minor literature as a "machine of expression," a tool for producing mere effects, with no center of gravity (*KML*, 18), thus divorcing it from any possible utopian dimension. Like minor literature, the arabesque is characterized by a lack of obligation to any sort of representation or mythic symbolism. Yet the arabesque does not discard the dream of a national utopia—indeed, it requires it: for the utopian dream creates a context and a target against which the arabesque can level its attack on uncritical, restrictive reductions. In fact, the arabesque undermines the dichotomy that (according to Deleuze and Guattari) any minor literature must address—a dichotomy between, on the one hand, an extreme *re*territorialization of language through symbols and archetypes (their example for the political results of this process is the Zionist dream) and, on the other, the process they ascribe to Kafka, a radical *de*territorialization of language "to the point of sobriety," culminating in "a perfect and unformed expression, a materially intense expression" (*KML*, 19). Shammas's Hebrew arabesque takes up at the socio-political level, the question Deleuze and Guattari had formulated at the linguistic level—that of evaluating "the degrees of territoriality, deterritorialization, and reterritorialization" (*KML*, 25) practiced in Hebrew (the mythic language informing the

genesis of Zionism) and other languages in a similar position. Faced
with these two conflicting demands—an extreme deterritorialization
"to the point of sobriety" vs. a concern for relative degrees of re- and
deterritorialization—the arabesque can suggest a dynamic middle
way. Shammas's paradigm concedes the importance of the concept of
a nation state, but only as articulated through the arabesque: not as an
absolute and rigid notion, defined once and for all, but in a much
more critical and flexible sense, as something evolving and responsive
to the dialectical process.

These differences between Shammas's model and Deleuze and Guattari's
construct in fact could serve to outline a theoretical discussion of the
principles implicit in the arabesque as a vehicle for minority discourse.
A good example of the especially pertinent advantages afforded by the
arabesque is the way Shammas turns to real advantage his own weakness as "slave" vis-á-vis an ambiguous "master." The Hebrew culture's battery of defense mechanisms, which thwarts the development
of a revolutionary consciousness, is appropriated by Shammas and
used for a different purpose: to illumine the quandary of the slave
forced to choose between assignment to a niche in the master culture,
thereby condemning himself to imitation, assimilation and loss of
identity, and adherence to his traditional culture, thus forcing him into
the position of a rejected "savage." Indeed, it is precisely within this
unique sort of majority culture, which pretends to be a minority culture and thereby absolves itself of its real responsibilities and commitments as the master culture, that Shammas can realize Derrida's ideal,
"to speak the other's language without renouncing [his] own."[16] We
should not forget that Hebrew Israeli culture, by virtue of being the
dominant majority's culture, acts as a magnet to the minorities who
must function within it. But when it represents itself as a minority culture, it undermines its own authority to reject whatever is defined as
the Other culture. Bar-On, who in his search for a literary subject shifts

---

16. Jacques Derrida, "Racism's Last Word," *Race, Writing, and Difference*, 333.
Shammas writes: "I feel like an exile within Arabic, the language of my blood. I feel
like an exile within Hebrew, my step-mother language." Unlike Jewish Hebrew writers
in Israel who "see Hebrew as a Jewish language being written in Israel," Shammas by
contrast "sees Hebrew and Arabic as two Israeli languages" ("Ashmat Ha-Babushka,"
45). His novel *Arabesques* deals with Hebrew culture and the future of Hebrew as an Israeli language. The fate of *Arabic* as an Israeli language, in light of the prevailing political asymmetry between Hebrew and Arabic, is another matter.

his attention from Shammas to the Palestinian from Nablus, compares the two. He himself admits to being troubled by Shammas's complex multiple identity, whose existence transcends the stereotype and violates the binary opposition between Bar-On and the Other: "But my previous hero [Shammas] does not define himself as my enemy, at least not in the accepted sense of the word. And this constitutes a difficulty for me. By contrast, I feel closer to the problems of this Palestinian, and I hope I will not be proved wrong, but my heart tells me that he is the one I will succeed in setting down in writing" (152).

Shammas's *Arabesques* places Israeli Jews in an uneasy position. On the one hand, they cannot just dismiss him or ignore him as someone totally Other especially in light of his virtuoso command of Hebrew as a literary medium and his vigorous participation in the Israeli mass media as journalist, polemicist, and author. On the other hand, Shammas's violation of the accepted boundaries of Hebrew culture makes it difficult for Israeli Jews to identify easily with him or adopt him as one of their own. This background shows how the novel forces a fundamental revision in some of the political assumptions underlying Israeli public discourse. The very fact that a novel like *Arabesques* exists at all undermines seriously the traditional view of Hebrew literature as a *Jewish national* literature. Through the special device of interweaving oral and folk elements into the narrative, the novel contributes to a process of deterritorialization, challenging the long-standing total coincidence of the Hebrew language with its Jewish subject matter. The Hebrew reader, unable to reject Shammas's challenge out of hand, must either undergo a kind of inner split or develop temporary defense mechanisms (for example, by putting folklore and politics in clearly separate boxes or by making the absurd demand that Shammas become a traditional Zionist). This phenomenon, of Arab authors writing in Hebrew, is still in its infancy, but the trend has already been joined by other writers, such as Na'im Araydi and Muhammad Ana'im. And on the Jewish side, it is noteworthy that parallel attempts to overthrow canonical linguistic boundaries have been made by the writers of Yoram Kanyuk and Yisrael Eliraz, who have actually published Hebrew works under Arab pseudonyms.

It is important now to turn our attention to the other side of the coin, shifting from the deterritorialization to the reterritorialization of Hebrew. "It is essential this time to have an Arab, as an answer to silence," Bar-On muses; "An Arab who speaks in the language of grace, as the exiled Florentine once termed Hebrew. Hebrew, as the language of grace, in contrast to the language of confusion which raged around the world with the fall of the Tower of Babel. My Arab will build his tower of confusion on my own lot. In the language of grace. In my opinion this is his one chance for salvation. Within the accepted limits, of course" (83). We have here a paradox, a simultaneous striving to speak in the Other's language without giving up one's own, as Derrida put it. Thus Hebrew, the old-new language which Shammas, following Dante, called the "language of grace" turns out to offer a political salvation for the Israeli Arab. But it can also suggest a political and existential solution to the confusion of "Jew" and "Israeli." The kind of synthetic Hebrew wielded so ably by Shammas, a popular and modern vernacular, is in fact also a new language, a language created by the Other. The very artificiality of Shammas's language, sometimes even verging on parody, undermines the "self-evident" presuppositions of the entire discourse and encourages the cultural and political reconceptualization so essential to the life and discourse of Israeli Jews. Curiously, this process reenacts, in a sense, the creation during the early days of Zionism of a national *Jewish* consciousness within the Hebrew literature of the late nineteenth and early twentieth centuries, as writers strove to re-create Hebrew as a new synthetic language and a source of modern national identity.[17] This work of linguistic invention now serves Shammas in his attempt to build a new-old language as a bridge toward the re-creation of an old-new nation. As an Arab writer, breaking into the linguistic and literary citadel of the Israeli Jews, Shammas calls into question their claim to exclusive possession of the language of traditional Zionism. For him Hebrew is simply the language of present-day Israelis. Acknowledging this revision in the canonical definition of Hebrew literature amounts to acknowledging the radical changes that the Zionist national subject must undergo to cope with the sharp contradictions besetting him in his new historical situation. The immediate (though not exclusive) expression of these changes is an admission of the need to force the values of the Jewish state to approximate better the concrete norms of a truly democratic society.

---

17. On the need for a new vocabulary to come to terms with the contradictions in present-day Israel, see Bial, *Power and Powerlessness in Jewish History*, 168-169.

Shammas's affair with Amira, the Jewish woman writer from Egypt, arouses Bar-On's anger. Bar-On sees in this love an intolerable threat to the established boundaries delimiting his national culture. But Amira has no material connection to the reality of Israel—and therefore for her, existing as a member of the Jewish minority in Alexandria, living in an Arabic and French milieu, Hebrew is indeed the language of the dead past. But for Shammas and Bar-On, Hebrew, as the language of Israel and the Israelis, is the "language of grace," a language capable of reconciling and uniting them. A Dutch author visiting the Writing Program wants to speak with Shammas about "this schizophrenia wherein Bar-On and [Shammas] are but a single individual" (130); and a Norwegian writer acknowledges "that they have not yet made up their minds which one is the other's ventriloquist" (130).

The language of grace, which is supposed to effect a fusion of Shammas and Bar-On, also reminds us of the way the arabesque maps out the future of this special confrontation between master and slave. As previously remarked, the possibility of this fusion is latent in the very ambivalence of the confrontation. Shammas's arabesque does not aim to liberate the slave through a reversal of roles whereby master and slave merely trade places. For, let us recall, a truly Hegelian freedom would involve an *Aufhebung* of the entire opposition. This is the promise held out by the arabesque's composition which "figure[s] forth eternity, presenting the infinite complexity and movement of existence and at the same time resolving it in total harmony of detail with detail and of part with whole so that all that movement is seen in overall repose. . . . The innumerable details are each felt as precious, *yet no one item stands out to dominate the whole*."[18]

But the dangers involved in a shift from Hebrew as the language of the past to Hebrew as "the language of grace" are not small. To be sure, the Israeli dream presented here is no Canaanite movement,[19] no apocalyptic vision of a liberation from the fetters of Judaism through an aggressive severing of historical roots. To the contrary: Shammas's Hebrew arabesque represents a utopia, emerging from a detailed critical

---

18. Hodgson, *The Venture of Islam*, 510; my emphasis.

19. The Canaanite Movement was a Jewish literary and political group active in Palestine (later in Israel) since the 1940s. It advocated shedding Jewish identity in favor of a return to pre-Juadaic, Hebrew, pagan culture presumably integral to the Semitic Middle East.

confrontation between the cultural demands of past and present. But the confrontation is fraught with danger. Indeed, when the husband of Shlomit, Shammas's Israeli Jewish lover, discovers Shammas's Hebrew love letters to his wife, their affair explodes, shattering a delicate and dangerous balance across both family and national boundaries (85). From a language of grace and redemption, Hebrew thus risks once again becoming a language of censure sanctioning racist fears of the Other, whose sexual prowess overcomes the "master's" wife.

The arabesque is a remarkable blend of two conceptions of temporality: a critical approach to time, having no necessary commitment to history or to any promise of progress toward redemption, with an adherence to a static and cyclical temporal continuum. Shammas's Israeli identity is constructed from multiple negations and a critical relationship to prevailing interpretations of the past and future. Shammas's arabesque appropriates the Hebrew language as the language of Israelis. This is an approximation of a relatively autonomous entity present and capable of bringing about a better future. In the current Israeli situation, the arabesque serves as a model for minority discourse, whose flexibility stands it in good stead even in a contradiction-ridden labyrinth that sometimes appears to have no exit. Shammas's book points the way to a utopian unification of the language of Arabs and Jews—a unification that is only a contingent possibility, subject to human and political constraints. And yet, coming as it does in the dark days of the occupation of the West Bank and Gaza, the deep sensitivity of Shammas's challenge may open a door to hope.

—translated by Orin D. Gensler

Gastarbeiterliteratur: The Other Speaks Back

Arlene Akiko Teraoka

M y essay has two beginnings. The first is the silence of the Turks in works of contemporary German drama. In the scene ironically titled "Foreigners' German" ("*Ausländerdeutsch*") in Franz Xaver Kroetz's *Furcht und Hoffnung der BRD* (1984), the Turk smiles, laughs, nods, shows hesitation, confusion, and even deliberation. But he never speaks.[1] The German woman who has invited him to her apartment "converses" with him about relationships between men and women in Turkey and in Germany, about intercultural marriage between Turkish men and German women, and, nervously and coyly, about the possibility of their own sexual relationship. Assured by his responses that he finds her desirable and would want to marry her even if they were in Turkey, she decides to go to bed with him, with the proviso that the Turk "be careful" (77); she is fearful, she explains, of becoming the mother of a Turkish child in Germany.

Kroetz's short scene depicts the development of a kind of trust on the part of the German woman. Her questions throughout express

---

1. Franz Xaver Kroetz, *Furcht und Hoffnung der BRD: Das Stück, das Material, das Tagebuch* (Frankfurt am Main: Suhrkamp, 1984), 73-77; further citations from this work will be included in the text. All translations from the German throughout this essay are my own.

stereotypical beliefs concerning the way Muslim men treat their women, while the seemingly thoughtful responses of the Turk work to soothe her apprehension. The decision at the end to sleep with her guest, with the belief that he will take care not to get her pregnant, in fact reverses the explicit rejection that opens the scene (she states at the outset, "No, I won't, because I'm not on the pill" [73]). It is part of Kroetz's craft that the reader also comes to sense the Turk's trustworthiness, and to attribute sensitivity and honesty to his nonverbal responses. Yet the Turk's ability to comprehend the woman's questions is never certain. When she asks, for example, "I'd never say that to you if you could understand me—can you understand me?" the response of the Turk remains deliberately ambiguous: he laughs (73). And the last line of the scene reinforces the sense of insecurity, as the text simply ends with the woman's question, "Right?" (77). The Turk remains mute, and his silence makes him indecipherable.

Botho Strauß's *Groß und klein* (1978), in the scene "Big and Little," offers another example of the Turkish riddle.[2] Again we are dealing with a Turkish man and a German woman, this time man and wife. Unlike Kroetz's silent Turk, however, Strauß's figure speaks, in both German and Turkish. What is of particular note is the manner in which these two languages are used. The Turk's German consists of monosyllabic words that he bellows out, "isolated screams" that sound "like military commands": "Bite," "Door," "Shit," "Beer," "One," "Come," and so forth (201-2). His German wife, interestingly enough, cannot make sense of his German words and can only guess at what her drunken husband is saying. It is his Turkish that she understands, and in his own language, her husband speaks what sounds like poetry: (she translates) "You are my wife and my darling . . . . You follow me . . . the thousand stone steps . . . down the stairs of life" (206). Strauß's fascinating scene presents the figure of a Turk who speaks a brutal and brutalized German that is indecipherable, while with the help of a translator, we are able to recognize a passionate, poetic Turkish soul beneath the drunken, incoherent exterior. As in Kroetz's text, the

---

2. Botho Strauß, *Trilogie des Wiedersehens/Groß und klein: Zwei Theaterstücke* (Munich: Deutscher Taschenbuch Verlag, 1980), 189-208; further citations from this work will be included in the text. Harald Weinrich discusses the scene briefly in his "Gastarbeiterliteratur in der Bundesrepublik Deutschland," *Zeitschrift für Literatur-wissenschaft und Linguistik*, no. 56 (1984): 12.

Turk cannot speak in German, which is to say that, except through the mediation of gestures or translation, he cannot speak—he cannot speak for himself.[3]

My second beginning is the remarkable work by Gilles Deleuze and Félix Guattari entitled (in English translation) *Kafka: Toward a Minor Literature*.[4] Drawing from Kafka's fascinating diary entry of 25 December 1911,[5] Deleuze and Guattari formulate the concept of a "small" or "minor" literature that is the collective and revolutionary literature of a minority writing in a major, dominant language (16-27). As a "minority" literature that is written within and against a dominating literary and cultural tradition, the *kleine Literatur* is structurally and politically related to the situation of the Third World vis-à-vis advanced industrial nations; Deleuze and Guattari, in fact, speak of "underdevelopment" and "linguistic Third World zones" (27). More important

3. The attitude that Turks or other foreign workers who cannot speak German are thus "speechless" can be found also in Irmgard Ackermann's "Nachwort" to the anthology *Türken deutscher Sprache: Berichte, Erzählungen, Gedichte*, ed. Irmgard Ackermann (Munich: Deutscher Taschenbuch Verlag, 1984). Ackermann states that the Turkish authors included in the volume, who write in German, possess a "capacity of articulation" that distinguishes them from other Turks "who remain mute in their suffering" (248); they thus become "spokesmen of the speechless" (251). Franco Biondi and Rafik Schami note the infrequent and clichéd treatment of guest workers in contemporary German literature, in "Mit Worten Brücken bauen! Bemerkungen zur Literatur von Ausländern," in *Türken raus? oder Verteidigt den sozialen Frieden: Beiträge gegen die Ausländerfeindlichkeit*, ed. Rolf Meinhardt (Reinbeck: Rowohlt, 1984), 69. Yüksel Pazarkaya notes the "disinterest" of contemporary German authors toward the topic of guest workers, in his "Stimmen des Zorns und der Einsamkeit in Bitterland: Wie die Bundesrepublik Deutschland zum Thema der neuen türkischen Literatur wurde," *Zeitschrift für Kulturaustausch* 35, no. 1 (1985): 19. Their observations are supported by Sargut Sölcün, "Türkische Gastarbeiter in der deutschen Gegenwartsliteratur," *Kürbiskern*, 1979, no. 3: 74–81; Helmut Scheuer, "Der 'Gastarbeiter' in Literatur, Film und Lied deutscher Autoren," *Zeitschrift für Literaturwissenschaft und Linguistik*, no. 56 (1984): 62–74; and Katharina Baudach, "Mehmet spielt nur die Rolle des Schatttens: In der deutschen Gegenwartsliteratur sind türkische Arbeitnehmer fast nur in Kinderbüchern bekannt," *Zeitschrift für Kulturaustausch* 31, no. 3 (1981): 319–21.
4. Gilles Deleuze and Félix Guattari, *Kafka: Toward a Minor Literature*, trans. Dana Polan, Theory and History of Literature, vol. 30 (Minneapolis: University of Minnesota Press, 1986); further citations from this work will be included in the text. The work has also appeared in German, as *Kafka: Für eine kleine Literatur*, trans. Burkhart Kroeber (Frankfurt am Main: Suhrkamp, 1976); original French title, *Kafka, Pour une littérature mineure* (Paris: Les Editions de Minuit, 1975).
5. Franz Kafka, *Tagebücher, 1910-1923*, ed. Max Brod (Frankfurt am Main: S. Fischer, 1948-49), 147-50.

here, they make the statement that minority status in a language and a culture that are not one's own ("the problem of a minor literature") is "the problem of immigrants, and especially of their children" (19).[6]

Here the two points of my beginning converge. From the German point of view, Turks have been an indecipherable, silent presence in West German society for the last twenty-five years.[7] A linguistic and cultural minority, economically oppressed and socially underprivileged, guest workers have nonetheless begun to produce and to publish literary works in German. When the silent Turk begins to speak in the dominant language, we can ask to what extent his words represent a collective and oppositional consciousness of the kind envisioned by Deleuze and Guattari, one that exists, to quote Deleuze and Guattari quoting Kafka, "[between] the impossibility of not writing, the impossibility of writing in German, [and] the impossibility of writing otherwise" (16).

Although foreign workers have been the subjects, if not also the authors, of works in their national languages since the 1960s, the so-called *Gastarbeiterliteratur* has been largely a phenomenon of the 1980s.[8]

---

6. The German translation uses the term *Gastarbeiter* (28).

7. There are now some 4.5 million foreigners (of a total population of approximately 62 million) in West Germany, a third of whom are Turkish. Turks were first recruited for work in West Germany in 1961. For general introductions to the history and present situation of the guest workers, see Ernst Klee, ed., *Gastarbeiter: Analysen und Berichte* (Frankfurt am Main: Suhrkamp, 1972); Verena McRae, *Die Gastarbeiter: Daten, Fakten, Probleme* (Munich: C.H. Beck, 1981); Pazarkaya, *Spuren des Brots: Zur Lage der ausländischen Arbeiter* (Zurich: Unionsverlag, 1983); Christian Habbe, ed., *Ausländer: Die verfemten Gäste*, Spiegel-Buch (Reinbek: Rowohlt, 1983); and Rolf Meinhardt, ed., *Türken raus? oder Verteidigt den sozialen Frieden* (Reinbek: Rowohlt, 1984).

8. Ackermann, in 1983, makes the following statement: "The literature which is at issue here, namely the texts written by foreigners about their own situation as *Gastarbeiter* in West Germany . . . , is a relatively recent occurrence in the literary field, as an independent literary form hardly more than four or five years old" (" 'Gastarbeiter' literatur als Herausforderung," *Frankfurter Hefte* 38 [1983] : 56). Cf. Peter Seibert, "Zur 'Rettung der Zungen': Ausländerliteratur in ihren konzeptionellen Ansätzen," *Zeitschrift für Literaturwissenschaft und Linguistik*, no. 56 (1984): 41-43; and Biondi and Schami, "Mit Worten Brücken bauen," 67-68 (see n.3 above). See Biondi on the development of Italian emigrant literature in the FRG, in his "Von den Tränen zu den Bürgerrechten: Ein Einblick in die italienische Emigranten-literatur," *Zeitschrift für Literaturwissenschaft und Linguistik*, no. 56 (1984): 75-100, esp. 77-81; cf. Biondi and Schami, "Literatur der Betroffenheit: Bemerkungen zur Gastarbeiter-literatur," in *Zu Hause in der Fremde: Ein bundesdeutsches Ausländer-Lesebuch*, ed. Christian Schaffernicht (Fischerhude: Verlag Atelier im Bauernhaus, 1981), 132. Pazarkaya discusses the development of Turkish literature from and about West

In addition to German publications by individual authors in such mainstream publishing houses as Deutscher Taschenbuch, Claassen, Rowohlt, and Fischer, the literary works of foreign workers have been made available to a German reading audience through a number of anthologies, some edited by these authors themselves, and special issues of journals such as the *Zeitschrift für Kulturaustausch* and *Kürbiskern*.[9] The sudden outpouring of literature from such an "improbable" segment of West German society has led one scholar and translator to exclaim, "We have before us not only a social phenomenon, but perhaps the most fascinating event in German literary history in the twentieth century."[10] One might disagree with this enthusiastic evaluation, but one thing seems certain: in the so-called *Gastarbeiterliteratur* the opaque Other has broken its silence and begun to speak to the West; moreover, in speaking "our" language, it has begun to speak *back*.

The predominant themes and issues addressed in this literature attest in fact to the intensity with which the authors feel the "Otherness" of their existence in Germany.[11] They write of their isolation as the seat

---

Germany, in "Stimmen des Zorns" (see n.3 above); Parzarkaya's essay is a slightly revised version of his "Türkiye, Mutterland — Almanya, Bitterland . . . : Das Phänomen der türkischen Migration als Thema der Literatur," *Zeitschrift für Literaturwissenschaft und Linguistik*, no. 56 (1984): 101-24. See also his " 'Ohne die Deutschen wäre Deutschland nicht übel': Der 'Gastarbeiter' und seine Erfahrungen als strittiges Thema der zeitgenössischen türkischen Literatur," *Zeitschrift für Kulturaustausch* 31, no. 3 (1981): 314-18.

9. Ackermann lists anthologies, special issues, and literary magazines and newspapers published by or for foreigners, in " 'Gastarbeiter' literatur als Herausforderung," 56-57. An excellent, but selected, bibliography of primary literature can be found in the special issue on *Gastarbeiterliteratur*, *Zeitschrift für Literaturwissenschaft und Linguistik*, no. 56 (1984): 142-47. The major literary anthologies upon which my essay is based are the following: Ackermann, ed., *Als Fremder in Deutschland: Berichte, Erzählungen, Gedichte von Ausländern* (Munich: Deutscher Taschenbuch Verlag, 1982); Biondi et al., eds., *Annäherungen*, Südwind Gastarbeiterdeutsch, vol. 3 (Bremen: Edition Con, 1982); Biondi et al., eds., *Im neuen Land*, Südwind Gastarbeiterdeutsch, vol. 1 (Bremen: Edition Con, 1980); Ackermann, ed., *In zwei Sprachen leben: Berichte, Erzählungen, Gedichte von Ausländern* (Munich: Deutscher Taschenbuch Verlag, 1983); Christian Schaffernicht, ed., *Zu Hause in der Fremde: Ein bundesdeutsches Ausländer-Lesebuch* (Fischerhude: Verlag Atelier im Bauernhaus, 1981); Biondi et al., eds., *Zwischen Fabrik und Bahnhof*, Südwind Gastarbeiterdeutsch, vol. 2 (Bremen: Edition Con, 1981); and Biondi et al., eds., *Zwischen zwei Giganten: Prosa, Lyrik und Grafiken aus dem Gastarbeiteralltag*, Südwind Gastarbeiterdeutsch, vol. 4 (Bremen: Edition Con, 1983). Topical special issues are *Kürbiskern*, 1979, no. 3, and *Zeitschrift für Kulturaustausch* 35, no. 1 (1985).

10. Gisela Kraft, "Türkische Literatur in deutscher Sprache: Übersetzernotizen zu Beginn der achtziger Jahre," *Sprache im technischen Zeitalter*, no. 82 (15 June 1982): 137.

11. For a general introduction to and an overview of the major themes of

beside them remains empty in an overcrowded streetcar; of the instant suspicion of their criminality when they are accused of murdering a man who has only fainted, or arrested for shoplifting when they try on a leather jacket in a department store; of the hatred they experience on a daily basis, observing time and again that dogs in Germany are treated with greater compassion than are the foreign workers. They write also of their feelings of alienation when they return as *Deutsche* to their native country. Those of the second generation, the immigrant children growing up in Germany, write of slowly losing their identity as they learn to accommodate themselves to their German environment, and of the social, cultural, and linguistic barriers against friendship and intimacy with Germans. Not only does this literature portray the "Otherness," the profound alienation of a significant portion of West German society; but as Harald Weinrich claims, "in this literature we [Germans] have the chance to experience ourselves as foreigners and Germany as a foreign country."[12]

Yet it would be naive to view the German literature of foreign workers in Germany as simply an instance of an exploited and marginalized group finally bringing its experiences into the German public sphere, or simply an opportunity for Germans to undergo a kind of cultural "alienation effect" and to examine their attitudes and behavior toward others. Rather, I would like to look at this literary phenomenon as something interpreted and constituted in often conflicting ways by various groups representing different cultural and political views. What is called *Gastarbeiterliteratur*, in other words, is really contested territory, and all claims made about or *on* it are profoundly strategic and political.

Gastarbeiterliteratur, I would recommend—with certain reservations that I elaborate later in this essay—the work by Irmgard Ackermann: in addition to " 'Gastarbeiter' literatur als Herausforderung," the essays "Integrationsvorstellungen und Integrationsdarstellungen in der Ausländerliteratur," *Zeitschrift für Literaturwissenschaft und Linguistik*, no. 56 (1984): 23-39; and "In der Fremde hat man eine dünne Haut . . . : Türkische Autoren der 'Zweiten Generation' oder Die Überwindung der Sprachlosigkeit," *Zeitschrift für Kulturaustausch* 35, no. 1 (1985): 28-32. See also Weinrich, "Gastarbeiterliteratur in der Bundesrepublik Deutschland" (see n.2 above).

12. Weinrich, "Gastarbeiterliteratur in der Bundesrepublik Deutschland," 12. Consider also Ackermann's plea: "It is equally obvious however that this literature is written also for Germans, in order to bring home to them the problems and the thoughts and views of the foreigners living among them, and at the same time, by presenting them critically from an outsider's point of view, to bring typical German habits and beliefs into question" (" 'Gastarbeiter' literatur als Herausforderung," 62).

For one thing, a reader of *Gastarbeiterliteratur* will soon realize that the term itself is more projection than description.[13] Franco Biondi, Rafik Schami, Jusuf Naoum, and Suleman Taufiq, the author-editors of several volumes of "guest worker literature," claim to adopt the term *Gastarbeiter* with full consciousness of the provocative irony implied. They write:

> We consciously use the term *Gastarbeiter* that has been imposed on us, in order to expose the irony within it. The ideologues have managed to shove together the concepts "guest" and "worker," although there have never been guests who worked. The provisional status that is supposed to be expressed in the word "guest" has been shattered by reality; *Gastarbeiter* are in fact an established segment of the West German population.[14]

The self-conscious use of the term *Gastarbeiterliteratur* exposes the bad faith and hypocrisy behind the euphemistic label "guest worker": the presence of immigrant laborers has become a permanent aspect of West German society and economy; further, these workers have experienced anything but the hospitality and generosity shown to proper "guests." There is no such thing, in short, as "guest" workers of a "guest worker literature."

There is also a second, and unintentional, irony. Not only is the term *Gastarbeiter* a socioeconomic contradiction; the concept of a literature written by or for these so-called guest workers is itself extremely problematic. The fact is striking, for example, that very few of the authors of *Gastarbeiterliteratur* are actually *Gastarbeiter* (or even *Arbeiter*) themselves. The Italian Franco Biondi came indeed as a guest worker to West Germany in 1965, but is now a certified psychologist. Likewise, Rafik Schami, who left Syria for Germany in 1971, began as a worker but went on to study and became a chemist. The Lebanese Jusuf Naoum began as a waiter, but after two years of unemployment was trained as a physical therapist. And Suleman Taufiq, the last of the editors of the series Südwind Gastarbeiterdeutsch, came to the Federal Republic of Germany specifically to study philosophy and comparative literature

---

13. Helmut Kreuzer discusses this and similar terms in "Gastarbeiter-Literatur, Ausländer-Literatur, Migranten-Literatur? Zur Einführung," *Zeitschrift für Literaturwissenschaft und Linguistik*, no. 56 (1984): 7-11.
14. Biondi and Schami, "Literatur der Betroffenheit," 134-35 n.1.

and in 1981 was teaching at a *Volkshochschule*.[15]

Thus anyone expecting to find a true workers' literature in *Gastarbeiterliteratur* may be disappointed that we are dealing here with a literature written at least in part by sympathetic intellectuals. Further, the possibility of guest workers as the intended audience of such a literature is also open to question. To my knowledge, studies have not been conducted on the extent and composition of the readership of guest worker literature. If the literature itself could be considered to present a reasonably accurate picture of the lives of *Gastarbeiter*, it becomes difficult to imagine that the Turks, Italians, and other foreign workers spend their leisure time reading the literature produced for them, much less literature produced for them in German. The second generation, the children who have been raised in Germany, might constitute a reading audience with the requisite command of German. One text, however, deals with a teacher's frustrated attempts to convince his Turkish schoolchildren of the value of reading even Turkish literature — "What's so important about this," they ask him, "can you make money with it, money?"[16] And one critic notes the publication of a dual-language volume of poetry in the Südwind series, two years after its founding with the explicit commitment to German as its sole language of publication: the series' decision to modify its initial stance was, Peter Seibert describes, a "concession to the actual level of German acquisition on the part of the foreign workers in West Germany."[17]

It would seem that the term *Gastarbeiterliteratur* does not refer unambiguously to a literature written either by or for "guest workers," although this is exactly what it claims to do. I would suggest that we

---

15. Biondi, Schami, Naoum, and Taufiq, however, insist that their Südwind anthologies present literature written by workers themselves: "In this volume the *Gastarbeiter* themselves have their say; they take a stand on issues that are crucial to them, they produce literature" ("In eigener Sache," *Zwischen Fabrik und Bahnhof*, 2). I take my information about the authors from the biographical sketches provided in the anthologies edited by Ackermann, and by Biondi et al.

16. Yusuf Ziya Bahadinli, "Lichtschimmer," *Zeitschrift für Kulturaustausch* 35, no. 1 (1985): 141.

17. Seibert, "Zur 'Rettung der Zungen,' " 46. Seibert quotes from the editors' preface: "The editors justify in their preface the establishment of a bilingual subseries with 'the fact that many foreign workers—even after a long period of residence here— write only in their native language' " (46 n.15). If the authors themselves are often unable to use German as a literary language, one can imagine that a German-reading literary audience of guest workers is equally problematic.

might understand this literature more accurately if we look not at its themes or even its authors, but rather examine the ways in which it has been represented and, to some extent, institutionalized. If a "guest worker literature" does not in fact exist as it is named, we need to look at the various and conflicting projections of its identity. That is, who is it that offers a definition, what definition is offered, and—the fundamental question that underlies these inquiries—what political interests are at stake in the argument over this contested literary territory?

There are three groups of spokesmen that dominate.[18] These are the Turkish author Yüksel Pazarkaya, who represents the position of cultural exchange and mutual understanding; the authors Franco Biondi, Rafik Schami, Jusuf Naoum, and Suleman Taufiq, founders and editors of the series Südwind Gastarbeiterdeutsch and proponents of a political literature aimed at fostering unity and solidarity among workers; and, finally, the German academics Irmgard Ackermann and Harald Weinrich, who through their literary contests for foreign German speakers bracket social, economic, and political differences in favor of a kind of aesthetic and linguistic homogeneity.

Yüksel Pazarkaya, one of the most important representatives of modern Turkish literature, went as a university student to West Germany, where he studied chemistry, and later earned an advanced degree in philosophy and *Germanistik*.[19] He claims, with justification, to be the first Turkish author to have written about *Gastarbeiter* and to have been the true "pioneer" in the field of *Gastarbeiterliteratur*.[20] In addition, Pazarkaya has been an extremely active translator of the masterpieces of Turkish literature into German, and is closely associated with the Ararat publishing house in West Berlin, which specializes not only in works dealing with the everyday lives of Turkish workers in Germany, but also in classical Turkish literature and Turkish folklore.[21]

---

18. Seibert in his "Zur 'Rettung der Zungen' " (see n.8 above) presents in tentative form some of the points I develop in the following discussion.

19. See the biographical information provided in Yasar Erdal and Wolfgang Grewel, comps., "Was sie berichten, wer sie sind . . . : Kleines Lexikon türkischer Autoren, die aus und über Deutschland schreiben," *Zeitschrift für Kulturaustausch* 35, no. 1 (1985): 159-60.

20. Other Turkish writers of note, Pazarkaya argues, were only occasional "visitors" to Germany and therefore either not intimately knowledgeable of the lives of the Turkish workers or so ideologically biased as to present distortions of another kind ("Stimmen des Zorns," 17-19).

21. On the Ararat program, see Seibert, "Zur 'Rettung der Zungen,' " 51, 53-54.

Pazarkaya's aim, which he has explicitly stated, is mutual cultural understanding—social as well as cultural "synthesis." The experience of Turkish workers has developed from an initial "culture shock" to the promising present state of imminent "cultural synthesis": Western Europe, Pazarkaya writes,

> can offer us a great deal from its history and also from its present, above all a wealth of experience. But we, who have not yet succumbed to the alienation and decadence of a technical and industrial world . . . who identify god with love, and prophet with friend, we have something to offer Western Europe as well.[22]

Elsewhere Pazarkaya speaks of the necessity of "mutual understanding," or of the desirability of integration "with mutual respect and the preservation of cultural identity and independence."[23] The profound humanism that underlies Pazarkaya's vision of mutual recognition and harmony comes to clear light in the following passage:

> A genuine synthesis is called for, whereby not only a profound acquaintance with both cultures is necessary, but also a kind of living incarnation into German culture, history, and contemporary life. Actually no one is capable of such a synthesis unless he has made Germany into his second homeland, and the German culture into his second culture. This is certainly a daring thesis which may well seem impossible to readers from both cultures. . . . But whoever thinks in global terms, and believes in human history [*Menschheitsgeschichte*] and human culture [*Menschheitskultur*] as a unity out of variety and difference, can expect great new syntheses to come from the pens of the "immigrant" Turkish authors in Germany, whether in Turkish, or in German.[24]

Terms of such lofty coinage as *Menschheitsgeschichte*, *Menschheitskultur*, and *Synthese* help to locate Pazarkaya's stance regarding guest worker literature: these are the ideals of the grand German tradition of the

---

22. Pazarkaya, "Vom Kulturschock zur Kultursynthese," in *Zu Hause in der Fremde*, 100.
23. Pazarkaya, "Stimmen des Zorns," 21; "Ohne die Deutschen wäre Deutschland nicht übel," 316.
24. Pazarkaya, "Ohne die Deutschen wäre Deutschland nicht übel," 317.

Enlightenment, of Herder and historicism, of German idealism and German classicism. In a poem entitled "german language" ("deutsche sprache"), Pazarkaya—who, we remember, was a student of German philosophy and literature—praises the language, "that i love without reservation," the language of "lessing and heine . . . schiller and brecht . . . leibniz and feuerbach . . . hegel and marx." He goes on in the same poem to claim that this high German culture, the German language that is his "second homeland" and "dwelling," does not properly belong to those native speakers who abuse the values of this tradition: "those who see in it a tool of humiliation / those who see in it a tool of exploitation / they are not in it not they."[25] True German culture, and the true possession of the German language, are thus elevated to a sphere of moral and humanistic understanding to which anyone, regardless of nationality or native language, can aspire—a Schillerian sphere of aesthetic understanding and harmony to which insightful Turkish writers can lead the way.[26] *Gastarbeiterliteratur*, as Pazarkaya would have it, emphasizes universal human values rather than cultural, national, or even class differences; it is, as he says, "global" in scope rather than local in focus and concern, and attempts to be unifying rather than oppositional.

A second, and radically different position, is taken by the authors of the Südwind Gastarbeiterdeutsch series. In place of harmony, Franco Biondi and his coworkers seek to inspire resistance; instead of appealing to the humanistic German tradition, they criticize existing problems

---

25. Pazarkaya, "deutsche sprache," in *Zu Hause in der Fremde*, 123; also published in *Zeitschrift für Kulturaustausch* 35, no. 1 (1985): 144.

26. Pazarkaya, born in 1940, is in many ways a typical intellectual of his generation. With the establishment of the modern Turkish state in 1923 under Kemal Atatürk, a massive effort was made to free the country from the Islamic traditions and influences of the Ottoman Empire. Among Atatürk's reforms, which included the adoption of the Roman alphabet and the Western calendar, was the institution of a vast project to translate the masterpieces of the European humanistic tradition—including the works of Lessing, Goethe, Schiller, Heine, and other major figures of the German literary and philosophical canon—into Turkish. European thought, understood as emancipatory, modern, and, in a strange way, "Turkish" as opposed to "Arab," was unquestioningly embraced and uncritically adopted. The generations of Turks educated from the late 1930s to the 1950s were steeped in this tradition. I thank Azade Seyhan for explaining this to me. For further reading, see Bernard Lewis, *The Emergence of Modern Turkey* (London: Oxford University Press, 1961). Günter Lorenz discusses the high regard traditionally held for German culture and technology in Turkey, in "Ein Freund gibt Grund zur Klage: Das Deutschlandbild in der Türkei oder Wie man einen guten Ruf aufs Spiel setzt," *Zeitschrift für Kulturaustausch* 35, no. 1 (1985): 9-13.

in present-day West German society; and they replace Pazarkaya's vision of cultural synthesis with a call for political solidarity.

These points may be illustrated by what will appear at first to be an unlikely example of *Gastarbeiterliteratur*: the short story "Sinbad's Last Journey: A Fairy Tale" by Jusuf Naoum. The example is unlikely because, as a work of folklore and fancy, it is in significant ways atypical of the kind of text usually published. Its very status as an exception, however, helps to foreground the essential aspects of guest worker literature as defined by the Südwind editors.

In Naoum's story, the legendary traveller Sinbad, along with his faithful donkey, takes a trip on his magic carpet to "a completely different region," present-day West Berlin.[27] En route Sinbad dreams of a land where lions are as tame as cats, big fish and little fish swim together peacefully, and Solomon's treasure lies for all to share; suddenly a giant black, scorpionlike animal appears, and Sinbad, terrified, awakens from his dream. A storm forces Sinbad and his donkey to land in the Grünewald lake. The magic carpet is lost, and after a long swim, a blackened Sinbad emerges from the murky, dirty water. He seeks the hospitality of the Germans living in the big white villas surrounding the lake, but they only slam their doors in his face or threaten to call the police. Sinbad and his donkey are taken in, eventually, by a Turkish worker in Kreuzberg.

Sinbad, who must now earn his plane fare home, experiences the problems of foreign workers: unable to obtain a work permit, he is forced to seek the services of an employment agent, who pockets half his wages. He learns that the people in the white houses who set their dogs after him are "the rich people" (154), while the grey, crumbling houses in Kreuzberg are inhabited by "us [Turks] and German workers" (153). He and his German coworker, although they communicate with gestures and the barest of vocabulary, are able to establish a relationship of friendship and trust (157). And Sinbad learns from his Turkish host of the importance of workers' unions: "The union is the organization of the workers. It represents their interests" (159). Finally, with his earnings supplemented by donations from friends and union members, Sinbad can plan his return flight. When he unexpectedly retrieves his magic carpet from a trash bin, he is able to invite friends and

---

27. Jusuf Naoum, "Sinbads letzte Reise: Ein Märchen," in *Als Fremder in Deutschland*, 147; further citations from this work will be included in the text.

comrades to a farewell celebration. And on the way home, Sinbad dreams again of the threatening black animal, but this time, with the help of friends, Sinbad kills the black scorpion.

Pazarkaya's lyric poem "deutsche sprache" invoked the names of Leibniz, Lessing, Schiller, and Hegel, to recapture a German tradition of humanism in which every individual, by virtue of his humanity, can participate. Naoum's text, in contrast, does not appeal to the values of a humanistic Enlightenment but concentrates rather on clarifying the everyday problems experienced by a largely foreign working class in Kreuzberg. The message of Naoum's critical text is solidarity among "guest" workers and German workers alike against "the rich" who live in villas and own factories. No real distinctions are made among workers of various nationalities, but all are shown to be subject to the same conditions. All must unite in order to protect and promote their interests, just as it is only with the help of his friends that Sinbad slays the evil black animal that haunts his dreams.

As Naoum's text suggests, the function of *Gastarbeiterliteratur* for the Südwind editors is largely critical and oppositional. Drawing upon the tradition of socialist workers' literature (*Arbeiterliteratur*),[28] Biondi, Schami, Taufiq, and Naoum conceive a literature of guest workers that is properly "multinational and committed" on the side of the workers.[29] The series Südwind Gastarbeiterdeutsch is founded to provide a "podium"

---

28. See Seibert, "Zur 'Rettung der Zungen,' " 48. Biondi was a member of the "Werkkreis Literatur der Arbeitswelt," founded in 1970. On the differences between the "Werkkreis" and Gruppe 61, with which Günter Wallraff is associated, see Reinhard Dithmar, " 'Arbeiterliteratur' nach 1945," *Frankfurter Hefte* 29 (1974): 667-79.

29. The quote is taken from the editorial statement "In eigener Sache: Der Südwind weht in der deutschen Literatur," from the anthology *Zwischen Fabrik und Bahnhof*, 2 (see n.9 above). Biondi and Schami state again, in a jointly written essay: "The stronger the attack on the *Gastarbeiter*, the more unequivocal, engaged, and determined their literature must be. It will not polish up the national pride that has been battered in an 'alien' country, but rather undertake the more courageous attempt to replace it with a consciousness of the multinational solidarity of all *Gastarbeiter*" ("Mit Worten Brücken bauen," 74). They claim in the same essay, "Mindful of the great things that bind us *Gastarbeiter* together without overlooking the differences among us, in a time when the hatred for foreigners is directed above all against our Turkish brethren, we all become Turks" (72). This premise of shared experience and solidarity is especially important for the Südwind editors, since, as Seibert points out, Biondi as an Italian belongs to a relatively respectable social group, and Schami, Taufiq, and Naoum, from Syria and Lebanon, respectively, do not represent typical immigrant populations ("Zur 'Rettung der Zungen,' " 52). Biondi et al. speak expressly of worker solidarity as a goal of *Gastarbeiterliteratur* in their "Vorwort," *Im neuen Land*, 4; "Literatur der Betroffenheit," 128, 133-34; and "Mit Worten Brücken bauen,"

for the development and promotion of this new "workers' literature,"[30] and further, the series editors raise the choice of German as its
sole language to a political imperative:

> The attempt will be made to carry on literary communication in-
> creasingly in German, i.e., to write increasingly in German. We
> wanted and want thereby to emphasize what we have in common,
> so that we may build bridges to the German citizens and to the
> various minorities of different linguistic backgrounds in West
> Germany. . . . The authors pay this price, because they are aware
> that only the combined action of all those affected will be able to
> eliminate the causes of their affliction.[31]

If the pioneer Pazarkaya reconciled economic and political differences
in an idealized sphere of cultural synthesis, Biondi and his group, in
contrast, subordinate aesthetic concerns to political ones and speak in
terms of cultural resistance.[32] The primacy of the political over the aesthetic is clear, for example, in Naoum's story, with its obvious and
overdetermined message of worker solidarity and its blatant political
sloganizing.[33]

But here the positions of Pazarkaya and Biondi begin, strangely, to
converge. The solidarity that the Südwind literature seeks to inspire,
despite its highly charged rhetoric, is not revolutionary, and the

72-74. Jörg Kuglin presents a pessimistic view of the development of such solidarity
among guest workers, in "Der 'Gastarbeiter' in der türkischen Literatur der
Gegenwart," *Kürbiskern*, 1979, no. 3: 85-86.

30. On the establishment and program of the Südwind series, see Biondi and
Schami, "Mit Worten Brücken bauen," 71-72, and their "Literatur der Betroffenheit,"
128-30, 133-34; Biondi, "Von den Tränen zu den Bürgerrechten," 80-81; the prefaces
("Vorwort") in *Im neuen Land* and *Zwischen zwei Giganten*; the statements "In eigener
Sache" in *Annäherungen* and *Zwischen Fabrik und Bahnhof*; and Seibert, "Zur 'Rettung der
Zungen'," 44-50.

31. Biondi and Schami, "Literatur der Betroffenheit," 134. See also Biondi and
Schami's "Mit Worten Brücken bauen": "Above all . . . the use of a common language
makes possible the development of a common, multinational identity. Therein lies the
beginning of a common perspective" (74).

32. See Biondi and Schami, "Literatur der Betroffenheit": "This [Südwind] series is
intended to help collect and promote this scattered, neglected, and oppressed literature. This cultural resistance is important and possible" (133). See also their remarks in
"Mit Worten Brücken bauen," 72-77.

33. Seibert makes the point that the marginalization of aesthetic issues for the
Biondi group is not only the result but also an indication and measure of the "authenticity" of their literature ("Zur 'Rettung der Zungen,' " 47).

similarity between *Gastarbeiterliteratur* and *Arbeiterliteratur* breaks down: the means of resistance, as the authors state, is "the sharpest, the *most peaceful*, the most humane weapon that exists . . . : the word" (emphasis mine).[34] Further, while the attitude taken by these texts toward conditions in present-day West German society is profoundly critical, the goal of the critique is not radical change, but—like Pazarkaya—a kind of mutual cultural accommodation and acceptance. The third volume of the Südwind series carries the significant banner *Conciliation (Annäherung)* as its title. There the editorial collective accordingly addresses its readers:

> In the present volume the authors describe their attempts at conciliation. A conciliation in which all sides wish to preserve their identity and to enrich their culture. It is a difficult attempt—and because we understand conciliation to be a process in which all sides approach one another, this volume includes contributions not only from *Gastarbeiter*, but from German authors as well.[35]

The theoretical oppositions between Pazarkaya and the Biondi group remain: Pazarkaya seeks to introduce the works of great Turkish writers into the German literary arena, and appeals to global understanding on the basis of a rejuvenated German tradition of Enlightenment humanism; Biondi and the political Südwind authors promote the relatively "minor" literature of a relatively vast group of foreigners in Germany, seeking thereby—aesthetic considerations aside—to instill a sense of solidarity in the multinational German working class. But Pazarkaya and the Südwind collective become unlikely allies on one fundamental point. Both argue ultimately for rapprochement and mutual acceptance between Germans and *Gastarbeiter*, whether inspired by ideals of *Menschheitskultur* and *Menschheitsgeschichte*, or on the grounds of common class interests. Thus Pazarkaya can speak of himself as "German," on the basis of his love of Lessing

---

34. Sandro Casalini, quoted by Biondi and Schami, in "Literatur der Betroffenheit," 125.

35. Biondi et al., "Liebe Leserinnen und Leser," *Annäherungen*, 5. See also Biondi's remarks on the necessity of creating "a place of encounter . . . a place of comparing, of debate and of reflection" that would offer the opportunity for "an exchange of ideas and experiences" among guest workers and Germans ("Von den Tränen zu den Bürgerrechten," 86).

and Hegel, and the series Südwind Gastarbeiterdeutsch can include, without contradiction, the works of native German writers.[36]

There is yet another position to add to this already complex field. While Pazarkaya and the Südwind editors are themselves immigrants to Germany, the third group of spokesmen for a German *Gastarbeiterliteratur* consists of sympathetic German academics at a research institute whose object of study is German as a second language.

Irmgard Ackermann and Harald Weinrich of the Institute for German as a Foreign Language (Institut für Deutsch als Fremdsprache) at Munich University have led the way among German scholars in focusing institutional attention on the literature written by foreign workers.[37] The titles of two articles, published in the widely circulating journals *Frankfurter Hefte* and *Merkur*, illustrate the fervor with which they would legitimize their subject: Ackermann views " 'Gastarbeiter' literature as a Challenge"; Weinrich writes "A Plea for a German Literature from Outside."[38] But Ackermann and Weinrich do more than create a new area of scholarship for themselves; as the editors of three volumes of literature published by Deutscher Taschenbuch Verlag, they have had the power, in essence, to define and control the literary phenomenon they study.[39]

---

36. At the same time, Biondi et al. warn against "integration" as "the dubious attempt to place a veil of harmony over a politics directed by economic calculation and at the same time the start of a process to destroy identity" ("Liebe Leserinnen und Leser," *Annäherungen*, 5), and criticize an *Ausländerpolitik* that seeks to turn foreigners into "well-assimilated, German-integrated individuals" in order to assure cheap labor power for the future ("Vorwort," *Zwischen zwei Giganten*, 2). Neither Pazarkaya nor Biondi seek cultural absorption.

37. Ackermann and Weinrich are the most important but not the only German academics to have dealt with *Gastarbeiterliteratur*, and I do not wish to suggest in what follows that they define "the German" point of view. Scholars at the Institut für Auslandsbeziehungen in Stuttgart, for example, have published three special issues of *Zeitschrift für Kulturaustausch* on the subject of guest workers and represent a very different approach (see *Zeitschrift für Kulturaustausch* 24, no. 3 [1974]; vol. 31, no. 3 [1981]; and vol. 35, no. 1 [1985]).

38. Ackermann, " 'Gastarbeiter' literatur als Herausforderung," 56-64; Weinrich, "Um eine deutsche Literatur von außen bittend," *Merkur* 37 (1983): 911-20.

39. This is especially true since, as Ackermann herself states, "the anthologies, because of the breadth of their spectrum, their representativeness, their echo, and their distribution, define the image of *Gastarbeiterliteratur* more than do the publications of individual authors" (" 'Gastarbeiter' literatur als Herausforderung," 57). The anthologies are *Als Fremder in Deutschland* (1982) and *In zwei Sprachen leben* (1983); the third, *Türken deutscher Sprache* (1984), includes material originally submitted to but judged inappropriate for *In zwei Sprachen leben*. In my discussion I focus on the first two volumes.

The Deutscher Taschenbuch volumes are the tangible result of literary contests sponsored by Weinrich and Ackermann's institute in 1980 and 1982, judged both times by a jury of all-German scholars and critics, on the themes "As a Foreigner in Germany" and "Living in Two Languages" ("Als Fremder in Deutschland," "In zwei Sprachen leben").[40] In a number of essays, the scholars explain the intentions of these contests. Weinrich's statement in *Merkur* is in this regard representative:

> A few years ago an idea came up in the Institute for German as a Foreign Language of Munich University. Through literary contests with various themes, we would stimulate foreigners for whom German is an acquired language to submit for publication the poems, stories, or other literary texts that they have written in German, or—better yet—we would get these people to start writing literary texts in German in the first place.[41]

The statement, seemingly straightforward and, I am sure, not in the least devious in its intent, projects in fact a view of non-native speakers that reflects the arrogance and power of the German. The "idea" of a German literature written by foreigners *originates* at a German university, and the literary contests that are sponsored are meant to "stimulate" (*anzuregen*) the foreigners who otherwise, it is implied, would remain idle and without literature. Without the enterprising Germans, these people would not write at all; the achievement of the German academics is "*diese Personen überhaupt erst dahin zu bringen, literarische Texte in deutscher Sprache zu schreiben*" (emphasis mine).[42] The implicit attitude of the German academics toward the foreigners seems in fact to approach the colonialist stereotype of the lazy, indolent natives

---

40. Jury members in both contests were Ackermann, Weinrich, Dietrich Krusche, Michael Krüger, and Hans Schwab-Felsch. The regulations and results of the literary contests of the institute are described in Ackermann, "Nachwort," *In zwei Sprachen leben*, 247-57; and "In zwei Sprachen leben: Ein literarisches Preisausschreiben für Ausländer," *Stimmen der Zeit*, July 1983: 443-54.

41. Weinrich, "Um eine deutsche Literatur von außen bittend," 919.

42. Ackermann characterizes the literary contests as having provided foreigners "an impetus" and "an impulse to write," and as an effort "to coax forth . . . literary expression" ("In zwei Sprachen leben: Ein literarisches Preisausschreiben für Ausländer," 443-44); see also her "Nachwort," *In zwei Sprachen leben*, 247. Always the Germans are active, the foreigners merely passive objects requiring an external impulse before they can act for themselves.

whose labor potential can be realized only under the external coercion of the advanced, culturally and technologically superior Europeans. The association is extreme, but not entirely unfair, as Weinrich himself compares the German *Gastliteratur*, as he calls it, to the English- and French-language literature produced by former British and French colonies.[43]

If Weinrich and Ackermann call a German-language literature of foreigners into being, just as—to stretch my point—one might establish a colony and promote a kind of colonial culture modeled after the European, we need to go on to ask how this new pseudocolonial literature is managed, controlled, and administered by its white experts.[44]

---

43. Weinrich writes:

We can call this literature, which—because it has not been nurtured—is only in its beginning stages, a German "guest literature." In choosing this word we remember at the same time that the British have dealt for a long time as a matter of course with an extremely noteworthy Commonwealth literature, and that even the French naturally appreciate the wealth that their literature owes not only to the Irishman Beckett and the Spaniard Arrabal, but also to the francophone Africans like Léopold Sédar Senghor or Sembène Ousmane.

["Vorwort," *Als Fremder in Deutschland*, 9]

Elsewhere Weinrich claims:

Just as the British look with pride upon their Commonwealth literature and the French as a matter of course consider the entire francophone literature as a part of their own, so do we Germans, who are less experienced in the world, have every reason to distance ourselves once and for all from the concept of a national literature in the nationalistic sense.

["Um eine deutsche Literatur von außen bittend," 920]

Biondi himself ties the emergence of *Gastarbeiterliteratur* to a colonial context, although for Biondi and the Südwind editors the guest worker literature represents a kind of *anti*colonialist cultural awakening; see "Literatur der Betroffenheit," 124; and Seibert, "Zur 'Rettung der Zungen'," 48-49.

44. Biondi and Schami put up some resistance here, although it is not directed specifically against Weinrich. See their remarks concerning the "archreactionary" views of some so-called experts on guest workers, in "Literatur der Betroffenheit," 134. Elsewhere they attack the "subtle sense of superiority and the patronizing attitude" perceptible in Dietrich Krusche's "Nachwort" to the volume *Als Fremder in Deutschland*, and claim that *Gastarbeiterliteratur* is discriminated against on the basis of its orgins, language, and content, pointing to the "condescending, patronizing pseudo arguments" of certain German critics; *Gastarbeiter*-authors, they claim, are "so to speak the subproletarians of German literature" ("Mit Worten Brücken bauen," 67, 75).

What we find is an uneasy, contradictory effort simultaneously to promote such a literature written by non-Germans and, by a number of different strategies, to defuse its potential political force.

While Biondi and the Südwind editors base their definition of a *Gastarbeiterliteratur* on the shared experience of foreign workers in Germany, there is little if anything that the authors in Ackermann and Weinrich's anthologies share except the experience of having learned the German language. The use of German as an acquired language, in fact, was the sole requirement for entry in the literary contests of the institute; Ackermann states, "The only stipulated requirements were that the participants, regardless of nationality, have learned German as a foreign language . . . and that the submitted texts be understood as *literary* contributions."[45] As a result, one can read in these anthologies, alongside texts written by authors belonging to the *Gastarbeiter*-milieu, entries by American, Irish, French, and Dutch students at German universities, and by professional *Germanisten* in New Zealand and the Peoples' Republic of China. The insistence on German as an acquired language as the sole focus of interest works to obscure, if not eliminate, economic, social, and political considerations from view. One cannot, except with deliberate blindness, group together the child of Turkish *Gastarbeiter* who grows up in Germany with the Stanford undergraduate who spends her junior year abroad in Bonn.[46]

The criteria for participation in the institute's contests set forth a second strategy for defusing critique. Although the themes "Als Fremder in Deutschland" and "In zwei Sprachen leben" might lend themselves to biographical or documentary accounts of actual experience in Germany, explicitly nonfictional writing is excluded by the demand that entries be understood as purely literary ("als *literarische* Beiträge

---

45. Ackermann, "Nachwort," *In zwei Sprachen leben*, 247-48.

46. Cf. Seibert's more reserved presentation of the institute's literary contests and anthologies, in his "Zur 'Rettung der Zungen,'" 56-60. Elsewhere Weinrich notes that *Gastarbeiterliteratur* is only one kind of *Ausländerliteratur* that exists in West Germany, and he lists as other relevant groups of authors the "refugees, emigrants, and asylum-seekers," and "persons who have come to our country of their own free will, such as students or trainees" ("Um eine deutsche Literatur von außen bittend," 917). Again, combining such disparate groups of foreigners into the *Ausländer* of an *Ausländerliteratur* works to eliminate the very real economic, social, and political differences among them from view and to distract attention from the specific situation of the *Gastarbeiter* in Germany. Biondi and Schami, in contrast, discuss the difference between "exile literature" and *Gastarbeiterliteratur* in "Literatur der Betroffenheit," 128-29.

verstanden werden sollten" [emphasis in original]). Whatever potential political and social criticism is contained in the texts submitted by foreign workers is thereby immediately subjectified, fictionalized, distanced; it must be understood as literature, not taken as reported fact.

The insistence on literariness explains also what appears at first to be a puzzling comparison: time after time, Weinrich honors Adelbert von Chamisso, the French count Louis Charles Adélaïde Chamisso de Boncourt who composed his beloved ballads in German, as an exemplary case of an author living between two languages and two cultures.[47] Again, it seems to me highly problematic to compare the tribulations of a French count, even one forced to Germany in exile as a result of the French Revolution, with the problems faced by Turkish immigrants, and to speak of the cultural and linguistic distance between France and Germany as though it were as immense as the distance between East Anatolia and Munich.

Another strategy that Weinrich and Ackermann employ to legitimize and to disarm the literature they study is to incorporate it within the German tradition—to regard it as fundamentally "German." Weinrich, for example, tries hard to explain to his German audience the reasons for the harsh critique of German society found in the texts of guest worker literature. There are diverse reasons, Weinrich says, including "hatred of foreigners" and the manifest errors of West German policies governing foreign residents, but Weinrich focuses on the conventions of literary history. His argument regarding this "simple literary fact" is worth quoting in full:

> the literature of the twentieth century, at least in the Western world, has imposed upon itself an almost unlimited ban on affirmation [*Affirmationsverbot*] . . . , from which a virtually superhuman effort is required to escape. There is practically no "optic for praise" left in the literary language of the twentieth century with which one could praise something, should there be something deserving

---

47. See Weinrich, "Vorwort," *In zwei Sprachen leben*, 9; "Vorwort," *Als Fremder in Deutschland*, 9; and "Um eine deutsche Literatur von außen bittend," 911. Weinrich was also instrumental in the establishment of the Adelbert von Chamisso Prize, awarded for the first time in 1985, for literary works either written in German or intimately connected with the life of foreigners in Germany, by authors whose native language is not German. See Heinz Friedrich, ed., *Chamissos Enkel: Zur Literatur von Ausländern in Deutschland* (Munich: Deutscher Taschenbuch Verlag, 1986).

of praise. It is therefore completely consistent in literary-historical terms that the *Gastarbeiter*-authors feel themselves bound to a poetics which they themselves call "literature of affliction." (*Literatur der Betroffenheit*)[48]

Again we find the tendency to reduce the literary production of foreigners in Germany to a purely literary phenomenon—here, after quickly mentioning German xenophobia and problems of government policy, Weinrich returns to relatively unpolitical turf, the broad generalizations of literary history, to offer an explanation for the themes and critical tone of *Gastarbeiterliteratur*.

The irony of it is that, as Weinrich himself must admit, this literary history is Western literary history—more precisely, the history of literature in advanced industrialized American and Western European countries. Weinrich, in other words, imposes the categories of a technologically (and culturally) dominant Western world upon the literary productions of a foreign minority. This, too, strikes me as colonialist. But the colonial parallel continues, as Weinrich goes on to reveal to us that—irony of ironies—this foreign territory was already essentially German to begin with:

> "Affliction" [*Betroffenheit*] is a unique and eminently German word for which there exists no proper equivalent in other languages. Two strands of meaning come together in this word. . . . The first comes out of the language of administration [*Verwaltungssprache*] and denotes the proper rubric for the particular matter at hand ("Re:") [*Betrifft*]. The other stems from a particular religious or quasi-religious experience which for example in Protestant theology is called "the existential affliction of belief" [*Betroffenheit des Glaubens*].

Weinrich concludes, "It seems to me remarkable how German the literature of guest workers is, in its innermost literary substance, to its advantage or disadvantage, when it strives to be a 'literature of affliction.' "[49]

---

48. Weinrich, "Gastarbeiterliteratur in der Bundesrepublik Deutschland," 21; cf. "Um eine deutsche Literatur von außen bittend," 915.
49. Weinrich, "Gastarbeiterliteratur in der Bundesrepublik Deutschland," 21-22; cf. "Um eine deutsche Literatur von außen bittend," 915-16. It is also extremely interesting

But *Gastarbeiterliteratur* as inherently *German?* The strategy of incorporation, intended to soften the challenge to German society expressed
in this literature, becomes itself threatening, and Weinrich, once he
has recognized the guest worker literature as profoundly German,
must go on to insist that it is nonetheless profoundly different.
Weinrich notes in particular the "simple and great art of storytelling"
which he finds neglected in German literature but prevalent in the
works of *Ausländerliteratur*; it is, he says, a kind of literature "that not so
much attacks the bastions of affluent German society with the literary
means of critical realism, but instead *naively or cunningly smuggles itself in*"
(emphasis mine).⁵⁰

The choice of words tells all: no matter how one looks at it, non-Germans in a German society, and non-German authors of German literature, are illegal aliens who have been smuggled in.⁵¹ In addition,
storytelling and storytellers are primitive, as Weinrich implies in the
following statement:

> The foreigners, especially those from the Balkans and from the
> Orient, still have a much more primitive [*ursprünglicheres*] relation-
> ship to narration, even to oral narration, and while we attempt to
> distill knowledge and learning by argumentation, they find practical
> wisdom [*Lebensklugheit*] in stories rich in experience. For the most
> part this narrative art is lost to us Germans in our industrial civili-
> zation.⁵²

(and somewhat amusing) to note what Weinrich claims are the essentially "German"
traditions—bureaucracy and Protestantism!—lying at the core of the guest worker literature of Italians, Turks, and others from the Mediterranean region.

50. Weinrich, "Betroffenheit der Zeugen—Zeugen der Betroffenheit: Einige Über-
legungen zur Ausländerliteratur in der Bundesrepublik Deutschland," *Zeitschrift für
Kulturaustausch* 35, no. 1 (1985): 15.

51. Ackermann seems to part company with Weinrich on this point as she argues in
the direction of a "multinational cultural landscape": "In doing so one would have to
take care that the culture of foreigners not be pushed into a ghetto, . . . but rather that
it be viewed as an integrated part of German culture, belonging to, enriching, and
helping to define the German cultural landscape" (" 'Gastarbeiter' literatur als
Herausforderung," 63-64). See also her "Integrationsvorstellungen und Integrations
darstellungen," 23-39, esp. 38.

52. Weinrich, "Betroffenheit der Zeugen—Zeugen der Betroffenheit," 15. In this
vein we might understand also Ackermann's observation that the German literature of
foreign authors contains a "special coloration" ("Nachwort," *In zwei Sprachen leben*,
250); cf. " 'Gastarbeiter' literatur als Herausforderung," 62.

The Orientals, who have maintained their intimate, "original" connection to an oral tradition of storytelling, are contrasted with the technologically advanced, rational and scientific Germans who "distill" their knowledge through logical argumentation—the prejudicial stereotyping of self and Other here is clear.

I began with the image of the silent Turk, the indecipherable foreign Other in works of contemporary German drama. The situation has changed now that, as Weinrich put it in his inimitable way, "among the millions of foreigners who live together with us Germans in this country, more than a few know not only how to handle a broom, but also how to handle a pen."[53] It is clear that with the emergence of a German *Gastarbeiterliteratur*, the problems, hopes, fears, anger, and frustration of two generations of immigrant workers have been made more directly accessible to the German-reading public. In my title and introduction I have spoken of this fascinating literary and social development in terms of the Other, previously silent and misrepresented, speaking back.

However, it is equally clear that what is generally called *Gastarbeiterliteratur* is a contested phenomenon. If there is an Other speaking back here, this "Other" is itself a subject that is defined, projected, or otherwise constructed in various ways by various interested parties. Whether defined as members of a global human community that overcomes local differences in a grand "cultural synthesis" (Pazarkaya), as members of a multinational working class (Biondi et al.), or as learners of German as a second language (Weinrich), the category of the "Other" is laden with political, social, historical, and cultural features. Its "speaking" also is never straightforward, direct, and unequivocal, but always mediated and controlled by translators, editors, and academics. There is in fact no silent Other as such who now begins to speak. Rather, we must speak in terms of groups with conflicting interests who, each in their own way, seek to produce and promote a *Gastarbeiterliteratur* of their own definition. The literary phenomenon of the 1980s—the sudden outpouring of German literature written by foreigners—is first and foremost a political battleground for recognition and for control; *Gastarbeiterliteratur* is contested territory.

I have tried in this essay to clarify the boundaries and claims of the

---

53. Weinrich, "Um eine deutsche Literatur von außen bittend," 912.

dispute. Overstating matters somewhat, I characterized the position of Pazarkaya as idealistic and humanistic, the program of Biondi and the Südwind editors as agitational and propagandistic, and the efforts of Weinrich and his institute as imperialistic. Weinrich's strategies are particularly interesting as he incorporates *Gastarbeiterliteratur* into the German literary tradition by arguing the peculiarly "German" nature of this literature, only then to distinguish this new acquisition, as primitive and alien, from what is "truly" German. But I wish to conclude by returning briefly to the efforts of the foreigners themselves, Pazarkaya and Biondi, who would also argue ultimately for a kind of rapprochement with, and inclusion among, the Germans.

The German language is his, Pazarkaya claims, when he honors the heritage of Leibniz, Lessing, Schiller, Heine, Hegel, and Marx; it is disowned by native Germans, he goes on to claim, when they employ it as an instrument of insult and oppression. Biondi and the editors of Südwind, drawing on the tradition of a socialist *Arbeiterliteratur*, call for solidarity among all workers in Germany, regardless of nationality. Both argue for common ground between foreigners and Germans, whether defined in terms of universal humanistic ideals, or shared class interests. It is interesting that both argue on the basis of particularly "German" traditions—the Enlightenment and idealism, and Marxism. But is this a kind of cultural submission, more evidence in support of Weinrich's claim that *Gastarbeiterliteratur*, with its sharp critique of West German society, is really actually "German" at heart?

The "minor literature" described by Deleuze and Guattari, we remember, is the collective effort of a minority writing in the dominant language, both within and against a major literary and cultural tradition. For Deleuze and Guattari, a minority literature that uses the language and traditions of the dominant society is not necessarily conciliatory or submissive, but potentially profoundly oppositional. And this, I would suggest, is the case when Pazarkaya and Biondi claim for themselves what they see as the best of the German tradition. It is one thing for those in power—as Weinrich is—to claim *Gastarbeiterliteratur* as German literature, and quite another when the claim is made by the *Gastarbeiter* themselves. One position is that of cultural hegemony, the other, that of critique and resistance. One tries to reassert its dominance, while the other seeks to alter the dominant structures altogether—"German" culture and society are no longer just for Germans; "racial purity" makes way for ethnic and cultural plurality. This, it seems to me, is the real challenge of *Gastarbeiter-literatur*.

Contentious Traditions:
The Debate on *Sati* in Colonial India

Lata Mani

T he abolition of *sati* by the British in 1829 has become a founding
moment in the history of women in modern India.[1] The legislative prohibition of *sati* was the culmination of a debate during which
8,134 instances of *sati* had been recorded mainly, though not exclusively, among upper caste Hindus, with a high concentration—63
percent—in the area around Calcutta City.[2] The debate, initiated primarily by colonial officials, is regarded as signifying the concern for the
status of women that emerges in the nineteenth century. Colonial rule,
with its moral civilizing claims, is said to have provided the contexts
for a thoroughgoing re-evaluation of Indian "tradition" along lines

1. This paper was orginally written for a forthcoming volume on women and culture
in modern India, to be edited by Kum Kum Sangari and Sudesh Vaid (New Delhi:
Kali). For their perceptive suggestions and careful reading of earlier versions of this pa-
per, I would like to thank James Clifford, Ruth Frankenberg, Inderpal Grewal, Donna
Haraway, Caren Kaplan, Katie King, Thomas Metcalf, Carla Petievich, Kum Kum
Sangari and Sudesh Vaid.

2. These figures are drawn from the *Parliamentary Papers on Hindoo Widows* (hereafter
PP). The 8,134 *satis* were recorded between 1815 and 1828. The proportion of burn-
ings in the Calcutta region is an average for this period. Breakdown of *satis* by caste was
tabulated in the PP for 1823: brahmin 234; kayasth 25; vaisya 14; sudra 292 (*PP*, 1825).
Sati was proportionately higher among brahmins.

more consonant with the "modern" economy and society believed to have been the consequence of India's incorporation into the capitalist world system.[3] In other words, even the most anti-imperialist amongst us has felt forced to acknowledge the "positive" consequences of colonial rule for certain aspects of women's lives, if not in terms of actual practice, at least at the level of ideas about "women's rights."

Among such reinterpreters of Indian tradition, Rammohun Roy holds a privileged place as the first nineteenth-century Indian figure to undertake publicly such a critical examination of Indian heritage, both in his stand against *sati* and also more generally in his attempts to reformulate Hinduism. There is an enormous body of literature on Rammohun as the father of the so-called Bengal Renaissance, ranging from adulation, to denunciation, to the more measured appreciation extended to him by Sumit Sarkar, Rajat Ray, and others, who have argued that Rammohun should be historicized.[4] Sarkar believes that Rammohun's modernity is contradictory and as such reflects the objective conditions of colonial subjugation, which in his view produces not a "full-blooded bourgeois modernity" but only a "weak and distorted caricature" of the same.[5] In other words, Sarkar sees colonialism as a partial modernizing force and warns against the simplistic application of narratives of progressive modernization to a study of nineteenth-century India. This is an important intervention in the debates on modernization. However, it leaves unproblematized the content of the concepts "tradition" and "modernity."

I will argue in this paper that part of the project of historically con-

---

3. There is considerable debate among political economists as to whether or not colonial rule produced conditions that were favorable to the development of capitalism in India. For instance, A.K. Bagchi has argued that colonial rule de-industrialized India; see his "De-industrialization in India in the Nineteenth Century: Some Theoretical Implications," *Journal of Development Studies* 12 (1975-76): 135-64. For a critical discussion of colonial economic historiography, see the special issue *Reinterpretation of Nineteenth-Century Indian Economic History* of *Indian Economic and Social History Review* 5, no. 1. This debate does not affect my argument here, for, whatever their analysis of the impact of colonialism on India's transition from feudalism to capitalism, all scholars agree that colonialism held the promise of modernity and inspired a critical self-examination of indigenous society and culture.

4. See V.C. Joshi, ed., *Rammohun Roy and the Process of Modernization in India* (New Delhi: Vikas, 1975), especially Sumit Sarkar, "Rammohun Roy and the Break with the Past," 46-68, and Rajat K. Ray's introduction to the volume, 1-20.

5. Sarkar, "Rammohun Roy and the Break with the Past," 63.

textualizing Rammohun and nineteenth-century debates on women in-cludes specifying the notion of tradition that they seek to reinterpret. For, as I will show through analysis of the debate on *sati*, the concep-tion of tradition that Rammohun contests, and that the orthodoxy de-fends, is one that is specifically "colonial." My concern with the debate on *sati* is thus not so much with who was for or against the practice but, rather, with how these ideological positions were argued. In other words, my interest is in the discursive aspects of the debate—what vari-ous sides assumed about *sati*, Indian society and the place of women in it, what they understood to be tradition, what counted as evidence, and so on. I will examine official and indigenous discourses on *sati* and will focus on three documents selected from a larger field of texts as exemplary registers of these discourses. Walter Ewer's letter to the Ju-dicial Department written in November 1818 will represent the official position. Rammohun Roy's 1830 tract in favor of the abolition of *sati* and the orthodox community's petition protesting the regulation will serve as examples of the "progressive" and "conservative" indigenous positions respectively.

I will also examine the constitution of official knowledge about *sati*. Official knowledge was generated through questioning pundits resi-dent at the courts. The interactions between pundits and judges, and pundits and magistrates, are invaluable for plotting the logic of official discourse. Analyzing them clarifies how the very formulation of official questions shapes the responses of pundits and how the answers of pundits are interpreted in specific ways by officials. Such moments thus provide the grounds both for naming the discourse as "colonial" and for questioning its premises.

Since the core argument is somewhat provocative and goes against the grain of the current historiography on social reform, I will present it first in the interest of clarity. It is crucial to add here that this paper is part of a longer project and that in the desire to debate further on the nature of the Bengal Renaissance, particularly its implications for women, I venture to include here claims that are at this stage speculative.

In this paper I will argue the following: first, that tradition is recon-stituted under colonial rule and, in different ways, women and brah-manic scripture become interlocking grounds for this rearticulation. Women become emblematic of tradition, and the reworking of tradi-tion is conducted largely through debating their rights and status in society. Despite this intimate connection between women and tradition, or perhaps because of it, these debates are in some sense not primarily about women but about what constitutes authentic cultural tradition. Brahmanic scriptures are increasingly seen to be the locus of this authenticity so that, for example, the legislative prohibition of *sati* becomes a question of scriptural interpretation. Contrary to the popular notion that the British were compelled to outlaw *sati* because of its barbarity, the horror of the burning of women is, as we shall see, a distinctly minor theme.

Second, this privileging of brahmanic scripture and the equation of tradition with scripture is, I suggest, an effect of a colonial discourse on India. By "colonial discourse," I mean a mode of understanding Indian society that emerged alongside colonial rule and over time was shared to a greater or lesser extent by officials, missionaries, and the indigenous elite,[6] although deployed by these various groups to different, often ideologically opposite ends. This discourse did not emerge from nowhere, nor was it entirely discontinuous with precolonial discourses in India. Rather, it was produced through interaction with select natives, though as I will show, officials clearly had power over the natives in question.

This greater power had several consequences. It meant that officials could insist, for instance, that brahmanic and Islamic scriptures were prescriptive texts containing rules of social behavior, even when the evidence for this assertion was problematic. Further, they could institutionalize their assumptions, as Warren Hastings did in 1772, by making these texts the basis of personal law. Official discourse thus had palpable material consequences, of which the constitution of personal law from religious texts is perhaps most significant from the point of view of women. The power underwriting official discourse also ensured its increasing normativity at least among the elite who were compelled, as we shall see, to take account of its key premises. I do not construe the elite as passive in this process, but as wresting these ideas to their own ends.

The claim that the discourse on *sati* is specifically colonial is approached

---

6. For my purposes the elite may be defined as well-to-do, urban, mercantile, and/or landed individuals whose business and social activities required them, in one way or another, to confront and negotiate the apparatus of the East India Company.

through examining the internal dynamics of the discourse, and also by drawing on the work done by Sumit Sarkar contrasting the radical rhetoric of Rammohun Roy in *Tuhfatul Muwahiddin* with that of his later writings.[7] Sarkar has discussed how Rammohun Ray moves from arguments based on reason in *Tuhfat* to arguments that are increasingly reliant on brahmanic scripture. I suggest that this trajectory of Rammohun might be understood as mapping the discursive shift that accompanies colonial rule. In other words, Rammohun's appeal to the scriptures in his later work might have more to do with the colonial insistence on the centrality of scripture to Indian society than on the "feudal" or "semifeudal" character of early nineteenth-century Bengal.[8] A claim that such a discursive shift occurred is, of course, far reaching and one that I can only begin to substantiate here. I hope, however, to make a convincing case that such an approach is fruitful and that it raises serious historiographical questions regarding the place of brahmanic scripture in precolonial India, the nature and functioning of precolonial legal systems and pre-British indigenous discourses on tradition and social reform. These issues seem to me to be especially compelling to an analysis of the consequences for women of such a discourse. For, as I will show, the equation of scripture, law and tradition, and the representation of women *as* tradition produced a specific matrix of constraints within which the question of *sati* was debated. This grid was fashioned out of the requirements of an expanding colonial power in need of systematic and unambiguous modes of governance, of law, for instance, and out of a particular view of Indian society. These twin features make intelligible the nature and scope of arguments about *sati* and the marginality of women to a discourse ostensibly about them.

A note on the focus and method adopted here is in order. This is not a social history of *sati*. I am not concerned here with what the practice of *sati* meant to those who undertook it,[9] but with the definition of it

---

7. Sarkar, "Rammohun Roy and the Break with the Past," 47-55.

8. I do not suggest here that nineteenth-century Bengal is neither feudal nor semifeudal but that Rammohun's use of scriptural arguments should be understood in terms of the emerging dominance of a colonial discourse on India, rather than as a "feudal residue."

9. For a very suggestive discussion that relates early nineteenth-century *sati* to socio-economic changes wrought by colonial rule, see A. Nandy, "Sati: A Nineteenth-Century Tale of Women, Violence, and Protest," in *Rammohun Roy and the Process of Modernization in India*, 168-94.

generated by colonial officials and with its place and function in debates on the status of women. Further, my reading of the debate is not chronological but discursive, examining that which is specifically colonial and which unifies the superficially different analyses of *sati* and Indian society advanced by proponents and opponents of legislative intervention.

Walter Ewer: An Instance of Official Discourse

Official discourse on *sati* was prompted by deliberation on whether it could be safely prohibited through legislation.[10] The concern with safety was premised on the belief that the practice had a basis in scripture and that interference in a religious matter might provoke indigenous outrage. Those opposed to abolition thus emphasized its "religious" basis and the dangers of intervention, while those in favor of outlawing *sati* stressed its "material" aspects (such as the family's desire to be rid of the financial burden of supporting the widow), and thus the safety of legislative prohibition. The two strategies were not mutually exclusive. For instance, abolitionists made both "religious" and "material" arguments for their position as did those in favor of tolerating *sati*. Indeed, the interplay between the two strategies was often quite complex.[11]

I have demonstrated elsewhere how, even though officials differed in their attitude to *sati*, both those in favor of abolition and those opposed to it were united in their analysis of Indian society and *sati*.[12] Stated briefly, I argued that officials advanced their positions from within a common discourse on India whose chief features were the centrality

---

10. This discussion of official discourse draws on the more detailed analysis presented in my article "The Production of an Official Discourse on *Sati* in Early Nineteenth-Century Bengal," *Economic and Political Weekly; Review of Women's Studies* (April 1986): 32-40. This article documents the legislative history of *sati* and includes a fuller discussion of the institutional context of the debate. Parts of it are included here since my arguments in this paper build on this earlier work. For Walter Ewer's letter, see PP 18 (1821), 521-23.

11. "Material" in official discourse refers to anything that can be shown to be without basis in or counter to scripture. Given British colonial assumptions regarding the hegemony of scriptural texts and the passive relation to them of indigenous people, this category often included actions that represented will, whether of individuals or groups. To say more here, however, would be to anticipate my argument.

12. Mani, "Production of Official Discourse on *Sati*," 34-36.

of brahmanic scriptures, unreflective indigenous obedience to these texts, and the religious nature of *sati*. In this paper I will draw on Walter Ewer, superintendent of police in the Lower Provinces, an abolitionist who epitomizes the official discourse on *sati*.

Ewer proposed that the contemporary practice of *sati* bore little resemblance to its scriptural model, which he defined as a voluntary act of devotion carried out for the spiritual benefit of the widow and the deceased. In reality, he argued, widows were coerced, and *sati* was performed for the material gain of surviving relatives. Ewer suggested that relatives might thereby spare themselves both the expense of maintaining the widow and the irritation of her legal right over the family estate. Also said to apply pressure on the widow by extolling the virtues and rewards of *sati* were "hungry brahmins" greedy for the money due to them for officiating such occasions.

Even if the widow succeeded in resisting the combined force of relatives and pundits, Ewer held that she would not be spared by the crowd. According to him, "the entire population will turn out to assist in dragging her to the bank of the river, and in keeping her down on the pile." Ewer thus concludes that "the widow is scarcely ever a free agent at the performance of the suttee" (*PP* [1821], 521). According to Ewer, scriptural transgressions, such as the coercion of widows or the performance of *sati* for material gain, could be the result of ignorance of the scriptures, or might reflect conscious design on the part of relatives and pundits. In the former case, *sati* could be abolished without provoking indigenous outrage; in the latter case, *sati* could not be considered a sacred act and could safely be prohibited.

Ewer's inference of the safety of abolition from instances of individuals acting by design suggests that in his view, when Hindus acted "consciously" they could not, by definition, be acting "religiously." "Religious" action is, in this perspective, synonymous with passive, unquestioning obedience. If the widow is thus construed as a victim of pundits and relatives, they in turn are seen by Ewer to act in two mutually exclusive ways: either "consciously," that is, "irreligiously," or "passively," that is, "religiously." Hence Ewer nowhere suggests that pundits and relatives could manipulate religion to their own ends. Ewer submitted that left to herself, the widow would "turn with natural instinct and horror from the thought of suttee" (*PP* [1821], 521). However, in his opinion, given the widow's ignorance and weak mental and physical capacity, it took little persuasion to turn any apprehension into a reluctant consent.

Having demonstrated that the actual practice bears no semblance to a religious rite, Ewer goes on to question the assumption of a scriptural sanction for *sati*. He points to the heterogeneity of the scriptures on the issue, demonstrating that Manu, "the parent of Hindoo jurisprudence," did not even mention *sati*, but instead glorified ascetic widowhood. It is important to note that what unites both the "temporal" and "scriptural" aspects of Ewer's arguments is the privileging of religion and the assumption of a complete native submission to its force.

The accent on "will" in Ewer's analysis signals the ambivalence which lies at the heart of the official attitude to *sati*. It suggests that within the general and avowed disapproval of the practice, there operated notions of "good" and "bad" *satis*. Good *satis* were those that were seen to be true to an official reading of the scriptures. It was this kind of reasoning that produced the 1813 regulation which defined *sati* as legal providing it met certain criteria, chief among which was that it be a voluntary act.[13] The Nizamat Adalat, or criminal court, accordingly instructed magistrates to pay close attention to the demeanor of the widow as she approached the pyre, so that officials could intercept at the merest suggestion of coercion. As a result, magistrates recorded in the annual returns on *sati* such remarks as the following: "the widow voluntarily sacrificed herself," "ascended the pyre of her own free will," burnt "without [sic] in any way inebriated and in conformity with the Shaster."

Official approval of *sati* as long as it was an act of free well was also reflected in a nonhorrified announcement of two *satis* in the *Calcutta Gazette* in 1827, at a time when it was officially maintained that fear of political repercussions was the only reason for tolerating *sati*. It described the widow as "having abandoned with cheerfulness and her own free will, this perishable frame," and as "having burnt herself with him in their presence with a swelling heart and a smiling countenance" (*PP* 23 [1828], 169). Of course, many officials conceded the possibility of such voluntary *satis* only in the abstract. Ewer, offered here as the paradigmatic example, insisted that in actuality widows were incapable of consenting and must therefore be protected from

---

13. For the legislative history of *sati*, see Mani, "Production of Official Discourse on *Sati*," 33-34.

pundits and crowds alike.

Analysis of official discourse makes it evident that arguments in favor of prohibiting *sati* were not primarily concerned with its cruelty or "barbarity," although many officials did maintain that *sati* was horrid even as an act of volition. It is also clear that officials in favor of legislative prohibition were not, as it has generally been conceived, interventionists contemptuous of aspects of indigenous culture, advocating change in the name of "progress" or Christian principles. On the contrary, officials in favor of abolition were arguing that such action was in fact consistent with upholding indigenous tradition, even that a policy of religious tolerance necessitated intervention. And indeed this was how the regenerating mission of colonization was conceptualized: not as the imposition of a new Christian moral order but as the recuperation and enforcement of the truths of indigenous tradition. C.B. Elliot, joint magistrate of Bellah, expressed this sentiment when he suggested that the preamble to *sati* regulation should include apposite quotations from the Hindu scriptures so that the indigenous subjects would

> rejoice in the mercy and wisdom of a government which blends humanity with justice, and consults at once the interests and prejudices of its subjects, by recalling them from practices revolting, and pronounced erroneous even by their own authorities. (*PP* 28 [1830], 918)

Official conception of colonial subjects held the majority to be ignorant of their "religion." Religion was equated with scripture. Knowledge of the scriptures was held to be the monopoly of brahmin pundits. Their knowledge was, however, believed to be corrupt and self-serving. The civilizing mission of colonization was thus seen to lie in protecting the "weak" against the "artful," in giving back to the natives the truths of their own "little read and less understood Shaster" (*PP* [1821], 532).

The arguments of officials in favor of abolition were thus developed within the ambit of "religion." The pros and cons of *sati* were systematically debated as considerations of brahmanic doctrines. In employing the scriptures to support their views, the officials were dependent on the *vyawasthas* of court pundits whose exegesis of the texts made them accessible to colonial officials. *Vyawasthas* were the written responses of pundits to questions put to them by colonial officials on various aspects of *sati*. However, as I shall demonstrate below, officials interpreted *vyawasthas* in particular ways so that the concept of *sati* produced by official discourse was specifically colonial.

Official discourse on *sati* rested on three interlocking assumptions: the hegemony of religious texts, a total indigenous submission to their dictates, and the religious basis of *sati*. These assumptions shaped the nature and process of British intervention in outlawing the practice. However, a close reading of the sources, attentive to the nature of evidence advanced for these ideas as well as the social relations of their production, makes it possible to contest this official view.

To begin with, I suggest that the insistence on textual hegemony is challenged by enormous regional variation in the mode of committing *sati*. The *vyawasthas* of pundits had elaborated differences by village and district, even by caste and occupation, in the performance of *sati*: "In certain villages of Burdwan, a district in Bengal, the following cermonies are observed," or "In certain villages situated in Benares, the following practices obtain among the widows of merchants and other traders" (*PP* [1821], 410, 411). Local influence predominated in every aspect of *sati*. For instance, the pundits pointed out, "She then proceeds to the place of sacrifice . . . having previously worshipped the peculiar dieties of the city or·village." In the face of such diversity court pundits concluded, "The ceremonies practically observed, differ as to the various tribes and districts" (*PP* [1821], 410-11, 412). Colonial officials acknowledged these differences and instructed magistrates to allow natives to follow local custom. However, such diversity was regarded as "peripheral" to the "central" principle of textual hegemony.

Similarly, regional variation in the incidence of *sati* did not serve to challenge the assumption of the hegemony of religion, even though it did count as evidence of a material basis for *sati*. Colonial officials did not ignore the fact of such variation. The regulation of 1813 had recognized that in some districts *sati* had almost entirely ceased, while in others it was confined almost exclusively to certain castes. Despite this, officials decided to continue tolerating it, since they believed that in most provinces "all castes of Hindoos would be extremely tenacious of its continuance" (*PP* [1821], 321). Whatever the justification for concluding thus in 1813, such insistence was hardly tenable once systematic data collection was begun in 1815. For it quickly became apparent that 66 percent of *satis* were carried out between the area surrounding Calcutta City and the Shahabad, Ghazipur and Sarun districts. This indicates that religion was not hegemonic. Officials, however, continued to make this assumption, interpreting such regional variation to imply that, although "material" factors might be at play, *sati* was primarily a religious practice.

If the hegemony of religious texts and its corollary, an unthinking obedience to scripture, is problematized by regional variation in the incidence and mode of performing *sati*, the representation of widows as perennial victims is similarly debatable. Colonial officials consistently conceptualized women as subjected, whether they were coerced or apparently willing to jump into the flames. The *Parliamentary Papers* contain several accounts of women resisting any attempt to prevent their immolation. Magistrates noted that widows would sometimes threaten relatives seeking to restrain them with the so-called legendary curse of the women about to commit *sati*.

It is difficult to know how to interpret these accounts, for we have no independent access to the mental or subjective states of widows outside of these overdetermined colonial representations of them. In any case, the meaning of consent in a patriarchal context is hard to assess. Still, it is fair to assume that the mental states of widows were complex and inconsistent. Some widows were undoubtedly coerced; the decisions of others would be difficult to reduce to "force."

What is surprising, though, is that officials persisted in describing as victims even those women who resisted attempts to force them into the pyre. The annual reports of *sati* include many instances of women being coerced. Representations of such incidents, however, do not stress the resistance of widows but the barbarity of hindu males in their coercion. The widow thus nowhere appears as a subject. If she resisted, she was seen to be dominated by hindu men. If she conceded, she was considered victimized by religion. Despite the difficulty of ascertaining the meaning of "willing" *satis*, given the absence of women's voices and the historical and cultural variability of such terms as "agency" and "subjecthood," it seems to me that the volition of some widows can justifiably be seen as equal to the resistance of others. Official response to this contradictory evidence, however, was typically to simplify it. Women were cast as either pathetic or heroic victims. The former

were portrayed as beaten down, manipulated, and coerced, the latter
as selflessly entering the raging flames oblivious to any physical pain.
Superslave or superhuman, women in this discourse remain eternal
victims.

Official representations further reinforced such a view of the widow
as helpless by "infantalizing" the typical *sati*. The widow is quite often
described as a "tender child." Here again, analysis of statistics on *sati*
compiled by officials between 1815 and 1829 fails to confirm such a
picture, for a majority of *satis* were undertaken by women well past
childhood. In 1818, for example, women in 64 percent of *satis* were
above forty years of age.

Finally, it is important to clarify that this criticism of the absence of
women's subjectivity in colonial accounts is not to argue either that
women died voluntarily or that I in any way condone *sati*. From my
perspective, the practice was and remains indefensible. My interest in
the representation of women is in the ways official discourse forecloses
any possiblity of women's agency, thus providing justification for "civilizing" colonial interventions.

Production of Official Knowledge on Sati: Interaction and Interrogation

It has been noted already that abolition of *sati* was made difficult by
official claims that it had a scriptural basis. Let us examine how officials concluded this. Information about *sati* was generated at the instance, or rather insistence, of colonial officials posing questions to
pundits resident at the courts. The pundits were instructed to respond
with "a reply in conformity with the scriptures" (*PP* [1821], 406). The
working of colonial power is nowhere more visible than in this process. It is worth examining one such interaction in detail.

In 1805, the question of scriptural sanction for *sati* was first put to
the pundits of the Nizamat Adalat. Specifically, they were asked:

> whether a woman is enjoined by the Shaster voluntarily to burn
> herself with the body of her husband, or is prohibited; and what
> are the conditions prescribed by the Shaster on such occasions?
> (*PP* [1821], 322)

The pundit responded as follows:

> Having duly considered the question proposed by the court, I now answer it to the best of my knowledge: every woman of the four castes (brahmin, khetry, bues and soodur) is permitted to burn herself with the body of her husband, provided she has not infant children, nor is pregnant, nor in a state of uncleanness, nor under the age of puberty; or in any of which cases she is not allowed to burn herself with her husband's body. (*PP* [1821], 322)

The pundit clarified that women with infant children could burn provided they made arrangements for the care of such infants. Further, he added that coercion, overt or subtle, was forbidden. In support of his opinion, he quoted the following texts:

> This rests upon the authority of Anjira, Vijasa and Vrihaspati Mooni. There are three millions and a half of hairs upon the human body, and every woman who burns herself with the body of her husband, will reside with him in heaven during a like number of years.
> In the same manner, as a snake-catcher drags a snake from his hole, so does a woman who burns herself, draw her husband out of hell; and she afterwards resides with him in heaven.
> The exceptions above cited, respecting women in a state of pregnancy or uncleanness, and adolescence, were communicated by Oorub and others to the mother of Sagar Raja." (*PP* [1821], 323)

The question posed to the pundit was whether *sati* was enjoined by the scriptural texts. The pundit responded that the texts did not enjoin but merely permitted *sati* in certain instances, drawing on quotes which spoke of the rewards *sati* would bring to widows and their husbands. That the scriptures permit *sati* can only be inferred from the above passage. Nevertheless, based on this response the Nizamat Adalat concluded:

> The practice, generally speaking, being thus recognized and *encouraged* by the doctrines of the Hindoo religion, it appears evident that the course which the British government should follow, according to the principle of religious tolerance . . . is to allow the

practice in those cases in which it is countenanced by their religion; and to prevent it in others in which it is by the same authority prohibited. (*PP* [1821], 325; emphasis mine)

Two moves have been made in reaching this conclusion. The pundit claims that he has answered the question "to the best of my knowledge." However, his response is treated as an altogether authoritative one. Further, permission by inference is transformed into scriptural recognition and encouragement of *sati*. The formulation of colonial policy on *sati* was based on the understanding of it produced by this interaction, for this encounter generated the only legislative enactment on *sati* until abolition. The statement itself was also repeatedly recalled by officals arguing against abolition. Certainly, permission to commit *sati* was more explicit elsewhere in the scriptures. However, at issue here is not the scriptural accuracy of the pundit's response so much as the arbitrariness so typical of the official interpretation of *vyawasthas*.

This example embodies many of the key principles by which a body of information about *sati* was generated. Questions to pundits were intended to establish clarity on all aspects of *sati*. Thus in 1813 Nizamat Adalat pundits were asked to specify the precise meaning of the phrase "of tender years" in their *vyawastha* which claimed that a woman with a child "of tender years" was not permitted *sati*. Clarification was sought by officials as to the age of the child and whether or not the child had to be weaned before its mother could commit *sati*.

Pundits were required to comb the scriptures and produce unambiguous scriptural support. Inferential conclusions or recourse to customary practice were acceptable only where explicit documentation was impossible. Thus Magistrate B.B. Gardiner appealed to the Sadr Nizamat Adalat for a clarification of the modes of burning appropriate for various castes, since the pundit at his court had referred only to customary evidence in his response to the question. The pundits at the superior court produced a *vyawastha* supported by scriptural evidence. Their *vyawastha* was forwarded to Gardiner by officials of the Sadr Nizamat Adalat with a reprimand to the district court pundit for having "referred to the custom of a country, upon a point expressly provided for by law" (*PP* [1821], 334).

Official insistence on clarity was crucial to enabling the constitution of "legal" and "illegal" *satis*. Through such continual and intensive questioning, criteria for an officially sanctioned *sati* were generated.

Sati had to be voluntary. Brahmin women were permitted only *sahamarana*, burning with the husband's corpse. Non-brahmin women could burn through *sahamarana* or *anoomarana* (burning with an article belonging to the husband). *Sati* was forbidden to women under sixteen and to women with infants less than three years old. Women of the *jogi* tribe were permitted to bury themselves.

Although scriptural authority was claimed for this model, a careful reading of the *Parliamentary Papers* suggests that such authority was dubious. For example, while officials treated *vyawasthas* as truthful exegeses of the scriptures in an absolute sense, it is clear from reading the *vyawasthas* that the pundits issuing them believed them to be interpretive.

Pundits attested to the interpretive nature of their *vyawasthas* in a number of ways. For one thing, they often characterized their replies as textual readings: "The authorities for the above opinion are as follows." The interpretive character of the *vyawasthas* was also evident from the way in which the scriptures were used: "In the above sentence by using the words she who ascends, the author *must have had in contemplation* those who declined to do so" and "From the above quoted passages of the Mitateshura *it would appear that* this was an act fit for all women to perform" (*PP* [1821], 407; emphasis mine). It is clear from these examples that *vyawasthas* claimed to pronounce neither scriptural truth nor the only possible response to a given question. The corpus of texts designated "the scriptures" made such a claim difficult to maintain. The scriptures were an enormous body of texts composed at different times. They included the Srutis, the Dharmashastras, or Smritis, and the commentaries. The fact that the texts were written at different periods accounted for their heterogeneity on many points, not least of which was the scriptural sanction for *sati*. Two pundits could thus issue *vyawasthas* on the same point and quote different texts or different passages from the same text to support their statement.

Official response to such heterogeneity took several forms. In general, the older the text the greater its stature was assumed to be. Thus *vyawasthas* citing Srutis or Smritis were treated more seriously than those that referred to more recent texts. (I shall return to this later.) Over and above this general principle, officials sometimes recognized diversity, as in the determination and enforcement of the appropriate modes of burning for brahmin and nonbrahmin women. At other times they acknowledged textual complexity but for practical reasons did not "resolve" it, as, for example, in the considered tolerance of regional variation in the mode of conducting *sati*: whether the widow's body was placed to the left or right of the corpse, the direction of the pyre and so on.

Yet another response was to marginalize certain *vyawasthas*. A telling example of such strategic marginalization was the fate of Mrityunjoy Vidyalankar's *vyawastha*.[14] Vidyalankar systematically called into question the colonial rationale of a scriptural sanction for *sati*. He questioned among other things its status as an act of virtue, since it was a practice undertaken not in the spirit of selfless absorption in the divine but with an end to reward. Although Vidyalankar was later to become vocal in his advocacy of *sati*, his *vyawastha* contained sufficient scriptural justification for its prohibition. It was, however, ignored. Such continual reinscription of *sati* into a scriptural tradition, despite evidence to the contrary, points to the specificity of meanings imposed by official reading of the *vyawasthas*, and to the production of a conception of *sati* that is specifically "colonial."

The aim of official policy prior to abolition was to ensure adherence to this "colonial" conception of a "scripturally authentic" *sati*. This desire was enabled by an unambiguous definition of *sati* which officials sought to ensure through scrutiny of the details of its practice. Official presence was required at each *sati*. Magistrates were asked to tabulate data on each case: personal data on the widow, and date, place, time and mode of burning. They were also given explicit instructions to "not allow the most minute particular to escape observation" (*PP* [1821], 327). Such details ensured that no shastric infraction, however small, whether on the part of natives or of the functionaries policing the proceedings, could escape the official eye. Thus we have instances of the Nizamat Adalat reprimanding officers for intervening in cases where the widow and family were well within their scriptural rights in committing *sati*. So much for official arguments that *sati* was horrid

---

14. Vidyalankar's *vyawastha* is included in the appendix to the 1817 proceedings of the Nizamat Adalat and appears to have been written by him after he became pundit of the Supreme Court in July 1816. It thus precedes Rammohun's first pamphlet on *sati*, which was published in 1818. Vidyalankar and Roy furnished officials with sufficient scriptural grounds for prohibiting *sati*; but abolition came over ten years later. Its timing was related to political factors and not primarily, as officials had claimed, to ambiguity of the scriptures; see Mani, "The Production of Official Discourse on *Sati*."

and the toleration of it merely strategic! In addition, whatever the official claims to religious noninterference, the process by which knowledge of *sati* was produced was specifically "colonial" and its vigilant enforcement thoroughly interventionist. As the examples above indicate, despite the involvement of brahmin pundits, the privilege of the final authoritative interpretation of their *vyawasthas* was appropriated by colonial officials. For it was the Nizamat Adulat judges, the governor-general and his council who determined which *vyawasthas* were "essential" and which "peripheral." The authority of the pundits was problematic: the fact of being native simultaneously privileged and devalued them as reliable sources. The pundits were essential to "unlocking" the scriptures for officials. But they were also believed by officials to be the "devious minority" against which it was the mission of colonization to protect the "simple majority."

Indigenous Progressive Discourse on Sati

Rammohun Roy's first pamphlet on *sati* was published in 1818, five years after the colonial administration had authorized a particular version of the practice and three years after systematic data collection on *sati* had begun.[15] By this time the main features of official discourse on *sati* had already taken shape. Between 1818 and his death in 1832, Rammohun wrote a great deal on *sati*. Here I will draw mainly, though not exclusively, on a tract published by him in 1830, a year after the abolition of *sati*, entitled "Abstract of the Arguments Regarding the Burning of Widows Considered as a Religious Rite."[16] In Rammohun's own view this pamphlet summarizes his main arguments over the years.[17]

As the title might imply, Rammohun's discussion of *sati* is grounded from the beginning in a discussion of scripture. As he puts it, "The first

---

15. Rammohun, "Translation of a Conference between an Advocate for and an Opponent of the Practice of Burning Widows Alive" (Calcutta, 1818). Two years later, Rammohun published "A Second Conference between an Advocate for and an Opponent of the Practice of Burning Widows Alive" (Calcutta, 1820). See *The English Works of Raja Rammohun Roy*, ed. J.C. Ghose, vol. 2 (New Delhi: Cosmo, 1982); hereafter "PBWA."

16. Rammohun, "Abstract of the Arguments Regarding the Burning of Widows Considered as a Religious Rite," *English Works*, 367-84; hereafter "BWRR."

17. Chronology is not significant here since the nature and structure of Rammohun's arguments remained essentially the same throughout his campaign against *sati*.

point to be ascertained is, whether or not the practice of burning widows alive on the pile and with the corpse of their husbands, is imperatively enjoined by the Hindu religion?" ("BWRR," 367). Rammohun suggests in answer to his own rhetorical question that "even the staunch advocates for Concremation must reluctantly give a negative reply," and offers Manu as evidence:

> Manu in plain terms enjoins a widow to *continue till death* forgiving all injuries, performing austere duties, avoiding every sensual pleasure, and cheerfully practicing the incomparable rules of virtue which have been followed by such women as were devoted to only one husband. ("BWRR," 367-68)

Rammohun produces similar proof from *Yajnavalkya* of the widow's right to live with her natal or marital family on the death of her husband. Having established that *sati* is not incumbent on the widow, Rammohun deliberates which option, *sati* or an ascetic life, is more meritorious. In this he draws on the Vedas, whose authority, he claims, is paramount: "From a desire during life, of future fruition, life ought not to be destroyed" ("BWRR," 368). This most "pointed and decisive" statement counters, in his view, the claims of advocates of *sati* who also refer to the Vedas, to a passage that Rammohun finds abstract and open to multiple interpretations. The sentence in question is the following:

> O fire, let these women, with bodies anointed with clarified butter, eyes coloured with collyrium and void of tears, enter thee, the parent of water, that they may not be separated from their husbands, themselves sinless, and jewels amongst women. ("BWRR," 368-69)

Rammohun points out that this passage nowhere enjoins women to commit *sati* and offers a reading of it as an allegory of the constellation of the moon's path. In this interpretation, butter signifies "the milky path," collyrium "the unoccupied space between one star and another," husbands "the more splendid of the heavenly bodies." Finally, allusions to ascending and entering the fire are understood as "the rise of the constellations through the southeast horizon, considered as the abode of fire" ("BWRR," 369). Rammohun thus dismisses this, at best inferential, Vedic support for *sati* in favor of statements from the Vedas that explicitly recommend ascetic widowhood.

Rammohun then considers the Smritis which he designates as "next in authority to the Vedas." The Smritis are seen to be ordered hierarchically, with *Manu* heading the list as the text "whose authority supercedes that of other lawgivers" ("BWRR," 369). Since *Manu* has already been shown to approve of ascetic widowhood, Rammohun turns his attention to those Smritis like *Ungira* and *Hareet* that do appear to place a positive value on *sati*. Rammohun notes a passage from *Ungira* exalting a widow who commits *sati* as equal to Arundhati, but dismisses its recommendation of *sati* as inferior since it is avowedly a "means to obtain carnal fruition," and as such occupies a lower rung in the spiritual hierarchy of acts" ("BWRR," 370).

Having demonstrated that *sati* is not commanded by the scriptures and having argued that, even where it is presented as an option, it is decidedly of inferior virtue as an act undertaken to procure rewards, Rammohun concludes his tract by considering "whether or not *the mode of* concremation prescribed by Hareet and others was ever duly observed" ("BWRR," 371). Rammohun points out that "these expounders of law" require the widow to ascend voluntarily the pyre and enter the flames. In his opinion, violation of either of these provisions "renders the act mere suicide, and implicates, in the guilt of the female murder, those that assist in its perpetration." Rammohun, like colonial officials, is here concerned with the thorny question of the widow's will. His view is similar to that of Ewer. He claims that "no widow ever voluntarily *ascended* on and *entered* into the *flames* in the fulfilment of this rite." No wonder, he says, that those in favor of *sati* have been "driven to the necessity of taking refuge in *usage*, as justifying both suicide and female murder, the most heinous of crimes" ("BWRR," 372).

It is clear even from this brief discussion that Rammohun's discourse shared key features with official discourse on *sati*. His case for abolition was grounded primarily in a discussion of the scriptures. Both his first and second pamphlets on *sati*, in which Rammohun stages dialogues between an advocate and opponent of *sati*, are debates on how the scriptures are to be interpreted. The opponent in both instances takes up, and seeks to demolish, the arguments put forward by advocates of the practice regarding its scriptural foundation. In

January 1830, Rammohun joined with three hundred Calcutta residents in presenting a petition to Governor-General William Bentinck in support of the regulation prohibiting *sati* that had been enacted on December 4, 1829.[18] The petition offers further evidence that *sati* is not legitimized by scripture. Rammohun and the petitoners argue that *sati* originated in the jealousy of certain Hindu princes who, to ensure the faithfulness of their widows, "availed themselves of their arbitrary power, and under the cloak of religion, introduced the practice of burning widows alive."[19] According to them, the princes then sought to legitimize the practice

> by quoting some passages from authorities of evidently inferior weight . . . as if they were offering female sacrifices in obedience to the dictates of the Shastras and not from the influence of jealousy.[20]

Elsewhere in his writings, Rammohun gives further evidence for regarding *sati* as a material practice, relating its greater incidence in Bengal to women's property rights under Dayabhaga law.[21] Rammohun suggests that such worldly interests are responsible for women being fastened onto the pyre in "gross violation" of the Shastras.

At first glance, it seems that Rammohun does not share the ambivalence that I have argued is characteristic of official attitudes to *sati*. This ambivalence, I have suggested, sorts *satis* into good and bad ones, the former being those that are properly voluntary, the latter those involving coercion. By contrast, there is neither qualified approval nor fascination for *sati* in Rammohun's writings. Indeed, Rammohun's analysis of Hindu women's status in society is extremely sophisticated for its understanding of what we now call "male domination." For

---

18. "Address to Lord William Bentinck" (16 January 1830), *English Works*, 475-77. This petition was specifically intended to counter the mobilizing efforts of the anti-*sati* lobby and was believed to have been drafted by Rammohun; see editor's note, *English Works*.

19. Ibid., 475.

20. Ibid., 476.

21. "A Pamphlet of Rammohun Roy Containing Some Remarks in Vindication of the Resolution Passed by the Government of Bengal in 1829 Abolishing the Practice of Female Sacrifices in India" (1831), in *Raja Rammohun Roy and Progressive Movements in India*, ed. J.K. Majumdar (Calcutta: Art Press, 1941), 186-87.

instance, in Rammohun's second conference between an advocate and opponent of *sati*, the opponent sharply criticizes the advocate for imputing faults to women "not planted in their constitution by nature" and then persuading others "to look down upon them as contemptible and mischievous creatures, whence they have been subject to constant miseries" ("PBWA," 360). The opponent also proposes that men have taken advantage of their greater physical strength relative to women, to deny "them those excellent merits that they are entitled to by nature, and afterwards they are apt to say that women are naturally incapable of acquiring those merits" ("PBWA," 360). Rammohun was thus clearly cognizant of the societal basis of female subjugation.

Yet, even in this rousing defense of the character of Hindu women, there is evident a certain ambivalence toward *sati*. *Sati* functions both as the act confirming the stoicism of women and as the practice that epitomizes their weakness. Thus, of the accusation that women lack resolve, the opponent has this to say:

> You charge them with want of resolution, at which I feel exceedingly surprised: for we constantly perceive, in a country where the name of death makes the male shudder, that the female from her firmness of mind offers to burn with the corpse of her deceased husband. ("PBWA," 361)

Here Rammohun seems to concede the possibility of "voluntary" *sati*. Not only that, he implies that women undertaking *sati* exhibit heroism and resolve, that *sati* exemplifies women's strength of mind and character. However, in the very next paragraph Rammohun cites the example of *sati* to make the opposite claim—the vulnerability of women.

> One fault they have, it must be acknowledged; which is by considering others equally void of duplicity as themselves, to give their confidence too readily, from which they suffer much misery, even so far that some of them are misled to suffer themselves to be burnt to death. ("PBWA," 361)

In this instance, *sati* is offered as testimony to women's naivete, a weakness that is said to make them overly trusting of others. In pointing to the way Rammohun draws on *sati* to make contradictory claims about women, I am not "accusing" Rammohun of "approving" of *sati*.

Rather, I suggest that, even for the staunchest abolitionist, the *idea* of *sati* continues to provoke ambivalence. This ambivalence is enabled by the construction of women as either supreme being or victim. It could not have been as credible given a more complex notion of female subjectivity. This discursive construction of *sati* and of women makes it possible to mobilize the practice to make diametrically opposite claims.

The Conservative Discourse on Sati: The Orthodox Petition to Bentinck

Whatever ambivalence may have marked "liberal" discourses on *sati* is strikingly absent from the conservative writings on the subject, which openly eulogize the practice as one willingly undertaken by devout Hindu widows.

> Under the sanction of immemorial usage as well as precept, Hindoo widows perform of their own accord and pleasure, and for the benefit of their husband's soul and their own, the sacrifice of self immolation called suttee, which is not merely a sacred *duty* but a high privilege to her who sincerely believes in the doctrines of their religion; and we humbly submit that any interference with a persuasion of so high and self-annihilating a nature, is . . . an unjust and intolerant dictation in matters of conscience . . . "[22]

Eulogy is, however, not the petition's main focus. The burden of the orthodox argument was to demonstrate that the East India Company's criminalizing of *sati* was based on an erroneous reading of the scriptures. This is hardly surprising since, as we have seen, the entire debate turned on the issue of *sati's* scriptural grounding. The orthodox argument did, however, differ in one respect from that of Rammohun and most colonial officials: it assigned a relatively greater weight to custom. The petition claimed that "the Hindoo religion is founded, like all other religions, on usage as well as precept, and one when immemorial is held equally sacred with the other" ("Petition," 156). Thus while Rammohun privileges scripture over custom, criticizing his opponents

---

22. "The Petition of the Orthodox Community Against the Suttee Regulation, Together With a Paper of Authorities, and the Reply of the Governor-General thereto" (14 January 1830) in *Raja Rammohun Roy and Progressive Movements in India*, 156; hereafter "Petition."

for "being driven to the necessity of taking refuge in *usage*" ("BWRR," 372), the orthodox petitioners argued that the antiquity of Hinduism implied an equal status for both. Nevertheless, despite this claim, they proceed to argue their case almost exclusively in terms of scripture.

The orthodox strategy was to undermine the credibility of scriptural interpreters held in esteem by the colonial administration, among them Rammohun, as well as the validity of their interpretations regarding the textual basis for the prohibition of *sati*. The petition charged the government with deriving its interpretations from apostates.

> But we humbly submit that in a question so delicate as the interpretation of our sacred books, and the authority of our religious usages, none but pundits and brahmins, and teachers of holy lives, and known learning, ought to be consulted . . . not . . . men who have neither any faith nor care for the memory of their ancestors or their religion. ("Petition," 157)

Pundits and brahmins are proposed as authoritative interpreters, and the differences of opinion between them are reduced to an opposition between believers and unbelievers. The petition was signed by eight hundred persons and included pundits of the Government Sanskirt College, Supreme Court, and Nizamat and Diwani Adalat. As we know, the claim that the government was dependent on unbelievers like Rammohun is without basis, since officials had relied primarily on heir pundits at the civil and criminal courts where many of the signatories were employed.

The petition was accompanied by a "paper of authorities" signed by 120 pundits presenting scriptural evidence in favor of *sati*, or, in the words of the petition, "the legal points declaring the practice of suttee lawful and expedient" ("Petition," 159). The enclosure sets out objections to the chief arguments of those who advocate the prohibition of *sati*: that asceticism has greater value than *sati*; that *sati* brings temporary rewards, while ascetic widowhood holds the promise of permanent bliss; and that Manu recommends asceticism and has priority over other Smritis since his text "is immediately originated from Sruti" ("Petition," 160).

In response to the suggestion that ascetic widowhood is more highly recommended than *sati*, the petition quotes *Manu* as cited in the

Nirnaya Sindhu: "On the death of her husband, if, by chance, a woman is unable to perform concremation, nevertheless she should preserve the virtue of widows." Here, the petitioners claim, "the order of meaning has preference over that of reading; in other words, ascetic widowhood is a secondary option and one intended for women unable to perform *sati*. Thus they conclude, clearly overstretching their case: "It appears from the Shastra that the first thing which a widow ought to do is to ascend the flaming pile" ("Petition," 160, 161).

The second objection to *sati* as producing only temporary bliss is countered with the observation that asceticism is also a "gradual step for final beatitude" and while *sati* involves only "short term suffering" and delivers "heavenly blessings," ascetic widowhood subjects women to "laboring under austerities for a long time" ("Petition," 161). The greater "spiritual" value of ascetic widowhood is thus contrasted negatively with what petitioners see as the greater and prolonged material suffering it implies for widows.

Finally, the following case is outlined for why the absence of a positive injunction to *sati* in *Manu* presents no particular problem for its scriptural status. First, it is pointed out that many acts currently performed in society such as *durga puja* or *dola jatra* have no basis in *Manu* and yet their performance is not believed to be inconsistent with scripture; indeed not performing them would be regarded as sinful. It is interesting to note that, although the petition begins with a general argument for regarding custom as equally important as scripture, this is the only point on which customary support is cited. In any case, the petition continues, the absence of *sati* in *Manu* cannot be construed as an argument against it. The *Dattaca Chandrika* is offered as positing the opposite: that "non-prohibition constitutes sanction." Finally, the petition ingeniously proposes, if copies of the *Institutes of Manu* in Bengal neglect to mention *sati*, this cannot be supposed to be the case generally, for it suggests,

> *the text has been omitted by the mistake of the printers*, for the authors of the *Nirnaya Sindhu* and other works, which are most prevalent in Dravira and other countries, quoted the following text of Manu: "A widow may either practice austerities or commit herself to the flame." ("Petition," 162)

A printing mistake is thus made accountable for the status of *sati* in

Manu's text in Bengal!

The petitioners wrap up their case for regarding *sati* as a scriptural practice by returning to a consideration of interpretive principles. They suggest that the fragment from the *Rig Veda*, "let not these women be widowed" (the passage that Rammohun debunks as obscure), implies that *sati* was comfortable to Sruti, and they propose that where Sruti and Smriti conflict, "the former has preference over the latter." Thus they conclude that "it is unobjectionable that concremation, being enjoined by the Sruti, which is the most prevalent authority and original of the Smritis, must be performed" ("Petition," 162). Where Rammohun prioritizes *Manu* as a founding text containing "the whole sense of the Veda" and insists that no code be approved that contradicted it, the orthodox petition argued the absolute priority of Sruti in every case, although within the Smritis, *Manu* is conceded a premier position.

A Common Discourse on Sati

It is evident from the foregoing discussion of the official and indigenous arguments for and against *sati* that, whatever their attitudes to the practice, all participants in the debate on abolition held in common certain key ideas about *sati* and Indian society and employed rather similar procedures for arguing their case. Advocates both for and against *sati* grounded their case in a discussion of brahmanic scriptures, with opponents endeavoring to prove that *sati* had no clear scriptural status and proponents contesting these conclusions. One could analyze these arguments for logical consistency and conclude that, by and large, the orthodox pro-*sati* lobby had a weak case and resorted to disingenuous and facile arguments to make its point. One could also conclude appropriately that the use of scripture was strategic: each side read the texts in a manner that supported its ideological position. However, given my interest in the discursive aspects of the debate, I will adopt a different focus. I will elaborate the internal logic and parameters of the discourse, examine the kinds of arguments admissible within it and the ideological implications of these for arguing for an improved status for women.

From this perspective, what is interesting is the fact that the entire issue was debated within the framework of scripture. In other words, however clumsy or unconvincing the use of scripture in a particular argument, what is significant is the explicit coding of arguments as scriptural. Even Rammohun, commonly regarded as the first modern champion of women's rights, did not base his support for abolition on the grounds that *sati* was cruel to women. He did, of course, develop critical analyses of the status of women in India of a more "secular" variety, but these are marginal to his arguments against *sati*.

Not only did colonial officials and the indigenous male elite consider the issue mainly in terms of religious texts, they also shared, with minor differences, remarkably similar ideas of what counted as evidence. Scriptural evidence was consistently treated as superior to evidence based on custom or usage. Thus officials ordered pundits to revise *vyawasthas* that depended on customary practice, and the orthodox petition abandoned customary evidence even though it claimed an equivalence between scripture and usage.

Officials and the indigenous elite also shared general principles for ordering the enormously heterogeneous and unwieldly corpus designated "the scriptures." These were ranked as follows: Srutis, Smritis (or Dharmashastras), and commentaries. The Srutis, including the Vedas and the Upanishads, were placed at the apex since they were believed to have been transcriptions of the revealed word of God. Thus the anti-*sati* petition describes the Sruti as "the most prevalent authority, and the original of all the Smritis" ("Petition," 162). Next in line were the Smritis or Dharmashastras, texts supposed to have been written by particular sages. *Manu* is conceived as the most important among these. Thus Rammohun quotes approvingly Sir William Jones's description of *Manu* as a

> system of duties, religious and civil, and of law, in all its branches, which the Hindoos firmly believe to have been promulgated in the beginning of time by Manu . . . a system so comprehensive and so minutely exact, that it may be considered as the institutes of Hindoo law.[23]

As we have seen, Ewer also regards Manu as "the parent of Hindoo Jurisprudence." The orthodox petitioners are less vociferous about the founding status of *Manu*, for their argument for *sati* was complicated

---

23. "A Pamphlet of Rammohun Roy Containing Some Remarks in Vindication of the Resolution," 188.

by the text's not having addressed the issue. However, they indirectly concede the importance of *Manu*, at least in this debate, by their great pains to prove that its neglect of the issue does not compromise the stature of *sati*, even going so far as to suggest that the text outside Bengal does contain references to concremation. The problematic status of *Manu* from their perspective also prompts the orthodox community to insist on the priority of Sruti over Smriti in case of conflict. By contrast, given the value of *Manu* to his position, Rammohun holds *Manu* to override Sruti, although elsewhere—in his reformulation of Hinduism for instance—it is to the Upanishads that he turns.

Another interpretive principle that marks the reading of scripture is the greater value assigned to passages that were explicit in their references to *sati*. The more literal a passage, the more authoritative its value as evidence. Thus, as we have seen, Rammohun rejects a passage from the *Rig Veda* for being too abstract, while colonial officials reject the testimony of pundits that are in their view based on "mere inference." The orthodox lobby is less committed to literalness since it does not serve them.

To recapitulate, whatever their stands on the prohibition of *sati*, colonial officials and the indigenous male elite agreed that scripture overrode custom, that explicit scriptural evidence had greater weight than evidence based on inference and that, in general, the older the text the greater its value. This privileging of the more ancient texts was tied to another discursive feature: the belief that Hindu society had fallen from a prior Golden Age. We have noted how the ideology of abolition conceived the prohibition of *sati* as a restorative act that returned to natives the "truths"of their own tradition. Bentinck spells this out in his response to the orthodox petition when he claimed that the regulation, by enabling ascetic widowhood, only enforced that which was

> commanded above other courses in books usually considered of the highest authority . . . and stated to be adapted to a better state of society; such as by the Hindoos, is believed to have subsisted in former times. ("Petition," 162)

Bentinck goes on to note that, by practicing ascetic widowhood, widows could be true both to the laws of government and "the purest precepts of religion." Further, according to Bentinck, the widows would provide "an example to the existing generation of that good conduct which is supposed to have distinguished the earlier and better times of the Hindoo people" ("Petition," 163).

Rammohun also subscribed to the notion that nineteenth-century Indian society represented a decline form an earlier greatness. In thanking Bentinck for the prohibition of *sati* he notes his satisfaction, "that the heinous sin of cruelty to females may no longer be committed, and that the ancient and purest system of Hindu religion should not any longer be set at nought by the Hindus themselves."[24] This notion of a fall from grace is also manifest in the claims made, by officials and by Rammohun, that the apparent scriptural legitimacy of *sati* was secured by tampering with the texts, or as Rammohun put it, by "interpolations and inventions, under the name of traditions."[25] According to Rammohun, this necessitated a return to the "original" texts, in this instance *Manu*, "the only safe rule to guard against endless corruptions, absurdities, and human caprices."[26] It can be argued that this desire to restore the original texts contributed to the general neglect in the debate on *sati* of the commentaries written between the eleventh and eigtheenth centuries. The theme of glorious past/degraded present is less prominent in the writings of the orthodoxy since their claim is that *sati* is part of the original canon and not an "accretion." Even so, this idea of a fall grew to be crucial to nineteenth-century indigenous discourses, "progressive" and "conservative," and was to intersect with the idea that Britain rescued Hindu India from Islamic tyranny, to produce specifically "Hindu" discourses of political and cultural regeneration. I will return to this issue below.

I would now like to relate this discussion of the details of the debate on *sati* to the argument set out at the beginning of this paper, namely, that the concept of tradition is reconstituted in the nineteenth century, that women and scripture are the terms of its articulation, and that this development is specifically colonial. So far, I have tried to demonstrate this historical specificity with reference to the process by which knowledge about *sati* was produced, the ideas that were central and

24. "Address to Lord William Bentinck," 477.
25. "A Pamphlet of Rammohun Roy Containing Some Remarks in Vindication of the Resolution," 188.
26. Ibid., 189.

marginal to this process, and the ways in which these ideas shaped the main arguments advanced by proponents and opponents of *sati*, both indigenous and official.[27]

My argument regarding the historical specificity of this discourse can also be made from another angle, by contrasting Rammohun's rhetoric in *Tuhfatul Muwahiddin* with that employed by him in the *sati* debate. I am drawing here on the excellent work of Sumit Sarkar, who has argued that the Bengal Renaissance should be regarded "not as a 'torch race,' but as a story of retreat and decline."[28] This decline is examined by Sarkar in terms of what he sees as the increasing conservatism of Rammohun's later writings. Sarkar discusses how Rammohun's argument for monotheism in *Tuhfat* is developed rigorously in terms of reason and the criterion of social comfort:

> Only three basic tenets common to all faiths and hence 'natural' are retained: belief in a single Creator (proved by the argument from design), in the existence of the soul, and faith in an afterworld where rewards and punishments will be duly awarded— and even the two latter beliefs are found acceptable only on utilitarian grounds. Everything else—belief in particular divinities . . . faith in divinely inspired prophets and miracles . . . 'the hundreds of useless hardships and privations regarding eating and drinking, purity and impurity, auspiciousness and inauspiciousness' is blown up with relentless logic . . .[29]

Sarkar observes that Rammohun in *Tuhfat* comes "perilously close to the vanishing point of religion," a position he draws back from in his post-1815 arguments for monotheism, which are primarily grounded in a reinterpretation of the Upanishads.[30] As Sarkar puts it, "the claims of

---

27. The argument that the scripturalizing of tradition is specifically colonial is also borne out in my analysis of Baptist missionary preaching narratives from this period. Here missionaries are to be found interrogating peasants on the scriptural authority for their "religious" practices and responding to their inability to answer such questions with the accusation that the peasants were ignorant of their own tradition! See Mani, "Early Missionary Discourse on India: The Journals of Carey, Marshman and Ward," unpublished ms.

28. Sarkar, "Rammohun Roy and the Break with the Past," 47.

29. Ibid., 49-50. It is important to note that reason here is located within the tradition of Islamic rationalism.

30. Ibid., 50.

reason are now balanced and increasingly limited by Upanishadic authority as well as by a conservative use of the social comfort criterion."[31]

From my perspective, what is significant is that the shift in Rammohun's rhetoric parallels his increasing involvement with colonial presence. It is known, for instance, that Rammohun did not know much English at the time of writing *Tuhfat* in 1803-4. He was at the time employed by Thomas Woodforde in a private capacity at Murshidabad. In 1805 he is said to have entered formally East India Company service under John Digby. There is much controversy over the chronology of key events in Rammohun's life,[32] and in any case problems of "influence" are complex and do not lend themselves to dating in any simple sense. However, one can agree with Rajat Ray, that the evidence suggests that the "three main influences in Rammohun's thought—Persian, Vedantic and occidental—were imbibed by him successively, strictly in that chronological order."[33] I would argue that, although this may have been the chronological order in which Rammohun encountered these various systems of thought, their influence on Rammohun was not cumulative; rather Rammohun reinterpreted his earlier ideas in terms of the occidental. In other words, the move from a trenchant critique of religion to a strategy which argued for social reform in terms of the scriptural was related to the emerging dominance of an official Western discourse on India, a discourse of moral superiority that acknowledged India's greatness but only in terms of her scriptural past.

This colonial discourse not only privileged brahmanic scriptures as the key to Indian society, it also distinguished sharply between the "Hindu" and the "Islamic," conceiving of these as mutually exclusive and autonomous heritages. Once again Rammohun's own history is suggestive, for as Sarkar points out:

> The Hindu intelligentsia of nineteenth century Bengal (and maybe Rammohun, too, to some extent, after he had mastered English) turned their backs entirely on . . . [the] . . . secularism, rationalism, and non-conformity [of] pre-British Muslim ruled India . . .[34]

31. Ibid., 53-54.
32. See the editors' comments in S.D. Collett, *The Life and Letters of Raja Rammohun Roy*, ed. D.K. Biswas and P.C. Ganguli (Calcutta: Sadharan Brahmo Samaj, 1962).
33. Ray, introduction to *Rammohun Roy and the Process of Modernization in India*, 7.
34. Sarkar, "Rammohun Roy and the Break with the Past," 52-53.

The centrality and importance given to brahmanic scripture by the British and the construction of "Hindu" law from these texts raise the question of the relationship between brahmanic scripture and society in pre-British India. The British saw themselves as resurrecting an ancient tradition that had been interrupted by the corruption of preceding centuries, but was this in fact the case? Were brahmanic scriptures the basis of law in precolonial India? D.D. Kosambi, among others, argues otherwise.[35] Kosambi is sharply critical of the British "brahmanising tendency" which ignored the laws enforced by caste *sabhas* and focused exclusively on brahmanic texts for the formulation of "Hindu" law.[36] It seems to me that we must pose the following questions. Have brahmanic texts always been prioritized as the source of law? To what extent have pundits been monopolists of scriptural knowledge as officials and Rammohun have claimed? Did this access to scripture give them social or political power? Put another way, did their access to scripture matter? What use of scripture was made by the caste councils that were said to have handled most cases? Is the development of a legal discourse on scripture a colonial phenomenon?[37]

There is interesting evidence in the materials presented here that in the beginning at least, the responses of pundits appointed to the court did not reflect the kind of authority that colonial officials had assumed, both for the texts and the pundits. As I have discussed, the *vyawasthas* did not claim to state scriptural truths. Pundits qualified their responses as opinions, their readings as interpretive. In other words, their authority was by their own admission circumscribed. Further, *vyawasthas* drew equally on custom as on scripture, although such responses were

---

35. D. D. Kosambi, "Combined Methods in Indology," in *D. D. Kosambi on History and Society*, ed. A.J. Syed (Bombay: University of Bombay, 1985), 1-2. There is, in addition, a rich body of literature on law in colonial India. For references, see Mani, "Production of Official Discourse," n. 9.

36. Kosambi's criticism of such textualism also extends to reformers like R.G. Bhandarkar arguing against widow remarriage in terms of the *Rig Veda* without reference to actual social practice, and to P.V. Kane whose *History of Dharmashastras* is castigated for restricting "the discussion to *smriti* documents, avoiding any disagreeable contact with anthropology, sociology or reality" (Kosambi, "Combined Methods of Indology," 2). Kosambi's criticism, rooted in a materialist conception of history, is well taken. I would, however, suggest that in addition the strategies of Bhandarkar and Kane should be historicized.

37. Needless to say, similar questions need to be posed regarding the constitution of Islamic personal law. Such an analysis would probably find parallel processes of codification at work, as well as similar ambivalences toward women.

invariably treated as marginal and pundits were required to revise them. By contrast there is nothing tentative about the 1830 orthodox petition; there are no qualifiers prefacing textual excerpts. To the petition is attached "a paper of authorities" described as a "translation of *a decision of the legal points* declaring the practice of suttee lawful and expedient" ("Petition," 159; emphasis mine). The *Asiatic Journal*, in reporting the submission of this petition to William Bentinck, remarks that it is *"accompanied by legal documents."*[38] Here the equation between scripture and law is complete.

Equally significant in its ideological consequences for women was the equation of tradition with scripture. As we have seen, colonial officials, Rammohun Roy and the orthodox Hindu community all deliberated the matter of *sati* in terms of religious texts. The scriptures, or rather various versions of them, provided the basis for arguments for and against this practice. Given that the debate on *sati* is premised on its scriptural and, consequently, its "traditional" and "legal" status, it is little wonder that the widow herself is marginal to its central concerns. The parameters of the discourse preclude this possibility. Instead, women become sites upon which various versions of scripture/ tradition/law are elaborated and contested. It is thus the alternatives to *sati* are also drawn from the scriptures. There is, after all, nothing necessarily logical or inevitable about ascetic widowhood as an option. Why widowhood? Why *ascetic* widowhood? Why not an argument for widow remarriage?[39]

The fundamental importance given to scripture in the debate on *sati* raises the following question: in what ways can it be regarded as an instance of a "modernizing" discourse? It is clear that the debate was not conducted along lines that are normally held to constitute the modern. It was not a secular discourse of reason positing a morality critical of "outmoded" practices and a new conception of "individual rights." To the contrary, as we have seen, at the ideological level the debate was a scriptural deliberation of the legitimacy of *sati* that was critical of its

38. *Asiatic Journal* (June 1830), in *Raja Rammohun Roy and Progressive Movements in India*, 172; emphasis mine.

39. In this respect it is interesting, as Sumit Sarkar notes, how Rammohun's painstaking detailing of the merits of ascetic widowhood was to complicate Vidyasagar's case for widow remarriage! Sarkar, "Rammohun Roy and the Break with the Past," 53.

contemporary form for not being, in a sense, "outmoded enough," not true to its original principles. (One must, of course, insist on the equally mythic status of this so-called original *sati*.)

The discussion of the rights of women as individuals is also absent except insofar as it is posed indirectly in context of the widow's will. As we have seen, this will is conceded primarily in the abstract and only reluctantly, and by a few in practice, thus justifying interventions on the widow's behalf, whether by the European official or the indigenous male social reformer. However, whatever the skepticism regarding the widow's subjecthood, this concern with individual will may itself be read as suggesting the modernity of this discourse.

But the discourse on *sati* was also modern in another more important sense: it was a modern discourse on tradition. It exemplifies late eigtheenth-century colonial discourses that elaborated notions of modernity against their own conceptions of tradition. I suggest, in other words, that what we have there is not a discourse in which pre-existing traditions are challenged by an emergent modern consciousness, but one in which both "tradition" and "modernity" as we know them are contemporaneously produced. The modernity of this discourse on tradition needs to be recognized more fully.

Tradition in this discourse is posited as a timeless and structuring principle of Indian society enacted in the everday lives of indigenous people. "Tradition," interchangeable for the most part with "religion" and "culture," is designated as a sphere distinct from material life. It is thus that officials can speak of returning to natives the truth of traditions that had been interrupted by the "Islamic interlude." This conception is also evident in Ewer's arguments that when Indians acted religiously they acted passively and in his legitimization of intervention in *sati*, given evidence for it as a material practice.[40]

There are two consequences to this concept of culture or tradition as a transhistorical and ubiquitous force acted out by people. First, it produces analyses of *sati* in purely "cultural" terms that empty it of both history and politics. Second, this notion of culture effectively erases the

---

40. This conception of tradition finds its clearest expression in descriptions of incidents of *sati* and in what Mary Pratt has elsewhere termed the "manners and customs" material, discussion of which is beyond the scope of this paper. See Mary Louise Pratt, "Scratches on the Face of the Country; or What Mr. Barrow Saw in the Land of the Bushmen," *Critical Inquiry* 12 (Autumn 1985): 119-43.

agency of those involved in such practices. However, as we noted in Ewer's description of how the widow is dragged to the river, not everyone involved in a *sati* is seen to be subjected equally to the imperatives of culture. Family members, especially the males, and the pundits present at the pyre are given alternate subject positions. The former are often seen to be acting in their own interest, the latter almost always so. Such interest is always coded as corrupt and to the detriment of the widow. Even so, within the general subjection of all indigenous people to "religion" or "tradition," men are offered some measure of will.

Not so the widow. She is consistently portrayed as either a heroine —entering the raging flames of the pyre with no display of emotion— or an abject victim—thrown upon the heap, sometimes fastened to it by unscrupulous family members or pundits. We saw both these in Rammohun's descriptions of *sati*. These poles, "heroine" and "victim," preclude the possibility of a complex female subjectivity. Indeed, given the definition of tradition operative in the discourse on *sati*, the portrayal of the immolated widow as heroine merely rewrites her as victim of a higher order: not of man but of God (or religion). This representation of the widow makes her particularly susceptible to discourses of salvation, whether these are articulated by officials or the indigenous elite. It thus comes as no surprise that both offer to intercede on her behalf, to save her from "tradition," indeed even in its name.

We can concede then, that women are not subjects in this discourse. Not only is precious little heard from them, but as I have suggested above, they are denied any agency. This does not, however, imply that women are the objects of this discourse, that this discourse is *about* them. On the contrary, I would argue that women are neither subjects nor objects, but rather the ground of the discourse on *sati*. For as we saw, analysis of the arguments of participants very quickly indicates that women themselves are marginal to the debate. Instead, the question of women's status in Indian society posed by the prevalence of widow burning becomes the occasion for struggle over the divergent priorities of officials and the indigenous male elite.

Indeed, as the nineteenth century progresses, at a symbolic level, the fate of women and the fate of the emerging nation become inextricably intertwined. Debates on women, whether in context of *sati*, widow remarriage, or *zenanas*, were not merely about women, but also instances in which the moral challenge of colonial rule was confronted and negotiated. In this process women came to represent "tradition" for all participants: whether viewed as the weak, deluded creatures who must be reformed through legislation and education, or the valiant keepers of tradition who must be protected from the first and be permitted only certain kinds of instruction. For the British, rescuing women becomes part of the civilizing mission. For the indigenous elite, protection of their status or its reform becomes an urgent necessity, in terms of the honor of the collective—religious or national. For all participants in nineteenth-century debates on social reform, women represent embarassment or potential. And given the discursive construction of women as either abject victims or heroines, they frequently represent both shame *and* promise.[41]

Tradition was thus not the ground on which the status of woman was being contested. Rather the reverse was true: women in fact became the site on which tradition was debated and reformulated. What was at stake was not women but tradition. Thus it is no wonder that, even reading against the grain of a discourse ostensibly about women, one learns so little about them. To repeat an earlier formulation: neither subject, nor object, but ground—such is the status of women in the discourse on *sati*.

I suggest that part of what enables this intimate interlocking of women and tradition is that this was a discourse of salvation: a recuperation of authenticity and purity, a vigorous protection of the weak and subordinated aspects of culture against their corrupt manipulation by the strong and dominant. We can see how easily this conception of tradition can intersect with patriarchal notions about women as pure, weak and submissive to produce a discourse in which both are intimately interwoven.

Epilogue

We have accepted for too long and at face value the view that colonization brings with it a more positive reappraisal of the rights of women. It is, of course, true that women become critical matter for public discourse in the nineteenth century. But does this signify concern for

---

41. For an excellent analysis of the ambivalent attitudes to women of social reformers active in the debate on widow remarriage, see Sudhir Chandra, "Widow Remarriage and Later Nineteenth-Century Literature," unpublished ms.

women, or do women become the currency, so to speak, in a complex set of exchanges in which several competing projects intersect? The contemporary example that illustrates an analogous situation—and one which also exemplifies the continuing persistence of colonial discourse—is the Shahbano case. On April 23, 1985, the Supreme Court of India in the *Mohammed Ahmed Khan vs. Shahbano Begum* case gave divorced Muslim women the right to lifelong maintenance. Mohammed Khan, Shahbano's ex-husband, had contested her claims for maintenance insisting that he had, according to Muslim personal law, supported her for three months after their divorce. The Supreme Court stressed that there was no conflict between its verdict and the provisions of Muslim personal law which, in its view, also entitled women to alimony if they were unable to maintain themselves. The judgment has sparked off nationwide controversy on the question of religious personal law and the desirability or otherwise of a uniform civil code. The Shahbano case dramatizes the working of the woman/tradition/law/scripture nexus, now complicated by a political environment that is blatantly communal.

The Shahbano affair has raised many of the same questions as the debate on *sati*: issues of scriptural interpretation, the relation between scripture and society, the role of protective legislation for women, the tension between Shahbano as an individual and Shahbano as a member of a community. Still current, though challenged by feminists and other progressives, is the notion of women and scripture as repositories of tradition. There are also important differences. Shahbano initiated legal action against her husband, while intercession in *sati* was undertaken not by widows but on their behalf. In addition, there has been active participation by women and feminists in the debate, and a successful pushing of the parameters of the discussion, so that it has not (unlike *sati*) developed merely, or even primarily, as a scriptural issue.

Despite this, elements of an earlier colonial discourse haunt the debate and entangle it. Communalism, whose emergence is inextricably linked with colonialism, conditions what strategies are appropriate in the case at the present time. We are required to maintain a delicate balance. On the one hand, we need to counter the arguments of Muslim fundamentalists who claim that "an attack on Muslim personal law is an attack on the Muslim community as such." (One can see in this claim, the equation between law, scripture, and the integrity of religious identity that underwrote the colonial ideology of so-called non-interference, an equation that was later key to the arguments of the indigenous orthodoxy in favor of *sati*.) Simultaneously, we need to challenge disingenuous Hindu fundamentalists and others who, carrying on the civilizing mission, are lamenting the fate of Muslim women and demanding that they be brought "into the twentieth century." (The echoes of colonial rhetoric here are too obvious to labor).

One progressive response to the Shahbano affair has been to defer the demand for a uniform civil code, given current communal tensions, and to seek instead reforms in specific aspects of personal law. Other progressives have persisted in the desire for a uniform civil code, suggesting that demands for legal reforms should be rooted in political principle and that political space should not be conceded to fundamentalists in either camp—hindu or muslim. Whatever one's strategy, we are all inscribed in the webs of a history whose claims on us are real and pressing. If Rammohun's arguments against *sati* were shaped by the discursive and political context of early nineteenth-century Bengal, we are faced with a situation that can be said to represent the unfolding of this same discursive and political history. And our interventions will in turn set precedents for the struggles to come.[42]

I believe it is important to write the history of colonial discourse, to trace its effects on the constitution of our systematic and common-sense knowledges of our tradition, culture and identity. Given the colonial privileging of scripture, is it any wonder that when we speak of tradition with a capital "T" it invariably refers to a textual tradition? Similarly, how far has the nineteenth-century location of culture and tradition in texts contributed to analyses that treat both as essentially unchanging? Such a perspective is implicit in statements regarding "the antiquity of Indian *culture*" or "the weight and persistence of tradition," or in discussions of the status of women in India that begin with unqualified references to *Manu* and the scriptures. Historically grounded analyses of nineteenth-century social reform that take seriously the notion of a colonial discourse on India can serve to preclude

---

42. I do not intend to suggest that communalism today is essentially the same as communalism in pre-independent India. Nor am I interested in blaming colonialism for all our current ills. The point here is to document the way colonial history shapes the present, to question the "post" in "postcolonial."

analytic complicity with this discourse, or its replication. Such work would clarify the continuities and discontinuities in the ideologies of colonial and postcolonial debates on women. Equally significant, it will problematize, once and for all, any insertion of these debates into narratives of progressive modernization in which the meaning of the terms "tradition" and "modernity" are assumed, not specified.

Deterritorializations: The Rewriting of Home and Exile in Western Feminist Discourse

Caren Kaplan

Women have a history of reading and writing in the interstices of masculine culture, moving between use of the dominant language or form of expression and specific versions of experience based on their marginality. Similarly, men and women who move between the cultures, languages, and the various configurations of power and meaning in complex colonial situations possess what Chela Sandoval calls "oppositional consciousness," the ability to read and write culture on multiple levels.[1] Such a view of cultural marginality necessitates the recognition of specific skills. As Bell Hooks writes:

> Living as we did — on the edge — we developed a particular way of seeing reality. We looked both from the outside in and from the inside out. We focused our attention on the center as well as the margin. We understood both . . . [2]

This location is fraught with tensions; it has the potential to lock the subject away in isolation and despair as well as the potential for critical innovation and particular strengths.

According to Immanuel Wallerstein, the political economy of margin and center relies on the relationship between the two terms.[3] Ulf

---

1. Chela Sandoval, (n.d.), "Women Respond to Racism: A Report on the National Women's Studies Association Conference, Storrs, Connecticut," Occasional Papers Series: *The Struggle Within* (Oakland, Ca.: Center for Third World Organizing).
2. Bell Hooks, *Feminist Theory: From Margin to Center* (Boston: South End Press, 1984).
3. Immanuel Wallerstein, *The Modern World System* (New York: Academic Press, 1974).

Hannerz has expanded this model to describe a "world system of cultures" where marginal societies (here one can insert the terms "third world" or "underdeveloped") are not the passive recipients of ready-made images and consumer goods. Rather, these are complex, sophisticated cultures which filter and mediate first world imports, recreating local meanings, producing hybrid cultural artifacts and subjects.[4]

A world which brings people, information, objects, and images across enormous distances at rapid speeds destabilizes the conventions of identity traditionally found in the culture of the first world during the first half of this century. "Deterritorialization" is one term for the displacement of identities, persons, and meanings that is endemic to the postmodern world system. Gilles Deleuze and Felix Guattari use the term "deterritorialization" to locate this moment of alienation and exile in language and literature. In one sense it describes the effects of radical distanciation between signifier and signified. Meaning and utterances become estranged. This defamiliarization enables imagination, even as it produces alienation, "to express another potential community, to force the means for another consciousness and another sensibility."[5] The paradoxical nature of this utopian moment in displacement can be realized in language or in the literature that Deleuze and Guattari designate as "minor." This is not a literature of "masters" or "masterpieces." Deleuze and Guattari assert: "We might as well say that minor no longer designates specific literatures but the revolutionary conditions for every literature within the heart of what is called great (or established) literature."[6] This writing dismantles notions of value, genre, canon, etc. It travels, moves between centers and margins.[7] Within the constructs of Deleuze and Guattari's theory, this process can be seen as

4. Ulf Hannerz, "The World System of Culture: The International Flow of Meaning and Its Local Management," mss., 1985. For a related discussion see James Clifford, "Histories of the Tribal and the Modern," *Art in America* (April 1985): 164-77, 215.

5. Gilles Deleuze and Felix Guattari, "What is a Minor Literature?" in *Kafka: Towards a Minor Literature*, trans. Dana Polan (Minneapolis: Univ. of Minnesota Press, 1986), 17.

6. Ibid., 18.

7. For an elaboration of the notion of the circulation of ideas and theories see Edward Said, "Traveling Theory" in *The World, the Text, the Critic* (Cambridge: Harvard Univ. Press, 1983), 226-47.

both deterritorialization and reterritorialization — not imperialism but nomadism.[8]

The value of this conception lies in the paradoxical movement between minor and major — a refusal to admit either position as final or static. The issue is positionality. In modern autobiographical discourses, for example, the self that is constructed is often construed to be evolving in a linear fashion from a stable place of origin towards a substantial present. In postmodern autobiographical writing such a singular, linear construction of the self is often untenable or, at the very least, in tension with competing issues.

Much of contemporary feminist theory proposes a strategy of reading and an analysis of positionality similar to Deleuze and Guattari's conception of "becoming minor." In working with issues of race, class, and sexualities, as well as gender, feminist discourses have come to stress difference and oscillation of margin and center in the construction of personal and political identities. In fact, the difficulty of defining and totalizing the full range of feminist concerns marks the enriched diversity of this field at this particular historical juncture.

For the first world feminist critic, therefore, the challenge at this particular time is to develop a discourse that responds to the power relations of the world system, that is, to examine her location in the dynamic of centers and margins. Any other strategy merely consolidates the illusion of marginality while glossing over or refusing to acknowledge centralities. Thus, the first world feminist critic may be marginal *vis à vis* the literary establishment or the academy that employs her, yet she may also be more closely linked to these institutions than a non-western or third world feminist critic. Interpretations based on dualities and dialectical oppositions may not provide adequate models for explaining our differences and our respective positions in full complexity.

How do we begin to make methods of describing, explaining, and understanding this world of differences in order to make the connec-

---

8. In his essay on Deleuze and Guattari's *Mille Plateaux* Stephen Muecke describes/cites their formulation of ex-centric nomad societies as models of "becoming and heterogeneity" as opposed to "the stable, the eternal, the identical and the constant." "It is a paradoxical 'model' of becoming." Cf. Stephen Muecke, "The Discourse of Nomadology: Phylums in Flux," *Art and Text* 14 (1984): 27.

tions necessary to change prevailing power relations? Deleuze and Guattari begin their investigation by focusing on the potential in language itself — "How many people live today in a language that is not their own?" they ask.[9] Displaced, marginal people — immigrants, subjects of external and internal colonialism, subjects of racial, gendered, or sexual oppression — recognize this issue in the full spectrum of affirmative and negative aspects. Gloria Anzaldua, an American writer who describes herself as a Chicana, a feminist, and a lesbian, describes the damage of this system as well as the possibility of developing a strategic response:

> Because white eyes do not want to know us, they do not bother to learn our language, the language which reflects us, our culture, our spirit. The schools we attended or didn't attend did not give us the skills for writing nor the confidence that we were correct in using our class and ethnic languages. I, for one, became adept at, and majored in English to spite, to show up, the arrogant racist teachers who thought all Chicano children were dumb and dirty. . . . And though I now write my poems in Spanish as well as English I feel the rip-off of my native tongue . . . [10]

Anzaldua's project has several dimensions: the recognition of a minor literature written from a viewpoint based on the experience of marginality, the full identification with that minor position, and the acknowledgement that her capacity to use the dominant or major language has strategic value. Ripped-off, defensive of her right to her native tongue, certainly embittered, Anzaldua writes through Sandoval's oppositional consciousness. Here she uses English for a purpose — stretching the language somewhat out of its major shape. In this instance, a major language has a minor use; it deconstructs its own preconditions in its very employment. Deleuze and Guattari explore this process when they write:

> This is the problem of immigrants, and especially of their children, the problem of minorities, the problem of a minor litera-

---

9.   Deleuze and Guattari, 19.
10.   Gloria Anzaldua, "Speaking in Tongues: A Letter to Third World Women Writers," in *This Bridge Called My Back: Writings by Radical Women of Color*, Cherrie Moraga and Gloria Anzaldua, eds. (Watertown, Ma.: Persephone Press, 1981), 165-66.

ture, but also a problem for all of us: how to tear a minor literature away from its own language, allowing it to challenge the language and making it follow a sober revolutionary path? How to
become a nomad and an immigrant and a gypsy in relation to
one's own language?[11]

When first world critics advocate a process of "becoming minor"
it is necessary to ask: where are we located in this movement of language and literature? What are we losing with such a move? What do
we stand to gain? Do we have freedom of movement and where does
this freedom come from? For example, I would have to pay attention
to whether or not it is possible for me to *choose* deterritorialization or
whether deterritorialization has chosen me. For if I choose deterritorialization, I go into literary/linguistic exile with all my cultural baggage intact. If deterritorialization has chosen me — that is, if I have
been cast out of home or language without forethought or permission, then my point of view will be more complicated. Both positions
are constructed by the world system but they are not equal. Of course,
Deleuze and Guattari are suggesting that we are all deterritorialized
on some level in the process of language itself and that this is a point of
contact between "us all." Yet we have different privileges and different
compensations for our positions in the field of power relations. My
caution is against a form of theoretical tourism on the part of the first
world critic, where the margin becomes a linguistic or critical vaca-
tion, a new poetics of the exotic. One can also read Deleuze and
Guattari's resistance to this romantic trope in their refusal to recognize a point of origin. Theirs is a poetics of travel where there is no return ticket and we all meet, therefore, en train. Reterritorialization
without imperialism? Can language provide a model of this process?
Who dares let go of their respective representations and systems of
meaning, their identity politics and theoretical homes, when it is, as
Kafka rightly noted, "a matter of life and death here?"[12]

What is lost in Deleuze and Guattari's formulation is the acknowledgement that oppositional consciousness (with its benefits and
costs) stems from the daily, lived experience of oppression. Language can constantly remind us of the differences encoded in social

---

11.   Deleuze and Guattari, 19.
12.   Ibid., 17.

relations. It may well be the site of the problem "for us all," but I am confused by the universalizing of the term "us." Who is the "us" that is circulating in the essay "What is a Minor Literature?"

I have found several more cogent discussions of deterritorialization and oppositional consciousness in the recent writings of some contemporary feminists. I will focus on two writers, in particular, to illustrate this method of feminist discourse, but there are many others who could easily be invoked for this discussion.[13] One writer I would like to discuss, Minnie Bruce Pratt, is a white American born in the South. Her essay "Identity: Skin Blood Heart" explores the difficulty and the costs of maintaining a notion of identity based on racist and heterosexual privilege. In the autobiographical process of memory and review in this essay Pratt questions the conditions of her "home" in the past and looks for a different representation of identity and location. In *Claiming an Identity They Taught Me to Despise* Michelle Cliff, born in Jamaica and writing in New York, constructs an autobiographical poetics that moves relentlessly towards a minor position. What is most interesting about both these memoirs is their inability to remain in any one position — past, utopian, present, minor, major — they explore the social relations that create all of these locations.

Location is a crucial metaphor in Pratt's considerations of identity. The first words we read are: "I live in a part of Washington D.C. that white suburbanites called 'the jungle' . . . "[14] Where Pratt as a white, lesbian feminist lives is always central to her description and explanation of a change in consciousness and way of being. She begins at the end of her story, in Washington D.C., her present location. But she soon moves us to Alabama where she grew up during the era of civil rights struggles. She simultaneously evokes the world of her childhood while dismantling the conditions of her early life. A desire

13.   See the work of: Cherrie Moraga, Audre Lorde, Elly Bulkin, Barbara Smith, Lillian Smith, Mitsuye Yamada, Chela Sandoval, Bernice Reagon, Adrienne Rich, Gloria Hull, Jewelle L. Gomez, Becky Birtha, Cheryl Clark, June Jordan, Katie King, Barbara Harlow, Nellie Wong, Bell Hooks, Osa Hidalgo, Lata Mani, Ruth Frankenberg, Lisa Bloom, Debbie Gordon, Biddy Martin, Chandra Talpade Mohanty, Alicia Partnoy, and many others.
14.   Minnie Bruce Pratt, "Identity: Skin Blood Heart," in *Yours in Struggle: Three Feminist Perspectives on Anti-Semitism and Racism*, Elly Bulkin, Minnie Bruce Pratt, and Barbara Smith, eds. (Brooklyn, N.Y.: Long Haul Press, 1984), 2.

to be and feel "at home" is examined in light of who and what made the conditions of security and contentment possible. In particular, Pratt focuses on the radical separation between people of different skin colors in her community. This separation was justified to her when she was a girl by a rigid system of racist explanation and rationalization. Pratt relates how she felt safe in this world, accepting its terms, never pushed to question the structure of its legitimation.

Protection and security come to be contextualized when Pratt finds herself feeling increasingly threatened by sexism and homophobia. Habituated to white southern gentility, Pratt has a rude awakening when she transgresses the boundaries of her culture. She finds that she no longer merits protection or consideration:

> Raised to believe that I could be where I wanted and have what I wanted, as a grown woman I thought I could simply claim what I wanted . . . . I had no understanding of the limits that I lived within, nor of how much my memory and my experience of a safe space was to be based on places secured by omission, exclusion, or violence, and on my submitting to the limits of that place.[15]

The incident which prompts this reflection involves the loss of Pratt's children in a custody battle. Her parents withdraw their emotional support from her at the same time. In this process of estrangement and loss, Pratt feels expelled from the warm circle of the home she had known. "I felt," she writes, "like my life was cracking around me."[16] Reflecting on the costs of the security she has taken for granted, she chooses to go another route — rather than return to the terms she had taken for granted, Pratt chooses to learn about the social relations that create the terms.

Pratt's autobiographical essay elaborates a dynamic feminist theory of location and positionality. Moving away from "home" to deconstruct the terms of social privilege and power, such a feminist practice favors the process of the move over the ultimate goal. The uncertainty of this situation is preferable, Pratt argues, to the sensation of being homesick while at "home."

---

15. Ibid., 25-26.
16. Ibid., 39.

For the first world feminist critic the process of becoming minor has two primary aspects. First, I must acknowledge that there are things that I do not know. Second, I must find out how to learn about what I have been taught to avoid, fear, or ignore. A critique of where I come from, my home location, takes me away from the familiar. Yet, there is no pure space of total deterritorialization. I must look carefully at what I carry with me that could help me with the process. This is crucial if I am to avoid appropriating the minor through romanticization, envy, or guilt. Becoming minor is not a process of emulation. As Pratt writes: "I am compelled *by my own life* to strive for a different place than the one we have lived in."[17]

This is work that feminists have to do for themselves — sometimes in concert with others, sometimes alone. What we gain from this process is an understanding of what connects us as well as how we are different from each other — here re-written as a refusal of the terms of radical separation. Exploring all the differences, keeping identities distinct, is the only way we can keep power differentials from masquerading as universals. We will have different histories, but we will often have similar struggles. To recognize with whom we need to work instead of against is a continual process.

The first stage in this process is refusing the privilege of universalizing theories. Some of us may experience ourselves as minor in a world that privileges the masculine gender. But our own centrality in terms of race, class, ethnicity, religious identity, age, nationality, sexual preference, and levels of disabilities is often ignored in our own work. All women are not equal, and we do not all have the same experiences (even of gender oppression). When we insist upon gender alone as a universal system of explanation we sever ourselves from other women. How can we speak to each other if we deny our particularities? Recognizing the minor cannot erase the aspects of the major, but as a mode of understanding it enables us to see the fissures in our identities, to unravel the seams of our totalities. First world feminist criticism is struggling to avoid repeating the same imperializing moves that we claim to protest. We must leave home, as it were, since our homes are often sites of racism, sexism, and other damaging social practices. Where we come to locate ourselves in terms of our specific histories and differences must be a place with room for what can be

---

17. Ibid., 48-49.

salvaged from the past and what can be made new. What we gain is a reterritorialization; we reinhabit a world of our making (here "our" is expanded to a coalition of identities — neither universal nor particular). In this spirit Pratt writes: "One gain for me as I change: I learn a way of looking at the world that is more accurate, complex, multi-layered, multi-dimensioned, more truthful: to see the world of overlapping circles . . . "[18]

In *Claiming an Identity They Taught Me to Despise* Michelle Cliff describes the process of finding a social space to inhabit that will not deny any of the complicated parts of her identity and history.[19] Radically deterritorialized from a Carribean culture and a race by a family conspiracy of silence and denial, she explores the parameters of identity and the limits of privilege. Separated from her home and family by geography, education, and experience, Cliff articulates the boundaries between homelessness and origin, between exile and belonging. She must, as she puts it, "untangle the filaments of my history."[20]

The first move Cliff makes in her autobiographical memoir is a return to the territory of her childhood. This trip into memory uncovers a primal injunction. "Isolate yourself," she was told:

> If they find out about you it's all over. Forget about your great-grandfather with the darkest skin . . . . Go to college. Go to England to study. Learn about the Italian Renaissance and forget that they kept slaves. Ignore the tears of the Indians. Black Americans don't understand us either . . . . Blend in . . . [21]

In order to understand her refusal to blend in, Cliff begins to explore what is at stake in her mother's efforts to obscure her racial identity. She has to learn the history of white, black, and mulatto people in Jamaica, the island where she was born. It is a history of divisions, violence, and suppression. A creole culture with no single origin, Jamaica exists in many levels and time periods. Cliff moves

---

18.   Ibid., 17.
19.   Michelle Cliff, *Claiming an Identity They Taught Me to Despise* (Watertown, Ma.: Persephone Press, 1980).
20.   Ibid., 7.
21.   Ibid.

through several of these identities. She rewrites her history to "claim" an identity through her powers of story-telling and imagination.

Turning her memories of childhood over and over, Cliff begins with the terrain of the island. Looking for a firm foundation for her identity she finds instead that the geography of that time is "obsolete." There is no possibility of return to that innocent land. Instead, she moves through each place she has lived, asking, "What is here for me: where do these things lead?"[22] At first Cliff discovers the pain that her family had struggled to spare her. Behind each nostalgic memory lies a history of oppression:

> Behind the warmth and light are dark and damp/ . . . behind the rain and river water, periods of drought/ underneath the earth are the dead/ . . . underneath the distance is the separation/ . . . behind the fertility are the verdicts of insanity/ . . . underlying my grandmother's authority with land and scripture is obedience to a drunken husband . . . [23]

Her new view of her past and her life has to contain all of these images and kinds of knowledge. They become materials for Cliff to discover and use, stories to listen to again, photographs to review, a landscape to rewrite. Mining her memories of both Jamaica and New York she is no longer able to remain separated from the full range of experiences and identities available to her in the past and present.

In the section of the text entitled "Against Granite" Cliff refines the possibilities of reterritorialization. Imagining an archive where historians are restoring "details of an unwritten past" she writes:

> Out back is evidence of settlement: a tin roof crests a hill amid mountains — orange and tangerine trees form a natural border. A river where women bathe can be seen from the historian's enclave. The land has been cultivated; the crops are ready for harvest. In the foreground a young black woman sits on grass which flourishes. Here women pick freely from the trees.[24]

---

22. Ibid., 20.
23. Ibid., 21.
24. Ibid., 29-30.

The inhabitants of this imaginary settlement are women, the "historians" who keep an eye on the border guards who threaten to invade their camp. Cliff names the threat to this vision of postcolonial feminist space: "slicers/suturers/invaders/abusers/sterilizers/infibulators/castrators/dividers/enclosers . . ."[25] Reflecting her new passion for historical specificity, Cliff's naming project becomes more explicit: "Upjohn, Nestle, Riker's, Welfare, Rockland State, Jesus, the Law of the Land — and yes, and also — Gandhi and Kenyatta." Cliff constitutes a kind of collective history based on gender as well as on race and class. It is a history of women who are threatened variously and complexly by forces ranging from an American drug company to the masculinist proponents of certain nationalist liberation struggles. This kind of epistemological shift helps to enact a politics of identity that is flexible enough to encompass the ironies and contradictions of the modern world system.

The notion of settlement delineated in this section of the text is a fictional terrain, a reterritorialization that has passed through several versions of deterritorialization to posit a powerful theory of location based on contingency, history, and change. One of the final images written in the text is a garden that resonates with many cultural associations, Western and non-Western. In Cliff's text the garden is a piece of land where she can work and live. The paramaters are fluid, there are no "slicers" or "dividers" here. "To garden is a solitary act," she writes.[26] Yet, this activity does not replicate the enclosed space of the modern ego, exiled from the world. The garden is, Cliff writes:

> Not a walled place — in fact, open on all sides.
> Not secret — but private.
> A private open space.[27]

This is a new terrain, a new location, in feminist poetics. Not a room of one's own, not a fully public or collective self, not a domestic realm — it is a space in the imagination which allows for the inside, the outside, and the liminal elements of inbetween. Not a romanticized pastoral nor a modernist urban utopia — Cliff's garden is the

---

25. Ibid., 30.
26. Ibid., 55.
27. Ibid., 52.

space where writing occurs without loss or separation. It is "next-to," or juxtaposed, to the other plots of postmodern fictions and realities. Feminist writing in this expanded sense of "minor" acts against the romanticization of solitude and the suppression of differences. It points towards a rewriting of the connections between different parts of the self in order to make a world of possibilities out of the experience of displacement.

Genet's Genealogy:
European Minorities and the
Ends of the Canon

David Lloyd

1. Minorities and Minor Status

"Orphans we are, and bastards of society."[1]

W hen I first conceived this essay, I could not have known that
its nominal subject would have passed away before its first
word was written. It is, then, only timely to recall that the late Jean
Genet knew better than any that the subject of writing is merely a
pretext from which the *process* of writing passes away, refusing the
production of identities, whether as epitaphs or passbooks. In Genet,
we have lost a figure but not an author, in the literary sense of the
word. For some time ago already Genet abandoned literature, and
with it the production of even those very texts which are so antagonistic to the literary canon and to its ends of identification. But in
abandoning literature, Genet did not cease to write, though his writing became increasingly the expression of his political solidarities.[2]
What he abandons is a literature which, in its irreconcilable antagonism to the canonical ends of aesthetic culture, still must accept its
own condemnation to minor status. Bringing this minor literature to

---

1. James Morrison, quoted in E.P. Thompson, *The Making of the English Working
Class* (New York: Vintage, 1966), 832.
2. See, for example, his recent, posthumously published work on the Palestinians,
Un Captif Amoureuse (Paris: Gallimard, 1986). I am indebted to Natalie Melas for drawing
my attention to essays which were later collected in this volume.

369

an end signals simultaneously the end of the canon: the major and the minor, after a long and antagonistic life, pass away in the same moment.

I am suggesting here that a specific phase in the history of western writing has come to an end in our own time, namely that phase which falls between the emergence of what I would term "aesthetic culture" and its current confrontation with the loss of the ethical function that legitimated it. It is within the discourse of aesthetic culture that the canon intended here is established, and from that discourse it derives the terms by which texts are distributed into major and minor categories, or even defined as literature at all. The end of the canon is not the end of writing, nor is the end of minor writing the same thing as the end of a distinct writing of or by minorities. The two phenomena, minor writing and the writing of minorities, frequently overlap, indeed, by the very terms which found the canon, *must* constantly overlap. But if, as I would argue, the hegemonic function of aesthetic culture has largely been superseded, it becomes all the more important to distinguish between a minor and a minority writing. In a sense, the latter continues where the former has passed away.

Accordingly, the question at stake here is: what is the historical relationship between a "minor literature" and the literature of "minorities?" In order to address this question, it is necessary to attend first to two prior conditions of any relationship that we may assert between these concepts. In the first place, how are minorities theoretically constituted as political and cultural categories, and, in addition, is there a relationship between the political and the cultural judgement? In the second place, how has that major literature historically been defined, in terms of function as in terms of properties, against which another writing has been adjudged minor?

The representation of certain groups of whatever kind as minorities requires in the first place the political constitution of states within which consensus is in theory reached through the mediation of conflicting interests to the benefit of a majority of the citizens. States so constituted emerge only in the wake of the bourgeois revolutions of the late eighteenth and early nineteenth centuries, but have rapidly imposed themselves globally as the proper model of political organization. To their virtually simultaneous emergence as *nation* states we will return.[3]

Given the claim that these revolutions establish universal equality of rights for all men, the provision for proper representation of minority interests within the constitution becomes essential to the theoretical legitimation of bourgeois hegemony. As John Stuart Mill puts it in his *Considerations on Representative Government* (1861):

> In a really equal democracy, any or every section would be represented, not disproportionately, but proportionately. A majority of the electors would always have a majority of the representatives; but a minority of the electors would always have a minority of the representatives. Man for man they would be as fully represented as the majority. Unless they are, there is not equal government, but a government of inequality and privilege: . . . contrary to all just government, but, above all, contrary to the principle of democracy, which professes equality as its very root and foundation.[4]

Mill provides here a fairly unexceptional account of the assumptions of "just government" and of the "principles of democracy." Further critical analysis of what is a classic account of liberal political theory will bring to light a number of assumptions which are crucial not only to the constitution but also to the domination of minorities.

Firstly, and in itself almost self-evidently, the theory of representative government, within which alone the existence of minorities makes sense, is applicable only to the more or less large nation state: it depends, in other words, on the necessity of representation, "since all cannot, in a community exceeding a single small town, participate personally but in some very minor portions of the public business" (*RG*, 217-18). Self-evident as this condition may be, the consequences which follow from it are less apparent. For it is not merely that representative government is a necessary compromise, consequent (though Mill is nowhere explicit about this) on the require-

---

3. See especially, out of a large body of writing on the subject, John Breuilly, *Nationalism and the State* (Manchester: Manchester Univ. Press, 1982), for a comprehensive overview of the subject.
4. John Stuart Mill, *Representative Government* in *Utilitarianism, Liberty, and Representative Government* (London: Dent, 1910), 257. Cited hereafter in the text as *RG*.

ment of developing capitalism that local variations in law and customs be progressively overridden in the interests of rationalizing both the labor and the commodity markets. Though this condition requires the mediation of an at first increasingly disparate set of local or partial interests, representative government is itself, in Mill's account, an institution intrinsically opposed to the spirit of locality:

> One of the strongest hindrances to improvement, up to a certain advanced stage, is an inveterate spirit of locality. Portions of mankind, in other respects capable of, and prepared for, freedom, may be unqualified for amalgamating into even the smallest nation. (*RG*, 222)

The initial subordination of localities by centralized power, by autocratic monarchies in other words, is an historical precondition of representative government on which it continues to draw and which it furthers. The dismantling of local centers of power by central government implies accordingly the incorporation into the state of a variety of laterally and vertically differentiated class and/or ethnic groups. Secondly, and consistent with that first condition, minorities within the large nation state are defined not merely by their numerical inferiority to the dominant ethnic or class groups that compose the nation, but moreover by the geographical dispersal which, in time with the eradication of local legal differences, capitalism requires of them as a condition of individual and collective economic survival. Unable to form a majority in any constituency, their unrepresented minority status is perpetuated by the very dislocations in which the modern state finds the conditions of its emergence.[5]

Confusion is virtually inevitable here, given the difference between the commonly accepted current usage of the term "minority" and the sense in which Mill employs the same term. It is essential to Mill's argument, and enabling to the direction which it takes, that the definition of minorities at this juncture be not only purely political

---

5.   *RG*, 264. It is for this reason that Marx, in "On the Jewish Question," ironically envisages all citizens of the modern state becoming "Jewish": "The *chimerical* rationality of the Jews is the rationality of the merchant, of the man of money in general." See Karl Marx, *Early Writings*, introd. Lucio Colletti, trans. Rodney Livingstone and Gregor Benton (New York: Vintage, 1978), 239.

but also purely formal. That is, Mill's usage of "minority" has reference only to *any* interest group whatsoever whose interests may not be those of the majority. There is no reference to minorities in the ethnic, cultural, or sexual sense. That this is so is crucial to the normative drive of his argument and to the notions of development which underpin it. Pointing out that, "though the Parliament of the nation ought to have as little as possible to do with purely local affairs," it will be necessary to have some provision for the representation of localities, Mill recognizes that in this case:

> It would be the minorities chiefly, who being unable to return the local member, would look elsewhere for a candidate likely to obtain other votes in addition to their own. (*RG*, 264)

This, however, does not lead Mill to argue for the provision of, say, a number of Jewish or Irish representatives open to election by their ethnic groups regardless of locality. Rather, he argues for just such a system to privilege the intellectuals or, as he is obliged to term them, "the instructed minority." Having recognized that geographical dispersal is one of the crucial factors excluding minorities from representation, he is enabled to argue that the most significant minority in the modern state is the body of intellectuals whose institutional functions require their dispersal throughout the nation.[6] Accordingly, it is essential to provide for special representation of the "instructed minority" within the legislative body. The arguments which justify this claim, and what may seem the even more outrageous claim that the "instructed" should be granted more votes than other citizens (*RG*, 285-90), constitute implicitly the legitimation for the perpetuation of the minority status of other groups and for the extension of western bourgeois hegemony globally.

Mill's contention is that his "instructed minority" would provide "a supplement, or completing corrective, to the instincts of a democratic majority" (*RG*, 268). This claim rests on two more or less ex-

---

6. Similarly, Coleridge regards the "clerisy" as the essential disseminating organ of cultivation in the political constitution of the state: see S.T. Coleridge, *On the Constitution of Church and State*, ed. John Colmer, Bollingen Series 25 (Princeton, N.J.: Princeton Univ. Press, 1976), 75. *Church and State* was clearly a direct influence on Mill's *Representative Government*.

plicit assumptions about the nature of intellectuals. In the first place, they can correct the potential abuses of majority power by a superior capacity for reflective rather than instinctive decision. In the second place, their interests will not coincide with that of the majority, or, where they do, their reflective capacities will allow them the uncommon capacity of laying their own interests in abeyance. The two arguments are distinct, but linked within the general narrative which underlies Mill's political theory. The minority status of intellectuals is consequent upon the same condition which makes them disinterested, namely, their unspoken detachment from any prior "organic" community: politically speaking, the intellectual no longer belongs to his or her class, local community, or other "natural" interest group. Dislocation is, in fact, the symptom of their disinterest. Dislocation and disinterest are seen, in fact, as the destiny of intellectuals, but as a legitimating destiny precisely insofar as it is also the ethical history of humankind. Within that history, intellectuals represent a kind of perpetual avant-garde which occupies the furthest point attained in the normative development of the human race.

This history of human development simultaneously describes the evolution of human beings to that stage at which they are capable of participating in representative government, which is "the ideal type of a perfect government" (*RG*, 218). Most significantly, it provides a model for both individual and cultural development, both individuals and cultures or societies passing through an ideal series of stages which prepare them ethically and politically for representative government:

> We have recognized in representative government the ideal type of the most perfect polity, for which, in consequence, any portion of mankind are better adapted in proportion to their degree of general improvement. As they range lower and lower in development, that form of government will be, generally speaking, less suitable to them; though this is not true universally: for the adaptation of a people to representative government does not depend so much upon the place they occupy in the general scale of humanity as upon the degree in which they possess certain special requisites; requisites, however, so closely connected with their general degree of advancement, that any variation between the two is rather the exception than the rule. (*RG*, 218)

The requisites referred to here are, in the final analysis, ethical, demanding the reconciliation in the individual, and, more generally, in "national character," of autonomy ("self-dependence") and self-subordination. Only an ethical disposition is capable of *freely* submitting to the general interest, and that disposition is one which is only developed through intellectual culture. Accordingly, in an argument profoundly influenced as is virtually all British cultural theory in the nineteenth century by the spectre of an empowered working class, Mill remarks that "universal teaching must precede universal franchise" (*RG*, 280). What is held to legitimate working class disenfranchisement within the framework of representative government is the contrast between the general level of development of the "national character" as represented by the intellectuals and the ethically deleterious effects of working class labor:

> Their work is a routine; not a labour of love, but of self-interest in the most elementary form, the satisfaction of daily wants; neither the thing done, nor the process of doing it, introduces the mind to thoughts or feelings extending beyond individuals; if instructive books are within their reach, there is no stimulus to read them; and in most cases the individual has no access to any person of cultivation much superior to his own. (*RG*, 216)

Under conditions of representative government, "public duty," even without franchise, prepares the way for full participation inasmuch as it provides ethical training in the "unselfish sentiment of identification with the public" (*RG*, 217). The working classes may be developed into the capacity for representing themselves.

But what is true internally to the state is equally true of humankind in general, with the proviso that at a lower stage of national development, individual ethical improvement cannot come about by minimal participations in public duty. The characteristics of the lowest stage of human development, the savage, are virtually identical with those of the working classes, and equally disabling, a fact which should serve to remind us of the extent to which a discourse of class continues to overlap with one of race:

> . . . a people in a state of savage independence, in which every one lives for himself, exempt, unless by fits, from any external control, is practically incapable of making any progress in civilization until it has learnt to obey. (*RG*, 197)

Though the disqualifying term, "self-interest," is the same, the consequence differs, since the working classes can be incorporated hegemonically through education and restricted participation in the affairs of the state, savages only by lessons in obedience. In turn this latter assertion becomes the inevitable legitimation for the disciplinary powers of dominant colonialism: primitive societies divide between two fundamental and fundamentally disabling characteristics, "savage independence" and the slavish obedience of the barbarian (*RG*, 197-99). Within Mill's universal narrative of human development, however, these characteristics are not synchronic. The slavish subjection of the barbarian is the necessary stage by which the savage mind can be improved, whether "to submit to the restraints of a regular and civilized government" (*RG*, 178) or to accept that "continuous labor" which is the price of civilization (*RG*, 198). Historically speaking, this explains the necessity of periods of despotism in the development of civilization; contemporaneously, it justifies the forceful subjection of native populations:

> Under a native despotism, a good despot is a rare and transitory accident: but when the dominion they are under is that of a more civilized people, that people ought to be able to supply it constantly. The ruling country ought to be able to do for its subjects all that could be done by a succession of absolute monarchs, guaranteed by irresistible force against the precariousness of tenure attendant on barbarous despotisms, and qualified by their genius to anticipate all that experience has taught to the more advanced nation. Such is the ideal rule of a free people over a barbarous or semi-barbarous one. (*RG*, 382)

The basic principle of external colonialism, that "improvement cannot come from themselves, but must be superinduced from without," contains also the model for the transition from dominant to hegemonic colonialism, the passage from "a government of will to one of law" (*RG*, 199). The judgement is at once historical and ethical in form, or, more precisely, it depends on an historiography which is already ethical, upon an ethics which is always historical.

Hence one notes the universality of its application as a legitimation of internal as well as external colonialism, and in terms of class as well as race relations. The specific constitution of minorities in the sense that concerns us here can be deduced from Mill's remark in his chapter on "Nationality." It has already been noted that the kind of state that Mill has always in mind is the *nation* state. But his chapter on the question of nationality comes late in the text and as if an incidental complication of the larger argument. It is necessary for us, accordingly, to stress what the concept of nationality implies within the historical schema that Mill everywhere invokes. Nation states are artificial entities, the creation in turn of the autocratic monarchies of Europe and of the need for an increasingly rationalized labor and commodity market under capitalism. But what is significant in the latter case is that in the absence of a self-legitimating autocratic power, an *internal* principle of legitimacy for the state must be found. This principle is generally racial, constituting the nation on grounds of ethnic identity. As Mill puts it:

> This feeling of nationality may have been generated by various causes. Sometimes it is the effect of identity of race and descent. Community of language, and community of religion, greatly contribute to it. Geographical limits are one of its causes. But the strongest of all is identity of political antecedents; the possession of a national history, and consequent community of recollections; collective pride and humiliation, pleasure and regret, connected with the same incidents in the past. (*RG*, 360)

Mill's argument here assumes ethnic identity within the historical production of identity, an assumption that becomes necessary from the moment that a *large* nation state must appeal for its unity to national identity, despite being composed of an aggregate of different ethnic groups.[7] But, as we have been seeing, history for Mill is the narrative of the ethical development of the race, defined precisely by ever-widening capacities for identification. Logically, therefore, his definition of nationality brings with it a valuable pay-off in relation to internal minorities, and one which can be efficiently transported,

---

7.   This is equally a problem for oppositional nationalisms which must forge a national political consciousness out of the divided loyalties of a population which only ever coheres as a "nation" in consequence of imperial domination. I have discussed this question at greater length in Chapter 2 of *Nationalism and Minor Literature: James Clarence Mangan and the Emergence of Irish Cultural Nationalism* (forthcoming, Berkeley: Univ. of California Press, 1987). See also Breuilly, *Nationalism and the State*, 115-16.

mutatis mutandi, to all modern western nation states. Mill turns to another "more purely moral and social consideration" than geographical bases for national boundaries:

> Experience proves that it is possible for one nationality to merge and be absorbed in another: and when it was originally an inferior and more backward portion of the human race the absorption is greatly to its advantage. (*RG*, 363)

He proceeds to laud the advantages for the Breton or the Basque of assimilating into that "highly civilized and cultivated people," the French, rather than "sulk[ing] on his own rocks, the half-savage relic of past times, revolving in his own little mental orbit, without participation or interest in the general movement of the world" (*RG*, 363-64). The same, of course, applies to the Celtic populations under English rule. "Admixture of nationalities" is, as a general principle, "a benefit to the human race" (*RG*, 364). But the apparent neutrality of Mill's assertion dissolves in the recognition that such admixture is in fact always the assimilation or incorporation of a less-developed (that is, technologically weaker) population into a more highly-developed one. And given that Mill's historical schema applies not only to the formal historical relations between different "national characters" but also, as in the case of the disenfranchisement of the working classes on educational grounds, to individuals and classes within any nation, the implication of his argument is that when the sulky Breton is absorbed into France he will not only constitute a "minority" in the purely statistical sense, but also a minority with diminished rights to political representation. The concept of representation invoked revolves crucially around an ethnocentric model of political and cultural development, and it is this developmental model which allows the easy transition between a liberal version of political representation and the legitimation of external and internal colonialism. The geographical centre can always be dissembled as representing a temporal moment of universal history.

2. Ends of an Aesthetic of Representation

What becomes clear from the logic of *Representative Government* is that the extension of proportional representation to minorities, however constituted, makes little difference while the concept of representation in play remains centred upon the cultural models of a European bourgeoisie. If the recognition of this fact will lead me to suggest the necessity of a critique of the aesthetic foundations of political representation, I should stress from the outset that I do not wish to imply in any way the sufficiency in itself of such a critique as a political intervention. Nonetheless, it does seem necessary to understand the intimate inter-involvement of aesthetic and political concepts of representation over the last two hundred years as mutually supporting aspects of a western discourse on "the human," conceived as universally valid but effectively ethnocentric. For it is insufficient to critique liberal theories of political representation without grasping their debt to the concept of an ethical subject formed by aesthetic culture, that in theory sublates otherwise irreconcilable political or economic interests. This concept is fundamental to Mill's whole argument; hence the central importance for him of the "instructed minority," that is, the intellectuals regarded as ethical subjects. In this ethical subject, the political and the aesthetic spheres intersect. Whether directed at political or aesthetic modes of representation, any critique will be deficient that does not address the nexal function of this representative instance.[8]

I have outlined elsewhere certain fundamental relationships between aesthetic and political concepts of representation and their grounding function in the establishment of the canon.[9] The main point that needs recapitulation here is that the domain of aesthetic culture provides a site of reconciliation which transcends continuing political differences and accordingly furnishes the domain of human freedom promised in theory by bourgeois states but belied in all but form by their practices. The aesthetic domain performs this function by virtue of the fact that, while bourgeois political theory postulates the essential identity of man, aesthetic works are held to furnish the

---

8. Thus interpretations of modernism which have addressed the breakdown of representation as an *aesthetic* concern are generally deficient to the extent that they ignore the relation of this *formal* phenomenon to contemporaneous crises in political representation and the dissolution of the representative role of high culture. The role of aesthetic culture could be said to have been efficiently taken over by the "culture industry."

9. See my article "Arnold, Ferguson, Schiller: Aesthetic Culture and the Politics of Aesthetics," *Cultural Critique* 2 (Winter 1986): 137-69.

representative instances of reconciliation which at once prefigure and produce an ethical subjectivity restored to identity with this universal human essence.[10] To contemplate aesthetic works of whatever kind is to be drawn into an ethical identification with this essence, which is crucially defined in terms of an inherently *formative* relationship between the human subject and its objects. Aesthetic theory provides consequently the formal paradigm for that "continuous labor" which both disciplines the subject and dominates the material world as a prerequisite to civilization.[11] Its notion of formation is accordingly developmental both in relation to the emergence of the ethical subject which it produces and in relation to the aesthetic products which are the objective signs of any culture's relative stage of civilization.

The canon which is framed by aesthetic theory can consequently be conceived in two interconnected aspects. One is historical, and consists of the ordering of an evolution of genres (*Gattungen*) in relation to the historical development of the species (*Gattung*). The classic instance of this is the sequence: song or ballad, epic, drama, lyric, which underpins romantic notions of generic evolution. The other is evaluative and concerns the discrimination between major and minor writing. A major writing can be broadly characterized as that which most effectively fulfills the function of aesthetic culture itself. Accordingly, it must be concerned with representative instances of the human, instances which may of course vary in relation to historical periods but are nonetheless contained within the historical schema that underwrites the evaluative principles of the canon. It should assist in the ethical formation of the subject, both by depicting the development of an identity to the point of identification with a more general humanity (the narrative of *Bildung*), and by eliciting the reader's similar identification with a character or a poetic subject. The famous "disinterest" of the aesthetic work is accordingly assured in two ways: by the claim that its fundamental patterns of development are universal in kind and by the claim that the universality of that de-

---

10.   See, for a striking instance, Thomas Paine, *Rights of Man*, ed. Henry Collins (Harmondsworth: Penguin, 1969), 87, where, in a founding moment for bourgeois political theory, he traces all political rights back to the original, singular figure of "Man."

11.   The terms are Mill's, in *RG*, 198.

velopment arises from a "common property" of humanity which the work instantiates and evokes. Key terms here are "autonomy" and "authenticity," concepts which anchor the free ethical development of the individual subject in the continuous reproduction of an original human essence.[12]

Any definition of "minor" writing is obliged to take into account its oppositional status *vis-à-vis* canonical or major literature thus described. For this reason, a too hasty identification of "minority" with "minor" literature will inevitably be inaccurate, and Deleuze and Guattari are thus far correct to remark in their study of Kafka that it is perfectly possible for a literature of minorities to "fulfill a major function."[13] One notable case in point would be the literature of nationalism which adopts the same aesthetic terms in order to forge an oppositional national identity. Deleuze and Guattari are equally correct to seek to differentiate a literature of minorities written in a "minority" language from a minor literature which would be that of minorities composed in a major language. For "minor literature" is so termed in relation to the major canon, and its characteristics are defined in opposition to those which define canonical writing. To enumerate them briefly and all too schematically, the characteristics of a minor literature would involve the questioning or destruction of the concepts of identity and identification, the rejection of representations of developing autonomy and authenticity, if not the very concept of development itself, and accordingly a profound suspicion of narratives of reconciliation and unification.

Deleuze and Guattari subsume these characteristics under the term "deterritorialization," a concept which, though often applied with such generality as to obscure the characteristics of particular historical instances, nonetheless relates quite specifically to the question of minor and minority literatures. Minority groups are so defined in consequence of a dislocation or deterritorialization which calls their collective identity in question and leads to their cate-

---

12. Thus Mill refers in "On Liberty," 122, to the "ever recurring originality" of those geniuses who, as the growth-points of culture, are also the "representative" individuals.

13. See Gilles Deleuze and Félix Guattari, "What is a Minor Literature?," Chapter 3 of *Kafka: Toward a Minor Literature*, trans. Richard Brinkley (Minneapolis: Univ. of Minnesota Press, 1986), 16-27.

gorization as instances of "underdevelopment": whether a minority group is defined in terms of gender, ethnicity, or any other typology, its status is never merely statistically established, but involves the aspersion of "minority" exactly in the sense of the common legal usage of the term for those too young to be out of "tutelage."[14] The hegemonic exercise of power replaces violent and exclusive apartheids with the concept of the "minority," defined no longer as bestial or subhuman, but as not yet fully developed, childlike, and subject to tutelage until assimilation is accomplished. Minority identity appears ill-formed by virtue of its supposedly arrested development. One response to such stereotyping, most frequently that of oppositional nationalism, resembles Mill's appropriation of minority status for intellectuals and his subsequent reterritorialization of that status within the model of developmental history. Nationalisms reterritorialize dislocated identities historically, and, despite their initially progressive intents, continue thereby to acquiesce in imperial hegemony even after "independence."[15] An alternative response is that represented by what we are terming minor literature, which refuses to reterritorialize identity, preferring to extend the critique of those developmental narratives which perpetuate hegemonic culture.

3. Genet's Genealogies

It is just such a process of rigorously pursued deterritorialization that Genet claims to have adopted deliberately in *The Thief's Journal*:

---

14.   Mill's comments, "On Liberty," 73, that "Liberty, as a principle, has no application to any state of things anterior to the time when mankind have become capable of being impressed by free and equal discussion," in fact summates his argument for excluding "minors" in the legal sense along with "backward states of society." Immanuel Kant (in *Anthropology from a Pragmatic Point of View*, trans. Mary J. Gregor [The Hague: Nijhoff, 1974], 79-80 and 97) argues the necessity of others representing those still in "tutelage" — namely, women, children, and the masses — and of emergence from tutelage as the ultimate goal of "enlightened" humanity.

15.   One could understand the theory of minor literature as seeking to make a contribution to cultural criticism similar to, if not on the same scale as, that made by "dependency theory" in the field of economics. Thus where Andre Gunder Frank argues in his early (1963) essay, *On Capitalist Underdevelopment* (Bombay: Oxford Univ. Press, 1975), for the necessity of socialism as the means to extricate third world nations from the dependency cycle, the theory of minor literature seeks to sketch a ground for breaking with forms and conventions which perpetuate the cultural dependency of "minorities."

The reasons for my choice, whose meaning is revealed to me only today perhaps because I have to write about it, were not clearly apparent. I think that I had to hollow out, to drill through, a mass of language in which my mind would be at ease. *Perhaps I wanted to accuse myself in my own language* . . . . Indeed, theft — and what is involved in it: prison sentences, along with the shame of the profession of thief — had become a disinterested undertaking, a kind of active and deliberate work of art which could be achieved only with the help of language, my language, and which would be confronted with the laws springing from this same language.[16]

Genet is here quite explicit as to the overlap, for him, between crime and the "disinterested work of art." Parodically, theft, which makes all property "common," and without which property itself could not exist, becomes equally the model for a work of art whose end is identity or, to invoke a forensic as well as aesthetic usage, identification, and which in its parody raises the spectre of the heteronomous demands which always inform the development of autonomy.

Jean-Paul Sartre has elaborated only too fully the extent to which Genet can be regarded as reappropriating identifications imposed on him by others, thereby restoring his existential freedom.[17] What Sartre is unable to acknowledge, however, is that the identities imposed upon Genet by others and by himself — bastard, thief, homosexual, vagabond — are all simultaneously terms for non-identity, precisely insofar as what they invoke is a certain failure to undergo proper ethical development. In this respect, it would be possible to adopt Genet as a representative "minority" figure, were it not that such adoption draws him back into the fold of a mode of "representation" with regard to which we have much reason for suspicion. Rather than insist upon the biographical circumstances which might make him a representative minority, we will insist on those processes of his writing which sustain a minorness resistant to the proprieties of representation.

---

16. Jean Genet, *The Thief's Journal*, trans. Bernard Frechtman (Harmondsworth: Penguin, 1965), 94-95. I use where necessary the French text, *Journal du Voleur* (Paris: Gallimard, 1949). These works are cited hereafter in the text as *TJ* and *JV* respectively.

17. Jean-Paul Sartre, *Saint-Genet: Actor and Martyr*, trans. Bernard Frechtman (New York: Pantheon, 1963), passim.

Such a procedure follows Genet's own prescriptions, which insist time and again that the events recounted in his nominal autobiography are merely the "pretext" to the writing which arises from them:

> We know that our language is incapable of recalling even the pale reflection of those bygone foreign states. The same would be true of this entire journal if it were to be the notation of what I was. I shall therefore make clear that it is to indicate what I am today, as I write it. It is not a quest of time gone by [*une recherche du temps passé*], but a work of art whose pretext-subtext is my former life. (*TJ*, 58; *JV*, 75-76)

This "autography" is, in other words, no autobiography, neither in the sense given by the Proustian reference to a "remembrance of things past" which seeks to restore the self-identity of the subject, nor in the sense of a writing which develops the image of an authentic and autonomous subjectivity. The term "pretext" is used in the fullest possible sense: the life recorded here is, Genet warns us, not to be taken as a truthful record, but rather as a ground for present writing, as something which gives rise, as he puts it later, "to a certain new emotion which I call poetry," and of which he is "no longer anything, only a pretext" (*TJ*, 98).

The narrative of this autobiography progressively eradicates not only past characters and events but also the present subject, transforming them all into pretexts. Moreover, theft itself, the ostensible subject of the work, becomes envisioned as no more than the "point de départ" for an aesthetic work which, in its devotion to achieving canonization, "sanctity," parodies gloriously the ethical intents of aesthetic culture. This expression, "point de départ," repeated frequently throughout Genet's writing, signals and embodies the processes of his writing. On the one hand, it designates the point of departure from which his writing "takes off," "se décolle," unfixes itself, and the events of the real world from which Genet's flights of fancy depart. On the other hand, this "départ" involves the partition of the words it gives rise to, as in this very phrase itself. Thus the name for Genet's chosen crime, theft, *le vol*, the crime against property, departs constantly from its "proper" sense to become the flight of the word, *le vol*: as words become unstuck (*décollés*) from their proper sense, they take off upon a trajectory of deterritorialization in which meaning oscillates in perpetual ambivalençe.

Ambivalence is the constant semantic and moral characteristic of Genet's writing, becoming a scandalous gesture which confuses identities and collapses distances, between cop and criminal, palace and prison, with gay abandon. The model for his ambivalent language can be found in the gay and criminal slang which he so frequently invokes, and whose transsexuality is not, as he points out, the sign of an inverted or alternative sexual identity, but rather the frisson of ambivalence:

> Men sometimes hail each other as follows:
>> 'Well, Old Gal?'
>> 'Hi, you Hen'
>> 'Is that you, Wench?'
> This usage belongs to the world of poverty and crime . . . . These salutations indicate the downfall of men who were once strong. Having been wounded, they can now bear the equivocal. They even desire it. The tenderness which makes them unbend is not femininity but the discovery of ambivalence. (*TJ*, 211)

Similarly, the transvestite slang and gestures of *Our Lady of the Flowers* engages in a play of division and grafting of word and movement, as well as a purely phonetic displacement of proper speech:

> These cries (Darling will say: "She's losing her yipes," as if he were thinking: "You're losing money," or, "You're putting on weight.") were one of the idiosyncracies of Mimosa I that Divine had appropriated. When they and a few others were together in the street or a queer cafe, from their conversations (from their mouths and hands) would escape ripples of flowers, in the midst of which they simply stood or sat about as casually as could be, discussing ordinary household matters.
>> "I really am, sure, sure, sure, the Quite Profligate."
>> "Oh, Ladies, I'm acting like such a harlot."
>> "You know [*tu sais*] (the *ou* was drawn out that that was all one noticed) *yoou know*, I'm the Consumed-with-Affliction [*tussé*]."
> . . .
> It was the same for gestures . . . . There was the elaborated ges-

ture, which was diverted from its initial goal, and the one that contained and completed it by grafting itself on just at the point where the first ceased.[18]

The "strange" and "hybrid" forms of fag slang and gesture open into the poetry of non-identity by way of a punning which erodes the propriety of naming. Always giving way to further flights, these puns perform for Genet not the reterritorializing function of the "Rabelaisian " joke in relation to the unconscious, but rather that of a poetry which "always pulls the ground away from under your feet and sucks you into the bosom of a wonderful night."[19]

Where Genet's hermetic prose becomes the sign of an otherness in the very constitution of identities, a paradox enters into the very heart of the relation between naming and identity. Like the ambivalently "feminine" names of the crooks in *The Thief's Journal*, the names of the transvestites and criminals of *Our Lady of the Flowers* are improper names: Mimosa, Divine, Darling Daintyfoot, First Communion, Persifanny. These improper names do not name the persisting identity of a legal subject, but gesture towards a performance of otherness and for others. At the same time, it must be understood that their "pretext," the subject ostensibly disguised by the improper name and costume of the transvestite, is erased: no authentic identity lies concealed beneath the mask; Divine is no more "Lou Culafroy" than Our Lady is properly "Adrien Baillon." When the transvestites are summoned as witnesses at Our Lady's trial, their interpellation by the law under their proper names does not reveal their proper identities as disguised males, but rather as even more artificial marionettes:

> Would it not have been better to have danced the entire dance with a simple wire? The question is worth examining. The faggots showed the framework that Darling discerned behind the

---

18. Jean Genet, *Our Lady of the Flowers*, trans. Bernard Frechtman, introd. Jean-Paul Sartre (New York: Grove, 1963), 112-13. I cite also *Notre-Dame des Fleurs*, in Jean Genet, *Oeuvres Complètes* (Paris: Gallimard, 1951), vol. 2. These works cited in the text hereafter as *OLF* and *NDF* respectively.

19. *OLF*, 242: Genet here overhears another convict's superb pun, to get a "Yard-on" ("l'envergué," *NDF*, 133) which makes him fantasize being "impaled by a broom."

silk and velvet of every armchair. They were reduced to nothing, and that's the best thing that's been done so far. (*OLF*, 281)

Such erosions of propriety and authenticity are crucial to Genet's writings, constantly preventing his works from falling back upon the constitution of a counter-identity such as Sartre seeks to evoke.

Divine's transvestitism is crucial here: the "truth" is not that she is a man in drag, the truth lies not in reversion to an original more authentic than the appearance, but rather in the "poetic conclusions" which we know to be flights stealing away from their pretexts:

> For though she felt as a "woman," she thought as a "man." One might think that, in thus reverting spontaneously to her true nature, Divine was a male wearing make-up, disheveled with make-believe gestures; but this is not a case of the phenomenon of recourse to the mother tongue in times of stress . . . . Her femininity was not *only* a masquerade. But as for thinking "woman" completely, her organs hindered her. . . . And all the "woman" judgments that she made were, in reality, poetic conclusions. (*OLF*, 224-25)

The "mother" is not the original model of woman for the queen precisely because the developmental model implied by a notion of maternal origins, which gives way to an assumed adult identity, is entirely irrelevant. The transvestite's identification is rather with woman in a structural relationship of power, with "her submission to the imperious male," and we can perceive that what underlies the identification of homosexual and woman is their common relegation by male theory to the general category of the "underdeveloped." The psychoanalytic theory of feminine sexuality refuses to women the possibility of ethical development, precisely because they always already lack the phallus by which the threat of castration can induce sublimation in the boy. Similarly, the homosexual subject suffers from arrested development, fixated on an anal eroticism which effectively precedes the genital organization which permits the dissolution of the oedipal complex. Though, to be sure, this identification takes place only within male theory, it signals the fact that for canonical theory women and homosexuals must always be in "subjection" since their development is always arrested at the point before which the subject's identity is formed. We can understand here the reasons for the constitution of gays and women as minorities.[20]

The anxiety of major, "male" theory stems from the recognition that the dissolution of identity is a model of pleasure, pleasure of performance, imitation, inauthenticity:

> It is customary to come in drag, dressed as ourselves. Nothing but costumed queens rubbing shoulders with child-pimps. In short, not a single adult. The make-up and the lights distort sufficiently, but often we wear black masks or carry fans for the pleasure of guessing who's who from the carriage of a leg, from the expression, the voice, the pleasure of fooling each other, of making identities overlap. (*OLF*, 218)

In the absence of either guilt or shame as mechanisms of proper socialization, the masked ball becomes the playground of a "sham culture." But the sham is not a pretence concealing a real ulterior motive; sham is the ostentatious end of these quasi-autobiographies, just as their models, their "points de départ," lie in the castigated culture of cheap sensational novels, which in turn give way to the "grace" of the imitative gesture:

> I continue my reading of cheap novels. It satisfies my love of hoodlums dressed up as gentlemen. Also my taste for imposture, my taste for the sham, which could very well make me write on my visiting cards: "Jean Genet, bogus Count of Tillancourt". . . . If from myself I make Divine, from them I make her lovers: Our Lady, Darling, Gabriel, Alberto, lads who whistle through their teeth and on whose heads you can, if you look closely, see, in the form of an aureole, a royal crown. . . . [T]hus the same gesture was common to a number of heroes, whom Darling suddenly became, and it always so happened that this gesture was the one that symbolized most forcefully the most graceful of males. (*OLF*, 258-59)

The "aureole" which invests Genet's sham characters and sham writings is the halo of a sanctity which, far from striving for an existential

<hr>

20. In the chapter "The So-Called Dependency Complex of the Colonized Peoples," in his *Black Skin, White Masks* (London: Pluto Press, 1986),83-108, Frantz Fanon attacks precisely this kind of psychoanalytic approach to the "mentality" of colonized peoples or minorities.

authenticity, models itself on the hollow plaster saints of Divine's childhood or on the priests whose rites are the consummation of transvestitism.

But if Genet lives "in the midst of an infinity of holes in the forms of men" (*OLF*, 174), it is without the nostalgic lament for wholeness that infuses Eliot's *Hollow Men*. Eliot's kind of canonization is not what he pursues. The destiny of the subjected is one which constantly reveals in parody the power which the aesthetic derives from its claim to reproduce the essential integrity of Man. That integrity is simultaneously policed and endangered by the spectre of castration, though we need always to recall that the psychic force of that metaphor derives from a culture devoted to the integrity of a property tied to the proper name of the father. It is thus worth pursuing the destiny of the wound and of the phallus among Genet's subjected. In the first place, what occupies his beggars in *The Thief's Journal* is the "cultivation of sores," *la culture des plaies* (*TJ*, 20; *JV*, 28). These wounds, the product of deliberate *culture*, have the singular property of being at once sham and real. It is in this culture that Genet learns, by way of a "recherche esthétique autant que morale," to give "un sens sublime á une apparence aussi pauvre." This sublimity is, however, transformed away from its Schillerian function of assuring the identity of man with his concept, freedom, to become rather the index of exquisite sham. A little later in the text, Stilitano, figure of male pride in whom Genet recognizes the "ped who hates himself," pins a bunch of plaster grapes inside his fly in a gesture that seeks at once to attract and to disgust. This bunch of plaster grapes restores to Stilitano, like the beggars' sores, the pride which a real wound, his amputated hand, destroys. It does so, however, by being a fake wound, "une plaie postiche" (*TJ*, 42-43; *JV*, 54-57). Stilitano is one of the "masculine" nodes of Genet's text, the literal bearer of a noble phallus — "je sais qu'il l'avait magnifique" — around which the *Journal* circulates in its pastiche play.

For all that, indeed, for this very reason, Genet's writing eludes phallocentricity. The destiny of the phallic figures in this writing is that of all origins, to become a fabulous pretext. Thus when Stilitano abandons Genet at one point:

> It was no longer even the memory of him that I carried away with me but rather the idea of a fabulous creature, the origin

and pretext of all desires, terrifying and gentle, remote and close
to the point of containing me . . . (*TJ*, 138)

A long parenthetical passage follows in which Genet once again returns to considering the generation of poetry by way of the attempt
to discharge it of its pretexts, in this case, of its "cultic" origins. The
passage, depicting this attempt, leads him to make his way "through
genealogical strata . . . in order to arrive at the Fable where all creation
is possible" (*TJ*, 139). This passage in turn gives way to a further representation of Stilitano, and is fixated upon two physical images: the
"veil of saliva" which always circulates round Stilitano's mouth, and
which Genet terms at one point "le voile du palais," and "the vision
of his prick . . . detached from him and standing upright and rigid,
like a leech . . . "

A network of subtle connections binds these apparently disjunc-
tive passages with each other and into the general economy of the
Journal. The phallus as object of desire, detached from its bearer,
who is, after all, the indifferent pretext of that desire, circulates
through the text incessantly. Its unveiling as "common property"
has the effect of uncovering identity beneath that "départage" which
differentiates the agents of the law from the outlaws:

> Criminals and the police are the most virile emanation of this
> world. You cast a veil over them. They are your shameful parts
> which, however, I call, as you do, noble parts. (*TJ*, 161)

As Sartre has pointed out, such analogies in Genet's work reveal
"deep identity," the identity which connects equally palace and prison, "one the root and the other the crest of a living system circulating between the two poles which contain it" (*TJ*, 72). But precisely as
it becomes the circulating sign of identity, the phallus is detached, its
unveiling becomes its transformation into the mark of a dissolution
of fixed identities. It is to just such a detachment from origins that
Genet traces both his capacity to dissolve the opposition between
palace and prison and the connections which draw together orphan-
age, theft, and homosexuality:

> Without thinking myself magnificently born, the uncertainty
> of my origin allowed me to interpret it. I added to it the peculiarity

of my misfortunes. Abandoned by my family, I already felt it was natural to aggravate this condition by a preference for boys, and this preference by theft, and theft by crime or a complacent attitude in regard to crime . . . . This almost gleeful rushing into the most humiliating situations is perhaps still motivated by my childhood imagination which invented for me . . . castles, parks peopled with guards rather than with statues . . . . Prison offers the same sense of security to the convict as does a royal palace to a king's guest. (*TJ*, 71)

In the absence of an origin, the origin becomes fabulous, "origin and pretext of all desire," of a desire indifferent to identity and constantly transforming its objects — Armand, Java, Stilitano — into pretexts. Hence the fascination of the "voilé du palais," a term which "departs" in the *sens double* of that which veils a "secret sense" and that which veils the site of power. In one sense, it is the words with which Genet veils his shame as originless orphan and which bring him back to his love for Stilitano:

But it is the abandoned urchin's amorous imaginings of royal magnificence that enables me to gild my shame, to carve it, to work it over like a goldsmith, until, through usage perhaps and the wearing away of the words veiling it, humility emerges from it. My love for Stilitano made me once again aware of so exceptional a disposition. (*TJ*, 73)

In another sense, it is analogous with the "plaie postiche," becoming, in its secret attractions as it revolves around Stilitano's lips, the "voile de la plaie" which distracts his lovers, male and female, from the fact that he too is one of Genet's "wounded men." Circulating sites of fascination, the detachable phallus and the veil of the palace operate both by concealment of an origin while appearing to be that origin. They seek by fixation to cover the mutilation of identity which is the condition of the "guilty," *le coupable*:

The wound I inflict upon this male compels me to a sudden respect, to new delicacies, and the dull, remote and almost narrow wound makes him languid, like the memory of the pains of childbirth . . . . But will he, later on, with his girl-friends, be able to forget what he was for me? What will it do to his soul? What ache never to be cured? Will he have, in this respect, the indifference of Guy, the same smile accompanying the shrug which he shakes off, letting it drift in the wake of his swift walk, that dull and heavy pain, the melancholy of the wounded male? (*TJ*, 196)

The mutilation of identity which provokes "the melancholy of the wounded male" lies at once in the discovering of homosexual desire in the proud male and in the arousal of a "memory of the pains of childbirth," of a maternal origin which perpetually erodes the vaunted autonomy of masculine identity. Accordingly, the singularity of "le coupable," contained by the society which seeks to reject him as "a wound from which flowed its blood, which it dared not shed itself" (*TJ*, 203), is contained equally within the semantic field of the word *bander*: *le bandit* is the one who, *tout en bandant* (getting an erection), enters the *bandes* (gangs) of criminals which *bandent* (bind/bandage) wounded males. In such male bonding, we perceive the perpetually veiled homosexual structure of social relations.

Criminal and homosexual social relations are condemned precisely because their parodic forms reveal the actuality of social relations as expropriation and male bonding concealed by homophobic law. That rationale recurs in the improper names of criminals and gays, names which gesture towards the ambivalence they discover. The absent mother is the sign, not the identity, of this ambivalence, mark of an irreducible "parturition" that is the simultaneous origin of identity and desire. Thus it is that Genet's genealogy is an affair of the mother, just as, in *Our Lady of the Flowers*, it is his/her mother's heritage that Culafroy/Divine pursues through the pages of Capefigue's history (*OLF*, 194-5): "It pleased Culafroy that the nobility belonged to Ernestine rather than to himself, and in this trait we may already see a sign of his destiny" (*OLF*, 195). And if that destiny is contained in the fact that even as a child, perhaps because a child, Culafroy who will be Divine "abandons himself" to genealogy "voluptuously, as he would have done to Art had he known it," it is because the sciences of genealogy and of philology find their poetry in the *division* of the name rather than in its unification in an essential origin (*OLF*, 197). The fabulous origin discovered beneath the layers of genealogy is parturition and ambivalence, source of all desires, after which all identities become merely the pretext for their own dissolution.

Genet's writing thus unwrites what is the recurrent founding movement of bourgeois political and aesthetic philosophy, the discovery already alluded to of the singular essence of man beneath the oppressive strata of hereditary privilege:

> The error of those who reason by precedents drawn from antiquity respecting the rights of man, is, that they do not go far enough into antiquity . . . . But if we proceed on, we shall at last come out right; we shall come to the time when man came from the hand of his Maker. What was he then? Man. Man was his high and only title and a higher cannot be given him.
>
> . . . . .
>
> Every history of the creation, and every traditionary account, whether from the lettered or unlettered world, however they may vary in their opinion or belief of certain particulars, all agree in establishing one point, *the unity of man* . . . [21]

As we have seen, the predication of an essential common identity of man inaugurates a universal history of development which always contains the realization of individual autonomy within a narrative so exclusive that it becomes the legitimation of an irreducible heteronomy. The path by which social identity is formed is the one which leads back from differentiation to identification with an imperial Man whose destiny is always the same. What Genet's writings discover is the logic of that law for which, secretly, both origin and end entail in fact the dissolution of singular identities into the uniform identity of western man. The "minoress" of his works lies in the fact that they are an incurable wound contained and covered by the body of that Man. It is the emergent literature of minorities which, refusing likewise the hegemonic narratives of identity, will dissolve the canonical form of Man back into the different bodies which it has sought to absorb.

---

21. Paine, *Rights of Man*, 87-88.

Culturalism as Hegemonic Ideology and Liberating Practice *

Arif Dirlik

This discussion argues the radicalism of cultural activity against efforts to subsume the question of culture within other, seemingly more radical activities upon which individuals attempting to change the world have increasingly focused their attention. In a world where economic necessity and political crisis confront us daily, this argument may seem superfluous or even self-indulgent. This is especially the case where the question of culture relates to the non-Western world (the primary focus of this discussion) where millions of lives await the urgent resolution of practical problems for their very survival. Yet I will argue in the face of necessity that the realm of culture, as the realm of activity that is bound up with the most fundamental epistemological questions, demands priority of attention.

The radicalism of the issue of culture lies in the fact that culture affords us ways of seeing the world, and if the latter have any bearing on our efforts to change the world, then it is essential that we confront our ways of seeing. The idea of culture has developed historically in juxtaposition to the idea of reason. However, it is also the only basis upon which we may comprehend the world rationally (if reason is to have any bearing on the world of the living) and make it more reasonable. Culture, in other words, is also a way to comprehend the rational, not an abstract rationality divorced from the world

*Earlier versions of this paper were presented in a seminar at the Department of Far Eastern Languages and Civilizations at the University of Chicago in February 1985 and the conference on "The Nature and Context of Minority Discourse" at the University of California, Berkeley, May 22-25, 1986. I would like to thank participants in both events for their valuable input.

of living people and set against the latter as its judge, but the rationality of the living. To avoid the question of culture is to avoid questions concerning the ways in which we see the world; it is to remain imprisoned, therefore, in a cultural unconscious, controlled by conditioned ways of seeing (even unto rationality), without the self-consciousness that must be the point of departure for all critical understanding and, by implication, for all radical activity.

To argue the radicalness of the question of culture is not to propound culturalism, that ideology which not only reduces everything to questions of culture, but has a reductionist conception of the latter as well. Thus the critique of culturalism as an ideology is a basic goal of this discussion. An authentically radical conception of culture forces our attention upon the contradictoriness of this concept itself. Culture is not only a way of seeing the world, but also a way of making and changing it. The first sense refers to the manner in which we usually understand and use the word, and it also signifies the cornerstone of culturalist ideology. It identifies for us entire peoples and eras in terms of the ways in which we think they see or saw the world. It helps us place them *vis-á-vis* one another, usually with ourselves at the center of the world and at the end of time. It is, in short, a way of organizing the world, its time and space.

This first definition of culture, seemingly commonsensical, mystifies its second sense, of which it is logically and historically the product, but to which it bears a contradictory relationship. Having organized the world in terms of culture, it seems easier to think of people as the creation of culture, rather than the reverse. The activity which produces and reproduces culture appears merely as one of the many ways in which people act according to their culture.

This mystification is crucial to understanding the role culture has played as an instrument of hegemony in social and political relations. To demystify this usage, to reassert the sense of culture as activity, makes possible the re-presentation of cultural activity also as liberating practice. Though culture is not reducible to ideology, the question of culture is nevertheless ideological in a fundamental sense. And though it is not reducible to socio-political relations, neither can it be apprehended critically (rather than ideologically) outside of these relations. Culture is not a thing, to paraphrase E.P. Thompson, but a relationship. It is not merely an autonomous principle that is expressive of the totality constituted by these relationships, a totality that, once it has been constituted, appears as a seamless web of which culture is the architectonic principle, exterior to the socio-political relations and logically prior to them. Rendering culture as such an autonomous principle requires an ideological operation that mystifies the priority of the socio-political relationships that go into its production. A critical reading of culture, one that exposes it as an ideological operation crucial to the establishment of hegemony, requires that we view it not merely as an attribute of totalities but as an activity that is bound up with the operation of social relations, that expresses contradiction as much as it does cohesion. Culture is an activity in which the social relations that are possible but absent, because they have been displaces or rendered impossible (or "utopian") by existing social relations, are as fundamental as the relations whose existence it affirms.

This requires, above all, that we confront culture in terms of its most basic contradiction, that is, as both an autonomous and a dependent activity. The culturalist assertion of the autonomy of culture reduces all realms of social experience (from the economy to ideology) to the question of culture; cultural change then appears as the key to all other change. It is not possible to counter such reductionism effectively with a counter-reductionism that dissolves the question of culture into these other constituents of social life, including ideology. Such a reductionism does not confront, but bypasses, the question of culture because it does not address the fundamental issue of hegemony raised by the question of culture.

The discussion below examines some related problems. First is the question of culturalism. In an earlier essay, "Culture, Society and Revolution: A Critical Discussion of American Studies of Chinese Thought," I described it as a hegemonic ideology.[1] I feel, however, that the dilemmas presented by culturalism cannot be fully appreciated unless we view it simultaneously as a liberating possibility that contradicts its hegemonic practice. In order to elucidate the contradictory possibilities and practices offered by culturalism, I will analyze briefly the conditions under which it appears as liberating practice. To this end, I will discuss at some length two works, one

---

1. Arif Dirlik, "Culture, Society and Revolution: A Critical Discussion of American Studies of Chinese Thought," *Working Papers in Asian/Pacific Studies* 1 (Durham: Asian/Pacific Studies Institute, Duke Univ., 1985).

from European history, the other by an Arab intellectual, that illustrate such practice: E.P. Thompson's *The Making of the English Working Class* and Abdallah Laroui's *The Crisis of the Arab Intellectual*. These works shed light on what has been called "culturalist Marxism" and what I have described in my essay on Chinese thought as a "social conception of culture."

Second, I would like to comment further on the question of culturalism as it has been viewed by Marxists, especially those from the Third World. Since culturalism as hegemonic ideology is central to bourgeois cultural assumptions, Marxism has been seen by many in the West and the non-West as the foremost ideological candidate in the struggle against culturalist hegemony. This, I think, has done more than anything else to underline the significance of Marxism as a cultural idea in contrast to its more economistic interpretation. Marxism, I will argue below, promises, but does not guarantee, to abolish the hegemonic practices associated with culturalism. Indeed, unless Marxism itself is examined critically from perspectives offered by culturalsim, it may serve as a tool of hegemonic practice by mystifying hegemonic relations between and within societies.

Finally, since the idea of culturalism contains potentially contradictory possibilities of practice, to discuss it at the abstract level of ideas, without reference to its social context, is not only to engage in intellectual mystification, but is socially irresponsible as well. Accordingly, I will comment further in this discussion on the role of intellectuals, particularly those in academia, as producers of ideologies, a question to which I have referred in the introduction to my earlier essay. Culturalism, I have suggested in that article, represents not so much a professional paradigm as the absorption into the profession of a discourse that is broadly social (a discourse that antedates and shapes the profession). Nevertheless, academic intellectuals have played a significant part in articulating and legitimizing hegemonic culturalism which otherwise might have remained a diffuse social prejudice. This point is forcefully made by Edward Said in *Orientalism*. I would like to stress here that the discursive practices of intellectuals acquire further clarity when viewed within the broader social context of their alienation. Culturalism is ideological practice in a fundamental sense: it does not merely reflect the social practice of intellectuals — it helps define such practice. This, I believe, is difficult to understand outside of the alienation that intellectual activity has undergone, for intellectuals, whatever their formal ideological professions, have been absorbed into structures of domination that represent alienated social power. Any consideration of culturalism as a liberating possibility, therefore, must take into account these relationships. I may illustrate this briefly here by suggesting that even a Marxist or Third Worldist ideology may be hegemonic if it does not divorce itself from existing structures of alienated power.

Culturalism and Marxist Culturalism

I would like to start this discussion with a few remarks on the way I use the concept of "culturalism" in "Culture, Society and Revolution." The closest I come to defining it is as an "ensemble of intellectual orientations that crystallize methodologically around the reduction of social and historical questions to abstract questions of culture" and as "responsible," therefore, "not only for legitimizing hegemonic relations between societies, but also for mystifying hegemonic relations of exploitation and oppression within societies." The identifying characteristic of a culturalist intellectual orientation, I have suggested in the above article, is a "preoccupation with the cultural gap" that separates societies and that "results [in] . . . a preoccupation with culture as the central datum" in the study of thought in Third World societies. I have also stated that "in the study of cultures alien to our own, historicism and culturalism are but two sides of the same coin: it is a reaffirmation, in the midst of global history, of the separateness of the society we study."[2] History here appears as cultural interpretation, and the historian as cultural interpreter. The notion of "tradition" is essential to culturalism since it becomes a way to identify the Other. Historical explanation, therefore, assumes as its task the analysis of the confrontation between native tradition and the West which, viewed from the perspective of the historian, translates into a confrontation between Us and the Other. The hegemonic function of culturalism rests in the latter because this juxtaposition leaves to the Other but one choice: escape into tradition (and, therefore, the past) or absorption into the West (which is the present and the future) — not much of an alternative since culture, viewed as tradi-

---

2.   Ibid., 55-56, 40, 44, 54.

tion, is little more than a congealed and therefore dead culture. The living belong to the West, native culture to the dead! The juxtaposition inevitably entails the "distancing" of the Other, if not into oblivion, then at best into the museum. Distancing in space is the most readily observable feature of culturalism, but, as Johannes Fabian argues in *Time and the Other*, it derives its hegemonic power from distancing in time, which is its inevitable accompaniment.[3]

Given the ways in which culture has been used to justify Western hegemony over the non-West, the concept of culture has become an embarrassment to the more radical students of these societies. Much of the reaction to the once popular (and still dominant in political practice) "modernization" approach to these societies, with its facile juxtaposition of the Modern (Western) against the Traditional (native), represents an effort to overcome the hegemonic implications of a Western logocentric view of the world. Not the least among these efforts are the various versions of "world-system" analysis which has found particular favor in recent years among radical students of non-Western societies. World-system analysis, which could with only slight unfairness be described as economism on a global scale, is inspired to a greater or lesser extent by Marxism and represents an essentially structuralist view of the world that in most uses bypasses the question of culture altogether.

These approaches, however, admirable their intention and significant their undertaking, do not resolve the question of hegemony but bypass its most fundamental aspects. They may, indeed, become sources themselves of a new hegemony. An economism, whether of bourgeois or Marxist variety, that reduces the globe to a uniform cultural field upon which economic forces play out their fate, still distances the Other by portraying it as a plaything in the hands of economic forces. If we are to challenge hegemonic culturalism, we must make an effort to confront directly the questions that it raises, especially its epistemological underpinnings which exist independently of and prior to the question of culture itself.

The question of culture, moreover, has been of immense significance to non-Western radicals. Revolutionary socialists in the Third World have repeatedly stated "cultural revolution" to be one of their

---

3. Johannes Fabian, *Time and the Other: How Anthropology Makes Its Object* (New York: Columbia Univ. Press, 1983), see especially chapter one.

central goals, the other being an economic revolution to secure liberation from capitalist domination. Third World revolutions have done much to dramatize the importance of the question of culture in Marxism not only because cultural transformation has emerged as a central issue of revolution in social environments that lack the cultural preconditions for socialism as envisaged initially in Marxist theory, but even more so because of questions raised by the imperatives of economic development. In a world dominated by capitalism, economic revolution in itself has promised not liberation from capitalist hegemony but a more intense incorpation within its scope. An exclusive preoccupation with questions of economic development inevitably ushers in economism, the ideology of the bourgeoisie, which gains strength along with economic development since the latter produces social groups and classes that identify themselves primarily with an economic rationale of social change.

Culture, under the circumstances, has had to carry the burden for the realization of socialism. In the revolutionary tradition created in the course of the struggle for social and political liberation, Third World socialists have seen (or hoped to see) the makings of a new culture which is neither of the West nor of the past, in other words, which can be national without being parochial and cosmopolitan without being alien — a new culture, the making of which must accompany the making of a new world, but without which the latter cannot be conceived. Even where economism has taken over, socialist leadership has found it difficult to abandon the hope of creating a new culture that would be contemporary without being Western or capitalist; the question may be even more crucial in such cases since a new anti-capitalist culture is essential to counteract the bourgeois hegemony that economism must produce. Without revolutionary social transformation upon which a new culture of liberation must rest, such hope may only result in an eclecticism that represents not a new culture but the illusion of one; however, we have no reason to doubt the authenticity of the quest itself.

For Western intellectuals to deny the importance of the question of culture in the name of the higher truth of a scientistic economism, then, is at best arrogant; at worst, it aids in the establishment of a new kind of hegemony — bourgeois hegemony represented by economism. The rejection of culture as a question, on the grounds that it has served to hegemonize the non-Western world, not only reveals a limited appreciation of the possibilities offered by culture, but also perpetuates other, even more powerful, bourgeois assumptions about the world. We need not reject either the past of non-Western societies or their present pecularities in order to challenge the premises of hegemonic culturalism. The point is to bring out the historical complexities of these societies (and to recognize the possibility of future diversity), not to perpetuate the image of them as undifferentiated cultural entities, this time so rendered in the name of economic truths. Challenges to culturalist hegemony that do not extend their criticism to this question perpetuate the most basic epistemological assumptions of such a hegemony.

The problem, therefore, is not whether the question of culture is a significant one, but rather how to conceive of a culture that may serve liberating rather than hegemonic purposes. Third World revolutionaries in their call for cultural revolution have suggested means, epistemological if not practical, for confronting this question. It is not likely that we will hear what they say, however, unless we take their questions seriously; indeed, it is more likely that we will be party to suppressing what they say, no matter how good our intentions. Before I discuss the critique of hegemony as it has appeared in the thinking of Third World intellectuals, I would like to examine the issue of hegemony as it has appeared in European Marxism. Debates within the latter, not involving issues of the Other, help enunciate clearly the epistemological questions raised by culturalism as hegemonic principle and liberating practice.

The question that arises here is whether or not we are justified in viewing culturalism merely as a feature of intellectual relations between the West and the Rest. I think not. Indeed, its presentation as an exclusive feature of this relationship not only imprisons the critique of culturalism itself in a culturalist discourse, but is socially and politically reactionary as well (all we need here is to remember that Western culturalism finds its counterpoint in native chauvinism!). Culturalism viewed as a global ideological phenomenon (not restricted to relations between the West and Others, but very much alive *within* Western societies themselves), on the other hand, brings into relief the problem of culture as it appears in the relationship between societies and makes possible a more thorough social critique of the hegemonic functions assumed by the concept of culture in the ideology of culturalism. This perspective also brings out with some clarity the possibilities implicit in culturalism as liberating practice, which contradicts its function as hegemonic principle. To elucidate this possibility, it is necessary to examine culturalism also as an attribute of relations between classes.

The question of culture has received considerable attention among Western Marxists in recent years, mainly in connection with problems presented by the debate over Marxist structuralism versus Marxist historicism. The nature of this question, as it pertains to historical work, may be illustrated through a brief discussion of E.P. Thompson's *The Making of the English Working Class*, a work that has exerted a seminal influence not only on Marxist thinking on culture in history, but on a whole generation of socio-historical writing. It has also provoked considerable controversy among Marxists over the question of agency versus structure in history, possibility the central question of Marxism in our day.

In an article entitled "Edward Thompson, Eugene Genovese, and Socialist Humanist History," Richard Johnson has pointed to *The Making of the English Working Class*, along with Genovese's *Roll Jordan Roll*, as outstanding examples of what he calls "culturalist Marxism." Johnson's use of the latter term in this context does not differ significantly from the way I have used it. Culturalism represents, according to Johnson, "A break away from . . . theoretical development and complex economism to an overriding concern with 'culture' and 'experience.' "[4] Thompson has rejected "absolutely" this suggestion that his work could be described as "culturalist."[5] As is typical of his various debates with his structuralist critics, Thompson's response to this is unduly defensive and intemperate; he is ready to throw out the baby with the bathwater. Culturalism in its non-Marxist sense has implications which must render the suggestion offensive to any Marxist since it implies an ideology of culture that sets it apart from and above the social relations in which any Marxist understanding of culture must rest. This, however, is not the point of Johnson's critique. It is indeed illuminating to view *The Making of the English Working Class* as a culturalist work *within* the context of Marxism, to juxtapose it to Marx-

---

4.   Richard Johnson, "Edward Thompson, Eugene Genovese, and Socialist Humanist History," *History Workshop* 6 (Autumn 1978): 81.

5.   E.P. Thompson, "Politics of Theory, " in *People's History and Socialist Theory*, ed. R. Samuel (London: Routledge & Kegan Paul, 1981), 396-408.

ist approaches that deny a significant, even semi-autonomous, role to culture in history. The two culturalisms share a common vocabulary, but they diverge radically in epistemology. The possibility of a Marxist culturalism brings into relief the epistemological foundations of hegemonic culturalism as a liberating practice (although this is not what Johnson does, because, essentially involved with structuralism, he misses the point about his own undertaking). In this, I think, lies the power of *The Making of the English Working Class*.

This Marxist culturalism, as its non-Marxist counterpart, is historicist, radically so. In Thompson's own eloquent words:

> But the fact is, again, the material took command of me, far more than I had ever expected. If you want a generalization I would have to say that the historian has got to be listening all the time. He should not set up a book or research project with a totally clear sense of exactly what he is going to be able to do. The material itself has got to speak through him. And I think this happens.[6]

This historicism has led culturalist Marxists to a suspicion of theory in favor of descriptive history. To quote Genovese this time:

> Many years of studying the astonishing effort of black people to live decently as human beings even in slavery has convinced me that no theoretical advance suggested in their experience could ever deserve as much attention as that demanded by their demonstration of the beauty and power of the human spirit under conditions of extreme oppression.[7]

Thompson's appreciation of theory, as he has stated repeatedly since *The Making of the English Working Class* in his debates with structuralist Marxists, is radically historicist. Theory to him, to quote Johnson, is merely "a moment in the historian's method." Thompson's approach to concepts is ruthlessly empirical. This is evident in his use of class, the central concept of his work, which has provoked considerable controversy. "Class," in Thompson's view, "is defined by men as they live their own history, and, in the end, this is its only defi-

---

6. Interview with E.P. Thompson, quoted in Johnson, 84.
7. Eugene Genovese, *Roll Jordan Roll: The World the Slaves Made* (New York: Pantheon Books, 1974), xvi.

nition."[8] Class is, we might add, what people do and how they think in "class ways."

Not surprisingly, tradition, too, plays a major part in this "culturalist Marxism." The first part of *The Making of the English Working Class* is devoted almost entirely to decoding the language of protest that is, as Thompson presents it, authentically and exclusively English. Particularly revealing in this respect is his apology to "Scottish and Welsh" readers in his preface: "I have neglected these histories, not out of chauvinism, but out of respect. It is because class is a cultural as much as an economic formation that I have been cautious as to generalizing beyond English experience."[9] The statement is reminiscent of the one used by some students of non-Western societies: to apply theory of Western origin to the analysis of non-Western societies is not only misleading but "imperialistic" as well!

Indeed, for the historian of China or of other non-Western societies, the conceptual apparatus that informs this "culturalist Marxism" is puzzlingly reminiscent of the one I have referred to as the source of culturalist hegemony in Western studies of non-Western thought and culture. Yet this is where the comparison stops. Both Thompson and Genovese are consciously anti-hegemonic in their intentions, Genovese more explicitly so since his work draws directly on Gramsci's critique of hegemony. And whatever we may think of the history/theory debate which their works have provoked (of which more later), none but the most ardent structuralist would deny that seemingly the same culturalism that appears as hegemonic principle in studies of non-Western societies manifests itself here as liberating practice.

This is not to suggest that culturalism appears as liberating practice within Western society and as hegemonic principle in relations between the West and the non-West, but to illustrate that culturalism in and of itself does not account for ideological hegemony. The parallel within the West to the hegemonic use of culture in studies of the Third World is to be found in the use of culture in establishing the ideological hegemony of one class over another. Here, too, culture

---

8. E.P. Thompson, "Eighteenth Century English Society: Class Struggle Without Class?" *Social History* 3, no. 2 (May 1978): 146.

9. E.P. Thompson, *The Making of the English Working Class* (New York: Vintage Books, 1963), 13.

has been utilized to distance the Other, if not in space (which is somewhat more problematic though by no means impossible) then at least in time, through the assertion of the ideological and cultural backwardness of the working classes, with similar hegemonic consequences, particularly in denying contemporary relevance to the culture of the Other. Culturalist hegemony is secured here by presenting the consequence of oppression, cultural impoverishment, as its cause, but above all by distancing the culture of the Other. Speaking of the emergence of the notion of the "masses" in nineteenth-century England, Raymond Williams writes:

> Masses are other people . . . There are in fact no masses; there are only ways of seeing people as masses. In an urban industrial society there are many opportunities for such ways of seeing. The point is not to reiterate the objective conditions but to consider, personally and collectively, what these have done to our thinking. The fact is, surely, that a way of seeing other people which has become characteristic of our kind of society, has been capitalized for the purposes of political or cultural exploitation. What we see, neutrally, is other people, many others, people unknown to us. In practice, we mass them, and interpret them, according to some convenient formula. Within its terms, the formula will hold. Yet it is the formula, not the mass, which it is our real business to examine. It may help us to do this if we remember that we ourselves are all the time being massed by others. To the degree that we find the formula inadequate for ourselves, we can wish to extend to others the courtesy of acknowledging the unknown. [10]

What then accounts for the contradictory consequences that issue from what is seemingly the same approach to history in terms of conceptual premises about the past and the present? The immediate answers would seem to be the humanism of Marxist culturalists or their sympathies for the oppressed, which enable them to turn the tables on hegemonic culturalists. While this is true to some extent, it explains differences only on a superficial level. Humanism is not sufficient to bridge the distances established by hegemonic culturalism between or within societies. Indeed, humanism may simply result in

---

10.   Raymond Williams, *Culture and Society, 1780-1950* (London: Penguin Books, 1968), 289.

a cultural relativism which, as Fabian has argued, does not overcome but confirms culturalist distancing. This is especially the case with cultural relativism within the context of relations between the West and the non-West and similarly with the notion of sympathy or even empathy for the oppressed. Sympathy neither precludes condescension, nor, at the least, a sense of the irrelevance of the Other, no matter how admired. Naipaul, in *A Bend in the River*, captures this problem in the figure of the Belgian priest Father Huysmans who, in love with Africa, views himself as the last witness to its dying civilization. This kind of sympathy that identifies with the Other and yet denies him "coevalness" (in Fabian's words) is essential, I think, to the "orientalizing" of the Other.

The differences, rather, must be sought in the fundamental epistemological divergence that underlies these seemingly identical conceptualizations of history. The liberating conclusions of Marxist culturalism as represented in the works of Thompson and Genovese (and to which Williams has made fundamental contributions) rest in going beyond expressions of sympathy for the working classes in order to counter their distancing in hegemeonic culturalism. As Thompson has explained his goals:

> I am seeking to rescue the poor stockinger, the Luddite cropper, the "obsolete" hand-loom weaver, the "utopian" artisan, and even the deluded follower of Joanna Southcott from the enormous condescension of posterity. Their crafts and traditions may have been dying. Their hostility to the new industrialism may have been backward-looking. Their communitarian ideals may have been fantasies. Their insurrectionary conspiracies may have been foolhardy. But they lived through these times of acute social disturbance, and we do not. Their aspirations are valid in terms of their own experience.[11]

This activity of "rescuing," I would like to suggest, entails more than simply bringing the benighted into the light of history. Thompson seeks not merely to remind us of the English working class, but to re-present it as the defender of the most central values of English society. As he puts it in the concluding lines of his book:

> Yet the working people should not be seen only as the lost myriads of

---

11.   Thompson, *The Making of the English Working Class*, 12-13.

eternity. They had also nourished, for fifty years, and with incomparable fortitude, the Liberty Tree. We may thank them for these years of heroic culture.[12]

The working people, then, did not merely contribute to the making of English society — their activities were central to the establishment of its most basic values.

This "centering" of the working people (the Other, in this instance) is crucial to understanding the epistemological under-pinnings of Marxist culturalism as liberating practice. The centering of the working class must of necessity be accompanied by the "decentering" of the ruling, or the hegemonic, class, since the two groups by definition make contradictory claims upon history. Thompson's goal, ultimately, is to show that the struggles of the working class in England, rather than being expressive of cultural backwardness or political irrelevance, helped preserve and promote the democratic values which the ruling class claimed for itself but was ever ready to compromise. From this perspective, the heroes of hegemonic history (the putative creators of democratic political values) appear as obstacles to the practice of democracy or, at the very least, lose their centrality in the creation and perpetuation of those values. If this does not necessarily replace the hegemonic class with the working class at the center of history (I do not believe this is Thompson's intention), it at least denies to history a center, without which culturalist hegemony is deprived of its frame of reference.

The same may be said of Thompson's use of tradition, which differs fundamentally from the use of this concept in hegemonic culturalism, to which the notion of tradition is crucial. Thompson (as well as Genovese) has an activist conception of tradition, which is consonant with the fundamental activist epistemology that underlies his work as a whole. He approaches tradition not as a burden of the past upon the present, an inert legacy that shapes the consciousness of people with its own prerogatives, but as an activity in the production of a past that is rooted in the social struggles over hegemony. An irrefutable tradition that defines the center of history is crucial to ruling-class history, and so is the presentation of that tradition as something prior to everyday life. Contrarily, in Thompson's presentation, tradi-

---

12. Ibid., 832.

tion does not shape social relations, rather it is produced and reproduces itself in the course of ongoing social activity. Traditions are unique (the past *does* make a difference for the present), but not the processes that produce traditions, for they are part and parcel of the structure of social conflict. The investigation of the language of protest in the English tradition is to Thompson both end and means: the language is important because it has shaped the way people have thought about social relations, but it must also be decoded in order to reveal the social conflict it signifies. The revelation of conflict, embedded in the very language of tradition, renders tradition problematic, raising immediate questions about its claims to centrality.

In raising questions about the center of history, Marxist culturalism appears as liberating practice. Hegemony requires a center, not only in space but also in time. The decentering of the hegemonic group, be it class or nation, deprives history of a center and the hegemonic group of its claims upon history. Culturalism that achieves this end points to a liberating possibility, if only as a possibility. This, I feel, is the intention, and the meaning, of Marxist culturalism.

This abolition of a center in the historical process is what Harootunian has in mind, I think, when he observes: "The social process has no center. . . . Instead, society is composed of multiple contradictions in relationships of overdetermination so as to create the potential for ideological conflict in the general effort to determine what is natural for groups and individuals."[13] What I would like to reflect on here is what this statement implies, not only for groups within history or society, but for historians and their relationship to history. Depriving history of a center, it seems to me, also deprives the historian of centrality. Without elaborating the implications of his observation, Johnson suggests that Althusser and the structuralists "intervene" in or "read" history; Thompson, on the other hand, "listens" while Genovese "tells." In the passage cited above, Thompson presents himself as the "mouthpiece" through which the people in history speak. Whether or not this is what he achieves is not as important a question here as his intention: to decenter the historians' discourse in order to

13. Harry Harootunian, "Ideology as Conflict," in *Conflict in Modern Japanese History: The Neglected Tradition*, T. Najita and V. Koschmann, eds. (Princeton: Princeton Univ. Press, 1982), 29.

make room at the center of history for its subjects whose "experiences" take precedence over the historian's discourse because they lived that history and the historian did not. The concession here, while fundamentally epistemological, is not merely so; it is a concession of the historian's hegemony over the past, the Other, as it were.

Historicism, Structuralism and Hegemony: The Alienation of Intellectuals and the Abstraction of Society

Such is the meaning of the historicism of culturalist Marxism; it explains why historicism appears here as a condition of culturalism as liberating practice. Ironically, structuralism may have provided a method that reveals the structuralist analysis of society as a hegemonic one. The use of categories or, more broadly, of abstractions, in history has emerged as the central issue around which the controversy between historicist and structuralist Marxists has revolved. I think it is naive to suppose that culturalist Marxism, because it is historicist, rejects the use of concepts and categories in social analysis. *The Making of the English Working Class* and *Roll Jordan Roll* take as their point of departure the concept of class, and they are fundamentally ideological in retaining this concept, especially so because their authors recognize the problematic nature of the concept. Still, there is an unbridgeable gap between Thompson and Genovese and their structuralist critics concerning the issue of concepts and theory in history (which makes efforts at conciliation rather naive). If I read these works correctly, what they reject are not concepts or theory, but the substitution of concepts or theory for lived experience: if the categories of the historian clash with the experiences of the historical subject, it is the former that must be abandoned in the name of the latter, and not the other way around. In other words, questions raised concerning abstract categories parallel at the level of epistemology questions raised concerning the historian's place *vis-à-vis* the historical subject: just as the historian is "de- centered" in favor of the historial subject, so are the categories of the historian's discourse "decentered" in favor of the subject's experience. Hence Thompson's insistence that the category of class should not be employed to conceptualize people in history who did not think of themselves in terms of this category.

Thompson has done much better at caricaturizing Althusser's structuralism (as with his "orrery of errors" which identifies structuralism with its vulgarization) than at dealing with the issues raised by structuralism. At times, his attacks on theory seem to deny it any place in analysis, which is not only obscurantist, but places his own work in basic contradiction since his own analysis is structured by highly theoretical concepts. Nevertheless, his work, in the presence it provides to the subjects of history, dramatizes the absence in structuralist analysis of the historical subject, in spite of theoretical claims to the contrary.

The controversy over abstractions, therefore, is at the same time a controversy over hegemony. Thompson feels categories are a means for distancing the Other, and he discusses Althusser's use of them: "a category . . . finds its definition only within a highly theorized structural totality, which disallows the real *experiential* historical process of class formation."[14] If this sounds unfair to Althusser, we may recall the observation of Poulantzas that "social classes are not empirical groups of individuals . . . . The class membership of the various agents depends on the class places they occupy."[15] Agent here is a misnomer because it does not make much sense to speak of agents when people have been rendered into categories. The immediate issue here is that such categorization represents little more than a taxonomic distancing. I am not sure that Thompson himself has ever suggested this directly, but the implication of his views is that categories, including that of class, are in themselves instruments of hegemony *if* they serve to distance the subjects of history from the historian; for surely "class" then becomes a counterpart (albeit viewed with sympathy by a Marxist) of Williams's "masses," a way of defining the Other whom we do not know, and who only exists in our minds as part of an internally undifferentiated totality.

The criticism of abstraction may, of course, be carried to the ridiculous and naive extreme of denying abstraction any part in understanding, which is the same as denying the latter any organization or direction. Indeed, the only consequence of rejecting abstractions may be acquiescence in tacit ideological premises which are present

---

14. E.P. Thompson, "Eighteenth-Century English Society," 148.

15. Nicos Poulantzas, *Classes in Contemporary Capitalism* (London: New Left Books, 1975), 17.

whether or not we wish to acknowledge them. This, obviously, does not characterize the thinking or the work of culturalist Marxists, but points to the difference between Marxist historicism, acutely aware of the ideological nature of historical discourses (within history or among historians), and an anti-theoretical historicism with its pretensions to truth.

Culturalist Marxism points to an epistemological issue with crucial social significance: abstractions, substituted for living people, may become tools of hegemony regardless of the goodwill or the professions of sympathy for the cause of liberation on the part of their practitioners. Abstractions inevitably create an ideological and, therefore, social distance between subject and object since their very purpose is to objectify human agency in history. If knowledge is power, as Foucault suggests, abstractions are the instruments of power which the knowing subject employs to establish control over understanding and over the known. This is most evident in the claims to comprehend society scientifically (not to be confused with systematically) which, whatever their ideological point of departure, presuppose that human agency must be reconstituted in accordance with "scientific principles" as understood by the "social scientist." The consciousness of the comprehending subject, in other words, takes precedence over the consciousness of the historical agent and constitutes the latter as its object in accordance with its own discourse. This, it should be obvious, licenses the comprehending subject to speak in the name of its object and, in case of opposition between the two, justifies the suppression of the latter in the name of higher truths, be they scientific or otherwise.

The historian, as a matter of practice, participates in three discourses: a discourse with the subjects of history, a discourse among historians, and a discourse with his social environment. To the extent that the historian assumes the prerogatives of the knowing subject, discourse among historians takes precedence over discourse with the subjects of history, and the latter is constituted in accordance with the prerogatives of the former. The result is the alienation of the historical subject through the abstractions that express the historian's discourse.

This alienation is an unavoidable consequence of professionalism. Intellectuals have been described by Gouldner as "speech communities."[16] This is all the more the case with professional intellectuals whose activity requires, nay demands, the creation of a language that defines professional activity. The historian's alienation from the historical subject is, in other words, a consequence of participation in a profession: it is a social alienation. This is the social price paid for expertise.

This alienation, however, is social in another, more fundamental, sense. Professions may not be tools of hegemonic social classes, but neither do they operate in isolation from the discourse of their environment with its hegemonic assumptions about society and the world. The validity of the learning produced by professionals is judged according to its resonance with these assumptions of the broader social discourse. The question of the participation of intellectuals in hegemonic practices assumes particular seriousness since the latter appear in the guise of what Gramsci calls "organic intellectuals," who are recruited into the service of "alienated social power," which I use here to denote not merely the state, as Marx had in mind, but the whole complex of institutions of power within the environment established by the state ("ideological state apparatuses," in Althusser's terms)[17] or, to put it less academically, the establishment. To the extent that professionalism is a socially desirable goal, professions are part of this alienated establishment. The alienation of the historian from the historical subject, it follows, finds its counterpart in the alienation of the historian as a professional from his immediate social environment. Hegemony over the historical subject is but an extension into the past of the hegemonic relationship the historian bears to his society as part of the establishment.

To the extent that expertise rather than political affiliation determines membership in the establishment, I might add, the struggle over hegemony ceases to be expressed simply as a struggle between right, middle, and left, or between conservative, liberal, and socialist, but as a struggle between the establishment and those who are marginalized (hegemonized) by the establishment.

---

16.   See Alvin Gouldner, *The Future of Intellectuals and the Rise of the New Class* (New York: Continuum Books, 1979).

17.   Louis Althusser, "Ideology and Ideological State Apparatuses," in *Lenin and Philosophy and Other Essays*, trans. Ben Brewster (New York: Monthly Review Press, 1971).

It is here, I think, that we find the social context for the struggle between culturalism as hegemonic principle and as liberating practice, between sociologism and historicism, between economism and humanism. Culturalist Marxism is the expression not so much of Marxism but of "decentered" intellectuals who have discovered in Marxist historicism a means to counter hegemony, past and present, by challenging the hegemonic practices of professional and therefore regnant assumptions of the dominant social discourse. None of this implies that culturalist Marxists are themselves immune to the social practices that they call into question. The challenge, nevertheless, is liberating in its rejection of a center to the historical and, therefore, social process.

The Third World Intellectual and Marxist Historicism

This is where Marxist culturalism has something of profound significance to tell us. Before we look at that, however, it will be helpful to distinguish the differences in the form that hegemonic culturalism takes in ideological relations between the West and the non-West from the form in which it appears in Western societies.

Simply stated, culturalist hegemony within the context of global relations is a "double-hegemony": it involves, in addition to the relationship between the West and the non-West, the hegemonic relations within non-Western societies. The interplay between these two creates a complexity over the question of hegemony that, while broadly recognized (at least since Lenin), continues to confound students of non-Western societies.

The question of hegemony between societies is perhaps the easiest to recognize because of its naked assumptions about Western centrality in the world. There are good reasons, moreover, not only intellectual but social, why Western students of non-Western societies should be well-prepared to recognize this form of hegemony. We all know that Western intrusion in the non-Western world displaces or "decenters" intellectuals in these societies who, as it were, learn to live in two cultural worlds without belonging in either one completely. This, to a lesser extent, also happens to intellectuals in the West who engage in the study of non-Western societies —Said's "orientalists." In our preoccupation with the hegemonic role these intellectuals play in relations between the West and the non-West, we fail to recognize sometimes that "orientalist" intellectuals are themselves "orientalized" by virtue of what they do because hegemonic culturalism, as it distances the non-Western world, also distances intellectually those who study it. We have all experienced at one time or another doubts on the part of our colleagues as to whether or not the work we are engaged in justifies complete integration into our disciplines! "Orientalists," in other words, have good reason to "decenter" Western hegemony and call an end to hegemonic relations between societies.

This does not in itself resolve the question of hegemony, however, but may itself serve as a cover for reactionary social attitudes, no matter how radical the claims. In order to be thorough, the critique of culturalist hegemony must be extended to the role culture plays as an instrument of hegemony *within* societies. As Third World Marxist critics of culturalist hegemony have long understood, this critique of internal hegemony is not only necessary if liberation from hegemony is to be total, extended beyond the elite to the people at large, but is also a precondition of cultural liberation of the society as a whole. Those Third World intellectuals who refuse to acknowledge this necessity and take recourse instead in the affirmation of a pre-Western tradition as a source of contemporary identity, or simply reject that tradition in favor of Westernism as an obstacle to development, only serve as grist for the mills of Western cultural hegemonism which finds confirmed in them its own tendency to view those societies as prisoners between the past and the West. To the extent that these intellectuals distance themselves from the present of their societies by taking refuge in the past or the West, they not only produce a hegemonic relationship between themselves and their societies, but facilitate the distancing of their societies in the hegemonic culturalism of the West.

This form of hegemony is somewhat more difficult to recognize. To the élitist "orientalist," it does not present itself as a problem, not only because it coincides with his own culturalist assumptions, but even more so because, given his hegemonic relationship to his own society, he does not recognize the question as a significant one. But there is also a more problematic radical "orientalism" that will allow the élite in Third World societies the kind of hegemonic behavior that it will not permit the élite in its own society. This kind of "orientalism," what we might call Third-Worldism, is in some ways more pernicious than the "orientalism" of the élites because it mystifies the question of hegemony in radical language. We often forget that the assumptions about other societies that go into the making of Western culturalist hegemony derive their plausibility from their coincidence with the assumptions held by chauvinistic nationalists about their own societies. The ruling classes in these societies, who uphold these assumptions, are not democratic by virtue of being a Third World ruling élite, but share in the social hegemonism of all ruling classes. Yet radical students of these societies have all too often been unwilling to criticize this kind of hegemony for fear of playing into the hands of Western imperialism.

In a discussion of this problem that is as cogent as it is honest and passionate, Abdallah Laroui in his *The Crisis of the Arab Intellectual* addresses the question of historical or cultural "retardation" that he believes must be part of non-Western intellectuals' confrontation with the West. The response to the intellectual crisis created by this sense of "retardation," Laroui argues, has been an uneasy eclecticism or an escape into tradition, which for Laroui, is not an abstract "thing" that "maintains itself by itself," but an ideological creation that "demands as much activity as progress." This activity, even if it provides the intellectual with some identity, only confirms retardation. Moreover, it is as alienating an activity as the escape into the West. In Laroui's words:

> Now there are two types of alienation: the one is visible and openly criticized, the other all the more insidious as it is denied on principle. Westernization indeed signifies an alienation, a way of becoming other, an avenue to self-division (though one's estimation of this transformation may be positive or negative, according to one's ideology). But there exists another form of alienation in modern Arab society, one that is prevalent but veiled: this is the exaggerated medievalization obtained through quasi-magical identification with the great period of classical Arabian culture.[18]

These two attitudes, "fundamentalist and liberal," Laroui suggests, "were opposed yet nonetheless complementary: liberalism was necessary but did not perforce imply a break with the past, traditionalism was tempting therapeutics but did not resolve urgent problems."[19]

---

18. Abdallah Laroui, *The Crisis of the Arab Intellectual: Traditionalism or Historicism?* (Berkeley: Univ. of California Press, 1976), 156.
19. Ibid., 121.

Alienation, as Laroui sees it, is not an abstract question but simply implies distancing of intellectuals from the present of their societies. How Westernization leads to this result does not need belaboring. Of traditionalism Laroui says:

> For all objective observers, the true alienation is this loss of self in the absolutes of language, culture, and the saga of the past. The Arab intellectual blithely plunges into them, hoping thus to prove his perfect freedom and to express his deepest personality. Here, then, are found the inward chains binding him to a present he yet claims to repudiate. Historical consciousness alone will allow him to free himself of them. Then he will see reality perhaps for the first time. He will see that the absolutes he worships are alien to him, for they may be interiorized only through intellectual analysis and synthesis, that is, through voluntary effort — never through inward understanding and intuition.[20]

Laroui's own solution to the problem is to suggest a radical Marxist historicism that he believes will reconnect the intellectual with the present.

> The historicism we are leading up to, one that is in many respects instrumental is not the passive acceptance of any past whatsoever and above all not the acceptance of one's own national past; rather, it is the voluntary choice of realizing the unity of historical meaning by the reappropriation of a selective past. This choice is motivated by pragmatic considerations, perhaps by modesty, above all by nationalism in the most natural sense of the word; the will to gain the respect of others by the shortest possible route. In this perspective we see clearly that it is not the moderate liberal who is being realistic, for he chooses to believe in the improbable equality of nations. Rather, it is the radical nationalist who is the realist; provided that he affirms his existence, he cares little if he loses his essence (his authenticity).[21]

This paragraph is problematic on a number of grounds; what concerns me here, however, is the clear link that Laroui establishes between the intellectual and the present of his society through the epistemology of historicism, specifically Marxist historicism, which, moreover, is connected in his mind to revolutionary activity in the

---

20. Ibid., 156-57.
21. Ibid., 99-100.

present. As he states in the very next paragraph: "Praxis therefore is historicism in action." And it should come as no surprise that all anti-historicism takes on an anti-praxis value. "An abstract universalism, expressing itself in economism, anthropology, or structuralism, knows nothing of involution and consequently takes no account of hegemony."[22]

I do not wish to read into Laroui's discussion issues that he does not address, not directly anyway. Nevertheless, in its advocacy of a radical historicism, as well as in the reasons it adduces for this advocacy, *The Crisis of the Arab Intellectual* has a direct bearing on questions raised by culturalism — both in its hegemonic and liberating practices. Laroui's idea of historicism draws heavily on Joseph Levenson's work on China, which I have depicted as an articulation of hegemonic culturalism,[23] but, on the other hand, his historicism is much closer in intention and implication to that of culturalist Marxists. The difference, I think, is the difference between historicism and Marxist historicism.

Levenson portrays the dilemma of Chinese intellectuals as a product of the necessity of choosing between the past and the West. His account of intellectual development in modern China is an account of the victory of its attraction to the West as opposed to its own ties to the past, which became increasingly emotional as the undeniable validity of Western ideas impressed itself upon the consciousness of Chinese intellectuals. Acceptance of the universality of Western values was accompanied by the inexorable historicization of Chinese values. The intellect/emotion bifurcation created by this confrontation was resolved by Marxism, which historicized Chinese values but salvaged their truth for the past (as the truth of a past mode of production), just as it legitimized acceptance of the West as the source of present truth while promising its eventual historicization (as the truth of an equally historical capitalism).

This dilemma is also the point of departure for Laroui, but it leads him in different directions. The fundamental difference is existential: Levenson is the American academic writing about the passing away of a culture he admired; Laroui is a Third World intellectual

---

22. Ibid., 100.
23. Joseph Levenson, *Confucian China and Its Modern Fate*, 3 vols. (Berkeley: Univ. of California Press, 1958-1965). For further discussion, see Dirlik, *op. cit.*

trying to rid his society of the hegemony of the past in order that the society itself may be salvaged. According to Levenson's analysis, he is indeed the object of the discourse striving to reassert himself as a subject of history. While Levenson sees the dilemma as a psychic one, that is, as the reintegration of the Chinese intellectual by overcoming the separation of value from history, Laroui sees it as a social problem: to reintegrate the intellectual within the society from which he has become alienated because he has identified himself with the past or the West. For Laroui, the confrontation between Arabs and the West is not merely an abstract confrontation between the ideas and values of civilizations removed from history, each with its own claims to truth, but a political and social confrontation as well: between oppressor societies and a society that has been "proletarianized" by the oppression. As he explains his idea of "New Nationalism":

> Where, in confrontation with Europe, the fundamentalist opposed a culture (Chinese, Indian, Islamic) and the liberal opposed a nation (Chinese, Turkish, Egyptian, Iranian), the revolutionary opposes a class — one that is often extended to include all that part of the human race exploited by the European bourgeoisie. One may refer to it as class nationalism that nevertheless retains many of the motifs of political and cultural nationalisms; hence the difficulties experienced by analysts who have attempted to define it. Revolutionary nationalism has three aspects: an exploited class, a dominated people, and a hard-pressed culture. The opposition to Europe also assumes a triple aspect.[24]

This is no longer the "Confucian China" of the Sinologist; it is the "proletarian" nation of revolutionary intellectuals (Li Dazhao, Sun Yat-sen, Mao Zedong come to mind immediately). If it does not bring the proletariat (or the oppressed classes) into the forefront of history, it at least makes them into a central component of the national struggle — as a referent against which the fate of ideas and values must be judged.

The idea of the "Proletarian nation," of course, still addresses only one aspect of the problem of hegemony, that between nations, but it does open up the possibility of dealing with the other aspect, that within societies. Laroui is quite aware (though this remains vague)

---

24. Laroui, 121-122.

that the ways in which Arab intellectuals have sought to resolve the dilemma of cultural choice (through recourse to the past or the West) has not only alienated them from the present of their societies, but also serves to distance society and guarantee the hegemony of intellectuals. The goal of cultural activity, therefore, must be to abolish this hegemony as well by reintegrating the intellectual within society. His, I think, is an idea of culture not significantly different from what I have called "a social concept of culture." For him, culture is the culture of everyday life, "quotidian temporality," as he puts it.[25]

The difference of Laroui's historicism from Levenson's does not rest merely in existential, but in ideological and epistemological, differences as well. It is ultimately a difference between historicism and Marxist historicism. To Levenson, Marxism, too, is an abstraction, an instrument that helps Chinese intellectuals rationalize their dilemma. For Laroui, Marxism is an epistemology that promises understanding and resolution: its significance lies not in the intellectual activity that distances the past and renders it irrelevant to the present, but in its relevance to praxis in the present. Marxism itself, moreover, must be refracted through the native present: it is not merely a means to historicize the native legacy; it itself must be historicized to serve the cause of present society. The distinction between historicist and structuralist Marxism, which is of no concern to Levenson since he distances Marxism as well, is of crucial significance to Laroui.

This distinction expresses an epistemological judgment that coincides with that of what we have called culturalist Marxism. This is not surprising; Laroui's intellectual forebears, as of culturalist Marxism in Europe, are Lukács and Gramsci and, through them, Lenin. And as with European culturalist Marxism, Laroui rejects the abstract in favor of the concrete. Abstractions are alienating; they also serve as tools of hegemony, regardless of whether or not they are of the liberal or the Marxist variety. In his Preface, he says:

> Those who criticize historicism as a philosophy — I refer in particular to the Frenchman L. Althusser— are interested primarily in a rationale of understanding: they take as models the exact sciences, which presume an eternal present and a homogenous milieu. A so-

---

25. Ibid., 70.

ciety that believes itself to be at the apogee of evolution and that strives to preserve the equilibrium it imagines it has attained will experience no difficulty in transposing such rationale to the social and human sciences. But a society that rejects its present, that lacks homogeneity, that feels itself to be different from those cultures that appear to be in the ascendant, will rediscover historicism as the theoretical justification for its course of action, sometimes in the guise of Marxism.[26]

Laroui's rejection of abstraction is rejection not of conceptual abstraction *per se*; given the complexity of the problems he deals with, his own argument proceeds at a very high, even opaque, level of abstraction. Indeed, one could argue that this argument, carried within the context of a cosmopolitan intellectual discourse, is inaccessible to the society with whom he would reconnect the intellectual and thus perpetuates the alienation that he himself criticizes. Nevertheless, it is important to note that he is critical of the alienating discourse that makes the subjects of history into its objects and that seeks to concretize culture in order to bring it to the level of everyday life. "The future of a given ideology," he tells us, "is not assured unless it offers the possibility of concretizing the frustrated hopes of a community."[27] Beneath all the opaqueness of his presentation, this is the message of his historicism.

The statement, "praxis is historicism in action," offers the key, I think, to understanding the coincidence in Laroui's analysis of an anti-abstractionist (not anti-theoretical) historicism and an empirical notion of culture with a dialectic of the present. It is through praxis that the basic contradiction in society is discovered or defined. Revolutionary political praxis does not confront culture as an external and therefore, abstract force, but only as a contradiction immanent in the structure of the social present. While theory may be crucial in disclosing this structure, moreover, theory (with its abstractions) is but a "moment" in the practice of politics, in the identification of political possibilities; for political praxis, if it is to avoid alienation, must comprehend society not abstractly but concretely, in terms of the empirical alignment of social forces. Political analysis, as Gramsci was well aware, parallels historical analysis; the difference between

---

26. Ibid., x.
27. Ibid., 108.

the two lies not in the method but in the object of analysis: politics is but practical history.

Laroui's activist epistemology finds in historicism the means to comprehend the present as a dialectical moment, a moment that is structured by the contradictory "inter-presence" of the native past and the West and that holds forth in the resolution of this contradiction the possibility of a future culture that is neither of the past nor of the West. Historicism for Laroui is not merely a heuristic device, but acquiescence in a globalized (or, "totalized," in Lukács's sense) historical consciousness that the decentering of intellectuals forces upon them, provided that they are willing to recognize themselves for what they are (regardless of their constant and alienating efforts to escape it) — the alienated products of this contradiction. This recognition presupposes a sense of history as an open-ended possibility, without a center to the historical process (Laroui is highly critical of evolutionism of whatever ideological persuasion), and of culture as an open-ended activity, without any central design, in which human agency creates the future out of the ingredients of the present, without any goals save the creation of a culture that is at once local and universal, without any centrality assigned to either. Laroui's historicism, nevertheless, is empirical without being empiricist and cosmopolitan without being relativist. It is a Marxist historicism in which the future is informed by the dialectic of the present. Future culture, which is to take form in the course of human activity, is the product neither of arbitrary eclecticism nor of abstract intellectual design, but of social praxis that seeks to eliminate the alienation of the intellectual and, with it, the existing structure of hegemony by abolishing the cultural distancing of the intellectual from his social present. The contradiction in culture, in other words, may be resolved only through social transformation since the problem of culture, as the expression of the problems of alienation and hegemony, is also a social problem. The resolution of one points the way to the resolution of the other, as a new society points to a new culture (or vice versa).

The dialectic of the present is ever present as the point of departure in the cultural thinking of Third World radical socialists who have stressed "cultural revolution" as a central project of socialist revolution. Unlike the hegemonic use of culture in culturalist ideology, where it appears as alienated (because determinative of the present as an external force), this radical conceptualization of culture resists alienation by positing the present as the focus of cultural activity. In the words of Mariategui, the Peruvian Marxist: "Peru's past interests us to the extent (that) it can explain Peru's present. Constructive generations think of the past as an origin, never as a program."[28] The words are echoed in Kwameh Nkrumah's philosophical declaration, *Consciencism*: "Consciencism is that philosophical standpoint which, taking its start from the present content of the African conscience, indicates the way in which progress is forged out of conflict in that conscience."[29]

While this resistance to the alienation of culture is motivated at least in part by a desire to deny the hegemonic claims of the ruling classes, the "keepers" of tradition, by challenging the contemporary relevance of the inherited culture upon which such claims are based, it does not follow that the inherited culture of the oppressed, substituted for that of the ruling classes, is sufficient source for the creation of a new culture. A romantic escape into popular culture, that of the oppressed, is another way of distancing the present, of which the past is a living part but which is not, therefore, identical with the past. As Franz Fanon puts it:

> A national culture is not a folklore, nor an abstract populism that believes it can discover the people's true nature. It is not made up of the inert dregs of gratuitous actions, that is to say actions which are less and less attached to the ever-present reality of the people. A national culture is the whole body of efforts made by a people in the sphere of thought to describe, justify and praise the action through which the people has created itself and keeps itself in existence. A national culture in under-developed countries should therefore take its place at the very heart of the struggle for freedom which these countries are carrying on.[30]

The insistence on the present as a new beginning implies more than a simple recognition that the present, defined by a historically unprecedented contradiction, contains the past only as a dialectical

---

28. José Carlos Mariategui, *Seven Interpretative Essays on Peruvian Reality* (Austin: Univ. of Texas Press, 1971), 274.

29. Kwameh Nkrumah, *Consciencism: Philisophy and Ideology for Decolonization and Development with Particular Reference to the African Revolution* (London: Heineman, 1964), 79.

30. Frantz Fanon, *The Wretched of the Earth* (New York: Grove Press, 1968), 188.

moment. It signifies not simply a denial of the hegemony of the past over the present, but a denial of the culturalist hegemony of the West which, in portraying the native present as a prisoner of the native past, parochializes not simply the native culture of the past but its very present. A present-oriented historicism, therefore, is not simply consistent with the cosmopolitan intention of radical socialism, but a very condition of the assertion by the Other of his "coevalness." The reaffirmation of the present as the only realm of cultural activity, in other words, is the assertion by the Other of his right to recognition as a subject of history. In a world where the native has been denied in ideology the very cosmopolitanism which has been forced upon him in reality, this reaffirmation of the present is the ultimate recognition of existence, radically opposite to the illusory search for an authenticity outside of that reality. This radical, present-oriented historicism is a pre-condition for the creation of an authentically cosmopolitan (Laroui prefers "universalistic") culture, a cosmopolitanism that is not defined in terms of the hegemonic culture of the West, but one that incorporates the native present (and the past) in the creation of a culture in which all are universal because all are equally parochial.

This activity of creating a new culture out of the dialectics of the present finally provides the means for transforming the intellectual from a plaything in the hands of the past or the West into an agent of cultural (that is to say social and political) change. Basic to radical socialism, with its cultural revolutionary intention, is the recognition that culture has at least a semi-autonomous role in revolutionary change: while the creation of a new culture must take as its point of departure the drastic overturning of existing social relations, the new culture thus created serves as the source of, or promotes, further social change. Revolution, in other words, is conceived here as a dialectical process where culture and society are structurally interrelated but are also autonomous moments of the dialectic. This presentation of the revolutionary process as a dialectic between culture and society presupposes a conception of revolution in which human activity plays a central role, where the revolutionary is at once the product and the subject of history. Mao Zedong in China had his counterpart in Che Guevara in Cuba who once stated that "the revolution is made by man, but man must forge his revolutionary spirit day by day."[31] While this brings the human agent into the center of the social process, it does not do so without profound ambiguity. While the revolutionary as subject of history has a sense of his direction, the latter provides no more than a tentative guideline, for ultimately the direction of revolution must emerge in the course of the struggle that *is* the revolution, just as its culture must be forged out of the relationship between the revolutionary and the revolutionized. In other words, the revolutionary, too, must be "listening" all the time and must not merely impose his abstractions upon the revolutionary process, which would merely involve the projection of his own alienation onto the latter. While the revolutionary is in the process of leading, in other words, his leadership must be defined in terms of the dialectic between the revolutionary consciousness and the consciousness of the social present with which he must integrate himself if the revolution is to issue in a new culture of liberation. This dialectic, too, has no center, and it is only to the extent that revolutionaries resist the temptation to establish such a center that revolution appears as a liberating possibility.

Culture, Hegemony and Liberation

Culturalism as hegemonic ideology mystifies the hegemonic role that culture plays in relationships between and within societies. A hegemonic culturalism abstracts culture from its social and political context in order to present it as an autochthonous attribute of entire groups and peoples that is exterior to, and independent of, social relationships. Culture, thus abstracted, is alienated from the social present, and is made into a timeless attribute of peoples that determines the character of the relationships into which they enter with others. It serves as a principle for organizing time and space, with the culture of the self at the center of space and the apogee of time. Abstraction is the epistemological starting point of culturalism as hegemonic ideology.

What makes culturalism truly hegemonic rather than nakedly oppressive (a distinction that we owe to Gramsci) is the participation of the hegemonized in this abstraction. Orientalism is inconceivable

---

31. Ernesto Che Guevara, *Socialism and Man* (New York: Pathfinder Press, 1978), 21.

without "self-orientalization." Laroui's argument provides us with a cogent critique of the participation of Third World intellectuals in this kind of abstraction which alienates them from their social present. Laroui owes a great deal for this insight to Joseph Levenson's work on China, which powerfully argues the defensive nature of this abstraction for Chinese intellectuals confronted with the West. What Laroui brings out, from his Marxist perspective, is that this abstraction is not merely defensive; it also serves the purposes of class hegemony within Third World societies.

The task of culturalism as liberating practice is defined by opposition to this practice of abstraction. What needs to be challenged in the opposition to culturalist hegemony is not the validity or relevance of the notion of culture, but the abstractionist epistemology that renders culture into an alien force ruling over living people. Whether or not culturalism is an entirely appropriate term for describing this oppositional activity is problematic. Obviously, as liberating practice it challenges the very basis of the understanding of culture in the ideology of hegemonic culturalism by concretizing it within the realm of social relations. It is a Marxist culturalism, in other words, whose understanding of culture is fundamentally different from that of culturalist ideology.

What justifies the usage, nevertheless, is a need to insist on the necessity of recognition of some autonomy, even priority, to the question of culture in any meaningful liberating practice. This is especially necessary in the case of Marxism which is vulnerable to a tendency toward an abstractionist epistemology that is contradictory to its liberating intention: Marxism, too, can (and has) become hegemonic by serving to distance the Other through its reduction of people to abstract categories. What we have described as culturalist Marxism (after Johnson) restores concreteness to social analysis by pointing to the particularity that not only recognizes the burden of history but, through that, the subjectivity of the historical agent that rests upon the particularity of social experience. This culturalist Marxism resists economistic reductionism by recognizing culture as a semi-autonomous realm: not merely a superstructural element or the organic expression of a totality, but an active element in history that exists in a dialectical relationship to other constituent elements of society that is at once a relationship of unity and contradiction. This is the meaning of culturalism *within* the context of Marxism.

In both of the texts discussed in detail above, this view of culture results in an activist epistemology, one that finds in praxis, rather than in theoretical speculation, the source of non-hegemonic understanding. This, it needs to be stressed, is not an epistemology the goal of which is to discover abstract truths, but an epistemology with an intention, one that seeks to overcome the alienation that is implicit in the notion of truth conceived abstractly. An epistemology that takes praxis as its point of departure calls attention to all knowable truth as historical truth. In the case of Thompson, this activist epistemology takes the form of recognizing the priority of the experiences of those who lived and made history. Laroui expresses it in his affirmation of existence over an alienating (because abstract) search for authenticity or essence. In any case, both authors discover in historicism the method of this epistemology.

This historicism, as with all Marxist historicism, is a post-theoretical, that is to say, a post-structuralist historicism; it takes for granted the prior existence of a theoretical epistemology which is implicit in the concepts that guide its historical analysis. As with all historicism, it represents history as a narrative, but unlike anti-theoretical historicism, with its pretensions to capturing the unadorned truth of history in narrative, the narratives of this historicism are cast around concepts, are intended, indeed, to demonstrate the realization of the concept in history. Its opposition to structuralism rests in its assimilation of theory to history, rather than the other way around as is the case with structuralism.

This is a historicism, in other words, that does not reject theory, but seeks to transcend its positivistic use, which, in its efforts to introduce the language of science into the study of society, not only results in an ideological reductionism, but also militates against an activist epistemology. The most significant concepts of social analysis, concepts that bear upon questions of political power (class, state, nation, democracy, socialism), are irreducible into abstractions without being rendered ideological. Abstractions are ideological not only because they represent "strategies of containment" in the definition of meaning, but because these strategies play a crucial role in the struggle for hegemony by suppressing alternative meanings that challenge hegemony. Concepts reduced to abstractions, moreover, lose their temporality, and hence their ability to explain and to guide change. An authentically critical practice must take as a central task

of social analysis the examination of the very concepts that make social analysis possible. Only then is it possible to reveal the interrela-
tionship of concepts and thus expose the ideological reductionism
that must accompany any abstraction of the concept from these relationships. Only in this fashion, furthermore, is it possible to retain
the concrete in the abstract, because the phenomena of life that concepts represent exist in the concrete not as isolated phenomena but
as relationships. To deny the admission into analysis the clutter of
social relations may salvage for analysis the elegance of simplicity,
but only at the cost of irrelevance or, worse, the ideological mystification of social relations. This is where historicism appears crucial. For
to assert the priority of the concrete in abstraction is to assert the
historicity of the conceptual, and historical concepts may be comprehended only historically. This is what Frederic Jameson has in mind
when he writes in a different context:

> . . . this very antithesis [theory vs. interpretive practice] marks out
> the double standard and the formal dilemma of all cultural study
> today . . . an uneasy struggle for priority between models and histo-
> ry, between theoretical speculation and textual analysis, in which
> the former seeks to transform the latter into so many mere exam-
> ples, adduced to support its abstract propositions, while the latter
> continues insistently to imply that the theory itself was just so much
> methodological scaffolding, which can readily be dismantled once
> the serious business of practical criticism is under way. These two
> tendencies —theory and literary history— have so often in Western
> academic thought been felt to be rigorously incompatible that it is
> worth reminding the reader, in conclusion, of the existence of a
> third position which transcends both. That position is, of course,
> *Marxism, which, in the form of the dialectic, affirms a primacy of theory which is
> at one and the same time a recognition of the primacy of History itself.* (Em-
> phasis mine)[32]

What are the conclusions that may be drawn from the coincidences
between culturalist Marxism and Marxist historicism as presented by
Laroui? Most striking is the coincidence of historicism as an activist
epistemology with the "decentering" of the intellectual. The Third

32. Fredric Jameson, *The Political Unconscious: Narrative as a Socially Symbolic Act* (Ithaca: Cornell Univ. Press, 1982), 13-14.

World intellectual, subject to the challenge of cultural domination by the West, experiences this "decentering" as a condition of existence. Traditionalism or Westernism may offer to some the promise of bringing the intellectual back to the center of intellectual and political life. Indeed, from a Western perspective, this effort is the easiest to comprehend since it fits in easily with the assumptions about the world of culturalist hegemony. These routes, nevertheless, alienate the intellectual from the present of his society, decenter him, in other words, *vis-à-vis* the present. It may bring power to intellectuals, but it does not bring them escape from culturalist hegemony (or, for that matter, political and social hegemony).

It follows that culturalism as liberating practice must resist this abstraction of culture and the intellectual. Hence the insistence on the necessity of reintegration of the intellectual within a present social reality that exists apart from a frozen tradition or a reified West and that is the object of hegemonic practice (as the location of "backwardness"). To recover that reality, nay to center it, is to decenter the hegemonic claims of the past or the West.

Historicism, in other words, rejects structure in the name of agency and restores the human subject to history. The decentered intellectual would appear in this discourse as a condition of liberating practice. Hegemonic culturalism (not to say a hegemonic political science) has long pointed to the alienation of intellectuals as a source of revolutionary activity. This is stating the obvious. The more important question, usually ignored, is from what are these intellectuals alienated. To that we may venture a simple answer: alienated social power that feeds upon those whom it hegemonizes.

By way of conclusion, I would like to return to a question that I raised earlier in this discussion: the status of Third Worldism as viewed from the perspective of culturalism as liberating practice. In recent years, a Third-Worldist establishment has come into being. Though still not universally recognized and highly vulnerable, this establishment raises new questions about the issues that I have discussed here. This establishment has found an institutional basis in various organizations of an international nature. It is strong in academia, where it has made its influence felt intellectually in the spread of challenges to older Western-centered "modernizationism" in the form of dependency theory and various versions of world-system analysis. Intellectually, it has made a significant impact in challenging a Western-centered view of the world through its advocacy of a global perspective.

This emergent establishment, if we may call it that, represents a radical alliance of the decentered intellectuals of both Western and non-Western societies. The challenge to Western cultural hegemonism may take the form here of a cultural-political relativism (with liberals); among radical Third-Worldists, it may on occasion be carried so far as to reverse the assumptions of earlier hegemonism; that is, non-Western societies may be held up as examples for the emulation of Western societies.

This development is a very significant one in terms of the hegemonic relations between Western and non-Western societies. Conservatives as usual have been quick to recognize the threat, as witnessed by recent attacks on UNESCO (the international cultural organization *par excellence*), as well as in the reaffirmation of the necessity of instilling in education a sense of the "Western tradition."

While its challenge to the power of a Western-centered leadership is quite evident, however, the relationship of this emergent Third-Worldist establishment to non-Western societies is highly problematic. To the extent that intellectuals of the Third World become part of such an establishment, with its own language and its own organizationally defined goals, they too are alienated from the constituencies in whose name they speak. That this establishment is predominantly economistic in its orientation is a case in point. While its appreciation of the world is global, moreover, it conceives of the globe in highly abstract structuralist terms. In this establishment, Third World intellectuals themselves produce an alienating ideology that distances them from their own societies, to which they of necessity come to bear a hegemonic relationship. Indeed, appearances to the contrary, it may be suggested that their participation in this establishment has contributed to the increasingly monolithic reality that oppression has come to assume in recent years: radical opposition to hegemony has been undercut by the incorporation of opposition into a new hegemonic structure of power. Ideologically, this is expressed in the abandonment of cultural opposition (or "cultural revolution") in favor of a supposedly more pragmatic economistic ideology.

What is at issue here is not the confounding of ideological identity, but the identification of what constitutes a liberating practice, which points to epistemological questions that cut across ideological divides. That Marxists should be participants in hegemonic practices is not surprising (nor is it a new phenomenon). Though ideological Marxism pretends to the contrary, Marxists are subject to the same ideological proposition that they apply to others: "it is not the consciousness of man that determines his social being, on the contrary, it is his social being that determines his consciousness." Marxism loses its critical edge and appears ideological to the extent that Marxists suppress the applicability of this proposition to themselves — or to the categories of Marxism. The assignment of a privileged position to the knowing subject over the subjects of history is parallelled at the level of thought by the privileging of theory over history. Whatever precision is thereby acquired, the gains are more than offset by the suppression of the temporality of categories that is the result of this disjuncture between history and theory, which alienates categories from their historical subject. The consequences are not merely intellectual but profoundly social: it renders Marxists into controllers of the hegemony and Marxism into a hegemonic ideology.

The question of culture derives its significance for liberating practice from the questions it raises concerning the historicity of theory or of a theoretical grasp of the world. Recalling culture in its double meaning, both as a "way of seeing" and as a way of making the world, returns the historical subject (or agent) to his dialectical temporality which, Jameson has suggested, decenters him from his privileged position in history. The dialectic, conceived in its "quotidian temporality" as the praxis which intermediates abstract design and social existence rather than as an excuse for an abstract evolutionism, offers the possibility of reintegrating the present and the future, theory and history, category and social subject but, above all, the knowing subject and the subject of history; in other words, there is the possibility of a truly liberating practice which can exist *only* as a possibility and which must take as its premise the denial of a center to the social process and of a predestined direction to history.

This is the reasoning that, I think, underlies the advocacy of cultural revolution in radical Marxist thinking in the Third World which, even more so than its counterpart in the West, has long recognized the insufficiency of economism as a condition of socialism or even as a basis for challenging capitalist hegemony. This radicalism has rested in the urge to reconnect the intellectual with the social present, not just to counter hegemonic alienation, but to create a new global culture that must be neither of the West nor of the past. The basic premise of this reasoning is that culturalist hegemony can be overcome only by the creation of a new culture that is at once universal and particular. Such a culture must be forged out of the ingredients of present society, for any other alternative must of necessity reintroduce alienation into the cultural process. In all cases, we find a coincidence of an activist epistemology (an anti-abstractionist historicism) with revolutionary practice. And, finally, common to all is the perception that true cosmopolitanism may be achieved only by moving from the particular to the universal (the latter is taken for granted) and not by imposing universals of whatever kind upon the particular.

This cultural revolutionary ideal appears more and more as an illusory utopianism in a world where necessity (economic *and* political) calls forth economism. It does not help either that the idea of cultural revolution has in practice created its own problems because its proponents have been unable to live up to the critical premises of their own reasoning. Nevertheless, we must continue to listen to their voices, if only as a constant reminder of the need to counter the mystification of the problem of liberation by self-professed radical alternatives which, out of cynicism or self-delusion, promise liberation but offer new forms of hegemony instead. To do otherwise would be no less than resignation to a profound fatalism that closes off all doors to the possibility of human liberation even as a vision.

On Disenchanting Discourse:
"Minority" Literary Criticism And Beyond

Sylvia Wynter

In order to introduce and integrate, within the space of this paper, several "new objects of knowledge" which cannot meaningfully exist within the discursive *vrai* (truth) of our present "fundamental arrangements of knowledge"[1] nor within the analogic of its "(ethico-) theoretical foundations,"[2] I shall make use of a series of epigraphs placed at different points of the argument. Their function will be to project the possibility of a "demonic observer" ground[3] *outside* the consolidated field of meanings of our present analogic, a ground in which these "new objects of knowledge" can find their efficient criterion/

---

1. See Michel Foucault, *The Order of Things: An Archaeology of the Human Sciences* (New York: Random House, 1973), 387.

2. The term *ethico-theoretical* is a progression on Derrida's usage of ethical-ontological distinction in "Limited Inc. abc" in *Glyph*, no. 2 (1977): 247.

3. In an article—"Demonic and Historical Models in Biology"—Alex Comfort coins the term "demonic models" to refer to "logical representations of reality which exclude a space-time oriented observer." We have adapted the concept here to suggest the possibility of an observer/site of observation that is non-analogically oriented, that is, one outside the present discursive formations and meaning "fields" of our present order and its related episteme. For Comfort's paper, see *The Journal of Social and Biological Structures* 3, no. 2 (April 1980): 207-216.

condition of truth.[4]

The new objects of knowledge to be presented here call equally for the construction of new conceptual tools and theoretical foundations, which this time go beyond *not* only the hegemonic paradigms of literary criticism but also beyond the grounding analogic of the episteme or "fundamental arrangements of knowledge" of which our present practice of literary criticism (in effect of normal "majority discourse") is an inter-connected component.[5] Our present arrangements of knowledge (and therefore their grounding analogic) were put in place in the nineteenth century as a function of the epistemic/discursive constitution of the "figure of Man." This represents, in our projected new terms, the first purely *secular criterion* of human being (or regulatory metaphysics) encoded in the "descriptive statement" of the human on the model of a natural organism and its related ontology. For our proposed new objects of knowledge to be receivable, we accordingly need to go beyond the ontology of the figure of man and the empowering *normalizing* discourses with which this "figure," as the projected model/criterion of being of the globally dominant Western-European bourgeoisie, is still enchantedly constituted—now dangerously, in the context of our post-atomic environment.

I shall propose in this paper, therefore, that the unifying goal of *minority* discourse, if the term *minority* and its related discourse is to constitute itself as the "institutional" (and therefore ontological) fact that it is rather than as the "brute"[6] or empirical fact that it is strategically[7] projected to be within the coercive analogic of our present onto-episteme,

---

4. Fernand Vandamme develops this concept convincingly in "Register Linguistics: A Nominalistic Language Interpretation and Its Implications for Some Central Problems in Glossogenesis" in *Glossogenetics: The Origin and Evolution of Language. Proceedings of the International Trans-disciplinary Symposium on Glossogenetics*, Eric de Grolier, ed. (New York: Harcourt Academic Publishers, 1983).

5. This concept is extrapolated from the new theory of cognition called *"connectionism"* developed by David E. Rumelhart, James L. McLelland and the P.D.P. Research Group in *Parallel Distributed Processing: Explorations in the Microstructure of Cognition*. Volume 1: *Foundations*, Volume 2: *Psychological and Biological Models* (Cambridge, Mass.: M.I.T. Press. 1986).

6. John R. Searle makes this distinction in *Speech Acts: An Essay on the Philosophy of Language* (London: Cambridge University Press, 1969), 51: "They (i.e., institutional facts) are indeed facts. But their existence, unlike the existence of brute facts, presupposes the existence of certain human institutions. It is only given the institution of knowledge that certain forms of behavior constitute Mr. Smith's marrying Jones."

7. The concept of discursive "strategy set" has been adapted from the use of the

will necessarily be to accelerate the conceptual "erasing" of the figure
of Man.[8] If it is to effect such a rupture, minority discourse must set
out to bring closure to our present order of discourse, as the nineteenth-century Western European bourgeoisie did from their parallel
ontologically subordinated status *vis à vis* the "enchanted" discourse of
the then hegemonic pre-industrial landed gentry.[9] But more, this must
occur as utterly as Ralph Ellison's novel *Invisible Man* has brought closure to the novel form as a meaningful existential genre, and therefore
to the first form of that secular mutation at the level of "regulatory human feelings"[10] which the novel's new generic onto-aesthetic field had
effected, in the moment of the originary rupture caused by Cervantes's
novel *Don Quixote.*

On Disenchanting Discourse: From The Semiotic Strings of Feudal Noble Blood to Those of Monarchical "Rational Nature"

> "You are right, Sancho," replied Don Quixote; "but I have told
> you already that there are many kinds of enchantments; and time
> may have changed the fashion from one kind to another. It may
> be usual now for people under a spell to do all that I do, although
> they did not before; so that there is no arguing or drawing conclu-
> sions against the customs of the times. I most certainly know that I
> am enchanted, and that is sufficient to ease my conscience, which
> would be greatly burdened if thought that I was not under a spell,
> and yet remained in this cage like an idler and a coward, defrauding
> the many distressed and needy of the succour I could give them."
>
> —Cervantes, *Don Quixote*

---

term "strategy set" by biologists. See, for example, Maynard Smith, "Game Theory and
the Evolution of Cooperation" in *Evolution from Molecules to Men*, D.S. Bendall, ed. (Cambridge: Cambridge University Press, 1983).

8. Michel Foucault, *The Order of Things*, 387.

9. For the implications of this usually non-recognized Event, see Foucault, *The Order
of Things*, Karl Polanyi, *The Great Transformation: The Political and Economic Origins of Our
Time* (Boston: Beacon Press, 1957), as well as J.G.A. Pocock, "Civic Humanism in Anglo American Thought" in *Politics, Language and Time: Essays on Political Thought and History* (New York: Athenaeum, 1973).

10. The interconnected concepts *onto-aesthetic fields* and order-specific *regulatory feelings* (or *feeling-sets*) have been coined on the basis of a central Darwinian point further
developed by M.T. Ghiselin, *The Economy of Nature and the Evolution of Sex* (Berkeley: University of California Press, 1974).

The exchange cited above takes place between *Don Quixote* and his squire, Sancho Panza, in part 1, chapter XLIX of the novel. In this episode, Don Quixote's friend, the Priest and the Barber, trying to get him home to his village, had disguised themselves, overpowered him while asleep, and shut him up in a cage, telling him that his imprisonment has been procured by a wicked enchanter and planned to last for a set period of time. Don Quixote has therefore resigned himself to his imprisonment, induced to do so by the fact that in the system of inference-making generated from the chivalric code/model of identity of the romances that he has read, enchanters, as counteragents of the supernatural, are the key explanatory device by which he manages to "save the appearances" of any event that contradicts the view of reality inferred from the mimetic model of the fictional knight-errants of romance.

Sancho, however, has caught sight of Don Quixote's friends and suspects the trick being played on his master. He tries to *disenchant* Don Quixote by a series of arguments designed to prove that he, Don Quixote, cannot be "enchanted"—that rather than being "under a spell" Don Quixote instead has been "humbugged and fooled."[11] His syllogistically argued[12] and seemingly irrefutable proof is that since it is commonly held that when under a spell people cannot eat, drink, or satisfy the urgent needs of nature and since his master has the desire to do all three, it follows that his master cannot be enchanted. But this proof is at once crushed by Don Quixote's irrefutable answer: that enchantments change their kind according to the "customs of the times." The exchange here functions both at the level of the disputes of the literary theory of the time and at the wider level of the abduction

---

11. See Miquel de Cervantes Saavedra. *The Adventures of Don Quixote*, trans. J.M. Cohen (Harmondsworth, Middlesex: Penguin Books, 1985), 431.

12. See Alban Forcione's discussion of this scene and of "the elements of parody in this *mock-discorso* between Sancho . . . and Don Quixote. As Forcione notes, Sancho, "in attempting to reveal the absurdity of his master's belief by subjecting it to the scrutiny demanded by the canon's principle of *Verisimilitude*," employs the syllogistic reasoning characteristic of the neo-Aristotelian theorists.

However, Rorcione's interpretation of the *mock-discorso* differs considerably from both Edwin Williamson's and my own. See Alban K. Forcione, *Cervantes, Aristotle and The Persiles* (Princeton: Princeton University Press, 1970). For an overview of the implications of the ethico-theoretical concepts of both the *marvellous* and of *verisimilitude*, as well as of the dispute between them (and which is central to the *mock-discorso*, as well as to the overall onto-aesthetic [our term] of the novel), see E.C. Riley, *Cervantes' Theory of the Novel* (Oxford: Clarendon Press, 1962).

schemas[13] or system of inference-making. The opposed schema were generated respectively from the explanatory schema of supernatural causality generic to the current of twelfth-century philosophical idealism whose discourse-system underlay both the aristocratic ethos and the romances of chivalry expressive of that mode of fantasy, and from the newly emergent emphasis on the explanatory hypothesis of natural causality. The latter schema establish equally the *"true* [vs. "legendary"] *history"* characteristic of the new monarchical ethos and the order of things of which ethos and its new discursive ideologic, the novel *Don Quixote*, was the innovative expression.

An epochal rupture has therefore taken place between the new genre of the novel and the old genre of chivalric romance, together with its enabling discourse of philosophical idealism and its still religiously guaranteed descriptive statement or criterion of being, in whose context the imitation of established traditional models had been projected as an ethico-aesthetic imperative. For the new genre was no longer to be based, as that of romance had been in the last instance, on a still pervasive theo-logic, but rather on the *ideologic* of a new order of discourse based on varieties of an ontologized "natural law," and its related secularizing variants/models of human being. These variants, beginning in the sixteenth/seventeenth centuries, were to realize their purely secular summa in the nineteenth/twentieth centuries with the emergence of the criterion of being encoded in the figure of man and its constitutive discourse of *biological idealism*.

At the level of literature, the rupture from *supernaturally guaranteeed* descriptive statements or criterial conceptions of being and the mutation to the first form of a now secularly guaranteed one were to be effected by the emergence of the new discourse of Neo-Aristotelian literary theory and poetics.[14] An equivalent rupture and mutation occurred at the level of the supernaturally guaranteed modes of verbal/semiotic symbol-matter information systems by means of which human

---

13. See Gregory Bateson, *Mind and Nature: A Necessary Unity* (New York: E.P. Dutton, 1979), where he develops this central concept of *abduction*, as a mode of thinking based on inference-making.

14. The term is adapted from the concept of organic *speciation* linked to the role played by regulatory genes that, by placing a limit on out-breeding, constitute the *interbreeding unit* as a "species." See Erik H. Erikson, *Toys and Reason* (New York: W.W. Norton, 1977), and E. Mayr, *Evolution and the Diversity of Life: Selected Essays* (Cambridge: Harvard University Press, 1976).

populations/orders are integrated as "composite wholes" in that process of pseudo (or fake) speciation first identified by Erikson as the mechanism at the level of human life through which the individual members of a group come to experience themselves as co-identifying conspecifics.[15]

The integrative analogic (or semantic closure principle) which underlay the religio-aesthetic system of the genre of romance and its chartering discourse was still based on the central Platonic concept "of a rationally and harmoniously ordered universe in which the Divine Idea expressed itself by means of imperishable and immutable forms, existing beyond the material world."[16] These *intelligible* forms were then prescribed as the *only ones* worthy of imitation, as distinct from the projected inferior forms/models of the antithetical world of historical actuality. With the chartering of the new analogic of neo-Aristotelian literary theory, however, the world of historical actuality and the actions of men within it were released from their earlier ontological subordination or "deferent" role.[17] For through this poetics, the "reality" of a now legitimated world of empirical action could be imitated so as to reveal the universal value expressed through it, by imitating, as Aristotle had advised, "according to a true idea." This concept of a true idea would be taken in a special didactic sense, one which led to a preoccupation with the *moral* in literature and to Cervantes's concept of the *exemplary novel*. Through the mediation of this master-concept, the "universal" ideas they expressed would not in any way contradict the true idea of the counter-Reformation faith, and the related ideologies of the Spanish monarchical-imperial state[18] would not be contrary to "good

---

15. An illuminating essay by Peter Dunn on the exemplary novels of Cervantes and their relation to the newly emergent Neo-Aristotelian literary theory/poetics, reveals the "endowment," which this theory helped to effect, of an entirely new secularizing attitude of both seeing and acting on the world, a new attitude *configured* in the novel form itself and in its founding generic analogic. See Peter N. Dunn "Las novelas ejemplare" in *Suma Cervantina*, J.B. Avalle-Arce and E.C. Riley, eds. (London: Tamesis Books, Ltd., 1973).

16. Ibid., 85.

17. The *intelligible/sensible* distinction was the philosophical expression or philosopheme of the feudal aristocratic code of symbolic "life" and "death."

18. In his prologue to *The Exemplary Novels*. See Cervantes, *Obras completas* (Madrid: A Valbuena Prat., 1956), 769-70. See, for a less onto-political, more strictly literary interpretation, Alban Forcione's Introduction in his *Cervantes and the Humanist Vision: A Study of Four Exemplary Novels* (Princeton: Princeton University Press, 1981).

customs" but would instead provide honest yet entertaining(*sabroso*) models of being/behaving appropriate to its way of life and the "true idea" about which the now hybridly religio-secular state integrated itself. Nor indeed would *Don Quixote*, the first fully achieved form of the novel as an existential genre, which gave expression to the analogic of the new literary theory by its fictional endowing of the particular experiences of its hero Don Quixote with representative (i.e., universal) value. For its emplotment led from the *parodic* life of a hero, governed by the mimetic non-true ideas of a text now projected as false and deluded, to the paragon death-bed conversion scene of a new text when, awakening to the "true idea" of his monarchical "rational nature," he comes exemplarily to his "true" self, his "true nature"[19] now as a Christian-monarchical subject of the same nature as his "real" text.

For the universalizing "true idea" of the new state form had entailed a relatively democratizing shift from the earlier purely supernaturally guaranteed descriptive statement and optimal signifier of "noble blood" to the first primarily statal-secular (although guaranteed in the last instance by the faith) descriptive statement, with the optimal criterion becoming that of "rational nature" and of degrees thereof. At the metaphysical/aesthetic level, lack of rational nature displaced lack-of-noble-blood, even if the latter continued to be partially hegemonic at the level of the social-systemic. To lack rational nature was to be governed by purely sensory nature with the latter defined as the "nature" common to men and animals. As such, this nature could not of itself be the basis of the ontologized natural law with its projected universally binding precepts. Instead this law was based on reason as the peculiar attribute of mankind (although already the humanist scholar Sepulveda denied this rational nature to the "Indians," as the native Ontological Other).[20]

19.See René Girard, *Deceit, Desire and the Novel: Self and Other in Literary Structure* (Baltimore: Johns Hopkins Press, 1965). Here Girard's innovative and original reading of the hero's awakening from *mimetic desire*, as the first expression of that *conversion* central to the novel form, errs only in one aspect—that is, he sees the hero as awakening to *truth*, in general, to his *true self*, rather than to a *specific mode* of the *self*, coherent with the monarchical historical-ensemble or system: that is, to a new secularizing mode which begins to project the concept of *"true nature"* as an absolute in place of Christian and other transcendent *natures*.

20. See Bernice Hamilton, *Political Thought in Sixteenth Century Spain: A Study of the Political Ideas of Vitoria, De Soto, Suarez and Molina* (Oxford: Clarendon Press, 1963).

Now the former behavior-orienting struggle between spirit and flesh became, for the new intellectual laity, the secularizing one between the individual's *sensory* nature as his appetitive nature expressed in an imaginative faculty capable of good (creation) or ill (seduction to act outside the universal "true idea" embodied in the religio-political order of state/faith). If *sensory nature/imaginative faculty* is to act for the good, it must therefore be curbed by rational nature which alone knows how to resist the temptation of falling into the new ontological threat represented by the contingency of fortune, and the instability of the particular.

Neo-Aristotelian literary theory, the first form of our present system of literary scholarship, and whose *prescriptive* rules functioned at the level of theory to replicate this governing binary code (rational/sensory nature) and its analogic of the level of the emerging field of secular literature, can therefore be seen here in its widest context as the expression of an epochal shift out of the earlier mythico-religiously and theologically guaranteed orders of discourse. For if, as Derrida argues, philosophic speech can only institute itself by the fettering and humiliation of another speech, projected as the new fool to the crowned king of its Logos,[21] with the device of "attaching lunacy" and transforming the earlier religio-aristocratic discourse into the fool of its now partly secularizing, partly religious statal/monarchical model of Being/Logos, Cervantes and the novel form effected that great discontinuity by which "rhetorical man" now enters.[22] His descriptive statements, or models of identity, are now guaranteed no longer by the religious but by the *aesthetic*; the "rhetorical man" brings with him what is to be for all humans a new historico-phenomenological space of being/discourse.

Whilst Don Quixote died exemplarily, the novel form which he, as hero, initiated was to transform itself, over the succeeding centuries. These transformations were to be effected through internal mutations with respect to the "sensory nature," tropological complex of the Renaissance schema of civic/monarchical humanism, including its tranumed "landed gentry" form. In this mutation the topos of "sensory

---

21. In the essay "Cogito and the History of Madness" in *Writing and Difference* (Chicago: University of Chicago Press, 1983), 61.

22. See R. Lanham, *The Motives of Eloquence: Literary Rhetoric in the Renaissance* (New Haven: Yale University Press, 1976).

nature" would now become that of a projected "primal nature" encoded, at the global level, in the *native* (with its zero degree signifier form as the *nigger*)[23] whose ideologic was to be disseminated by the mode of the novel and by its founding discourse of biological idealism. And this new discourse was to be projected about the new exemplary bourgeois "figure of man" just as the empowering discourse of philosophical idealism had been projected about the then exemplary figure of the chivalric-aristocratic figure of the Knight.

Attaching "Blindness" To The Controllers of Reality. Disenchanting the "Figure of Man"

> And that a little black man with an assumed name should die because a big black man in his hatred and confusion over the nature of a reality that seemed controlled by whites whom I knew to be as blind as he was, was just too much, too outrageously absurd. And I knew that it was better to live out one's absurdity than to die for that of others whether that of Ras or Jack's.
> —Ellison, *Invisible Man*

If *Don Quixote* laughed away the ideal Christian-chivalric model of the human, Ellison's *Invisible Man* attaches the ironic metaphor of *blindness* to the characters who embody the three differing variants of the contemporary order of discourse of biological idealism. Of the three variants, the first is that of Liberal Positivism embodied in Norton and Emerson: Norton, a pragmatic philanthropist who plays God to southern Blacks by giving money to Southern Black colleges designed to

---

23. The "figure of the nigger" was to function as the negative signifier of the mode of being embodied in the bourgeois "figure of man" (as the *mad* had functioned in the "rational nature" order of the landed gentry, and within its empowering analogic or discourse of humanism). Whilst the *mad* embodied the extreme form of a projected subordination to *sensory nature*, the nigger would project the extreme form of an ostensibly "primal human" which had remained subordinated by the processes of evolutionary natural selection, as such subordinated to natural necessity, and as such *non-autonomous*. Note that the word *nigger* projects the human as *pure object*, the antonym of the pure ostensible autonomously willing "figure of man." If the *mad* functioned to signify its opposite as *normal* reason, the *nigger* does so to signify its opposite as normal *being*. "Racism" is a behavioral competence of this analogic. See in this respect the book by Jacob Pandian, *Anthropology and the Western Tradition: Towards an Authentic Anthropology* (Prospect Heights, Illinois: Waveland Press, Inc., 1985).

provide a second-level education for a secondary Black middle class, the other a "concerned" liberal for whom "poor Blacks" are the means by which to realize his liberal "concern," just as Don Quixote needed the "many distressed and needy" to succour in order to realize his knight-errantry. The second is that of Marxism-Leninism with its "true idea" imaged in Brother Jack, Hambro, and the leadership of the Brotherhood. The third is the Black variant of the discourse of "Romantic Nationalism" which is embodied in *Ras*, the fictional projection of Marcus Garvey and his movement.[24]

Yet all three discourses are generated as phenotexts from the same founding genotextual discourse which is itself generated from the underlying *archia* or descriptive statement of the model of the human as a "natural organism."[25] And whilst the version imaged in the character of Norton is original and *projective* in that it encodes the new origin "beliefs" and related ontological schema, this is not so with the versions of Brother Jack's Stalinist-Marxism nor with that of Ras's Black romantic nationalism. For these are both *reactive* to the *systemically* functioning economic rationality and morality encoded by Norton's Liberal Positivism in that, by taking the ontological "facts" of class and of race as if they were "brute" facts, they remain trapped in the context and the code of the hegemonic order of discourse and its system of motivation.

Both movements were therefore to prefigure the temptation that

---

24. The real life challenge of Marcus Garvey to the "*class first*" empowering discourse of the Marxian Euroamerican intelligentsia (and its black fellow-members of the intelligentsia) functioned on two levels. At the first level (the level enacted by Ellison) it functioned within the nineteenth-century discourse-model of Romantic nationalism. At another level, it challenged *the ontological subordination* of the black within the overall analogic of the nineteenth-century model of being. The contradiction of Garveyism derived therefore from this duality of discourse/praxis as it both assimilated to, and broke from the dominant schema and mode of mimetic desire, and as such dually functioning within the bourgeois analogic, whilst moving towards post-western and post-bourgeois cultural forms and modes of self-organization. And whilst Marxism's theory of *economic* subordination provided a dazzling set of explanatory hypotheses, the more foundational concept of *ontological* subordination (reacted against empirically by the Garvey movement) had/has yet to find its "theoretic frame" (Cruse). This thesis is developed more fully in an ongoing work entitled *By means of a Creature: Essays Towards a Science of the Human.*

25. See Foucault, *The Order of Things*, 310. See also Ernesto Grassi, *Rhetoric and Philosophy: The Humanist Tradition* (University Park, Pa.: Pennsylvania State University Press, 1980) for the concept of *archia* which we have linked to the idea of a founding "descriptive statement" (Bateson) or *analogic*. See also G. Bateson, "Conscious Purpose vs. Nature" in *The Dialectics of Liberation*, D. Cooper, ed. (Harmondsworth, Middlesex: Penguin, 1968).

confronts minority discourse at this juncture, the same temptation to which the differing *isms* that emerged in the Sixties and Seventies all succumbed: that is, of taking the ontological "facts" of ethnicity (non-White and White) as well as of gender, sexuality, and culture as if these were things-in-themselves, rather than "totemic" signifiers in an overall system of resemblances and differences.[26] Taken as such, these terms are only meaningful within their reinforcing systemic function as the "specifying" negative Ontological Others of the first purely secular and therefore non-transcendentally guaranteed model of human being/identity.

For if Marx had zeroed in on the economic opposition between owners/non-owners of capital, he had overlooked the ontological aspect of the opposition between them. He overlooked, that is, the Ontological Other coding role in which those groups categorized under the signifier Labor functioned as the antithesis[27] that verified, through ostensive negation, the new archia by which the industrializing bourgeoisie self-signified itself by its ownership of capital as the incarnated embodiment of the new metaphysics of life/death, which now constituted the generalities of the post-landed gentry ordering of "real life." For in this new metaphysic/code, projected in the "figure of man"[28] and its ordering discourse-system and episteme, a transumption had been made from the earlier code in which "ownership of land," put forward in the Anglo-American variant of the discourse of "civic humanism" as the single matrix and source of both empirical and metaphysical well-being, had functioned to legitimate the exclusive control of decision-making power in the hands of the then hegemonic gentry. The counter-discourse of the new figure of man, generated from a model of being projected from the life-activity of the rising industrial bourgeoisie, had posited the analogic of a counter-metaphysical schema, one no longer based on the landed gentry's

---

26. See C. Levi-Strauss, *Totemism* (Hammondsworth: Penguin, 1969).

27. The oversight of this signifying ontological function of the "working classes" in addition to their role in economic production has enabled the intelligentsia to use the category/projection of the "figure of the proletarian" for their own group empowerment. Ellison catches this discursive sleight of hand powerfully in his portrayal of Brother Jack and of Hambro in relation to their group strategy set of "scientific objectivity."

28. The proposal here is that the "figure of man" encodes the bourgeois criterion of being as the "figure of the *yeoman*" did that of the "landed gentry" and the "figure of the *proletarian*," that of the education owning/information controlling intelligentsia-as-a-social category.

topos of the "natural benevolence of the land" but rather on the inversion of that topos, the new topos of the "avarice of nature" and the "natural scarcity" of the land.[29] It was on the basis of this new topos of causality that the new master-discipline of economics was to be erected, together with the other disciplines of its complex, including that of literary criticism/literary studies.

In Ellison's *Invisible Man,* Mr. Norton incarnates the exemplary activity of the autonomous, decision-taking investor/speculator whose calculative intelligence is projected as rationality-in-general, and not as a systemically constituted *relative* mode of intelligence. A central "blindness" with respect to a reality which the decision-making of men like Norton was now supposed to control would therefore be functional to the behavior-inducing order of discourse which underlay the new mode of life just as another variant of blindness had been centrally functional to that of the landed gentry. Thus the inferential logic of the new discourse by which the Nortons of the world regulated their behaviors would have to *invisibilize* those aspects of reality which contradicted this system-functional mode of perception. Most crucially, of all, if the contribution of accumulated "moveable wealth" or *capital* were to continue to be perceived as the symbolic *source* of the "surplus-value" of material "life," then both the existence of the multiple other factors which contributed to the always systemically produced surplus-value and of the concrete flesh and blood human whose life-activities and culturally coded needs/desires are the causal source of these processes would have to be overseen and controlled. For this human with its always culturally determined desires existed concretely outside the procrustean *conception of the human*, that is, outside a conception that was essential to the system of inference making of the discourse of *biological idealism*.

As J.F. Danielli hypothesizes, an internal reward system (I.R.S.) should be seen as functioning as the central mechanism by which human individuals are motivated to sacrifice their individual interest for that of others with whom they are co-identified—in effect for the sake of the common good.[30] The pleasure centers and the functioning of the euphoria-inducing family of substances would "reward" behaviors which further "altruistic" integration (good) and inhibit dysfunctional

---

29. See Foucault, *The Order of Things*, 256–57.

30. J.F. Danielli, "Altruism: The Opium of the People," *Journal of Social and Biological Structures* 3, no. 2 (April 1980): 87–94.

behaviors (evil/deilos), thus providing "the rudiments of a physiological basis for some aspects of motivation." However, he points out, what still remains missing to complete the hypothesis is "any knowledge of the *social* conditioning of the I.R.S.," that is, of how it functions "so that *rewards are provided which relate to the necessary or desirable roles of an individual in a specific society*."[31]

Danielli's "missing components of knowledge" can be both linked to and understood in the context of the macro-metaphor of *blindness* which Ellison attaches to the first purely secular and *guaranteed* post-landed gentry criterion of being, embodied in the character of Norton.

Through the formidable conceptual instruments of Mandeville, Adam Smith, and Ricardo, on the one hand, and of Malthus/Darwin, on the other, allied to a new fiction which functioned at the level of the onto-aesthetic field of "regulatory feelings," the bourgeoisie had disenchanted the discourse-system of the order of the landed gentry. The *grounding premise* of a criterion of being attached to the ownership of land was revealed and displaced along with the criterion-specific and "participatory" nature[32] of the classical episteme in whose system of inference they themselves were ontologically subordinated and proscribed as the owners of unstable, "moveable wealth." They nevertheless found themselves confronted with a major problem. Whilst the solution to this problem would be found, it would be found only at the price of the specific kind of "blindness" exemplified in Norton and in the revelatory fiction of Ellison's *Invisible Man*.

The problem was that of finding the necessarily non-transcendental mechanism by which the first purely secular criterion of being, projected by the Western European industrializing bourgeoisie to take the place of that of the landed gentry, could now be *absolutized*. For only by means of such a mechanism of absolutization could the metonymic process, by which the new criterion of being about which our global order still auto-hierarchizes and auto-regulates itself, be stably attached to the euphoric reward system of "feeling good." Only by this could the new post-landed gentry order be literally "enchanted" and "rewards" provided "which, by relating to the necessary or desirable

31. Ibid., 90.

32. See Francisco Varela's theory of the "participatory" nature of all human modes of knowledge as developed in his book, *Principles of Biological Autonomy* (New York: North Holland Series in General Systems Research, 1979).

roles of individuals" (Danielli) in our specific power-prestige order, would ensure its stable replication.

For the now purely secular order of the western bourgeoisie a series of signifying others remaining in their prescribed places would now function as the "real/empirical model"—like that of Freud's *mimetic* anatomical model[33]—whose existential reality now functioned to *absolutize* the secular criteria of being of which they were the ostensive negation. Hence the analogic with which, in the case of Ellison's Mr. Norton and the other "normal" characters of the novel, the series of multiple Others would have to be regularly "invisibilized" so as to be "seen," discoursed upon, and treated, not as they were, but as they were "needed to be" within the a priori inferential logic of the collective "inner eyes" constituted by the discourse of biological idealism. To these inner eyes *Invisible Man* now attaches the label of "blindness":

> I am an invisible man. No, I am not a spook like those who haunted Edgar Allan Poe; nor am I one of your Hollywood-movie ectoplasms. I am a man of substance, of flesh and bone, fiber and liquids—and I might even be said to possess a mind. I am invisible, understand, simply because people refuse to see me. When they approach me, they see only my surroundings, themselves, or figments of their imagination—indeed, everything and anything except me . . .
>
> Nor is my invisibility exactly a matter of a biochemical accident to my epidermis. That invisibility to which I refer occurs because of a peculiar disposition of the eyes of those with whom I come in contact. A matter of the construction of their *inner* eyes, those eyes with which they look through their physical eyes upon reality.[34]

To disenchant his hero's invisibility, Ellison here attaches to an ostensibly autonomous seeing/willing model of being/perceiving the label of a pre-determined mode of inner eyes which controls how its subjects see and act upon reality. He shows these inner eyes to be constituted by a system of inference, determined by the specifications of the mimetic model of being (or "reigning conception of man's hu-

---

33. In Luce Irigaray, *Speculum of the Other Woman* (Ithaca: Cornell University Press, 1985), 15.

34. Ralph Ellison, *The Invisible Man* (New York: Random House, 1972), 3.

manity") which the systemic subjects—like the narrator of *The Invisible Man*—struggle above all else to achieve. These specifications are absolutized and embodied negatively in an empirical series of Ontological Other categories which, taken together, signify *damnation* in the new secular motivational schema in which salvation is equated with freedom from natural necessity both at the material and cultural levels. The "thematic object" of the narrator's sought-after "briefcase" in *The Invisible Man* embodies this new ideal of being as Don Quixote's "helmet" did for him.

Both function as Danielli's opiate-inducing signifiers; both intoxicate their heroes to the point of 'blind' madness. The socio-systemic ontological category of the "Poor" (for whom, as in the case of Trueblood, the signifier of the briefcase is an impossibility) is the embodied category now central both to motivating escape from poverty (newly projected as a metaphysical evil) and to the negative specification of freedom as freedom in its bourgeois modality. For the category of the poor/Trueblood now functions to incarnate the signifier of metaphysical "death" in the new governing code of the bourgeois "formation of human existence," providing the secular-empirical yet ontological "place of the damned" in the systemic apparatus of motivation by which order-maintaining behaviors on the part of its subjects (keep the Nigger Boy running!) are stably generated. The category of the Poor (and the poverty archipelagoes) would therefore have to be produced as such a systemic category, that is, *as a system-maintaining function* of the order's stable autopoesis.

If the category of the Poor functioned as a hypher-sign within the "natural unit" of the nation at the level of the *family*, the Ontological Other slot was filled by the category of gender, of the woman, appearing at this level as one bearer-category of the lack of bourgeois rationality embodied normally in the *male* as the signifier of rationality. Here, the ontologically privileged male receives, as Virginia Woolf noted as early as the 1920s, the opiate reward (*cocaine* in her words) of the narcissistic advantage of a prescribed feeling of innate supremacy.[35]

However, at the global level of the new ordering of things, the central Ontological spot of the *Poor* at the level of the nation, and of the *woman* at the level of the family, was filled by the category of the *native* as the projection not only of the lack of bourgeois-occidental rationality but

---

35. In her essay, *A Room of One's Own* (New York: Harcourt Brace & World, Inc., 1929).

also of the lack of metaphysical Being. The *natives*, nevertheless, also constituted a hierarchy of projected degrees of lack, measured both by nearness to the ultimate *evolved* mode of Indo-European physiognomy and ideal-type culture[36] and by degrees of distance from the ultimate zero degree category of an ostensibly *"primal"* human nature whose differentiation from a lurking *bestiality* was dangerously imprecise and uncertain, so uncertain as to call for a question mark to be placed with respect to the humanity of this zero-degree category. Like the woman in the male/female relationship, this enabled the experiencing of euphoric supremacy at the level of race and culture—that euphoric supremacy that it is above all the function of South African apartheid to protect. For the Ontological Other slot of this ultimate negative specification of the bourgeois conception of human being was/is filled by the empirical reality of *Africa/the Negro* and the related tropological complex of representation projected in the emergent philosophical discourse of nineteenth-century Europe. The Negro represents the Negative Signifier of an allegedly "primal" human being totally subordinated to "natural necessity."[37] As such, the tropology of *Africa/The Negro* was to provide a foundational constant of the system of inference-making of biological idealism and to be constantly projected, as Chinua Achebe notes, as "the antonymic foil to Europe's spiritual grace," as the projection of that primal/near bestial nature which Europe and the bourgeoisie had overcome in themselves. And they had done so, the analogic runs, by means of their material development as well as of their creation of "high Cultures."

Both these empirical activities functioned not only as markers of an ontological difference in bio-substance between the two groups, thereby making conceptualizable our present ordering principle of differential degrees of human genetic value, but also, and even more so, as markers of the vast difference which now separated the West's refined "cultivated sensibility" from the primal human nature which still threat-

36. See George L. Mosse, *Towards the Final Solution: A History of European Racism* (New York: Howard Ferhg, 1978), where he traces the processes by which the aesthetic criteria of Greek classical culture, "whose villains outside the tribe" were the Jews and the Blacks, was developed by nineteenth-century European scholars and provided the basis for the Nazis' Aryan "myth of origin."

37. See M. G. Gillespie, *Hegel, Heidegger and the Ground of History* (Chicago: University of Chicago Press, 1984), where the latter traces the role played by this concept, both in Kant and later in Hegel's philosophy.

ened ontologically in the form of *Africa/the Negro*, into which, unless presented by a bourgeois mode of being/feeling/knowing, one could atavistically relapse.

Attaching Non-Autonomy to the Autonomous, "Blindness" to Scientific Objectivity, Futility to Romantic Nationalism: Not Who but What Controls?

> To study Metaphysics as they have always been studied, appears to me to be like puzzling at astronomy without mechanics . . . . He who understand baboon [sic] would do more towards metaphysics than Locke.
> — Darwin, *Notebooks*, 1838

> "When Marx said that 'religion is the opiate of the people,' he spoke with greater accuracy than he realized. The . . . decline of religion . . . [has] . . . tended to transform society so that we could now say that 'Ideology is the opium of the people.' What none of us has realized until the last few years is that . . . unless society provides mechanisms for the release of endogenous opiates, i.e., for activating the I.R.S. . . . social cohesion is lost and collapse . . . may be imminent."
> —J. F. Danielli, 1980

It is this enchanting "opiate inducing" system of figuration that Ellison ironically reverses in his portrayal of the encounter between Norton as the bearer of the "cultivated sensibility code of High Culture" and Trueblood. For Trueblood is here the bearer of 'Field Niggerism,' projected in the overall schema as the negation of High Culture and introjected though the overall conditioning apparatus of the official representation system as primal and backward. He represents the Black Southern American culture from which the young, upwardly mobile narrator, in order to "be" in the "reigning conception of humanity," must develop a "learned" aversion, must run and run, never responding to the subversive rhythms of its sounds, always religiously choosing the signifiers of toast and orange juice over Ontologically Other pork chops and grits, never relapsing into eating Field Niggerism's hot baked yams out in the life of its streets, into exchanging that "signifying" repartee of the dozens that heretically defines the human as "life that has speech," but instead must run and run in order to "be" according to the specifications of the mimetic model of being of the bourgeoisie, running from everything that the Narrator's historical people have been and are: Keep this Nigger Boy running! For, in the dominant order of discourse in the U.S., Field Niggerism functions as the analogue of Africa/the Negro. As such it places a question mark on the Narrator's humanity, a question mark reinscribed by the very "High Culture" taught at the school, from which all "taint" of an antithetical Field Niggerism is excluded. And its "cultivated sensibility code" is incarnated in rich white trustees like Norton, whom the young Narrator, still caught up in his borrowed desire, chauffeurs reverentially around as the incarnation of that "true" model of human "life" to which he aches mimetically to attain.

The first of the series of confrontations/experiences which, like Don Quixote's pratfalls, will lead to the Narrator's eventual "awakening" and conversion/revolt against the hegemonic order of discourse and its behavior-directing signs, is the encounter between Norton and Trueblood, an encounter which the Narrator's mistake precipitates, and of which he is the helpless and horrified witness. For the strange bond which emerges between Norton and Trueblood is the fact that the latter has breached the *normative* sexual code and its prohibition of incest, which, like the prohibition of non-genital sexuality, functions to constitute such sexual practices as signifiers of an ostensible relapse into that "bestiality" that threatens ontologically to overwhelm the distance which the bourgeois ideal model of being struggles to place between itself and an ostensibly primal human.

Norton has long had an incestuous sexual attraction to his daughter, but one repressed because of the simultaneously physical and metaphysical nature of his desire: his daughter as a white woman is also the bearer of the bourgeois conception of ontological "purity," of which the "sexually promiscuous" black woman is the negation.[38] He is fascinated by Trueblood, whose attraction to his daughter is purely physical, because the latter has, while half-asleep, inadvertently committed incest with her and yet remains unashamed, since his concept of being a "man" differs so profoundly from the dominant conception embodied in Norton for whom being in charge, always in conscious

---

38. I have developed this thesis more fully in an essay entitled "After Feminism: Towards a Theoria for Our Times" in *Black Women Writing: Political and Cultural Imperatives*, J.M. Braxton and Andree Nicole McLaughlin, eds. (Rutgers University Press, forthcoming).

control, is the major imperative.

As Norton listens, stirred and seduced by Trueblood's narrating of the episode, he is overcome by his aroused sexual urges towards his own "pure" daughter, loses control and faints. In the scene that follows, Ellison attaches not the "stuff of lunacy," as Cervantes did to the chivalric code, but, rather, in the context of the new order of discourse, the stuff of non-control over urges that have ostensibly been "tamed" and refined out of existence; and even more of non-control over a will that is ostensibly autonomous, free from subordination to natural necessity, and as such empowered to make decisions which determine the collective destiny of the peoples of the global order. In this scene, Ellison uses Trueblood's narration to reveal that Norton's will/desires are mediated by speech/rhetoric/discourse, that for the human it is discourse and its system of inference which determine. For they do so, once in place, beyond subjective consciousness, by giving system-specific *verbal* shape and form to the originary dynamics of the genetic motivation system of our purely physiological heritage. This is transferred to the third level of existence, human life, by the strategies of opiate-inducing rhetoric which exist at the interface between the symbol-matter information system of the genome and the linguistic symbol-matter information systems by which all human modes of being effect their autopoesis as systemic forms of always symbolic codes of life/death.[39] For in the *human* beginning it was indeed the Word.

Here, therefore, Ellison disenchants the ordering systemic discourse which Norton incarnates by attaching both the labels of "blindness" and of non-autonomy of desire. He shows Norton here as never really "seeing" Trueblood, but rather only *inferring* him as an abstraction on which to project the desires which he, like the Narrator, *must* firmly repress in order to realize himself in the dominant conception of being. Again, Norton, the criterion/model-of-being, canonized in "real life" as the bearer of exemplary life activity, that of freedom from subordination to the "iron laws of nature" (i.e., natural necessity, natural scarcity), is here shown as bereft of that pure autonomy which in the

---

39. For the concept of "symbol matter information systems," see H.H. Pattee, "Clues from Molecular Symbol Systems" in *Signed and Spoken Launguage: Biological Constraints on Linguistic Forms*, U. Bellugi and M. Studdert-Kennedy, eds. (Berlin: Verlag Chemic, 1980), 261-274, and "Laws and Constraints, Symbols and Languages" in *Towards a Theoretical Biology*, C.H. Waddington, ed. (Edinburgh, University of Edinburgh Press, 1972), 248-258.

governing behavior-regulatory analogic of our present order confers on him the right of decision-making as to when and where to invest in accord with the calculative mode of intelligence which makes these decisions on the basis of the analogically *True Idea*/criterion of their return-on-investment potential. Hence the paradox: Norton's absolute power over processes of decision-making determines the negative destinies of others like Trueblood and condemns their lives, stigmatized as lacking in bottom-line "return-on-investment-potential," to the poverty archipelagoes that are as inferentially logical to the ordering discourse of Logical Positivism/Liberal Humanism as the Auschwitz archipelagoes were to that of Nazism and its a priori criterion of *genetic* inferiority/superiority, or the Gulag archipelagoes to that of Stalinism and its a priori of "scientific truth" versus "ideology," and of the superiority of the Party-line criterion of "true" Proletarian origin over non-Proletarian origin; yet Norton's autonomy of desire is an autonomy itself coded by the discursively constituted conception of being.

Thus if it is clear that Trueblood, as the *Lumpen* underclass, exists *outside* the dominant order of discourse and its reigning "conception of man's humanity," Brother Jack and Ras, whom the Narrator will later confront in a further series of painful, humiliating experiences, are themselves paradoxically caught up in the very conception of man's humanity against which they fight, one in the name of "class," the other in the name of "race."

For Jack, and his discourse-variants, the unskilled, jobless lumpen Blacks in Harlem are the discursive antithesis of the "deserving" destined ruling class of the *workers*, within the analogic of Marxist theory whose new criterion of being is "labor" or the projected source of surplus-value, and for which surplus-value is generated *only* in the process of production,[40] and which, therefore, finds its ideal model of being in the "*Proletarian*" in place of Man. The jobless lumpen are necessarily "outside history." As such they are metaphysically irredeemable, a force only fit to be deployed in carefully staged riots, allowed to function only within the tightly controlled overall master-plan of the Brotherhood. Hence, in a series of brutal experiences, the Narrator must learn the terrifying truth that he has been used to make his own

---

40. See Samir Amin, *The Law of Value and Historical Materialism* (New York, Monthly Review Press, 1978), and Abdel-Malek, "Historical Surplus-Value" in *Review* III, no. 1 (1979). See also, Jean Baudrillard, *The Mirror of Production* (St. Louis: Telos Press, 1975).

people into a sacrifice, this time in the interests of Jack and the Brotherhood, as the price of his own honorary incorporation into the party structures of power as a pseudo-cosmopolitan, non-lumpen, secondary intelligentsia member, hired to *talk* but not to *think*. Even more tellingly, he must learn too, that for Brother Jack, blinded by the inferential logic of his scientific objectivity, Blacks are only abstractions, mere ciphers in Jack's as in Norton's group's particular projects which they represent as universals. The price to be paid for his upward mobility in the context of either one of the exemplary projects of these two men, both of whom are "blind" (Brother Jack has a glass eye) to the reality which they have set out to control, is his betrayal of the Black lumpen Harlem majority. For this lumpen proletariat is stigmatized as outside the productive economy and as such "like discarded machinery" in the system of inference of one project and "outside history" in that of the other. In both it is finally expendable, only useful, on the one hand, as voting power or, on the other, as cannon fodder in the "spontaneous riots" orchestrated by the New Class of the Brotherhood in their non-conscious thrust to hegemony over against the bourgeoisie.

In the series of scenes in which the scales fall from the Narrator's eyes, the revelation of the purely instrumental abstraction that the Blacks of Harlem are for the Brotherhood is central to his own final self-disenchantment and to his own eventual holing up underground in his basement. Here he takes refuge from an entire order of being, pledging to go up tomorrow, yet never actually going up, holding out in the name of all invisible humans—"perhaps in the lower frequencies I speak for you"—the possibility of their/our recognition of this imposed "invisibility," which leads to a new demand for another concept of freedom, another possibility of livable being that culminates in his recognition of his "alterity:"

> . . . And now I . . . saw Jack and Norton and Emerson . . . each attempting to force his picture of reality upon me and neither giving a hoot in hell for how things looked to me. I was simply a material, a natural resource to be used. I had switched from the arrogant absurdity of Norton and Emerson to that of Jack and the Brotherhood, and it all came out the same—except I now recognized my invisibility.[41]

---

41. Ellison, *Invisible Man*, 497.

Whilst Don Quixote dies after his moment of lucidity, the Narrator has to confront the world again from the perspective of his disenchanted view before he can regain safety in his "hole." But before he does so, he finds himself caught in the conflict between the "scientific objectivity" of Jack and the Romantic nationalism of Ras. Ras's discourse variant does *not* deal in Jack's abstractions, since he shares with the Lumpen-Black the same humiliating experiences, and his semi-millenarian discourse comes much nearer to recognizing the ontological coding function to which Blacks are subordinated, since it inverts and attacks the grounding symbolic template of the order, challenging the metaphysics of the figure of "man" for which the figure of the Negro is the imperative antithesis. Nevertheless, in taking "Race" as an in-itself, as against the more sophisticated class analysis of Jack, Ras remains blinded to the realities of the powerful forces grouped against any possible realization of his empirical, empowering Back-to-Africa-dream. He remains "blinded," too, to the fact that without what Cruse calls a "theoretic frame" of superior explanatory power to that of Logical Positivism and of Marxism-Leninism, one that is able to disenchant their discourses, the attempt at violent *physical* resistance by vastly outgunned Blacks could only end in futility. And because both Brother Jack and Ras overlook the reciprocally reinforcing *systemic* function of "class" and "race"—and indeed of "gender," "culture," "sexuality," etc.—and because each, as members of the emerging new class, controllers of the means of information rather than owners of capital, logically struggle to project the "priority" of his own "*ism*," the clash which erupts between their "proletarian" and Lumpen forces—a transposition of the "real life" competitive clash between Marcus Garvey and the Communists—entraps the now disenchanted Narrator in the final conflict between the two over the absolute truth of their respective versions of reality, over which category is to take primacy, "class" first or "Race/Nation" first.[42]

The passage just cited, therefore, reveals the narrator confronted by Ras, who is determined to kill him at the very moment when his experiences have led him to opt out of the normalizing discourses, at the

---

42. The *Race first/class first* clash is now being re-enacted in the *race first/gender first* clash, with both generated from the ostensible *universality* of the *class* and *gender* categories, projected from a Western-European/Euramerican perspective. The category of "race" necessarily functions as the "deferent" category in both cases.

very moment when he has stumbled onto the new question: not *who* controls reality but *what?*

Fiction as a Higher Level of *"Truth:"*
Obtaining Access to What Controls Reality To Our Cognitive Domain

The idea of a dynamic structure of desire which transcends rhetorical conventions, even historical cultures, but which nevertheless is truly constitutive of the literary works which are our objects of study, cannot be seen as a Freudian idea, since it clashes head on with psychoanalysis. And it clashes head on also with all the actual forms of literary criticism, whose evaluative and classificatory criteria it must necessarily reject, transgressing all its principles.

Basically, this reformulation suggests that literary works defined as works of genius . . . may well conceptualize in a manner superior to our own . . . such a reformulation cannot therefore be made either in the name of science, nor in the name of literature as both are understood today.

—René Girard, 1975

The above epigraph suggests that it is by means of a new approach to narrative discourse that we might best explore the question as to what controls "reality," what in effect determines the specifications of those "inner" eyes or modes of systemic consciousness by means of which we know the world, orienting our behaviors by this knowledge within shared uniform parameters of perception and motivation.

The epigraph puts forward René Girard's seminal proposal with respect to the "objective" functioning of the *dynamics of desire*—which is parallel to Deleuze and Guattari's concept of the systemic functioning of a machinery of desiring production.[43] It is this dynamics that we have put forward as the proposed *rhetorical motivation system*, the analogue for humans of the genetic motivation system for organic species. In this context, Girard's dynamics of desire suggests a possible explanatory key that may at last elucidate the laws of functioning of the directive signs that govern human behavior in the same way as genetic "directive signs" govern the dynamics of the behaviors of organic species.

---

43. In G. Deleuze and F. Guattari, *Anti-Oedipus: Capitalism and Schizophrenia* (New York: Viking Press, 1977).

We propose here further that the dynamics of desire exists "objectively" as a *transferred* human variant of the "desire" for reproductive potency that functions as the proximate mechanism by means of which the stable and optimal replication of species-specific organic modes of life are secured. Desire is shifted by means of the process of discursive regulation by which humans are conditioned to desire the signifier-criterion of well-being or governing code of symbolic "life." Accordingly, what Girard calls the "dynamic structure of desire" is none other than the "fake" motivational system by means of which the desire for the signifier of potency specific to each culture or form of life, once enculturated in its systemic subjects as an opiate-inducing signifier in the context of the analogic of founding narrative schemas, functions to induce the collective set of behaviors of human subjects, behaviors which in turn bring each criterion/model of being into autopoetic living existence.

Here we differ from Girard in one crucial respect. For we propose that it is precisely by means of *rhetorical conventions* encoded in narrative orders of discourse that each system-specific signifier of potency is constituted as an opiate-inducing signifier of desire. Here we link Girard's concept of the determining functioning of an "objective" dynamics of desire—knowledge of which is most lucidly provided by fictional narrative—to Frantz Fanon's parallel concept of the systemic functioning of an inculcated *mimetic* model of aversion by which his Black patients had come to be aversive to their own existential selves, desiring to "be" in the mode of a whiteness that is systemically invested with all that is desirable.[44] Fanon's further exploration of the role of discourses such as that of psychiatric medicine and their regulatory functioning in the inculcation of learned self-aversion, when linked to Girard's proposed dynamics of desire, and illuminated in the light of *Don Quixote* and *Invisible Man,* suggests that human discourse is never neutral. It is everywhere a *function* of the maintaining in being of the systemic *rhetorical motivational systems* which, rather than the autonomous "inner man" or will of the individual subject, determine and orient the parameters of our ultimately system-maintaining behaviors: a function of the maintaining-in-being, then, of the dynamics of desire (aversion being a mode of desire). This dynamic, rather than objective reason out there, determines the mode of rationality or "participatory

---

44. See Frantz Fanon, *Black Skin, White Masks* (New York: Grove Press, 1964), 146-51.

epistemology"through which the always already systemic human subjects must necessarily know self, other, and world.

All genetic motivation systems of *organic* species are constituted through regulatory criteria of well being/ill-being which select and judge self and world in relation to what is good or bad for the survival/realization of the mode of the species. All human rhetorical motivational systems are themselves constituted on the basis of an underlying ontological schema or regulatory metaphysis which functions as the analogue of the genetically programmed regulatory criterion of well being/ill-being of organic life.[45] The ordering discourse of these ontological schemas should function, at a rhetorico-linguistic level, so as to parallel the functioning of the neurophysiological/electro-chemical reward-punishment apparatus of the brain, and therefore to define *good* as that which is good for the overall survival/realization of the discursively constituted model of being, and *evil* as its antithesis. They therefore institute themselves as *amoral* systems of inference (abduction schemas)[46] based on specific conceptions of life/death, conceptions which then function both as the specification for being and as the specifications for the shared mode of "mind" (Ellison's "inner eyes") by which each individual member is made conspecific with each other and able to function in an "integrated composite human population" or human system. This system then functions as a higher level unit with its own autopoetic intentionality transcending that of the individual subject.

However, the problem here, as Varela has posed it, is that whilst the "autonomy of the higher level of the systemic level gives a vantage point from which the individuality of components in the next lower level is seen in perspective," the obstacle that confronts us is that "we do not have access to the domain of interaction of the unit to which *we* belong."[47] And the answer to the *what* would call for such access to the domain of "the cognitive processes of the autonomous unit of which we are participants and components." Yet if, as we counter-propose, the modes of desire/aversion (R.M.S.) specific to each descriptive statement of human being (that is the R.M.S. which gives living expression to that statement) are everywhere constituted by rhetorical devices/

---

45. See Robert Boyd and Peter J. Richardson, *Culture and the Evolutionary Process* (Chicago: University of Chicago Press, 1985), 14.

46. Gregory Bateson, *Mind and Nature*, 142-144.

47. Varela, 274.

strategies, which are then inculcated by our order of discourse, and most "deep-structurally" of all by the fictional narrative/poetry whose function is to induce stably shared system-maintaining "regulatory sentiments" at the psycho-affective (aesthetic) level of being, then analysis of such rhetorical devices/strategies should provide us with precisely such access, and, by extension, access to the answer to the *what* controls reality. Here Girard's proposal for a total rupture with our present approaches to literary scholarship would then prefigure the kind of rupture that "minority" literary criticism must make both with our present discipline and more far-reachingly with the episteme of which it is an expression in order to take these rhetorical devices as the object of a diagnostic, rather than merely exegetical, analysis.

Literary Criticism From a Craft to a Science: The Role of Minority Discourse.

—"We follow the laws of reality so we make sacrifices . . ."
—"So the weak must sacrifice for the strong . . . ?"
—"No, a part of the whole is sacrificed—until a new society is formed . . ."
—"But who is to judge? Jack, the committee?"
—"We judge through cultivating scientific objectivity . . ."
—"Don't kid yourself . . . The only scientific objectivity is a machine."

—Ellison, *Invisible Man*

"But what can be *our* place in the symbolic contract? If the social contract, far from being that of equal men (humans), is based on an essentially sacrificial relationship of . . . *articulation of differences which in this way* produces communicable meaning, what is our place in this order of sacrifice and/or language."

—Kristeva, 1979

"The woman is accused of poisoning her husband with her menstrual blood. The myth then leads from menstrual blood which flows downwards—as a *natural* privilege of women, but a privileged *marked negatively*, to the tobacco smoke which rises upwards as the *cultural* privilege of the men, *which is marked positively*, that is to say, from the signifier of procreation to the signifier of religion.

—Lucien Scubla, 1982

The constant of the human governing codes is always a "deferent" relation between the menstrual signifier of procreation, that is, of "mere" biological life, to the tobacco smoke signifier of "true symbolic life," with the latter being the only life that humans live. And in the analogic of our present governing code/totemic set of the onto-theoretical distinctions which articulate the mode of symbolic life, the term *minority* necessarily bears an ontological relation to the term *majority*. As such it must function axiomatically as mere biological life to the true symbolic life generated by the mainstream discourses of literary criticism, as the signifier *menstrual blood*, then, to the signifier *tobacco smoke*; or, as the signifier of the *negroid* peoples to the opiate-inducing *Caucasian/Asian* signifier complex, or, in terms of our economic variant, as the owners of capital-as-moveable wealth to the non-owners. As such, the category *minority* is always already a subordinated category within the organizing principle of difference/deference of our present "symbolic contract" and of the mode of particular "nature" to which its specific secular ontology "ties us down" metaphysically.[48] As a result we are just as restricted to our negative signifier function (i.e., functioning to constitute majority discourse as an opiate-inducing signifier so that it can maintain its "narcissistic advantage"[49]) as the category of women is restricted in the traditional myth deciphered by Scubla.

In order to call in question this ontologically subordinated function, "minority discourse" can *not* be merely another voice in the present ongoing conversation or order of discourse generated from our present episteme and its disciplinary triad—biology, economics, philology (linguistics and literary scholarship)—inherited from the nineteenth century's industrial ordering of words/things and its founding analogic. Rather, it should bring closure to a conversation which is now as conceptually and imaginatively exhausted in our post atomic, post-bio-technological order of reality as was the conversation of philosophical idealism, which, through the outworn genre of chivalric romances, had also continued to disseminate an illusionary and anachronistic chivalresque model of being/behaving/desiring. The rise of the novel form and of the practice of institutionalized literary scholarship, beginning

---

48. See A.T. de Nicolas, "Notes on the Biology of Religion" in *Journal of Social Biological Structures* 3, no. 2 (April 1980).

49. See Julia Kristeva, "Women's Time" in *Signs* 7 no. 1 (1981-1982).

with Neo-Aristotelian Poetics, was itself part of what Blumenberg refers to as the "counter-exertion" that brought in the modern age,[50] and, accordingly, the present closure of the novel form, effected in "counter-novels" such as *The Invisible Man*, points towards the emergence in our day of a parallel movement of "counter-exertion," one that will entail the transformation both of literary scholarship and of our present organization of knowledge.[51]

If the *Quixote* opened the process of self-assertion over against the objectified form of purely theological absolutism of the medieval age, it is this second phase of objectification, based on the hardening of what Foucault calls the constraints of our present orders of "true discourse," that the closure of the novel form in *The Invisible Man*, together with the rise of new critical praxes such as structuralism, semiotics, and deconstruction, have begun to assault, in another concerted movement of counter-exertion, one capable, in Cornel West's phrase, of opening onto new cultural forms in the context of a post-Industrial, post-Western and truly global civilization.[52]

The major proposal here is that it is only as a leading thrust in this new movement of "counter-exertion" that Minority Discourse is imperatively necessary, because linked to the motives of general human self-interest, rather than to the particular interests of specific groups. For if, as the range of articles in the Minority Discourse issues suggests, the category of minority includes the sub-category "women," then we are here confronted with the anomaly that it is *we* who constitute the *numerical majority*. Yet such is the force of the shared semantic charter through which we interdepend, that we all know what we mean when we use the category *minority* to apply to an empirical *majority*.[53] This is because the term is being used here to designate a fact which

---

50. See Hans Blumenberg, *Legitimacy of the Modern Age* (Cambridge, Mass.: M.I.T. Press, 1983), 177–178.

51. See also Stratford Beer's point in Varela, *Principles of Biological Autonomy*, with respect to the urgent need for the "rewriting of knowledge."

52. In an essay, "The Dilemma of the Black Intellectual" in *Cultural Critique*, no. 1 (Fall 1985), 122.

53. Bill Strickland was the first scholar to note, in a talk given at Stanford in 1980, the strategic use of the term *minority* to *contain* and defuse the *Black* challenge of the Sixties to both the founding analogic and to our present epistemic/organizations of knowledge. The term *minority*, however, is an *authentic* term for hitherto repressed Euroamerican ethnic groups who, since the sixties, have made a bid to displace Anglo-American cultural dominance with a more inclusive Euroamerican mode of hegemony.

depends for its "truth" on a specific institutional system. And since these terms function to signify a relation of relative power to power-lessness, it is clear here that *Women and Minorities*, taken together as a systemic category, constitute the set of negative Ontological Others by means of which the descriptive statement of man-as-a-natural-organism, encoded in the figure of *man*, is stably brought into systemic being. This is the descriptive statement which our present organization of knowledge, including the discipline of literary criticism, was put in place to replicate. That is to say, the present forms of literary criticism and indeed all the disciplinary practices of our present episteme must accept, as its non-questioned but founding presupposition, our encoding as the systemic set of negative Ontological Others by means of which the specifications of our present model of being, the figure of man (in place of the landed gentry's ideal Figure of the Yeoman), is maintained in being.

It is from our shared identity as the systemic set of negative Ontological Others and from our complementary systemic role that we can derive potentially innovative contributions to the de-objectification of our present systems of theoretical absolutism and to the urgently needed transformation of our present episteme and its now objectified mode of rationalistic knowledge. That negative identity entails for us a spearheading role in the counter-exerting thrust to regain the now lost motives of the self-interest of the human species. In other words, it is the very liminality (on the threshold, both *in* and *outside*) of our category-structure location within the present "field of play" of the *discursive* symbol-matter information system that gives us the cognitive edge with respect to such a far-reaching transformation.

For the "grounding premise" of our present majority/minority code as generated in its contemporary modality is itself a transumed post-Sixties form of the same grounding premise which, in the field of the nineteenth-century episteme, virtually partitioned off "the Humanities" as the discourse of the universal Human Self from "anthropology" as the discourse on the particular "native" Other.[54] In other words,

---

54. Wole Soyinka, in his Introduction to a book of essays *Myth, Literature and the African World* (Cambridge: Cambridge University Press, 1976), vii, tells of his experiences at Cambridge University. During a one year visiting appointment there the Department of English refused to allow him to teach African literature as a part of the department's offerings. Classifying non-consciously, according to underlying analogic/archia

our present incorporation within literary scholarship as "brute" terminologies, (i.e., as *Afro-Americans/Blacks, Chicanos, Women, Native Americans, Asian Americans*, etc.) still incorporates us within new forms of the same Universal/Particular, objective/subjective order of value that was once at work in the more directly "Manichean allegory" of the Man/Native relation.[55]

Our constitution as "natives" by the discipline of anthropology, fenced, separated off, from the Humanities, functioned to signify that the "figure of man," embodied in the Indo-European, incarnated the ideal prototype of the secular human, its own epistemic organization of knowledge being in turn projected as isomorphic with an objective reality out there. Thus the present definition, *majority/minority*, if accepted as a brute fact, empowers mainstream literary scholarship to continue to see itself, and the parochial nature of its investigation into the functioning of human narrative discourse, as so ordered by the given nature of things rather than secured by the institutionalized directive signs of an order of discourse.

Most importantly, were we to accept *minority discourse* as a brute fact domain-in-itself, which would function as a kind of supra-*ism*, incorporating all *minorities* (as Feminism incorporates all women under the category of *gender*, Marxism, all workers under the category of *class*, Black Nationalism, all Blacks under the category of Pan-Africans) we would be unable to escape the fate of these *isms*. We would end up with some *minorities*, those less burdened with zero-degree signifiers, becoming increasingly more equal than the others by the automatic functioning of the directive signs of a new discourse based on the presupposition of minority status both as a brute and as an isolated fact rather than as a component of a negative Ontological Other category set defined by the *liminality* of our location. For it is precisely as such liminal subjects, able to experience to varying degrees the injustices *"inherent in structure,"* that we are able, in the words of the anthropologist Legesse, to "disenchant" our fellow systemic subjects from the "structure's cate-

---

of our present episteme, the English Department insisted that his lectures of African literature should be given in the Department of Anthropology.

55. See Abdul JanMohamed, *Manichean Aesthetics: The Politics of Literature in Colonial Africa* (Amherst, Ma.: University of Massachusetts Press, 1983) and "The Economy of Manichean Allegory: The Function of Racial Difference in Colonialist Literature," *Critical Inquiry* 12, no. 1 (Autumn 1985): 58-87.

gories and prescriptions."[56]

This point made by Legesse is central to our proposal. For our cognitive edge cannot be defined in *moralistic* terms—that is, we ourselves as intellectuals are not the "victims" of oppression, nor of wicked exploiters, and it is neither our intention to set out to "reclaim the true value" of our "minority" being nor, indeed, to establish a "dictatorship of the Minoriat." Such a *moralistic* approach is the logical result of taking our *isms* as isolated rather than systemic facts. Rather, we are constituted as a negative ontological category by the systemically functioning directive signs of an order of discourse generated from the descriptive statement of man on the model of a natural organism, an order of discourse which it is our task to *disenchant*.

We cannot, however, effect this disenchantment by establishing a "truer discourse," i.e., of minority discourse as such. As Foucault suggests and Ellison images, all "true discourses" contain "strategy sets" based on a non-conscious politics of replacing a new group hegemony for old group hegemonies. And, as Derrida further points out, what we might call in our terms the system-enabling Logos of each human order can only speak itself as an order of discourse definable as "rational" by "imprisoning" the differing varieties of "madness" of its discursive others. Thus the loss here for us, in our status as "knowers," that is, as specific intellectuals[57] for whom our "job" identity takes precedence over our intermediate *status*, would be cognitively far-reaching. For the role of a minority discourse which sees itself as a utopian discourse, in Ricoeur's sense,[58] the kind of new discourse that can only be generated from groups who accept their liminality to the systemically functioning order, would be given up if we accepted our role as that of constituting just another "true" discourse. Indeed the "Beyond" of my title is intended to suggest that we need to begin our praxis by

---

56. See Asmarom Legesse, *Gada: Three Approaches to the Study of an African Society* (New York: Free Press, 1973), 271.

57. For the use and definition of this term, see Michel Foucault, "Interview: Truth and Power" in *Power/Knowledge: Selected Interviews and Other Writings, 1972-1977* (New York: Pantheon Books), 109-133. There he makes the distinction between the intellectual as "bearer of a truth," just and true for all, "and the intellectual who, in effecting the specific tasks of his job, comes upon truth which is genuinely subversive of the prevailing "regime of truth."

58. See Paul Ricoeur, "Ideology and Utopia as Cultural Imagination" in *Being Human in a Technological Age*, D.M. Borchert and David Stewart, eds. (Athens, Ohio: Ohio University Press, 1980).

casting a critical eye on the systemic-functional role that the permitted incorporation of such a projected *true* discourse is intended to play, and the price at the level of emancipatory knowledge that would have to be paid for our newly licensed functioning within the present organization of rational knowledge.

For the potential role of a minority discourse as the discourse of the category of Ontological Other to the systemic figure of *man* is not only that of transforming the grounding premise on whose basis its existential discourse is made possible. It involves in addition an even more extensive shift which has to do with the liberation of the literary humanities themselves from the secondary role to which they have been logically relegated in our present episteme. The transformation of our present episteme requires the conversion of our present practice of literary criticism from a highly sophisticated yet system-functional craft into a science, making use both of Valesio's proposed disciplinary practice of a *rhetorics*,[59] of Todorov's proposed *symbolics of language*,[60] and of the conscious deciphering of figurative practices initiated by deconstruction.

From Biology and "Life" as a New Object of Knowledge to Human "Life" and a New Order of Knowledge

Western culture has constituted under the name of Man, a being who by one and the same interplay of reasons must be *a positive domain* of knowledge, and cannot be an object of science.
— Foucault, 1973

The "sudden appearance" at the turn of the nineteenth century of the arrangement of knowledge that was to constitute our present episteme was generated from a parallel large-scale movement of socio-historical forces active down to our own times, a parallel self-movement of the historical system-ensemble.[61] It was these forces and their challenge to the landed gentry's order of things which caused the crumbling of the

59. See Paolo Valesio, *Nova Antigua: Rhetorics as a Contemporary Theory* (Bloomington, Indiana: Indiana University Press, 1980).

60. See T. Todorov, *Theories of the Symbol* (Ithaca, N. Y.: Cornell University Press, 1977).

61. The term is used by Kurt Hubner in *Critique of Scientific Reason* (Chicago: University of Chicago Press, 1983).

Classical ordering of knowledge. Its epistemic frame found itself unable to answer the new questions and solve the new problems which had arisen out of the solutions that it had found and the behaviors it had oriented in response to the questions which it in its own time had arisen to confront. Thus the enormous question of the rationalization of industrial production at the national level, for example, could not be solved within the disciplinary frame of mercantilism's "analysis of wealth." It called instead for a new frame, in whose context the mode of truth of the "analysis of wealth" could be replaced by the new behavior-orienting discipline of *economics* as the master-discipline in place of *politics*.

For this to happen, however, the self-representation of the human that underpinned the system of rational knowledge of the classical episteme had itself to be transformed. The new representation, that of the human on the model of the natural organism, came into being with the shift, at the level of the episteme, from natural history to the study of a new object of knowledge, life, within the new disciplinary frame of *biology*. The third shift was from the analysis of *general grammar* to the new discipline of *philology* as the study of the historical evolution of changes impelled by the interior mechanisms in languages which now came to serve an evolutionary "genetic" function for the projection of human populations as "language families," that is, as groups whose "essence" was defined by their language rather than by their self-representations, including that of being defined in their "primordial" essence by their shared languages.[62]

In the ideologic of this new epistemic frame, the study of what was specific to human life as distinct from organic life was made secondary. Sociology, psychology, and the new humanities (literary criticism), as the disciplines which had the *potential* to constitute the founding models of being as a new object of knowledge, that is, human life as a hybridly organic and meta-organic third level of existence, were logically marginalized as the realm of the "subjective." In other words, the model of the human as a natural organism logically calls for the active marginalization of those areas of knowledge able to posit human life, its models of being and relative epistemes as new objects of knowledge of an entirely different code of knowledge which would parallel in our time the constitution of the discipline of biology and its new object, life,

---

62. See Foucault, *The Order of Things*, 290.

outside of the frame of the then classical episteme.

From "Parricide" and Western Metaphysics to Literary Criticism as a Science

> Ultimately it would appear that . . . men and women have never been any one particular thing or have had any particular nature to tie them down metaphysically . . . . [Humans] become through their powers of embodiment, a multiplicity of theories that became human because man has the capacity to turn theory into flesh. Insofar as the past conditions the present . . . [the] biological study of religion could liberate humans from codings in the nervous system which if not known as *conditioning*, might be taken as liberation when in every case they are only the shackles on human freedom.
>
> —Antonio T. de Nicolas, 1981

Because of our coding function in the order of discourse of biological idealism and its regulatory metaphysics, and because of our *experiential* knowledge of the empirical effects of this function, human discourse can no longer be seen by us as neutral, unmotivated, or disinterested but, rather, because system-functional, as everywhere potentially *amoral* to those who are outside what Helen Fein defines as the "common universe of obligation."[63] Thus, whilst majority discourse, in its most advanced positions, can aim, in the words of J. Hillis Miller, at committing "parricide" by and through the deconstruction of Western metaphysics, the role of Minority Discourse must go beyond this to call in question the grounding premises from which the metaphysical discourses of *all* population groups, *all* human systems—including that of the West—are generated. It is this calling in question which impels our going beyond the boundaries of our present episteme into a new constitutive domain of knowledge that we have called a science of human systems, a move which impels also our transformation of literary criticism into a science of human discourse, a new science which makes use of the insights of the biological sciences only to go beyond their limits.

Since it is these enculturating discourses, based on the "grounding

---

63. See Helen Fein, *Accounting for Genocide: National Responses and Jewish Victimization during the Holocaust* (Chicago: University of Chicago Press, 1979).

premise" of the metaphysical conception of life/death, and their related "codings in the nervous system" or systems of inference that enable what René Girard calls "the dynamic structure of desire" to bring
into being differing modes of the *human* (as distinct from the biological
hominid), the question becomes that of finding a meta-discourse
able to constitute the discourse of its own order as an object of knowledge and thus to allow us "access to our cognitive domain."

As Girard implies, all literature, indeed all human narrative, functions to encode the dynamics of desire at the deep structural level of
the order's symbolic template. It is, in consequence, precisely through
fiction, ritual, and art that we can have access to the higher level units
of our system-specific modes of mind and to the "enchanted" order of
discourse which must everywhere function, in the last instance, to conserve the grounding premises of its mode of inferential analogic from
which its system-maintaining "truths" are stably generated.

Here Girard's point that fictional works of genius can afford us access to a kind of knowledge superior to our "rational" one, if linked to
Grassi's concept of the rhetorical speech that underlies all our systems
of rational knowledges, suggests that the higher level of knowledge afforded by fiction, as indeed by religious ritual, myths of origin, etc., in
effect provides access precisely to knowledge of those modes of rhetorical speech on whose basis all human orders are discursively erected.
For it is through literature and art that these speeches are both "incarnated," that is, constructed, and deconstructed, as our readings of the
processes of discourse-disenchantment in *Don Quixote* and *The Invisible
Man* illustrate.

Like the narrator of *The Invisible Man,* we as "Minority" scholars find
ourselves confronting a reality deeply enchanted by the post-atomic
functioning of anachronistic true discourses inherited from an industrial order now past and gone. In order to effect a gesture parallel to
that by which the ancient Egyptians went from their rule-of-thumb
measuring of the post-flood marshes to the theorems of geometry, it is
necessary that we now go from our present art and craft of discourse to
a new science of that third level of existence, human life, of whose
bringing-into-being all orders of discourse, and the behavioral directive signs which they encode, are a function.

This projected transformation of literary criticism from a craft to a
science is therefore based on the transgression of the present division

between the humanities and the neurosciences which study the functioning of the neurophysiological machinery and electro-chemical messenger systems of the brain. For orders of discourse and their rhetorical strategies/devices, that is, their semiotic strings, "cannot be understood in their behavior-motivating/regulating power unless the discursive orders are seen as functioning at the physiological level in tandem with the functioning of the electro-chemical systems" (Danielli's I.R.S.) and overall neurophysiological machinery of the human brain. For it is their concerted praxis that constitutes the specific (verbal) symbol-matter information systems generated from Grassi's founding rhetorical speech and that thereby enables the configuring both of shared regulatory sentiments (the aesthetic) and of shared modes of "mind" (the cognitive) that are integrative and specific to those human systems that we anthropomorphically call "cultures." Their praxis that regulates the "codings in our nervous system," while seeming to us like liberation, can be really only shackles on our human freedom.[64]

There are no Birds of Yesteryear in this Year's Nest: To Disenchant Discourse

[M]en will turn once more to . . . wonderment; . . . will explore the vast reaches of space within . . . .
                                        —Ishmael Reed, *Mumbo-Jumbo*

To disenchant discourse will therefore be to desacralize our "cultures" and their systems of rationality by setting upon our literary and cultural heritages and their orders of discourse rather than by continuing to adapt to their generating premises and non-conscious systems of inference as we do now. The "setting upon" process of disenchantment—parallel to Heidegger's definition of "technology" as expressive of the human's new setting upon physical nature rather than adapting to it—will be effected by "bringing into unconcealedness" the non-autonomous function played by all human discourse; by the revealing of the transindividual role of discourse in the functioning of the dynamic structure of desire or of the machinery of desiring-production by means of which our present human system brings itself autopoetically

---

64. A.T. de Nicolas, "Notes on the Biology of Religion" in *Journal of Social and Biological Structures* 3, no. 2 (April 1980): 225.

into being through the collective behaviors of the systemic subjects which the order of discourse unconsciously orients and regulates.

This proposal redefines the dynamics of desire as a new meta-biological object of knowledge constituted by discourse, as the acquired rhetorical motivation systems which are the uniquely human parallel of the species-specific motivation systems characteristic of all mammalian forms of life up to and including the different species of the prehuman hominid. These systems regulate all facets of species-specific behavior, cognitive and actional, in non-human mammals and linguistically speciated, i.e., group-specific, behaviors in human. It is these acquired/rhetorically coded, rather than innate/genetically coded, motivation systems that constitute the psychic unity of the human species. Like Mendel's new object of knowledge, *hereditary traits*, which functioned as an object irreducible to the species and to the "sex transmitting them,"[65] rhetorical motivation systems whose function is to bring differing modalities of "human being" into being, by means of enculturating discourses generated from the grounding premise of an environmentally "fit" conception of life/death, must also necessarily decenter the human subjects whose behaviors enable the stable replication of their own autopoesis as systems. That is to say, their own intentionality and autonomy as autopoetic systems, once put into discursive play, whilst largely compatible with, are not reducible to that of their individual subjects.

The discursive system of each human order functions as the enculturating machinery by and through which the motivational system which dictates the behaviors needed if a specific mode of the human is to be brought into dynamic being and stably replicated (even if and where these behaviors are contradictory to the self-realization of human individuals or groups: cf. *Black Skins/White Masks*, minority skins, majority masks). Thus orders of discourse must function so as to "enchant" their human subjects into desiring in the mode of desiring needed, into acquiescing to the effecting of the intentionality of the R.M.S. in question, even at the cost of not affirming their own. Hence the great moments of Girardian *conversion*, from *Don Quixote* to *The Invisible Man*, arise where the novelistic hero wakes up, rejecting the non-conscious "mimetic" quality of his former inculcated mode of motivation/desire.

It is in the disenchanting of the discourses which brings into being

---

65. Foucault, *The Archaeology of Knowledge*, trans. A. M. Sheridan Smith (New York: Pantheon, 1972), 224.

an existential reality experienced as if it were objectively outside our human control that Minority Discourse will both find and go beyond its own paradoxical rationale. For if, as Derrida argues, the "very idea of reason as dominant . . . in human nature is also a fiction" since consciousness or reason are "effects, traces, the detritus of will" and "man lacks the capacity—to know without motive,"[66] it is only through the "disenchanting" of our true discourses that we will come to know the grounding premise that determines this ostensibly autonomous "will" or "motive" and to determine then consciously what now determines us, determining how we know and act upon the world: to disenchant the human, then, enabling her/his Girardian "waking up" to a consciously chosen intentionality. With this emerges the possibility of a science of human behavior, and of what Gellner calls the extra-territoriality, at last, of human cognition.

In doing this of course we would only follow in the wake of the *Pilgrim's Progress* from "enchantment" to "conversion," into a space that the frontiers of revelatory fiction have already opened out before us.

> . . . "(A)nd I no hero, but short and dark with only a certain eloquence and a bottomless capacity for being a fool to mark me from the rest; saw them, recognized them at last as those whom I had failed and of whom I was now, just now, a leader, though leading them, running ahead of them, only in the stripping away of my illusionment."[67]

Some 350 years before:

> "Let us go gently, gentlemen" said Don Quixote, "for there are no birds this year in last year's nests. I was mad, but I am sane now. I was Don Quixote de la Mancha, but today as I have said, I am Alonso Quixano the Good."[68]

To paraphrase Ellison: "Perhaps in the lower frequencies, they speak for us."[69]

---

66. As cited by Berel Lang, *Philosophy and the Art of Writing: Studies in Philosophical and Literary Style* (Lewisburg: Bucknell University Press, 1983), 228.

67. Ellison, *Invisible Man*, 546.

68. Cervantes, *Don Quixote*, 938.

69. Ellison, *Invisible Man*, 568.

Contributors

Barbara Christian is Associate Professor in the Afro-American Studies Department at University of California, Berkeley. She is author of *Black Women Novelists: The Development of a Tradition, In Search of Our Past,* and *Teaching Guide to Black Foremothers.*

Arif Dirlik is an Associate Professor of History at Duke University. He is the author of *Revolution and History: Origins of Marxist Historiography in China, 1919–1937* and other studies of twentieth-century Chinese historical and political thought. He has recently completed a study of the origins of the Communist Party of China.

Henry Louis Gates, Jr. is professor of English, Comparative Literature, and African American Studies at Duke University. He is the author of *The Signifying Monkey* and *Figures in Black,* as well as the editor of *The Slave's Narrative* and *In the House of Osugbo.*

Nancy Hartsock is associate professor of Political Science and Women Studies at the University of Washington. She is author of *Money, Sex, and Power: Toward a Feminist Historical Materialism,* has co-edited *Women and Poverty,* and is working on a book tentatively entitled *Postmodernism and Political Change.*

Hannan Hever teaches in the Department of Poetics and Comparative Literature at Tel-Aviv University. He has published articles on modern Hebrew literature, focusing on its political and social dimensions, and has co-edited an anthology of protest poetry against the Lebanon war, *Fighting and Killing Without End.*

Abdul R. JanMohamed teaches in the English department at the University of California, Berkeley. His publications include *Manichean Aesthetics: The Politics of Literature in Colonial Africa.* He is currently working on the confluence of the politics of racial and sexual oppression in the fiction of Richard Wright.

Caren Kaplan teaches in the English Department at Georgetown University. Her translation of a section of *Buenos Aires* by Alicia Dujovne Oritz

470

has been published along with her essay, "The Poetics of Displacement in *Buenos Aires*," in *Discourse*.

Elaine H. Kim is a member of the Asian American Studies Department at University of California, Berkeley. Her writings include *Asian American Literature: An Introduction to the Writings and Their Social Context*.

Josaphat B. Kubayanda teaches in the Spanish Department at Ohio State University in Columbus. He has published several articles in a variety of journals including *Estudios Hispanicos, Afro-Hispanic Review, Plantation Society in the Americas, West Africa,* and *Legon Journal of the Humanities*.

David Lloyd is a member of the English department at the University of California, Berkeley. His writings include *Nationalism and Minority Literature: James Clarence Mangan and the Origins of Irish Cultural Nationalism*.

Lata Mani teaches in the Anthropology Department at the University of California, Davis. Her research explores constructions of woman and tradition in colonial India.

Nora Pauwels is a printmaker currently working in Berkeley, California. She studied in Antwerp and Ghent, Belgium, and has had exhibitions in Belgium and California. She has done the prints for the past three issues of *Cultural Critique*.

José Rabasa is Associate Professor of Spanish and Portuguese at the University of Maryland, College Park. He is currently completing a book-length study of New World Spanish historiography.

R. Radhakrishnan teaches critical theory in the English Department at the University of Massachusetts at Amherst. He has published essays in *boundary 2* and *Works and Days,* and has forthcoming articles in journals such as *Poetics Today* and *Social Text*.

Renato Rosaldo is a member of the Department of Anthropology at Stanford University. He has written extensively on the status of history in anthropological work, on discourses of domination in the Philippines, and on Mayan and Chicano studies. He is working on a collection of essays on ethnographic rhetorics and strategies that reassess the role of experience and emotion in cultural interpretation.

Kumkum Sangari teaches at Indraprastha College, University of Delhi, India. She is the author of numerous articles on Third World literature and culture.

Allogan Slagle, a California attorney, formerly taught in the Native American Studies department at the University of California, Berkeley and is a visiting lecturer at Stanford Law School. He is Chairman of California Indian Legal Services and Secretary of the Urban Indian Health Board, Inc. and serves on the Association on American Indian Affairs' Advisory Board on Federal Acknowledgment.

Arlene Teraoka teaches in the German department at the University of

Minnesota, Twin Cities campus. Her publications include *The Silence of Entropy of Universal Discourse: The Postmodernist Poetics of Heiner Muller* and she is currently working on a book on post-war German writers' appropriation of Third World cultures.

Sylvia Wynter teaches at Stanford University in the department of Spanish and Portuguese and the Program of African and Afro-American Studies. She is currently at work on a book entitled *By Means of a Creature: Essays Towards a Science of Human "Life."*